Seventh Edition

CompTIA Security+

Guide to Network Security Fundamentals

MARK CIAMPA, PH.D.

INFORMATION SECURITY

Cengage

Australia • Brazil • Canada • Mexico • Singapore • United Kingdom • United States

CompTIA® Security+ Guide to Network Security Fundamentals, Seventh Edition
Mark Ciampa

SVP, Higher Education Product Management: Erin Joyner

VP, Product Management: Thais Alencar

Product Team Manager: Kristin McNary

Associate Product Manager: Danielle Klahr

Product Assistant: Tom Benedetto

Director, Learning Design: Rebecca von Gillern

Senior Manager, Learning Design: Leigh Hefferon

Learning Designer: Natalie Onderdonk

Vice President, Marketing – Science, Technology, & Math: Jason Sakos

Senior Marketing Director: Michele McTighe

Marketing Manager: Cassie Cloutier

Product Specialist: Mackenzie Paine

Director, Content Creation: Juliet Steiner

Senior Manager, Content Creation: Patty Stephan

Senior Content Manager: Brooke Greenhouse

Director, Digital Production Services: Krista Kellman

Digital Delivery Lead: Jim Vaughey

Developmental Editor: Lisa Ruffalo

Production Service/Composition: SPi

Design Director: Jack Pendleton

Designer: Erin Griffin

Cover Image(s): iStockPhoto.com/phochi

For product information and technology assistance, contact us at
**Cengage Customer & Sales Support, 1-800-354-9706
or support.cengage.com.**

For permission to use material from this text or product,
submit all requests online at **www.copyright.com.**

Library of Congress Control Number: 2020920904

ISBN-13: 978-0-357-42437-7
Loose-leaf Edition: 978-0-357-42438-4

Cengage
200 Pier 4 Boulevard
Boston, MA 02210
USA

Cengage is a leading provider of customized learning solutions with employees residing in nearly 40 different countries and sales in more than 125 countries around the world. Find your local representative at: **www.cengage.com.**

To learn more about Cengage platforms and services, register or access your online learning solution, or purchase materials for your course, visit **www.cengage.com.**

Printed at CLDPC, USA, 09-23

BRIEF CONTENTS

TABLE OF CONTENTS

INTRODUCTION

The number of cyberattacks has reached epidemic proportions. According to one report, the number of new malware releases every month exceeds 20 million, and the total malware in existence is approaching 900 million variants. More than 11.5 billion records have been exposed through data breaches since 2005. In 2019, four out of every five organizations experienced at least one successful cyberattack, and more than one-third suffered six or more successful attacks.[1] It is estimated that by 2021, a business will fall victim to a ransomware attack once every 11 seconds. Cybercrime will cost the world $6 trillion annually by 2021, an increase of 100 percent in just six years, representing the greatest transfer of economic wealth in human history.[2] Compounding the problem, 85 percent of organizations are experiencing a shortfall of skilled security professionals.[3]

The need to identify and defend against these continual attacks has created an essential workforce that is now at the very core of the information technology (IT) industry. Known as information security, these professionals are focused on protecting electronic information. Various elements of information security, such as application security, infrastructure security, forensics and malware analysis, and security leadership, along with several others, make up this workforce. The demand for certified professionals in information security has never been higher.

When filling cybersecurity positions, an overwhelming majority of enterprises use the Computing Technology Industry Association (CompTIA) Security+ certification to verify security competency. Of the hundreds of security certifications currently available, Security+ is one of the most widely acclaimed security certifications. Because it is internationally recognized as validating a foundation level of security skills and knowledge, the Security+ certification has become the foundation for today's IT security professionals. The value for an IT professional who holds a CompTIA security certification is significant. On average, an employee with a CompTIA certification commands a salary between 5 and 15 percent higher than their counterparts with similar qualifications but lacking a certification.

The CompTIA Security+ certification is a vendor-neutral credential that requires passing the current certification exam SY0-601. A successful candidate has the knowledge and skills required to identify attacks, threats, and vulnerabilities; design a strong security architecture; implement security controls; be knowledgeable of security operations and incident response; and be well versed in governance, risk, and compliance requirements.

Certification provides job applicants with more than a competitive edge over their noncertified counterparts competing for the same IT positions. Some institutions of higher education grant college credit to students who successfully pass certification exams, moving them further along in their degree programs. For those already employed, achieving a new certification increases job effectiveness, which opens doors for advancement and job security. Certification also gives individuals interested in careers in the military the ability to move into higher positions more quickly.

CompTIA® Security+ Guide to Network Security Fundamentals, Seventh Edition, is intended to equip learners with the knowledge and skills needed to be information security IT professionals. Yet it is more than an "exam prep" book. While teaching the fundamentals of cybersecurity by using the CompTIA Security+ exam objectives as its framework, the book takes a comprehensive view of security by examining in depth today's attacks against networks and endpoints and what is needed to defend against these attacks. *Security+ Guide to Network Security Fundamentals*, Seventh Edition, is a valuable tool for those who want to learn about security and enter the field of information security. It also provides the foundation that will help prepare for the CompTIA Security+ certification exam. For more information on CompTIA Security+ certification, visit the CompTIA website at *comptia.org*.

INTENDED AUDIENCE

This book is designed to meet the needs of students and professionals who want to master basic information security. A fundamental knowledge of computers and networks is all that is required to use this book. Those seeking to pass the CompTIA Security+ certification exam will find the text's approach and content especially helpful; all Security+ SY0-601 exam objectives are covered in the text (see Appendix A). *Security+ Guide to Network Security Fundamentals*, Seventh Edition, covers all aspects of network and computer security while satisfying the Security+ objectives.

The book's pedagogical features are designed to provide a truly interactive learning experience to help prepare you for the challenges of network and computer security. In addition to the information presented in the text, each module includes Hands-On Projects that guide you through implementing practical hardware, software, network, and Internet security configurations step by step. Each module also contains case studies that place you in the role of problem solver, requiring you to apply concepts presented in the module to achieve successful solutions.

MODULE DESCRIPTIONS

The following list summarizes the topics covered in each module of this course:

Module 1, "Introduction to Security," introduces the cybersecurity fundamentals that form the basis of the Security+ certification. The module begins by defining information security and identifying attackers. It also looks at vulnerabilities in systems and the types of attacks that take advantage of the vulnerabilities.

Module 2, "Threat Management and Cybersecurity Resources," looks at threat management as it pertains to penetration testing and vulnerability scans. The module also explores cybersecurity standards, regulations, frameworks, and configuration guidelines.

Module 3, "Threats and Attacks on Endpoints," focuses on network-connected hardware devices, better known as endpoints. It begins by looking at attacks using various types of malware and then surveys application attacks. It also examines adversarial artificial intelligence attacks.

Module 4, "Endpoint and Application Development Security," describes different sources of threat intelligence information. The module also explores securing endpoint devices and creating and deploying secure applications to run on those devices.

Module 5, "Mobile, Embedded, and Specialized Device Security," looks at securing mobile devices. As users have embraced mobile devices, so too have attackers embraced them as targets. This module also explores embedded systems and the Internet of Things devices. Finally, it examines keeping specialized devices secure.

Module 6, "Basic Cryptography," explores how encryption can be used to protect data. The module covers what cryptography is and how it can be used for protection, and then examines how to protect data using three common types of encryption algorithms: hashing, symmetric encryption, and asymmetric encryption. It also covers how to use cryptography on files and disks to keep data secure.

Module 7, "Public Key Infrastructure and Cryptographic Protocols," examines how to implement cryptography and use digital certificates. It also looks at public key infrastructure and key management. This module covers cryptographic protocols to see how cryptography is used on data that is being transported and concludes with how to implement cryptography.

Module 8, "Networking Threats, Assessments, and Defenses," begins a study of network attacks and defenses. First, the module explores some of the common attacks that are launched against networks today. Then it looks at tools for assessing and defending networks. Finally, it examines physical security defenses that can be used to protect network technology devices.

Module 9, "Network Security Appliances and Technologies," examines security appliances that provide resilience to attackers—such as firewalls, proxy servers, deception instruments, and other security appliances. It also explores security technologies such as access technologies, technologies for monitoring and managing networks, and principles for designing a secure network.

Module 10, "Cloud and Virtualization Security," looks at both cloud computing and virtualization. It examines what both of these technologies are, how they function, and how they can be secured. Because cloud computing relies on secure network connections, it also discusses secure network protocols.

Module 11, "Wireless Network Security," explores the attacks on wireless devices that are common today. It also identifies vulnerabilities in wireless security and examines several secure wireless protections.

Module 12, "Authentication," defines authentication and the secure management techniques that enforce authentication. This module looks at the types of authentication credentials that can be used to verify a user's identity and the techniques and technology used to manage user accounts in a secure fashion.

Module 13, "Incident Preparation, Response, and Investigation," focuses on the plans that must be made for when a cybersecurity incident occurs. These plans cover incident preparation, incident response, and then a follow-up investigation as to how the incident occurred and how similar future events can be mitigated.

Module 14, "Cybersecurity Resilience," explores the capacity of an organization to recover quickly from difficulties and spring back into shape. This module defines business continuity and why it is important. Next, it investigates how to prevent disruptions through redundancy. Finally, it explains how business policies can help provide resilience to an organization.

Module 15, "Risk Management and Data Privacy," examines two elements of cybersecurity that are of high importance to both enterprises and users. The first involves risk and the strategies for mitigating risks. It also explores data privacy and the issues that surround it.

Appendix A, "CompTIA SY0-601 Certification Examination Objectives," provides a complete listing of the latest CompTIA Security+ certification exam objectives and shows the modules and headings in the modules that cover material associated with each objective, as well as the Bloom's Taxonomy level of that coverage.

Appendix B, "Two Rights & a Wrong: Answers," contains the answers to the "Two Rights and a Wrong" assessment questions.

FEATURES

The course's pedagogical features are designed to provide a truly interactive learning experience and prepare you to face the challenges of cybersecurity. To aid you in fully understanding computer and network security, this course includes many features designed to enhance your learning experience.

- **Maps to CompTIA Objectives.** The material in this text covers all the CompTIA Security+ SY0-601 exam objectives.
- **Module Objectives.** Each module lists the concepts to be mastered within that module. This list serves as a quick reference to the module's contents and as a useful study aid.
- **Front-Page Cybersecurity.** This section opens each module and provides an explanation and analysis of some of the latest attacks and defenses related to topics that are covered in the module. The sections establish a real-world context for understanding cybersecurity.
- **Illustrations, Tables, and Bulleted Lists.** Numerous full-color diagrams illustrating abstract ideas and screenshots of cybersecurity tools help learners better visualize the concepts of cybersecurity. In addition, the many tables and bulleted lists provide details and comparisons of both practical and theoretical information that can be easily reviewed and referenced in the future.
- **Module Summaries.** Each module reading concludes with a summary of the concepts introduced in that module. These summaries revisit the ideas covered in each module.
- **Key Terms.** All of the terms in each module that were introduced with bold text are gathered in a Key Terms list, providing additional review and highlighting key concepts. Key Term definitions are included in the Glossary at the end of the text.
- **Review Questions.** The end-of-module assessment begins with a set of review questions that reinforce the ideas introduced in each module. These questions help you evaluate and apply the material you have learned. Answering these questions will ensure that you have mastered the important concepts and provide valuable practice for taking CompTIA's Security+ exam.
- **Hands-On Projects.** Projects at the end of each module give you the opportunity to apply in practice what you have just learned. These projects include detailed step-by-step instructions to walk you through endpoint security configuration settings and demonstrate actual security defenses using websites or software downloaded from the Internet. In addition, instructions are provided regarding how to perform these projects in a protected sandbox or virtual machine environment so that the underlying computer is not impacted.

- **Case Projects.** Although it is important to understand the theory behind cybersecurity technology, nothing beats real-world experience. To this end, each module includes several case projects aimed at providing practical implementation experience as well as practice in applying critical thinking skills to reinforce the concepts learned throughout the module.

New to this Edition

- Maps fully to the latest CompTIA Security+ exam SY0-601
- Completely revised and updated with expanded coverage on attacks and defenses
- New module units: Security Fundamentals, Endpoint Security, Cryptography, Network Security, and Enterprise Security
- All new "Front-Page Cybersecurity" opener in each module
- Two Rights & a Wrong self-assessments that give you opportunities to quickly assess your understanding of the topics
- All new virtual machine labs that help you refine the hands-on skills needed to master today's cybersecurity toolset
- New and updated Hands-On Projects cover some of the latest security software
- All new introductions to the Hands-On Projects provide time estimates, Security+ objective mappings, and project descriptions
- New cybersecurity consultant and assurance service scenarios in which you serve as an intern and gain practical experience regarding what you might encounter on the job
- New Information Security Community Site activities allow you to interact with other learners and security professionals from around the world through a regularly updated blog, discussion boards, and other features
- All SY0-601 exam topics fully defined
- Linking of each exam subdomain to Bloom's Taxonomy (see Appendix A)

Text and Graphic Conventions

Wherever appropriate, additional information and exercises have been added to this book to help you better understand the topic at hand. Icons throughout the text alert you to additional materials. The following icons and elements are used in this textbook:

NOTE 1

Note elements draw your attention to additional helpful material related to the subject being described.

 **CAUTION**　The Caution icons warn you about potential mistakes or problems and explain how to avoid them.

TWO RIGHTS & A WRONG

The "Two Rights & a Wrong" elements let you quickly assess your understanding of the topics. The answers to these assessments appear in Appendix B.

 **VM LAB**　The VM Lab icons alert you to live, virtual machine labs that reinforce the material in each module.

 **CERTIFICATION**

Certification icons indicate CompTIA Security+ objectives covered under major module headings.

INSTRUCTOR MATERIALS

Everything you need for your course is in one place. This collection of book-specific lecture and class tools is available online. Please visit *login.cengage.com* and log in to access instructor-specific resources on the Instructor Resources, which includes the Guide to Teaching Online; Instructor Manual; Solutions to the textbook, lab manual, and live, virtual machine labs; Test Bank files; PowerPoint Presentations; Syllabus; and Student Downloads.

- **Guide to Teaching Online.** The Guide to Teaching Online includes two main parts. Part 1 offers general technological and pedagogical considerations and resources, and Part 2 provides discipline-specific suggestions for teaching when you can't be in the same room with students.
- **Electronic Instructor Manual.** The Instructor Manual that accompanies this textbook includes the following items: additional instructional material to assist in class preparation—including suggestions for lecture topics, additional projects, and class discussion topics.
- **Solutions Manuals.** The instructor resources include solutions to all end-of-module material, including review questions and case projects. The Lab Manual Solutions include answers to the review questions found in the lab manual modules. The Live, Virtual Machine Labs Solutions include examples of correct screenshots and answers to the inline questions found within the labs.
- **Test Banks with Cengage Testing Powered by Cognero.** This flexible, online system allows you to do the following:
  - Author, edit, and manage test bank content from multiple Cengage solutions.
  - Create multiple test versions in an instant.
  - Deliver tests from your LMS, your classroom, or wherever you want.
- **PowerPoint Presentations.** This book comes with a set of Microsoft PowerPoint slides for each module. These slides are meant to be used as a teaching aid for classroom presentations, to be made available to students on the network for module review, or to be printed for classroom distribution. Instructors are also at liberty to add their own slides for other topics introduced.
- **Syllabus.** The sample syllabus provides an example of a template for setting up a 14-week course.
- **Student Downloads.** The student downloads include Accessible Launch Text for MindTap Lab Simulations and Accessible Launch Text for MindTap Live Virtual Machine Labs.

Total Solutions for Security

To access additional course materials, please visit *www.cengage.com*. At the *cengage.com* home page, search for the ISBN of your title (from the back cover of your book) using the search box at the top of the page. This will take you to the product page where these resources can be found.

MindTap

MindTap for *Security+ Guide to Network Security Fundamentals*, Seventh Edition, is a personalized, fully online digital learning platform of content, assignments, and services that engages students and encourages them to think critically while allowing you to easily set your course through simple customization options.

MindTap is designed to help students master the skills they need in today's workforce. Research shows employers need critical thinkers, troubleshooters, and creative problem solvers to stay relevant in our fast-paced, technology-driven world. MindTap helps you achieve this with assignments and activities that provide hands-on practice, real-life relevance, and certification test prep. Students are guided through assignments that help them master basic knowledge and understanding before moving on to more challenging problems.

All MindTap activities and assignments are tied to defined learning objectives. Readings support course objectives, while Security for Life activities encourage learners to read articles, listen to podcasts, or watch videos to stay current with what is happening in the field of IT and cybersecurity. You can use these activities to help build student interest in the field of information security as well as lifelong learning habits.

Reflection activities encourage self-reflection and open sharing among students to help improve their retention and understanding of the material. Visualize Videos help explain and illustrate difficult information technology concepts.

Lab simulations provide students with an opportunity for hands-on experience and problem-solving practice with automatic feedback. The live, virtual machine labs provide hands-on practice and give students an opportunity to troubleshoot, explore, and try different real-life solutions in a secure, private sandbox environment.

Test Prep questions in the ATP app allow students to quiz themselves on specific exam domains, and the pre- and post-course assessments measure exactly how much they have learned. CNOW quizzes provide test questions in the style of the Security+ certification exam and help you measure how well learners mastered the material after completing each MindTap module.

MindTap is designed around learning objectives and provides the analytics and reporting to easily see where the class stands in terms of progress, engagement, and completion rates.

Students can access eBook content in the MindTap Reader—which offers highlighting, note taking, search, and audio, as well as mobile access. Learn more at *www.cengage.com/mindtap/*.

Instant Access Code: (ISBN: 9780357424407)
Printed Access Code: (ISBN: 9780357424414)

Lab Manual

Hands-on learning is necessary to master the security skills needed for both CompTIA's Security+ Exam and for a career in network security. Included only in the MindTap, *Security+ Guide to Network Security Fundamentals Lab Manual*, 7th Edition, contains hands-on exercises that use fundamental networking security concepts as they are applied in the real world. Each module offers review questions to reinforce your mastery of network security topics and to sharpen your critical thinking and problem-solving skills.

Bloom's Taxonomy

Bloom's Taxonomy is an industry-standard classification system used to help identify the level of ability that learners need to demonstrate proficiency. It is often used to classify educational learning objectives into different levels of complexity. Bloom's Taxonomy reflects the "cognitive process dimension." This represents a continuum of increasing cognitive complexity, from remember (lowest level) to create (highest level).

There are six categories in Bloom's Taxonomy as seen in Figure A.

In all instances, the level of coverage the domains in *Security+ Guide to Network Security Fundamentals*, Seventh Edition, meets or exceeds the Bloom's Taxonomy level indicated by CompTIA for that objective. See Appendix A for more detail.

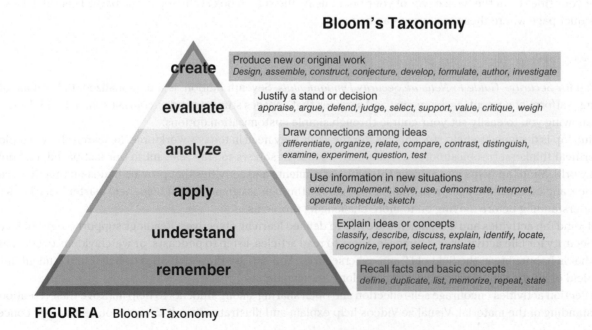

Bloom's Taxonomy

create — Produce new or original work
Design, assemble, construct, conjecture, develop, formulate, author, investigate

evaluate — Justify a stand or decision
appraise, argue, defend, judge, select, support, value, critique, weigh

analyze — Draw connections among ideas
differentiate, organize, relate, compare, contrast, distinguish, examine, experiment, question, test

apply — Use information in new situations
execute, implement, solve, use, demonstrate, interpret, operate, schedule, sketch

understand — Explain ideas or concepts
classify, describe, discuss, explain, identify, locate, recognize, report, select, translate

remember — Recall facts and basic concepts
define, duplicate, list, memorize, repeat, state

FIGURE A   Bloom's Taxonomy

Information Security Community Site

Stay secure with the Information Security Community Site. Connect with students, professors, and professionals from around the world, and stay on top of this ever-changing field. Visit *http://community.cengage.com/Infosec2/* to

- **Ask** authors, professors, and students the questions that are on your mind in the Discussion Forums.
- **See** up-to-date news, videos, and articles.
- **Read** regular blogs from author Mark Ciampa.
- **Listen** to podcasts on the latest Information Security topics.
- **Review** textbook updates and errata.

Each module's Case Projects include information on a current security topic and specific projects ask the learner to post reactions and comments to the Information Security Community Site. This allows users from around the world to interact and learn from other users as well as security professionals and researchers.

WHAT'S NEW WITH COMPTIA SECURITY+ CERTIFICATION

The CompTIA Security+ SY0-601 exam was updated in November 2020. Several significant changes have been made to the exam objectives. The exam objectives have been significantly expanded to reflect current security issues and knowledge requirements more accurately. These exam objectives place importance on knowing "how to" rather than just knowing or recognizing security concepts.

The following are the domains covered on the new Security+ exam:

Domain	% of Examination
1.0 Attacks, Threats, and Vulnerabilities	24%
2.0 Architecture and Design	21%
3.0 Implementation	25%
4.0 Operations and Incident Response	16%
5.0 Governance, Risk, and Compliance	14%
Total	100%

About the Author

Dr. Mark Ciampa is Professor of Information Systems in the Gordon Ford College of Business at Western Kentucky University in Bowling Green, Kentucky. Previously, he was Associate Professor and Director of Academic Computing at Volunteer State Community College in Gallatin, Tennessee, for 20 years. Mark has worked in the IT industry as a computer consultant for businesses, government agencies, and educational institutions. He has published more than 25 articles in peer-reviewed journals and is also the author of more than 25 technology textbooks, including *CompTIA Guide to CySA+, CWNA Guide to Wireless LANs 3e, Guide to Wireless Communications, Security Awareness: Applying Practical Security In Your World 5e,* and *Networking BASICS.* Dr. Ciampa holds a PhD in technology management with a specialization in digital communication systems from Indiana State University, and he has certifications in security and health care.

Acknowledgments

A large team of dedicated professionals all contributed to this project, and I am honored to be part of such an outstanding group of professionals. First, thanks go to Cengage Product Managers Amy Savino and Danielle Klahr for providing me the opportunity to work on this project and for providing their continual support. Thanks also to Senior Content

CompTIA.

Becoming a CompTIA Certified IT Professional is Easy

It's also the best way to reach greater professional opportunities and rewards.

Why Get CompTIA Certified?

Growing Demand

Labor estimates predict some technology fields will experience growth of over 20% by the year 2020.* CompTIA certification qualifies the skills required to join this workforce.

Higher Salaries

IT professionals with certifications on their resume command better jobs, earn higher salaries and have more doors open to new multi-industry opportunities.

Verified Strengths

91% of hiring managers indicate CompTIA certifications are valuable in validating IT expertise, making certification the best way to demonstrate your competency and knowledge to employers.**

Universal Skills

CompTIA certifications are vendor neutral—which means that certified professionals can proficiently work with an extensive variety of hardware and software found in most organizations.

 Learn  Certify  Work

Learn more about what the exam covers by reviewing the following:

- Exam objectives for key study points.
- Sample questions for a general overview of what to expect on the exam and examples of question format.
- Visit online forums, like LinkedIn, to see what other IT professionals say about CompTIA exams.

Purchase a voucher at a Pearson VUE testing center or at CompTIAstore.com.

- Register for your exam at a Pearson VUE testing center:
- Visit pearsonvue.com/CompTIA to find the closest testing center to you.
- Schedule the exam online. You will be required to enter your voucher number or provide payment information at registration.
- Take your certification exam.

Congratulations on your CompTIA certification!

- Make sure to add your certification to your resume.
- Check out the CompTIA Certification Roadmap to plan your next career move.

Learn more: **Certification.CompTIA.org/securityplus**

Manager Brooke Greenhouse for answering all my questions, to Learning Designer Natalie Onderdonk for her valuable input, and to Danielle Shaw for her technical reviews. I would like to give special recognition to developmental editor Lisa Ruffolo. Although this was our first major project together, it was like we had worked together for many years because she knew exactly what I needed. Lisa provided numerous helpful suggestions, made excellent comments, and expertly managed all the pieces that this fast-moving project required. I also appreciated the significant contributions of the reviewers for this edition: Joyce Thompson, Professor of Computer Science and GIS at Lehigh Carbon Community College, and Jeffrey Koch, Professor of Computer Science at Tarrant County College. To everyone on the team I extend my sincere thanks.

Finally, I want to thank my wonderful wife, Susan. Her patience, support, and love were, as always, there from the first page to the last. I could not have done it without her.

Dedication

To Braden, Mia, Abby, Gabe, Cora, Will, and Rowan.

TO THE USER

This book should be read in sequence, from beginning to end. Each module builds on those that precede it to provide a solid understanding of networking security fundamentals. The book may also be used to prepare for CompTIA's Security+ certification exam. Appendix A pinpoints the modules and sections in which specific Security+ exam objectives are covered.

Hardware and Software Requirements

Following are the hardware and software requirements needed to perform the end-of-module Hands-On Projects.

- Microsoft Windows 10
- An Internet connection and web browser
- Microsoft Office

Free Downloadable Software Requirements

Free, downloadable software is required for the Hands-On Projects in the following modules.

Module 1:

- Microsoft Safety Scanner
- Oracle VirtualBox

Module 3:

- Refog Keylogger
- EICAR AntiVirus Test File

Module 4:

- ConfigureDefender

Module 5:

- Prey
- BlueStacksNorton Security (Android app)

Module 6:

- OpenPuff Steganography
- HashCalc
- Jetico BestCrypt

Module 7:

- Adobe Reader

Module 9:

- GlassWire

Module 10:

- VMware vCenter Converter

Module 11:

- NirSoft WifiInfoView
- Vistumbler

Module 12:

- BioID Facial Recognition Authenticator
- KeePass

Module 13:

- Directory Snoop

Module 14:

- UNetbootin
- Linux Mint

Module 15:

- Browzar

References

1. "2020 Cyberthreat defense report," *Cyberedge Group*, accessed Apr. 20, 2020, https://cyber-edge.com/cdr/.
2. Morgan, Steve, "2019 official annual cybercrime report," *Cybersecurity Ventures*, accessed Apr. 20, 2020, www
   .herjavecgroup.com/wp-content/uploads/2018/12/CV-HG-2019-Official-Annual-Cybercrime-Report.pdf.
3. "2020 Cyberthreat defense report," *Cyberedge Group*, accessed Apr. 20, 2020, https://cyber-edge.com/cdr/.

SECURITY FUNDAMENTALS

Relentless is perhaps the best way to describe today's cyberattacks. These attacks, directed against devices ranging from huge cloud computing servers to tiny Internet of Things (IoT) sensors, are designed to steal or manipulate the sensitive data stored in them. The modules in Part 1 introduce security and outline the causes of these attacks. The modules also discuss how to perform security evaluations to identify the weaknesses that need to be addressed to repel attacks.

MODULE 1
INTRODUCTION TO SECURITY

MODULE 2
THREAT MANAGEMENT AND CYBERSECURITY RESOURCES

PART 1

INTRODUCTION TO SECURITY

After completing this module, you should be able to do the following:

1. Define information security and explain why it is important
2. Identify threat actors and their attributes
3. Describe the different types of vulnerabilities and attacks
4. Explain the impact of attacks

Front-Page Cybersecurity

Threat actors have a long history of using current events to take advantage of distracted and unsuspecting users. For example, whenever a natural disaster such as a hurricane or flood occurs, unscrupulous attackers send out email messages with tempting subject lines such as "Contribute to Disaster Relief Here" or "These Flood Pictures Are Unbelievable!" These messages are, of course, intended to trick a user to open an email attachment that contains malware or click a hyperlink that redirects them to a malicious website.

The 2020 pandemic caused by the coronavirus disease (COVID-19) was no exception. Threat actors used this tragic worldwide event as cover for their attacks. A variety of campaigns distributed malware, stole user credentials, and scammed victims out of their money.

Many email scams offered to sell hard-to-find face masks or even medication to cure COVID-19 infections. Some scams asked for investments in fake companies that claimed to be developing vaccines, while other email scams asked for donations to fictitious charities, such as the World Health Community. (This organization does not exist, but the name is similar enough to the World Health Organization to cause confusion.)

Some malicious emails were designed to infect a victim's computer with malware. Email subject lines such as a "Breaking Coronavirus News Update" or "You Must Do This Right Now!" were common and caused anxious victims to open an attachment that infected their computer. Often emails that pretended to come from the Centers of Disease Control and Prevention (CDC) claimed to contain a list of new COVID-19 cases in the vicinity and included the instructions, "You are instructed to immediately read this list of cases to avoid potential hazards." Unfortunately, opening the attachment installed malware on the computer and stole user passwords.[1]

In one particularly egregious email attack, the threat actors claimed to have access to personal information about the email recipient, including where they lived. The attackers threatened to visit the user to infect them and their family with COVID-19 unless a ransom was paid online. Over a span of two days, this attack was detected more than 1,000 times.

Perhaps the award for the most innovative attack goes to the AI Corona Antivirus website. This site advertised "Corona Antivirus—World's best protection." Downloading and installing its digital "AI Corona Antivirus" would protect the computer from digital malware infections and keep the user from being infected by the biological COVID-19. In case someone might be skeptical that downloading and installing computer antivirus software would protect them from COVID-19, the website claimed proof that their product actually worked: "Our scientists from Harvard University have been working on a special AI development to combat the virus using a Windows app. Your PC actively protects you against the coronaviruses while the app is running."

However, downloading the AI Corona Antivirus software on a computer did not protect the user from the biological COVID-19—though it took several other actions. It turned the computer into a launching pad to attack other computers. It also took screenshots of what was displayed on the monitor, stole web browser cookies and saved passwords, installed a program to capture keystrokes, and even took any Bitcoin wallets saved on the computer.[2]

How many cyberattacks have you heard about over the past month? The past week? Even today? The number of attacks has reached astronomical proportions. According to one report, the number of new malware releases every month exceeds 20 million, and the total malware in existence is approaching 900 million instances.[3] In 2019, four out of every five organizations experienced at least one successful cyberattack, and more than one-third suffered six or more successful attacks.[4] It is estimated that by 2021, a business will fall victim to a ransomware attack once every 11 seconds. Cybercrime will cost the world $6 trillion annually by 2021, an increase of 100 percent in just six years, representing the greatest transfer of economic wealth in human history.[5] Compounding the problem, 85 percent of organizations are experiencing a shortfall of skilled security professionals.[6] The dismal numbers go on and on.

The need to identify and defend against these constant attacks has created an essential workforce that is now at the core of the information technology (IT) industry. Known as *information security,* personnel in this field are focused on protecting electronic information. Various elements of information security—such as *application security, infrastructure security, forensics and malware analysis,* and *security leadership*, along with several others—make up this workforce.

The information security workforce is usually divided into two broad categories. Information security *managerial personnel* administer and manage plans, policies, and people, while information security *technical personnel* are concerned with designing, configuring, installing, and maintaining technical security equipment. Within these two broad categories are four generally recognized types security positions:

- *Chief information security officer (CISO).* This person reports directly to the chief information officer (CIO). (Large enterprises may have more layers of management between this person and the CIO.) The CISO is responsible for assessing, managing, and implementing security.

- *Security manager.* The security manager reports to the CISO and supervises technicians, administrators, and security staff. Typically, a security manager works on tasks identified by the CISO and resolves issues identified by technicians. This position requires an understanding of configuration and operation but not necessarily technical mastery.

- *Security administrator.* The security administrator has both technical knowledge and managerial skills. A security administrator manages daily operations of security technology and may analyze and design security solutions within a specific entity as well as identifying users' needs.

- *Security technician.* This position is generally entry level for a person who has the necessary technical skills. Technicians provide technical support to configure security hardware, implement security software, and diagnose and troubleshoot problems.

NOTE 1

The job outlook for security professionals is exceptionally strong. According to the U.S. Bureau of Labor Statistics (BLS) "Occupational Outlook Handbook," the job outlook for information security analysts through 2024 is expected to grow by 18 percent, much faster than the average job growth rate.[8] One report states that by the end of the decade, demand for security professionals worldwide will rise to 6 million, with a projected shortfall of 1.5 million unfilled positions.[9]

As noted earlier, organizations have a desperate need for trained security personnel. The number of unfilled cybersecurity positions has increased by 50 percent since 2015.[7] By some estimates, 3.5 million positions will open by 2021.

When filling cybersecurity positions, an overwhelming majority of enterprises use the Computing Technology Industry Association (CompTIA) Security+ certification to verify security competency. Of the hundreds of security certifications currently available, Security+ is one of the most widely acclaimed security certifications.

Because it is internationally recognized as validating a foundation level of security skills and knowledge, the Security+ certification has become the foundation for today's IT security professionals.

NOTE 2

The value for an IT professional who holds a CompTIA security certification is significant. On average, an employee with a CompTIA certification commands a salary from 5 to 15 times higher than their counterparts with similar qualifications but lacking a certification.[10]

The CompTIA Security+ certification is a vendor-neutral credential that requires passing the current certification exam, SY0-601. A successful candidate has the knowledge and skills required to identify attacks, threats, and vulnerabilities; design a strong security architecture; implement security controls, be knowledgeable of security operations and incident response; and be well versed in governance, risk, and compliance requirements.

NOTE 3

The CompTIA Security+ certification meets the ISO 17024 standard and is approved by U.S. Department of Defense (DoD) to fulfill multiple levels of the DoD 8140 directive, which is an expansion of and replacement for the earlier DoD 8570 directive. This directive outlines which cybersecurity certifications are approved to validate the skills for certain job roles.

This module introduces the security fundamentals that form the basis of the Security+ certification. It begins by defining information security and then examines the attackers and how they function. It also covers vulnerabilities, categories of attacks, and the impacts of attacks.

WHAT IS INFORMATION SECURITY?

The first step in a study of information security is to define exactly what it is. This involves examining the definition of security and how it relates to information security.

Understanding Security

What is *security*? The word comes from Latin, meaning *free from care*. Sometimes security is defined as *the state of being free from danger*, which is the *goal* of security. It is also defined as the *measures taken to ensure safety*, which is the *process* of security. Since complete security can never be fully achieved, the focus of security is more often on the process instead of the goal. In this light, security can be defined as *the necessary steps to protect from harm*.

The relationship between *security* and *convenience* is *inversely proportional* (the symbol α), as illustrated in Figure 1-1: as security is increased, convenience is decreased. That is, the more secure something is, the less convenient it may become to use. Consider a house in which the homeowner installs an automated alarm system. The alarm requires a resident to enter a code on a keypad within 30 seconds of entering the house. Although the alarm system makes the house more secure, it is less convenient to race to the keypad than to casually walk into the house.

NOTE 4

Security is often described as *sacrificing convenience for safety.*

Defining Information Security

Several terms describe security in an IT environment: *computer security, IT security, cybersecurity,* and *information assurance*, to name just a few. Whereas each has its share of proponents and slight variations of meanings, the term *information security* may be the most appropriate because it is the broadest: protecting information from harm. Information security is often used to describe the tasks of securing digital information, whether it is manipulated by a microprocessor (such as on a personal computer), preserved on a storage device (such as a hard drive or USB flash drive), or transmitted over a network (such as a local area network or the Internet).

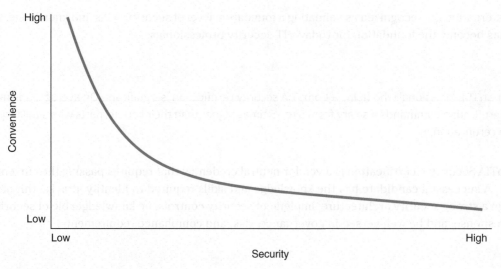

Figure 1-1   Relationship of security to convenience

> **⚠ CAUTION**   Information security should not be viewed as a war to win or lose. Just as crimes such as burglary can never be completely eradicated, neither can attacks against technology devices. The goal is not achieving complete victory but instead maintaining equilibrium: as attackers take advantage of a weakness in a defense, defenders must respond with an improved defense. Information security is an endless cycle between attacker and defender.

Information security cannot completely prevent successful attacks or guarantee that a system is totally secure, just as the security measures taken for a house can never guarantee complete safety from a burglar. The goal of information security is to ensure that protective measures are properly implemented to ward off attacks, prevent the total collapse of the system when a successful attack does occur, and recover as quickly as possible. Thus, information security is first *protection*.

Second, information security is intended to protect *information* that provides value to people and enterprises. Known as the *CIA Triad*, three protections must be extended over information:

1. *Confidentiality.* Only approved individuals should be able to access sensitive information. For example, the credit card number used to make an online purchase must be kept secure and unavailable to unapproved entities. *Confidentiality* ensures that only authorized parties can view the information. Providing confidentiality can involve several security tools, ranging from software to encrypt the credit card number stored on the web server to door locks to prevent access to those servers.

2. *Integrity. Integrity* ensures that the information is correct and no unauthorized person or malicious software has altered the data. In the example of an online purchase, an attacker who could change the amount of a purchase from $10,000.00 to $1.00 would violate the integrity of the information.

3. *Availability.* Information has value if the authorized parties who are assured of its integrity can access the information. *Availability* ensures that data is accessible to only authorized users and not to unapproved individuals. For example, the total number of items ordered as the result of an online purchase must be made available to an employee in a warehouse so that the correct items can be shipped to the customer, but the information should not be available to a competitor.

Because information is stored on computer hardware, manipulated by software, and transmitted by communications, each of these areas must be protected. The third objective of information security is to protect the integrity, confidentiality, and availability of information *on the devices that store, manipulate, and transmit the information*.

Protection is achieved through a process that combines three entities. As shown in Figure 1-2, information and hardware, software, and communications are protected in three layers: *products*, *people*, and *policies and procedures*. The procedures enable people to understand how to use products to protect information.

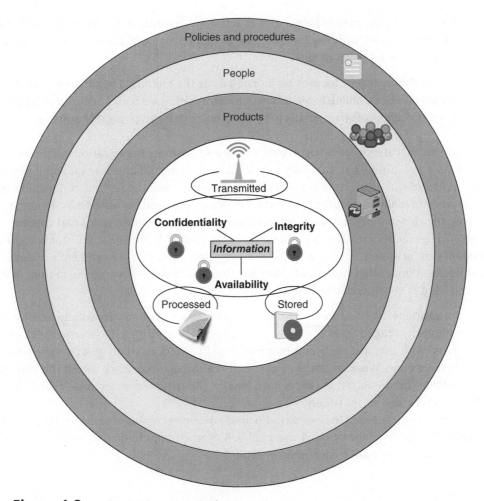

Figure 1-2 Information security layers

Thus, information security may be defined as *that which protects the integrity, confidentiality, and availability of information through products, people, and procedures on the devices that store, manipulate, and transmit the information.*

TWO RIGHTS & A WRONG

1. A security manager works on tasks identified by the CISO and resolves issues identified by technicians.
2. Since 2015, the number of unfilled cybersecurity positions has increased by 10 percent.
3. The relationship between security and convenience is inversely proportional: as security is increased, convenience is decreased.

See Appendix B for the answer.

WHO ARE THE THREAT ACTORS?

 CERTIFICATION

1.5 Explain different threat actors, vectors, and intelligence sources.

In cybersecurity, a **threat actor** (also called a *malicious actor*) is an individual or entity responsible for cyber incidents against the technology equipment of enterprises and users. The generic term *attacker* is also commonly used.

The very first cyberattacks were mainly for the threat actors to show off their technology skills (*fame*). However, that soon gave way to threat actors with the focused goal of financial gain (*fortune*). Financial cybercrime is often divided into three categories based on its targets:

- *Individual users*. The first category focuses on individuals as the victims. The threat actors steal and use stolen data, credit card numbers, online financial account information, or Social Security numbers to profit from their victims or send millions of spam emails to peddle counterfeit drugs, pirated software, fake watches, and pornography.
- *Enterprises*. The second category focuses on enterprises and business organizations. Threat actors attempt to steal research on a new product so that they can sell it to an unscrupulous foreign supplier who then builds an imitation model of the product to sell worldwide. This deprives the legitimate business of profits after investing hundreds of millions of dollars in product development, and because these foreign suppliers are in a different country, they are beyond the reach of domestic enforcement agencies and courts.
- *Governments*. Governments are also the targets of threat actors. If the latest information on a new missile defense system can be stolen, it can be sold—at a high price—to that government's enemies. In addition, government information is often stolen and published to embarrass the government in front of its citizens and force it to stop what is considered a nefarious action.

The **attributes**, or characteristic features, of the groups of threat actors can vary widely. Some groups have a high level of power and complexity (called **level of capability/sophistication**) with a massive network of resources, while others are "lone wolves" with minimal skills and no resources. In addition, some groups have deep **resources and funding** while others have none. Whereas some groups of threat actors may work within the enterprise (**internal**), others are strictly outside the organization (**external**). Finally, the **intent/motivation**—that is, the reason for the attacks—of the threat actors also varies widely.

In the past, the term **hacker** referred to a person who used advanced computer skills to attack computers. Because that title often carried a negative connotation, it was qualified in an attempt to distinguish between different types of the attackers. The types of hackers are summarized in Table 1-1.

Table 1-1   Types of hackers

Hacker Type	Description
Black hat hackers	Threat actors who violate computer security for personal gain (such as to steal credit card numbers) or to inflict malicious damage (corrupt a hard drive).
White hat hackers	Also known as *ethical attackers*, they attempt to probe a system (with an organization's permission) for weaknesses and then privately provide that information back to the organization.
Gray hat hackers	Attackers who attempt to break into a computer system without the organization's permission (an illegal activity) but not for their own advantage; instead, they publicly disclose the attack in order to shame the organization into taking action.

However, these broad categories of hackers no longer accurately reflect the differences between attackers. Today threat actors are classified in more distinct categories, such as script kiddies, hacktivists, state actors, insiders, and others.

Script Kiddies

Script kiddies are individuals who want to perform attacks, yet lack the technical knowledge to carry them out. Script kiddies instead do their work by downloading freely available automated attack software (*scripts*) and use it to perform malicious acts. Figure 1-3 illustrates a widely available software package that launches a sophisticated attack when a user simply makes selections from a menu. Due to their lack of knowledge, script kiddies are not always successful in penetrating defenses, but when they are, they may end up causing damage to systems and data instead of stealing the data.

Figure 1-3   Menu of attack tools

Hacktivists

Individuals that are strongly motivated by ideology (for the sake of their principles or beliefs) are **hacktivists** (a combination of the words *hack* and *activism*). Most hacktivists do not explicitly call themselves "hacktivists," but the term is commonly used by security researchers and journalists to distinguish them from other types of threat actors.

In the past, the types of attacks by hacktivists often involved breaking into a website and changing its contents as a means of making a political statement. (One hacktivist group changed the website of the U.S. Department of Justice to read *Department of Injustice*.) Other attacks were retaliatory: hacktivists have disabled a bank's website because the bank stopped accepting online payments deposited into accounts belonging to groups supported by the hacktivists. Today many hacktivists work through disinformation campaigns by spreading fake news and supporting conspiracy theories.

NOTE 5

Hacktivists were particularly active during the coronavirus disease (COVID-19) pandemic of 2020. One large group of what were considered far-right neo-Nazi hacktivists embarked on a months-long disinformation campaign designed to weaponize the pandemic by questioning scientific evidence and research. In another instance, thousands of breached email addresses and passwords from U.S. and global health organizations—including the U.S. National Institutes of Health, CDC, and the World Health Organization—were distributed on Twitter by these groups to harass and distract the health organizations.

State Actors

Instead of using an army to march across the battlefield to strike an adversary, governments are increasingly employing their own state-sponsored attackers for launching cyberattacks against their foes. These attackers are known as **state actors**. Their foes may be foreign governments or even citizens of their own nation that the government considers hostile or threatening. A growing number of attacks from state actors are directed toward businesses in foreign countries with the goal of causing financial harm or damage to the enterprise's reputation.

Many security researchers believe that state actors might be the deadliest of any threat actors. When fortune motivates a threat actor, but the target's defenses are too strong, the attacker simply moves on to another promising target with less effective defenses. State actors, however, have a specific target and keep working until they are successful. They are highly skilled and have enough government resources to breach almost any security defense.

State actors are often involved in multiyear intrusion campaigns targeting highly sensitive economic, proprietary, or national security information. The campaigns have created a new class of attacks called **advanced persistent threat (APT)**. The attacks use innovative tools (*advanced*) and once a system is infected, they silently extract data over an extended period of time (*persistent*). APTs are most commonly associated with state actors.

Insiders

Another serious threat to an enterprise comes from its own employees, contractors, and business partners, called *insiders*, who pose an **insider threat** of manipulating data from the position of a trusted employee. For example, a healthcare worker disgruntled about being passed over for a promotion might illegally gather health records on celebrities and sell them to the media, or a securities trader who loses billions of dollars on bad stock bets could use her knowledge of the bank's computer security system to conceal the losses through fake transactions. These attacks are harder to recognize because they come from within the enterprise, yet they may be costlier than attacks from the outside.

Six out of 10 enterprises reported being a victim of at least one insider attack during 2019. The focus of the insiders was intellectual property (IP) theft (43 percent), sabotage (41 percent), and espionage (32 percent).[11] Because most IP thefts occur within 30 days of an employee resigning, the insiders may believe that either the IP belongs to them instead of the enterprise or that they were not properly compensated for their work on the IP. In recent years, government insiders have stolen large volumes of sensitive information and then published it to alert its citizens of clandestine governmental actions.

Other Threat Actors

Other categories of threat actors are summarized in Table 1-2.

Table 1-2   Descriptions of other threat actors

Threat Actor	Description	Explanation
Competitors	Launch attacks against an opponent's system to steal classified information.	May steal new product research or a list of current customers to gain a competitive advantage.
Criminal syndicates	Move from traditional criminal activities to more rewarding and less risky online attacks.	Usually run by a small number of experienced online criminal networks that do not commit crimes themselves but act as entrepreneurs.
Shadow IT	Employees become frustrated with the slow pace of acquiring technology, so they purchase and install their own equipment or resources in violation of company policies.	Installing personal equipment, unauthorized software, or using external cloud resources can create a weakness or expose sensitive corporate data.
Brokers	Sell their knowledge of a weakness to other attackers or governments.	Individuals who uncover weaknesses do not report it to the software vendor but instead sell them to the highest bidder who is willing to pay a high price for the unknown weakness.
Cyberterrorists	Attack a nation's network and computer infrastructure to cause disruption and panic among citizens.	Targets may include a small group of computers or networks that can affect the largest number of users, such as the computers that control the electrical power grid of a state or region.

 **CAUTION**   Often the perception of an attacker by the general public is a "hacker in a hoodie," a disgruntled teenager looking for an easy target. Nothing could be further from the truth. Threat actors today generally have excellent technology skills, are tenacious, and have strong financial backing. Attackers have even modeled their work after modern economic theories (such as finding the optimum "price point" in which victims will pay a ransom) and software development (attack tools that threat actors sell are often software suites that receive regular updates). It is a serious mistake to underestimate modern threat actors.

TWO RIGHTS & A WRONG

1. Script kiddies are responsible for the class of attacks called advanced persistent threats.
2. Hacktivists are strongly motivated by ideology.
3. Brokers sell their knowledge of a weakness to other attackers or a government.

See Appendix B for the answer.

VULNERABILITIES AND ATTACKS

 **CERTIFICATION**

1.1 Compare and contrast different types of social engineering techniques.

1.5 Explain different threat actors, vectors, and intelligence sources.

1.6 Explain the security concerns associated with various types of vulnerabilities.

When exploiting vulnerabilities, threat actors use several avenues for their attacks. However, one of the most successful types of attack—social engineering—does not even exploit technology vulnerabilities. Regardless of how attacks occur, each successful attack has serious ramifications.

Vulnerabilities

A *vulnerability* (from Latin meaning *wound*) is defined as the state of being exposed to the possibility of being attacked or harmed. Cybersecurity vulnerabilities can be categorized into platforms, configurations, third parties, patches, and zero-day vulnerabilities.

Platforms

Several vulnerabilities are the result of the *platform* being used. (A computer platform is a system that consists of the hardware device and an operating system (OS) that runs software such as applications, programs, or processes.) Although all platforms have vulnerabilities to some degree, some platforms by their very nature have more serious vulnerabilities. These include legacy platforms, on-premises platforms, and cloud platforms.

Legacy Platforms   One type of platform that is well known for its vulnerabilities is a legacy platform. A legacy platform is no longer in widespread use, often because it has been replaced by an updated version of the earlier technology. Although legacy hardware introduces some vulnerabilities, more often vulnerabilities result from legacy software, such as an OS or program.

Modern OS software, such as Microsoft Windows, Apple macOS, and Linux, continually evolve and are updated with new enhancements and—most critically—fixes to uncovered vulnerabilities. For a variety of reasons—limited hardware capacity, an application that only operates on a specific OS version, or even neglect—an OS may not be updated, thus depriving it of these security fixes. This creates a legacy platform just asking to be attacked.

NOTE 6

Prior to Microsoft Windows 10, all versions of the OS had a *Fixed Lifecycle Policy* with published end-of-support dates. For instance, Windows 7 was first released in October 2009, it was no longer available for purchase in October 2016, and all support ceased in January 2020. Windows 10, however, introduced the *Modern Lifecycle Policy* in which Windows 10 versions receive continuous support and servicing.

On-Premises Platforms   Another platform that has significant vulnerabilities is the on-premises platform. On-premises ("on-prem") is the software and technology located within the physical confines of an enterprise, which is usually consolidated in the company's *data center*. At one time, the on-premises platform was considered the secure model of computing: an organization's servers and data were protected behind its firewalls to prevent attacks.

However, this model proved to be faulty. Organizations found that they had to add more servers, network resources, support for remote access, and new software to support emerging business processes and user needs. This often resulted in a hodgepodge of resources that were quickly provisioned but not adequately configured for security. In addition, numerous entry points from the outside into the on-premises platform (through USB flash drives, wireless network transmissions, mobile devices, and email messages, for example) made protecting the on-premises platform an ever-changing and never-ending challenge.

Cloud Platforms   Forty years ago, as computing technology became widespread, enterprises employed an on-premises model, in which they purchased all the hardware and software necessary to run the organization. As more resources were needed, more purchases were made, and more personnel were hired to manage the technology. Because this resulted in spiraling costs, some enterprises turned to *hosted services*.

In a hosted services environment, servers, storage, and the supporting networking infrastructure are shared by multiple enterprises over a remote network connection that has been contracted for a specific period of time. As more resources are needed (such as additional storage space or computing power), the enterprise contacts the hosted service, negotiates an additional fee, and signs a new contract for those new services.

Today a new model is gaining widespread use. Known as a cloud platform, this is a pay-per-use computing model in which customers pay only for the online computing resources they need. As computing needs increase or decrease, cloud computing resources can be scaled up or scaled back.

However, cloud platforms have proven to have significant vulnerabilities. The vulnerabilities are most often based on misconfigurations by the company personnel responsible for securing the cloud platform. Cloud resources are, by definition, accessible from virtually anywhere, putting cloud computing platforms constantly under attack from threat actors probing for vulnerabilities.

Configurations

Modern hardware and software platforms provide an array of features and security settings that must be properly configured to repel attacks. However, the configuration settings are often not properly implemented, resulting in weak configurations. Table 1-3 lists several weak configurations that can result in vulnerabilities.

Table 1-3   Weak configurations

Configuration	Explanation	Example
Default settings	Default settings are predetermined by the vendor for usability and ease of use (not for security) so the user can immediately begin using the product.	A router comes with a default password that is widely known.
Open ports and services	Devices and services are often configured to allow the most access so that the user can close ports that are specific to that organization.	A firewall comes with FTP ports 20 and 21 open.
Unsecured root accounts	A root account can give a user unfettered access to all resources.	A misconfigured cloud storage repository could give any user access to all data.

(continues)

Table 1-3   Weak configurations *(continued)*

Configuration	Explanation	Example
Open permissions	Open permissions are user access over files that should be restricted.	A user could be given *Read, Write*, and *Execute* privileges when she should have only *Read* privileges.
Unsecure protocols	Also called *insecure protocols,* this configuration uses protocols for telecommunications that do not provide adequate protections.	An employee could use devices that run services with unsecure protocols such as *Telnet* or *SNMPv1*.
Weak encryption	Users choosing a known vulnerable encryption mechanism.	A user could select an encryption scheme that has a known weakness or a key value that is too short.
Errors	Human mistakes in selecting one setting over another without considering the security implications.	An employee could use deprecated settings instead of current configurations.

Third Parties

Almost all businesses use external entities known as **third parties**. Examples of third parties are marketing agencies, landscapers, shredding contractors, and attorneys.

Many enterprises also use IT-related third parties due to their elevated level of expertise. For example, organizations often contract with third parties to assist them in developing and writing a software program or app. This is called **outsourced code development**. Also, many organizations rely on third-party **data storage** facilities for storing important data. This helps to reduce the capital expenditures associated with purchasing, installing, and managing new storage hardware and software but also can provide remote access to employees from almost any location.

With the sheer number of third parties used, it can be difficult to coordinate their diverse activities with the organization. **Vendor management** is the process organizations use to monitor and manage the interactions with all of their external third parties.

Almost all third parties today require access to the organization's computer network. Access gives external entities the ability to perform their IT-related functions (such as outsourced code development) and even do basic tasks such as submitting online invoices. Connectivity between the organization and the third party is known as **system integration**. However, the organization's systems are often not compatible with the third party's systems, requiring "workarounds," which can create vulnerabilities. In addition, not all organizations are equipped with the expertise to handle system integration (**lack of vendor support**).

One of the major risks of third-party system integration involves the principle of the weakest link. That is, if the security of the third party has any weaknesses, it can provide an opening for attackers to infiltrate the organization's computer network. This can be illustrated by a 2013 attack on the Target retail chain. A refrigeration, heating, and air-conditioning third-party subcontractor that worked at a number of Target stores and other top retailers was provided access to Target's corporate computer network. The access was intended to allow the subcontractor to monitor energy consumption and temperatures in the stores to save on costs and to alert store managers if the temperatures fluctuated outside of an acceptable range. However, threat actors were able to gain access to the third party's computer network and then pivot into the Target network, where they stole 40 million credit card numbers.

Patches

Early OSs were simply program loaders whose job was to launch applications. As more features and graphical user interfaces (GUIs) were added, OSs became more complex. The increased complexity introduced unintentional vulnerabilities that

NOTE 7

One of the most alarming recent unsecured root account vulnerabilities was revealed in 2017 on the Apple macOS High Sierra OS. A user could enter the word *root* in the username field of a login prompt, move the insertion point to the password field, and then press Enter. The user would then be logged in with root privileges.

NOTE 8

Microsoft's first operating system, MS-DOS v1.0, had 4,000 lines of code, while Windows 10 is estimated to have up to 50 million lines.

could be exploited by attackers. In addition, new attack tools made vulnerable what were once considered secure functions and services in operating systems.

To address the vulnerabilities in OSs that are uncovered after the software has been released, software developers usually deploy a software "fix." A fix can come in a variety of formats. A security **patch** is an officially released software security update intended to repair a vulnerability.

However, as important as patches are, they can create vulnerabilities:

- *Difficulty patching firmware.* **Firmware**, or software that is embedded into hardware, provides low-level controls and instructions for the hardware. Updating firmware to address a vulnerability can often be difficult and requires specialized steps. Furthermore, some firmware cannot be patched.
- *Few patches for application software.* Outside of the major application software such as Microsoft Office, patches for applications are uncommon. In most cases, no automated process can identify which computers have installed the application, alert users to a patch, or to distribute the patch.
- *Delays in patching OSs.* Modern operating systems—such as Red Hat Linux, Apple macOS, Ubuntu Linux, and Microsoft Windows—frequently distribute patches. These patches, however, can sometimes create new problems, such as preventing a custom application from running correctly. Many organizations test patches when they are released to ensure that they do not adversely affect any customized applications. In these instances, the organization delays installing a patch from the developer's online update service until the patch is thoroughly tested.

NOTE 9

A variation on a zero-day vulnerability is when the software developer is actively working on a patch, but the vulnerability is discovered by the threat actors who launch an attack before the patch is completed. This could occur when an independent security investigator instead of the software developer uncovers the vulnerability and then alerts the developer who begins work on a patch. However, in the interim, the information about the vulnerability leaks out or is even sold to attackers, who exploit the vulnerability while the developers rush to patch it.

Zero Day

As noted earlier, patches are created and distributed when the software developer learns of a vulnerability and corrects it. What happens if it is not the developer who uncovers the vulnerability, but a threat actor who finds it first? In this case, the vulnerability can be exploited by attackers before anyone else even knows it exists. This type of vulnerability is called a **zero day** because it provides zero days of warning.

Zero-day vulnerabilities are considered extremely serious: systems are open to attack with no specific patches available. However, other protections can mitigate a zero-day attack. For example, some protections use machine learning to collect data from previously detected exploits and create a baseline of safe system behavior that may help detect an attack based on a zero-day vulnerability.

Attack Vectors

An **attack vector** is a pathway or avenue used by a threat actor to penetrate a system. Although there are many specific types of attacks, like vulnerabilities, attack vectors can be grouped into the following general categories:

- *Email.* Almost 94 percent of all malware is delivered through email to an unsuspecting user.[12] The goal is to trick the user to open an attachment that contains malware or click a hyperlink that takes the user to a fictitious website.
- *Wireless.* Because wireless data transmissions "float" through the airwaves, they can be intercepted and read or altered by a threat actor if the transmission is not properly protected.
- *Removable media.* A removable media device, such as a USB flash drive, is a common attack vector. Threat actors have been known to infect USB flash drives with malware and leave them scattered in a parking lot or cafeteria. A well-intentioned employee will find the drive and insert it into his computer to determine its owner. However, once inserted, the USB flash drive will infect the computer.
- *Direct access.* A **direct access** vector occurs when a threat actor can gain direct physical access to the computer. Once the attacker can "touch" the machine, she can insert a USB flash drive with an alternative operating system and reboot the computer under the alternate OS to bypass the security on the computer.

- *Social media.* Threat actors often use social media as a vector for attacks. For example, an attacker may read social media posts to determine when an employee will be on vacation and then call the organization's help desk pretending to be that employee to ask for "emergency" access to an account.
- *Supply chain.* A **supply chain** is a network that moves a product from the supplier to the customer and is made up of vendors that supply raw material, manufacturers who convert the material into products, warehouses that store products, distribution centers that deliver them to the retailers, and retailers who bring the product to the consumer. Today's supply chains are global in scope: manufacturers are usually thousands of miles away overseas and not under the direct supervision of the enterprise selling the product. The fact that products move through many steps in the supply chain—and that some steps are not closely supervised—has opened the door for malware to be injected into products during their manufacturing or storage (called *supply chain infections*). Supply chains also serve as third-party vulnerabilities.

> **⊘ CAUTION** Supply chain infections are considered especially dangerous. Users are receiving infected devices at the point of purchase, unaware that a brand-new device may be infected. Also, there is rarely any way to contact users and inform them of an infected device. Because it is virtually impossible to closely monitor every step in the global supply chain, these infections cannot be easily prevented.

- *Cloud.* As enterprises move their computing resources to remote cloud servers and storage devices, threat actors take advantage of the complexity of these systems to find security weaknesses.

Social Engineering Attacks

Not all attacks rely on technology vulnerabilities; in fact, some cyberattacks use little if any technology to achieve their goals. **Social engineering** is a means of **eliciting information** (gathering data) by relying on the weaknesses of individuals. Information elicitation may be the goal of the attack, or the information may then be used for other attacks. Social engineering is also used as **influence campaigns** to sway attention and sympathy in a particular direction. These campaigns can be found exclusively on social media (**social media influence campaign**) or may be combined with other sources (**hybrid warfare influence campaign**).

Social engineering attacks usually rely on psychological principles. They also can involve physical procedures.

Psychological Principles

Many social engineering attacks rely on psychology to affect others mentally and emotionally rather than physically. At its core, social engineering relies on an attacker's clever manipulation of human nature to persuade the victim to provide information or take actions. Several basic principles make psychological social engineering highly effective. These are listed in Table 1-4 with the example of an attacker pretending to be the chief executive officer (CEO) calling the organization's help desk to reset a password.

Table 1-4   Social engineering effectiveness

Principle	Description	Example
Authority	To impersonate an authority figure or falsely cite their authority	"I'm the CEO calling."
Intimidation	To frighten and coerce by threat	"If you don't reset my password, I will call your supervisor."
Consensus	To influence by what others do	"I called last week, and your colleague reset my password."

(continues)

Table 1-4 Social engineering effectiveness *(continued)*

Principle	Description	Example
Scarcity	To refer to something in short supply	"I can't waste time here."
Urgency	To demand immediate action	"My meeting with the board starts in five minutes."
Familiarity	To give the impression the victim is well known and well received	"I remember reading a good evaluation on you."
Trust	To inspire confidence	"You know who I am."

Another technique is called **prepending**, which is influencing the subject before the event occurs. A common general example is a preview of a soon-to-be-released movie that begins with the statement, "The best film you will see this year!" By starting with the desired outcome ("The best film"), the statement influences the listener to think that way. Threat actors use prepending with social engineering attacks, such as including the desired outcome in a statement that uses the urgency principle, as in "You need to reset my password immediately because my meeting with the board starts in five minutes."

Because many of the psychological approaches involve person-to-person contact, attackers use a variety of techniques to gain trust. For example:

- *Provide a reason.* Many social engineering threat actors are careful to add a reason along with their request. Giving a rationalization and using the word "because" makes it more likely the victim will provide the information. For example, *I was asked to call you because the director's office manager is out sick today.*
- *Project confidence.* A threat agent is unlikely to generate suspicion if she enters a restricted area by calmly walking through the building as if she knows exactly where she going (without looking at signs, down hallways, or reading door labels) and even greeting people she sees with a friendly *Hi, how are you doing?*
- *Use evasion and diversion.* When challenged, threat agents might evade a question by giving a vague or irrelevant answer. They could also feign innocence or confusion, or keep denying allegations, until the victim eventually believes his suspicions are wrong. Sometimes a threat agent can resort to anger and cause the victim to drop the challenge. *Who are you to ask that? Connect me with your supervisor immediately!*
- *Make them laugh.* Humor is an excellent tool to put people at ease and to develop a sense of trust. *I can't believe I left my badge in my office again! You know, some mistakes are too much fun to make only once!*

Social engineering psychological approaches often involve impersonation, phishing, redirection, spam, hoaxes, and watering hole attacks.

Impersonation   Social engineering **impersonation** (also called **identity fraud**) is masquerading as a real or fictitious character and then playing the role of that person with a victim. For example, an attacker could impersonate a help desk support technician who calls the victim, pretends that there is a problem with the network, and asks for her username and password to reset the account. Sometimes the goal of the impersonation is to obtain private information (**pretexting**).

 **CAUTION**   Common roles that are often impersonated include a repair person, an IT support technician, a manager, or a trusted third party. Often attackers impersonate individuals whose roles are authoritative because victims generally resist saying "no" to anyone in power. Users should exercise caution when receiving a phone call or email from these types of people asking for something suspicious.

To impersonate real people, the threat actor must know as much about them as possible to appear genuine. This type of **reconnaissance** is called **credential harvesting** and is typically carried out by Internet and social media searches.

Phishing   One of the most common forms of social engineering is phishing. **Phishing** is sending an email message or displaying a web announcement that falsely claims to be from a legitimate enterprise in an attempt to trick the user into surrendering private information or taking action. Users are asked to respond to an email message or are directed to a website where they are requested to update personal information, such as passwords, credit card numbers, Social Security numbers, bank account numbers, or other information. However, the email or website is actually an imposter site set up to steal the information the user enters. Users may also receive a fictitious overdue invoice that demands immediate payment and, in haste, make the payment (called an **invoice scam**).

Whereas at one time phishing messages were easy to spot due to misspelled words and obvious counterfeit images, that is no longer the case. In fact, one reason that phishing is so successful today is that the emails and the fake websites are difficult to distinguish from legitimate ones: logos, color schemes, and wording seem to be almost identical. Figure 1-4 illustrates an actual phishing email message that looks like it came from a legitimate source.

> **NOTE 10**
>
> The word *phishing* is a variation on the word "fishing," to reflect the idea that bait is thrown out knowing that while most will ignore it, some will bite.

Figure 1-4 Phishing email message

Source: Email message sent to Dr. Mark Revels

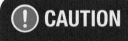 **CAUTION** Phishing is also used to validate email addresses. A phishing email message can display an image retrieved from a website and requested when the user opens the email message. A unique code links the image to the recipient's email address, which then tells the phisher that the email address is active and valid. This is the reason most email today does not automatically display images received in emails. Users should be cautious in displaying images in email messages.

The following are several variations on phishing attacks:

- *Spear phishing*. Whereas phishing involves sending millions of generic email messages to users, **spear phishing** targets specific users. The emails used in spear phishing are customized to the recipients, including their names and personal information, to make the message appear legitimate.
- *Whaling*. One type of spear phishing is **whaling**. Instead of going after the "smaller fish," whaling targets the "big fish"—namely, wealthy individuals or senior executives within a business who typically have large sums of money in a bank account that an attacker could access if the attack is successful. By focusing on this smaller

group, the attacker can invest more time in the attack and finely tune the message to achieve the highest likelihood of success.

- *Vishing.* Instead of using email to contact the potential victim, attackers can use phone calls. Known as **vishing** (*v*oice ph*ishing*), an attacker calls a victim who, upon answering, hears a recorded message that pretends to be from the user's bank stating that her credit card has experienced fraudulent activity or that her bank account has had unusual activity. The victim is instructed to call a specific phone number immediately (which has been set up by the attacker). When the victim calls, it is answered by automated instructions telling her to enter her credit card number, bank account number, Social Security number, or other information on the phone's keypad.
- *Smishing.* A variation on vishing uses short message service (SMS) text messages and callback recorded phone messages. This is known as **smishing**. The threat actors first send a text message to a user's cell phone that pretends to come from their bank saying that their account has been broken into or their credit card number has been stolen. Along with the text message is a callback telephone number the customer is instructed to call immediately. That phone number plays a recording telling the customer to enter their Social Security number or credit card number for verification. The attackers then simply capture the information the user enters.

Phishing continues to be a primary weapon used by threat actors. Phishing is considered to be one of the largest and most consequential cyber threats facing both businesses and consumers. During the third quarter of 2019, phishing attacks increased by 46 percent from the previous quarter and almost doubled the number recorded during the fourth quarter of the previous year. One nation saw a 232 percent increase in phishing during 2019.[13] It is estimated that these trends will continue.

 **CAUTION**
> Although most web browsers automatically block known phishing websites, because so many sites are appearing so rapidly, it is difficult for the browsers to stay up to date. Users should remain constantly vigilant to guard against phishing attacks.

NOTE 11

The cost of typo squatting is significant because of frequent misspellings. In one month, the typo squatting site *goggle.com* received almost 825,000 unique visitors. It is estimated that typo squatting costs the 250 top websites $285 million annually in lost sales and other expenses.[14]

NOTE 12

An increasing number of registered attacker domains are the result of bitsquatting, such as *aeazon.com* (for *amazon .com*) and *microsmft.com* (for *microsoft.com*). Security researchers found that 20 percent of a sample of 433 registered attacker domains were the result of bitsquatting.[15]

Redirection If threat actors cannot trick a user to visit a malicious website through phishing, they can use other tactics to redirect the user.

What happens if a user makes a typing error when entering a uniform resource locator (URL) address in a web browser, such as typing *goggle.com* (a misspelling) or *google.net* (incorrect domain) instead of the correct *google.com*? In the past, an error message like *HTTP Error 404 Not Found* would appear. However, today the user is often directed to a fake lookalike site filled with ads for which the attacker receives money for traffic generated to the site. These fake sites exist because attackers purchase the domain names of sites that are spelled similarly to actual sites. This is called **typo squatting**. A well-known site such as *google.com* may have to deal with more than 1,000 typo squatting domains.

Enterprises have tried to preempt typo squatting by registering the domain names of close spellings of their website. At one time, top-level domains (TLDs) were limited to .com, .org, .net, .int, .edu, .gov, and .mil, so it was fairly easy to register close-sounding domain names. However, today there are more than 1,200 generic TLDs (gTLDs), such as .museum, .office, .global, and .school. Organizations must now attempt to register many sites that are a variation of their registered domain name.

In addition to registering names similar to the actual names (like *goggle.com* for *google.com*), threat actors are registering domain names that are *one bit* different. The billions of devices that are part of the Internet have multiple instances of a domain name in a domain name server (DNS) memory at any time, increasing the likelihood of a RAM memory error that involves a bit being "flipped." Figure 1-5 illustrates that the change of one bit in the letter *g* (0110011*1*) results in the change of the entire character from *g* to *f*. In this example, a threat agent would register the domain *foo.gl* as a variation of the actual *goo.gl*.

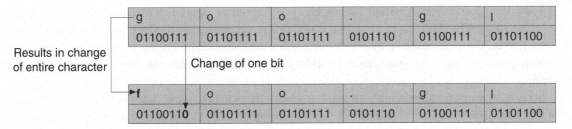

Figure 1-5   Character change by bit flipping

Another redirection technique is pharming. Pharming attempts to exploit how a URL such as www.cengage.com is converted into its corresponding IP address *69.32.308.75*. A threat actor may install malware on a user's computer that redirects traffic away from its intended target to a fake website instead. Another technique is to infect a DNS that would direct multiple users to inadvertently visit the fake site.

Spam   Spam is unsolicited email that is sent to a large number of recipients. Users receive so many spam messages because sending spam is lucrative. It costs spammers very little to send millions of spam email messages. Almost all spam is sent from botnets, and a spammer who does not own his own botnet can lease time from other attackers ($40 per hour) to use a botnet of up to 100,000 infected computers to launch a spam attack. Even if spammers receive only a small percentage of responses, they still make a large profit. For example, if a spammer sent spam to 6 million users for a product with a sale price of $50 that cost only $5 to make, and if only 0.001 percent of the recipients responded and bought the product (a typical response rate), the spammer would still make more than $270,000 in profit.

Text-based spam messages that include words such as *Viagra* or *investments* can easily be trapped by filters that look for these words and block the email. Because of the increased use of these filters, spammers have turned to *image spam*, which uses graphical images of text in order to circumvent text-based filters. Image spam cannot be filtered based on the textual content of the message because it appears as an image instead of text. These spam messages often include nonsense text so that it appears the email message is legitimate (an email with no text can prompt the spam filter to block it). Figure 1-6 shows an example of an image spam.

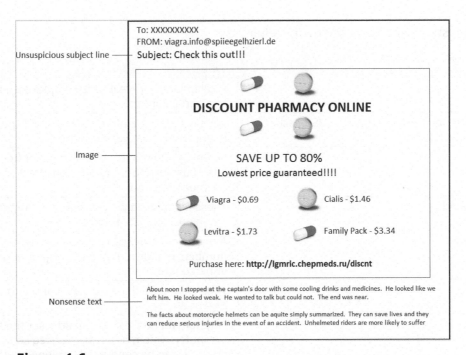

Figure 1-6   Image spam

Spim is spam delivered through instant messaging (IM) instead of email. For threat actors, spim can have even more impact than spam. The immediacy of instant messages makes users more likely to reflexively click embedded links in a spim. Furthermore, because spim may bypass some antimalware defenses, spim can more easily distribute malware. As antispam measures for email are more widely implemented, more spammers may be inclined to migrate to sending spim.

Beyond being annoying and interfering with work productivity as users spend time reading and deleting spam messages, spam and spim can be security vulnerabilities. This is because they can be used to distribute malware. Messages sent with attachments that contain malware are common means by which threat actors distribute their malware today.

Hoaxes   Threat agents can use hoaxes as a first step in an attack. A **hoax** is a false warning, often contained in an email message claiming to come from the IT department. The hoax purports that there is a "deadly virus" circulating through the Internet and that the recipient should erase specific files or change security configurations and then forward the message to other users. However, changing configurations allows an attacker to compromise the system. And erasing files may make the computer unstable, prompting the victim to call the phone number in the hoax email message for help, which is actually the phone number of the attacker.

Watering Hole Attack   In the natural world, similar types of animals are known to congregate around a pool of water for refreshment. In a similar manner, a **watering hole attack** is directed toward a smaller group of specific individuals, such as the major executives working for a manufacturing company. These executives all tend to visit a common website, such as that of a parts supplier to the manufacturer. An attacker who wants to target this group of executives tries to determine the common website that they frequent and then infects it with malware that will make its way onto the group's computers.

Physical Procedures

While some social engineering attacks rely on psychological manipulation, other attacks rely on physical acts. These attacks take advantage of user actions that can result in compromised security. Three of the most common physical procedures are dumpster diving, tailgating, and shoulder surfing.

Dumpster Diving   **Dumpster diving** involves digging through trash receptacles to find information that can be useful in an attack. Table 1-5 lists the different items that can be retrieved—many of which appear to be useless—and how they can be used.

Table 1-5   Dumpster diving items and their usefulness

Item retrieved	Why useful
Calendars	A calendar can reveal which employees are out of town at a particular time.
Inexpensive computer hardware, such as USB flash drives or portal hard drives	These devices are often improperly disposed of and might contain valuable information.
Memos	Seemingly unimportant memos can often provide small bits of useful information for an attacker who is building an impersonation.
Organizational charts	These identify individuals within the organization who are in positions of authority.
Phone directories	A phone directory can provide the names and telephone numbers of individuals in the organization to target or impersonate.
Policy manuals	These may reveal the true level of security within the organization.
System manuals	A system manual can tell an attacker the type of computer system that is being used so that other research can be conducted to pinpoint vulnerabilities.

An electronic variation of physical dumpster diving is to use the Google search engine to look for documents and data posted online that can be used in an attack. This is called *Google dorking*, and it uses advanced Google search techniques to look for information that unsuspecting victims have carelessly posted on the web.

For example, to find on the web any Microsoft Excel spreadsheets (.xlsx) that contain the column heading "SSN" (Social Security number), the Google search term *intext:"SSN" filetype:xlsx* can be used, or to find any Microsoft Word documents (.docx) that contained the word "passwords" as part of the title, the Google search term *allintitle: "passwords" filetype:docx* is used.

NOTE 13

Google dorking is from a slang term that originally was used to refer to someone who is not considered intelligent (a *dork*) and later came to refer to uncovering security vulnerabilities that are the result of the actions of such a person.

Tailgating   Organizations can invest tens of thousands of dollars to install specialized doors that permit access only to authorized users who possess a special card or who can enter a specific code. These automated access control systems are designed to restrict entry into an area. However, a weakness of these systems is that they cannot always control *how many* people enter the building when access is allowed; once an authorized person opens the door, one or more individuals can follow behind and also enter. This is known as tailgating.

The following are several ways tailgating can occur:

- A tailgater waits at the end of the sidewalk until an authorized user opens the door. She then calls out to him to "Please hold the door!" as she hurries to enter. In most cases, good etiquette wins out over good security practices, and the door is held open for the tailgater.
- A tailgater waits near the outside of the door and then quickly enters once the authorized employee leaves the area. This technique is used most commonly during weekends and at nights, where the actions of the more overt tailgater would be suspicious.
- A tailgater stands outside the door and waits until an employee exits the building. He then slips behind the person as he is walking away and grabs the door just before it closes to gain access to the building.
- An employee conspires with an unauthorized person to allow him to walk in with him through the open door (called *piggybacking*).

Shoulder Surfing   If an attacker cannot enter a building as a tailgater without raising suspicion, an alternative is to watch an individual entering the security code on a keypad. Known as shoulder surfing, this technique can be used in any setting that allows an attacker to casually observe someone entering secret information, such as the security codes on a door keypad. Attackers are also using webcams and smartphone cameras to "shoulder surf" users of ATM machines to record keypad entries.

> 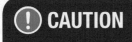 **CAUTION**   A defense against shoulder surfing is an application that uses the computer's web cam to watch if anyone nearby is looking at the computer screen. If someone is detected, the user can be alerted with a popup window message or the screen will automatically blur so that it cannot be read.

Impacts of Attacks

A successful attack always results in several negative impacts. These impacts can be classified as data impacts and effects on the organization.

Data Impacts

Whereas the goal of some attacks may be harm to a system, such as manipulating an industrial control system to shut down a water filtration facility, most attacks focus on data as the primary target. The consequences of a successful attack on data are listed in Table 1-6.

Effects on the Enterprise

A successful attack can also have grave consequences for an enterprise. First, the attack may make systems inaccessible (availability loss). This results in lost productivity, which can affect the normal tasks for generating income (financial loss).

Table 1-6 Consequences of data attack

Impact	Description	Example
Data loss	Destroying data so that it cannot be recovered	Maliciously erasing patient data used for cancer research
Data exfiltration	Stealing data to distribute it to other parties	Taking a list of current customers and selling it to a competitor
Data breach	Stealing data to disclose it in an unauthorized fashion	Stealing credit card numbers to sell to other threat actors
Identity theft	Taking personally identifiable information to impersonate someone	Stealing a Social Security number to secure a bank loan in the victim's name

One of the most devastating effects is on the public perception of the enterprise (**reputation**). If an organization is the victim of an attack that steals customer data, the public blames the organization and forms a serious negative impression. Many current customers will become disgruntled at the perceived lack of security at the organization and move their business to a competitor.

TWO RIGHTS & A WRONG

1. Spear phishing targets specific users.
2. "I'm the CEO calling" is an example of the psychological principle of authority.
3. The goal of impersonation is often prepending, which is obtaining private information.

See Appendix B for the answer.

VM LAB   You're now ready to complete the live, virtual machine labs for this module. The labs can be found in each module in the MindTap.

SUMMARY

- Attacks against information security have grown astronomically in recent years. Eighty percent of organizations have experienced at least one successful attack in a single year, with many organizations suffering multiple successful attacks annually. Compounding the problem is a serious shortfall of skilled security professionals.
- The information security workforce is usually divided into two broad categories. Information security managerial personnel administer and manage plans, policies, and people, while information security technical personnel are concerned with designing, configuring, installing, and maintaining technical security equipment.
- The CompTIA Security+ certification is a vendor-neutral credential that requires passing the current certification exam, SY0-601. A successful candidate has the knowledge and skills required to identify attacks, threats, and vulnerabilities; design a strong security architecture; implement security controls, be knowledgeable of security operations and incident response; and be well versed in governance, risk, and compliance requirements.
- Security can be defined as the necessary steps to protect from harm. The relationship between security and convenience is inversely proportional: as security is increased, convenience is decreased. Information security protects the integrity, confidentiality, and availability of information through products, people, and procedures on the devices that store, manipulate, and transmit the information.
- The threat actors, or individuals behind computer attacks, fall into several categories and exhibit different attributes. Some groups have a high level of power and complexity with a massive network of resources,

while others work alone and have minimal skills and no resources. Some groups have deep resources and funding while others have none. Certain threat actors are internal and work within the enterprise, and others are strictly outside the organization. The intent and motivation, or the reasons for the attacks, vary widely.

- Script kiddies do their work by downloading automated attack software from websites and then using it to break into computers. Hacktivists are strongly motivated by their ideology and often attack to make a political statement. State actors are employed by governments as state-sponsored attackers for launching computer attacks against foes. Other threat actors include competitors, criminal syndicates, shadow IT, brokers, and cyberterrorists.

- Cybersecurity vulnerabilities are often categorized into five broad categories: platforms, configurations, third parties, patches, and zero-day vulnerabilities. Several vulnerabilities are the result of the platform being used. Legacy or outdated platforms have not been updated and are prime targets for attacks. On-premises platforms are located within the physical confines of an enterprise, which are usually consolidated in the company's data center. Due to the rapid provisioning of resources, on-premises platforms are often not adequately configured for security. Cloud platforms are proven to have significant vulnerabilities. These vulnerabilities are most often based on misconfigurations by company personnel responsible for securing the cloud platform.

- Modern hardware and software platforms provide a wide array of features and security settings, and these must be properly configured to repel attacks. Unfortunately, the configuration settings are not always properly implemented, resulting in weak configurations. Many enterprises also use IT-related third parties due to their elevated level of expertise. Almost all third parties require access to the organization's computer network. However, often the organization's systems are not compatible with the third party's systems and require work-arounds, which can create vulnerabilities. A security patch is an officially released software security update intended to repair a vulnerability. However, as important as patches are, they can create vulnerabilities. A zero-day vulnerability has no advance warning because there has been no previous knowledge of the vulnerability.

- An attack vector is a pathway or avenue used by a threat actor to penetrate a system. Although there are many specific types of attacks, vectors can be grouped into general categories. These include email, wireless, removable media, direct access, social media, supply chain, and cloud.

- Social engineering is a means of eliciting information (gathering data) by relying on the weaknesses of individuals. Information elicitation may be the goal of the attack, or the information may be used for other attacks. Many social engineering attacks rely on psychology, which involves taking a mental and emotional approach—rather than a physical approach—to gathering data. At its core, social engineering relies on an attacker's clever manipulation of human nature to persuade the victim to provide information or take actions. Social engineering psychological approaches often involve impersonation, phishing, redirection, spam, hoaxes, and watering hole attacks. Some social engineering attacks rely on physical acts. These attacks take advantage of user actions that can result in compromised security. Three of the most common physical procedures are dumpster diving, tailgating, and shoulder surfing.

- A successful attack always results in several negative impacts. Most attacks focus on data as the primary target. The consequences of a successful attack on data are data loss, data exfiltration, data breach, and identity theft. A successful attack can also have significant consequences for an enterprise. Systems may be rendered inaccessible, which results in lost productivity and impacts the normal tasks for generating income. One of the most devastating effects is on the public perception of the enterprise, or its reputation. An organization that is the victim of an attack in which customer data is stolen faces a serious negative impression in the eye of the public.

Key Terms

advanced persistent threat (APT)	competitors	data storage
attack vector	consensus	default settings
attributes	credential harvesting	direct access
authority	criminal syndicates	dumpster diving
availability loss	data breach	eliciting information
black hat hackers	data exfiltration	errors
cloud platforms	data loss	external

familiarity
financial loss
firmware
gray hat hackers
hacker
hacktivists
hoax
hybrid warfare influence campaign
identity fraud (also called
   impersonation)
identity theft
impersonation (also called
   identity fraud)
influence campaigns
insider threat
intent/motivation
internal
intimidation
invoice scam
lack of vendor support
legacy platform

level of capability/sophistication
on-premises platform
open permissions
open ports and services
outsourced code development
patch
pharming
phishing
prepending
pretexting
reconnaissance
reputation
resources and funding
scarcity
script kiddies
shadow IT
shoulder surfing
smishing
social engineering
social media influence campaign
spam

spear phishing
spim
state actors
supply chain
system integration
tailgating
third parties
threat actor
trust
typo squatting
unsecure protocols
unsecured root accounts
urgency
vendor management
vishing
watering hole attack
weak configurations
weak encryption
whaling
white hat hackers
zero day

Review Questions

1. After Bella earned her security certification, she was offered a promotion. As she reviewed the job responsibilities, she saw that in this position she will report to the CISO and supervise a group of security technicians. Which of these generally recognized security positions has she been offered?
   a. Security administrator
   b. Security technician
   c. Security officer
   d. Security manager

2. Which of the following is false about the CompTIA Security+ certification?
   a. Security+ is one of the most widely acclaimed security certifications.
   b. Security+ is internationally recognized as validating a foundation level of security skills and knowledge.
   c. The Security+ certification is a vendor-neutral credential.
   d. Professionals who hold the Security+ certification earn about the same or slightly less than security professionals who have not achieved this certification.

3. Which of the following is true regarding the relationship between security and convenience?
   a. Security and convenience are inversely proportional.
   b. Security and convenience have no relationship.

   c. Security is less important than convenience.
   d. Security and convenience are equal in importance.

4. Which of the following of the CIA Triad ensures that information is correct, and no unauthorized person has altered it?
   a. Confidentiality
   b. Integrity
   c. Availability
   d. Assurance

5. Which of the following is *not* used to describe those who attack computer systems?
   a. Threat actor
   b. Hacker
   c. Malicious agent
   d. Attacker

6. Which of the following is *not* true regarding security?
   a. Security is a goal.
   b. Security includes the necessary steps to protect from harm.
   c. Security is a process.
   d. Security is a war that must be won at all costs.

7. Luna is reading a book about the history of cybercrime. She read that the very first cyberattacks were mainly for what purpose?
   a. Fortune
   b. Fame

    c. Financial gain

    d. Personal security

8. Which of the following ensures that only authorized parties can view protected information?

    a. Authorization

    b. Confidentiality

    c. Availability

    d. Integrity

9. Which type of hacker will probe a system for weaknesses and then privately provide that information back to the organization?

    a. Black hat hackers

    b. White hat hackers

    c. Gray hat hackers

    d. Red hat hackers

10. Complete this definition of information security: *That which protects the integrity, confidentiality, and availability of information* _____.

    a. *on electronic digital devices and limited analog devices that can connect via the Internet or through a local area network.*

    b. *through a long-term process that results in ultimate security.*

    c. *using both open-sourced as well as supplier-sourced hardware and software that interacts appropriately with limited resources.*

    d. *through products, people, and procedures on the devices that store, manipulate, and transmit the information.*

11. Which of the following groups have the lowest level of technical knowledge?

    a. Script kiddies

    b. Hacktivists

    c. State actors

    d. Insiders

12. Which of the following groups use advanced persistent threats?

    a. Brokers

    b. Criminal syndicates

    c. Shadow IT

    d. State actors

13. Which of the following is *not* a reason a legacy platform has not been updated?

    a. Limited hardware capacity

    b. An application only operates on a specific OS version

    c. Neglect

    d. No compelling reason for any updates

14. How do vendors decide which should be the default settings on a system?

    a. Those that are the most secure are always the default settings.

    b. There is no reason specific default settings are chosen.

    c. Those settings that provide the means by which the user can immediately begin to use the product.

    d. The default settings are always mandated by industry standards.

15. Which tool is most commonly associated with state actors?

    a. Closed-Source Resistant and Recurrent Malware (CSRRM)

    b. advanced persistent threat (APT)

    c. Unlimited Harvest and Secure Attack (UHSA)

    d. Network Spider and Worm Threat (NSAWT)

16. What is the term used to describe the connectivity between an organization and a third party?

    a. System integration

    b. Platform support

    c. Resource migration

    d. Network layering

17. What is an objective of state-sponsored attackers?

    a. To right a perceived wrong

    b. To amass fortune over of fame

    c. To spy on citizens

    d. To sell vulnerabilities to the highest bidder

18. Which of the following is *not* an issue with patching?

    a. Difficulty patching firmware

    b. Few patches exist for application software

    c. Delays in patching OSs

    d. Patches address zero-day vulnerabilities

19. Which of the following is *not* a recognized attack vector?

    a. Supply chain

    b. Social media

    c. On-prem

    d. Email

20. What is the category of threat actors that sell their knowledge of vulnerabilities to other attackers or governments?

    a. Cyberterrorists

    b. Competitors

    c. Brokers

    d. Resource managers

Hands-On Projects

Project 1-1: Examine Data Breaches—Visual

Time Required: 15 minutes

Objective: Explain the security concerns associated with various types of vulnerabilities.

Description: In this project, you use a visual format to view the biggest data breaches resulting in stolen information.

1. Open your web browser and enter the URL **www.informationisbeautiful.net/visualizations/worlds-biggest-data-breaches-hacks/** (If you are no longer able to access the site through this web address, use a search engine to search for "Information Is Beautiful World's Biggest Data Breaches & Hacks.")

2. This site will display a visual graphic of the data breaches, as shown in Figure 1-7.

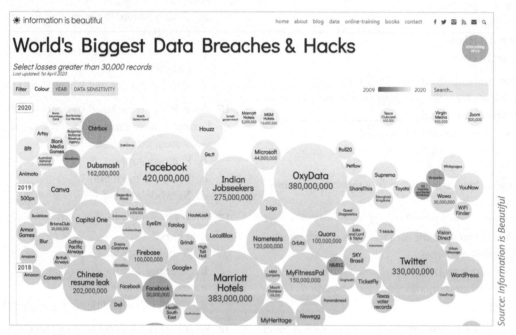

Figure 1-7   World's biggest data breaches & hacks webpage

Source: Information is Beautiful

3. Scroll down the page to view the data breaches by year. Note that the size of the breach is indicated by the size of the bubble.

4. Scroll back up to the top.

5. Hover over several of the bubbles to read a quick story of the breach.

6. Note the color of the bubbles that have an "Interesting Story." Click one of the bubbles and read the story. When finished, close only the interesting story tab in your browser.

7. Click the **Data Sensitivity** button on the World's Biggest Data Breaches & Hacks page. Note the color legend from Low to High that indicates how sensitive the data was.

8. Click the **Year** button to return to the original screen.

9. Click the **Filter** button to display the filter menu.

10. Under Sector, click **healthcare** to view those breaches related to the healthcare industry.

11. Click one of the bubbles and read the story.

12. Click **Reset** in the filter menu.

13. Select the sector **financial**.

14. Select the method **poor security**.

15. Click one of the bubbles and read the story.

16. Create your own filters to view different types of breaches. Does this graphic convey a compelling story of data breaches?

17. How does this visualization help you with the understanding of threats?

18. Close all windows.

Project 1-2: Scan for Malware Using the Microsoft Safety Scanner

Time Required: 15 minutes

Objective: Given a scenario, analyze potential indicators to determine the type of attack.

Description: In this project, you download and run the Microsoft Safety Scanner to determine if there is any malware on the computer.

1. Determine which system type of Windows you are running. Click **Start**, **Settings**, **System**, and then **About**. Look under System type for the description.
2. Open your web browser and enter the URL *docs.microsoft.com/en-us/windows/security/threat-protection/intelligence/safety-scanner-download* (If you are no longer able to access the site through the URL, use a search engine to search for "Microsoft Safety Scanner.")
3. Select either **Download Microsoft Safety Scanner (32-bit)** or **Download Microsoft Safety Scanner (64-bit)**, depending upon which system type of Windows you are running.
4. When the **MSERT.exe** program finishes downloading, launch this program by double-clicking it.
5. If a warning dialog box appears, click **Run anyway**.
6. If a User Account Control dialog box appears, click **Yes.**
7. Click the check box to accept the license terms for this software. Click **Next**.
8. Click **Next**.
9. Select **Quick scan** if necessary.
10. Click **Next**.
11. Depending on your computer, this scan may take several minutes. Analyze the results of the scan to determine if it found any malicious software in your computer.
12. If you have problems, you can click **View detailed results of the scan**. After reviewing the results, click **OK**. If you do not find any problems, click **Finish**.
13. If any malicious software was found on your computer, run the scan again and select **Full scan**. After the scan is complete, click **Finish** to close the dialog box.
14. Close all windows.

Project 1-3: Configure Microsoft Windows Sandbox

Time Required: 15 minutes

Objective: Given a scenario, implement host or application security solutions.

Description: A *sandbox* is an isolated virtual machine: anything run within a sandbox will impact only the virtual machine and not the underlying computer. The Microsoft Windows Sandbox first became available in Windows 10 Version 1903 released in 2019, and additional features have been added with recent Windows 10 updates to provide even more control.

NOTE 14

Although separate programs can perform a sandbox function, the Windows Sandbox has the advantages of being included as part of Windows, so nothing has to be downloaded and installed. It relies on the Microsoft hypervisor to run a separate kernel that isolates the Windows Sandbox from the host. This makes it more efficient since it can take advantage of the Windows integrated kernel scheduler, smart memory management, and a virtual GPU. Once you close the Windows Sandbox, nothing remains on your computer; when you launch Windows Sandbox again, it is as clean as new.

In this project you will configure the Windows Sandbox to use with this book.

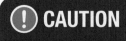 **CAUTION** You must be running Windows 10 Professional, Enterprise, or Education (not Home) Version 1903 or higher. To determine which version you are running, click Settings, then System, and then About. If you are not using the correct version, skip to the next project to create a different virtual machine.

1. First check if your system has virtualization turned on. Right-click the taskbar (at the bottom of the screen) and select **Task Manager**.
2. Click the **Performance** tab.
3. Under Virtualization, it must say "Enabled." If it says "Disabled," you will need to reboot and enter your BIOS or UEFI and turn on virtualization.

NOTE 15

With older BIOS, you may also need to disable other settings, such as Hyper-threading.

4. Now enable Windows Sandbox. In the Windows search box on the taskbar, enter **Windows Features** to open the Windows Features window.
5. Click the **Windows Sandbox** check box to turn on this feature.
6. To launch Windows Sandbox, click **Start**, and scroll down to Windows Sandbox, and then click **Windows Sandbox**. A protected virtual machine sandbox that looks like another Windows instance will start, as shown in Figure 1-8.

Source: Used with permissions from Microsoft

Figure 1-8   Windows sandbox

7. Explore the settings and default applications that come with the Windows Sandbox.
8. You can download a program through the Microsoft Edge application in Windows Sandbox. (Edge is included within Windows Sandbox along with a handful of other Windows applications, including access to OneDrive.) Open Edge and go to **www.google.com** to download and install the Google Chrome browser in the Windows Sandbox.

NOTE 16

You can also copy an executable file from your normal Windows environment and then paste it to the Windows Sandbox desktop to launch it.

9. After the installation is complete, close the Windows Sandbox.
10. Now relaunch the Windows Sandbox. What happened to Google Chrome? Why?
11. Close all windows.

Project 1-4: Create a Virtual Machine of Windows 10 for Security Testing—Part 1

Time Required: 25 minutes

Objective: Given a scenario, implement host or application security solutions.

Description: If you were unable to install the Windows Sandbox in Project 1-3, a different virtual machine can be created in which new applications can be installed or configuration settings changed without affecting the base computer. In a virtual machine environment, the "host" computer runs a "guest" operating system. Security programs and testing can be conducted within this guest operating system without affecting the regular host operating system. In this project, you create a virtual machine using Oracle VirtualBox software.

1. Open a web browser and enter the URL **www.virtualbox.org** (If you are no longer able to access the site through this web address, use a search engine to search for "Oracle VirtualBox download.")
2. Click **Downloads** (or a similar link or button).
3. Under VirtualBox binaries, select the latest version of VirtualBox to download for your specific host operating system. For example, if you are running Windows, select the version for "Windows hosts."
4. Under VirtualBox x.x.x Oracle VM VirtualBox Extension Pack, click **All supported platforms** to download the extension package.
5. Navigate to the folder that contains the downloads and launch the VirtualBox installation program **VirtualBox-xxx-nnnnn-hhh.exe**.
6. Accept the default configurations from the installation wizard to install the program.
7. If you are asked "Would you like to install this device software?" on one or more occasions, click **Install**.
8. When completed, click **Finish** to launch VirtualBox.
9. Now install the VirtualBox extensions. Click **File** and then click **Preferences**.
10. Click **Extensions**.
11. Click the **Add a package** icon on the right side of the screen.
12. Navigate to the folder that contains the extension pack downloaded earlier to select that file. Click **Open**.
13. Click **Install**. Follow the necessary steps to complete the default installation.
14. Remain in VirtualBox for the next project to configure VirtualBox and install the guest operating system.

Project 1-5: Create a Virtual Machine of Windows 10 for Security Testing—Part 2

Time Required: 20 minutes

Objective: Given a scenario, implement host or application security solutions.

Description: After installing VirtualBox, the next step is to create the guest operating system. For this project, Windows 10 will be installed. Different options are available for obtaining a copy of Windows:

- A retail version of the software can be purchased.
- If you or your school is a member of the Microsoft Azure Dev Tools for Teaching program, the operating system software and a license can be downloaded. See your instructor or lab supervisor for more information.
- A 90-day evaluation copy can be downloaded and installed from the Microsoft TechNet Evaluation Center (**www.microsoft.com/en-US/evalcenter/evaluate-windows-10-enterprise**).

1. Obtain the ISO image of Windows 10 using one of the preceding options and save it on the hard drive of the computer.
2. Launch VirtualBox.
3. Click **New**.
4. In the Name: box, enter **Windows 10** as the name of the virtual machine.
5. Be sure that the Type: box displays **Microsoft Windows** and the Version: box changes to **Windows 10 (xx-bit)**. Click **Next**.
6. Under Memory size, accept the recommended size or increase the allocation if you have sufficient RAM on your computer. Click **Next**.
7. Under Hard disk, accept **Create a virtual hard drive now**. Click **Create**.
8. Under Hard drive file type, accept the default **VID (VirtualBox Disk Image)**. Click **Next**.
9. Under Storage on physical hard drive, accept the default **Dynamically allocated**. Click **Next**.
10. Under File location and size, accept **Windows 10**. Click **Create**.

11. Now the configuration settings for the virtual machine are set. Next you will load the Windows 10 ISO image. Click **Settings**.
12. In the left pane, click **Storage**.
13. Under Controller: click **Empty**.
14. In the right page under Attributes, click the icon of the optical disc.
15. Click **Choose Virtual Optical Disk File**.
16. Navigate to the location of the Windows 10 ISO file and click **Open**.
17. Click **OK**.
18. Click **Start** to launch the Windows 10 ISO.
19. Follow the Windows 10 installation wizard to complete the installation.
20. To close the Windows 10 guest operating system in VirtualBox, click **File** and then click **Exit**.
21. Close all windows.

Case Projects

Case Project 1-1: Personal Attack Experiences

What type of computer attack have you (or a friend or another student) experienced? When did it happen? What type of computer or device was involved? What type of damage did it inflict? What had to be done to clean up following the attack? How was the computer fixed after the attack? What could have prevented it? List the reason or reasons you think that the attack was successful. Write a one-page paper about these experiences.

Case Project 1-2: Security Podcasts or Video Series

Many security vendors and security researchers now post weekly audio podcasts or video series on YouTube on security topics. Locate two different podcasts and two different video series about computer security. Listen and view one episode of each. Then write a summary of what was discussed and a critique of the podcasts and videos. Were they beneficial to you? Were they accurate? Would you recommend them to someone else? Write a one-page paper on your research.

Case Project 1-3: Phishing Simulators

Search the Internet for three different phishing simulators. Take the phishing challenge on each simulator to determine if you can identify the phishing attacks. Then create a table that lists the features of the phishing simulators, their ease of use, and how accurate you think they were. Would these simulators be helpful in training users about phishing? Write a one-paragraph summary along with your table.

Case Project 1-4: Sources of Security Information

The following is a partial overall list of some of the sources for security information:

- Security content (online or printed articles that deal specifically with unbiased security content)
- Consumer content (general consumer-based magazines or broadcasts not devoted to security but occasionally carry user security tips)
- Vendor content (material from security vendors who sell security services, hardware, or software)
- Security experts (IT staff recommendations or newsletters)
- Direct instruction (college classes or a workshop conducted by a local computer vendor)
- Friends and family
- Personal experience

Create a table with each of these sources and columns that list Advantages, Disadvantages, Example, and Rating. Use the Internet to complete the entire table. The Rating column is a listing from 1 to 7 (with 1 being the highest) of how useful each of these sources is in your opinion. Compare your table with other learners.

Case Project 1-5: Information Security Community Site Activity

The Information Security Community Site is an online companion to this textbook. It contains a wide variety of tools, information, discussion boards, and other features to assist learners. In order to gain the most benefit from the site, you will need to set up a free account.

Go to **community.cengage.com/infosec2**. Click **Join the Community**. On the Join the Community page, enter the requested information to create your account.

NOTE 17

Your instructor may have a specific naming convention that you should use, such as the name of your course followed by your initials. Check with your instructor before creating your sign-in name.

Explore the various features of the Information Security Community Site and become familiar with it. Visit the blog section and read the blog postings to learn about some of the latest events in IT security.

Case Project 1-6 North Ridge Security

North Ridge Security provides security consulting and assurance services to over 500 clients in more than 20 states and a wide range of enterprises. A new initiative at North Ridge is for each of its seven regional offices to provide internships to students who are in their final year of the security degree program at the local college.

As part of National Cybersecurity Awareness Month, North Ridge is visiting local high schools to talk about careers in cybersecurity. You have been asked to present an introductory session on the need for cybersecurity workers, the types of jobs that are available, what a cybersecurity professional does each day, and the value of security certifications.

1. Use the Internet to research information about working in the cybersecurity field. Then create a PowerPoint presentation that explains why cybersecurity employees are needed, what they do, and the value of security certifications. Your presentation should be seven to 10 slides in length.
2. As a follow-up to your presentation, create a Frequently Asked Questions (FAQ) sheet that outlines working in cybersecurity. Write a one-page FAQ about security employment.

References

1. Shi, Fleming, "Threat spotlight: Coronavirus-related phishing," *Barracuda*, Mar. 26, 2020, accessed Apr. 19, 2020, https://blog.barracuda.com/2020/03/26/threat-spotlight-coronavirus-related-phishing/.
2. "Fake 'Corona Antivirus' distributes BlackNET remote administration tool," *MalwareBytes Labs*, Mar. 23, 2020, accessed Apr. 19, 2020, https://blog.malwarebytes.com/threat-analysis/2020/03/fake-corona-antivirus-distributes-blacknet-remote-administration-tool/.
3. "McAfee Labs threats report," Dec. 2018, accessed Apr. 21, 2019, www.mcafee.com/enterprise/en-us/assets/reports/rp-quarterly-threats-dec-2018.pdf.
4. "2020 cyberthreat defense report," *Cyberedge Group*, accessed Apr. 20, 2020, https://cyber-edge.com/cdr/.
5. Morgan, Steve, "2019 official annual cybercrime report," *Cybersecurity Ventures*, accessed Apr. 20, 2020, www.herjavecgroup.com/wp-content/uploads/2018/12/CV-HG-2019-Official-Annual-Cybercrime-Report.pdf.
6. "2020 cyberthreat defense report," *Cyberedge Group*, accessed Apr. 20, 2020, https://cyber-edge.com/cdr/.
7. Hospelhorn, Sarah, "Solving the cybersecurity skills shortage within your organization," *Varonis*, Mar. 29, 2020, accessed Apr. 20, 2020, https://www.varonis.com/blog/cybersecurity-skills-shortage/.
8. "Information security analysts," *Bureau of Labor Statistics*, Apr. 10, 2020, accessed Apr. 30, 2020, www.bls.gov/ooh/computer-and-information-technology/information-security-analysts.htm.

9. Morgan, Steve, "One million cybersecurity job openings in 2016," *Forbes*, Jan. 2, 2016, accessed Feb. 16, 2017, www.forbes.com/sites/stevemorgan/2016/01/02/ one-million-cybersecurity-job-openings-in-2016/#1118fc737d27.

10. "How CompTIA certifications can earn you higher salary and better opportunities," *Simplilearn*, Aug. 5, 2019, accessed Apr. 20, 2020, www.simplilearn.com/ how-comptia-certification-can-earn-higher-salary-rar409-article.

11. "2019 insider threat report," *NucleusCyber*, retrieved Apr. 21, 2020, https://info.nucleuscyber. com/2019-insider-threat-report.

12. Fruhlinger, Josh, "Top cybersecurity facts, figures and statistics for 2020," *CSO*, Mar. 9, 2020, accessed Apr. 21, 2020, www.csoonline.com/article/3153707/top-cybersecurity-facts-figures-and-statistics.html.

13. "Phishing activity trends report," *Anti-Phishing Working Group*, accessed Apr. 25, 2020, https://apwg.org/trendsreports/.

14. McNichol, Tom, "Friend me on Facebook," *Bloomberg Businessweek*, Nov. 7, 2011.

15. Domabirg, Artem, "Bitsquatting: DNS hijacking without exploitation," *Diaburg.org*, accessed Mar. 27, 2017, dinaburg.org/bitsquatting.html.

THREAT MANAGEMENT AND CYBERSECURITY RESOURCES

After completing this module, you should be able to do the following:

1. Explain what a penetration test is
2. Identify the rules of engagement and how to perform a pen test
3. Define vulnerability scanning
4. Describe different cybersecurity resources

Front-Page Cybersecurity

"Bug bounties" are monetary rewards given for uncovering a software vulnerability. Although these programs have been in existence since 1995, when Netscape first offered cash to anyone who could find security vulnerabilities in its Netscape Navigator web browser, in recent years bug bounty programs have changed significantly. Not only are exceptionally large rewards now offered, but those paying for rewards are no longer only software developers who want to fix the bugs. The large bounties have resulted in fierce competition over bugs.

Google is typical of the software developers who have bug bounty programs. Starting its program in 2010, Google now pays anywhere from $100 to $31,337 per bug found in their basic software. To date, Google has paid more than $21 million for bug bounties. Google also maintains a leaderboard of the top 10 recipients of bounties. (It is called the "0x0A Leaderboard" because "0x0A" is the number 10 in hexadecimal.) Once a security researcher finds a vulnerability and reports it, Google then immediately works to patch the bug.

Recently, several other players beside software developers have started offering bug bounties. The European Commission (EC), which is part of the European Union (EU) and is responsible for essentially managing the daily affairs of the EU, now offers bug bounties for security vulnerabilities that are uncovered in some of the most popular free and open source software. The EC, which itself has been a victim of cyberattacks that resulted in thousands of diplomatic cables being stolen and published, says that it wants to protect EU citizens (and itself) from attacks by uncovering bugs. Their bug bounties range from €25,000 to €90,000 ($28,600–$103,000).

An entirely new player offering bug bounties is Zerodium. Founded in 2015, Zerodium calls itself the "leading exploit acquisition platform for premium zero-days and advanced cybersecurity capabilities." Zerodium buys bug information and then sells it to "mainly government organizations in need of specific and tailored cybersecurity capabilities and/or protective solutions to defend against zero-day attacks." In other words, the governments may use the knowledge of these zero-day bugs to defend themselves from future attacks—or they may instead use the information to launch silent attacks against their citizens and other nations. But the price that Zerodium pays has been nothing like the software developers: Zerodium pays up to $2 million for certain types of bugs in Apple products and $1 million for Microsoft Windows bugs.

This has resulted in a price war over bugs. In late 2019, Apple expanded its bug bounty program by opening it to anyone who found a bug. (Previously, Apple's program was invitation-only: they would only accept and pay a bounty from preapproved security researchers.) Apple now pays from $200,000 to $1.5 million per bug and adds a 50 percent bonus on top of the regular payout for any bug reported in an Apple beta release. Other software developers have also raised their prices.

In order to secure an organization from attacks, a concept known as *threat management* is often used. The goal of threat management is to take the appropriate steps needed to minimize hostile cyber actions. It seeks to answer the question, "What threat can take advantage of a vulnerability to bypass our defenses, and how can we prevent it?"

One of the first steps in threat management is to test the defenses to find any weaknesses. However, tests should never be "one-and-done" or conducted only periodically. Instead, because of the nature of today's security attacks, a regular cycle of scans must be conducted. In addition to these tests and scans for defenses, a wealth of cybersecurity information can also be used for defenses.

In this module, you will learn about threat management as it pertains to penetration testing and vulnerability scans. You will also explore cybersecurity standards, regulations, frameworks, and configuration guidelines.

PENETRATION TESTING

CERTIFICATION

1.8 Explain the techniques used in penetration testing.

Studying penetration testing involves defining what it is and why such a test should be conducted. It also examines who should perform the tests and the rules for engagement. Finally, knowing how to perform a penetration test is also useful.

Defining Penetration Testing

Penetration testing attempts to exploit vulnerabilities just as a threat actor would. This helps to uncover new vulnerabilities, provide a clearer picture of their nature, and determine how they could be used against the organization. Kali Linux, a popular penetration testing tool, is shown in Figure 2-1.

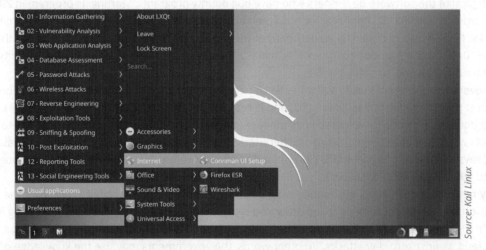

Figure 2-1   Kali Linux penetration testing tool

It is generally recognized that the most important element in a "pen test" (short for "penetration test") is the first step: *planning*. A lack of planning can result in a flawed penetration test that tries to do too little or too much. It can also result in *creep*, which is an expansion beyond the initial set of the test's limitations. In penetration testing, it is often tempting to exploit a vulnerability "down a rabbit hole" and waste valuable time and resources without gaining any significant value.

Yet, the most dangerous result of poor planning is creating unnecessary legal issues. Because the nature of penetration testing is to exploit vulnerabilities, an outsider can easily perceive the testing to be the work of a real threat actor. Breaking into an organization's network and exploiting vulnerabilities is a clear violation of state and national laws. This could easily put a penetration tester in legal peril unless proper planning takes place first.

 **CAUTION**   The importance of planning a penetration test should never be underestimated. Planning a pen test is essential; in fact, no pen test should ever occur without a detailed planning phase.

Why Conduct a Test?

By its very nature, a penetration test attempts to uncover vulnerabilities and then exploit them, just as a threat actor would. This involves a significant amount of time and resources. So sometimes asked is the question, "Why spend the time and effort to perform a penetration test? Why can't we just do a scan of our network defenses to find vulnerabilities?"

While a scan of network defenses can help find vulnerabilities, the *type* of vulnerabilities revealed is different from a penetration test. A scan usually finds only *surface* problems to be addressed. This is because many scans are entirely *automated* and provide only a limited verification of any discovered vulnerabilities. A penetration test, on the other hand, can find *deep* vulnerabilities. Penetration tests go further and attempt to exploit vulnerabilities using *manual* techniques.

These deep vulnerabilities can only be exposed through *actual attacks that use the mindset of a threat actor*. Both elements are important. First, the attacks must be the same (or remarkably similar) as those used by a threat actor; anything less will not uncover the deep vulnerabilities that an attacker can find. Second, the attacks should follow the thinking of threat actors. Understanding their thinking helps to better perceive what assets they are seeking, how they may craft the attack, and even how determined they are to obtain assets. Without having an attacker's mindset, it is difficult to find deep vulnerabilities.

NOTE 1

Some security professionals believe organizations that do not have a solid cybersecurity defense should not consider a pen test as the first step. Instead, a general scan should first be conducted to reveal and address surface vulnerabilities. Once this analysis is completed, a more thorough pen test can be performed.

Who Should Perform the Test?

One of the first questions to answer is who should conduct the penetration test. Should it be conducted by in-house employees or an external consultant? Is there another option? What are the advantages and disadvantages to each approach?

Internal Security Personnel

Using internal employees to conduct a penetration test has advantages in some cases. First, there is little or no additional cost. Also, the test can be conducted much more quickly. Finally, an in-house penetration test can be used to enhance the training of employees and raise the awareness of security risks.

When conducting an in-house pen test, an organization often divides security employees into opposing teams to conduct a "war game" scenario. Table 2-1 lists the composition and duties of the teams in a pen test war game.

However, using internal security employees to conduct a penetration test has several disadvantages:

- *Inside knowledge*. Employees often have in-depth knowledge of the network and its devices. A threat actor, on the other hand, would not have the same knowledge, so an attack from employees would not truly simulate that of a threat actor.

Table 2-1   Penetration testing war game teams

Team Name	Role	Duties	Explanation
Red Team	Attackers	Scans for vulnerabilities and then exploits them	Has prior and in-depth knowledge of existing security, which may provide an unfair advantage.
Blue Team	Defenders	Monitors for Red Team attacks and shores up defenses as necessary	Scans log files, traffic analysis, and other data to look for signs of an attack.
White Team	Referees	Enforces the rules of the penetration testing	Makes notes of the Blue Team's responses and the Red Team's attacks.
Purple Team	Bridge	Provides real-time feedback between the Red and Blue Teams to enhance the testing	The Blue Team receives information that can be used to prioritize and improve their ability to detect attacks while the Red Team learns more about technologies and mechanisms used in the defense.

- *Lack of expertise*. Employees may not have the credentials needed to perform a comprehensive test. Their lack of expertise may result in few deep vulnerabilities being exposed.
- *Reluctance to reveal*. Employees may be reluctant to reveal a vulnerability discovered in a network or system that they or a fellow employee has been charged with protecting.

NOTE 2

Sometimes organizations add an incentive called a *capture the flag (CTF)* exercise. A series of challenges with varying degrees of difficulty are outlined in advance. When one challenge is solved, a "flag" is given to the pen tester, and the points are totaled once time has expired. The winning player or team is the one that earns the highest score. CTF events are often hosted at information security conferences or by schools.

External Pen Tester Consultants

Contracting with an external third-party pen testing consultant to conduct a penetration test offers the following advantages:

- *Expertise*. External contractors that conduct penetration tests have the technical and business expertise to conduct a thorough test.
- *Credentials*. Pen test contractors usually employ people who hold several security certifications to validate their pen testing knowledge and experience.
- *Experience*. Because they have conducted numerous penetration tests, contractors know what to look for and how to take advantage of a vulnerability.
- *Focus*. Reputable penetration testing firms generally deliver expert security services and are highly focused on the task.

Penetration testing using external consultants is often classified based on the level of information and access provided in advance of the pen test. These levels are described in Table 2-2.

A disadvantage of using an external consultant is the usage of the information that is uncovered. A contractor who conducts a pen test will not only learn about an organization's network and system vulnerabilities but may also receive extremely sensitive information about these systems and how to access them. Such knowledge could be sold to a competitor by an unscrupulous employee of the third-party contractor. As a protection, most penetration testing contracts contain a *nondisclosure agreement (NDA)* that states all client information related to the test will be treated as highly confidential and that at the end of the test, all data and storage media is either destroyed or given back to the client.

Table 2-2   Penetration testing levels

Level Name	Description	Main Task	Advantages	Disadvantages
Black box	Testers have no knowledge of the network and no special privileges	Attempt to penetrate the network	Emulate exactly what a threat actor would do and see	If testers cannot penetrate the network, then no test can occur
Gray box	Testers are given limited knowledge of the network and some elevated privileges	Focus on systems with the greatest risk and value to the organization	More efficiently assess security instead of spending time trying to compromise the network and then determining which systems to attack	This head start does not allow testers to truly emulate what a threat actor may do
White box	Testers are given full knowledge of the network and the source code of applications	Identify potential points of weakness	Focus directly on systems to test for penetration	This approach does not provide a full picture of the network's vulnerabilities

Crowdsourced Pen Testers

A **bug bounty** is a monetary reward given for uncovering a software vulnerability. Most software developers offer some type of bug bounty, ranging from several thousands of dollars to millions of dollars. Bug bounty programs take advantage of *crowdsourcing*, which involves obtaining input into a project by enlisting the services of many people through the Internet.

Recently some third-party organizations have begun offering crowdsourced pen testing. Instead of contracting with a single external pen tester consulting organization, crowdsourced pen testing involves a large group of individuals who are not regular employees of the contractor. These handpicked crowdsourced members of the security community test the security of the client. Some of the advantages of crowdsourced pen testers are the following:

- Faster testing, resulting in quicker remediation of vulnerabilities
- Ability to rotate teams so different individuals test the system
- Option of conducting multiple pen tests simultaneously

Rules of Engagement

The **rules of engagement** in a penetration test are its limitations or parameters. Without these parameters, a penetration test can easily veer off course and not accomplish the desired results, take too long to produce timely results, or test assets that are not necessary to test. The categories for the rules for engagement are timing, scope, authorization, exploitation, communication, cleanup, and reporting.

Timing

The *timing* parameter sets when the testing will occur. The first consideration for timing is the start and stop dates of the test. When using an external third party, these dates are based on estimates provided by the tester and directly tied to the experience of a tester in a certain area. However, during a penetration test, several events can occur that may slow the testing process. For example, a significant vulnerability may be found that requires immediate attention; multiple meetings may then be necessary with different levels of management and security personnel to address the vulnerability. Such meetings can significantly affect the original estimated completion date. Many pen testers recommend adding up to 20 percent more time to the end date to provide a cushion if any interruptions occur in testing.

The second timing consideration involves when the pen testing should take place. Should the active portions of the pen test—scanning and exploitation—be conducted during normal business hours, which could cause unforeseen interruptions to normal activities? Some organizations choose to have penetration testing conducted after business hours or only on weekends to minimize any impact.

Scope

For a pen test, the *scope* is what should be tested. Scope involves several elements that define the relevant test boundaries. These elements include the following technical boundaries:

- *Environment.* Should the pen test be conducted on the live production environment? This option has the advantage of producing the most accurate test. However, the disadvantage is that it will likely disrupt normal business operations. As an alternative, a simulated environment could be created, but this option comes with additional work and costs.
- *Internal targets.* Before starting a penetration test, all internal targets must be clearly identified for an external third-party gray box test or white box test. (Black box testers are responsible for finding internal targets.) These internal targets are owned by the customer, and information about them may include specific IP addresses, network ranges, or domain names. Also, the scope of internal targets must account for systems such as firewalls, intrusion detection systems, intrusion prevention systems, and networking equipment between the tester and the final target.

 **CAUTION**   Before starting a pen test, all internal targets should be validated to ensure that they are actually owned by the customer. There could be serious legal consequences if a pen tester attacked and successfully penetrated a system—only to discover that it belonged to another organization.

- *External targets.* In some situations, a pen test may include testing a service or an application hosted by a third party. These targets may include cloud service providers or Internet service providers (ISPs).
- *Target locations.* Because laws vary among states, provinces, and countries, testing planners must identify the physical location of the targets and, if necessary, adjust the scope of the test. For instance, countries in the European Union (EU) have more stringent laws surrounding personal privacy, which can change how a social engineering engagement would be executed.
- *Other boundaries.* In addition to technical boundaries, other boundaries should be considered. For example, does the pen test include physical security, such as fencing, cameras, and guards? Are there limitations on who should be targeted by social engineering attacks (such as excluding specific C-suite executives)? Should there be limits on spear-phishing messages, such as those that contain offers for drugs or pornographic material?

 **CAUTION**   The importance of determining the scope of pen testing can be illustrated by an event in 2019. Two security contractors from Coalfire, a penetration testing company that frequently does security assessments for federal agencies and for state and local governments, were arrested in Adel, Iowa, as they attempted to gain access to the Dallas County Courthouse. They claimed to be conducting a penetration test to determine how vulnerable county court records were and to measure law enforcement's response to a break-in. However, because the Iowa state court officials who ordered the test never told county officials about it, the penetration testers were arrested and went to jail. The state officials later apologized to Dallas County, citing confusion over just what Coalfire was going to test, although later both parties said there were "different interpretations" of the scope of the pen test.

Authorization

Authorization is the receipt of prior written approval to conduct the pen test. A formal written document *must* be signed by all parties before a penetration test begins. Naturally, this approval includes people within the organization being tested. However, other levels of authorization are frequently overlooked.

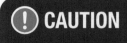 **CAUTION**   Before performing a pen test against cloud service providers and ISPs, remember that while permission may have been granted by the customer to perform a pen test on external targets, permission must also be obtained from the external targets themselves. Many external targets have specific procedures for penetration testers to follow and may require request forms, scheduling, and explicit permission before testing can begin.

Exploitation

The *exploitation level* in a pen test should also be part of the scope that is discussed in the planning stages. When a vulnerability is uncovered, should it always be exploited? Or are specific areas considered "off limits" so that the tester should not view the related data?

Communication

Communication in penetration testing is particularly important. The pen tester should communicate with the organization on several occasions during the process. These include the following:

- *Initiation*. Once the pen test has started, the organization should be notified that the process has begun.
- *Incident response*. If a pen tester can complete the initial vulnerability assessment without triggering the organization's incident response mechanism, then a critical gap in the security structure has been identified.
- *Status*. Instead of waiting until the pen test is completed, it is better to provide periodic status reports to the organization's management.
- *Emergency*. If the pen tester uncovers a critical vulnerability, it should be immediately reported to the organization's management while the penetration test is paused.

Cleanup

Following the exploitation of the systems outlined in the scope, the pen tester must ensure that everything related to the pen test has been removed. This is called the **cleanup** phase of a pen test and should be clearly outlined in the rules of engagement. Cleanup involves removing all software agents, scripts, executable binaries, temporary files, and backdoors from all affected systems. Also, any credentials that were changed should be restored, and any additional usernames created should be removed. In short, the systems should be returned to their preengagement state.

Reporting

Once the pen test is completed, a report should be generated to document its objectives, methods used, and results. The report should be divided into two parts based on two separate audiences.

The first part of the report should be an executive summary designed for a less technical audience—namely, those who are in charge of the oversight and strategic vision of the security program as well as any members of the organization who may be affected by the identified threats. The executive summary often contains a section that identifies the overall risk of the organization and a breakdown of the types of vulnerabilities that were exploited, as shown in Figure 2-2.

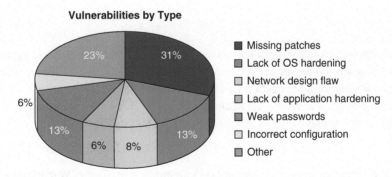

Figure 2-2   Types of vulnerabilities

The second part of the report should be technical in nature and written for security professionals. It should describe in detail the scope of the pen test, the vulnerabilities uncovered, how the vulnerabilities were exploited, the results, and suggested remediation for each vulnerability.

Performing a Penetration Test

Despite how movies portray the ease and speed of breaking into the technology assets of an organization, this is rarely the case in real life. Rather, a great deal of effort and time are needed for performing a penetration test. Many first-time pen testers find the work more difficult than first envisioned.

A key ingredient necessary for performing a successful penetration test is persistence, which is defined as *determination, resolve*, and *perseverance*. Pen testers should be prepared for spending long hours and even days searching for vulnerabilities that they might not discover.

Although a variety of actions take place when performing a penetration test, they can be grouped into two phases: reconnaissance and penetration.

Phase 1: Reconnaissance

The first task of the black box and gray box tester is to perform preliminary information gathering from outside the organization. This reconnaissance is called footprinting.

Testers gather this information using two methods. Active reconnaissance involves directly probing for vulnerabilities and useful information, much like a threat actor would do. For example, unprotected wireless data transmissions from wireless local area networks or Wi-Fi can often be used to gather information or even circumvent security protections. There are different means by which this wireless information can be gathered through active reconnaissance. One means is through war driving. War driving is searching for wireless signals from an automobile or on foot while using a portable computing device. To maximize the ability to detect wireless signals, several tools are necessary. These tools are listed in Table 2-3.

Table 2-3   War driving tools

Tool	Purpose
Mobile computing device	A mobile computing device with a wireless NIC can be used for war driving. This includes a standard portable computer, a pad computer, or a smartphone.
Wireless NIC adapter	Many war drivers prefer an external wireless NIC adapter that connects into a USB or other port and has an external antenna jack.
Antenna(s)	Although all wireless NIC adapters have embedded antennas, attaching an external antenna will significantly increase the ability to detect a wireless signal.
Software	Because client utilities and integrated operating system tools provide only limited information about a discovered Wi-Fi, pen testers use more specialized software.
Global positioning system (GPS) receiver	Although this is not required, it does help to pinpoint the location more precisely.

NOTE 3

War driving was originally derived from the term *war dialing*. When telephone modems were popular in the 1980s and 1990s, an attacker could program the device to randomly dial telephone numbers until a computer answered the call. This random process of searching for a connection was known as war dialing, so the word for randomly searching for a wireless signal became known as war driving. However, pen test war driving is not randomly searching for any Wi-Fi signal but is much more focused at finding those associated with the target organization.

However, a more efficient means of discovering a Wi-Fi signal is war flying. War flying uses drones, which are officially known as unmanned aerial vehicles (UAVs). Because they can quickly cover a wider area, are not limited to streets and sidewalks, and can easily fly over security perimeters such as fences, drones are the preferred means for finding a Wi-Fi signal. A drone is shown in Figure 2-3.

The disadvantage of active reconnaissance in a pen test is that the probes are likely to alert security professionals within the enterprise who do not know about the pen test that something unusual is occurring. This may result in them "locking down" the network to become more restrictive and thus more difficult to probe.

In contrast with active reconnaissance, passive reconnaissance takes an entirely different approach: the tester uses tools that do not raise any alarms. This may include searching online for publicly accessible information called open source intelligence (OSINT) that can reveal valuable insight about the system.

Source: Kletr/Shutterstock.com

Figure 2-3   Drone

NOTE 4

Active reconnaissance relies on traffic being sent to the targeted system, while passive reconnaissance calls for testers to quietly "make do" with whatever information they can accumulate from public sources.

Phase 2: Penetration

Because a pen test is intended to simulate the actions of a threat actor, the question becomes, "What do threat actors do when they uncover a vulnerability through reconnaissance?" Generally, threat actors follow these steps in an actual attack:

1. The threat actors first conduct reconnaissance against the systems, looking for vulnerabilities.
2. When a path to a vulnerability is exposed, they gain access to the system through the vulnerability.
3. Once initial access is gained, the threat actors attempt to escalate to more advanced resources that are normally protected from an application or user. This is called **privilege escalation**.
4. With the advanced privileges, the threat actors tunnel through the network looking for additional systems they can access from their elevated position (called **lateral movement**).
5. Threat actors install tools on the compromised systems to gain even deeper access to the network.
6. Threat actors may install a backdoor that allows them repeated and long-term access to the system in the future. The backdoors are not related to the initial vulnerability, so access remains even if the initial vulnerability is corrected.
7. Once the backdoor is installed, threat actors can continue to probe until they find their ultimate target and perform their intended malicious action, such as stealing R&D information, password files, or customer credit card numbers.

The initial system that was compromised—the system through which the attackers first gained entry—most often does not contain the data that is the goal of the attack. Rather, this system only serves as a gateway for entry. Once

NOTE 5

Threat actors can exploit *any* vulnerability they uncover, not just a vulnerability on the ultimate target. This means they are not defeated if they cannot find a vulnerability on the target; rather, a remote vulnerability can be used to pivot to the final target.

they are inside the network, the threat actors **pivot**, or turn, to other systems to be compromised, with the goal of reaching the ultimate target.

Several lessons can be learned from how threat actors work, and those lessons can be applied to a penetration test. First, when a vulnerability is discovered during a penetration test, the work is not finished. Instead, the pen tester must determine how to pivot to another system using another vulnerability to continue moving toward the target. Second, vulnerabilities that are not part of the ultimate target can still provide a gateway to that target. This means that no vulnerability is insignificant for a pen tester. Third, unlike some types of automated vulnerability scanning, penetration tests are manual. Therefore, a pen tester needs to design attacks carefully. Finally, because threat actors are patient and persistent, pen testers must also be patient and persistent. A pen test is not a task that should be scheduled for completion quickly; rather, a good pen test may take an extended amount of time to uncover all weaknesses.

> **(!) CAUTION** Whereas the work of attackers (and pen testers) has generally required manual effort for lateral movement and pivoting, some attackers are now automating their lateral movements within a compromised system.

TWO RIGHTS & A WRONG

1. The Purple Team is made up of the referees who enforce the rules of a pen test.
2. One advantage of using external pen testing consultants is their credentials.
3. White box testers are given full knowledge of the network.

See Appendix B for the answer.

VULNERABILITY SCANNING

- -
1.7 Summarize the techniques used in security assessments.
- -

Like penetration testing, vulnerability scanning is considered an important task in maintaining a cybersecurity defense; in fact, vulnerability scanning in some ways complements pen testing. Studying vulnerability scanning involves understanding what it is, how to conduct a scan, how to use data management tools, and how threat hunting can enhance scanning.

What Is a Vulnerability Scan?

Older model cars typically have a "Needs Service" light on the dashboard that turns on after the car has been driven a certain number of miles, indicating that service such as an oil change is needed. While performing the oil change, a mechanic could note that additional repairs are needed. Newer model cars, on the other hand, usually track mileage automatically. Dealers send the owner monthly email reminders of when the next service is due and even indicate if something is not working properly so the owner can have it taken care of immediately.

The difference between older and newer cars is similar to the difference between a penetration test and a vulnerability scan. A penetration test is a single event using a manual process often performed only after a specific amount of time has passed, such as once a year (and sometimes only to comply with regulatory requirements). A **vulnerability scan**, on the other hand, is a frequent and ongoing process, usually automated, that continuously identifies vulnerabilities and monitors cybersecurity progress. In other words, a vulnerability assessment is a cyclical process of ongoing scanning and continuous monitoring to reduce the attack surface. Table 2-4 contrasts a vulnerability scan with a penetration test.

Table 2-4   Vulnerability scan vs. penetration test

	Vulnerability Scan	Penetration Test
Purpose	Reduces the attack surface	Identifies deep vulnerabilities
Procedure	Scans to find weaknesses and then mitigate them	Acts like a threat agent to find vulnerabilities to exploit
Frequency	Usually includes ongoing scanning and continuous monitoring	Tests when required by regulatory body or on a predetermined schedule
Personnel	Uses internal security personnel	Uses external third parties or internal security personnel
Process	Usually is automated, with a handful of manual processes	Uses an entirely manual process
Goal	Aims to identify risks by scanning systems and networks	Aims to gain unauthorized access and exploit vulnerabilities
Final report audience	Includes an executive summary for less technical audiences and technical details for security professionals	Includes several different audiences

NOTE 6

A vulnerability scan and a penetration test are similar in some ways. For example, both should be conducted following a data breach, the launch of a new application, or a major change to the network. However, because a vulnerability scan is continuous, it may only need to focus on the new application or change to the network.

Conducting a Vulnerability Scan

Conducting a vulnerability scan involves knowing what to scan and how often, along with selecting a type of scan and interpreting vulnerability information. All vulnerability scans require a close examination of the results.

When and What to Scan

It might seem that the optimum approach for vulnerability scanning is simply to scan all systems all the time. However, that approach is usually not practical. There are two primary reasons for not conducting around-the-clock vulnerability scans:

- *Workflow interruptions.* Continual vulnerability scans may impact the response time of a system so that its daily workflow or normal business processes are hindered. Moving the scans to "off hours" such as nights or weekends can limit interruptions.
- *Technical constraints.* Limitations based on technology can dictate how frequently a scan may be performed. For an organization with a large network that contains many devices, it simply may not be possible to scan the entire network within a desired time period. Other technical constraints include limitations on network bandwidth and vulnerability scan software license limitations. When dealing with technical constraints, spreading out the scans to run at specific times may be a necessary alternative.

When considering what to scan, the temptation to scan everything is again not practical. Some organizations may instead choose to scan the network, applications, and web applications on a rotating basis. However, running a full vulnerability scan of just the network can take a significant amount of time to find all assets and assess their vulnerabilities.

A more focused approach is to know the location of data so that specific systems with high-value data can be scanned more frequently. Organizations can create a list of systems to be scanned by creating and then consulting an *asset inventory*, a list of all significant assets. If no asset inventory is available, then most vulnerability scanning tools allow for an inventory scan that only searches for devices attached to the network instead of conducting a full vulnerability scan. Figure 2-4 shows the hardware asset management screen of the vulnerability scanner Nessus. Software assets should also be identified and scanned; Figure 2-5 shows the Nessus software asset management screen.

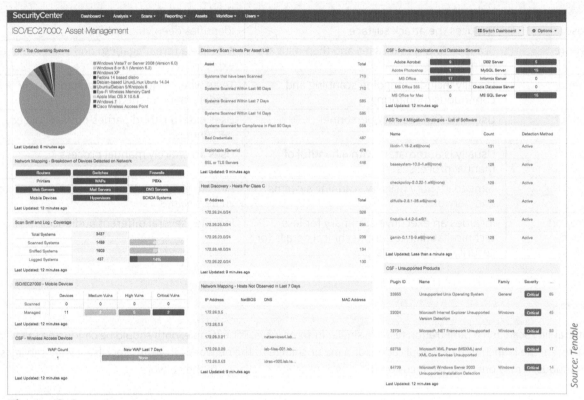

Source: Tenable

Figure 2-4   Nessus hardware asset management

Source: Tenable

Figure 2-5   Nessus software asset management

NOTE 7

While several vulnerability scanning tools are available, Nessus is perhaps the best-known and most widely used vulnerability scanner. It is a product of Tenable and contains a wide array of pre-built templates. Nessus advertises that new information about vulnerabilities are available as soon as 24 hours after a new vulnerability is disclosed. Nessus has a free version called Nessus Essentials that scans 16 IP addresses.

Because a vulnerability scan should be limited, a **configuration review** of the software settings should be conducted. This may include the following tasks:

- Define the group of target devices to be scanned, which may include a range of hosts or subnets.
- Ensure that a scan should be designed to meet its intended goals. If a specific vulnerability for Windows 10 computers is being targeted in the scan, for example, it makes sense to scan only Windows 10 systems.
- Determine the *sensitivity level* or the depth of a scan—in other words, the type of vulnerabilities being searched for. While a general scan may search for all vulnerabilities, a scan often looks for a specific type of vulnerability.
- Specify the data types to be scanned. Like the sensitivity level, this setting can be used to "drill down" when searching for a specific vulnerability in a known file type instead of searching all files on a system.

NOTE 8

A configuration review can also reduce the vulnerability scan's impact on overall network performance.

Types of Scans

There are several types of vulnerability scans. Two of the major types of scans are credentialed scans and intrusive scans.

Credentialed vs. Non-credentialed Scans   In a **credentialed scan**, valid authentication credentials, such as usernames and passwords, are supplied to the vulnerability scanner to mimic the work of a threat actor who possesses these credentials. A **non-credentialed scan** provides no such authentication information. Figure 2-6 shows the credentials that can be entered for a credentialed scan.

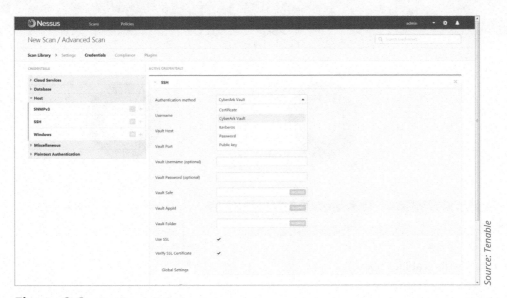

Source: Tenable

Figure 2-6   Credentialed scan

NOTE 9

Non-credentialed scans run faster because they perform fundamental actions such as looking for open ports and finding software that will respond to requests. Credentialed scans are slower but can provide a deeper insight into the system by accessing a fuller range of the installed software and examining the software's configuration settings and current security posture.

Intrusive vs. Nonintrusive Scans   An **intrusive scan** attempts to employ any vulnerabilities that it finds, much like a threat actor would. A **nonintrusive scan** does not attempt to exploit the vulnerability but only records that it was discovered. While intrusive tests are more accurate, they can impair the target system. In some cases, the system may even become unstable and unusable. However, a nonintrusive scan cannot determine for certain if an installed service is truly vulnerable; rather, it can only indicate that it *might* be vulnerable.

Vulnerability Information

Vulnerability scanning software looks for a vulnerability by comparing the software it scans against a set of known vulnerabilities. Such monitoring requires access to an updated database of vulnerabilities along with a means of actively comparing and matching to known vulnerabilities.

Vulnerability information is available to provide updated information to scanning software about the latest vulnerabilities. Several sources are available. However, the most popular vulnerability feed is the Mitre **Common Vulnerabilities and Exposures (CVE)**. The CVE identifies vulnerabilities in operating systems and application software.

Examining Results

Consider a vulnerability scan that produces the 20 vulnerabilities listed in Figure 2-7. Although the list includes no critical vulnerabilities, others are categorized as high, medium, and low. When addressing these vulnerabilities, where do you begin? Do you start with the high vulnerabilities and work your way down, or is there a better approach to take? How do you know that each is indeed a true vulnerability?

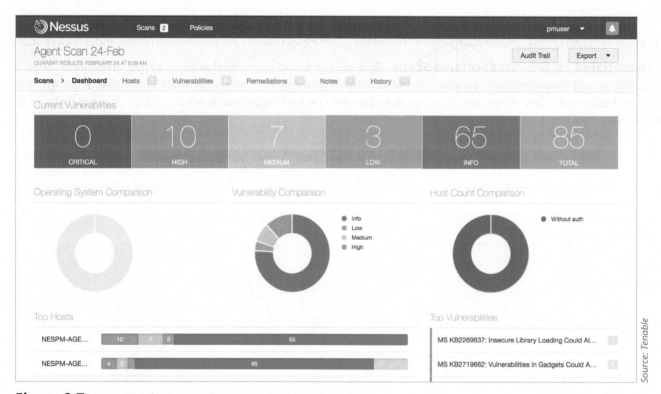

Figure 2-7   Results of vulnerability scan

When examining the results of a vulnerability scan, you should assess the importance of vulnerability as well as its accuracy.

Importance   Many new security personnel are surprised to learn *it is rarely possible, and often not desirable, to address all vulnerabilities*. Not all vulnerabilities are as potentially damaging as others. Also, although a scanner might assign a medium rating to a vulnerability, not all organizations react to the rating in the same way. To one company, this vulnerability may be critical, but to another, it is not worth the effort to fix. Because many vulnerabilities are complex to unravel and take an extended amount of time to address, organizations may not have enough time to solve all of them. So, beginning with the high vulnerabilities and working down through the low ones may not always be the best plan of action.

Instead, vulnerabilities need to be prioritized so that the most important ones are addressed early on, while others are delayed until later or are not even addressed. Several criteria are used for prioritizing vulnerabilities.

First, a numeric score is usually assigned to a vulnerability based on the Common Vulnerability Scoring System (CVSS). The numeric scores are generated using a complex formula that considers variables such as the access vector, attack complexity, authentication, confidentiality of the data, and the system's integrity and availability. The vulnerabilities with the highest CVSS scores are generally considered to require early attention.

However, the vulnerabilities with higher CVSS scores may not always be the ones that should be addressed first. Instead, look at scores and the entire vulnerability scan in the context of the organization. These questions about a vulnerability may help in identifying which ones need early attention:

- Can the vulnerability be addressed in a reasonable amount of time, or would it take several days or even a week to fix?
- Can the vulnerability be exploited by an external threat actor, or would exploitation require that the person be sitting at a computer in a vice president's office?
- If the vulnerability led to threat actors infiltrating the system, would they be able to pivot to more important systems, or would they be isolated?
- Is the data on the affected device sensitive or is it public?
- Is the vulnerability on a critical system that runs a core business process, or is it on a remote device that is rarely used?

Prioritizing vulnerabilities is an inexact and sometimes difficult process. However, attention should first be directed toward vulnerabilities deemed to be critical (those that can cause the greatest degree of harm to the organization). Another part of prioritizing is making sure that the difficulty and time for implementing the correction is reasonable.

Accuracy Another consideration when examining results of a vulnerability scan is to review its accuracy. First, be sure to identify false positives. A false positive is an alarm raised when there is no problem; a false negative is the failure to raise an alarm when there is an issue. Vulnerability scans may produce false positives for several reasons; for example, scan options may not have been well defined or may have been missed in a configuration review, or the scanner might not recognize a control that is already in place to address an existing vulnerability. Security professionals should attempt to identify false positives in a scan report, especially those that would require extensive effort to address.

One means of identifying false positives is to correlate the vulnerability scan data with several internal data points. The most common are related log files. Because a log is simply a record of events that occur, system event logs document any unsuccessful events and the most significant successful events. The types of information recorded might include the date and time of the event; a description of the event; its status, error codes, and service name; and the user or system that was responsible for launching the event. Log reviews, or an analysis of log data, can be used to identify false positives.

Logs can be particularly helpful internal data points when correlating with vulnerability scan results. For example, if a scan indicates that a vulnerability in a software application was found on a specific device, but a follow-up investigation revealed that the application was no longer vulnerable, log files could indicate whether that program's configuration had been changed between the time of the scan and the follow-up analysis.

Data Management Tools

In addition to logs, each of the tools for monitoring the security of a network—such as resource monitors, firewalls, and routers—also generate security alerts continuously because an enterprise is the target of continual attacks. How can these alerts, all from different sources and generated at different times, be monitored and managed while searching for evidence of vulnerabilities and attacks?

Two data management tools are used for collecting and analyzing this data. These tools are Security Information and Event Management (SIEM) and Security Orchestration, Automation and Response (SOAR).

Security Information and Event Management (SIEM)

A **Security Information and Event Management (SIEM)** product (usually pronounced *seem* instead of *sim*) consolidates real-time security monitoring and management of *security information* with analysis and reporting of *security events*. A SIEM product can be a separate device, software that runs on a computer, or even a service provided by a third party. A SIEM dashboard is shown in Figure 2-8.

Figure 2-8   SIEM dashboard

The starting point of a SIEM is the data input. Data feeds into a SIEM are the standard packet captures of network activity and log collections. Because of the numerous network devices producing logs, SIEMs also perform log aggregation. A SIEM typically has the following features:

- *Aggregation. SIEM aggregation* combines data from multiple data sources—such as network security devices, servers, and software applications—to build a comprehensive picture of attacks.
- *Correlation.* The *SIEM correlation* feature searches the data acquired through SIEM aggregation to look for common characteristics, such as multiple attacks coming from a specific source.
- *Automated alerting and triggers. SIEM automated alerting and triggers* can inform security personnel of critical issues that need immediate attention. A sample trigger may be *Alert when a firewall, router, or switch indicates 40 or more drop/reject packet events from the same IP source address within 60 seconds.*
- *Time synchronization.* Because alerts occur over a wide spectrum of time, *SIEM time synchronization* can show the order of the events.
- *Event duplication.* When the same event is detected by multiple devices, each generates an alert. The *SIEM event duplication* feature can help filter the multiple alerts into a single alarm.
- *Logs. SIEM logs* or records of events can be retained for future analysis and to show that the enterprise has been in compliance with regulations.

However, a SIEM goes beyond collecting and aggregating data. A SIEM can perform **user behavior analysis**. User behavior analysis looks at the normal behavior of users and how they interact with systems to create a picture of typical "everyday" activity. A user's account suddenly acting in an unusual fashion, such as a lateral movement between assets, could indicate that a threat actor has compromised that account. A SIEM can generate an alert for further investigation.

SIEMs can also perform **sentiment analysis**. Sentiment analysis is the process of computationally identifying and categorizing opinions, usually expressed in response to textual data, to determine the writer's attitude toward a particular topic. In other words, sentiment analysis is the interpretation and classification of emotions (positive, negative, and neutral) within text data using text analysis techniques. Sentiment analysis has been used when tracking postings threat actors make in discussion forums with other attackers to better determine the behavior and mindset of threat actors. This type of information can be valuable in determining their goals and actions and has even been used as a predictive power to alert against future attacks.

NOTE 10

Sentiment analysis is often used by businesses while conducting online chats with customers or examining Twitter and other social media posts to identify customer sentiment toward products, brands, and services.

Security Orchestration, Automation, and Response (SOAR)

A **Security Orchestration, Automation, and Response (SOAR)** product is similar to a SIEM in that it is designed to help security teams manage and respond to security warnings and alarms. However, SOARs take it a step further by combining more comprehensive data gathering and analytics to automate incident response. While a SIEM tends to generate more alerts than a security team may be able to respond to, a SOAR allows a security team to automate incident responses.

Threat Hunting

It is common today for threat actors to invade a network by slipping past defenses. These threat actors then quietly lurk in "stealth" mode, evading detection, looking for confidential material or stealing login credentials to infiltrate laterally across the network. Attackers can remain unnoticed for weeks, months, and even years before they finally find their valuable treasure.

Vulnerability scans and the SIEM and SOAR tools that provide dashboards of security incidents are considered as *reactive*: during or after an event occurs, something is noticed, and alarms are sounded.

What if instead of being reactive, security tools could be more *proactive*? That is, rather than waiting for an attack to take place, what if the threats could be identified before they occur? That is the principle behind threat hunting. **Threat hunting** is proactively searching for cyber threats that thus far have gone undetected in a network.

Threat hunting begins with a critical major premise: *threat actors have already infiltrated our network*. It proceeds to find unusual behavior that may indicate malicious activity. One means of finding this unusual behavior is for the threat hunter himself to conduct unusual behavior, called **maneuvering**. For example, passwords on an administrator's account are changed every two hours (not a normal activity) to determine if a hidden threat actor is making internal password-cracking attempts. Another maneuver is to clear Domain Name Server (DNS) caches regularly to help detect if the hidden attacker is trying to communicate with an external server.

Threat hunting investigations often use crowdsourced attack data. This data includes *advisories and bulletins*, cybersecurity **threat feeds**, which are data feeds of information on the latest threats, and information from a **fusion center**, which is a formal repository of information from enterprises and the government used to share information on the latest attacks. By learning from others who have been successfully attacked, threat hunters can use this attack data for insight into the attacker's latest tactics, techniques, and procedures. Threat hunting also uses advanced data analytics to sift massive amounts of data to detect irregularities that may suggest potential malicious activity. These anomalies then become hunting leads that skilled analysts investigate to identify the silent threats.

TWO RIGHTS & A WRONG

1. The purpose of a vulnerability scan is to reduce the attack surface.
2. SIEMs generate alerts and automate incident response.
3. The Common Vulnerabilities and Exposures (CVE) vulnerability feed identifies vulnerabilities in operating systems and application software.

See Appendix B for the answer.

CYBERSECURITY RESOURCES

✅ CERTIFICATION

1.5 Explain different threat actors, vectors, and intelligence sources.

5.2 Explain the importance of applicable regulations, standards, or frameworks that impact organization security posture.

It would be a sobering task for an organization to attempt to mount a defense against threat actors by itself. Fortunately, that is not necessary. A variety of external cybersecurity resources are available that defenders have at their disposal to help ward off attacks. These resources include frameworks, regulations, legislation, standards, benchmarks/secure configuration guides, and information sources.

Frameworks

A cybersecurity **framework** is a series of documented processes used to define policies and procedures for implementing and managing security controls in an enterprise environment. About 84 percent of U.S. organizations use a security framework, and 44 percent use multiple frameworks.[1] The most common frameworks are from the National Institute of Standards and Technology (NIST), International Organization for Standardization (ISO), American Institute of Certified Public Accountants (AICPA), Center for Internet Security (CIS), and Cloud Security Alliance (CSA).

National Institute of Standards and Technology (NIST)

The National Institute of Standards and Technology (NIST), operating under the U.S. Commerce Department, created the NIST cybersecurity frameworks as a set of guidelines for helping private companies identify, detect, and respond to cyberattacks. These frameworks also include guidelines for how to prevent and recover from an attack.

The NIST cybersecurity frameworks are divided into three basic parts. The first part is the *framework core*, which defines the activities needed to attain different cybersecurity results. The framework core is further subdivided into four elements, which are listed in Table 2-5.

Table 2-5   Cybersecurity framework core elements

Element Name	Description	Example
Functions	The most basic cybersecurity tasks	Identify, protect, detect, respond, and recover
Categories	Tasks to be carried out for each of the five functions	To protect a function, organizations must implement software updates, install antivirus and antimalware programs, and have access control policies in place
Subcategories	Tasks or challenges associated with each category	To implement software updates (a category), organizations must be sure that Windows computers have auto-updates turned on
Information Sources	The documents or manuals that detail specific tasks for users and explain how to accomplish the tasks	A document is required that details how auto-updates are enabled on Windows computers

The second part of the NIST cybersecurity frameworks is the *implementation tiers*. The NIST framework specifies four implementation tiers that help organizations identify their level of compliance: the higher the tier, the more compliant the organization.

The third and final part is *profiles*. Profiles relate to the current status of the organization's cybersecurity measures and the "road maps" toward compliance with the NIST cybersecurity framework. Profiles are like an executive summary of everything an organization has done for the NIST cybersecurity framework, and they can help demonstrate how each function, category, or subcategory can increase security. These profiles allow organizations to see their vulnerabilities at each step; once the vulnerabilities are mitigated, the organization can move up to higher implementation tiers. There are two widely used NIST frameworks:

- *Risk Management Framework (RMF).* The NIST Risk Management Framework (RMF) is considered a guidance document designed to help organizations assess and manage risks to their information and systems. It is viewed as comprehensive road map that organizations can use to seamlessly integrate their cybersecurity, privacy, and supply-chain risk management processes.
- *Cybersecurity Framework (CSF).* The NIST Cybersecurity Framework (CSF) is used as a measuring stick companies can use to compare their cybersecurity practices to the threats they face. The elements of the CSF are shown in Figure 2-9.

Figure 2-9   NIST Cybersecurity Framework (CSF) functions

International Organization for Standardization (ISO)

The International Organization for Standardization (ISO) has created a wide array of cybersecurity standards. The ISO 27000 is a family of 72 standards designed to help organizations keep information assets secure. ISO 27001 is a standard that provides requirements for an information security management system (ISMS). An ISMS is a systematic approach to managing sensitive assets so that they remain secure. These assets include the people, processes, and IT systems used to manage risk. ISO 27002 is a code of practice for information security management within an organization and contains 114 control recommendations. ISO 27701, an extension to ISO 27001, is a framework for managing privacy controls to reduce the risk of privacy breach to the privacy of individuals. ISO 31000 contains controls for managing and controlling risk.

American Institute of Certified Public Accountants (AICPA)

The American Institute of Certified Public Accountants (AICPA) is the national professional organization for Certified Public Accountants (CPAs) in the United States. The AICPA has created a series of Statements on Standards for Attestation Engagements (SSAE). (An "attestation engagement" is technically "an arrangement with a client where an independent third party investigates and reports on subject matter created by a client" but is better known as an internal controls report or audit.) One AICPA SSAE is a suite of services called the System and Organization Controls (SOCs), which are service offerings that Certified Public Accountants (CPAs) may provide in connection with system-level controls of a service organization or entity-level controls of other organizations. The two primary SOCs that relate to cybersecurity are the following:

- *SSAE SOC 2 Type II.* The SSAE SOC 2 Type II report is an internal controls report that reviews how a company safeguards customer data and how well those controls are operating. As an audit, it looks at internal controls, policies, and procedures that directly relate to the security of a system at a service organization. The SOC 2 report is designed to determine if service organizations are compliant with the categories of security, availability, processing integrity, confidentiality, and privacy.
- *SSAE SOC 2 Type III.* The SSAE SOC 2 Type III report is the same as a SOC 2 Type II except for its distribution. A SOC 3 report can be freely distributed, whereas a SOC 2 can only be read by the user organizations that rely on the services. While a SOC 3 does not give a description of the service organization's system, it can provide interested parties with the auditor's report on whether an entity maintained effective controls over its systems.

Center for Internet Security (CIS)

The Center for Internet Security (CIS) is a nonprofit community-driven organization. It has created two recognized frameworks. The *CIS Controls* are controls for securing an organization and consist of more than 20 basic and advanced cybersecurity recommendations. The *CIS Benchmarks* are frameworks for protecting 48 operating systems and application software.

NOTE 11

Other security frameworks include ISACA Control Objectives for Information and Related Technology (COBIT), Sherwood Applied Business Security Architecture (SABSA), Open Group Architecture Framework, and AXELOS IT Infrastructure Library (ITIL).

Cloud Security Alliance

The **Cloud Security Alliance (CSA)** is an organization whose goal is to define and raise awareness of best practices to help secure cloud computing environments. Its **Cloud Controls Matrix** is a specialized framework (*meta-framework*) of cloud-specific security controls. These controls are mapped to the leading standards, best practices, and regulations regarding cloud computing and are generally regarded as the authoritative source of information (**reference architecture**) about securing cloud resources. The current version of the Cloud Controls Matrix is v3.0.1 and was released in August 2019.

Regulations

Another cybersecurity resource are *regulations,* and the process of adhering to them is called *regulatory compliance.* Industry **regulations** are typically developed by established professional organizations or government agencies using the expertise of seasoned security professionals. These regulations are followed by companies that have similar business processes, resulting in a common set of tested and approved regulations that are under continual review and revision. Almost every industry has its own set of regulations, and cybersecurity is no exception; several regulations relate to IT and specifically to cybersecurity.

However, organizations face significant challenges to achieve regulatory compliance. First, virtually all organizations must follow multiple regulations from different regulatory bodies. For example, this is a small sample of cybersecurity regulations or related regulations that an organization may be required to follow:

- *Broadly applicable regulations.* Sarbanes-Oxley Act (SOX or Sarbox), Payment Card Industry Data Security Standard (PCI DSS), Gramm-Leach-Bliley (GLB) Act, Electronic Fund Transfer Act, Regulation E (EFTA), Customs-Trade Partnership Against Terrorism (C-TPAT), Free and Secure Trade Program (FAST), Children's Online Privacy Protection Act (COPPA), Fair and Accurate Credit Transaction Act (FACTA), including Red Flags Rule, Federal Rules of Civil Procedure (FRCP), Computer Fraud and Abuse Act (CFAA), Federal Privacy Act of 1974, Federal Intelligence Surveillance Act (FISA) of 1978, Electronic Communications Privacy Act (ECPA) of 1986, Communications Assistance for Law Enforcement Act (CALEA) of 1994, and the USA Patriot Act of 2001
- *Industry-specific regulations.* Federal Information Security Management Act (FISMA), North American Electric Reliability Corp. (NERC) standards, Title 21 of the Code of Federal Regulations (21 CFR Part 11) Electronic Records, Health Insurance Portability and Accountability Act (HIPAA), The Health Information Technology for Economic and Clinical Health Act (HITECH), Patient Safety and Quality Improvement Act (PSQIA, Patient Safety Rule), and H.R. 2868: The Chemical Facility Anti-Terrorism Standards Regulation
- *U.S. state regulations.* Massachusetts 201 CMR 17, Nevada Personal Information Data Privacy Encryption Law NRS 603A
- *International regulations.* Personal Information Protection and Electronic Documents Act (PIPEDA) in Canada, Federal Law on the Protection of Personal Data Held by Private Parties in Mexico and Safe Harbor Act. An international regulation that has received worldwide attention is the **European Union General Data Protection Directive (GDPR)**. The GDPR is a regulation regarding data protection and privacy in the EU and the European Economic Area (EEA). Its aim is to give individuals control over their personal data, to address the transfer of personal data to areas outside the EU and EEA, and to simplify the regulatory environment for international business by creating a single regulation across all EU members.

 **CAUTION**   With so many regulations that must be followed, organizations often find it difficult to meet all of the requirements. Also, it is not unusual for a requirement in one regulation to adversely impact—or, in some instances, even negate—a requirement in another regulation.

Legislation

Specific legislation or laws can also be enacted by governing bodies that can provide a cybersecurity resource. These include national, territorial, and state laws. However, with the number of different entities involved in passing multiple—and even contradictory—legislation, this often leads to a hodgepodge of legislation and is not always a good cybersecurity resource.

As an example, consider legislation regarding notification for a specific type of cyber incident. The United States does not have a federal law that requires a notification. In that absence, states have legislative mandates for communication. California's Database Security Breach Notification Act was passed in 2003, and by 2018, all other states had passed similar notification laws. Although there is a common core of definitions about personal information and what constitutes a breach of security, due to a lack of comprehensive federal regulations for data breach notification, many states have amended their breach notification laws from the basic definitions shown here. As a result, no two state laws are the same. Table 2-6 lists some of the deviations from these basic definitions, along with examples of states where the deviations occur and expanded definitions of the laws.

Table 2-6   Deviations in state laws from basic definitions

Deviation	Example State	Expanded Definition
Broader definition of personal information	Alabama	A tax identification number; passport number; military identification number; other unique identification number issued on a government document used to verify the identity of a specific individual; any information about an individual's medical history, mental or physical condition, or medical treatment or diagnosis by a healthcare professional; health insurance policy number or subscriber identification number and any unique identifier used by a health insurer to identify the individual; a username or email address in combination with a password or security question and answer.
Notification triggered by access to data and not documented theft	Florida	"Breach of security" means unauthorized access to personal information in electronic format.
Breach must satisfy risk-of-harm analysis	Arkansas	Notification is not required if, after a reasonable investigation, the business determines that there is no reasonable likelihood of harm to customers.
Expanded notification beyond impacted citizens	Colorado	Additional notice must be provided to the state attorney general.
Includes encryption safe harbor	Alaska	The statute only applies to unencrypted information or encrypted information when the encryption key has also been disclosed.
Covers other forms of data	Hawaii	The statute applies to personal information in any form, whether computerized, paper, or otherwise.

Standards

A **standard** is a document approved through consensus by a recognized standardization body. It provides for frameworks, rules, guidelines, or characteristics for products or related processes and production methods. Strictly speaking, compliance is not mandatory, but there may be restrictions for those organizations that do not comply.

One cybersecurity standard is the **Payment Card Industry Data Security Standard (PCI DSS)**. The PCI DSS compliance standard was introduced to provide a minimum degree of security for handling customer card information. Requirement 11 of the latest standard (PCI DSS 3.2.1) states that organizations must *regularly test security systems and processes* using both vulnerability scans and penetration tests. A partial list of the PCI DSS Requirement 11 standards is shown in Table 2-7.

Table 2-7   PCI DSS Requirement 11 standards

Standard	Description	Frequency
11.1	Implement processes to test for the presence of wireless access points (802.11) and detect and identify all authorized and unauthorized wireless access points.	Quarterly
11.2	Run internal and external network vulnerability scans to address vulnerabilities and perform rescans as needed until passing scans are achieved. External scans must be performed by an Approved Scanning Vendor (ASV), while scans conducted after network changes and internal scans may be performed by internal staff.	At least quarterly and after any significant change in the network
11.3	Develop and implement a methodology for penetration testing that includes external and internal testing. If segmentation is used to reduce PCI DSS scope, perform penetration tests to verify that the segmentation methods are operational and effective. Service providers using segmentation must confirm PCI DSS scope by performing penetration testing on segmentation controls.	At least annually and after any significant upgrade or modification; service providers must perform penetration testing at least every six months and after making changes to controls

Benchmarks/Secure Configuration Guides

Benchmark/secure configuration guides are usually distributed by hardware manufacturers and software developers. These serve as guidelines for configuring a device or software so that it is resilient to attacks. Usually, these are platform/vendor-specific guides that only apply to specific products. Guides are available for network infrastructure devices, OSs, web servers, and application servers.

Information Sources

There are a variety of information sources that can provide valuable in-depth information. Generic sources include

- Vendor websites
- Conferences
- Academic journals
- Local industry groups
- Social media

There are also specialized research sources that apply specifically to cybersecurity. Requests for comments (RFCs) are white papers documents that are authored by technology bodies employing specialists, engineers, and scientists who are experts in those areas. These RFCs describe methods, behaviors, research, or innovations applicable to cybersecurity. *Data feeds* are continually maintained databases of the latest cybersecurity incidences. Common cybersecurity data feeds include vulnerability feeds that provide information on the latest vulnerabilities and threat feeds that outline current threats and attacks. The adversary tactics, techniques, and procedures (TTP) is a database of the behavior of threat actors and how they orchestrate and manage attacks.

TWO RIGHTS & A WRONG

1. The two NIST frameworks are the NIST Risk Management Framework (RMF) and NIST Cybersecurity Framework (CSF).
2. The Center for Internet Security (CIS) has published a Cloud Controls Matrix.
3. The European Union General Data Protection Directive (GDPR) is a regulation regarding data protection and privacy in the EU and the European Economic Area (EEA).

See Appendix B for the answer.

 **VM LAB** You're now ready to complete the live virtual machine labs for this module. The labs can be found in each module in the MindTap.

SUMMARY

- Penetration testing attempts to exploit vulnerabilities just as a threat actor would. This helps to uncover new vulnerabilities, provide a clearer picture of their nature, and determine how they could be used against the organization. The most important element in a pen test is the first step of planning. A lack of planning can result in a flawed penetration test that tries to do too little or too much. A scan of network defenses can help find vulnerabilities, but the types of vulnerabilities revealed are different from a penetration test. A scan usually finds only surface problems to be addressed. This is because many scans are entirely automated and provide only a limited verification of any discovered vulnerabilities. A penetration test can find deep vulnerabilities. Penetration tests go further and attempt to exploit vulnerabilities using manual techniques.

- Using internal employees to conduct a penetration test has advantages in some cases. First, there is little or no additional cost. Also, the test can be conducted much more quickly. However, these employees may lack expertise or have too much inside knowledge to be able to perform a valid pen test. External pen tester consultants have the credentials and experience for conducting a test. Recently, some third-party organizations have begun offering crowdsourced pen testing. Instead of contracting with a single external pen tester consulting organization, crowdsourced pen testing involves a large group of individuals who are not regular employees of an organization.

- The rules of engagement in a penetration test are its limitations or parameters. Without these parameters, a penetration test may not accomplish the desired results, may take too long to produce timely results, or may test assets that are not necessary to test. The categories for the rules for engagement are timing, scope, authorization, exploitation, communication, cleanup, and reporting.

- The first phase of a penetration test is reconnaissance, also called footprinting. Active reconnaissance involves directly probing for vulnerabilities and useful information, much like a threat actor would do. Passive reconnaissance takes an entirely different approach: the tester uses tools that do not raise any alarms. The second phase is penetration by simulating the actions of an attacker. After the initial system is compromised, threat actors then pivot or turn to other systems to be compromised, with the goal of reaching the ultimate target.

- A penetration test is a single event using a manual process that is usually performed only after a specific amount of time has passed, such as once a year (and sometimes only to comply with regulatory requirements). However, a vulnerability scan is a frequent and ongoing process, often automated, that continuously identifies vulnerabilities and monitors cybersecurity progress. A vulnerability assessment is a cyclical and continual process of ongoing scanning and continuous monitoring to reduce the attack surface.

- The best approach for vulnerability scanning is not to scan all systems all the time. Usually, it is not practical to do so. A more focused approach is to know the location of data so that specific systems with high-value data can be scanned more frequently. There are several types of vulnerability scans. A credentialed scan is a scan in which valid authentication credentials, such as usernames and passwords, are supplied to the vulnerability scanner to mimic the work of a threat actor who possesses these credentials. A non-credentialed scan provides no such authentication information. An intrusive scan attempts to employ any vulnerabilities it finds, much like a threat actor would. A nonintrusive scan does not attempt to exploit the vulnerability but only records that it was discovered.

- Vulnerability information is available to provide updated information to scanning software about the latest vulnerabilities. The Mitre Common Vulnerabilities and Exposures (CVE) identifies vulnerabilities in operating systems and application software. When examining the results of a vulnerability scan, you should assess the importance of vulnerability as well as its accuracy.

- Two data management tools are used for collecting and analyzing this data. The first is the Security Information and Event Management (SIEM) tool. It consolidates real-time security monitoring and management of security information with analysis and reporting of security events. A SIEM product can be a separate device, software that runs on a computer, or even a service provided by a third party. A Security Orchestration, Automation, and Response (SOAR) tool is similar to a SIEM in that it is designed to help security teams manage and respond to the very high number of security warnings and alarms. However, SOARs combine more comprehensive data gathering and analytics in order to automate incident response. Threat hunting is proactively searching for cyber threats that thus far have gone undetected in a network.

- There are a variety of external cybersecurity resources available that defenders have at their disposal to help ward off attacks. A cybersecurity framework is a series of documented processes used to define policies and procedures for implementation and management of security controls in an enterprise environment. The most common frameworks are from the National Institute of Standards and Technology (NIST), International Organization for Standardization (ISO), American Institute of Certified Public Accountants (AICPA), Center for Internet Security (CIS), and Cloud Security Alliance (CSA). Regulations are another cybersecurity resource. Industry regulations are typically developed by established professional organizations or government agencies using the expertise of seasoned security professionals. These regulations are followed by companies that have similar business processes, resulting in a common set of tested and approved regulations that are under continual review and revision. Specific legislation or laws can also be enacted by governing bodies that can provide a cybersecurity resource.

- A standard is a document approved through consensus by a recognized standardization body. It provides for frameworks, rules, guidelines, or characteristics for products or related processes and production methods. Strictly speaking, compliance is not mandatory, but there may be restrictions for those organizations that do not comply. Benchmark/secure configuration guides are usually distributed by hardware manufacturers and software developers. These serve as a guideline for configuring a device or software so that it is resilient to attacks. Usually these are platform/vendor-specific guides that only apply to specific products. A variety of information sources can provide valuable information. Some are generic sources while others are specific to cybersecurity.

- Deep vulnerabilities can only be exposed through actual attacks that use the mindset of a threat actor. First, the attacks must be the same (or remarkably similar) as those used by a threat actor; anything less will not uncover the deep vulnerabilities that an attacker can find. Second, the attacks should follow the thinking of threat actors. Understanding their thinking helps to better perceive what assets they are seeking, how they may craft the attack, and even how determined they are to obtain assets. Without having an attacker's mindset, it is difficult to find these deep vulnerabilities.

Key Terms

active reconnaissance
adversary tactics, techniques, and
  procedures (TTP)
benchmark/secure configuration
  guides
Black box
Blue Team
bug bounty
Center for Internet
  Security (CIS)
cleanup
Cloud Controls Matrix
Cloud Security Alliance (CSA)
Common Vulnerabilities and
  Exposures (CVE)

Common Vulnerability Scoring
  System (CVSS)
configuration review
credentialed scan
drone
European Union General Data
  Protection Directive (GDPR)
false negative
false positive
footprinting
framework
fusion center
Gray box
intrusive scan
ISO 27001

ISO 27002
ISO 27701
ISO 31000
lateral movement
log
log reviews
maneuvering
NIST Cybersecurity
  Framework (CSF)
NIST Risk Management
  Framework (RMF)
non-credentialed scan
nonintrusive scan
open source intelligence (OSINT)
passive reconnaissance

Payment Card Industry Data
  Security Standard (PCI DSS)
penetration testing
persistence
pivot
platform/vendor-specific
  guides
privilege escalation
Purple Team
Red Team
reference architecture

regulations
request for comments (RFC)
rules of engagement
Security Information and Event
  Management (SIEM)
Security Orchestration,
  Automation and Response
  (SOAR)
sentiment analysis
SSAE SOC 2 Type II
SSAE SOC 2 Type III

standard
threat feeds
threat hunting
unmanned aerial vehicle (UAV)
user behavior analysis
vulnerability feeds
vulnerability scan
war driving
war flying
White box
White Team

Review Questions

1. Ebba has received a new initiative for her security team to perform an in-house penetration test. What is the first step that Ebba should undertake?
   a. Approval
   b. Budgeting
   c. Planning
   d. Documentation

2. Which of the following is NOT a characteristic of a penetration test?
   a. Automated
   b. Finds deep vulnerabilities
   c. Performed occasionally
   d. May use internal employees or external consultants

3. Linnea has requested to be placed on the penetration testing team that scans for vulnerabilities to exploit them. Which team does she want to be placed on?
   a. Blue Team
   b. Purple Team
   c. White Team
   d. Red Team

4. Lykke's supervisor is evaluating whether to use internal security employees to conduct a penetration test. Lykke does not consider this a good idea and has created a memo with several reasons they should not be used. Which of the following would NOT be part of that memo?
   a. The employees could have inside knowledge of the network that would give them an advantage.
   b. There may be a lack of expertise.
   c. Employees may have a reluctance to reveal a vulnerability.
   d. They would have to stay overnight to perform the test.

5. What penetration testing level name is given to testers who have no knowledge of the network and no special privileges?
   a. Black box
   b. Gray box
   c. White box
   d. Purple box

6. Which of the following is NOT an advantage of crowdsourced penetration testing?
   a. Faster testing
   b. Less expensive
   c. Ability to rotate teams
   d. Conducting multiple tests simultaneously

7. Tilde is working on a contract with the external penetration testing consultants. She does not want any executives to receive spear-phishing emails. Which rule of engagement would cover this limitation?
   a. Scope
   b. Exploitation
   c. Targets
   d. Limitations and exclusions

8. Which is the final rule of engagement that would be conducted in a pen test?
   a. Cleanup
   b. Communication
   c. Reporting
   d. Exploitation

9. What is another name for footprinting?
   a. High-level reconnaissance
   b. Active reconnaissance
   c. Modeling
   d. Revealing

10. When researching how an attack recently took place, Nova discovered that the threat actor, after penetrating the system, started looking to move through the network with their elevated position. What is the name of this technique?
    a. Jumping
    b. Twirling
    c. Squaring up
    d. Lateral movement

11. What are documents that are authored by technology bodies employing specialists, engineers, and scientists who are experts in those areas?
    a. Cybersecurity feeds
    b. White notebooks
    c. Blue papers
    d. Requests for comments (RFCs)

12. Which of the following is not a general information source that can provide valuable in-depth information on cybersecurity?
    a. Twitter
    b. Conferences
    c. Local industry groups
    d. Vendor websites

13. Which of the following is a standard for the handling of customer card information?
    a. DRD STR
    b. OSS XRS
    c. RMR CDC
    d. PCI DSS

14. Which of the following are developed by established professional organizations or government agencies using the expertise of seasoned security professionals?
    a. Legislation
    b. White papers
    c. Regulations
    d. Benchmarks

15. Which group is responsible for the Cloud Controls Matrix?
    a. CSA
    b. CIS
    c. OSINT
    d. NIST

16. Tuva's supervisor wants to share a recent audit outside the organization. Tuva warns him that this type of audit can only be read by those within the organization. What audit does Tuva's supervisor want to distribute?
    a. SSAE SOC 2 Type II
    b. SSAE SOC 2 Type III
    c. SSAE SOC 3 Type IV
    d. SSAE SOC 3.2 Type X

17. Which ISO contains controls for managing and controlling risk?
    a. ISO XRS
    b. ISO 31000
    c. ISO 271101
    d. ISO 27555

18. Which premise is the foundation of threat hunting?
    a. Cybercrime will only increase.
    b. Threat actors have already infiltrated our network.
    c. Attacks are becoming more difficult.
    d. Pivoting is more difficult to detect than ever before.

19. Which of the following can automate an incident response?
    a. SIEM
    b. SOAR
    c. CVCC
    d. SOSIA

20. Which of the following is NOT something that a SIEM can perform?
    a. User behavior analysis
    b. Sentiment analysis
    c. Log aggregation
    d. Incident response

Hands-On Projects

Project 2-1: Exploring Common Vulnerabilities and Exposures (CVE)

Time Required: 20 minutes

Objective: Summarize the techniques used in security assessments.

Description: Vulnerability feeds are available to provide updated information to scanning software about the latest vulnerabilities. One of the most highly regarded vulnerability feeds is the Mitre Common Vulnerabilities and Exposures (CVE). Feeds can also be manually examined for information on the latest vulnerabilities. In this project, you will learn more about CVE and view CVE information.

1. Open your web browser and enter the URL **https://cve.mitre.org/** (if you are no longer able to access the site through this web address, use a search engine to search for "Mitre CVE").
2. Click **About**.
3. Click **About CVE**.
4. This page gives a brief overview of CVE. Read through the information regarding CVE. In your own words, how would you describe it? How does it work? What advantages does it provide?
5. Point to **About**.
6. Click **FAQs** to display more detailed information on CVE. Who is behind CVE? Who owns it? How is it used? How does CVE compare to a vulnerability database? How would you answer the argument that threat actors could use CVE?
7. Scroll down to **CVE Entries**. Describe the three elements that make up a CVE Entry.
8. Scroll down to **CVE List Basics**. What is the process by which a vulnerability becomes a CVE listing? Who is involved in this process?
9. Click the link **CVE Data Feeds**. Scroll through the newest CVE entries feed. Were you aware of these vulnerabilities? How does the CVE distribute its information? Would you consider it sufficient? How can this be used by security personnel?
10. Click **Search CVE List**.
11. Enter a generic vulnerability such as **passwords** to display the CVE entries. How many are there that relate to this topic?
12. Select several of the CVE entries and read through the material.
13. Locate a CVE entry that contains the tag *Disputed*. Click this entry. Under *Description* click ****DISPUTED**** to read about what constitutes a disputed CVE. Who would dispute a CVE? Why?
14. Click **Search CVE List**.
15. Enter a different vulnerability and select several entries to read through its details.
16. Close all windows.

Project 2-2: Exploring the National Vulnerability Database

Time Required: 20 minutes
Objective: Explain different threat actors, vectors, and intelligence sources.
Description: The National Vulnerability Database (NVD) is managed by the U.S. government as a repository for vulnerability management data and contains software flaws, misconfigurations, product names, and their impacts. In this project, you will explore the NVD.

1. Open your web browser and enter the URL **https://nvd.nist.gov/** (if you are no longer able to access the site through this web address, use a search engine to search for "NIST NVD").
2. Click the plus sign next to **General**.
3. Click **FAQ**.
4. Click **General FAQs**.
5. Read through the material. In your own words, how does the Mitre CVE compare with the NIST NVD? When would you use the CVE? When would you use the NVD? How frequently is the NVD updated? Is this often enough?
6. Return to the home page by clicking the back button as many times as necessary.
7. Click the plus sign next to **General**.
8. Click **NVD Dashboard** to view the latest information. Do the numbers surprise you? How does the number of vulnerabilities under the score distribution compare? Is that what you would have expected?
9. Scroll through the *Last 20 Scored Vulnerability IDs & Summaries*. Have you heard of any of these vulnerabilities? How will they be distributed to the public at large?
10. Return to the home page.
11. Click the plus sign next to **General**.
12. Click **Visualizations** to display graphical information.
13. Click **Vulnerabilities – CVE**.

14. Click **Description Summary Word** to display a bar graph of the most common words used as part of a vulnerability description, as seen in Figure 2-10. Hover over the three highest bars to view the three most frequent words used. Is this what you would have expected?

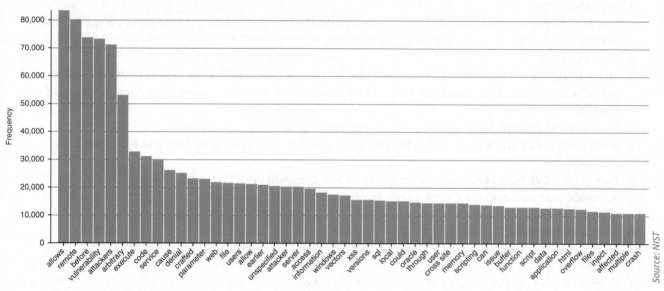

Figure 2-10 NVD Description Summary Word Frequency

15. Return to the Vulnerability Visualizations page. Select each of the other graphs and study the information presented. How could this information be used by a security professional?

16. Return to the NVD Visualizations page. Click **Products – CPE**. Which vendor has the highest number of total products that appears in the NVD? View other vendors by hovering over the bars. What do you find interesting about this distribution?

17. Return to the home page by clicking the back button as many times as necessary.

18. Click the plus sign next to **Other Sites**.

19. Click **Checklist (NCP) Repository**.

20. This page displays a form you can use to search for benchmarks/secure configuration guides. Select different parameters to view different guides, and then select one to view in detail. Is this information helpful?

21. Return to the home page by clicking the back button as many times as necessary.

22. Click the plus sign next to **Search**.

23. Click **Vulnerability Search**.

24. Enter **passwords**. How many vulnerabilities are found? Select several of these to read through the information.

25. Select a different vulnerability to search the NVD database. How useful is this information?

26. Close all windows.

Project 2-3: Sentiment Analysis

Time Required: 20 minutes

Objective: Summarize the techniques used in security assessments.

Description: Sentiment analysis is the process of computationally identifying and categorizing opinions, usually expressed in response to textual data, in order to determine the writer's attitude toward a particular topic. It has been used when tracking postings threat actors make to determine the behavior and mindset of threat actors and has even been used as a predictive power to alert against future attacks. In this project, you will experiment with sentiment analysis to learn of its capabilities.

1. Open your web browser and enter the URL **https://monkeylearn.com/** (if you are no longer able to access the site through this web address, use a search engine to search for "MonkeyLearn").

2. Click **RESOURCES** and then **Guides**. This webpage helps show how sentiment analysis fits into the context of artificial intelligence.

3. Click **Sentiment Analysis** and read through what it is, how it is useful, and how it can be performed.

4. Now create an account. Go to **https://app.monkeylearn.com/accounts/register/** and follow the instructions to create a MonkeyLearn account, and then sign in.

5. Click **Explore**.

6. Click **Sentiment Analysis**.

7. Enter the text **I like sunshine.** and click **Classify Text**. What tag does it provide, and what is the confidence level?

8. Enter several random phrases and perform an analysis on each.

9. Return to the Explore screen.

10. Select **Hotel Aspect**.

11. Search the Internet for two reviews of a hotel—one that you consider would be positive and another that would be negative—and paste the first review into the text box. Click **Classify Text**. Would you agree with the analysis? Then do the same with the second review.

12. Return to the Explore screen.

13. Select **Sentiment Analysis**.

14. Use a search engine to search the Internet for *cybersecurity quotations.* Cut and paste several of these into the text box and analyze them.

15. Now enter statements from threat actors. Go to Google Images (**https://images.google.com**).

16. Enter the search word **ransomware**.

17. Locate ransomware screens that contain messages from threat actors and enter these into the Sentiment Analysis text box for analysis. What is the sentiment analysis for these quotations from threat actors?

18. How could sentiment analysis be useful in identifying a threat actor's mindset? Do you think it could be used for predicting attacks?

19. Close all windows.

Case Projects

Case Project 2-1: False Positives and False Negatives

Use the Internet to research false positives and false negatives. Which is worse? If a doctor gives information to a patient about the results of a diagnostic test, is a false positive or a false negative worse? What about facial recognition scanning for a criminal? Which is worse for a vulnerability scan, a false positive or a false negative? Write a one-page paper on your findings and analysis.

Case Project 2-2: Pen Test Products

Use the Internet to research pen test scanners. Select three scanners and create a table that compares their features. Be sure to include such elements as how often they are updated, the systems they run on, and available tools. Based on your analysis, which would you recommend? Why?

Case Project 2-3: Vulnerability Scanners

Search the Internet for information on Nessus. Then search for two other vulnerability scanners. Create a table that compares their features. Which would you choose? Why?

Case Project 2-4: Threat Actor Tactics

Most users are unaware of how threat actors work and their various tactics. Read the article *Tales From the Trenches; a Lockbit Ransomware Story* at **www.mcafee.com/blogs/other-blogs/mcafee-labs/tales-from-the-trenches-a-lockbit-ransomware-story/**. This article contains detailed information about the tactics of threat actors for a particular strain of ransomware. Although some of the information is very technical in nature, it does give a good picture of the advanced skills and strategies used today. Write a one-paragraph summary of what you have learned about their tactics.

Case Project 2-5: Information Security Community Site Activity

The Information Security Community Site is an online companion to this textbook. It contains a wide variety of tools, information, discussion boards, and other features to assist learners. In order to gain the most benefit from the site, you will need to set up a free account.

Go to **community.cengage.com/infosec2**. Create a posting about what you have learned in Module 2. What were your biggest surprises? What did you already know? How could you use this information in your first security job?

Case Project 2-6: North Ridge Security

North Ridge Security provides security consulting and assurance services to more than 500 clients in more than 20 states for a wide range of enterprises. A new initiative at North Ridge is for each of its seven regional offices to provide internships to students who are in their final year of the security degree program at the local college.

North Ridge is preparing a request for proposal (RFP) for a potential new client to perform a penetration test. You have been asked to develop a first draft on the rules of engagement for pen testing a web server running the Apache OS and Apache Tomcat.

1. Use the Internet to research information about Apache OS and Apache Tomcat. Then create a rules of engagement document that contains your recommendations for the seven engagement rules found in this module.
2. As a follow-up to your rules of engagement document, create a PowerPoint presentation for the potential customer on why they should use North Ridge Security instead of internal security personnel or crowdsourced pen testers. Your presentation should be at least seven slides in length.

References

1. Watson, Melanie, "Top 4 Cybersecurity Frameworks," *IT Governance*, Jan. 17, 2019, accessed Sep. 13, 2019, www.itgovernanceusa.com/blog/top-4-cybersecurity-frameworks.

ENDPOINT SECURITY

An *endpoint* is any hardware device connected to a network. This includes stationary devices (desktop computers and printers), mobile devices (laptops, smartphones, and tablets), and specialized hardware (Internet of Things (IoT) devices). The modules in this second part identify the threats and attacks directed at endpoints and the security that should be applied to these devices and their applications.

MODULE 3
THREATS AND ATTACKS ON ENDPOINTS

MODULE 4
ENDPOINT AND APPLICATION DEVELOPMENT SECURITY

PART 2

THREATS AND ATTACKS ON ENDPOINTS

After completing this module, you should be able to do the following:

1. Identify the different types of attacks using malware
2. Define application attacks
3. Explain how threat actors use application attacks
4. Define adversarial artificial intelligence attacks

Front-Page Cybersecurity

Despite the skyrocketing number of ransomware attacks in the past five years, ransomware has been used for more than 30 years. The first known ransomware attack was initiated in 1989 by an AIDS researcher. He carried out his attack by distributing 20,000 floppy disks to other AIDS researchers in more than 90 countries with an accompanying message that the disks contained a program that analyzed an individual's risk of acquiring AIDS. However, the disk also contained ransomware that remained dormant until the computer had been turned on 90 times. At the next startup, the ransomware displayed a message demanding a payment of $189 (plus $378 for use of the program).

Today, ransomware attacks are running rampant. There were an estimated 184 million ransomware attacks in 2018. In 2019, attackers using ransomware turned their sights on government agencies, educational institutions, and even healthcare providers. But these incidents were not just expensive inconveniences; the disruption they caused put health, safety, and even lives at risk. Ransomware attacks on healthcare providers resulted in emergency patients being redirected to other hospitals, inaccessible medical records, cancelled surgical procedures, postponed lab tests, and suspended hospital admissions. Emergency responder and law enforcement agencies were also common victims so that emergency 911 services were interrupted, police were unable to access details about criminal histories or active warrants, and jail doors could not be opened.[1]

What is fueling the rapid rise of ransomware? Is it a growing sophistication of attackers? Misguided users? More powerful ransomware? The answer, according to some, is none of these but something entirely unexpected.

The rapid rise of ransomware is attributed to cyber insurance.

Cyber insurance started 20 years ago by Lloyd's of London, and today it is an $8 billion industry. About 80 percent of Lloyd's cyber insurance is written for U.S. entities. A cyber insurance policy is not cheap. The city of Houston is now taking out three $10 million policies from three different insurance companies for a total of $30 million in coverage. For this, Houston will pay $471,400 annually in premiums. Another Texas city, Fort Worth, has only a $5 million policy, but it costs $99,570 in annual premiums.

How can the blame be placed on cyber insurance agencies for the rapid growth of ransomware?

Following a ransomware attack, enterprises and government agencies need to get back to normal as quickly as possible. Every minute they are locked out of their computers because of ransomware, they are losing money or putting individuals at risk. Cyber insurers claim that it makes more financial sense to pay the ransom and get the key to unlock encrypted files so that organizations can get back to normal quickly.

However, paying the ransom is actually an advantage to the cyber insurance agencies. By paying the ransom, cyber insurance agencies hold down their overall costs. They do not have to pay for lost revenue due to downtime brought on by ransomware or pay for third-party security consultants to aid in the data recovery. But when insurers reward attackers by paying the ransom, they might actually be encouraging more ransomware attacks because attackers know they will be paid. In addition, an increase in the number of ransomware attacks could frighten more businesses and government agencies into buying cyber insurance policies.

But doesn't paying the ransom cost the cyber insurance agencies money? No. Cyber insurance is a very lucrative business. The "loss ratio" is an industry standard for comparing premiums paid for insurance (what comes in) against insurance claims (what goes out). For all property and casualty insurance, like auto insurance and homeowner insurance, that loss ratio is about 62 percent (or for every dollar of premiums, about 62 cents are paid out in claims). However, for cyber insurance, it is only 35 percent, meaning that the cyber insurance agencies pay 35 cents in claims for each dollar of premiums.

Some researchers claim that cyber insurance is increasing number of ransomware attacks. In fact, the chief technology officer for a well-known antivirus company has said, "Cyber insurance is what's keeping ransomware alive today."[2]

Throughout the years, different words have been used to describe network-connected hardware devices. Thirty years ago, when the TCP/IP protocol was becoming popular, the word *host* referred to any communicating device on the network (networks were made up of hosts). Twenty years ago, as servers became more popular, the word *client* was used (clients made requests to servers).

Today, a different word is commonly used when referring to network-connected hardware devices: *endpoints*. This change reflects the fact that devices that are connected to a network today are far more than a computing device with a keyboard and monitor. Instead, devices ranging from mobile smartphones and tablets to wearable fitness trackers, industrial control system sensors, automotive telematics units, and even personal drones are all network-connected hardware devices. The word endpoint has become an accurate description of today's end-user technology devices.

This change in terminology also reflects the increased risks that have multiplied—exponentially—with the increase of these new devices. Instead of protecting hosts or clients located inside a network security perimeter, today each endpoint is a target for attackers to attempt to steal or manipulate their data. And because the endpoints are connected to the network, a vulnerability on an endpoint can result in an attack that penetrates the network and infects all other endpoints. In short, today *every endpoint is a potential entry point*.

This module examines threats and attacks on endpoints. It begins by looking at attacks using various types of malware and then looks at application attacks. It concludes by examining adversarial artificial intelligence attacks.

ATTACKS USING MALWARE

 CERTIFICATION

1.2 Given a scenario, analyze potential indicators to determine the type of attack.

In a legal setting, a "computer contaminant" is defined as any set of computer instructions that is designed to modify, damage, destroy, record, or transmit information within a computer, computer system, or network without the intent or permission of the owner of the information, computer system, or network.[3] This legal definition is the basis for the definition of the cybersecurity word **malware** (*mal*icious soft*ware*), which is software that enters a computer system without the user's knowledge or consent and then performs an unwanted and harmful action. Malware is most often used as the general term that refers to a wide variety of damaging software programs.

Malware is continually evolving to avoid detection by improved security measures. According to one report, the number of new malware releases every month exceeds 20 million, and the total malware in existence is approaching 900 million instances.[4] Yet no standard has been established for the classification of the different types of malware so that like malware can be grouped together for study.

One attempt at classifying the diverse types of malware can be to examine the primary action that the malware performs and then group those together with similar actions. These malware actions used for groupings are imprison, launch, snoop, deceive, and evade.

Imprison

A prison is a building or location housing individuals who have been deprived of their freedom. Some types of malware attempt to take away the freedom of the user to do whatever they want on their computer. The types of malware that imprisons are ransomware and cryptomalware.

Ransomware

One of the fastest-growing types of malware is ransomware. **Ransomware** prevents a user's endpoint device from properly and fully functioning until a fee is paid; that is, it takes away a user's freedom from freely using their computer until the ransom is transacted. The ransomware embeds itself onto the computer in such a way that it cannot be bypassed, and even rebooting causes the ransomware to launch again.

Ransomware became widespread around 2010. This earliest ransomware displays a screen and prevents the user from accessing the computer's resources (called *blocker ransomware*). The screen contains instructions that pretends to be from a reputable third party, giving a "valid" reason for blocking the user's computer. One example is ransomware that purports to come from a law enforcement agency. This message, using official-looking imagery, states that the user performed an illegal action such as downloading pornography and must immediately pay a fine online by entering a credit card number. Figure 3-1 shows a blocker ransomware message.

NOTE 1

The popular vulnerability feed Mitre Common Vulnerabilities and Exposures (CVE) assigns a CVE ID number, brief description, and any pertinent references but does not try to group common vulnerabilities together. Likewise, the National Vulnerability Database (NVD) does not attempt to classify vulnerabilities. Both CVE and NVD are covered in Module 2.

NOTE 2

Some malware has more than one of these actions. However, in terms of classification, the *primary* action of the malware is used here.

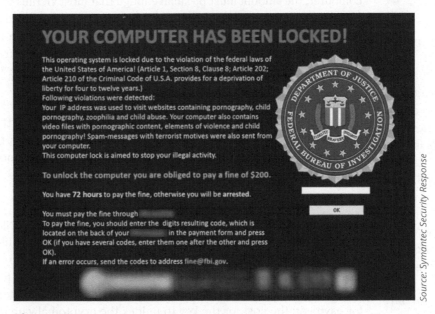

Source: Symantec Security Response

Figure 3-1 Blocker ransomware message

Another variation of this type of ransomware pretends to come from a software vendor and displays a fictitious warning that a software license has expired or there is a problem with the computer such as imminent hard drive failure or—in a touch of irony—a malware infection. This ransomware variation tells users that they must immediately renew their license or purchase additional software online to fix a nonexistent problem. The ransomware example in Figure 3-2 uses color schemes and icons like those found on legitimate software.

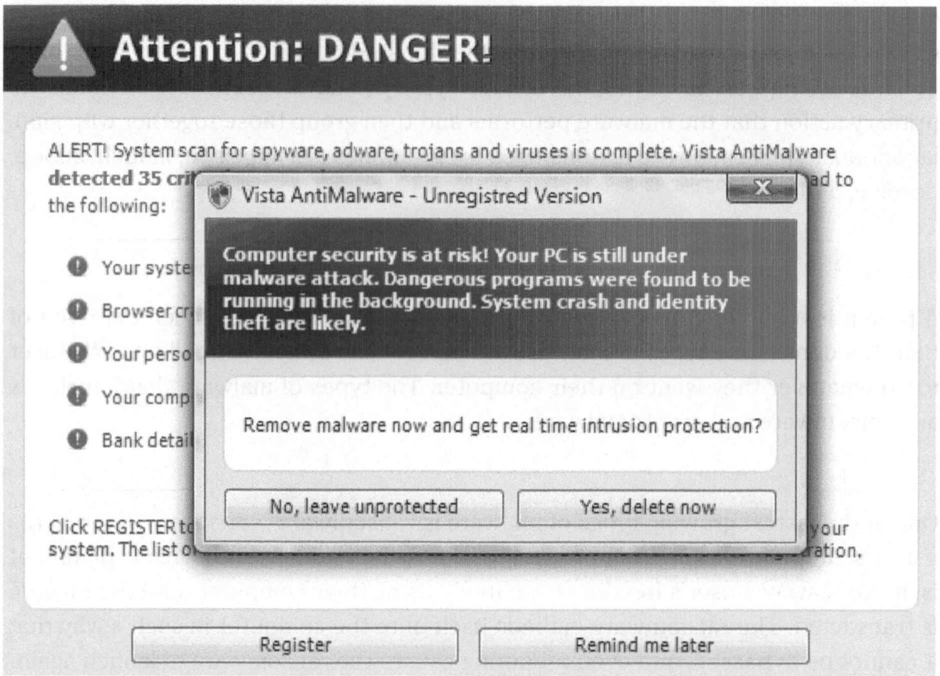

Source: Used with permissions from Microsoft

Figure 3-2   Ransomware computer infection

NOTE 3

Researchers have developed an entirely new means of detecting a ransomware infection, and it works even if the type of ransomware is new and has never been seen before. When ransomware begins to encrypt files, the computer's temperature, power consumption, and voltage levels experience a surge. Sensors can detect these surges and immediately halt the encryption process, stopping ransomware dead in its tracks.

NOTE 4

Originally, the FBI did not support paying a ransom in any circumstances. It said, "The FBI does not advocate paying a ransom, in part because it does not guarantee an organization will regain access to its data ... Paying ransoms emboldens criminals to target other organizations and provides an alluring and lucrative enterprise to other criminals." But in late 2019, the FBI seemingly softened its stance by adding, "However, the FBI understands that when businesses are faced with an inability to function, executives will evaluate all options to protect their shareholders, employees, and customers."[8]

As ransomware became more widespread, the threat agents dropped the pretense that the ransomware was from a reputable third party. Instead, they simply blocked the user's computer and demanded a fee for its release. Ransomware attackers have determined what they consider the optimal price point for payment to unblock a computer: the amount must be small enough that most victims will begrudgingly pay to have their systems unblocked, but large enough that when thousands of victims pay up, the attackers can garner a handsome sum. For individuals, the ransom is usually around $500. However, for enterprises, the price has increased dramatically: the average ransom paid for one type of malware was more than $1.3 million, and the average ransom for all ransomware has increased by one-third.[5]

Ransomware continues to be a serious threat to users. Threat actors have now shifted their sights to state and local governments that typically have weaker security. In 2019, two-thirds of ransomware attacks targeted state and local governments;[6] to date, more than 350 of these governments have been the victims of successful attacks.[7]

Cryptomalware

In recent years, a more malicious form of ransomware has arisen. Instead of just blocking users from accessing the computer, it encrypts all the files on the device so that none of them can be opened. This is called **cryptomalware**. A screen appears telling the victims that their files are now encrypted, and a fee must be paid to receive a key to unlock them. In addition, threat actors have increased the urgency for payment: the cost for the key to unlock the cryptomalware increases every few hours or days. On some occasions, the threat actors claim that a growing number of the encrypted user files will be deleted until the ransom is paid; if the ransom is not paid promptly, the key to unlock the files can never be purchased. Figure 3-3 shows a cryptomalware message.

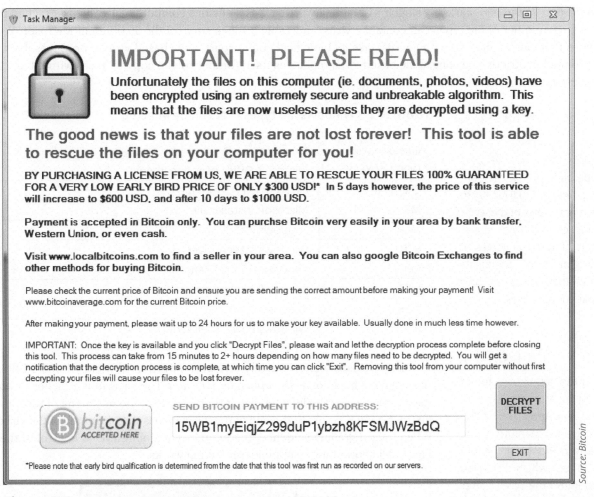

Figure 3-3   Cryptomalware message

In addition to encrypting files on the user's local hard drive, new variants of cryptomalware encrypt all files on *any* network or attached device connected to that computer. This includes secondary hard disk drives, USB hard drives, network-attached storage devices, network servers, and even cloud-based data repositories. Thus, if a user's computer in an enterprise is infected with cryptomalware, potentially *all* files for the enterprise—and not just those on one computer—can be locked.

Launch

Another category of malware is that which infects a computer to launch attacks on other computers. This includes a virus, worm, and bot.

Virus

There are two types of viruses: a file-based virus and a fileless virus.

File-Based Virus   A biological virus is composed of tiny bits of genetic material enclosed by a protective shell. By themselves, viruses are lifeless and inert as they wait for a favorable environment in which to reproduce. When a virus encounters a host cell, the virus attaches itself to the outer wall of the cell, enters inside, travels to the cell's genome, merges with its genes, and then tricks the host's genome into make copies of itself.

NOTE 5

With early cryptomalware attacks, threat actors only delivered the decryption key fewer than half of the times that a ransom was paid. However, this resulted in some victims not paying a ransom since the risk was high of not getting the key. Threat actors have since learned that there is more to gain in the long run of making the key available after a ransom is paid. Today, when victims pay the ransom, a decryption tool is delivered 99 percent of the time. However, the key only works about 96 percent of the time. This is because specific variants of ransomware have a tendency to corrupt data when it is encrypted.[9]

A *file-based virus* is remarkably similar to a biological virus. It is malicious computer code that is attached to a file. A very large number of file types can contain a virus, and Table 3-1 lists some of the 50 different Microsoft Windows file types that can be infected with a virus. Like its biological counterpart, a file-based virus reproduces itself on the same computer. Strictly speaking, a file-based virus replicates itself (or an evolved copy of itself) without any human intervention.

NOTE 6

When the host cell is infected by a virus, the virus takes over the operation of that cell, converting it into a virtual factory to make more copies of the virus. The host cell rapidly produces millions of identical copies of the original virus. Biologists often say that viruses exist only to make more viruses.

Table 3-1   Windows file types that can be infected

File extension	Description
DOCX or XLSX	Microsoft Office user documents
EXE	Executable program file
MSI	Microsoft installer file
MSP	Windows installer patch file
SCR	Windows screen saver
CPL	Windows Control Panel file
MSC	Microsoft Management Console file
WSF	Windows script file
PS1	Windows PowerShell script

NOTE 7

One of the first viruses found on a microcomputer was written for the Apple II in 1982. Rich Skrenta, a ninth-grade student in Pittsburgh, wrote "Elk Cloner," which displayed his poem on the screen after every 50th use of the infected floppy disk. Unfortunately, the virus leaked out and found its way onto the computer used by Skrenta's math teacher. In 1984, the mathematician Dr. Frederick Cohen introduced the term *virus* based on a recommendation from his advisor, who came up with the name from reading science fiction novels.

Early viruses were relatively straightforward in how they infected files. One basic type of infection is the *appender infection*. The virus first attaches or appends itself to the end of the infected file. It then inserts at the beginning of the file a *jump* instruction that points to the end of the file, which is the beginning of the virus code. When the program is launched, the jump instruction redirects control to the virus. Figure 3-4 shows how an appender infection works.

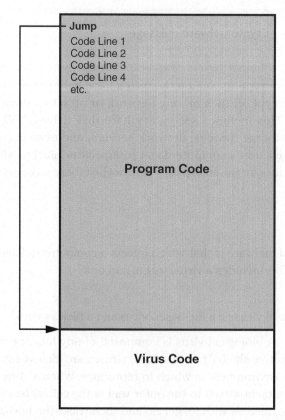

Figure 3-4   Appender infection

However, these types of viruses could be detected by virus scanners relatively easily. Later file-based viruses went to greater lengths to avoid detection; this type of virus is called an *armored file-based virus*. Some of the armored virus infection techniques include the *split infection* (it split the malicious code itself into several parts and then these parts are placed at random positions throughout the program code) and the *mutation* (the virus changes its internal code to one of a set number of predefined mutations whenever it is executed).

Each time the infected program is launched or the data file is opened—either by the user or the computer's operating system (OS)—the virus first unloads a payload to perform a malicious action (such as to corrupt or delete files, prevent programs from launching, steal data to be sent to another computer, cause a computer to crash repeatedly, or turn off the computer's security settings). Then the virus reproduces itself by inserting its code into another file, but only on the same computer. A virus can only replicate itself on the host computer where it is located; it cannot automatically spread to another computer by itself. Instead, it must rely on the actions of users to spread to other computers. Because viruses are attached to files, they are spread when a user transfers those files to other devices. For example, a user might send an infected file as an email attachment or copy an infected file to a USB flash drive and give the drive to another user. Once the virus reaches a new computer, it begins to infect it. Thus, a virus must have two carriers: a file to which it attaches and a human to transport it to other computers.

Fileless Virus   A fileless virus, on the other hand, does not attach itself to a file. Instead, fileless viruses take advantage of native services and processes that are part of the OS to avoid detection and carry out its attacks. These native services used in a fileless virus are called *living-off-the-land binaries (LOLBins)*. For a computer running Microsoft Windows, some of commonly exploited LOLBins are listed in Table 3-2.

Table 3-2   Microsoft Windows common LOLBins

Name	Description
PowerShell	A cross-platform and open source task automation and configuration management framework
Windows Management Instrumentation (WMI)	A Microsoft standard for accessing management information about devices
.NET Framework	A free, cross-platform, open source developer platform for building different types of applications
Macro	A series of instructions that can be grouped together as a single command to automate a complex set of tasks or a repeated series of tasks, can be written by using a macro scripting language, such as Visual Basic for Applications (VBA), and is stored within the user document (such as in an Excel .xlsx workbook or Word .docx file)

Unlike a file-based virus, a fileless virus does not infect a file and wait for that file to be launched. Instead, the malicious code of a fileless virus is loaded directly in the computer's random access memory (RAM) through the LOLBins and then executed.

There are several advantages of a fileless virus over a file-based virus:

- *Easy to infect*. A fileless virus does not require that a specific type of file be stored on the computer's hard drive for the virus to infect. Instead, a common delivery method is through malicious webpages that the user visits. These pages silently send a script to the victim's web browser, which invokes a scripting language such as JavaScript. The browser passes instructions to a LOLBin such as PowerShell, which reads and executes the commands.

NOTE 8

Some armored viruses scan for the presence of files that security researchers typically use. If those files are present, the virus assumes it is being examined for weaknesses and automatically self-destructs by deleting itself.

NOTE 9

Several similarities between biological and computer viruses exist: both must enter their host passively (by relying on the action of an outside agent), both must be on the correct host (a horse virus cannot make a human sick, just as an Apple Mac virus cannot infect a Windows computer), both can only replicate when inside the host, both may remain dormant for a period of time, and both types of viruses replicate at the expense of the host.

NOTE 10

Microsoft Windows LOLBins are often categorized into binaries (programs that end in .EXE), libraries (.DLL), and scripts (.VBS). By some estimates 115 Windows LOLBins can be exploited by a fileless virus, while UNIX/Linux systems have 185 LOLBins.

- *Extensive control.* Several LOLBins have extensive control and authority on a computer. For example, PowerShell has full access to the core OS of a Windows computer, so it can undermine existing security features. PowerShell can also manipulate user accounts and password protection.
- *Persistent.* A program that is loaded into RAM for execution will terminate once the computer is shut down or rebooted. However, fileless viruses often write their script into the *Windows Registry*, which is a database that stores settings for the Windows OS and application programs. Each time the computer is restarted or on a set schedule, the script of the fileless virus is again launched.
- *Difficult to detect.* Files that are infected with a file-based virus can be scanned by an antivirus tool for detection. However, because a fileless virus loads into RAM, no telltale file can be scanned. Also, by using LOLBins, there is no evidence of other tools being used. And some LOLBins like PowerShell run in a section of system memory that cannot be queried or searched, making its activities virtually impossible to detect.
- *Difficult to defend against.* To fully defend against a fileless virus, it would be necessary to turn off all the potential LOLBins, which would cripple the OS and cause it to not properly function. Also, these LOLBins are loaded by default when the OS starts so that any attempt to turn selected LOLBins off would already be too late.

Worm

A second type of malware that has as its primary purpose to spread is a worm. A **worm** is a malicious program that uses a computer network to replicate. (Worms are sometimes called *network viruses*.) A worm is designed to enter a computer through the network and then take advantage of a vulnerability in an application or an OS on the host computer. Once the worm has exploited the vulnerability on one system, it immediately searches for another computer on the network that has the same vulnerability.

NOTE 11

One of the first wide-scale worm infections occurred in 1988. This worm exploited a misconfiguration in a program that allowed commands emailed to a remote system to be executed on that system. The worm also carried a payload containing a program that attempted to determine user passwords. Almost 6,000 computers, or 10 percent of the devices connected to the Internet at that time, were affected. The threat actor responsible was later convicted of federal crimes in connection with this incident.

Early worms were relatively benign and designed simply to spread quickly but not corrupt the systems they infected. These worms slowed down the network through which they were transmitted by replicating so quickly that they consumed all network resources. Today's worms can leave behind a payload on the systems they infect and cause harm, much like a virus. Actions that worms have performed include deleting files on the computer or allowing the computer to be remotely controlled by an attacker.

NOTE 12

Although viruses and worms are said to be automatically self-replicating, *where* they replicate is different. A virus self-replicates *on* the host computer but does not spread to other computers by itself. A worm self-replicates *between* computers (from one computer to another).

Bot

Another popular payload of malware is software that allows the infected computer to be placed under the remote control of an attacker for the purpose of launching attacks. This infected robot computer is known as a **bot** or *zombie*. When hundreds, thousands, or even millions of bot computers are gathered into a logical computer network, they create a *botnet* under the control of a *bot herder*.

NOTE 13

Due to the multitasking capabilities of modern computers, a computer can act as a bot while carrying out the tasks of its regular user. Users are completely unaware that their computer is being used for malicious activities.

Table 3-3 lists some of the attacks that can be generated through botnets.

Table 3-3   Uses of botnets

Type of attack	Description
Spamming	Botnets are widely recognized as the primary source of spam email. A botnet consisting of thousands of bots enables an attacker to send massive amounts of spam.
Spreading malware	Botnets can be used to spread malware and create new bots and botnets. Bots can download and execute a file sent by the attacker.
Ad fraud	Threat actors earn money by generating a high number of "clicks" on advertisements at targeted websites, using a bot to mimic the mouse clicks of a user.
Mining cryptocurrencies	Also called "cryptomining," this is a process in which transactions for various forms of cryptocurrency are verified, earning the "miner" a monetary reward. Botnets combine the resources of millions of bots for mining cryptocurrencies.

Infected bot computers receive instructions through a **command and control (C&C)** structure from the bot herders regarding which computers to attack and how. There are a variety of ways for this communication to occur, including the following:

- A bot can receive its instructions by automatically signing in to a bot-herding website where information has been placed that the bot knows how to interpret as commands.
- Bots can sign in to a third-party website; this has an advantage of the bot herder not needing to have a direct affiliation with that website.
- Commands can be sent via blogs, specially coded attack commands through posts on Twitter, or notes posted in Facebook.
- Bot herders are increasingly using a "dead drop" C&C mechanism by setting up a Google Gmail email account and then creating a draft email message that is never sent but contains commands the bot receives when it logs in to Gmail and reads the draft. Because the email message is never sent, there is no record of the commands. All Gmail transmissions are protected so that outsiders cannot view them.

Snoop

Another category of malware "snoops" or spies on its victims. The two common types of snooping malware are spyware and keyloggers.

Spyware

Spyware is tracking software that is deployed without the consent or control of the user. Spyware can secretly monitor users by collecting information without their approval through the computer's resources, including programs already installed on the computer, to collect and distribute personal or sensitive information. Table 3-4 lists different technologies used by spyware.

Table 3-4   Technologies used by spyware

Technology	Description	Impact
Automatic download software	Downloads and installs software without the user's interaction	Could install unauthorized applications
Passive tracking technologies	Gathers information about user activities without installing any software	Could collect private information such as websites a user has visited
System modifying software	Modifies or changes user configurations, such as the web browser home page or search page, default media player, or lower-level system functions	Changes configurations to settings that the user did not approve
Tracking software	Monitors user behavior or gathers information about the user, sometimes including personally identifiable or other sensitive information	Could collect personal information that can be shared widely or stolen, resulting in fraud or identity theft

>  **CAUTION** Not all spyware is necessarily malicious. For example, spyware monitoring tools can help parents keep track of the online activities of their children.

Keylogger

Another type of spying is done with a **keylogger** that silently captures and stores each keystroke that a user types on the computer's keyboard. The threat actor can then search the captured text for any useful information such as passwords, credit card numbers, or personal information. A keylogger can be a software program or a small hardware device.

Software keyloggers are programs installed on the computer that silently capture sensitive information. However, software keyloggers, which conceal themselves so that the user cannot detect them, go far beyond capturing a user's keystrokes. These programs can also capture everything on the user's screen and silently turn on the computer's web camera to record images of the user. A software keylogger is illustrated in Figure 3-5.

NOTE 14

An advantage of software keyloggers is that they do not require physical access to the user's computer because they can be installed remotely. They can routinely send captured information back to the attacker through the victim's own Internet connection.

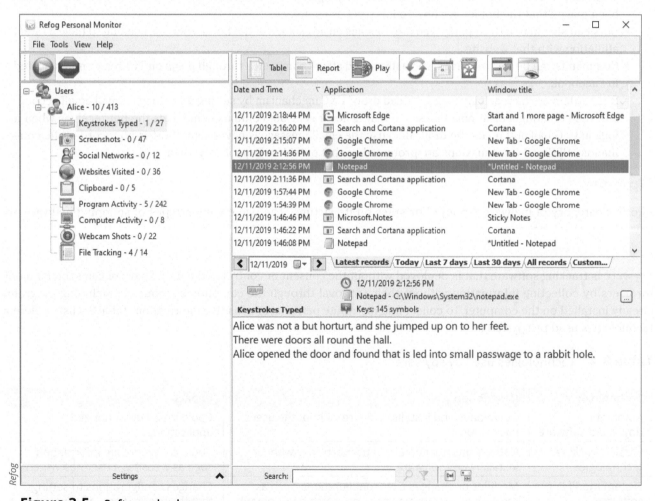

Figure 3-5   Software keylogger

For computers that are in a public location such as a library or computer lab but are "locked down" so that no software can be installed, a hardware keylogger can be used instead. These keyloggers are hardware devices inserted between the computer keyboard connection and USB port, as shown in Figure 3-6. Because the device resembles an ordinary keyboard plug and the computer keyboard USB port is often on the back of the computer, a hardware keylogger can easily go undetected. In addition, the device is beyond the reach of the computer's antimalware scanning software and thus raises no alarms. A disadvantage of a hardware keylogger is that the threat actor must install and then later return to physically remove the device in order to access the information it has stored, each time being careful not to be detected.

Hardware
keylogger

Figure 3-6   Hardware keylogger

Deceive

Some malware attempts to deceive the user and hide its true intentions. Software in this category includes potentially unwanted programs (PUPs), Trojans, and remote access Trojans (RATs).

Potentially Unwanted Program (PUP)

A broad category of software that is often more annoying than malicious is called **potentially unwanted programs (PUPs)**. A PUP is software that the user does not want on their computer. PUPs often become installed along with other programs and are the result of the user overlooking the default installation options on software downloads, as seen in Figure 3-7.

Figure 3-7   Default installation options

NOTE 15

The term PUP was created by an Internet security company because marketing firms objected to having their products being called "spyware."

PUPs may include software that is pre-installed on a new computer or smartphone and cannot be easily removed (if at all). Other examples of PUPs are advertising that obstructs content or interferes with web browsing, pop-up windows, pop-under windows, search engine hijacking, home page hijacking, toolbars with no value for the user, and settings that redirect to competitors' websites, alter search results, and replace ads on webpages.

Trojan

According to ancient legend, the Greeks won the Trojan War by hiding soldiers in a large hollow wooden horse that was presented as a gift to the city of Troy. Once the horse was wheeled into the fortified city, the soldiers crept out of the horse during the night and attacked the unsuspecting defenders.

A computer **Trojan** is an executable program that masquerades as performing a benign activity but also does something malicious. For example, a user might download what is advertised as a calendar program, yet in addition to installing the calendar, it also installs malware that scans the system for credit card numbers and passwords, connects through the network to a remote system, and then transmits that information to the attacker.

Remote Access Trojan (RAT)

A special type of Trojan is a **remote access Trojan (RAT)**. A RAT has the basic functionality of a Trojan but also gives the threat agent unauthorized remote access to the victim's computer by using specially configured communication protocols. This creates an opening into the victim's computer, allowing the threat agent unrestricted access. The attacker can not only monitor what the user is doing but also change computer settings, browse and copy files, and even use the computer to access other computers connected on the network.

Evade

The final category of malware attempts to help malware or attacks evade detection. This includes backdoor, logic bomb, and rootkit.

Backdoor

A **backdoor** gives access to a computer, program, or service that circumvents any normal security protections. Backdoors installed on a computer allow the attacker to return later and bypass security settings.

Creating a legitimate backdoor is a common practice by developers, who may need to access a program or device on a regular basis, yet do not want to be hindered by continual requests for passwords or other security approvals. The intent is for the backdoor to be removed once the application is finalized. However, in some instances, backdoors have been left installed, and attackers have used them to bypass security.

Logic Bomb

A **logic bomb** is computer code that is typically added to a legitimate program but lies dormant and evades detection until a specific logical event triggers it. Once it is triggered, the program then deletes data or performs other malicious activities.

NOTE 16

Many logic bombs have been planted by disgruntled employees. For example, a Maryland government employee tried to destroy the contents of more than 4,000 servers by planting a logic bomb script that was scheduled to activate 90 days after he was terminated.

Logic bombs are difficult to detect before they are triggered. This is because logic bombs are often embedded in very large computer programs, some containing hundreds of thousands of lines of code, and a trusted employee can easily insert a few lines of computer code into a long program without anyone detecting it. In addition, these programs are not routinely scanned for containing malicious actions.

Rootkits

A **rootkit** is malware that can hide its presence and the presence of other malware on the computer. It does this by accessing "lower layers" of the operating system or even using undocumented functions to make alterations. This enables the rootkit and any accompanying software to become undetectable by the operating system and common antimalware scanning software that is designed to seek and find malware.

NOTE 17

The risks of rootkits are significantly diminished today due to protections built into operating systems. These protections include preventing unauthorized kernel drivers from loading, stopping modifications to certain kernel areas used by rootkits to hide, and preventing rootkits from modifying the bootloader program.

TWO RIGHTS & A WRONG

1. It is a common tactic for cryptomalware attackers to not send the decryption key after the ransom has been paid.
2. Fileless viruses take advantage of native services and processes that are part of the operating system (OS) to avoid detection and carry out its attacks, and these native services used in a fileless virus are called living-off-the-land binaries (LOLBins).
3. A remote access Trojan (RAT) can monitor what the user is doing, change computer settings, browse and copy files, and use the computer to access other computers connected on the network.

See Appendix B for the answer.

APPLICATION ATTACKS

 **CERTIFICATION**

1.3 Given a scenario, analyze potential indicators associated with application attacks.

Attacks using malware typically add malicious software to an endpoint. Another category of attacks specifically targets software applications that are already installed and running on the device. These attacks look for vulnerabilities in the application or manipulate the application in order to compromise it. While on occasion threat actors target applications running on a user's endpoint like a personal computer, more often, their sights are set on compromising applications that can provide many more potential victims than a single computer user. The more common targets of attackers using application attacks are Internet web servers.

A web server provides services that are implemented as "web applications" through software applications running on the server. A typical web application infrastructure is shown in Figure 3-8. The client's web browser makes a request using the Hypertext Transport Protocol (HTTP) to a web server, which may be connected to one or more web application servers. These application servers run the specific "web apps," which in turn are directly connected to database servers on the internal network. Information from these database servers is retrieved and returned to the web server so that the information can be sent back to the user's web browser.

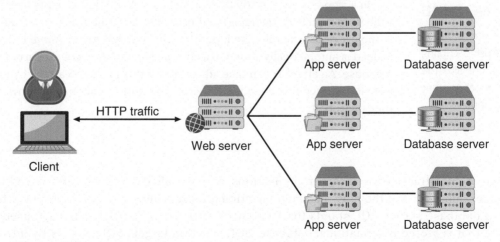

Figure 3-8   Web server application infrastructure

The multiple elements in a web application infrastructure provide multiple attack points: a single vulnerability could expose many other users who are accessing the web server. An attack could also compromise backend databases and app servers, and the connected network infrastructure.

Application attacks include scripting attacks, injection attacks, request forgery attacks, and replay attacks. These attacks typically target how the applications function. In addition, attacks directly focused on vulnerabilities in the software applications are common.

Scripting

Most web applications create dynamic content based on input from the user. Figure 3-9 illustrates a fictitious web application that allows friends to share their favorite bookmarks with each other online. Users can enter their name, a description, and the URL of the bookmark and then receive a personalized "Thank You" screen. In Figure 3-10, the code that generates the "Thank You" screen is illustrated.

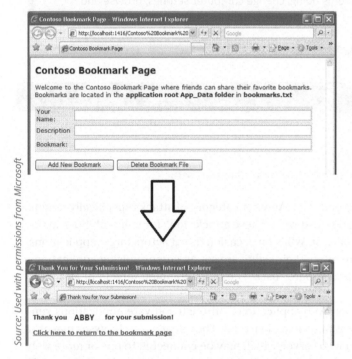

Source: Used with permissions from Microsoft

Figure 3-9 Bookmark page that accepts user input

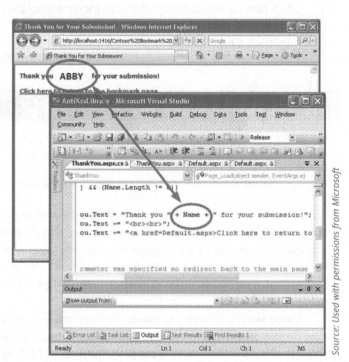

Source: Used with permissions from Microsoft

Figure 3-10 Input used in response

In a **cross-site scripting (XSS)** attack, a website that accepts user input without validating it (called *sanitizing*) and uses that input in a response can be exploited. In the previous example, the input that the user enters for *Name* is not verified but instead is automatically added to a code segment that becomes part of an automated response. An attacker can take advantage of this in an XSS attack by tricking a valid website into feeding a malicious script to another user's web browser, which will then execute it.

Injection

In addition to cross-site attacks on web server applications, attacks called **injections** also introduce new input to exploit a vulnerability. One of the most common injection attacks, called **SQL injection**, inserts statements to manipulate a database server. SQL stands for **Structured Query Language**, a language used to view and manipulate data that is stored in a relational database. SQL injection targets SQL servers by introducing malicious commands into them.

Consider a webpage that offers a solution for users who have forgotten their password. An online form asks users to enter their username, which is also their email address that is already on file. The submitted email address is compared to the stored email address, and if they match, a reset URL is emailed to that address.

If the email address entered by the user into the form is stored in the variable *$EMAIL*, then the underlying SQL statement to retrieve the stored email address from the database would be similar to this:

```
SELECT fieldlist FROM table WHERE field = '$EMAIL'
```

The *WHERE* clause is meant to limit the database query to only display information when the condition is considered true (that is, when the email address in *$EMAIL* matches an address in the database).

An attacker using an SQL injection attack would begin by first entering a fictitious email address on this webpage that included a single quotation mark as part of the data, such as *braden.thomas@fakemail.com'*. If the message *E-mail Address Unknown* is displayed, it indicates that user input is being properly filtered and an SQL attack cannot be rendered on the site. However, if the error message *Server Failure* is displayed, it means that the user input is not being filtered and all user input is sent directly to the database. This is because the *Server Failure* message is due to a syntax error created by the additional single quotation mark in the fictitious email address.

Armed with the knowledge that input is sent unfiltered to the database, the attacker knows that anything he enters as a username in the form would be sent to and then processed by the SQL database. Now, instead of entering a user name, the attacker would enter this command, which would let him view all the email addresses in the database: *whatever' or 'a'='a*. This command is stored in the variable *$EMAIL*. The expanded SQL statement would read

```
SELECT fieldlist FROM table WHERE field = 'whatever' or 'a'='a'
```

These values are the following:

- *'whatever'*. This can be anything meaningless.
- *or*. The SQL *or* means that as long as either of the conditions are true, the entire statement is true and will be executed.
- *'a'='a'*. This is a statement that will always be true.

Because *'a'='a'* is always true, the *WHERE* clause is also true. It is not limited as it was when searching for a single email address before it would become true. The result can be that *all* user email addresses will then be displayed.

By entering crafted SQL statements as user input, information from the database can be extracted or the existing data can be manipulated. SQL injection statements that can be entered and stored in *$EMAIL*, and their pending results are shown in Table 3-5.

Table 3-5 SQL injection statements

SQL injection statement	Result
'whatever' AND email IS NULL;	Determine the names of different fields in the database
'whatever' AND 1= (SELECT COUNT(*) FROM tabname);	Discover the name of the table
'whatever' OR full name LIKE '%Mia%';	Find specific users
'whatever'; DROP TABLE members;	Erase the database table
'whatever'; UPDATE members SET email = ' attacker-email@ evil.net' *WHERE email = '* Mia@good.com';	Mail password to attacker's email account

In addition to using SQL to view and manipulate data that is stored in a relational database, other types of databases not using SQL (called *NoSQL databases*) are also used. One popular type of NoSQL database manipulates data using the **eXtensible Markup Language (XML)**. Like the markup language Hyper Text Markup Language (HTML) used for webpages, XML is not a processing language but instead is designed to store information. A NoSQL database that uses XML for data manipulation is also subject to an injection attack like SQL injection if the input is not sanitized. This is called an **XML injection**.

Request Forgery

Although some attacks have confusing names, that is not the case with the category of *request forgery*. As its name suggests, it is a request that has been fabricated. There are two types of request forgeries. These are a cross-site request forgery (CSRF) and a server-site request forgery (SSRF).

Cross-Site Request Forgery (CSRF)

A **cross-site request forgery (CSRF)** takes advantage of an authentication "token" that a website sends to a user's web browser. If a user is currently authenticated on a website and is then tricked into loading another webpage, the new page inherits the identity and privileges of the victim, who may then perform an undesired function on the attacker's behalf. Figure 3-11 illustrates a cross-site request forgery. Because a CSRF takes place on the client site, it is sometimes called a **client-side request forgery**.

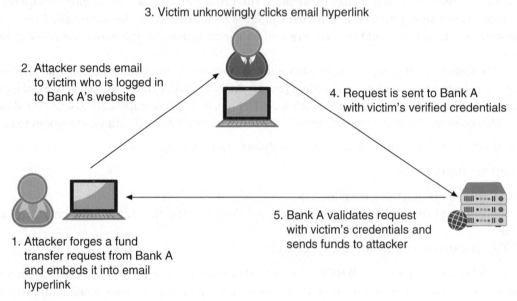

3. Victim unknowingly clicks email hyperlink

2. Attacker sends email to victim who is logged in to Bank A's website

4. Request is sent to Bank A with victim's verified credentials

1. Attacker forges a fund transfer request from Bank A and embeds it into email hyperlink

5. Bank A validates request with victim's credentials and sends funds to attacker

Figure 3-11   Cross-site request forgery

NOTE 19

In other words, in a CSRF attack a *request* to a website is not from the authentic user but is a *forgery* that involves *crossing sites*.

Server-Side Request Forgery (SSRF)

A **server-side request forgery (SSRF)** takes advantage of a trusting relationship between web servers (as opposed to a CSRF, which manipulates the trust from a user's browser to a server). SSRF attacks exploit how a web server processes external information received from another server. Some web applications are designed to read information from or write information to a specific URL. If an attacker can modify that target URL, they can potentially extract sensitive information from the application or inject untrusted input into it. Table 3-6 outlines the differences between a CSRF and a SSRF.

Table 3-6   CSRF and SSRF differences

Attack name	Attack target	Purpose of attack
CSRF	User	Force target to take action for attacker while pretending to be authorized user
SSRF	Web server	Gain access to sensitive data or inject harmful data

Replay

Whereas some attacks try to capture data sent between two users, a **replay** attack copies data and then uses it for an attack. Replay attacks are commonly used against digital identities—after intercepting and copying data, the threat actor retransmits selected and edited portions of the copied communications later to impersonate the legitimate user. Many digital identity replay attacks are between a user and an authentication server.

Attacks on Software

Other attacks are directly focused on vulnerabilities in the software applications. These include exploiting memory vulnerabilities, improper exception and error handling, and external software components.

Memory Vulnerabilities

Several attacks are directed at vulnerabilities associated with how a program uses RAM. These are often the result of poor techniques (or laziness) by the software developer.

Some memory-related attacks are called **resource exhaustion attacks** because they "deplete" parts of memory and thus interfere with the normal operation of the program in RAM. This may allow the threat actor access to the underlying OS in a way that it could be exploited by bypass security settings. An example is a **memory leak**. An application normally dynamically allocates memory, but due to a programming error, it may not free that memory when finished using it. An attacker can then take advantage of the unexpected program behavior resulting from a low memory condition.

Other memory-related attacks attempt to manipulate memory contents. Again, these are made possible by poor programming practices. These types of attacks include buffer overflow attacks and integer overflow attacks.

Buffer Overflow   Consider a teacher working in his office who manually grades a lengthy written examination by marking incorrect answers with a red pen. Because he is frequently interrupted in his grading by students, the teacher places a ruler on the test question he is currently grading to indicate his "return point," or the point at which he should resume the grading. Suppose that two devious students enter his office as he is grading examinations. While one student distracts him, the second student silently slides the ruler down from question 4 to question 20. When the teacher returns to grading, he will resume at the wrong "return point" and not look at the answers for questions 4 through 19.

This scenario is similar to how a buffer overflow attacker attempts to compromise a computer. A storage buffer on a computer typically contains the memory location of the software program that was being executed when another function interrupted the process; that is, the storage buffer contains the "return address" where the computer's processor should resume once the new process has finished. Attackers can substitute their own "return address" in order to point to a different area in the computer's memory that contains their malware code.

A **buffer overflow attack** occurs when a process attempts to store data in RAM beyond the boundaries of a fixed-length storage buffer. This extra data overflows into the adjacent memory locations (a *buffer overflow*). Because the storage buffer typically contains the "return address" memory location of the software program being executed when another function interrupted the process, an attacker can overflow the buffer with a new address pointing to the attacker's malware code. A buffer overflow attack is shown in Figure 3-12.

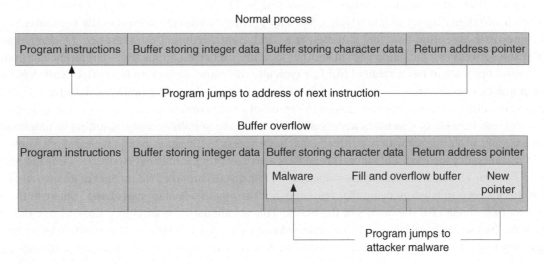

Figure 3-12   Buffer overflow attack

NOTE 20

The "return address" is not the only element that can be altered in a buffer overflow attack, but it is one of the most commonly altered elements.

Integer Overflow   Consider a digital clock that can display the hours only as *1* to *12*. What happens when the time moves past *12:59*? The clock then "wraps around" to the lowest hour value of *1* again.

On a computer, an *integer overflow* is the condition that occurs when the result of an arithmetic operation—such as addition or multiplication—exceeds the maximum size of the integer type used to store it. When this integer overflow occurs, the interpreted value then wraps around from the maximum value to the minimum value. For example, an eight-bit signed integer has a maximum value of 127 and a minimum value of −128. If the value 127 is stored in a variable and 1 is added to it, the sum exceeds the maximum value for this integer type and wraps around to become −128.

In an **integer overflow attack**, an attacker changes the value of a variable to something outside the range that the programmer had intended by using an integer overflow. This type of attack could be used in the following situations:

- An attacker could use an integer overflow attack to create a buffer overflow. If an integer overflow could be introduced during the calculations for the length of a buffer when a copy is occurring, it could result in a buffer that is too small to hold the data. An attacker could then use this to create a buffer overflow attack.

NOTE 21

An extreme example of an integer overflow attack would be withdrawing $1 from an account that has a balance of 0, which could cause a new balance of $4,294,967,295!

- A program that calculates the total cost of items purchased would use the number of units sold times the cost per unit. If an integer overflow were introduced when tallying the number of items sold, it could result in a negative value and a resulting negative total cost, indicating that a refund is due the customer.
- A large positive value in a bank transfer could be wrapped around by an integer overflow attack to become a negative value, which could then reverse the flow of money: instead of adding this amount to the victim's account, it could withdraw that amount and later transfer it to the attacker's account.

Improper Exception Handling

Other attacks on software, like memory vulnerabilities, are the result of poor coding on the part of software developers. This is commonly the case when the program does not properly check for exceptions that may occur when the program is running.

Software that allows the user to enter data but has **improper input handling** features does not filter or validate user input to prevent a malicious action. For example, a webpage on a web server with improper input handling that asks for the user's email address could allow an attacker to instead enter a direct command that the server would then execute.

Other software may not properly trap an error condition and thus provides an attacker with underlying access to the system. This is known as incorrect **error handling**. Suppose an attacker enters a string of characters that is much longer than expected. Because the software has not been designed for this event, the program could crash or suddenly halt its execution and then display an underlying OS prompt, giving an attacker access to the computer.

Another improper exception handling situation is a NULL **pointer/object dereference**. (A *dereference* obtains from a pointer the address of a data item held in another location.) When an application dereferences a pointer that it expects to be valid but instead has a value of NULL, it typically will cause a program to crash or exit. A NULL pointer/object dereference can occur through a number of flaws, including simple programming omissions.

A NULL pointer/object dereference can also be the result of a race condition. A **race condition** in software occurs when two concurrent threads of execution access a shared resource simultaneously, resulting in unintended consequences. For example, in a program with two threads that have access to the same location in memory, Thread #1 stores the value *A* in that memory location. But since Thread #2 is also executing, it may overwrite the same memory location with the value *Z*. When Thread #1 retrieves the value stored, it is given Thread #2's *Z* instead of its own *A*. The software checks the state of a resource before using that resource, but the resource's state can change between the check and the use in a way that invalidates the results of the check. This is called a **time of check/time of use** race condition. This condition is often security-relevant: a threat actor who can influence the state of the resource between check and use can negatively impact a number of shared resources such as files, memory, or variables in multithreaded programs.

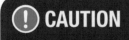 **CAUTION**   Time of check/time of use often appears as time of check to time of use (TOCTTOU). A typo of TOCTTOU is TOCCTOU and has been used in some influential documents, so the typo is repeated fairly frequently.

Attacks on External Software Components

In addition to attacking the software directly, threat actors also target external software components. These include the following:

- *Application program interface (API).* An *application program interface (API)* is a link provided by an OS, web browser, or other platform that allows a developer access to resources at a high level. An example of an API is when a user visits a website and the message "This site wants to know your location" appears. The website is attempting to the use geolocation API available in the web browser. APIs relieve the developer from the need to write code for specific hardware and software. Because APIs provide direct access to data and an entry point to an application's functions, they are attractive targets for attackers looking for vulnerabilities in the API in an **application program interface (API) attack**.

- *Device driver.* A *device driver* is software that controls and operates an external hardware device that is connected to a computer. Device drivers are specific to both the OS and the hardware device. Threat actors may attempt to alter a device driver for use in an attack (called **device driver manipulation**). An attacker may use **shimming**, or transparently adding a small coding library that intercepts calls made by the device and changes the parameters passed between the device and the device driver. This **refactoring** (changing the design of existing code) can be difficult to detect yet serves as a real threat.

- *Dynamic-link library (DLL).* A *dynamic-link library (DLL)* is a repository of both code and data that can be used by more than one program at the same time. For example, in the Windows operating systems, the Comdlg32.DLL performs common dialog box related functions. Attackers use a technique called **DLL injection** for inserting code into a running process through a DLL to cause a program to function in a different way than intended.

> **NOTE 22**
>
> API vulnerabilities are particularly attractive because they can have a broad impact and may take a long time to discover. In 2018, Facebook found a vulnerability in its API code that made it possible for attackers to steal access tokens and take over the accounts of 30 million users. It took Facebook 14 months before they discovered the API vulnerability. It is predicted that by 2022, API abuses will become the most common type of web application attack resulting in a data breach.[10]

TWO RIGHTS & A WRONG

1. In an XSS attack, a website that accepts user input without sanitizing it and uses that input in a response can be exploited.
2. An SSRF takes advantage of a trusting relationship between a web browser and web servers.
3. A time of check/time of use is a vulnerability that causes a race condition.

See Appendix B for the answer.

ADVERSARIAL ARTIFICIAL INTELLIGENCE ATTACKS

 CERTIFICATION

1.2 Given a scenario, analyze potential indicators to determine the type of attack.

Artificial intelligence is being used worldwide in a wide variety of applications, ranging from the mundane to the very sophisticated. Cybersecurity is likewise using these innovative technologies to enhance the detection of malicious behavior and advanced threats. However, there are significant vulnerabilities and risks with using these new tools. Understanding them includes knowing what the tools are and what they can do, how these tools are used in cybersecurity, and their potential risks.

What Are Artificial Intelligence (AI) and Machine Learning (ML)?

Consider the following scenario. Junaid's team leader asks him to fly to another branch of the company tomorrow morning to assist with its new direct marketing campaign. He agrees and books online an airplane reservation for early the next morning. As Junaid awakens, his smartphone buzzes. His phone alerts him about the weather at his destination and makes recommendations about the clothes to pack for his trip. It also tells him what time to leave for the airport based on local traffic and the length of time needed to pass through airport security. When Junaid pulls his car out of his driveway, he receives another message on his phone explaining that an accident is slowing traffic on the main road to the airport and directing him to take an alternate route. After his flight, Junaid arrives at the hotel and suddenly remembers that he volunteered to help plan a birthday party for his niece on Saturday. Using the smart speaker in his hotel room, he logs in to his account and tells the voice assistant what he needs. After a few minutes, he has arranged for the party invitations to be sent to select individuals in his contact list, ordered a birthday present based on what is popular with other children the same age as his niece, and has set a reminder for him to pick up the cake after he arrives back home. The next morning, Junaid arrives at the remote office to help with a direct marketing campaign. He begins by demonstrating to a college intern how to use the company's new smart assistant to segment their customers into groups to receive targeted messaging in order to increase the response rates.

NOTE 23

The original goal of AI was to make computers more useful and more capable of independent reasoning. Most historians trace the birth of AI to a Dartmouth research project in 1956 that explored problem solving and symbolic methods. In the 1960s, the U.S. DoD became interested in this research and worked on training computers to imitate human reasoning. Some projects that came from the DoD were a street-mapping project in the 1970s and intelligent personal assistants in the early 2000s.

Just a few years ago, this scenario would have been nothing more than science fiction. Today, however, it is commonplace and occurs multiple times every day in our work and personal lives. This is based on tools that provide genuine human-to-machine interaction.

The foundation behind this interaction is called *artificial intelligence (AI)*. Although definitions of AI vary, at its core, AI may be defined as technology that imitates human abilities. Although the practical use of AI has only appeared recently, it has a long history dating back to the first large-scale computers.

A recognized subset of AI is *machine learning (ML)*. Humans learn by direct commands of someone older and wiser, but this requires the other person to always be present. Humans also learn through experiences (such as touching a hot stove results in a painful burn). ML is defined as "teaching" a technology device to "learn" by itself without the continual instructions of a computer programmer. ML also involves learning through repeated experience: that is, if something attempted does not work, then it determines how it could be changed to make it work.

NOTE 24

The relationship between AI and ML is AI applies ML to solve problems without being explicitly programmed what to do.

Uses in Cybersecurity

Cybersecurity AI allows organizations to detect, predict, and respond to cyberthreats in real time using ML. AI is already being used broadly in cybersecurity defenses. Virtually all email systems use some type of AI to block phishing attacks by examining obvious clues (such as the URL of the link that the victim is being tempted to click) but also subtle clues (such as the tense and voice of words in the email). AI using ML can analyze these to continually learn to distinguish and block phishing emails while allowing genuine emails to reach the user's inbox.

The prime advantages of using AI to combat threats are continual learning and greater speed in response. By relying on data from previous similar attacks, AI can predict and prevent future attacks. ML learning algorithms can quickly apply complex pattern recognition techniques to spot and thwart attacks much faster than humans can.

The use of AI in cybersecurity is widespread. About one in five organizations used cybersecurity AI before 2019, increasing to two out of three organizations planning to deploy it by the end of 2020. Telecommunications providers use cybersecurity AI more than any other sector: 80 percent of telecom companies said that they would not be able to respond to cyberattacks without using AI.[11] Figure 3-13 illustrates where AI cybersecurity is used in specific areas within an enterprise.

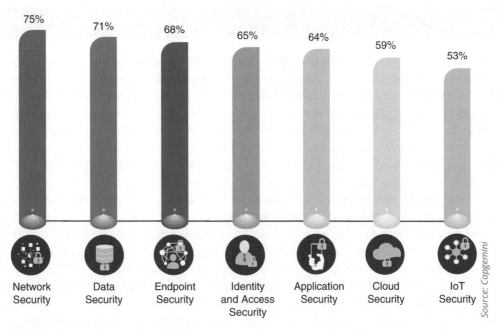

Figure 3-13   How AI cybersecurity is used

Risks in Using AI and ML in Cybersecurity

Although the use of AI in cybersecurity is growing, there are risks associated with using AI and ML in cybersecurity. This is called **adversarial artificial intelligence**. The first risk is the **security of the ML algorithms**. Just as all hardware and software is subject to being infiltrated by threat actors, AI-powered cybersecurity applications and their devices likewise have vulnerabilities. These could be attacked and compromised, allowing threat actors to alter algorithms to ignore attacks, much like a rootkit can instruct an OS to ignore malicious actions.

Another risk is **tainted training data for machine learning**. Attackers can attempt to alter the training data that is used by ML in order to produce false negatives to cloak themselves.

⊘ CAUTION   Another concern is that threat actors themselves will turn to using AI for attacks in order to circumvent defenses.

TWO RIGHTS & A WRONG

1. Artificial intelligence (AI) may be defined as technology that imitates human abilities.
2. AI is already being used broadly in cybersecurity defenses.
3. A recognized subset of ML is AI.

See Appendix B for the answer.

 **VM LAB**   You're now ready to complete the live, virtual machine labs for this module. The labs can be found each module in the MindTap.

SUMMARY

- The word "endpoint" is commonly used when referring to network-connected hardware devices. Devices that are connected to a network today include traditional desktop computers, mobile smartphones, tablets, wearable fitness trackers, and even personal drones. The word endpoint reflects the risks that have increased with using these devices. Instead of protecting devices located inside a network security perimeter, today each endpoint is a target for attackers to attempt to steal or manipulate their data. Every endpoint is a potential entry point for attackers.

- Malware (malicious software) is software that enters a computer system without the user's knowledge or consent and then performs an unwanted and harmful action. There has been no standard established for the classification of the different types of malware so that like malware can be grouped together for study. One attempt at classifying the diverse types of malware can be to examine the primary action that the malware performs and then group those together with similar actions.

- Some types of malware attempt to take away the freedom of users to do whatever they want on their computer. These types of malware "imprison" the user. One of the fastest-growing types of malware is ransomware, which takes away users' freedom from using their computer until the ransom is transacted. Early ransomware pretended to be from a reputable third-party, giving a "valid" reason for blocking the user's computer. As ransomware became more widespread, the threat agents dropped the pretense that the ransomware was from a reputable third party. Instead, they simply blocked the user's computer and demanded a fee for its release. In recent years, a more malicious form of ransomware has arisen. Instead of just blocking the user from accessing the computer, it encrypts all the files on the device so that none of them can be opened. This is called cryptomalware.

- Another category of malware infects a computer to then launch attacks on other computers. A file-based virus is remarkably similar to a biological virus. It is malicious computer code that is attached to a file. Like its biological counterpart, a file-based virus reproduces itself on the same computer. Early viruses were relatively straightforward in how they infected files. Later file-based viruses went to greater lengths to avoid detection; this type of virus is called an armored file-based virus. A fileless virus does not attach itself to a file but takes advantage of native services and processes that are part of the OS to avoid detection and carry out its attacks. These native services used in a fileless virus are called living-off-the-land binaries (LOLBins). There are several advantages of a fileless virus over a file-based virus. These include ease of infection, extensive control, persistence, difficulty in detection, and difficulty in defense. A worm is a malicious program that uses a computer network to replicate. It is designed to enter a computer through the network and then take advantage of a vulnerability in an application or an OS on the host computer. An infected computer that is under the remote control of an attacker for the purpose of launching attacks is called a bot or zombie. When large numbers of bot computers are gathered into a logical computer network, they create a botnet. Infected bot computers receive instructions through a command and control (C&C) structure.

- Another category of malware "snoops" or spies on its victims. Spyware is tracking software that is deployed without the consent or control of the user. Spyware typically secretly monitors users by collecting information without their approval using the computer's resources, including programs already installed on the computer, to collect and distribute personal or sensitive information. A keylogger silently captures and stores each keystroke that a user types on the computer's keyboard so that the attacker can later search the captured text for any useful information. A keylogger can be a software program or a small hardware device.

- Some malware attempts to deceive the user and hide its true intentions. A broad category of software that is often more annoying than malicious is called potentially unwanted programs (PUPs), or software that the user does not want on their computer. PUPs often become installed along with other programs when the user overlooks the default installation options on software downloads. A computer Trojan is an executable program that masquerades as performing a benign activity but also does something malicious. A special type of Trojan is a remote access Trojan (RAT). A RAT has the basic functionality of a Trojan but also gives the threat agent unauthorized remote access to the victim's computer by using specially configured communication protocols.

- Some malware attempts to evade detection. A backdoor gives access to a computer, program, or service that circumvents any normal security protections. When installed on a computer, a backdoor allows the attacker to return later and bypass security settings. A logic bomb is computer code that is typically added to a legitimate program but lies dormant and evades detection until a specific logical event triggers it. Once it is triggered, the program then deletes data or performs other malicious activities. Logic bombs are difficult to detect before they are triggered because they are often embedded in very large computer programs. A rootkit is malware that can hide its presence and the presence of other malware on the computer. It does this by accessing "lower layers" of the operating system or even using undocumented functions to make alterations.

- Another category of attacks specifically targets software applications that are already installed and running on the device. These attacks look for vulnerabilities in the application or manipulate the application in order to compromise it. In a cross-site scripting (XSS) attack, a website that accepts user input without validating (sanitizing) it and uses that input in a response can be exploited. Another type of attack called injections introduces new input to exploit a vulnerability. One of the most common injection attacks, called SQL injection, inserts statements to manipulate a database server. By entering crafted SQL statements as user input, information from the database can be extracted or the existing data can be manipulated. In addition to using SQL, other types of databases are used, such as those containing the eXtensible Markup Language (XML), which can also be used for data manipulation similar to an SQL injection. This is called an XML injection.

- A cross-site request forgery (CSRF) takes advantage of an authentication "token" that a website sends to a user's web browser. If a user is currently authenticated on a website and is then tricked into loading another webpage, the new page inherits the identity and privileges of the victim, who may then perform an undesired function on the attacker's behalf. A server-side request forgery (SSRF) takes advantage of a trusting relationship between web servers. SSRF attacks exploit how a web server processes external information received from another server. A replay attack copies data and then uses it for an attack.

- Several attacks are directed at vulnerabilities associated with how a program uses RAM. Some of these memory-related attacks are called resource exhaustion attacks because they "deplete" parts of memory and thus interfere with the normal operation of the program in RAM. This may allow the threat actor access to the underlying OS in a way that it could be exploited by bypassing security settings. A memory leak occurs when an application, instead of normally dynamically allocating memory, does not free that memory when finished using it. An attacker can then take advantage of the unexpected program behavior resulting from a low memory condition. A buffer overflow attack occurs when a process attempts to store data in RAM beyond the boundaries of a fixed-length storage buffer, and this extra data overflows into the adjacent memory locations. An attacker can overflow the buffer with a new address pointing to the attacker's malware code. An integer overflow attack occurs when an attacker changes the value of a variable to something outside the range that the programmer had intended by using an integer overflow.

- Software that allows the user to enter data but has improper input handling features does not filter or validate user input to prevent a malicious action. Other software may not properly trap an error condition and thus provides an attacker with underlying access to the system. This is known as incorrect error handling. When an application dereferences a pointer that it expects to be valid but instead has a value of NULL, it typically will cause a program to crash or exit. A NULL pointer/object dereference can occur through a number of flaws, including simple programming omissions. It can also be the result of a race condition, in which two concurrent threads of execution access a shared resource simultaneously.

- In an application program interface (API) attack, a threat actor looks for vulnerabilities in the API, a link provided by an OS, web browser, or other platform that allows a developer access to resources at a high level. A device driver is software that controls and operates an external hardware device that is connected to a computer and is specific to both the OS and the hardware device. Threat actors may attempt to alter a device driver for use in an attack (called device driver manipulation). A dynamic link library (DLL) is a repository of both code and data that can be used by more than one program at the same time. Attackers use a technique called DLL injection for inserting code into a running process through a DLL to cause a program to function in a way other than intended.

- Artificial intelligence (AI) is technology that imitates human abilities. Although the practical use of AI has only appeared recently, it has a long history dating back to the first large-scale computers. A recognized subset of AI is machine learning (ML). ML is defined as "teaching" a technology device to "learn" by itself without the continual instructions of a computer programmer and also to learn through repeated experience. Cybersecurity AI allows organizations to detect, predict, and respond to cyberthreats in real time using ML. There are risks associated with using AI and ML in cybersecurity called adversarial artificial intelligence. One risk is the security of the ML algorithms: just as all hardware and software is subject to being infiltrated by threat actors, AI-powered cybersecurity applications and their devices likewise have vulnerabilities. Another risk is tainted training data for machine learning. Attackers can attempt to alter the training data that is used by ML in order to produce false negatives to cloak themselves.

Key Terms

adversarial artificial intelligence	fileless virus	replay
application program interface (API) attack	improper input handling	resource exhaustion attacks
	injections	rootkit
backdoor	integer overflow attack	security of the ML algorithms
bot	keylogger	server-side request forgery (SSRF)
buffer overflow attack	logic bomb	shimming
client-side request forgery	malware	spyware
command and control (C&C)	memory leak	SQL injection
cross-site request forgery (CSRF)	pointer/object dereference	Structured Query Language
cross-site scripting (XSS)	potentially unwanted programs (PUPs)	tainted training data for machine learning
cryptomalware		
device driver manipulation	race condition	time of check/time of use
DLL injection	ransomware	Trojan
error handling	refactoring	worm
eXtensible Markup Language (XML)	remote access Trojan	XML injection

Review Questions

1. What word is the currently accepted term to refer to network-connected hardware devices?
   a. Host
   b. Endpoint
   c. Device
   d. Client

2. Which of the following is NOT a characteristic of malware?
   a. Deceive
   b. Launch
   c. Imprison
   d. Diffusion

3. Gabriel's sister called him about a message that suddenly appeared on her screen that says her software license has expired and she must immediately pay $500 to have it renewed before control of the computer will be returned to her. What type of malware has infected her computer?
   a. Persistent lockware
   b. Blocking ransomware
   c. Cryptomalware
   d. Impede-ware

4. Marius's team leader has just texted him that an employee, who violated company policy by bringing in a file on her USB flash drive, has just reported that her computer is suddenly locked up with cryptomalware. Why would Marius consider this a dangerous situation?
   a. It sets a precedent by encouraging other employees to violate company policy.

   b. Cryptomalware can encrypt all files on any network that is connected to the employee's computer.
   c. The organization may be forced to pay up to $500 for the ransom.
   d. The employee would have to wait at least an hour before her computer could be restored.

5. Which type of malware relies on LOLBins?
   a. PUP
   b. File-based virus
   c. Fileless virus
   d. Bot

6. Which of the following is known as a network virus?
   a. TAR
   b. Worm
   c. Remote exploitation virus (REV)
   d. C&C

7. Josh is researching the different types of attacks that can be generated through a botnet. Which of the following would NOT be something distributed by a botnet?
   a. LOLBins
   b. Spam
   c. Malware
   d. Ad fraud

8. Which of the following is NOT a means by which a bot communicates with a C&C device?
   a. Signing in to a website the bot herder operates
   b. Signing in to a third-party website
   c. Email
   d. Command sent through Twitter posts

9. Randall's roommate is complaining to him about all of the software that came pre-installed on his new computer. He doesn't want the software because it slows down the computer. What type of software is this?
   a. Spyware
   b. BOT
   c. PUP
   d. Keylogger

10. What is the difference between a Trojan and a RAT?
   a. There is no difference.
   b. A RAT gives the attacker unauthorized remote access to the victim's computer.
   c. A Trojan can carry malware while a RAT cannot.
   d. A RAT can infect only a smartphone and not a computer.

11. Which of these would NOT be considered the result of a logic bomb?
   a. Send an email to Rowan's inbox each Monday morning with the agenda of that week's department meeting.
   b. If the company's stock price drops below $50, then credit Oscar's retirement account with one additional year of retirement credit.
   c. Erase the hard drives of all the servers 90 days after Alfredo's name is removed from the list of current employees.
   d. Delete all human resource records regarding Augustine one month after he leaves the company.

12. Which of the following attacks is based on a website accepting user input without sanitizing it?
   a. RSS
   b. XSS
   c. SQLS
   d. SSXRS

13. Which of the following attacks is based on the principle that when a user is currently authenticated on a website and then loads another webpage, the new page inherits the identity and privileges of the first website?
   a. SSFR
   b. DLLS
   c. CSRF
   d. DRCR

14. Which of the following manipulates the trusting relationship between web servers?
   a. SSRF
   b. CSRF

   c. EXMAL
   d. SCSI

15. Which type of memory vulnerability attack manipulates the "return address" of the memory location of a software program?
   a. Shim overflow attack
   b. Factor overflow attack
   c. Integer overflow attack
   d. Buffer overflow attack

16. What race condition can result in a NULL pointer/object dereference?
   a. Conflict race condition
   b. Value-based race condition
   c. Thread race condition
   d. Time of check/time of use race condition

17. Which of the following attacks targets the external software component that is a repository of both code and data?
   a. Application program interface (API) attack
   b. Device driver manipulation attack
   c. Dynamic-link library (DLL) injection attack
   d. OS REG attack

18. What term refers to changing the design of existing code?
   a. Library manipulation
   b. Shimming
   c. Refactoring
   d. Design driver manipulation

19. Which of the following is technology that imitates human abilities?
   a. AI
   b. ML
   c. RC
   d. XLS

20. Which statement regarding a keylogger is NOT true?
   a. Software keyloggers can be designed to send captured information automatically back to the attacker through the Internet.
   b. Hardware keyloggers are installed between the keyboard connector and computer keyboard USB port.
   c. Software keyloggers are generally easy to detect.
   d. Keyloggers can be used to capture passwords, credit card numbers, or personal information.

Hands-On Projects

Project 3-1: Analyze File and URL for File-Based Viruses Using VirusTotal—Part 1

Time Required: 25 minutes

Objective: Given a scenario, analyze potential indicators to determine the type of attack.

Description: VirusTotal is a free online service that analyzes files and URLs to identify potential malware. VirusTotal combines 70 antivirus scanners and URL/domain blacklisting services along with other tools to identify malware. A wide range of files can be submitted to VirusTotal for examination, such as user data files and documents, executable programs, PDFs, and images. One of the uses of VirusTotal is to provide a "second opinion" on a file or URL that may have been flagged as suspicious by other scanning software. In this project, you use VirusTotal to scan a file and a URL.

1. First view several viruses from 20 years ago and observe their benign but annoying impact. Open your web browser and enter the URL **archive.org/details/malwaremuseum&tab=collection** (if you are no longer able to access the site through the web address, use a search engine to search for "Malware Museum").
2. All of the viruses have been rendered ineffective and will not harm a computer. Click several of the viruses and notice what they do.
3. When finished, close your web browser.
4. Use Microsoft Word to create a document that contains the preceding paragraph description about VirusTotal. Save the document as **VirusTotal.docx**.
5. Exit Word.
6. Open your web browser and enter the URL **www.virustotal.com** (if you are no longer able to access the site through the web address, use a search engine to search for "Virus Total").
7. If necessary, click the **File** tab.
8. Click **Choose File**.
9. Navigate to the location of **VirusTotal.docx** and click **Open**.
10. Click **Confirm upload**.
11. Wait until the upload and analysis are completed.
12. Scroll through the list of antivirus (AV) vendors that have been polled regarding this file. A green checkmark means no malware was detected.
13. Click the **DETAILS** tab and read through the analysis.
14. Use your browser's Back button to return to the VirusTotal home page.
15. Now you will analyze a website. Click **URL**.
16. Enter the URL of your school, place of employment, or another site with which you are familiar.
17. Wait until the analysis is completed.
18. Click the **DETAILS** tab and read through the analysis.
19. Click Scroll through the list of vendor analysis. Do any of these sites indicate **Unrated site** or **Malware site**?
20. How could VirusTotal be useful to users? How could it be useful to security researchers? Could it also be used by attackers to test their own malware before distributing it to ensure that it does not trigger an AV alert? What should be the protections against this?
21. Close all windows.

Project 3-2: Analyze Virus File Using VirusTotal—Part 2

Time Required: 20 minutes

Objective: Given a scenario, analyze potential indicators to determine the type of attack.

Description: What happens when VirusTotal detects a file-based virus? In this project, you will download a file that has a "signature" of a file-based virus into a sandbox in order to upload it to VirusTotal.

NOTE 25

None of the actions in this project will harm the underlying fomputer.

1. Open your web browser.
2. Enter the URL **www.eicar.org/?page_id=3950**.
3. Scroll down to **Download area using the standard protocol http**.
4. Click **eicar.com** to start the download.
5. Your antimalware software on your personal computer should immediately flag this file as malicious and not allow you to download it. Because it cannot (and should not) be downloaded on your regular computer, you will instead want to use the Windows Sandbox or VMware sandbox you created in Module 1.

NOTE 26

Refer to Project 1-3 and Project 1-4 of Module 1 for creating these sandboxes.

6. If you are using the Windows Sandbox, click **Start**, scroll down to Windows Sandbox, and then click **Windows Sandbox**.
7. First you will turn off the security protections in Windows Sandbox. Click **Start** and then **Windows Security**.
8. Click the three horizontal lines at the left of the screen to display the menu options.
9. Click **App & browser control**.
10. For each of the categories, click the **Off** button to turn off security. Remember this will only impact the security within the Windows Sandbox and will have no impact on the underlying computer.
11. Open Internet Explorer in the Windows Sandbox.

NOTE 27

Be sure to use the web browser in the Windows Sandbox and not the web browser in the underlying computer.

12. Enter the URL **www.eicar.org/?page_id=3950**.
13. Scroll down to **Download area using the standard protocol http**.
14. Click **eicar.com** to start the download.
15. The antimalware software within Windows Sandbox will now allow the file to be downloaded into the Sandbox.
16. Open another tab on the Internet Explorer web browser in the Windows Sandbox, and enter the URL **www.virustotal.com** (if you are no longer able to access the site through the web address, use a search engine to search for "Virus Total").
17. If necessary, click the **File** tab.
18. Click **Choose File**.
19. Navigate to the location of **eicar.com** and click **Open**.
20. Click **Confirm upload**.
21. Wait until the upload and analysis are completed.
22. Scroll through the list of AV vendors that have been polled regarding this file. A green checkmark means no malware was detected.
23. Click the **DETAILS** tab and read through the analysis.
24. Close the Windows Sandbox. This will delete the **eicar.com** file and reset the security settings to normal.

Project 3-3: Explore Ransomware Sites

Time Required: 15 minutes
Objective: Given a scenario, analyze potential indicators to determine the type of attack.
Description: A variety of sites provide information about ransomware along with tools for counteracting some types of infection. In this project, you explore different ransomware sites.

1. Open your web browser and enter the URL **www.nomoreransom.org** (if you are not able to access this site open a search engine and search for "**Nomoreransom.org**").
2. Click the **No** button.
3. Read through the Prevention Advice. Do you think it is helpful?
4. Click **Crypto Sheriff**. How could this be useful to a user who has suffered a ransomware infection?
5. Click **Ransomware: Q&A**. Read through the information. Which statements would you agree with? Which statements would you disagree with?

6. Click **Decryption Tools**. This contains a list of different tools that may help restore a computer that has been infected by a specific type of ransomware.

7. Click one of the tools and then click **Download** to download. Note that these tools change frequently based on the latest types of ransomware that is circulating.

8. Run the program to understand how these decryption tools function. Note that you will not be able to complete the process because there are no encrypted files on the computer. Close the program.

9. Now visit another site that provides ransomware information and tools. Open your web browser and enter the URL **id-ransomware.malwarehunterteam.com**.

10. What features does this site provide?

11. How could these sites be useful?

12. Close all windows.

Project 3-4: Use a Software Keylogger

 **CAUTION**   The purpose of this activity is to provide information regarding how these programs function in order that adequate defenses can be designed and implemented. These programs should never be used in a malicious fashion against another user.

Time Required: 25 minutes

Objective: Given a scenario, analyze potential indicators to determine the type of attack.

Description: A keylogger program captures everything that a user enters on a computer keyboard. In this project, you download and use a software keylogger.

1. Open your web browser and enter the URL **refog.com** (if you are no longer able to access the program through the URL, use a search engine to search for "Refog Keylogger").

2. Click **Features** to see the features of the product.

3. Click **Home**.

4. Click **Download**.

5. Click **Create an account** and enter the requested information.

6. Click **Download**.

7. When the file finishes downloading, run the installation program. Note that you may have to enter the password on the previous page to extract the files.

8. When prompted with **I'm going to use this software to monitor:** select **My own computer**.

9. Click **Hide program icon from Windows tray**. Click **Next**.

10. Click **I Agree**.

11. Click **Select All** and then **Next**.

12. Create a login and password for the online dashboard. Click **Activate**.

13. You will receive a message that the subscription has expired. Click **Yes** to install in offline mode.

14. Click **Install**.

15. Click **Restart Now**.

16. After the computer has restarted, use the keystroke combination **Ctrl + Alt + Shift + K** to launch Refog Keylogger.

17. Click **Tools** and then click **Settings**.

18. Note the default settings regarding what is captured.

19. Click **Back to log**.

20. Minimize Refog Keylogger.

21. Use your computer normally by opening a web browser to surf to a website. Open Microsoft Word and type several sentences. Open and close several programs on the computer.

22. Maximize Keylogger and note the information that was captured.

23. In the left pane, click through the different items that were captured.

24. Under Settings, click **Websites Visited**.

25. Under Websites Visited, click **Make website screenshots**.

26. Click **Apply**.

27. Open a web browser and surf to multiple websites.
28. Under Users, click **Websites visited**. Note the screen captures of the different sites.
29. What type of information would a software keylogger provide to a threat actor? How could it be used against the victim?
30. Click **File** and then **Exit** to close Keylogger.
31. You may uninstall Keylogger if you wish.
32. Close all windows.

Case Projects

Case Project 3-1: Biological and File-Based Viruses

The word virus comes from Latin, meaning a slimy liquid, poison, or poisonous secretion. In late Middle English, it was used for the venom of a snake. The word later evolved from the discharge to the substances within the body that caused the infectious diseases that produced the discharge. In 1799, Edward Jenner published his discovery that the cowpox virus could actually be used as a vaccine against smallpox. As biological science continued to advance, the word "virus" became even more specific when referring to tiny infectious agents—even smaller than bacteria—that replicate in living cells. This new field of virology exploded in the 1930s, when electronic microscopes allowed scientists to see viruses for the first time. Since then, scientists have continued to identify and name new biological viruses. Combating viruses by developing vaccines has many parallels to how malicious file-based viruses are identified and removed from a computer. Using the Internet, research these two types of viruses and find the similarities between combating biological and computer viruses. Write a one-to-two-paragraph summary of your research.

Case Project 3-2: Living-off-the-Land Binaries (LOLBins)

Fileless viruses take advantage of native services and processes that are part of the OS to avoid detection and carry out their attacks. These native services used in a fileless virus are called living-off-the-land binaries (LOLBins). Use the Internet to research fileless viruses and LOLBins. When did fileless viruses first appear? How do they compare with file-based viruses? What are the defenses against fileless viruses? Write a one-page paper on your research.

Case Project 3-3: Infamous Logic Bombs

Search the Internet for examples of logic bombs. Select four logic bombs and write a report about them. Who was responsible? When did the bombs go off? What was the damage? What was the penalty for the person responsible? Did the organization make any changes after the attack? How can they be prevented?

Case Project 3-4: Cybersecurity AI

The use of AI in cybersecurity is growing rapidly. Use the Internet to research the latest developments in cybersecurity AI. How does it work? What platforms are using it? What are some examples of it? How is it being improved? How can adversarial AI attacks be defended against? Write a one-page paper of what you have learned.

Case Project 3-5: Information Security Community Site Activity

The Information Security Community Site is an online companion to this textbook. It contains a wide variety of tools, information, discussion boards, and other features to assist learners. In order to gain the most benefit from the site, you will need to set up a free account.

Go to **community.cengage.com/infosec2**. Search the blogs on the topic "Ransomware." What did you learn? What were your biggest surprises? What did you already know? How could you use this information in your first security job?

Case Project 3-6: North Ridge Security

North Ridge Security provides security consulting and assurance services. You have recently been hired as an intern to assist them. North Ridge is preparing a presentation to the monthly meeting of IT programmers and has asked you to do research on attacks on software.

1. Create a PowerPoint presentation on memory leaks, buffer overflow, integer overflow, pointer/object dereference, and attacks using API, device drivers, and DLLs. Your presentation should be at least nine slides in length.
2. As a follow-up to your presentation, you have been asked to write a one-page report on race conditions. Use the Internet to research race conditions and how they can best be addressed.

References

1. "The state of ransomware in the US: Report and statistics 2019," *Emisoft*, Dec. 12, 2019, accessed May 6, 2020, https://blog.emsisoft.com/en/34822/the-state-of-ransomware-in-the-us-report-and-statistics-2019/.
2. Dudley, Renee, "The extortion economy: How insurance companies are fueling a rise in ransomware attacks," *ProPublica*, Aug. 27, 2019, accessed Oct. 27, 2019, www.propublica.org/article /the-extortion-economy-how-insurance-companies-are-fueling-a-rise-in-ransomware-attacks.
3. "Definition of computer contaminant," *Law Insider*, accessed May 9, 2020, www.lawinsider.com /dictionary/computer-contaminant.
4. "McAfee Labs Threats Report," Dec. 2018, accessed Apr. 21, 2019, www.mcafee.com/enterprise/en-us /assets/reports/rp-quarterly-threats-dec-2018.pdf.
5. "Ransomware payments up 33% as Maze and Sodinokibi proliferate in Q1 2020," *Coveware*, accessed May 5, 2020, www.coveware.com/blog/q1-2020-ransomware-marketplace-report.
6. Soare, Bianca, "This year in ransomware payouts (2019 edition)," *Heimdal Security*, Dec. 11, 2019, accessed May 9, 2020, https://heimdalsecurity.com/blog/ransomware-payouts/.
7. "Ransomware attacks map," *Statescoop,* accessed May 9, 2020, https://statescoop.com/ransomware-map/.
8. "High-impact ransomware attacks threaten U.S. businesses and organizations," *Public Service Announcement Federal Bureau of Investigation*, Oct 2, 2019, accessed May 9, 2020, www.ic3.gov /media/2019/191002.aspx.
9. "Ransomware payments up 33% as Maze and Sodinokibi proliferate in Q1 2020," *Coveware*, accessed May 5, 2020, www.coveware.com/blog/q1-2020-ransomware-marketplace-report.
10. Zumerle, Dioisio, D'Hoinne, Jeremy, and O'Neill, Mark, "How to build an effective API security strategy," *Gartner Research*, Dec. 8, 2017, accessed May 12, 2020, www.gartner.com/en/documents/3834704.
11. "Reinventing cybersecurity with artificial intelligence: The new frontier in digital security," *Capgemini Research Institute,* accessed May 13, 2020, www.capgemini.com/wp-content/ uploads/2019/07/AI-in-Cybersecurity_Report_20190711_V06.pdf.

ENDPOINT AND APPLICATION DEVELOPMENT SECURITY

After completing this module, you should be able to do the following:

1. Describe different threat intelligence sources
2. List the steps for securing an endpoint
3. Explain how to create and deploy SecDevOps

Front-Page Cybersecurity

Suppose you were to uncover a zero-day vulnerability that nobody else knew about. What could you do with it?

You could be a broker and sell your knowledge of the vulnerability to a willing buyer. Governments often serve as buyers of zero-day vulnerabilities to protect their citizens or attack their enemies. Other willing buyers are third-party "acquisition platforms" who buy and then resell the vulnerability information to a government or a software developer. Very willing buyers are also threat actors who would craft their own attacks based on the vulnerability.

However, a more responsible option would be for you to privately disclose the vulnerability to the developer of the software, allowing the developer to fix it before an attacker uncovers and takes advantage of it. Not all zero-day vulnerabilities are discovered by individuals. Many organizations have internal security teams who look for vulnerabilities in their own code and in programs from other developers. When they find a problem, they privately contact the software developer with the information so the developer can patch it.

What happens if developers drag their feet and do not patch the vulnerability within a reasonable period of time? Delaying can keep the door open for a threat actor to find the zero-day vulnerability and exploit it.

Faced with the conundrum of trying to give developers time to create a patch and the public's right to protection from attacks, organizations have come up with "disclosure deadlines," or the time that the software developer is given to patch a vulnerability before it is publicly disclosed. These disclosure deadlines generally range from 45 days to 120 days.

Google started Project Zero in 2014 to look for zero-day vulnerabilities in its code and code from other software developers. Many developers responded quickly to a private alert of a zero-day vulnerability. As soon as the patch was available, Project Zero released information about it. However, not all developers moved quickly: in some instances, it took six months for the software developers to issue a patch.

Google's Project Zero set a disclosure deadline of 90 days, after which it would go public with information about the vulnerability. Going public would alert the user base to be aware of the vulnerability and possibly stop using the software while shaming the developer into a faster response. The next year, Project Zero added a 14-day grace period: after the 90-day deadline, a developer could request two additional weeks to make a patch available. Beyond 14 days, however, Google would go public with the information. Project Zero said that by 2019, 97.7 percent of vulnerabilities uncovered were fixed within 90 days.

However, in early 2020, Project Zero announced a trial tweak to their disclosure deadline. The limit is still 90 days. But Project Zero sometimes found that software developers were rushing to fix the zero-day vulnerability to meet the 90-day deadline, and this sometimes resulted in a rushed and flawed patch that introduced another vulnerability into the code. With Project Zero's new trial tweak, software developers will now have the full 90 days to create a patch for the vulnerability, and Project Zero will say nothing until the end of the 90 days. Even if the developer can fix the vulnerability in just 20 days, Google will still say nothing until 90 days have elapsed. However, the developer and Google can make a mutual disclosure before the 90-day deadline if both sides agree on the early disclosure.

Why the change? Project Zero says that faster patch development, while still important, is not the exclusive goal anymore. Instead, thorough patch development—not sticking a bandage on it but actually finding the underlying problem and correcting it—and improved patch adoption are also important. In the words of Project Zero, "End user security doesn't improve when a bug is found, and it doesn't improve when a bug is fixed. It improves once the end user is aware of the bug and typically patches their device."

Attacks using malware, application attacks, and adversarial artificial intelligence attacks against endpoints continue around the clock every day. What defenses can be used to ward off these attacks?

First, it is important to access threat intelligence sources in order to be aware of the latest types of attacks and how to defend against them. With that information at hand, securing devices through boot integrity, protecting endpoints, and hardening endpoints can then effectively be used. But deploying these defenses is still considered "after the fact." A growing chorus of security professionals today are demanding that it is the responsibility of the software developers to create and deploy software using secure application development coding techniques.

In this module, you will learn about securing endpoint devices and creating and deploying secure applications. But first you will explore the sources of threat intelligence information.

THREAT INTELLIGENCE SOURCES

CERTIFICATION

1.5 Explain different threat actors, vectors, and intelligence sources.

At one time, organizations were reluctant to share information about attacks on their networks and endpoints, often because they were concerned about "bad publicity" that might arise from this disclosure. Today that is no longer the case. Organizations are pooling their experiences and knowledge gained about the latest attacks with the broader security community. Sharing this type of information has become an important aid to help other organizations shore up their defenses.

One type of shared information is the evidence of an attack. Most organizations monitor their networking environment to determine what normally occurs. They use this data to create a database of *key risk indicators (KRIs)*. A KRI is a metric of the upper and lower bounds of specific indicators of normal network activity. These indicators may include the total network logs per second, number of failed remote logins, network bandwidth, and outbound email traffic. A KRI exceeding its normal bounds could be (but is not always) an **indicator of compromise (IOC)**. An IOC shows that a malicious activity is occurring but is still in the early stages of an attack.

NOTE 1

Like radar that shows the enemy approaching, predictive analysis helps determine when and where attacks may occur.

Making IOC information available to others can prove to be of high value as it may indicate a common attack that other organizations are also experiencing or will soon experience. This information aids others in their **predictive analysis** or discovering an attack before it occurs.

Threat intelligence sources fall into several categories, as do the sources from which threat intelligence information can be gathered.

Categories of Sources

The two categories of threat intelligence sources are open source and closed source.

Open Source Information

The phrase **open source** has its roots in the computer industry. Initially, it referred to software for which the *source code* was open for anyone to examine. Over time, "open source" was used to refer to anything that could be freely used without restrictions, such as an *open source film* or *open source curriculum*.

NOTE 2

The phrase "open source" came out of a strategy session in 1998 by about a half dozen Linux software developers who wanted to take advantage of an announcement by Netscape that it was planning to give away the source code of its browser. The developers wanted to persuade the corporate world about the superiority of an open software development process but found that the phrase "free software" that had been used previously carried a stigma of being inferior. After a brainstorming session, the label "open source" was agreed upon.

Open source threat intelligence information that is freely available, often called open source intelligence (OSINT), has become a vital resource. This information is often collected and then disseminated through **public information sharing centers**. A typical sharing center is the U.S. Department of Homeland Security (DHS) Cyber Information Sharing and Collaboration Program (CISCP). The CISCP "enables actionable, relevant, and timely unclassified information exchange through trusted public-private partnerships across all critical infrastructure sectors." With the DHS serving as the coordinator, the CISCP enables its members (called "partners") to not only share threat and vulnerability information but also take advantage of the DHS's cyber resources. Some of the CISCP services include the following:

- *Analyst-to-analyst technical exchanges.* Partners can share and receive information on threat actor tactics, techniques, and procedures (TTPs) and emerging trends.
- *CISCP analytical products.* A portal can be accessed through which partners can receive analysis of products and threats.
- *Cross industry orchestration.* Partners can share lessons learned and their expertise with peers across common sectors.
- *Digital malware analysis.* Suspected malware can be submitted to be analyzed and then used to generate malware analysis reports to mitigate threats and attack vectors.

NOTE 3

The CISCP program is free to join and use. Those interested must agree to a Cyber Information Sharing and Collaboration Agreement (CISCA), which enables DHS and its partners to exchange anonymized information. Once partners sign the agreement, DHS coordinates an on-boarding session to customize how DHS and the organization can exchange information.

The two concerns around public information sharing centers are the privacy of shared information and the speed at which the information is shared.

Privacy   A concern about using public information sharing centers is that of privacy. An organization that is the victim of an attack must be careful not to share proprietary or sensitive information when providing IOCs and attack details.

As a safeguard, most public information sharing centers have protections in place to prevent the disclosure of proprietary information. For example, Table 4-1 lists the privacy protections of the CISCP.

Speed   Threat intelligence information must be distributed as quickly as possible to others. To rely on email alerts that require a human to read them and then react takes far too much time. As an alternative, **Automated Indicator Sharing (AIS)** can be used instead. AIS enables the exchange of cyberthreat indicators between parties through computer-to-computer communication, not email communication. Threat indicators such malicious IP addresses or the sender address of a phishing email can be quickly distributed to enable others to repel these attacks.

NOTE 4

Those participating in AIS generally are connected to a managed system controlled by the public information sharing center that allows bidirectional sharing of cyberthreat indicators. Not only do participants receive indicators, but they can also share indicators they have observed in their own network defenses to the public center, which then distributes them to all participants.

Table 4-1 CISCP privacy protections

Protection	Explanation	Example
Cybersecurity Information Sharing Act (CISA)	CISA is a federal law passed in 2015 that provides authority for cybersecurity information sharing between the private sector, state, and local governments and the federal government.	CISA requires a non-federal entity to remove any information from a cyberthreat indicator that it knows at the time of sharing to be personal information of a specific individual or information that identifies a specific individual that is not directly related to a cybersecurity threat.
Freedom of Information Act (FOIA)	FOIA was passed in 1967 and provides the public the right to request access to records from any federal agency.	Although federal agencies are required to disclose any information requested under the FOIA, they offer nine exemptions, one of which protects interests such as personal privacy.
Traffic-Light Protocol (TLP)	TLP is a set of designations used to ensure that sensitive information is shared only with the appropriate audience.	TLP uses four colors (red, amber, green, and white) to indicate the expected sharing limitations the recipients should apply.
Protected Critical Infrastructure Information (PCII)	The PCII Act of 2002 protects private sector infrastructure information that is voluntarily shared with the government for the purposes of homeland security.	To qualify for PCII protections, information must be related to the security of the critical infrastructure, voluntarily submitted, and not submitted in place of compliance with a regulatory requirement.

NOTE 5

APIs are covered in Module 3.

Two tools facilitate AIS. **Structured Threat Information Expression (STIX)** is a language and format used to exchange cyberthreat intelligence. All information about a threat can be represented with objects and descriptive relationships. STIX information can be visually represented for a security analyst to view or stored in a lightweight format to be used by a computer. **Trusted Automated Exchange of Intelligence Information (TAXII)** is an application protocol for exchanging cyberthreat intelligence over Hypertext Transfer Protocol Secure (HTTPS). TAXII defines an *application protocol interface (API)* and a set of requirements for TAXII clients and servers.

Closed Source Information

NOTE 6

AIS is used more extensively with public information sharing centers than private centers.

Closed source is the opposite of open source. It is *proprietary*, meaning it is owned by an entity that has an exclusive right to it. Organizations that are participants in closed source information are part of **private information sharing centers** that restrict both access to data and participation. Whereas private sharing centers are similar to public sharing centers in that members share threat intelligence information, insights, and best practices, private sharing centers are restrictive regarding who may participate. All candidates must go through a vetting process and meet certain criteria.

Sources of Threat Intelligence

Several sources of threat intelligence are useful. These include the following:

- *Vulnerability databases*. A **vulnerability database** is a repository of known vulnerabilities and information as to how they have been exploited. These databases create "feeds" of the latest cybersecurity incidences. Common cybersecurity data feeds include *vulnerability feeds* that provide information on the latest vulnerabilities and *threat feeds* that outline current threats and attacks. The *adversary tactics, techniques, and procedures (TTP)* is a database of the behavior of threat actors and how they orchestrate and manage attacks.

> **NOTE 7**
>
> Data feeds, vulnerability feeds, threat feeds, and TTP are covered in Module 2.

- *Threat maps*. A cybersecurity **threat map** illustrates cyberthreats overlaid on a diagrammatic representation of a geographical area. Figure 4-1 illustrates a threat map. Threat maps help in visualizing attacks and provide a limited amount of context of the source and the target countries, the attack types, and historical and near real-time data about threats.

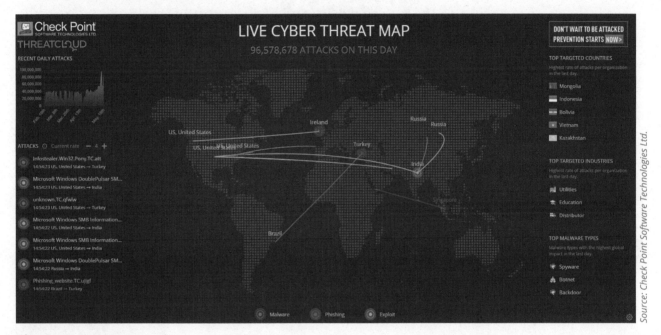

Source: Check Point Software Technologies Ltd.

Figure 4-1   Threat map

 **CAUTION**   Threat maps may look impressive, but in reality, they provide limited valuable information. Many maps claim that they show data in real time, but most are simply a playback of previous attacks. Because threat maps show anonymized data, it is impossible to know the identity of the attackers or the victims. Also, threat actors usually mask their real locations, so what is displayed on a threat map is incorrect. As a result, many cybersecurity professionals question the value of threat maps.

- *File and code repositories*. **File and code repositories** are another source of threat intelligence. Victims of an attack can upload malicious files and software code that can then be examined by others to learn more about the attacks and craft their defenses. Several entities of the U.S. government—including the Federal Bureau of Investigation (FBI), the Cybersecurity and Infrastructure Security Agency (CISA), and the Department of Defense (DoD) U.S. Cyber Command—are particularly active in posting to file and code repositories. Often samples of recently discovered malware variants are uploaded to the VirusTotal malware aggregation repository along with published detailed malware analysis reports (MARs) containing IOCs for each malware variant.

> **NOTE 8**
>
> The Hands-On Projects 3-1 and 3-2 in Module 3 provide you with experience using VirusTotal.

- *Dark web*. The web has three levels, as illustrated in Figure 4-2: the *clear web*, which includes ordinary websites (social media, ecommerce, news, etc.) that most users access regularly and can be located by a search engine; the *deep web*, which includes exclusive and protected websites (corporate email, material behind a digital paywall, cloud hosting services, etc.) that are hidden from a search engine and cannot be accessed without valid credentials; and the dark web. The dark web is like the deep web in that it is beyond the reach of a normal search engine, but it is the domain of threat actors. Using special software such as *Tor or I2P (Invisible Internet Project)* this software will mask the user's identity to allow for malicious activity such as selling drugs and stolen personal information and buying and selling malicious software used for attacks. Some security professionals and organizations use the dark web on a limited basis to look for signs that information critical to that enterprise is being sought out or sold on the dark web.

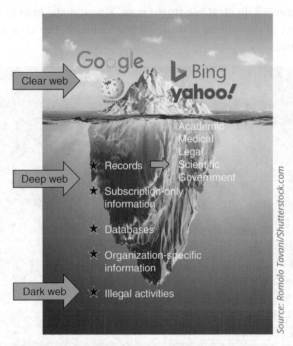

Figure 4-2   Dark web

(!) CAUTION   Finding information on the dark web is difficult. First, it requires using Tor or IP2, which prevents a device's IP address being traced. Second, although some dark web search engines are available, they are unlike regular search engines such as Google. The dark web search engines are difficult to use and notoriously inaccurate. One reason is because merchants who buy and sell stolen data or illicit drugs are constantly on the run, and their dark websites appear and then suddenly disappear with no warning. Finally, dark websites use a naming structure that results in URLs such as *p6f47s5p3dq3qkd.onion*. All of these are hurdles that keep out anyone who does not understand these inner workings.

TWO RIGHTS & A WRONG

1. Two concerns about public information sharing centers are the privacy of shared information and the speed at which the information is shared.
2. Two tools that facilitate AIS are STIX and TAXII.
3. Security professionals consider threat maps a vital source of information.

See Appendix B for the answer.

SECURING ENDPOINT COMPUTERS

✔ CERTIFICATION

3.2 Given a scenario, implement host or application security solutions.

4.4 Given an incident, apply mitigation techniques or controls to secure an environment.

Despite the fact that endpoint devices like smartphones, tablets, and wearable fitness trackers receive the bulk of attention today, the "workhorse" of technology remains the personal computer. More than 260 million computers are sold annually in the United States[1] compared to 160 million smartphones sold each year.[2] While all endpoints must be protected from attacks, endpoint desktop and laptop computers must be secured because they are connected to corporate networks and its data, they contain data stored locally, and they can be used as a springboard to attack other endpoints.

Securing endpoint computers primarily involves three major tasks: *confirming* that the computer has started securely, *protecting* the computer from attacks, and then *hardening* it for even greater protection.

Confirm Boot Integrity

One of the steps that is often overlooked in securing endpoint computers is to confirm that the computer has started without any malicious activity taking place. Ensuring secure startup involves the Unified Extensible Firmware Interface (UEFI) and its boot security features.

Unified Extensible Firmware Interface (UEFI)

Early cowboys and workhands were known for wearing tall, tight-fitting boots. These boots had a tab or loop at the top through which a tool called a boot hook could be inserted to assist in pulling on the boot. In the mid-1800s, the expression *pull yourself up by your own bootstraps* was used to describe an impossible task of lifting oneself off the ground by pulling on the bootstrap. The phrase later came to mean to improve your situation by your own efforts without any external help.

Computers adopted this language to describe the process of starting a computer when it has been powered off. Because a computer is unable to rely on external assistance when powered on, starting a computer is called *booting up* or just *booting*.

The booting process on early personal computers, both Apple Mac and Windows PC, used firmware called the *BIOS (Basic Input/Output System)*. The BIOS was a chip integrated into the computer's motherboard. When the computer was powered on, the BIOS software would "awaken" and perform the following steps in a *legacy BIOS boot*:

1. The BIOS would first test the various components of the computer to ensure that they were functioning properly (called the *POST* or *Power-On Self-Test*).

2. Next, the BIOS would reference the *Master Boot Record* (*MBR*) that specified the computer's *partition table*, which instructed the BIOS where the computer's operating system (OS) could be located.

3. Finally, the BIOS passed control to the installed boot loader, which launched the OS.

Originally, BIOS firmware was stored in a *ROM* (*read-only memory*) chip on the motherboard, supplemented by a *CMOS* (*complementary metal-oxide-semiconductor*) chip that stored any changes to the BIOS. Later computer systems stored the BIOS contents in *flash memory* so it could be easily updated. This provided the ability to update to the BIOS firmware so new features could be added.

NOTE 9

Although BIOS chips were nonvolatile (they retained the information even when the computer was turned off), CMOS needed its own dedicated power source, which was a lithium-ion battery about the size of a coin that could hold a charge for up to 10 years before needing to be replaced. If the CMOS battery died, the BIOS settings were not lost but instead were reset to their default settings.

To add functionality, an improved firmware interface was developed to replace the BIOS. Known as **UEFI (Unified Extensible Firmware Interface)**, it provides several enhancements over BIOS. This includes the ability to access hard drives that are larger than two terabytes (TB), support for an unlimited number of primary hard drive partitions, faster booting, and support for networking functionality in the UEFI firmware itself to aid in remote troubleshooting. UEFI also has a more advanced user interface for configurations and information, as seen in Figure 4-3.

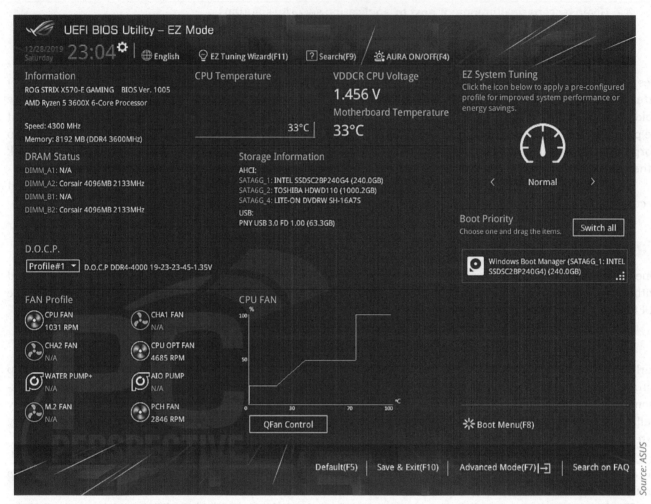

Figure 4-3   UEFI user interface

Source: ASUS

Boot Security

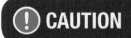

NOTE 10

Legacy BIOS boot support from motherboard manufacturers ended in 2020 and UEFI is now the standard.

Another significant improvement of UEFI over BIOS relates to boot security. The ability to update the BIOS in firmware also opened the door for a threat actor to create malware to infect the BIOS. Called a *BIOS attack*, it would exploit the update feature of the BIOS. Because the BIOS resides in firmware and an infected BIOS would then persistently re-infect the computer whenever it was powered on, BIOS attacks were difficult to uncover and hard to disinfect. UEFI, used along with other components, is designed to combat these BIOS vulnerabilities and provide improved boot security.

> **CAUTION**   UEFI by itself does not provide enhanced boot security. It must be paired with other boot security functions.

Boot security involves validating that each element used in each step of the boot process has not been modified. This process begins with the validation of the first element (boot software). Once the first element has been validated, it can then validate the next item (such as software drivers) and so on until control has been handed over to the OS.

This is called a *chain of trust*: each element relies on the confirmation of the previous element to know that the entire process is secure.

But how does the chain begin? What if a threat actor were to inject malware prior to start of the chain of trust? If the starting point is software, it can be replaced or modified. That would then compromise each element of the chain. To prevent this, a chain of trust requires a strong starting point.

The strongest starting point is hardware, which cannot be modified like software. This is known as the **hardware root of trust**. Security checks are "rooted" in (begin with) hardware checks. Because this chain of trust begins with a hardware verification, each subsequent check can rely upon it (called **boot attestation**).

Several techniques can be used to assure boot security, all of which rely on UEFI; some also rely on the hardware root of trust. Boot security modes are listed in Table 4-2.

Table 4-2   Boot security modes

Name	Description	Advantages	Disadvantages
Legacy BIOS Boot	Uses BIOS for boot functions	Compatible with older systems	No security features
UEFI Native Mode	Uses UEFI standards for boot functions	Security boot modules can be patched or updated as needed.	No validation or protection of the boot process
Secure Boot	Each firmware and software executable at boot time must be verified as having prior approval.	All system firmware, bootloaders, kernels, and other boot-time executables are validated.	Custom hardware, firmware, and software may not pass without first being submitted to system vendors like Microsoft.
Trusted Boot	Windows OS checks the integrity of every component of boot process before loading it.	Takes over where Secure Boot leaves off by validating the Windows 10 software before loading it	Requires using Microsoft OS
Measured Boot	Computer's firmware logs the boot process so the OS can send it to a trusted server to assess the security.	Provides highest degree of security	Could slow down the boot process

 **CAUTION**   The Secure Boot security standard is designed to ensure that a computer boots using only software that is trusted by the computer manufacturer. Manufacturers can update the list of trusted hardware, drivers, and OS for a computer, which are stored in the Secure Boot database on the computer. Although it is possible for the user to disable Secure Boot to install hardware or run software or OS that have not been trusted by the manufacturer, this makes it difficult or impossible to reactivate Secure Boot without restoring the computer back to its original factory state.

Protect Endpoints

Once boot security has been established; the computer endpoints must be actively protected. The protection can be done through software installed on the endpoint, such as antivirus software, antimalware, web browser protections, and monitoring and response systems.

Antivirus

One of the first software protections was **antivirus (AV)** software. This software can examine a computer for file-based virus infections as well as monitor computer activity and scan new documents that might contain a virus. (Scanning is typically performed when files are opened, created, or closed.) If a virus is detected, options generally include cleaning the file of the virus, quarantining the infected file, or deleting the file. Log files created by AV products can also provide beneficial information regarding attacks.

NOTE 11

Viruses are covered in Module 3.

Many AV products use signature-based monitoring, also called *static analysis*. The AV software scans files by attempting to match known virus patterns against potentially infected files (called *string scanning*). Other variations include *wildcard scanning* (a wildcard is allowed to skip bytes or ranges of bytes instead of looking for an exact match) and *mismatch scanning* (mismatches allow a set number of bytes in the string to be any value regardless of their position in the string).

>  The weakness of signature-based monitoring is that the AV vendor must constantly be searching for new viruses, extracting virus signatures, and distributing those updated databases to all users. Any out-of-date signature database could result in an infection.

NOTE 12

One AV heuristic monitoring technique used is *code emulation* in which a virtual environment is created that simulates the CPU and memory of the computer. Any questionable program code is executed in the virtual environment (no actual virus code is executed by the real CPU) to determine if it is a virus.

A newer approach to AV is heuristic monitoring (called *dynamic analysis*), which uses a variety of techniques to spot the characteristics of a virus instead of attempting to make matches. The difference between static analysis and dynamic analysis detection is similar to how airport security personnel in some nations screen for terrorists. A known terrorist attempting to go through security can be identified by comparing his face against photographs of known terrorists (static analysis). What about a new terrorist with no photograph? Security personnel can look at the person's characteristics—holding a one-way ticket, not checking any luggage, showing extreme nervousness—as possible indicators that the individual may need to be questioned (dynamic analysis).

Antimalware

Instead of only protecting against file-based viruses as with AV, **antimalware** is a suite of software intended to provide protections against multiple types of malware, such as ransomware, cryptomalware, and Trojans.

NOTE 13

Bayesian filters generally trap a much higher percentage of spam than other techniques.

Some antimalware software protects against spam that has evaded the corporate email gateway and monitors emails for spam and other unwanted content. Antimalware spam protection is often performed using a technique called *Bayesian filtering*. The software divides email messages that have been received into two piles, spam and nonspam. The filter then analyzes every word in each email and determines how frequently a word occurs in the spam pile compared to the nonspam pile. A word such as "the" would occur equally in both piles and be given a neutral 50 percent ranking. A word such as "report" may occur frequently in nonspam messages and would receive a 99 percent probability of being a nonspam word, while a word like "sex" may receive a 99 percent probability of being a spam word. Whenever email arrives, the filter looks for the 15 words with the highest probabilities to calculate the message's overall spam probability rating.

NOTE 14

A pop-up blocker can be part of an antimalware package, a separate program, or a feature incorporated within a browser that stops pop-up advertisements from appearing.

Another component of an antimalware suite is *antispyware*, which helps prevent computers from becoming infected by spyware. One common technique is to use a *pop-up blocker*. A *pop-up* is a small web browser window that appears over a webpage. Most pop-up windows are created by advertisers and launch as soon as a new website is visited. Using a pop-up blocker, users can often select the level of blocking, ranging from blocking all pop-ups to allowing specific pop-ups.

Web Browsers

Web browsers have a degree of security that can protect endpoint computers. This security includes secure cookies and HTTP headers.

Secure Cookies The Hypertext Transfer Protocol (HTTP) is the Internet-based protocol that is the foundation of all data exchanges on the web. It is a client-server protocol so that requests are initiated by the recipient or client, usually a web browser, to a web server.

One of the limitations of HTTP is that it is a *stateless protocol*. Unlike a *stateful protocol*, which "remembers" everything that occurs between the browser client and the server, a stateless protocol "forgets" what occurs when the session is interrupted or ends. Three ways the stateless protocol HTTP can mimic a stateful protocol include the following:

- Using a URL extension so the state is sent as part of the URL as a response
- Using "hidden form fields" in which the state is sent to the client as part of the response and returned to the server as part of a form's hidden data
- Storing user-specific information in a file on the user's local computer and then retrieve it later in a file called a *cookie*.

Websites use several types of cookies. A *first-party cookie* is created from the website that a user is currently viewing; whenever the user returns to this site, that cookie is used by the site to view the user's preferences and better customize the browsing experience. Some websites attempt to place additional cookies on the local hard drive. These cookies often come from third parties that advertise on the site and want to record the user's preferences. These cookies are called *third-party cookies*. A *session cookie* is stored in random-access memory (RAM), instead of on the hard drive, and only lasts for the duration of visiting the website.

Cookies can pose security risks as well as privacy risks. First-party cookies can be stolen and used to impersonate the user, while third-party cookies can be used to track the browsing or buying habits of a user. When multiple websites are serviced by a single marketing organization, cookies can be used to track browsing habits on all the client's sites.

As a means of protection for cookies, a web browser can send a **secure cookie**. This cookie is only sent to the server with an encrypted request over the secure HTTPS protocol. This prevents an unauthorized person from intercepting a cookie that is being transmitted between the browser and the web server.

NOTE 15

A cookie can contain a variety of information based on the user's preferences when visiting a website. For example, if a user inquires about a rental car at the car agency's website, that site might create a cookie that contains the user's travel itinerary. In addition, it may record the pages visited on a site to help the site customize the view for any future visits. Cookies can also store any personally identifiable information (name, email address, work address, telephone number, and so on) that was provided when visiting the site; however, a website cannot gain access to private information stored on the local computer.

HTTP Response Headers   When users visit a website through their web browser, the web server answers back with **HTTP Response Headers**. These headers tell the browser how to behave while communicating with the website. Several HTTP Response Headers can improve security; these are listed in Table 4-3.

Table 4-3   HTTP response headers

HTTP response header	Description	Protection
HTTP Strict Transport Security (HSTS)	Forces browser to communicate over more secure HTTPS instead of HTTP	Encrypts transmissions to prevent unauthorized user from intercepting
Content Security Policy (CSP)	Restricts the resources a user is allowed to load within the website	Protects against injection attacks
Cross Site Scripting Protection (X-XSS)	Prohibits a page from loading if it detects a cross-site scripting attack	Prevents XSS attacks
X-Frame-Options	Prevents attackers from "overlaying" their content on the webpage	Foils a threat actor's attempt to trick a user into providing personal information

Monitoring and Response Systems

The three types of monitoring and response systems for endpoint computers are host intrusion detection systems (HIDS), host intrusion prevention systems (HIPS), and endpoint detection and response (EDR).

Host Intrusion Detection Systems (HIDS)   A **host intrusion detection system (HIDS)** is a software-based application that runs on an endpoint computer and can detect that an attack has occurred. The primary function of a HIDS is automated detection, which saves someone from sorting through log files to find an indication of unusual behavior. HIDS can quickly detect evidence that an intrusion has occurred. Figure 4-4 shows a HIDS dashboard.

Figure 4-4   HIDS dashboard

A HIDS relies on agents installed directly on the endpoint, and these agents work closely with the OS to observe activity. HIDSs typically monitor these types of endpoint computer functions:

- *System calls.* Each operation in a computing environment starts with a *system call*. A system call is an instruction that interrupts the program being executed and requests a service from the operating system. HIDS can monitor system calls based on the process, mode, and action being requested.
- *File system access.* System calls usually require specific files to be opened to access data. A HIDS works to ensure that all file openings are based on legitimate needs and are not the result of malicious activity.
- *Host input/output.* HIDS monitors all input and output communications to watch for malicious activity. For example, if the system never uses instant messaging (IM) and suddenly a threat attempts to open an IM connection from the system, the HIDS would detect this as anomalous activity.

Host Intrusion Prevention Systems (HIPS)   As its name implies, an intrusion *prevention* system not only monitors to detect malicious activities but also attempts to stop them. A host intrusion prevention system (HIPS) monitors endpoint activity to immediately block a malicious attack by following specific rules. Activity that a HIPS watches for includes an event that attempts to control other programs, terminate programs, and install devices and drivers. When a HIPS blocks action, it then alerts the user so an appropriate decision about what to do can be made.

 **CAUTION**   One of the drawbacks to a HIPS is a high number of false positives can be generated. Both legitimate and malicious programs often access the same resource, and each can cause a HIPS to then block the action.

Endpoint Detection and Response (EDR)   Endpoint detection and response (EDR) tools have a similar functionality to HIDS of monitoring endpoint events and of HIPS of taking immediate action. However, EDR tools are considered more robust than HIDS and HIPS. First, an EDR can aggregate data from multiple endpoint computers to a centralized database so that security professionals can further investigate and gain a better picture of events occurring across multiple endpoints instead of just on a single endpoint. This can help determine if an attack is more widespread across the enterprise and if more comprehensive and higher-level action needs to be taken. Second, EDR tools can perform more sophisticated analytics that identify patterns and detect anomalies. This can help detect unusual or unrecognized activities by performing baseline comparisons of normal behavior.

NOTE 16

Many EDRs also allow for a manual or user analysis of the data.

Harden Endpoints

After boot security has been established and the endpoints have been protected, the next step is to harden the endpoints for further protection. Hardening endpoints involves patch management and OS protections.

Patch Management

One of the most important steps in securing an endpoint computer is to promptly install patches. Threat actors often watch for the release of a patch and then immediately craft an attack around the vulnerability the patch addresses, knowing that many users and organizations are lax in applying patches.

Effective patch management involves two types of patch management tools to administer patches. The first type includes tools for patch distribution, while the second type involves patch reception.

Patch Distribution   Modern operating systems—such as Red Hat Linux, Apple macOS, Ubuntu Linux, and Microsoft Windows—frequently distribute patches. A growing number of application and utility software developers are also distributing patches for their products (**third-party updates**).

These patches, however, can sometimes create new problems, such as preventing a custom application from running correctly. Organizations that have these types of applications usually test patches when they are released to ensure that they do not adversely affect any customized applications. In these instances, the organization delays the installation of a patch from the vendor's online update service until the patch is thoroughly tested. But how can an organization prevent its employees from installing the latest patch until it has passed testing and still ensure that all users download and install necessary patches?

The answer is an *automated patch update service*. This service is used to manage patches within the enterprise instead of relying upon the vendor's online update service. An automated patch update service typically consists of a component installed on one or more servers inside the corporate network. Because these servers can replicate information among themselves, usually only one of the servers must be connected to the vendor's online update service, as seen in Figure 4-5.

Advantages of using an automated patch update service include the following:

- Downloading patches from a local server instead of using the vendor's online update service can save bandwidth and time because each computer does not have to connect to an external server.
- Administrators can approve or decline updates for client systems, force updates to install by a specific date, and obtain reports on what updates each computer needs.
- Administrators can approve updates for "detection" only; this allows them to see which computers require the update without installing it.

Patch Reception   Early versions of OSs allowed the user to configure how they receive patches. For example, prior to Windows 10, Microsoft users had several options regarding accepting or even rejecting patches. These options included *Install updates automatically, Download updates but let me choose whether to install them, Check for updates but let me choose whether to download and install them,* and *Never check for updates.* However, this approach frequently resulted in important security patches being ignored by users and putting their computers at risk.

Today users have fewer—if *any*—options regarding patches: usually patches are automatically downloaded and installed whenever they become available. This is called **auto-update**, and it ensures that the software is always up to date.

Microsoft Windows 10 is typical of the enhancements of patch reception. Figure 4-6 shows the Windows 10 Advanced options. These options include the following:

- *Forced updates.* Users can no longer refuse or indefinitely delay security updates. By default, all updates will be downloaded and installed automatically. However, users can defer the "quality updates" (those with security patches) but only for seven days (Windows 10 Home edition) or 35 days (all other versions). New feature updates (those without security patches) can be delayed for 35 days (Windows 10 Home edition) or 365 days (all other versions).

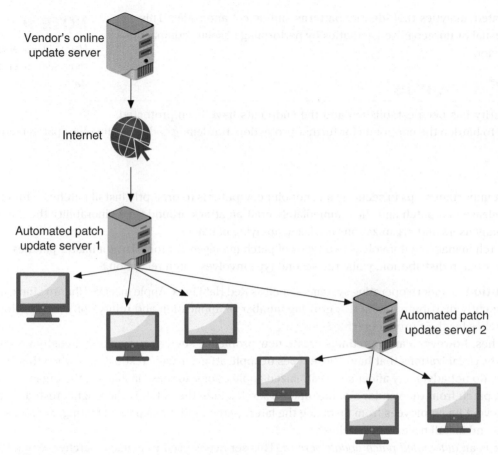

Figure 4-5 Automated patch update service

- *No selective updates.* Unlike in previous versions of Windows, users cannot select individual Windows updates to download and install. However, users can select if they want to receive updates for other installed Microsoft products (such as Office).
- *More efficient distribution.* If many Windows 10 devices are connected to a network, each device does not have to download the updates over the Internet individually. Instead, once one device has downloaded the updates, they can then be distributed to the other devices across the local network. In addition, Windows will not download updates on mobile devices unless that device is connected to an unrestricted Wi-Fi network (so that it does not use the cellular data connections that users pay for).

Operating Systems

There are different types and uses of operating systems. Several of the major types are listed in Table 4-4.

Although protections within the OS are designed to provide security for the endpoint device, the OS itself must be protected. Securing an OS involves proper security configurations and using confinement tools.

Security Configuration The security of an OS depends upon the proper configuration of its built-in security features. Modern operating systems have hundreds of security settings. A typical OS security configuration should include the following:

- *Disabling unnecessary ports and services.* One of the primary OS security configurations involves **disabling unnecessary open ports and services**, or "turning off" any service that is not being used, such as Microsoft Windows ASP.NET State Service, Portable Device Enumerator Service, and Apple macOS Spotlight Indexing. In addition, closing any unnecessary TCP ports can also enhance security.
- *Disabling default accounts/passwords.* Another important disabling function is disabling default accounts and passwords. Some OSs include unnecessary accounts. For example, Microsoft Windows 10 includes a *built-in Administrator account* that can be used for those building new computers to run programs and applications

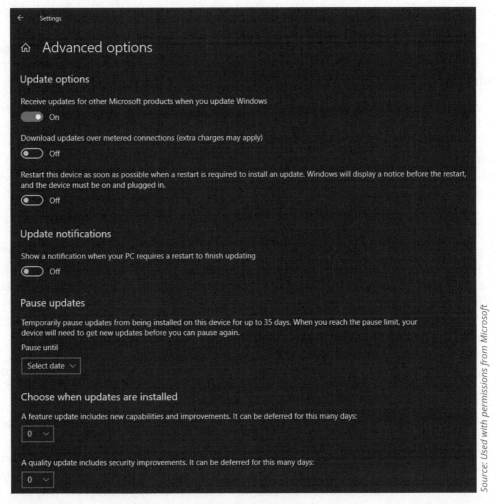

Source: Used with permissions from Microsoft

Figure 4-6   Microsoft Windows 10 Advanced options

Table 4-4   Types of OSs

OS type	Uses	Examples
Network OS	Software that runs on a network device like a firewall, router, or switch	Cisco Internetwork Operating System (IOS), Juniper JUNOS, MikroTik RouterOS
Server OS	Operating system software that runs on a network server to provide resources to network users	Microsoft Windows Server, Apple macOS Server, Red Hat Linux
Workstation OS	Software that manages hardware and software on a client computer	Microsoft Windows, Apple macOS, Ubuntu Linux
Appliance OS	OS in firmware that is designed to manage a specific device like a digital video recorder or video game console.	Linpus Linux
Kiosk OS	System and user interface software for an interactive kiosk	Microsoft Windows, Google Chrome OS, Apple iOS, Instant WebKiosk, KioWare (Android)
Mobile OS	Operating system for mobile phones, smartphones, tablets, and other handheld devices	Google Android, Apple iOS, Apple iPadOS

before a user account is created. In addition, some accounts may come with default passwords that should be changed.

- *Employing least functionality.* The concept of "least functionality" states a user should only be given the minimum set of permissions required to perform necessary tasks; all other permissions should be configured as not available to the user. For example, a user should not have the ability to modify system security features.

Instead of recreating the same security configuration on each endpoint computer, tools can be used to automate the process. In Microsoft Windows, a *security template* is a collection of security configuration settings. These settings typically include account policies, user rights, event log settings, restricted groups, system services, file permissions, and registry permissions. Once a single endpoint computer has been configured properly, a security template from that device can be developed and used for deploying to other systems. Predefined security templates are also available to be imported, and these settings then can be modified to create a unique security configuration for all endpoints.

NOTE 17

Although a Microsoft Windows security template can be deployed manually, this requires an administrator to access each computer and apply the security template either through using the command line or a *snap-in*, which is a software module that provides administrative capabilities for a device. A preferred method is to use *Group Policy*, which is a feature that provides centralized management and configuration of computers and remote users who are using specific Microsoft directory services known as *Active Directory (AD)*. Group Policy allows a single configuration to be set and then deployed to many or all users.

NOTE 18

Tamper Protection also prevents changes to security settings by programs, Windows command line commands, or through Group Policy.

NOTE 19

Instead of managing security options on an OS that has been deployed, in some cases, it is necessary to tighten security during the design and coding of the OS. This is called OS hardening. An OS that has been designed in this way to be secure is a *trusted OS*.

For a Microsoft Windows endpoint computer, it is also important to secure the registry, which is a database that contains low-level settings used by the Windows OS and for those applications that use the registry. Threat actors who can modify the registry could be able to disable antivirus and antimalware protections, disable any cloud-delivered protection, and remove security updates.

To mitigate this risk, the Windows 10 Tamper Protection security feature prevents Windows security settings from being changed or disabled by a threat actor who modifies the registry. Instead, the security settings can only be accessed directly through the Windows 10 user interface or through enterprise management software.

In addition to Tamper Protection, a Group Policy setting can prevent access to the tool that can alter the registry. This setting is *Prevent access to registry editing tools* and is shown in Figure 4-7.

Confinement Tools Several tools can be used to "confine" or restrict malware. These tools include the following:

- *Application whitelisting/blacklisting.* An increasingly popular approach to client OS security is to employ application whitelisting/blacklisting. Whitelisting is approving in advance only specific applications to run on the OS so that any item not approved is either restricted or denied ("default-deny"). The inverse of whitelisting is blacklisting, creating a list of unapproved software so that any item not on the list of blacklisted applications can run ("default-allow"). Application whitelisting/blacklisting requires preapproval for an application to run or not run.

NOTE 20

The elite Tailored Access Operations (TAO) section of the National Security Agency (NSA) is responsible for compromising networks owned by hostile nations to spy on them. The head of the TAO spoke at a security conference about the best practices of security from the NSA's perspective (in his own words, "what can you do to defend yourself to make my life hard?"). One of the most important steps was to employ whitelisting for the software that runs on servers. A similar step is to whitelist a predefined set of websites to which users can connect to prevent malware from accessing a C&C or to exfiltrate stolen information.[3]

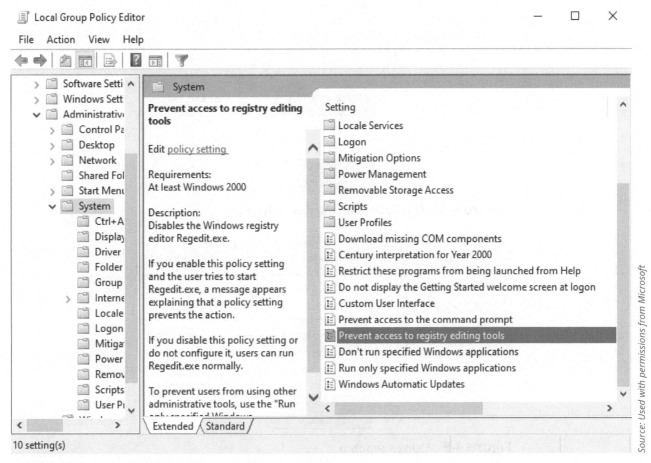

Source: Used with permissions from Microsoft

Figure 4-7   Prevent access to registry editing tools

- *Sandbox.* Figure 4-8 illustrates a conceptual view of applications that interact with an OS. A **sandbox** is a "container" in which an application can be run so that it does not impact the underlying OS, as illustrated in Figure 4-9. Anything that occurs within the sandbox is not visible to other applications or the OS outside the sandbox. Also, the contents of the sandbox are not saved when the sandbox is closed. Sandboxes are often used when downloading or running suspicious programs to ensure that the endpoint will not become infected.

- *Quarantine.* Whereas a sandbox is used to contain an *application*, **quarantine** is a process that holds a suspicious *document*. Quarantine is most commonly used with email attachments. When an attachment is received, the quarantine process removes the attachment and, depending upon the policy set by the organization, either sends to the user sent a sanitized version of the attachment (such as a Word DOCX document that has been converted to a PDF document) or a URL to the document on a restricted computer so that the user can view, print, or delete the attachment.

NOTE 21

A sandbox is not the same as a virtual machine. A virtual machine is a "computer within a computer" in which an entire OS runs as an application on top of the regular OS. However, its contents can be saved for future use.

NOTE 22

Microsoft Office documents that are received as attachments, opened from an Internet location, or opened from an unsafe location are by default quarantined. The documents are displayed in Protected View, which is a read-only mode with most editing functions disabled. If the file needs to be saved or printed, the user can click the "Enable Editing" button to open the document as normal.

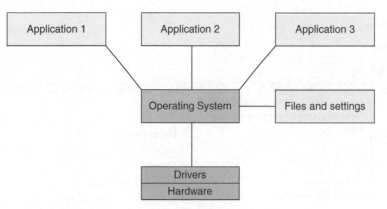

Figure 4-8   Applications interacting with an OS

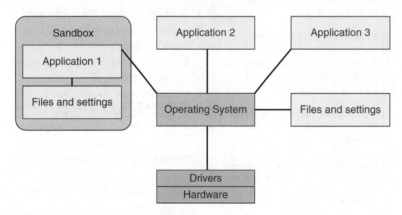

Figure 4-9   Using a sandbox

TWO RIGHTS & A WRONG

1. In a Trusted Boot, the endpoint's firmware logs the boot process to the OS can send it to a trusted server to assess the security.
2. Dynamic analysis uses heuristic monitoring.
3. Cookies are a workaround of the stateless protocol HTTP.

See Appendix B for the answer.

CREATING AND DEPLOYING SECDEVOPS

 **CERTIFICATION**

2.3 Summarize secure application development, deployment, and automation concepts.

3.2 Given a scenario, implement host or application security solutions.

Confirming boot integrity, protecting endpoints, and hardening endpoints are all essential steps in securing an endpoint computer. But an additional element that is also critical is creating and deploying secure applications. Because endpoint computers run applications, the best endpoint boot security, antivirus and antimalware, patch management, and OS security configurations can all be negatively impacted—and sometimes negated—by an application that contains vulnerabilities. An unsecure application can open the door for attackers to exploit the application, the data that it uses, and even the underlying OS. Table 4-5 lists attacks that can be launched using vulnerabilities in applications.

Table 4-5   Attacks based on application vulnerabilities

Attack	Description	Defense
Executable files attack	Trick the vulnerable application into modifying or creating executable files on the system	Prevent the application from creating or modifying executable files for its proper function
System tampering	Use the vulnerable application to modify special sensitive areas of the operating system (Microsoft Windows registry keys, system startup files, etc.) and take advantage of those modifications	Do not allow applications to modify special areas of the OS
Process spawning control	Trick the vulnerable application into spawning executable files on the system	Take away the process spawning ability from the application

One particularly dangerous attack can be the result of a vulnerability in an application. The *root directory* is a specific directory on a web server's file system, and users who access the server are usually restricted to the root directory and directories and files beneath the root directory, but they cannot access other directories. For example, the default root directory of Microsoft's Internet Information Services (IIS) web server is *C:\Inetpub\wwwroot*. Users have access to this directory and subdirectories beneath this root (*C:\Inetpub\wwwroot\news*) if given permission, but they do not have access to other directories in the file system, such as *C:\Windows\System32*. A **directory traversal** attack takes advantage of vulnerability in the web application program or the web server software so that a user can move from the root directory to other restricted directories. The ability to move to another directory could allow an unauthorized user to view confidential files or even enter commands to execute on a server known as *command injection*. A directory traversal attack is illustrated in Figure 4-10. Other dangerous weaknesses in an application can create vulnerabilities in computer memory or buffer areas that can be easily exploited. These poor **memory management** vulnerabilities result in attacks such as buffer overflow, integer overflow, pointer/object deference, and DLL injection attacks.

NOTE 23

Buffer overflow, integer overflow, pointer/object deference, and DLL injection attacks are all covered in Module 3.

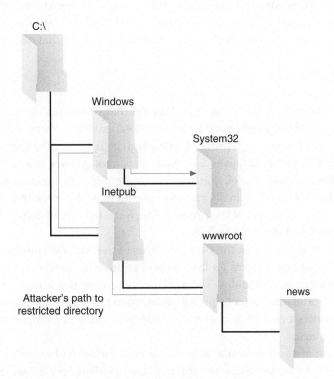

Figure 4-10   Directory traversal attack

The cause of most unsecure applications is usually the result of how the application was designed and written. Creating and developing secure software involves understanding application development concepts, secure coding techniques, and code testing.

Application Development Concepts

The two levels of application development concepts include general concepts that apply to all application development and those that apply to a more rigorous security-based approach.

General Concepts

Developing an application requires completing several stages. These stages include the following:

- *Development*. At the **development stage**, the requirements for the application are established, and it is confirmed that the application meets the intended business needs before the actual coding begins.
- *Testing*. The **testing stage** thoroughly tests the application for any errors that could result in a security vulnerability.
- *Staging*. The **staging stage** tests to verify that the code functions as intended.
- *Production*. In the **production stage** the application is released to be used in its actual setting.

Often application development will involve **software diversity**. Software diversity is a software development technique in which two or more functionally identical variants of a program are developed from the same specification but by different programmers or programming teams. The intent is to provide error detection, increased reliability, and additional documentation. It also can reduce the probability that errors created by different **compilers**, which are programs that create **binary** machine code from human source code, will influence the end results.

Another concept regarding application development involves how the completed application will be used in the context of the larger IT footprint of the enterprise. **Provisioning** is the enterprise-wide configuration, deployment, and management of multiple types of IT system resources, of which the new application would be viewed as a new resource. **Deprovisioning** in application development is removing a resource that is no longer needed.

Integrity measurement is an "attestation mechanism" designed to be able to convince a remote party (external to the coding team) that an application is running only a set of known and approved executables. Whenever a file is called in an executable mode, such as when a program is invoked or a sharable library is mapped, the integrity measurement tool generates a unique digital value of that file. On request, the tool can produce a list of all programs run and their corresponding digital values. This list can then be examined to ensure that no unknown or known vulnerable applications have been run.

SecDevOps

An *application development lifecycle model* is a conceptual model that describes the stages involved in creating an application. Most projects use one of two major application development lifecycle models.

The *waterfall model* uses a sequential design process: as each stage is fully completed, the developers move on to the next stage. This means that once a stage is finished, developers cannot go back to a previous stage without starting all over again. For example, in the waterfall model, **quality assurance (QA)**—verification of quality—occurs only after the application has been tested and before it is finally placed in production. However, this makes any issues uncovered by QA difficult to address since it is at the end of the process. The waterfall model demands extensive planning in the very beginning and requires that it be followed carefully.

The *agile model* was designed to overcome the disadvantages of the waterfall model. Instead of following a rigid sequential design process, the agile model takes an incremental approach. Developers might start with a simplistic project design and begin to work on small modules. The work on these modules is done in short (weekly or monthly) "sprints," and at the end of each sprint, the project's priorities are again evaluated as tests are being run. This approach allows for software issues to be incrementally discovered so that feedback and changes can be incorporated into the design before the next sprint is started.

One specific type of software methodology that follows the agile model and heavily incorporates **secure coding practices and techniques** to create secure software applications is called *SecDevOps*. SecDevOps (also known as DevSecOps and DevOpsSec) is the process of integrating secure development best practices and methodologies into application software development and deployment processes using the agile model. It is a set of best practices designed to help organizations implant secure coding deep in the heart of their applications.

SecDevOps is often promoted in terms of its **elasticity** (flexibility or resilience in code development) and its **scalability** (expandability from small projects to very large projects). However, the cornerstone of SecDevOps is automation. With standard application development, security teams often find themselves stuck with time-consuming manual tasks. SecDevOps, on the other hand, applies what is called **automated courses of action** to develop the code as quickly and securely as possible. This automation enables **continuous monitoring** (examining the processes in real time instead of at the end of a stage), **continuous validation** (ongoing approvals of the code), **continuous integration** (ensuring that security features are incorporated at each stage), **continuous delivery** (moving the code to each stage as it is completed), and **continuous deployment** (continual code implementation).

NOTE 24

The SecDevOps methodology also includes concepts such as *immutable systems* (once a value or configuration is employed as part of an application, it is not modified; if changes are necessary, a new system must be created), *infrastructure as code* (managing a hardware and software infrastructure using the same principles as developing computer code), and *baselining* (creating a starting point for comparison purposes in order to apply targets and goals to measure success).

Table 4-6 lists sources of recommendations for SecDevOps.

Table 4-6   Secure SDLC sources

Source	Description	Materials available
OWASP (Open Web Application Security Project)	A group that monitors web attacks	Maturity models, development guides, testing guides, code review guides, and application security verification standards
SANS (SysAdmin, Audit, Network and Security Institute)	A company that specializes in cybersecurity and secure web application development	White papers, research reports, and best practices guidelines
CIS (Center for Internet Security)	Not-for-profit organization that compiles CIS security controls	Training, assessment tools, and consulting services

Because SecDevOps is based on the agile method, it involves continuous modifications throughout the process. With these continual changes, it is important to use tools that support change management or creating a plan for documenting changes to the application. One tool for change management is **version control** software that allows changes to be automatically recorded and, if necessary, "rolled back" to a previous version of the software.

Secure Coding Techniques

Several coding techniques should be used to create secure applications and limit **data exposure** or disclosing sensitive data to attackers. These techniques include determining how encryption will be implemented and ensuring that memory management is handled correctly so as not to introduce memory vulnerabilities. Other techniques are summarized in Table 4-7.

Code Testing

Testing is one of the most important steps in SecDevOps. Instead of testing only after the application is completed, testing should be performed much earlier during the implementation and verification phases of a software development process. Testing involves static code analysis and dynamic code analysis.

NOTE 25

Edsger W. Dijkstra, a famous software engineer, once said, "Program testing can be used to show the presence of bugs, but never to show their absence!"

Table 4-7 Secure coding techniques

Coding technique	Description	Security advantage
Proper input validation	Accounting for errors such as incorrect user input (entering a file name for a file that does not exist).	Can prevent Cross-site scripting (XSS) and Cross-site request forgery (CSRF) attacks
Normalization	Organizing data within a database to minimize redundancy.	Reduces footprint of data exposed to attackers
Stored procedure	A subroutine available to applications that access a relational database.	Eliminates the need to write a subroutine that could have vulnerabilities
Code signing	Digitally signing applications.	Confirms the software author and guarantees the code has not been altered or corrupted
Obfuscation/ camouflaged code	Writing an application in such a way that its inner functionality is difficult for an outsider to understand.	Helps prevent an attacker from understanding a program's function
Dead code	A section of an application that executes but performs no meaningful function.	Provides an unnecessary attack vector for attackers
Server-side execution and validation or Client-side execution and validation	Input validation generally uses the server to perform validation but can also have the client perform validation by the user's web browser.	Adds another validation to the process
Code reuse of third-party libraries and SDKs	Code reuse is using existing software in a new application; a software development kit (SDK) is a set of tools used to write applications.	Existing libraries that have already been vetted as secure eliminate the need to write new code

Static Code Analysis

Analysis and testing of the software should occur from a security perspective before the source code is even compiled. These tests are called **static code analysis**. Figure 4-11 illustrates an automated static code analysis tool.

Automated static code analysis may also be accompanied by **manual peer reviews**. In these reviews, software engineers and developers are paired together or grouped in larger teams to laboriously examine each line of source code, looking for vulnerabilities.

Dynamic Code Analysis

Security testing should also be performed after the source code is compiled (a process called **dynamic code analysis** or *run-time verification*) and when all components are integrated and running. This testing typically uses a tool or suite of pre-built attacks or testing tools that specifically monitor the application's behavior for memory corruption, user privilege issues, and other critical security problems.

Some of the most common dynamic code analysis tools use a process called **fuzzing**. Fuzzing provides random input to a program in an attempt to trigger exceptions, such as memory corruption, program crashes, or security breaches. An advantage of fuzzing is that it produces a record of what input triggered the exception so it can be reproduced to track down the problem within the code. Fuzzing test software consists of an *execution engine* and an *input generator*, which usually allows the tester to configure the types of inputs (see Figure 4-12).

 **CAUTION** A single pass of a fuzzer is unlikely to find all exceptions in software due to the randomness in the fuzzing process. The mutation of the inputs relies on randomness to determine where to mutate input and what to mutate. Fuzzers require multiple trials and statistical tests.

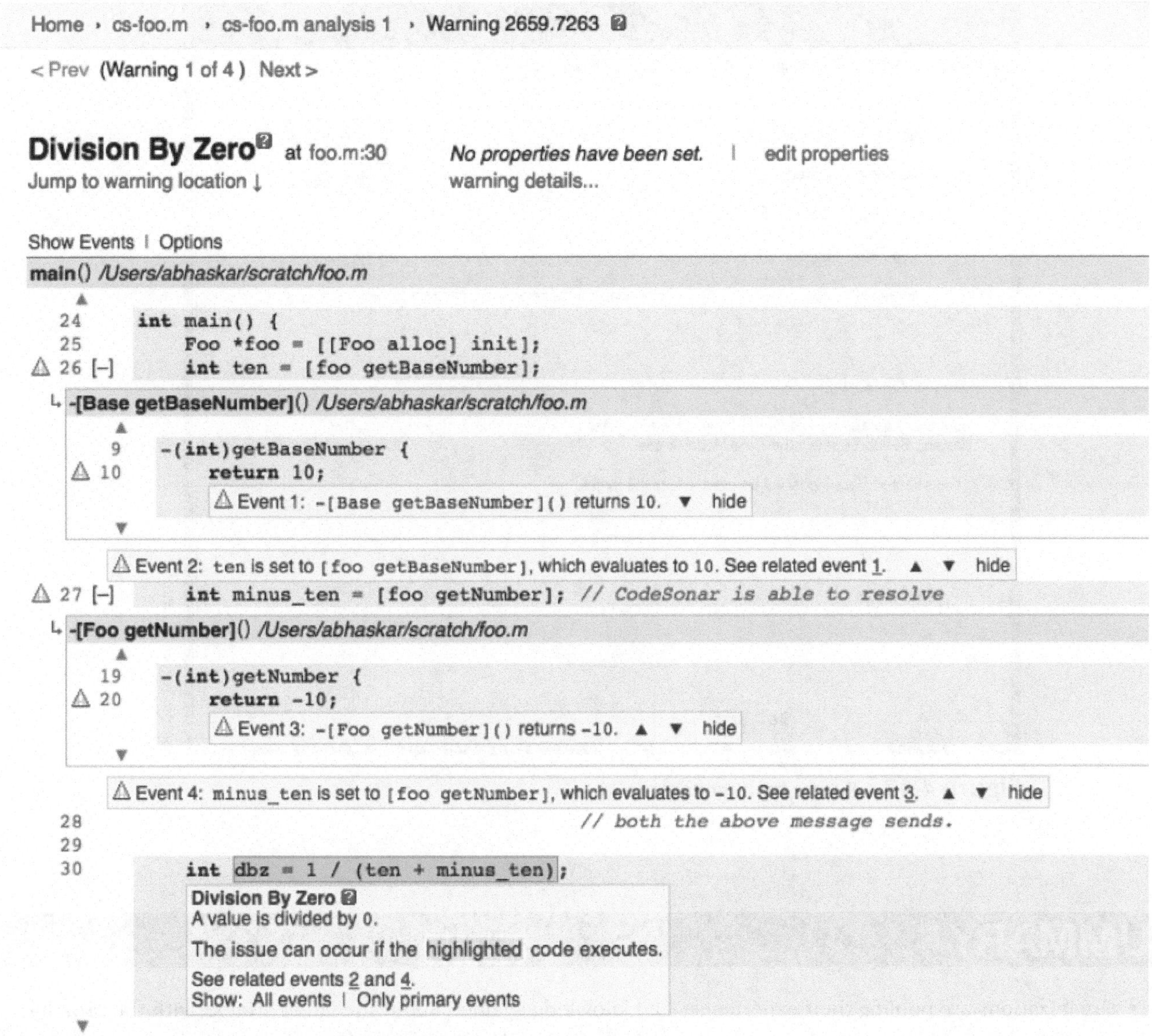

Home › cs-foo.m › cs-foo.m analysis 1 › Warning 2659.7263 ▣

< Prev (Warning 1 of 4)   Next >

Division By Zero▣ at foo.m:30   *No properties have been set.* | edit properties
Jump to warning location ↓   *warning details...*

Show Events | Options

main() */Users/abhaskar/scratch/foo.m*

```
   24      int main() {
   25          Foo *foo = [[Foo alloc] init];
△ 26 [–]      int ten = [foo getBaseNumber];
```

└ **-[Base getBaseNumber]**() */Users/abhaskar/scratch/foo.m*

```
    9      -(int)getBaseNumber {
△ 10          return 10;
                △ Event 1: -[Base getBaseNumber]() returns 10.  ▼  hide
```

△ Event 2: ten is set to [foo getBaseNumber], which evaluates to 10. See related event 1. ▲ ▼ hide

```
△ 27 [–]      int minus_ten = [foo getNumber]; // CodeSonar is able to resolve
```

└ **-[Foo getNumber]**() */Users/abhaskar/scratch/foo.m*

```
   19      -(int)getNumber {
△ 20          return -10;
                △ Event 3: -[Foo getNumber]() returns -10.  ▲  ▼  hide
```

△ Event 4: minus_ten is set to [foo getNumber], which evaluates to -10. See related event 3. ▲ ▼ hide

```
   28                                    // both the above message sends.
   29
   30          int dbz = 1 / (ten + minus_ten);
```

Division By Zero ▣
A value is divided by 0.

The issue can occur if the highlighted code executes.

See related events 2 and 4.
Show: All events | Only primary events

Source: GrammaTech

Figure 4-11   Automated static code analysis tool

TWO RIGHTS & A WRONG

1. A goal of software diversity is to reduce the probability that errors created by different compilers will influence the end results.
2. Provisioning is removing a resource that is no longer needed.
3. SecDevOps has elasticity and scalability.

See Appendix B for the answer.

📱 **VM LAB**   You're now ready to complete the live virtual machine labs for this module. The labs can be found in each module in the MindTap.

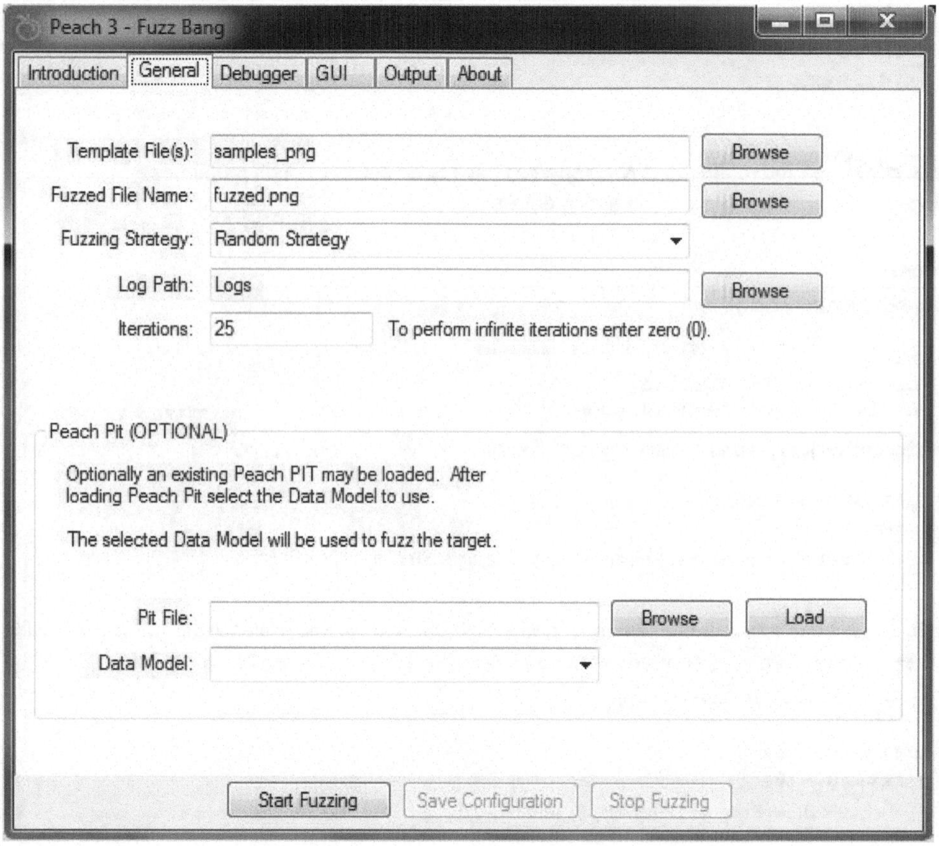

Figure 4-12   Fuzzer input generator

Source: Déjà vu Software

SUMMARY

- Organizations are pooling their experiences and knowledge gained about the latest attacks with the broader security community because sharing this type of information has become an important aid to help other organizations shore up their defenses. Open source threat intelligence information that is freely available, often called open source intelligence (OSINT), has become a vital resource. This information is often collected and then disseminated through public information sharing centers. The two concerns around public information sharing centers are the privacy of shared information and the speed at which the information is shared. Closed source is the opposite of open source. Organizations that are participants in closed source information are part of private information sharing centers that restrict both access to data and participation.

- Several sources of threat intelligence are useful. A vulnerability database is a repository of known vulnerabilities and information as to how they have been exploited. These databases create "feeds" of the latest cybersecurity incidences. A cybersecurity threat map illustrates cyberthreats overlaid on a diagrammatic representation of a geographical area. Threat maps help in visualizing attacks and provide a limited amount of context of the source and the target countries, the attack types, and historical and near real-time data about threats, although they provide limited valuable information. File and code repositories are used by victims of an attack who can upload malicious files and software code that can then be examined by others to learn more about these attacks and craft their defenses. The dark web is the domain of threat actors and beyond the reach of a normal search engine. Malicious activity such as selling drugs and stolen personal information and buying and selling malicious software used for attacks occurs on the dark web. Some security professionals and organizations use the dark web on a limited basis to look for signs that information critical to that enterprise is being sought out or sold on the dark web.

- One of the steps that is often overlooked in securing endpoint computers is to confirm that the computer has started without any malicious activity taking place. The booting process on early personal computers used firmware called the BIOS (Basic Input/Output System). Although the ability to update the BIOS firmware enabled new features to be added, it also opened the door for threat actors to create malware to infect the BIOS. To combat this vulnerability and add functionality, UEFI (Unified Extensible Firmware Interface) was developed, in conjunction with the Secure Boot security standard. Several techniques can be used to assure boot security by taking advantage of the features in UEFI.

- Antivirus (AV) software can examine a computer for any file-based virus infections and monitor computer activity and scan new documents that might contain a virus. A new approach to AV is dynamic analysis, which uses a variety of techniques to spot the characteristics of a virus instead of attempting to make matches. Antimalware is a suite of software intended to provide protections against multiple types of malware, such as ransomware, cryptomalware, Trojans, spam, and spyware.

- Web browsers have a degree of security that can protect endpoint computers. User-specific information stored in a file on the user's local computer is called a cookie. There are several types of cookies. As a means of protection for cookies, a web browser can send a secure cookie. This cookie is only sent to the server with an encrypted request over the secure HTTPS protocol. When a user visits a website through their web browser, the web server answers back with HTTP Response Headers. These headers tell the browser how to behave while communicating with the website. Several HTTP Response Headers can improve security.

- A host intrusion detection system (HIDS) is a software-based application that runs on an endpoint computer and can detect that an attack has occurred. The primary function of a HIDS is automated detection, which saves someone from sorting through log files to find an indication of unusual behavior. A HIDS relies on agents installed directly on the endpoint, and these agents work closely with the OS to observe activity. A host intrusion prevention system (HIPS) monitors endpoint activity to immediately react to block a malicious attack by following specific rules. Activity that a HIPS watches for includes an event that attempts to control other programs, terminate programs, and install devices and drivers. Endpoint detection and response (EDR) tools have a similar functionality to HIDS of monitoring endpoint events and of HIPS of taking immediate action. However, EDR tools are considered more robust than HIDS and HIPS.

- One of the most important steps in securing an endpoint computer is to promptly install patches. Modern operating systems—such as Red Hat Linux, Apple macOS, Ubuntu Linux, and Microsoft Windows—frequently distribute patches. A growing number of application and utility software developers are also distributing patches called third-party updates. An automated patch update service is used to manage patches within the enterprise instead of relying upon the vendor's online update service. Early versions of OSs allowed users to configure how they receive patches; however, today patches are usually automatically downloaded and installed whenever they become available.

- An unsecure application can open the door for attackers to exploit the application, the data that it uses, and even the underlying OS. The cause of most unsecure applications is usually the result of how the application was designed and written. Developing an application requires several stages. An application development lifecycle model is a conceptual model that describes the stages involved in creating an application. The waterfall model uses a sequential design process: as each stage is fully completed, the developers move on to the next stage. The agile model was designed to overcome the disadvantages of the waterfall model. Instead of following a rigid sequential design process, the agile model takes an incremental approach. One specific type of software methodology that follows the agile model and heavily incorporates secure coding practices and techniques to create secure software applications is called SecDevOps. Several coding techniques should be used to create secure applications and limit data exposure or disclosing sensitive data to attackers. These techniques include determining how encryption will be implemented and ensuring that memory management is handled correctly so as to not introduce memory vulnerabilities.

- Testing is one of the most important steps in SecDevOps. Yet, instead of testing only after the application is completed, testing should be performed much earlier during the implementation and verification phases of a software development process. Analysis and testing of the software should occur from a security perspective before the source code is even compiled. These tests are called static code analysis. Security testing should also be performed after the source code is compiled (a process called dynamic code analysis).

Key Terms

antimalware

antivirus (AV)

application whitelisting/
  blacklisting

automated courses of action

Automated Indicator Sharing
  (AIS)

auto-update

binary

blacklisting

boot attestation

client-side execution and
  validation

closed source

code reuse of third-party libraries
  and SDKs

code signing

compilers

continuous delivery

continuous deployment

continuous integration

continuous monitoring

continuous validation

dark web

data exposure

dead code

deprovisioning

development stage

directory traversal

disabling unnecessary open ports
  and services

dynamic code analysis

elasticity

endpoint detection and response
  (EDR)

file and code repositories

fuzzing

hardware root of trust

host intrusion detection system
  (HIDS)

host intrusion prevention system
  (HIPS)

HTTP Response Headers

indicator of compromise (IOC)

integrity measurement

manual peer reviews

Measured Boot

memory management

normalization

obfuscation/camouflaged code

open source

OWASP (Open Web Application
  Security Project)

predictive analysis

private information sharing
  centers

production stage

proper input validation

provisioning

public information sharing centers

quality assurance (QA)

quarantine

registry

sandbox

scalability

secure coding practices and
  techniques

secure cookie

server-side execution and
  validation

software diversity

staging stage

static code analysis

stored procedure

Structured Threat Information
  Expression (STIX)

testing stage

third-party updates

threat map

Trusted Automated Exchange
  of Intelligence Information
  (TAXII)

UEFI (Unified Extensible Firmware
  Interface)

version control

vulnerability database

whitelisting

Review Questions

1. An IOC occurs when what metric exceeds its
   normal bounds?
   a. IRR
   b. LRG
   c. EXR
   d. KRI

2. What are the two concerns about using public
   information sharing centers?
   a. Cost and availability
   b. Privacy and speed
   c. Security and privacy
   d. Regulatory approval and sharing

3. Which privacy protection uses four colors
   to indicate the expected sharing limitations
   that are to be applied by recipients of the
   information?
   a. CISA
   b. FOIA

   c. TLP
   d. PCII

4. Oskar has been receiving emails about critical
   threat intelligence information from a public
   information sharing center. His team leader has
   asked him to look into how the process can
   be automated so that the information can feed
   directly into the team's technology security. What
   technology will Oskar recommend?
   a. Automated Indicator Sharing (AIS)
   b. Bidirectional Security Protocol (BSP)
   c. Linefeed Access
   d. Lightwire JSON Control

5. Which of the following is an application protocol
   for exchanging cyberthreat intelligence over
   HTTPS?
   a. STIX
   b. AIP-TAR

c. TAXII

d. TCP-Over-Secure (ToP)

6. What are the two limitations of private information sharing centers?

a. Access to data and participation

b. Government approval and cost

c. Timing of reports and remote access

d. Bandwidth and CPU

7. Which of the following is NOT a limitation of a threat map?

a. Many maps claim that they show data in real time, but most are simply a playback of previous attacks.

b. Because threat maps show anonymized data, it is impossible to know the identity of the attackers or the victims.

c. They can be difficult to visualize.

d. Threat actors usually mask their real locations, so what is displayed on a threat map is incorrect.

8. Luka has been asked by his supervisor to monitor the dark web for any IOCs concerning their organization. The next week, Luca reports that he was unable to find anything because looking for information on the dark web is different from using the regular web. Which of the following is FALSE about looking for information on the dark web?

a. It is necessary to use Tor or IP2.

b. Dark web search engines are identical to regular search engines.

c. Dark web merchants open and close their sites without warning.

d. The naming structure is different on the dark web.

9. Which of the following is NOT an improvement of UEFI over BIOS?

a. Stronger boot security

b. Networking functionality in UEFI

c. Access larger hard drives

d. Support of USB 3.0

10. Which boot security mode sends information on the boot process to a remote server?

a. UEFI Native Mode

b. Secure Boot

c. Trusted Boot

d. Measured Boot

11. Which of the following is NOT an important OS security configuration?

a. Employing least functionality

b. Disabling default accounts

c. Disabling unnecessary services

d. Restricting patch management

12. Which stage conducts a test that will verify the code functions as intended?

a. Production stage

b. Testing stage

c. Staging stage

d. Development stage

13. Which model uses a sequential design process?

a. Secure model

b. Agile model

c. Rigid model

d. Waterfall model

14. Which of the following is NOT an advantage of an automated patch update service?

a. Downloading patches from a local server instead of using the vendor's online update service can save bandwidth and time because each computer does not have to connect to an external server.

b. Administrators can approve updates for "detection" only; this allows them to see which computers require the update without installing it.

c. Users can disable or circumvent updates just as they can if their computer is configured to use the vendor's online update service.

d. Administrators can approve or decline updates for client systems, force updates to install by a specific date, and obtain reports on what updates each computer needs.

15. What type of analysis is heuristic monitoring based on?

a. Dynamic analysis

b. Static analysis

c. Code analysis

d. Input analysis

16. Which of these is a list of preapproved applications?

a. Greenlist

b. Redlist

c. Blacklist

d. Whitelist

17. What is the advantage of a secure cookie?

a. It cannot be stored on the local computer without the user's express permission.

b. It is sent to the server over HTTPS.

c. It is analyzed by AV before it is transmitted.

d. It only exists in RAM and is deleted once the web browser is closed.

18. Which of the following tries to detect and stop an attack?

a. HIDS

b. HIPS

c. RDE

d. SOMA

19. What does Windows 10 Tamper Protection do?

    a. Limits access to the registry.

    b. Prevents any updates to the registry until the user approves the update.

    c. Compresses and locks the registry.

    d. Creates a secure backup copy of the registry.

20. Which of the following is FALSE about a quarantine process?

    a. It holds a suspicious application until the user gives approval.

    b. It can send a sanitized version of the attachment.

    c. It can send a URL to the document that is on a restricted computer.

    d. It is most often used with email attachments.

Hands-On Projects

 **CAUTION**   If you are concerned about installing any of the software in these projects on your regular computer, you can instead install the software in the Windows in the Microsoft Sandbox or a virtual machine created in the Module 1 Hands-On Projects. Software installed within the virtual machine will not impact the host computer.

Project 4-1: Using the Microsoft Online Security Bulletins

Time Required: 20 minutes

Objective: Explain different threat actors, vectors, and intelligence sources.

Description: Microsoft has made its security bulletins available in a searchable online database. All security professionals need to be familiar with using this database. In this project, you will explore the online database.

1. Open your web browser and enter the URL **portal.msrc.microsoft.com/en-us/**. (The location of content on the Internet may change without warning. If you are no longer able to access the program through this URL, use a search engine to search for "Microsoft Security Response Center.")
2. Click **Read the Security Update Guide FAQ**.
3. Click **Expand all** to read through the information.
4. Click the link **www.icasi.org/cvrf/** (or enter it into another tab in your browser). What is the Common Vulnerability Reporting Framework (CVRF)? How is it used?
5. Return to the Microsoft Security Update Guide and then the MSRC main page.
6. Click the **Go to the Security Update Guide** button.
7. If no security updates appear, adjust the **From** date to the first day of the previous month.
8. Scroll through the list of security updates.
9. Click the first link under **Article**.
10. Read through this information.
11. Now return to the previous page and select another article to read.
12. How useful is this information? Is it presented in a format that is helpful?
13. Now click the CVE link under **Details** and read this information. Note the detail of this information.
14. Read the information under **Exploitability Assessment** (if the exploit you selected does not list an Exploitability Assessment, then select another that does include the assessment). What does this mean? Open another tab on your web browser, and search for **Microsoft Exploitability Index**. Read through the description that you find and keep this tab open.
15. Return to the Microsoft Security Update Guide and view the **Exploitability Assessment**. How serious is this security vulnerability?
16. How important is this information to a security professional? How easy is this online database to use?
17. Now compare the Microsoft database with Apple's. Enter the URL **support.apple.com/en-us/HT201222**. (The location of content on the Internet may change without warning. If you are no longer able to access the program through the above URL, use a search engine to search for "Apple Security Updates.")
18. Scroll down through the list of Apple security updates. How does this list compare with the updates from Microsoft?
19. Select a recent event under **Name and information link**.

20. Read the information about the update. How does this information compare with Microsoft's information? Why is there such a difference? Which provides better information for security professions?

21. Close all windows.

Project 4-2: Setting Windows Local Security Policy

Time Required: 20 minutes

Objective: Given a scenario, implement host or application security solutions.

Description: The Local Group Policy Editor is a Microsoft Management Console (MMC) snap-in that gives a single user interface through which all the Computer Configuration and User Configuration settings of Local Group Policy objects can be managed. The Local Security Policy settings are among the security settings contained in the Local Group Policy Editor. An administrator can use these to set policies that are applied to the computer. In this project, you will view and change local security policy settings.

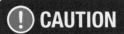 **CAUTION** You will need to be an administrator to open the Local Group Policy Editor.

1. Click **Start**.
2. Type **secpol.msc** into the Search box, and then click **secpol**.

NOTE 26

If your computer is already joined to a domain then searching for secpol.msc might not launch the application. If this is the case, click **Start** and type **mmc.msc**. On the File menu, click **Add/Remove** snap-in, and then click **Add**. In **Add Standalone Snap-in**, double-click **Group Policy Object Editor**.

3. First create a policy regarding passwords. Expand **Account Policies** in the left pane, and then expand **Password Policy**.
4. Double-click **Enforce password history** in the right pane. This setting defines how many previously used passwords Windows will record. This prevents users from "recycling" old passwords.
5. Change **passwords remembered** to **4**.
6. Click **OK**.
7. Double-click **Maximum password age** in the right pane. The default value is 42, meaning that a user must change his password after 42 days.
8. Change **days** to **30**.
9. Click **OK**.
10. Double-click **Minimum password length** in the right pane. The default value is a length of eight characters.
11. Change **characters** to **10**.
12. Click **OK**.
13. Double-click **Password must meet complexity requirements** in the right pane. This setting forces a password to include at least two opposite case letters, a number, and a special character (such as a punctuation mark).
14. Click **Enabled**.
15. Click **OK**.
16. Double-click **Store passwords using reversible encryption** in the right pane. Because passwords should be stored in an encrypted format, this setting should not be enabled.
17. If necessary, click **Disabled**.
18. Click **OK**.
19. In the left pane, click **Account lockout policy**.
20. Double-click **Account lockout threshold** in the right pane. This is the number of times that a user can enter an incorrect password before Windows will lock the account from being accessed. (This prevents an attacker from attempting to guess the password with unlimited attempts.)
21. Change **invalid login attempts** to **5**.
22. Click **OK**.
23. Note that the Local Security Policy suggests changing the **Account lockout duration** and the **Reset account lockout counter after** values to 30 minutes.

24. Click **OK**.
25. Expand **Local Policies** in the left pane, and then click **Audit Policy**.
26. Double-click **Audit account logon events**.
27. Check both **Success** and **Failure**.
28. Click **OK**.
29. Right-click **Security Settings** in the left pane.
30. Click **Reload** to have these policies applied.
31. Close all windows.

Project 4-3: Configuring Microsoft Windows Security—Part 1

Time Required: 15 minutes

Objective: Given a scenario, implement host or application security solutions.

Description: It is important that security settings be properly configured on a computer in order to protect it. In this project, you examine several security settings on a Microsoft Windows 10 computer using the Windows interface.

>  **CAUTION**   This project shows how to configure Windows security for a personal computer. If this computer is part of a computer lab or office, these settings should not be changed without the proper permissions.

1. Click **Start** and **Settings**.
2. Click **Update and security**.
3. If necessary, click **Windows Update** in the left pane.
4. Click **Pause updates for 7 days**. What warning are you given?
5. Click **Resume updates**.
6. Click **View update history**.
7. Expand each area and select one update to review. Read through the information on the update. How detailed is this information?
8. Return to the **View update history** page.
9. Return to the **Windows Update** page.
10. Click **Advanced options**.
11. Be sure that **Receive updates for other Microsoft products when you update Windows** is set to **On**. This will allow for updates for Microsoft software such as Office to also be updated.
12. Read the information under **Pause updates**. Why would you select this option?
13. Click the down arrow under **A quality update includes security improvements. It can be deferred for this many days:**. How many days can you defer security updates?
14. Return to the **Windows Update** page.
15. In the left pane, click **Windows Security**.
16. Click **Virus & threat protection**.
17. Click **Scan options** and be sure that **Quick scan** is selected.
18. Now perform a Quick scan of the most essential files. Click **Scan now**. Depending upon your system, it may take several minutes to complete. What was the result of the scan?
19. Return to the Virus & threat protection page. Under **Virus & threat protection settings**, click **Manage settings**.
20. Read through the details of the options. Are there any that you would change? Why?
21. Close all windows.

Project 4-4: Configuring Microsoft Windows Security—Part 2

Time Required: 15 minutes

Objective: Given a scenario, implement host or application security solutions.

Description: As seen from Project 4-3, Windows security settings are found across several different screens. This can make it easy to overlook important settings and time consuming to fine-tune the settings, especially when configuring the Windows Defender virus and threat protection product. A third-party tool called ConfigureDefender provides an easier interface. In this project, you will download and use the ConfigureDefender product.

NOTE 27

ConfigureDefender is not installed on the computer but runs as a stand-alone application.

1. Open your web browser and enter the URL **github.com/AndyFul/ConfigureDefender** (if you are no longer able to access the program through the URL, use a search engine to search for "ConfigureDefender").
2. Find the latest version of ConfigureDefender (the program is compressed in a ZIP file). Click the filename.
3. Click **Download**.
4. After the file has downloaded, unpack it, and then launch the program.
5. Click the **Info about Defender** button to see the computer's Defender settings. When finished, close the window.
6. Click the **Defender Security Log** button. Read the log file about recent actions. Does anything surprise you? When finished, close the window.
7. Scroll down and read the different settings. Were you aware that there were so many different options for Windows Defender?
8. Hover over the **DEFAULT** button and read the information.
9. Now hover over the **HIGH** button and read the information.
10. Click the **HIGH** button, and then close the pop-up box.
11. Scroll down through the settings. How much stronger are they than from the Default settings?
12. Now hover over the **MAX** button and read the information.
13. Click the **MAX** button, and then close the pop-up box.
14. Scroll down through the settings. How much stronger are they?
15. Finally click either the **DEFAULT** or **HIGH** button to set your computer at the security level that you choose.
16. How easy is ConfigureDefender to use? Would you recommend it to others?
17. Close all windows.

Case Projects

Case Project 4-1: AV Comparison

Select four antivirus products, one of which is a free product, and compare their features. Create a table that lists the features. How do they compare with the AV software you currently use? Which would you recommend to others? Why? Create a report on your research.

Case Project 4-2: Threat Maps

Locate four online cybersecurity threat maps. Compare their real-time results. Why are these results different? What type of information do they provide? How easy or hard are they to use? How could they be used? How should they not be used? What are the strengths? What are the weaknesses? What recommendations would you make for improving host security? Write a one-page paper on your analysis.

Case Project 4-3: Application Patch Management

Select four third-party applications (not OSs) that you frequently use. How does each of them address patch management? Visit their websites to determine how they alert users to new vulnerabilities. Are the patch management systems adequate? Should patch management be required of all third-party applications? What are the advantages? What are the disadvantages? Write a one-page paper on your findings.

Case Project 4-4: UEFI

Use the Internet to research UEFI. What are its advantages? What are its disadvantages? What criticisms have been leveled against it? Do you agree with the criticism? Write a one-page paper on your findings.

Case Project 4-5: STIX and TAXII

Research the Internet to find information on STIX and TAXII. How are they used? What formats do they provide? How widely are they used? What are their strengths and weaknesses? Write a one-page paper on your findings.

Case Project 4-6 Information Security Community Site Activity

The Information Security Community Site is an online companion to this textbook. It contains a wide variety of tools, information, discussion boards, and other features to assist learners. In order to gain the most benefit from the site, you will need to set up a free account.

Go to **community.cengage.com/infosec2**. Post your thoughts about the following: *Should the dark web be shut down?* What would be the advantages? What would it take for this to happen? What would threat actors do if it were suddenly unavailable? Is there any impact on free speech? Does free speech protect criminal enterprises? What do you think?

Case Project 4-7 North Ridge Security

North Ridge Security provides security consulting and assurance services. You have recently been hired as an intern to assist this organization.

You have been asked to prepare a presentation on SecDevOps for a group of students studying programming at a local college.

1. Create a PowerPoint presentation on SecDevOps, how it compares to standard application development, how it is different, and how it works. Your presentation should be at least seven slides in length.
2. As a follow-up to your presentation, you have been asked to write a one-page report on fuzzing. Use the Internet to research fuzzing, how it can be used, its strengths and weaknesses, and your recommendations.

References

1. Porter, Jon, "The PC market just had its first year of growth since 2011," *The Verge*, Jan. 14, 2020, retrieved May 20, 2020, www.theverge.com/2020/1/14/21065100/ pc-market-shipments-idc-gartner-growth-2019-laptops-desktops-windows-7-10.
2. O'Dea, S., "Number of smartphone unit shipments In the United States from 2013 to 2023 (In millions)," *Statista*, Feb. 27, 2020, retrieved May 20, 2020, www.statista.com/statistics/619811/ smartphone-unit-shipments-in-the-us/.
3. Horowitz, Michael, "The head of NSA TAO advises on defensive computing for networks," *Computerworld*, Feb. 1, 2016, accessed May 11, 2017, www.computerworld.com/article/3028025/security/defending-a-network-from-the-nsa.html.

MOBILE, EMBEDDED, AND SPECIALIZED DEVICE SECURITY

After completing this module, you should be able to do the following:

1. List and compare the different types of mobile devices and how they are deployed
2. Explain the ways to secure a mobile device
3. Describe the vulnerabilities and protections of embedded and specialized devices
4. Explain the issues surrounding securing specialized devices

Front-Page Cybersecurity

Standardized testing dates back thousands of years. An ancient Chinese government conducted standardized testing to help select candidates for government jobs. In 1806, England also started using written testing for its civil service positions. In 1845, the educational pioneer Horace Mann suggested using a written test instead of an annual oral test given to Boston Public School children to measure their achievement. The written test was intended to eliminate bias because the oral test graders knew the child.

It was not long until standardized tests were being used in elementary, secondary, and college educational systems. However, unlike Mann's tests, which were designed to measure achievement *after* completing instruction, standardized school tests became a way to measure a student's ability *before* instruction. This form of standardized testing was promoted as a means to identify students who showed a high ability for success. Later the same tests were also used to evaluate the effectiveness of the teacher and institution.

One drawback of standardized tests was that manually grading was tedious and prone to error. In 1935, IBM introduced automated scoring to produce more reliable results. Automated scoring was expensive and even required the use of special pencils to record answers; however, as the technology evolved, computerized scoring became less expensive, more widely available, and more convenient, as students could use standard #2 pencils to fill in answer bubbles.

In the mid-1980s, computer-based testing was introduced as an electronic version of the traditional pencil-and-paper method. As computer-based standardized testing evolved, it provided the ability to determine what questions to ask each student. Today many standardized tests use a test taker's response on one question to determine the difficulty level of the next question.

However, as long as people have participated in standardized testing, there has been cheating on tests. At one time, cheating took the form of looking at another student's responses or writing answers on the back of the test taker's hand. Today, cheating is high-tech, with cheaters using mobile and specialized devices. Answers can be stored and retrieved from a programmable calculator or recorded on a smartphone and then displayed on a wearable smartwatch.

Like many countries, the Algerian nation has faced an epidemic of cheating among the more than 700,000 students who take Algeria's baccalaureate (four-year bachelor's degree) exit test. Test questions and answers started to appear on social media sites almost immediately after the start of the exam by students who used their smartphones to post the information while taking the test. Test latecomers could see the questions and answers before entering one of Algeria's 2,100 exam centers. The problem became so widespread in 2016 that the Algerian Education Ministry declared several exams void and required more than 500,000 students to retake the exam with new questions. Thirty-one people were arrested, including several Education Ministry employees.

In 2017, the Ministry installed mobile phone jammers in the exam centers and blocked access to Facebook, Twitter, and Instagram. Students who arrived late were banned from taking the exam but had to later attend an exam session at an alternative test center. This practice did not completely prevent test cheating.

In 2018, all exam centers installed metal detectors to prevent students from smuggling in smartphones. All teachers and test proctors also had to surrender their phones, tablets, and electronic devices. Devices for jamming wireless signals and video surveillance cameras were also installed.

Algeria took one more drastic step: it shut down all access to the Internet. Not only was Internet access unavailable to students in testing centers: the Internet was turned off all across the entire country.

By order of the Algerian government, private Internet service providers (ISPs) and the public telephone operator that provides much of the Internet access turned off the Internet for up to three hours per day during testing week. There were three one-hour blackouts on Wednesday and two each on Thursday through Monday. For everyone in Algeria, every kind of Internet or mobile connection, from wired to cellular to Wi-Fi, went dark while students were tested.

Algeria was not alone in this drastic action. The nations of Syria, Iraq, Mauritania, Uzbekistan, and several Indian states also blocked all access to the Internet during testing. Ethiopia shut down access to social media during the times of testing. China deployed drones carrying radio scanners to catch students who were using electronic devices during tests. Today most schools and testing centers ban all forms of electronic equipment, especially mobile devices such as smartphones and smartwatches, from all testing facilities.

If time travelers living 20 years ago could be transported to today's world, they likely would be shocked at how mobile devices have dramatically changed daily life in just a short period of time. Watching cars pass on the road, they would observe a high percentage of drivers talking or sending text messages on their mobile phones, often in violation of laws that prohibit it. Sitting in a classroom, the time travelers would see that almost all students use their mobile devices to read e-textbooks, access online files, and take notes. In the few remaining malls, shoppers scan bar codes on their smartphones to determine if the same item is offered at another mall store at a lower price or if it would be cheaper to immediately order it online. These dramatic changes might discourage the time travelers from jumping ahead another 20 years to see what a world filled with even more mobile devices would be like.

The statistics confirm that mobile devices have changed—and are continuing to change—our everyday lives. About 96 percent of 18- to 29-year-olds own a smartphone (the remaining 4 percent own a basic cell phone), and 81 percent of all Americans own a smartphone, compared with only 35 percent in 2011. Half of the public now owns a tablet computer (tablet ownership in 2010 was a mere 3 percent).[1] The average daily time spent consuming online media on a mobile device is 203 minutes compared to 128 minutes on desktop computers.[2]

However, just as users have flocked to mobile devices, so too have attackers. Because mobile devices have become the primary, if not exclusive, computing devices for a growing number of users, attacks directed at mobile device have increased dramatically.

In this final module on endpoint security, you will explore mobile, embedded, and specialized device security. You begin by looking at securing mobile devices and then survey embedded systems and the Internet of Things devices. Finally, you will examine how to keep specialized devices secure.

SECURING MOBILE DEVICES

✔ CERTIFICATION

1.2 Given a scenario, analyze potential indicators to determine the type of attack.

3.5 Given a scenario, implement secure mobile solutions.

Each type of mobile device faces several cybersecurity risks. Security professionals can use a variety of techniques and technologies for securing mobile devices.

Introduction to Mobile Devices

Of the many types of mobile devices, each can connect to networks using different technologies. Enterprises also use different ways to deploy mobile devices to their employees.

Types of Mobile Devices

Most mobile devices have a common set of core features that differentiate them from other computing devices. Many, but not all, mobile devices extend their core features to include additional tools and technologies. Both types of features are listed in Table 5-1.

Table 5-1   Mobile device core and additional features

Core features	Additional features
Small form factor	Global Positioning System (GPS)
Mobile operating system	Microphone and/or digital camera
Wireless data network interface for accessing the Internet, such as Wi-Fi or cellular telephony	Wireless cellular connection for voice communications
Stores or other means of acquiring applications (apps)	Wireless personal area network interfaces such as Bluetooth or near field communications (NFC)
Local nonremovable data storage	Removable storage media
Data synchronization capabilities with a separate computer or remote servers	Support for using the device itself as removable storage for another computing device

Mobile devices include tablets, smartphones, wearables, and portable computers.

Tablets   *Tablets* are portable computing devices first introduced in 2010. Designed for user convenience, tablets are thinner, lighter, easier to carry, and more intuitive to use than other types of computers. Tablets are often classified by their screen size. The two most common categories of tablet screen sizes are 5–8.5 inches (12.7–21.5 cm) and 8.5–10 inches (12.7–25.4 cm). The weight of tablets is generally less than 1.5 pounds (0.68 kg), and they are less than 1/2 inch (1.2 cm) thick. Figure 5-1 shows a typical tablet device.

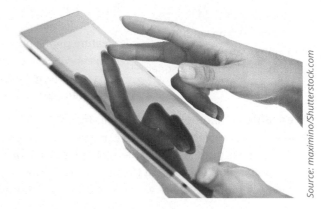

Source: maximino/Shutterstock.com

Figure 5-1   Tablet device

NOTE 1

Tablets have a sensor called an accelerometer that detects vibrations and movements. It can determine the orientation of the device so that the screen image is always displayed upright.

Tablets generally lack a built-in keyboard or mouse. Instead, they rely on a touch screen that users manipulate with touch gestures to provide input. Table 5-2 lists the touch gestures for an Apple tablet.

Table 5-2   Apple touch gestures

Gesture name	Action	Usage
Tap	Lightly strike the screen	Make a selection
Double tap	Two quick taps in succession	Zoom in or out of content or an image
Flick	Place finger on the screen and quickly "swipe" in the desired direction	Scroll or pan quickly
Drag	Place finger on the screen and move it in the desired direction	Scroll or move the viewing area
Pinch open	Place thumb and finger close together on the screen and move them apart	Zoom in
Pinch close	Place thumb and finger a short distance apart on the screen and move them toward each other	Zoom out
Touch and hold	Touch the screen until the action occurs	Display an information bubble or magnify content
Two-finger scroll	Move two fingers together in the same direction	Scroll content in an element with overflow capability

Although tablets are primarily display devices with limited computing power, they have proven to be popular. Besides their portability, a primary reason for their popularity is that tablet computers have an operating system (OS) that allows them to run third-party apps. The most popular OSs for tablets are Apple iOS and iPadOS, Google Android, and Microsoft Windows.

Smartphones   Earlier models of cellular telephones were called *feature phones* because they included a limited number of features, such as a camera, an MP3 music player, and ability to send and receive text messages. Many feature phones were designed to highlight a single feature, such as cameras for taking high-quality photos or a large amount of memory for music storage.

NOTE 2

Because of the ability to run apps, smartphones are essentially handheld personal computers.

The feature phone has given way to today's *smartphone*, which has all the tools of a feature phone plus an OS that allows it to run apps and access the Internet. Because it has an OS, a smartphone offers a broader range of functionality. Users can install apps to perform tasks for productivity, social networking, music, and so forth, much like a standard computer.

Wearables   Another class of mobile technology consists of devices that can be worn by the user instead of carried. Known as *wearables*, the devices can provide even greater flexibility and mobility.

The most popular wearable technology is a *smart watch*. Early smart watches were just a means to receive smartphone notifications on the user's wrist. However, today wearables have evolved to much more sophisticated devices. A modern smart watch can still receive notifications of phone calls and text messages, but it can also be used as a fitness tracker, a contactless payment system, and safety monitor that calls emergency services if the watch detects the user has fallen. Figure 5-2 displays a smart watch.

Another popular type of wearable is a *fitness tracker*. Originally designed to monitor and record physical activity, such as counting steps, they likewise have evolved into sophisticated health-monitoring devices. Modern fitness trackers can provide continuous heart rate monitoring, GPS tracking, oxygen consumption, repetition counting (for weight training), and sleep monitoring.

Portable Computers   As a class, *portable computers* are devices that closely resemble standard desktop computers. Portable computers have similar hardware (keyboard, hard disk drive, and RAM, for example) and run the same OS (Windows, Apple macOS, or Linux) and applications (such as Microsoft Office and web browsers) as general-purpose desktop computers. The primary difference is that portable computers are smaller, self-contained devices that can easily be transported from one location to another while running on battery power.

Source: Alexey Boldin/Shutterstock.com

Figure 5-2   Smart watch

NOTE 3

Many fitness trackers and smart watches use two colors of LED lights on the underside of the device to read vital signs on the human body and then measure the light absorption with photodiodes. They use green LED lights when the wearer is exercising (such as running or bicycle riding) by flashing green light onto the wrist hundreds of times per second. Human blood absorbs green light, so the heart rate can be determined by measuring the changes in green light absorption (a method called photoplethysmography, or PPG). Red LED lights are used when the wearer is not exercising. Human blood reflects red light, so about every 10 minutes, the red LEDs flash to measure the resting heart rate. The reason for having two colors of LED lights is due to accuracy and battery life. Green LEDs are more accurate, which is more important when assessing a rapid heart rate than a sedentary heart rate. But since green LEDs require more power, red LEDs are also used to save battery life.

A *laptop* computer is regarded as the earliest portable computer. A laptop is designed to replicate the abilities of a desktop computer with only slightly less processing power yet is small enough to be used on a lap or small table. A *notebook* computer is a smaller version of a laptop and is considered a lightweight personal computer. Notebook computers typically weigh less than laptops and are small enough to fit inside a briefcase. A *subnotebook* computer is even smaller than standard notebooks and use low-power processors and solid-state drives (SSDs). A *2-in-1* computer (also called a *hybrid* or *convertible*) can be used as either a subnotebook or a tablet. The devices have a touch screen and a physical keyboard; they can be transformed from a subnotebook to a tablet through a folding design or as a slate with a detachable keyboard, as shown in Figure 5-3.

A new type of computing device that resembles a laptop computer is a *web-based computer*. It contains a limited version of an OS and a web browser with an integrated

Source: Chesky/Shutterstock.com

Figure 5-3   2-in-1 computer with slate design

media player. Web-based computers are designed to be used while connected to the Internet. No traditional software applications can be installed, and no user files are stored locally on the device. Instead, the device accesses online web apps and saves user files on the Internet. The most common OSs for web-based computers are the Google Chrome OS and Microsoft Windows 10 in S Mode.

NOTE 4

One of the first mobile devices was a *personal digital assistant (PDA)*, a handheld mobile device intended to replace paper systems. Most PDAs had a touch screen for entering data while others had a rudimentary keyboard that contained only a numeric keypad or thumb keyboard. Popular in the 1990s and early 2000s, PDAs fell out of favor as smartphones gained in popularity.

Mobile Device Connectivity Methods

Methods for connecting mobile devices to networks include the following:

- *Cellular.* Many mobile devices rely on **cellular telephony** for connectivity. The coverage area for a cellular telephony network is divided into cells; in a typical city, the hexagon-shaped cells measure 10 square miles (26 square kilometers). At the center of each cell is a transmitter that mobile devices in the cell use to send and receive signals. The transmitters are connected through a mobile telecommunications switching office (MTSO) that controls all of the transmitters in the cellular network and serves as the link between the cellular network and the wired telephone world. This configuration is illustrated in Figure 5-4.

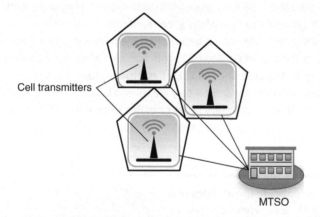

Cell transmitters

MTSO

Figure 5-4 Cellular telephony network

- *Wi-Fi.* A *wireless local area network (WLAN)*, commonly called *Wi-Fi*, is designed to replace or supplement a wired local area network (LAN). Devices such as tablets, laptop computers, and smartphones within range of a centrally located connection device can send and receive data at varying transmission speeds.
- *Infrared.* Instead of using radio frequency (RF) as the communication media, some devices can use light. All the types of light that travel from the sun to the Earth make up the light spectrum, and visible light is a small part of that entire spectrum. (All other types of lights—such as X-rays, ultraviolet rays, and microwaves—are invisible to the human eye.) **Infrared** light is next to visible light on the light spectrum and, although invisible, has many of the same characteristics of visible light. At one time, infrared data ports were installed on laptop computers, printers, cameras, watches, and other devices so that data could be exchanged using infrared light. However, due to its slow speed and other limitations, infrared capabilities in mobile devices are rarely found today.

NOTE 5

Other types of connectivity methods for mobile devices include Bluetooth and NFC. These are covered in detail in Module 11.

- *USB connections.* Different types and sizes of **Universal Serial Bus (USB) connectors** on mobile devices are used for data transfer. These include standard-size connectors, mini connectors, and micro connectors, all of which are available as either type A (flat) or type B (square).

Enterprise Deployment Models

Due to the widespread use of mobile devices, it is not always feasible to require employees to carry company-owned smartphones along with their own personal cell phones. Many organizations have adopted an enterprise deployment model for mobile devices. These are listed in Table 5-3.

Table 5-3   Enterprise deployment models

Model name	Description	Employee actions	Business actions
Bring your own device (BYOD)	Employees use their own personal mobile devices for business purposes.	Employees have full responsibility for choosing and supporting the device.	This model is popular with smaller companies or those with a temporary staff.
Corporate owned, personally enabled (COPE)	Employees choose from a selection of company-approved devices.	Employees are supplied the device chosen and paid for by the company, but they can also use it for personal activities.	Company decides the level of choice and freedom for employees.
Choose your own device (CYOD)	Employees choose from a limited selection of approved devices but pay the upfront cost of the device while the business owns the contract.	Employees are offered a suite of choices that the company has approved for security, reliability, and durability.	Company often provides a stipend to pay monthly fees to wireless carrier.
Virtual desktop infrastructure (VDI)	Stores sensitive applications and data on a remote server accessed through a smartphone.	Users can customize the display of data as if the data were residing on their own mobile device.	Enterprise can centrally protect and manage apps and data on server instead of distributing to smartphones.
Corporate owned	The device is purchased and owned by the enterprise.	Employees use the phone only for company-related business.	Enterprise is responsible for all aspects of the device.

Several benefits of the BYOD, COPE, and CYOD models include the following for the enterprise:

- *Management flexibility*. BYOD and CYOD ease the management burden by eliminating the need to select a wireless data carrier and manage plans for employees.
- *Less oversight*. Businesses do not need to monitor employee telecommunications usage for overages or extra charges.
- *Cost savings*. Because employees are responsible for their own mobile device purchases and wireless data plans (BYOD) or receive a small monthly stipend (CYOD), the company can save money.
- *Increased employee performance*. Employees are more likely to be productive while traveling or working away from the office if they are comfortable with their device.
- *Simplified IT infrastructure*. By using the existing cellular telephony network, companies do not have to support a remote data network for employees.
- *Reduced internal service*. BYOD, COPE, and CYOD reduce the strain on IT help desks because users will be primarily contacting their wireless data carrier for support.

In addition, users are eager to accept the flexibility of these models. The user benefits include the following:

- *Choice of device*. Users like the freedom of choosing the type of mobile device with BYOD, COPE, and CYOD instead of being forced to accept a corporate device that may not meet their individual needs (corporate owned).
- *Choice of carrier*. Most users have identified a specific wireless data carrier they want to use and often resist being forced to use a carrier with whom they have experienced a poor past relationship.
- *Convenience*. Because almost all users already have their own device, the BYOD, COPE, and CYOD models provide the convenience of carrying only a single device.

Mobile Device Risks

Like all endpoints, mobile devices have security vulnerabilities and are at risk of being compromised. Many attacks directly target mobile devices, which has a profound impact on organizations. In a recent survey, almost 40 percent of organizations admitted to suffering a compromise due to a mobile device. Half of the incidents resulted in the loss of data, and more than one-third were described as major incidents with lasting repercussions. Threat actors often use compromised mobile devices to pivot to other targets: 58 percent of the attacks on mobile devices led to the compromise of other devices. Almost half of respondents reported that their organizations sacrificed mobile security to perform work more quickly.[3]

 **CAUTION** The survey summarized by saying, "We found that many companies are failing to protect their mobile devices. And we're not talking about some almost-impossible-to-achieve gold standard. We're talking about companies failing to meet even a basic level of preparedness."[4]

Security risks associated with using mobile devices include mobile device vulnerabilities, connection vulnerabilities, and accessing untrusted content.

Mobile Device Vulnerabilities

Mobile device vulnerabilities include physical security, limited updates, location tracking, and unauthorized recording.

Physical Security   The greatest asset of a mobile device—its portability—is also one of its greatest vulnerabilities. Mobile devices are frequently lost or stolen. Unlike desktop computers, mobile devices by their very nature are designed for use in a variety of locations, both public (coffee shops, hotels, and conference centers) and private (employee homes and cars). These locations are outside of the enterprise's normal protected physical perimeter of walls, security guards, and locked doors. One-quarter of all laptop thefts occurred from unattended cars or while traveling on airplanes and trains, 15 percent of thefts occurred in airports and hotels, and 12 percent occurred in restaurants.[5] However, due to the portable nature of a mobile device, even a strong physical perimeter does not always provide protection from theft. Almost half of all laptop thefts occur from school offices and classrooms.[6]

Unless properly protected, any data on a stolen or lost device could be retrieved by a thief. Of greater concern may be that the device itself can serve as an entry point into corporate data. On average, every employee at an organization has access to 17 million files and 1.21 million folders. The average organization has more than half a million sensitive files, and 17 percent of all sensitive files are accessible to each employee.[7]

Limited Updates   Currently there are two dominant OSs for mobile devices. Apple iOS, developed by Apple for its mobile devices, is a closed and proprietary architecture. Google Android is not proprietary but is open for any original equipment manufacturer (OEM) to install or even modify. (However, modifications must adhere to Google's criteria to access all Google services.) Many OEMs worldwide make mobile devices that use Android because it is freely available.

Security patches and updates for these two mobile OSs are distributed through firmware over-the-air (OTA) updates. Though they are called "firmware" OTA updates, they include modifying the device's firmware and updating the OS software. Apple commits to providing OTA updates for at least four years after the OS is released. Users can set iOS updates to occur automatically or manually, either through the device itself or by connecting it to a computer through which the update is downloaded.

However, OTA updates for Android OSs vary considerably. Mobile hardware devices developed and sold by Google receive Android OTA updates for three years after the device is first released. Other OEMs are required to provide OTAs for at least two years. However, after two years, many OEMs are hesitant to distribute Google updates because it limits their ability to differentiate themselves from competitors if all versions of Android start to look the same through updates. Also, because OEMs want to sell as many devices as possible, they have no financial incentive to update mobile devices that users would then continue to use indefinitely.

Whereas users once regularly purchased new mobile devices about every two years, that is no longer the case. Due to the high cost of some mobile devices, users are keeping their devices for longer periods of time. This can result in people using mobile devices that no longer receive OTA security updates and thus have become vulnerable.

Location Tracking The **Global Positioning System (GPS)** is a satellite-based navigation system that provides information to a GPS receiver anywhere on (or near) the Earth with an unobstructed line of sight to four or more GPS satellites. Mobile devices with GPS capabilities typically support **geolocation**, or identifying the geographical location of the device. When finding a person carrying a mobile device, geolocation also identifies the location of a close friend or displays the address of the nearest coffee shop. Location services are used extensively by social media, navigation systems, weather systems, and other mobile-aware applications.

However, mobile devices using geolocation are at increased risk of targeted physical attacks. An attacker can determine where users with mobile devices are currently located and use that information to follow them and steal the mobile devices or inflict physical harm. In addition, attackers can craft attacking by compiling a list of people with whom the users associate and the types of activities they perform.

A related risk is **GPS tagging** (also called **geo-tagging**), which is adding geographical identification data to media such as digital photos taken on a mobile device. A user who, for example, posts a photo on a social networking site may inadvertently identify a private location to anyone who can access the photo.

Unauthorized Recording Video cameras ("webcams") and microphones on mobile devices have been a frequent target of attackers. By infecting a device with malware, a threat actor can secretly spy on an unsuspecting victim and record conversations or videos.

Connection Vulnerabilities

Vulnerabilities in mobile device connections can also be exploited by threat actors. These vulnerabilities are summarized in Table 5-4.

Table 5-4 Connection vulnerabilities

Name	Description	Vulnerability
Tethering	A mobile device with an active Internet connection can be used to share that connection with other mobile devices through Bluetooth or Wi-Fi.	An unsecured mobile device may infect other tethered mobile devices or the corporate network.
USB On-the-Go (OTG)	An OTG mobile device with a USB connection can function as either a host (to which other devices may be connected such as a USB flash drive) for **external media access** or as a peripheral (such as a mass storage device) to another host.	Connecting a **malicious flash drive** infected with malware to a mobile device could result in an infection, just as using a device as a peripheral while connected to an infected computer could allow malware to be sent to the device.
Malicious USB cable	A USB cable could be embedded with a Wi-Fi controller that can receive commands from a nearby device to send malicious commands to the connected mobile device.	The device will recognize the cable as a Human Interface Device (similar to a mouse or keyboard), giving the attacker enough permissions to exploit the system.
Hotspots	A hotspot is a location where users can access the Internet with a wireless signal.	Because public hotspots are beyond the control of the organization, attackers can eavesdrop on the data transmissions and view sensitive information.

Accessing Untrusted Content

Normally users cannot download and install unapproved apps on their iOS or Android device. Instead, users must access the Apple App Store or Google Play Store (or other Android store) to download and install an app on a mobile device; in fact, Apple devices can only download from the App store. However, users can circumvent the

NOTE 6

Banks are expanding the use of geolocation to help reduce bank card fraud. When a user makes a purchase at a store, the bank can immediately check the location of the user's authorized cell phone. If the cell phone and the bank card are in the same place, then the purchase may be considered legitimate. But if the cell phone is in Nashville and someone is trying to make a purchase in a store in Tampa, then the payment may be rejected. Geolocation can also help prevent rejecting valid purchases. One credit card issuer says that it can reduce unnecessary declines by as much as 30 percent.[8]

built-in installation limitations on their smartphone (called **jailbreaking** on Apple iOS devices or **rooting** on Android devices) to download from an unofficial **third-party app store** (called **sideloading**) or even write their own **custom firmware** to run on their device. Because the apps have not been vetted, they may contain security vulnerabilities or malicious code.

> **⓵ CAUTION**   Jailbreaking and rooting give access to the underlying OS and file system of the mobile device with full permissions. For example, a jailbreak on an Apple iPhone gives users access to a UNIX shell with root privileges, essentially allowing them to do anything on the device.

Jailbreaking and rooting are not the same as **carrier unlocking**. Originally almost all cell phones were connected ("locked") to a specific wireless carrier so that neither the phone nor the phone number could be transferred to another carrier. The restriction was enforced by a 2012 decision from the Library of Congress that cell phone unlocking was a violation of the Digital Millennium Copyright Act. However, in 2015, the Unlocking Consumer Choice and Wireless Competition Act was passed to approve carrier unlocking.

Untrusted content can also invade mobile devices through **short message service (SMS)**, which are text messages of a maximum of 160 characters; **multimedia messaging service (MMS)**, which allows text message to include pictures, video, and audio; and **rich communication services (RCS)**, which can convert a texting app into a live chat platform and supports pictures, videos, location, stickers, and emojis. Threat actors can send SMS messages containing links to untrusted content or specially crafted MMS or RCS videos that can introduce malware into the device.

Mobile devices can also access untrusted content that other types of computing devices generally cannot access. One example is a *Quick Response (QR)* code. A QR code is a matrix or two-dimensional barcode consisting of black modules (square dots) arranged in a square grid on a white background. QR codes can store website URLs, plain text, phone numbers, email addresses, or virtually any alphanumeric data up to 4,296 characters, which can be read by an imaging device such as a mobile device's camera. A QR code for *www.cengage.com* is illustrated in Figure 5-5.

Figure 5-5   QR code

An attacker can create an advertisement listing a reputable website, such as a bank, but include a QR code that contains a malicious URL. Once the user snaps a picture of the QR code using the camera on a mobile device, the code directs the web browser on the mobile device to the attacker's imposter website or to a site that immediately downloads malware.

Protecting Mobile Devices

Users can take steps to secure a mobile device. These include configuring the device and using mobile management tools.

Device Configuration

Several configurations should be considered when setting up a mobile device for use. These include using strong authentication, managing encryption, segmenting storage, and enabling loss or theft services.

Use Strong Authentication   Verifying that the authentic user of a mobile device involves requiring a strong passcode and restricting unauthorized users with a screen lock.

Passcode.   Almost all mobile devices have options for configuring a passcode that must be entered before access will be granted. Although passwords are the most secure option, most users unfortunately opt not to configure their device with a password. This is primarily due to the time needed to enter the password and the difficulty of entering a complex password on the device's small on-screen keyboard.

Another option is to use a **personal identification number (PIN)**. Unlike a password that can be comprised of letters, numbers, and characters, a PIN is made up of numbers only. Although the length of the PIN can usually range from four to 16 numbers, many users choose to set a short four-digit PIN, like those used with a bank's automated teller machine (ATM). However, short PIN codes provide only a limited amount of security. An analysis of 3.4 million users' four-digit (0000–9999) PINs that were compromised revealed that users create predictable PIN patterns. The PIN *1234* was used in more than one out of every 10 PINs. Table 5-5 lists the five most common PINs and their frequency of use. Of the 10,000 potential PIN combinations, 26.83 percent of all PINs could be guessed by attempting the top 20 most frequent PINs.[9]

Table 5-5 Most common PINs

PIN	Frequency of use
1234	10.71%
1111	6.01%
0000	1.88%
1212	1.19%
7777	0.74%

NOTE 7

The research also revealed that the least common PIN was *8068*, which appeared in only 25 of the 3.4 million PINs.

A third option is to use a fingerprint to unlock the mobile device. Several smartphone devices have the fingerprint sensor on the back of the phone. This allows the user to access the fingerprint reader without moving their index finger from the back of the phone (where the index finger is normally located while holding the phone).

A final option is to draw or swipe a specific pattern connecting dots to unlock the device, as illustrated in Figure 5-6. Swipe patterns can be detected by threat actors who watch a user draw the pattern or observe any lingering "smear" on the screen.

Screen Lock. A **screen lock** prevents the mobile device from being accessed until the user enters the correct passcode, permitting access. Lock screens should be configured so that whenever the device is turned on or is inactive for a period, the user must enter the passcode. Most mobile devices can be set to have the screen automatically lock after anywhere from 5 seconds to 50 minutes of inactivity.

Some mobile devices can be configured so that the device automatically unlocks and stays unlocked (ignoring the inactivity setting) until a specific action occurs. This is called **context-aware authentication**, which is using a contextual setting to validate the user. An example of context-aware authentication is in the Google Android OS, which has a feature called Smart Lock that can be configured depending on the context. These contexts are listed in Table 5-6.

Manage Encryption Early versions of mobile devices using Apple iOS or Google Android did not provide native encryption, so third-party apps had to be installed to encrypt data. However, later versions of both OSs encrypt all user data on their mobile devices (**full disk encryption**) by default when the device is locked.

NOTE 8

Accessing a device through fingerprint, face, or voice is called *biometrics* and is covered in Module 12.

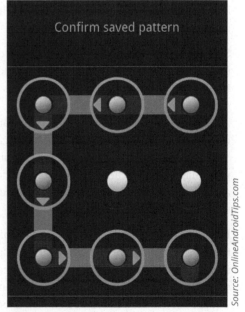

Source: OnlineAndroidTips.com

Figure 5-6 Swipe pattern

NOTE 9

Android provides an encryption option called *file-based encryption*, which is considered more secure than full disk encryption. File-based encryption encrypts each file with a different key so that files can be unlocked independently without decrypting an entire partition at once. The device can decrypt and use files needed to boot the system and process critical notifications while not decrypting personal apps and data.

Table 5-6 Android Smart Lock configuration options

Configuration name	Explanation	Comments
On-body detection	Device turns on and remains on when it is on the user's body in a pocket or purse.	On-body detection learns the pattern of how the user walks, and if it detects a different walk style, it locks the device.
Trusted places	Can set a specific location where the phone will turn on and then off when the user leaves the location.	Device will remain unlocked in an 80-meter radius around a building; users can also designate a specific building at a single address.
Trusted devices	Device will unlock whenever it is connected to another specific device.	Common trusted devices are Bluetooth watches, fitness trackers, or car systems; users should avoid trusted devices that are always with the device such as a Bluetooth mouse.
Trusted face	Whenever the device is turned on, it will search for the designated face and unlock if it recognizes the user.	This is the least secure configuration option because the device could be tricked by someone who looks similar.
Trusted voice	If a user says, "OK Google," voice commands can be issued without unlocking the device.	Trusted voice does not completely unlock the device as with other options but only gives the ability to issue some voice commands.

Although user data on a mobile device—*local* data-at-rest—is encrypted so that unauthorized users cannot access it, mobile device data can still be accessed through *remote* data-at-rest.

Data from mobile devices is routinely backed up to Apple's iCloud or to a Google server. Although the data on the servers is encrypted, Apple and Google possess the decryption keys necessary to unlock the data on their servers. Because the data is encrypted on the user's device and is inaccessible to outside parties, courts routinely serve orders to Apple and Google to provide the same data stored on their servers using their decryption keys. Those users who are concerned about maintaining the highest level of security on their data often turn off backups to iCloud or Google servers.

Segment Storage   With the exception of corporate-owned devices, each of the other enterprise deployment models (BYOD, COPE, and CYOD) permit the owner of a mobile device to use it for both business and personal needs. However, this usage may comingle critical business data with personal photos, downloads, and SMS text messages, which is not desirable to the enterprise or the user.

An option on mobile devices that contain personal and corporate data is **storage segmentation**, or separating business data from personal data. Users can apply **containerization**, or separating storage into business and personal "containers" and managing each appropriately. Segmenting storage on a mobile device used for both business and personal needs has advantages. It helps companies avoid data ownership privacy issues and legal concerns regarding a user's personal data stored on the device. In addition, it allows companies to delete only business data when necessary without touching personal data.

Enable Loss or Theft Services   One of the greatest risks of a mobile device is the loss or theft of the device. Unprotected devices can be used to access corporate networks or view sensitive data stored on them. If a mobile device is lost or stolen, several security features can be used to locate the device or limit the damage. Many of these features can be configured through the OS or an installed third-party app. The features are listed in Table 5-7.

If a lost or stolen device cannot be located, it may be necessary to perform a **remote wipe**, which will erase sensitive data stored on the mobile device. A remote wipe ensures that even if a thief accesses the device, no sensitive data will be compromised.

To reduce the risk of theft or loss, users should consider the following best practices:

- Keep the mobile device out of sight when traveling in a high-risk area.
- Avoid becoming distracted by what is on the device. Always maintain an awareness of your surroundings.
- When holding a device, use both hands to make it more difficult for a thief to snatch.
- Do not use the device on escalators or near transit train doors.

- White or red headphone cords may indicate they are connected to an expensive device. Consider changing the cord to a less conspicuous color.
- If a theft does occur, do not resist or chase the thief. Instead, take note of the suspect's description, including any identifying characteristics and clothing, and then call the authorities. Also contact the organization or wireless carrier and change all passwords for accounts accessed on the device.

Table 5-7   Security features for locating lost or stolen mobile devices

Security feature	Explanation
Alarm	The device can generate an alarm even if it is on mute.
Last known location	If the battery is charged to less than a specific percentage, the device's last known location can be indicated on an online map.
Locate	The current location of the device can be pinpointed on a map through the device's GPS.
Remote lockout	The mobile device can be remotely locked and a custom message sent that is displayed on the login screen.
Thief picture	Thieves who enter an incorrect passcode three times will have their picture taken through the device's on-board camera and emailed to the owner.

Mobile Management Tools

When using mobile devices in the enterprise, several support tools can facilitate the management of the devices. These include mobile device management, mobile application management, mobile content management, and unified endpoint management.

Mobile Device Management (MDM)   Mobile device management (MDM) tools allow a device to be managed remotely by an organization. MDM typically involves a server component, which sends out management commands to the mobile devices, and a client component, which runs on the mobile device to receive and implement the management commands. An administrator can then perform OTA updates or change the configuration on one device, groups of devices, or all devices.

Some features that MDM tools provide include the following:

- Apply or modify default device settings.
- Approve or quarantine new mobile devices.
- Configure email, calendar, contacts, and Wi-Fi profile settings.
- Detect and restrict jailbroken and rooted devices.
- Display an acceptable use policy that requires consent before allowing access.
- Distribute and manage public and corporate apps.
- Enforce encryption settings, antivirus updates, and patch management.
- Enforce geofencing, which is using the device's GPS to define geographical boundaries where an app can be used.
- Securely share and update documents and corporate policies.
- Selectively erase corporate data while leaving personal data intact.
- Send SMS text messages to selected users or groups of users (called push notification services).

NOTE 10

MDM provides a high degree of control over the device but a lower level of control on the apps, whereas MAM gives a higher level of control over apps but less control over the device.

Mobile Application Management (MAM)   Whereas MDM focuses on the device, mobile application management (MAM) covers application management, which comprises the tools and services responsible for distributing and controlling access to apps. The apps can be internally developed or commercially available apps.

Mobile Content Management (MCM)   Content management supports the creation and subsequent editing and modification of digital content by multiple employees. It can include tracking editing history, version control (recording changes and "rolling back" to a previous version if necessary), indexing, and searching. A **mobile content management (MCM)** system is tuned to provide content management to hundreds or even thousands of mobile devices used by employees in an enterprise.

Unified Endpoint Management (UEM)   All the capabilities in MDM, MAM, and MCM can be supported by **unified endpoint management (UEM)**. UEM is a group or class of software tools with a single management interface for mobile devices as well as computer devices. It provides capabilities for managing and securing mobile devices, applications, and content.

TWO RIGHTS & A WRONG

1. Due to its slow speed and other limitations, infrared capabilities in mobile devices are rarely found today.
2. COPE allows users to use their own personal mobile devices for business purposes.
3. Circumventing the installed built-in limitations on an Apple iPhone is called jailbreaking.

See Appendix B for the answer.

EMBEDDED SYSTEMS AND SPECIALIZED DEVICES

✅ CERTIFICATION

2.6 Explain the security implications of embedded and specialized systems.

Not all computing systems are desktop or mobile devices designed for human input. Computing capabilities can be integrated into appliances and other devices. An **embedded system** is computer hardware and software contained within a larger system designed for a specific function. A growing trend is to add the capabilities to devices that have never had computing power before. These devices can pose security risks.

Types of Devices

Categories of embedded and specialized devices include the hardware and software that can be used to create these devices, specialized systems, industrial systems, other devices, and IoT devices.

Hardware and Software

Hardware and software components are easily available for industrious users to create their own specialized device. One of the most common hardware components is the **Raspberry Pi**. This is a low-cost, credit-card-sized computer motherboard, as shown in Figure 5-7. The motherboard has hardware ports that can connect to a range of peripherals. Figure 5-8 shows the Raspberry Pi ports. The Raspberry Pi can perform almost any task that a standard computer device can, such as browsing the Internet, playing high-definition video, creating spreadsheets, and playing games. It can also be used to control a specialized device.

A device similar to the Raspberry Pi is the **Arduino**. Unlike the Raspberry Pi, which can function as a complete computer, the Arduino is designed as a controller for other devices: it has an eight-bit microcontroller instead of a 64-bit microprocessor on the Raspberry Pi, a limited amount of RAM, and no operating system. In addition, it can only run programs compiled for the Arduino platform, most of which

Source: Raspberry Pi Foundation

Figure 5-7   Raspberry Pi

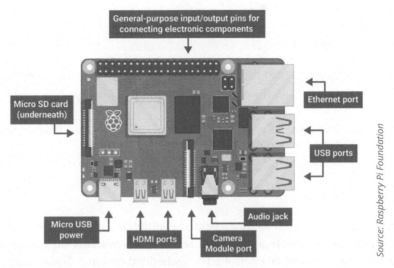

Source: Raspberry Pi Foundation

Figure 5-8   Raspberry Pi ports

must be written in the C++ programming language. Although the Raspberry Pi and Arduino can be used to interact with other specialized devices—such as control a robot, build a weather station, broadcast an FM radio signal, or build an automatic plant-watering device—the Arduino is generally considered a better solution. It has only a single USB port, a power input, and a set of input/output pins for connections but consumes little power.

Although the Raspberry Pi and Arduino are small motherboards, a **field-programmable gate array (FPGA)** is a hardware "chip" or integrated circuit (IC) that can be programed by the user ("field programmable") to carry out one or more logical operations (ICs on standard computers as well as a Raspberry Pi and Arduino cannot be user programmed). Specifically, a FPGA is an IC that consists of internal hardware blocks with user-programmable interconnects to customize operations for a specific application. A user can write software that loads onto the FPGA chip and executes functions, and that software can later be replaced or deleted.

An even smaller component than the Raspberry Pi or Arduino is a **system on a chip (SoC)**. A SoC combines all the required electronic circuits of the various computer components on a single IC chip. (The Raspberry Pi and Arduino are tiny motherboards that contain ICs, one of which is an SoC.) SoCs often use a **real-time operating system (RTOS)**, an OS specifically designed for an SoC in an embedded or specialized system. Standard computer systems, such as a laptop with a mouse and a keyboard or a tablet with a touch screen, typically receive irregular "bursts" of input data from a user or a network connection. Embedded systems, on the other hand, receive large amounts of data very quickly, such as an aircraft preparing to land on a runway at night during a storm. An RTOS is tuned to accommodate high volumes of data that must be immediately processed for critical decision making.

> **NOTE 11**
>
> FPGAs are used in aerospace and defense, medical electronics, digital television, consumer electronics, industrial motor control, scientific instruments, cybersecurity systems, and wireless communications. Microsoft is now using FPGAs in its data centers to run Bing search algorithms.

Specialized Systems

Several types of specialized systems are designed for specific applications. One example measures the amount of utilities consumed. Traditionally, households have had utilities such as electricity and water measured by an analog meter that records the amount of electricity or water being used. An employee from the utility must visit each home and read from the meter the amount that was consumed for the month so that a bill can be send to the occupant. Analog meters are being replaced by digital **smart meters**. Smart meters have several advantages over analog meters, and these are listed in Table 5-8.

Other specialized systems include medical systems, aircraft, and vehicles. The progression of specialized systems in automobiles is an example of how the systems have dramatically changed human-to-machine interaction. The first automobile embedded systems appeared in mass-production vehicles in the mid-1970s in response to regulations calling for higher fuel economy and emission standards. They handled basic functions such as engine ignition timing

Table 5-8   Analog meters vs. smart meters

Action	Analog meter	Smart meter
Meter readings	Employee must visit the dwelling each month to read the meter.	Meter readings are transmitted daily, hourly, or even by the minute to the utility company.
Servicing	Annual servicing is required in order to maintain accuracy.	Battery replacement every 20 years.
Tamper protection	Data must be analyzed over long periods to identify anomalies.	Can alert utility in the event of tampering or theft.
Emergency communication	None available	Transmits "last gasp" notification of a problem to utility company.

and transmission shifting. By the 1980s, more sophisticated computerized engine-management systems enabled the use of reliable electronic fuel-injection systems, and later active safety systems such as antilock braking and traction and stability control features were added, all controlled by embedded systems. Today, embedded systems in cars use sonar, radar, and laser emitters to control brakes, steering, and the throttle to perform functions such as blind spot and pedestrian collision warnings, automated braking, safe distance keeping, and fully automated parking. Some of the embedded systems in cars are shown in Figure 5-9.

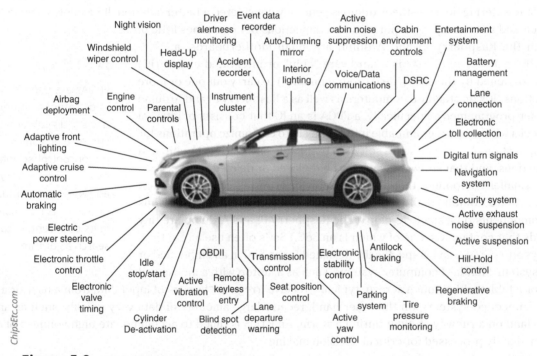

Figure 5-9   Embedded systems in cars

Industrial Systems

Industrial control systems (ICSs) in local or at remote locations collect, monitor, and process real-time data so that machines can directly control devices such as valves, pumps, and motors without human intervention. ICSs are managed by a larger **supervisory control and data acquisition (SCADA)** system. SCADA systems are crucial today for industrial organizations. They help to maintain efficiency and provide information on issues to help reduce downtime.

Other Specialized Systems

Other examples of specialized systems include **heating, ventilation, and air conditioning (HVAC)** environmental systems, which provide and regulate heating and cooling.

A **multifunctional printer (MFP)** combines the functions of a printer, copier, scanner, and fax machine. These peripheral devices are essentially special-purpose computers with a CPU; a hard drive that stores all received print jobs, faxes, and scanned images; a LAN or wireless LAN connection; a telephone connection for faxes; and a USB port to allow users to print documents stored on that device. *Smart MFDs* even have an OS that allows additional applications to be installed that extend the abilities of the MFD.

An **unmanned aerial vehicle (UAV)**, commonly known as a **drone**, is an aircraft without a human pilot on board to control its flight. Drones can be controlled by a remote human operator, usually on the ground, or autonomously by preprogramming the onboard computers. While drones were originally used in military applications, today they have expanded into commercial, scientific, agricultural, and recreational uses. They are commonly used for policing and surveillance, product deliveries, aerial photography, infrastructure inspections, and even drone racing. A drone is shown in Figure 5-10.

Source: Den Rozhnovsky/Shutterstock.com

Figure 5-10   Drone

For several years, different forms of digital communications have been unified into a single mode of transmission by shifting to an all-digital technology infrastructure. One of the most visible unification efforts is the convergence of voice and data traffic over a single Internet Protocol (IP) network. Using IP, various services such as voice, video, and data can be combined (*multiplexed*) and transported under a universal format. Known as **voice over IP (VoIP)**, it uses a data-based IP network to add digital voice clients and new voice applications onto the IP network.

> **NOTE 12**
>
> The term drone was first used to refer to unmanned aircraft that were used for target practice by battleships in the 1920s.

Internet of Things

The Telecommunication Standardization Sector of the International Telecommunication Union (ITU-T) defines the **Internet of Things (IoT)** as *a global infrastructure for the information society, enabling advanced services by interconnecting (physical and virtual) things based on existing and evolving interoperable information and communication technologies.*[10] More simply put, the IoT is connecting any device to the Internet for the purpose of sending and receiving data to be acted upon. Although this definition could encompass laptop computers and tablets, more often IoT refers to devices that heretofore were not considered as computing devices connected to a data network. IoT devices include wearable technology and multifunctional devices as well as many everyday home automation items such as thermostats, coffee makers, tire sensors, slow cookers, keyless entry systems, washing machines, electric toothbrushes, headphones, and light bulbs, to name just a few. It is estimated that, by 2025, there will be more than 25 billion IoT devices, of which more than half will be consumer devices.[11]

An example of IoT and the great promise it holds can be seen in devices that can be used for *body area networks (BAN)*, which is a network system of IoT devices in close proximity to a person's body that cooperate for the benefit of the user. Sensors are placed on the human body to monitor electrocardiogram (EKG) impulses, blood pressure, glucose, and other human biological functions. The readings are transmitted via computer or smartphone to a third-party physician who can make decisions regarding any medications to prescribe or lifestyle changes to recommend. This is called a *managed body sensor network (MBSN)*.

> **NOTE 13**
>
> IoT BAN sensors that continuously monitor body temperature are being proposed to help stem the spread of viruses among humans. The sensors could help to shut down emerging viruses before a pandemic can take hold.

A more robust approach is the *autonomous body sensor network (ABSN)*. Instead of only reading and transmitting information, an ABSN introduces actuators in addition to the sensors so that immediate effects can be made on the human body. Dozens of IoT micro-stimulator implant devices can be used to treat paralysis and other conditions. These devices take in signals from the human nervous system and then stimulate nerves through electrical charges that cause muscles to contract and limbs to move, bypassing areas of the nervous system that have been impaired by strokes or spinal cord or brain injuries. The ABSN can expand the use of functional electric stimulation to restore sensation, mobility, and function to those persons with paralyzed limbs and organs. Another ABSN being tested installs "stretchy" microprocessors on the tips of cardiac catheters, which are threaded through arteries into the heart. The catheters will be used to monitor the heart's electrical activity to pinpoint the location of irregular heartbeats and, if necessary, can treat the heart by "zapping" the tissue that is malfunctioning.

Security Issues

Although embedded systems and specialized devices are widely used and will continue to grow exponentially, they introduce significant security issues.

Consider the following actual incidents involving embedded systems and specialized devices:

- A worm was discovered that was actively targeting Windows computers that managed large-scale SCADA systems—which are often found in military installations, oil pipeline control systems, manufacturing environments, and even nuclear power plants. Named Stuxnet, the malware attempted to gain administrative access to other computers through the network to control the SCADA system. It appears that Stuxnet's primary target was nuclear reactors at the Bushehr nuclear power plant. Located in southwestern Iran near the Persian Gulf, Bushehr was a source of tension between Iran and the West (including the United States) because of fear that spent fuel from the reactor could be reprocessed elsewhere in the country to produce weapons-grade plutonium for use in nuclear warheads. Stuxnet was ultimately not successful in its attack.[12]
- Marc G. was in the kitchen when he began to hear strange sounds coming from the nursery of his two-year-old daughter Allyson. Marc and his wife entered the nursery and heard a stranger's voice calling out Allyson's name, cursing at her, and calling her vile names. The parents discovered that the voice was coming from the electronic baby monitor in Allyson's room that contained a camera, microphone, and speaker connected to their home Wi-Fi network. Because they did not have any security set on their wireless network, the attacker had been able to take control of the baby monitor from an unknown remote location. When Marc and his wife stepped in front of the camera, the attacker turned his verbal attack toward them. They quickly unplugged the device. The parents surmised that the attacker knew their daughter's name because he saw "Allyson" spelled out on the wall in her room. This situation is not unique: it is estimated that hundreds of thousands of wireless IoT cameras can easily be exploited because they have virtually no security.

These incidents illustrate the lack of security in embedded systems and specialized devices and can result in a wide range of attacks. Several **constraints** (limitations) make security a challenge for these systems and specialized devices. These security constraints are listed in Table 5-9.

Table 5-9 Security constraints for embedded systems and specialized devices

Constraint	Explanation
Power	To prolong battery life, devices and systems are optimized to draw very low levels of power and thus lack the ability to perform strong security measures.
Compute	Due to their size, small devices typically possess low processing capabilities, which restricts complex and comprehensive security measures.
Network	To simplify connecting a device to a network, many device designers support network protocols that lack advanced security features.
Cryptography	Encryption and decryption are resource-intensive tasks that require significant processing and storage capacities that these devices lack.
Inability to patch	Few, if any, devices have been designed with the capacity for being updated to address exposed security vulnerabilities.
Authentication	To keep costs at a minimum, most devices lack authentication features.
Range	Not all devices have long-range capabilities to access remote security updates.
Cost	Most developers are concerned primarily with making products as inexpensive as possible, which means leaving out all security protections.
Implied trust	Many devices are designed without any security features but operate on an "implied trust" basis that assumes all other devices or users can be trusted.
Weak defaults	User names (such as "root," "admin," and "support") and passwords ("admin," "888888," "default," "123456," "54321," and even "password") for accessing devices are often simple and well known.

Over several years, many industry-led initiatives have attempted to address security vulnerabilities in IoT and embedded devices. However, the initiatives were scattered and did not represent a comprehensive solution to the problem. To address security in these devices, governments have begun to propose or enact legislation to require stronger security on embedded systems and specialized devices. The *Internet of Things (IoT) Cybersecurity Improvement Act of 2019* was legislation introduced in the U.S. Senate in May 2019 with the following requirements:

- Require the National Institute of Standards and Technology (NIST) to issue recommendations addressing, at a minimum, secure development, identity management, patching, and configuration management for IoT devices.
- Direct the Office of Management and Budget (OMB) to issue guidelines for each agency that are consistent with the NIST recommendations, and charge OMB with reviewing the policies at least every five years.
- Require any Internet-connected devices purchased by the federal government to comply with those recommendations.
- Direct NIST to work with cybersecurity researchers and industry experts to publish guidance on coordinated vulnerability disclosure to ensure that vulnerabilities related to agency devices are addressed.
- Require contractors and vendors providing IoT devices to the U.S. government to adopt coordinated vulnerability disclosure policies so that if a vulnerability is uncovered, that information is disseminated.

California and Oregon passed state laws addressing IoT security that went into effect in January 2020. Both state laws require that connected devices be equipped with "reasonable security features" appropriate for the nature and function of the device and the information the device collects, contains, or transmits. Devices must be designed to protect both the device itself and any information contained within the device from unauthorized access, destruction, use, modification, or disclosure.

 **CAUTION** When defining a "reasonable security feature," both California and Oregon laws say that such a feature may consist of a preprogrammed password unique to each device manufactured. An alternative is a security feature that requires a user to create a new means of authentication before accessing a device for the first time. Beyond this example, however, neither law provides clear guidance as to what else could constitute a "reasonable security feature."

TWO RIGHTS & A WRONG

1. Multiple SCADAs are controlled by an ICS.
2. Power, compute, and network are all security constraints for embedded systems and specialized devices.
3. An RTOS is tuned to accommodate very high volumes of data that must be immediately processed for critical decision making.

See Appendix B for the answer.

 **VM LAB** You're now ready to complete the live virtual machine labs for this module. The labs can be found in each module in the MindTap.

SUMMARY

- There are several types of mobile devices. Tablet computers are portable computing devices smaller than portable computers, larger than smartphones, and focused on ease of use. Tablets generally lack a built-in keyboard and rely on a touch screen. A smartphone includes an operating system that allows it to run apps and access the Internet, and it offers a broad range of functionality. A new class of mobile technology is wearable technology, devices that can be worn by the user instead of being carried.

- Portable computers are devices that closely resemble standard desktop computers. A laptop is designed to replicate the abilities of a desktop computer with only slightly less processing power yet is small enough to be used on a lap or small table. A notebook computer is a smaller version of a laptop computer that is designed to include only the most basic frequently used features of a standard computer in a smaller size that is easy to carry. A subnotebook computer is even smaller than the standard notebook. A 2-in-1 computer can be used as either a subnotebook or a tablet. Web-based computers are designed to be used primarily while connected to the Internet.

- Connectivity methods used to connect mobile devices to networks include cellular telephony, which divides the coverage area into cells. Wi-Fi is a wireless local area network standard. USB connectors on mobile devices are used for data transfer.

- It is not always feasible to require an employee to carry a company-owned smartphone along with a personal cell phone. Many organizations have adopted an enterprise deployment model as it relates to mobile devices. Bring your own device (BYOD) allows users to use their own personal mobile devices for business purposes. Corporate owned, personally enabled (COPE) gives employees a choice from a selection of company approved devices. Choose your own device (CYOD) gives employees a limited selection of approved devices, though the employee pays the upfront cost of the device while the business owns the contract. A virtual desktop infrastructure (VDI) allows users to customize the display of data as if it were residing on their mobile device. Corporate-owned devices are purchased and owned by the enterprise.

- Several risks are associated with using mobile devices. Mobile devices are used in a wide variety of locations outside of the organization's normal physical perimeter. Devices can easily be lost or stolen, and any unprotected data on the device can be retrieved by a thief. As mobile devices age, they may no longer receive security updates. Geolocation, or the process of identifying the geographical location of a device, can be helpful but also is a security risk because it can identify the location of a person carrying a mobile device. Video cameras and microphones on mobile devices have been used by attackers to secretly "spy" on an unsuspecting victim. Vulnerabilities in mobile device connections can also be exploited by threat actors.

- Mobile devices have the ability to access untrusted content that other types of computing devices generally do not have. Users can circumvent the installed built-in limitations on their smartphone (jailbreaking on Apple iOS devices or rooting on Android devices) to download from an unofficial third-party app store (sideloading) or even write their own custom firmware to run on their device. Because these apps have not been approved, they may contain security vulnerabilities or even malicious code. Other means by which untrusted content can invade mobile devices include short message service (SMS), multimedia messaging service (MMS), and rich communication services (RCS).

- Users should consider security when initially setting up a mobile device. Mobile devices have options for configuring different types of passcodes that must be entered as authentication credentials. Although passwords are the most secure option, many users instead opt for a weaker personal identification number (PIN) or fingerprint reader, or they draw or swipe a specific pattern connecting dots to unlock the device. Although later versions of both iOS and Android encrypt all data on mobile devices, threat actors can access mobile device data that has been backed up to Apple or Google servers. Personal and corporate data can be separated into different containers and each can be managed appropriately. If a mobile device is lost or stolen, several security features can be used to locate the device or limit the damage.

- Several support tools can facilitate the management of mobile devices in the enterprise. Mobile device management (MDM) tools allow a device to be managed remotely by an organization. Mobile application management (MAM) covers application management, which comprises the tools and services responsible for distributing and controlling access to apps. A mobile content management (MCM) system provides content management to mobile devices used by employees in an enterprise. All of the capabilities in MDM, MAM, and MCM can be supported by unified endpoint management (UEM).

- Embedded and specialized devices can be classified into several categories. Hardware and software components are easily available for an industrious user to create their own specialized device. The Raspberry Pi is a low-cost credit-card-sized computer motherboard with hardware ports that can connect to a range of peripherals. Unlike the Raspberry Pi, which can function as a complete computer, the Arduino is designed as a controller for other devices. A field-programmable gate array (FPGA) is a hardware integrated circuit (IC) that can be programed by the user. A system on a chip (SoC) combines all the required electronic circuits of the various computer components on a single IC chip. SoCs often use a real-time operating system (RTOS) that is specifically designed for an SoC in an embedded or specialized system.

- Specialized systems designed for specific applications include a smart meter, which is a digital meter for measuring the consumption of utilities. Industrial control systems (ICSs) control locally or at remote locations by collecting, monitoring, and processing real-time data so that machines can directly control devices such as valves, pumps, and motors without the need for human intervention. Multiple ICSs are managed by a larger supervisory control and data acquisition (SCADA) system. Heating, ventilation, and air conditioning (HVAC) environmental systems provide and regulate heating and cooling. A multifunctional device (MFD) combines the functions of a printer, copier, scanner, and fax machine. An unmanned aerial vehicle (UAV), commonly known as a drone, is an aircraft without a human pilot on board to control its flight. Voice over IP (VoIP) uses a data-based IP network to add digital voice clients and new voice applications onto the IP network. The Internet of Things (IoT) is connecting any device to the Internet for the purpose of sending and receiving data to be acted upon.
- Security in embedded systems and specialized devices is lacking and can result in a wide range of attacks. Several constraints make security a challenge for these systems. To address security in these devices, governments have begun to propose or enact legislation to require stronger security on embedded systems and specialized devices.

Key Terms

application management
Arduino
bring your own device (BYOD)
carrier unlocking
cellular telephony
choose your own device (CYOD)
constraints
containerization
content management
context-aware authentication
corporate owned, personally enabled (COPE)
corporate owned
custom firmware
drone
embedded system
external media access
field-programmable gate array (FPGA)
firmware OTA updates
full disk encryption
geofencing
geolocation

Global Positioning System (GPS)
GPS tagging (geo-tagging)
heating, ventilation, and air conditioning (HVAC)
hotspot
industrial control systems (ICS)
infrared
Internet of Things (IoT)
jailbreaking
malicious flash drive
malicious USB cable
mobile application management (MAM)
mobile content management (MCM)
mobile device management (MDM)
multifunctional printer (MFP)
multimedia messaging service (MMS)
personal identification number (PIN)
push notification services
Raspberry Pi

real-time operating system (RTOS)
remote wipe
rich communication services (RCS)
rooting
screen lock
short message service (SMS)
sideloading
smart meters
storage segmentation
supervisory control and data acquisition (SCADA)
system on a chip (SoC)
tethering
third-party app store
unified endpoint management (UEM)
Universal Serial Bus (USB) connectors
unmanned aerial vehicle (UAV)
USB On-the-Go (OTG)
virtual desktop infrastructure (VDI)
voice over IP (VoIP)

Review Questions

1. Akira is explaining to his team members the security constraints that have made it a challenge for protecting a new embedded system. Which of the following would Akira NOT include as a constraint?
   a. Authentication
   b. Cost
   c. Power
   d. Availability

2. Agape has been asked to experiment with different hardware to create a controller for a new device on the factory floor. She needs a credit-card-sized motherboard that has a microcontroller instead of a microprocessor. Which would be the best solution?
   a. Arduino
   b. Raspberry Pi
   c. SoC
   d. FPGA

3. Hakaku needs a tool with a single management interface that provides capabilities for managing and securing mobile devices, applications, and content. Which tool would be the best solution?
   a. MCCM
   b. MDM
   c. UEM
   d. MMAM

4. In her job interview, Xiu asks about the company policy regarding smartphones. She is told that employees may choose from a limited list of approved devices but that she must pay for the device herself; however, the company will provide her with a monthly stipend. Which type of enterprise deployment model does this company support?
   a. CYOD
   b. COPE
   c. BYOD
   d. Corporate owned

5. Aoi has been asked to provide research regarding adding a new class of Android smartphones to a list of approved devices. One of the considerations is how frequently the smartphones receive firmware OTA updates. Which of the following reasons would Aoi NOT list in her report as a factor in the frequency of Android firmware OTA updates?
   a. OEMs are hesitant to distribute Google updates because it limits their ability to differentiate themselves from competitors if all versions of Android start to look the same through updates.
   b. Because many of the OEMs have modified Android, they are reluctant to distribute updates that could potentially conflict with their changes.
   c. Wireless carriers are reluctant to provide firmware OTA updates because of the bandwidth the updates consume on their wireless networks.
   d. Because OEMs want to sell as many devices as possible, they have no financial incentive to update mobile devices that users would then continue to use indefinitely.

6. What is the process of identifying the geographical location of a mobile device?
   a. Geotracking
   b. Geolocation
   c. GeoID
   d. Geomonitoring

7. Which of these is used to send SMS text messages to selected users or groups of users?
   a. Pull notification services
   b. Replay notification distribution (RND)
   c. Push notification services
   d. MAM mass SMS

8. Enki received a request by a technician for a new subnotebook computer. The technician noted that he wanted USB OTG support and asked Enki's advice regarding it. Which of the following would Enki NOT tell him?
   a. A device connected via USB OTG can function as a peripheral for external media access.
   b. A device connected via USB OTG can function as a host.
   c. USB OTG is only available for connecting Android devices to a subnotebook.
   d. Connecting a mobile device to an infected computer using USB OTG could allow malware to be sent to that device.

9. Banko's sister has just downloaded and installed an app that allows her to circumvent the built-in limitations on her Android smartphone. What is this called?
   a. Rooting
   b. Sideloading
   c. Jailbreaking
   d. Ducking

10. Which of the following technologies can convert a texting app into a live chat platform?
    a. MMS
    b. QR
    c. SMS
    d. RCS

11. What prevents a mobile device from being used until the user enters the correct passcode?
    a. Swipe identifier (SW-ID)
    b. Screen lock
    c. Screen timeout
    d. Touch swipe

12. Hisoka is creating a summary document for new employees about their options for different mobile devices. One part of his report covers encryption. What would Hisoka NOT include in his document?
    a. All modern versions of mobile device OS encrypt all user data by default.
    b. Encryption occurs when the mobile device is locked.
    c. Apple uses file-based encryption to offer a higher level of security.
    d. Data backed up to an Apple or Google server could be unlocked by a court order.

13. What does containerization do?
    a. It splits operating system functions only on specific brands of mobile devices.
    b. It places all keys in a special vault.
    c. It slows down a mobile device to half speed.
    d. It separates personal data from corporate data.

14. What allows a device to be managed remotely?
    a. Mobile device management (MDM)
    b. Mobile application management (MAM)
    c. Mobile resource management (MRM)
    d. Mobile wrapper management (MWM)

15. Which of these is NOT a security feature for locating a lost or stolen mobile device?
    a. Remote lockout
    b. Last known good configuration
    c. Alarm
    d. Thief picture

16. What enforces the location in which an app can function by tracking the location of the mobile device?
    a. Location resource management
    b. Geofencing
    c. GPS tagging
    d. Graphical Management Tracking (GMT)

17. Which of these is considered the strongest type of passcode to use on a mobile device?
    a. Password
    b. PIN
    c. Fingerprint swipe
    d. Draw connecting dots pattern

18. Which of the following is NOT a context-aware authentication?
    a. On-body detection
    b. Trusted places
    c. Trusted devices
    d. Trusted contacts

19. Which tool manages the distribution and control of apps?
    a. MAM
    b. MDM
    c. MCM
    d. MFM

20. Which type of OS is typically found on an embedded system?
    a. SoC
    b. RTOS
    c. OTG
    d. COPE

Hands-On Projects

 **CAUTION**   If you are concerned about installing any of the software in these projects on your regular computer, you can instead use the Windows Sandbox or install the software in the Windows virtual machine created in the Module 1 Hands-On Projects. Software installed within the virtual machine will not impact the host computer.

Project 5-1: Creating and Using QR Codes

Time Required: 15 minutes

Objective: Given a scenario, implement secure mobile solutions.

Description: Quick Response (QR) codes can be read by an imaging device such as a mobile device's camera or online. However, they pose a security risk. In this project, you create and use QR codes.

1. Use your web browser to go to **www.qrstuff.com**. (If you are no longer able to access the program through this URL, use a search engine to search for "Qrstuff.")
2. First create a QR code. Under **DATA TYPE**, be sure that **WEBSITE URL** is selected.
3. Under **CONTENT**, enter the URL **www.cengage.com**. Watch how the **QR CODE PREVIEW** changes as you type.
4. Under **Encoding Options**, select **Static-Embed URL into code as-is**.
5. Under **QR CODE PREVIEW**, click **DOWNLOAD QR CODE** to download an image of the QR code.
6. Navigate to the location of the download and open the image. Is there anything you can tell by looking at this code? How could threat actors use this to their advantage? Where could malicious QR codes be used? Is there any protection for the user when using QR codes?
7. Now use an online reader to interpret the QR code. Use your web browser to go to **blog.qr4.nl/Online-QR-Code_Decoder.aspx**. (The location of content on the Internet may change without warning. If you are no longer able to access the program through this URL, use a search engine and search for "Free Online QR Code Reader.")
8. Click **Choose File**.
9. Navigate to the location of the QR code that you downloaded on your computer and click **Open**.
10. Click **Upload**.
11. What does the text box display? How could an attacker use a QR code to direct a victim to a malicious website?
12. Use your web browser to go to **qrcode-monkey.com**. (If you are no longer able to access the program through this URL, use a search engine to search for "qrcodemonkey.")
13. Click **LOCATION**.
14. On the map, drag the pointer to an address with which you are familiar. Note how the **Latitude** and **Longitude** change.
15. Click **Create QR Code**.
16. Click **Download PNG** to download this QR code to your computer.
17. Navigate to the location of the download and open the image. How does it look different from the previous QR code? Is there anything you can tell by looking at this code?
18. Use your web browser to return to **blog.qr4.nl/Online-QR-Code_Decoder.aspx**.
19. Click **Choose File**.
20. Navigate to the location of the map QR code that you downloaded on your computer and click **Open**.
21. Click **Upload**.
22. In the text box, a URL will be displayed. Paste this URL into a web browser.
23. What does the browser display? How could an attacker use this for a malicious attack?
24. Return to **www.qrstuff.com**.
25. Click each option under **DATA TYPE** to view the different items that can be created by a QR code. Select three and indicate how they could be used by an attacker.
26. Close all windows.

Project 5-2: Using Software to Locate a Missing Laptop

Time Required: 20 minutes

Objective: Given a scenario, implement secure mobile solutions.

Description: If a mobile device is lost or stolen, there are several security features that can be used to locate the device or limit the damage. Many of these can be used through an installed third-party app. In this project, you download and install software that can locate a missing laptop computer. Note that for this project, a portable computer or desktop computer can be used.

1. Open your web browser and enter the URL **preyproject.com**. (The location of content on the Internet may change without warning. If you are no longer able to access the program through this URL, use a search engine and search for "Prey Project.")

2. Click **Features** and then **Tracking and Location**.

3. Read through the information so you will understand what Prey does.

4. Click **Download**.

5. Select the latest version for your computer.

6. When the file finishes downloading, run the program and follow the default installation procedures.

7. Click **Finish** to configure the Prey settings.

8. Be sure that **New user** is selected. Click **Next**.

9. Enter your information to create an account and click **Create**.

10. Go to **panel.preyproject.com**.

11. Enter your login information, and on the **All your devices** page, click the name of your recently added device.

12. You will then receive in your email information about this added device.

13. Notice that your device is shown on a map regarding its current location. How accurate is this?

14. Click **Hardware information**. How accurate is this information?

15. Click **Map and actions**.

16. Under **Actions** in the right pane, click **Sound alarm**. Read the pop-up window about this function. How would it be useful? Depending upon your setting, either click **Close** (to cancel this) or **Confirm** (to sound the alarm).

17. Under **Actions** in the right pane, click **Send message**. Click **Confirm**. Notice that the message appears on the screen. Is this wording strong enough to compel the person to return a missing laptop? Should a reward be offered? How would you frame this message?

18. Close the message.

19. Under **Actions** in the right pane, click **Lock device**. Read about the function this will perform. How useful would this be? Depending upon your setting, either click **Close** (to cancel this) or **Confirm** (to lock the device).

20. Click **Activity log**. Read through the list of events that have occurred.

21. Click **Set device to missing** and read through what occurs when this is selected. Click **Advanced Options**. How helpful would it be to have a photo of the person who is using the device and a screen capture of what they are doing on the device?

22. Click **Yes, my device is missing**. It may take up to 10 minutes for the alarm to sound depending on how frequently the device checks into Prey.

23. When a report is generated, click **Reports**, and read the information about the location of the device. Would this be sufficient information to find the missing device?

24. Change the settings so that your device is no longer registered as missing.

25. Close all windows.

Project 5-3: Installing BlueStacks Android Emulator

Time Required: 20 minutes

Objective: Given a scenario, implement secure mobile solutions.

Description: In this project, you install an Android emulator on a personal computer to test different tools. Note that you will need a Google account to access these tools.

1. Use your web browser to go to **www.bluestacks.com**. (The location of content on the Internet may change without warning. If you are no longer able to access the program through this URL, use a search engine and search for "BlueStacks.")

2. Click **Download BlueStacks**.

3. When the download is complete, launch the installation file and accept the defaults to install BlueStacks.

4. Click **Sign in with Google**.

5. Enter your Google account information.

6. Click **Done**.

7. Click the right arrow in the window.

8. Click **Continue**.

9. If necessary, sign in with your Google account.

10. Click **OK**.

11. Click the right arrow in the window.

12. If necessary, personalize the information and click the right arrow in the window.
13. Click **Finish**.
14. Click **Got it**.
15. Remain in BlueStacks for the next project.

Project 5-4: Installing Security Apps Using BlueStacks

Time Required: 20 minutes
Objective: Given a scenario, implement secure mobile solutions.
Description: In this project, you download and install Android apps to test different antimalware tools.

1. Click **Search apps**.
2. In the search bar enter **Antivirus**.
3. Select **Norton Security**.
4. Click **Install**.
5. Click **Accept**.
6. After the app has installed, click **OPEN**.
7. If the button **Agree and launch** appears, click it to start the app.
8. After the app has loaded and scanned, click through the various options for this app. Would you consider this antivirus app one that you would use on your Android device?
9. Click **Play Store**.
10. Click the magnifying glass to start another search.
11. In the search bar, enter **Antivirus**.
12. This time select a different antivirus product. Install it and then view the different options.
13. Click **Play Store**.
14. Click the magnifying glass to start another search.
15. Enter **Security** and press **Enter**.
16. Scroll down through the different apps available.
17. Select a different security app and install it.
18. How easy were these apps to install and configure? How do they compare with comparable desktop antimalware apps?
19. Close all windows.

Case Projects

Case Project 5-1: Unified Endpoint Management Tools

Use the Internet to identify and compare three different unified endpoint management tools. Create a table that lists their various features. Which of the tools would you recommend for a small business with 10 employees who use smartphones but has a single person managing IT services? Why?

Case Project 5-2: Enterprise Deployment Model Comparison

Research the different enterprise deployment models listed in Table 5-3. Create a detailed table listing their typical features, how they are used, and their advantages and disadvantages to both the enterprise as well as to the employee. Which of them is the most secure option? Which is the least secure option? Which of them is most advantageous for the enterprise? Which would you prefer to use? Which would you recommend for your school or place of employment? Why? Create a one-paragraph summary along with your table.

Case Project 5-3: Raspberry Pi and Arduino

Research information on the Raspberry Pi and the Arduino. What are the strengths of each platform? What are the weaknesses? How much do they cost? What additional peripherals are needed for each platform? How difficult are they to program and use? What are some interesting uses for each? Create a one-page document of your comparisons.

Case Project 5-4: Rooting and Jailbreaking

Research Android rooting and Apple jailbreaking. What privileges can be obtained by rooting and jailbreaking? What are the advantages? What are the disadvantages? Can a device that has been broken return to its default state? If so, how? Finally, create a list of at least five reasons why rooting and jailbreaking are considered harmful in a corporate environment.

Case Project 5-5: MFPs

MFPs are widely used in corporate environments. Use the Internet to research MFPs. Identify three MFPs, and list their features. What are the security risks of an MFP? How should they be protected? Write a one-page paper on your research.

Case Project 5-6: Internet of Things

Use the Internet to research the Internet of Things (IoT). In your own words, what is IoT? How is it being used today? How will it be used in the near future? What impact will IoT have on technology, society, and the economy over the next five years? What are its advantages and disadvantages? Finally, identify five of the most unusual IoT devices that you can find described online. Write a one-page paper on the information that you find.

Case Project 5-7: North Ridge Security Consulting

North Ridge Security provides security consulting and assurance services to more than 500 clients in more than 20 states for a wide range of enterprises. A new initiative at North Ridge is for each of its seven regional offices to provide internships to students who are in their final year of the security degree program at the local college.

The Carlyle-Stedman Museum provides patrons with mobile devices that contain prerecorded information that can be listened to while viewing the museum's artifacts. Recently, an incident occurred in which a patron circumvented the security on the device and, because it was not examined after it was turned in, the next patron who tried to use it was exposed to inappropriate content. The executive board of Carlyle-Stedman decided that something must be done to prevent this from recurring and wants to ensure that all employee mobile devices are also secure. They have asked North Ridge to make a presentation about mobile device security, and you have been given this assignment.

1. Create a PowerPoint presentation for the staff about the security risks of mobile technology and steps to be taken to secure mobile devices. Be sure to cover these from the perspective of the organization, the IT department, and the user. Your presentation should contain at least eight slides.
2. After the presentation, the IT director at the museum has asked North Ridge for recommendations on using MDM, MAM, MCM, and/or UEM. Write a one-page memo listing the features of these tools and how they could be used to help the museum.

Case Project 5-8: Information Security Community Site Activity

The Information Security Community Site is an online companion to this textbook. It contains a wide variety of tools, information, discussion boards, and other features to assist learners. Go to *community.cengage.com/infosec2* and click the *Join or Sign in* icon to log in, using your login name and password that you created in Module 1. Click **Forums (Discussion)** and click **Security+ Case Projects (7th edition)**. Read the following case study.

Read again the information in the module regarding the security risks of data-in-transit and remote data-at-rest. What are your feelings regarding the ability of the government to access data on iCloud and Google servers? Do you believe this is a safeguard for the nation, or is it a serious violation of personal privacy? What are the advantages and the risks of a government that has these powers? How could they be abused? Post your thoughts about app data sharing on the discussion board.

References

1. "Mobile fact sheet," *Pew Research Center*, Jun. 12, 2019, accessed May 26, 2020, www.pewresearch.org/internet/fact-sheet/mobile/.

2. "Mobile vs. desktop usage (latest 2020 data)," *BroadbandSearch*, accessed May 26, 2020, www.broadbandsearch.net/blog/mobile-desktop-internet-usage-statistics.

3. "Mobile security Index - 2020 report," *Verizon Wireless*, accessed May 26, 2020, https://enterprise.verizon.com/resources/reports/2020-msi-report.pdf.

4. Constantin, Lucian, "One In three organizations suffered data breaches due to mobile devices," *CSO*, Mar. 5, 2019, accessed May 26, 2020, www.csoonline.com/article/3353560/one-in-three-organizations-suffered-data-breaches-due-to-mobile-devices.html.

5. "Survey: IT Security and Laptop Theft," *Kensington*, Aug. 2016, accessed May 15, 2017, www.kensington.com/a/283005.

6. "Laptop and mobile device theft awareness," *University of Pittsburgh*, accessed May 27, 2020, www.technology.pitt.edu/security/laptop-theft.

7. "Data gets personal: 2019 global data risk report from the Varonis data lab," *Veronis*, accessed May 27, 2020, www.varonis.com/2019-data-risk-report/.

8. "Visa Tech Matters," *Visa*, Feb. 12, 2015, accessed May 26, 2017, http://visacorporate.tumblr.com/post/110835709353/visatechmatters-visa-launches-mobile-location.

9. "Pin analysis," *DataGenetics*, accessed Mar. 10, 2014, http://datagenetics.com/blog/september32012/index.html.

10. "Overview of the Internet of things, Series y: Global information infrastructure, internet protocol aspects and next-generation networks: Next Generation Networks; Frameworks and functional architecture models," Jun. 2012, Retrieved May 18, 2017, www.itu.int/rec/T-REC-Y.2060-201206-I.

11. "Forecast number of IoT connected objects worldwide from 2018 to 2025, by type," *Statista*, retrieved May 28, 2020, www.statista.com/statistics/976079/number-of-iot-connected-objects-worldwide-by-type/.

12. Kushner, David, "The real story of Stuxnet," *IEEE Spectrum*, Feb. 26, 2013, retrieved May 26, 2017, http://spectrum.ieee.org/telecom/security/the-real-story-of-stuxnet.

CRYPTOGRAPHY

This part introduces you to an essential element of modern security, that of cryptography. The importance of cryptography has increased over time to become a key defense in securing data from threat actors. Module 6 defines cryptography, explains cryptographic algorithms, looks at attacks on cryptography, and shows how cryptography is implemented. Module 7 continues with more advanced cryptography topics such as digital certificates, public key infrastructure (PKI), and transport encryption algorithms.

MODULE 6
BASIC CRYPTOGRAPHY

MODULE 7
PUBLIC KEY INFRASTRUCTURE AND CRYPTOGRAPHIC PROTOCOLS

PART 3

BASIC CRYPTOGRAPHY

After completing this module, you should be able to do the following:

1. Define cryptography
2. Describe hash, symmetric, and asymmetric cryptographic algorithms
3. Explain different cryptographic attacks
4. List the various ways in which cryptography is used

Front-Page Cybersecurity

It has long been recognized that the Allies' ability to read the encrypted transmission codes of Germany during World War II was a decisive key to victory. Yet this does not mean that the Allies could simply listen in and hear the conversations taking place, much like listening to a voice conversation over a telephone. The encryption keys used for encoding the messages were changed daily, so that each day, codebreakers had to work to determine the new key for that day before reading any messages. The transmissions were not voice communications but Morse code (dots and dashes). So, the Allies' attempts to read encrypted transmissions was a daily endeavor that continued throughout the war, not always successfully.

An often-overlooked aid in breaking the encoded messages was the complexity of sending the messages themselves.

At the start of World War II, the Germans used a cipher machine called Enigma, which had rotor settings and wiring schemes that were changed daily. Later Germany implemented an additional scheme called Double Playfair. This was an even more complex system than Enigma: it used a five-by-five grid with two separate keys, and each pair of letters had to be encrypted not once but twice. An overlaying stencil also changed daily as with the Enigma settings. Double Playfair was used on the front lines to send information about immediate military plans, and often by the time the message could be deciphered by the Allies, it was too late to take advantage of it.

The complexity of Double Playfair became its own worst enemy.

Due to the difficulty of coding messages with Double Playfair, the German radio operators often made mistakes in encrypting messages, and they were then forced to immediately send corrected messages. Thus, the same message with only minor corrections was sent multiple times. Repeating the same message with slight variations to correct errors was a tremendous aid to the codebreakers trying to crack the message because it revealed a detectable pattern that made the code much easier to break.

Other seemingly innocent actions by German radio operators also helped the codebreakers. Morse code messages are generally transmitted by a hand-operated device such as a telegraph key. Operators differ in how they tap out the dots and dashes on the key: they may use a slightly shorter or longer dash or gap between each tap, and they may even do so only for particular characters. This tendency is called their unique "fist." Experienced listeners can recognize specific senders based on their fist alone.

The fist of the German radio operators could help identify the sender. Over time, the Allies could pinpoint where the sender was located based on the content of the messages. Information about the transmitted military plans could even be narrowed to the specific region or town where the plans would be carried out. Some German radio operators also sent more gossip than others did, so over time, message content also helped to identify the sender.

Another aid to identify senders was that many of them, like all humans, were creatures of habit. They might use a girl-friend's name each time they sent a test message or end each message with the same phrase. This repeated content helped the Allies detect patterns and crack the codes.

The complexity of Double Playfair and repeating the same words regularly from habit were all helpful in breaking the German's code during World War II. Some of the same principles hold true today. While it may be hard to crack an encryption cipher itself, if the process by the user is poorly implemented, then encryption suddenly becomes very weak.

Consider attorneys who need to protect important documents stored at their office. They may erect a fence surrounding the property, install strong door locks, and place cameras over the doors in order to deter thieves. Yet, as important as physical defenses are, they nevertheless could be breached—and, in some cases, rather easily. For the attorneys to securely safeguard the documents, as a second line of defense, they would likely store the documents in a safe protected by a combination lock. Even if thieves could climb over the fence, break the door locks, and circumvent the cameras to enter the office, the intruders would have to break the code to the combination lock before reaching the documents. The effort would require a much higher level of time and expertise and generally would defeat all but the most sophisticated and determined thieves.

Information security uses the approach to protect data. Physical and technical security, such as motion detection devices and firewalls, help to keep out data thieves. For high-value data that must be fully protected, security professionals use a second level of protection: encryption. Even if attackers penetrate the device and reach the data, they still must uncover the key to unlock the encrypted contents, a virtually impossible task if the encryption is properly applied.

In this module, you will learn how encryption can be used to protect data. You will first look at what cryptography is and how it is used. You will also examine cryptographic attacks and, finally, see how to use cryptography.

DEFINING CRYPTOGRAPHY

 **CERTIFICATION**

2.1 Explain the importance of security concepts in an enterprise environment.

2.8 Summarize the basics of cryptographic concepts.

Defining cryptography involves understanding what it is and how it is used. It also involves knowing the limitations of cryptography.

What Is Cryptography?

As early as 600 BC, the ancient Greeks wrestled with how to keep messages sent by couriers from falling into enemy hands. One early method was to tell the message to a courier so he could later repeat it when he arrived at his destination. However, couriers often paraphrased the message in their own words, which resulted in omissions or variations due to forgetfulness. In some cases, couriers even intentionally altered the message if they had been bribed or blackmailed by the enemy.

Written dispatches, on the other hand, accurately conveyed the message without the courier knowing its contents, thus reducing the risk of a security breach. But enemies could uncover written messages if they found and searched the courier, so the Greeks contrived ingenious ways of disguising and concealing documents. News of an imminent

Persian invasion early in the fifth century BC was sent by writing the message in ink on wooden tablets and then covering them with wax, the normal medium for written messages. An innocuous message was written on the wax, which hid the underlying secret message. Other techniques included messages disguised in the form of a wound dressing, hidden in an earring, written as a tattoo, or concealed in a sandal or a mule's hoof.

Although these strategies made the message more difficult to find, if it were discovered, the contents could be read easily. The ancient Greeks then turned to making their messages intelligible only to the desired recipient. One technique was to substitute one letter for another (in English, *A = M, B = N, C = O*, etc.), though this was fairly easy to decipher. The Greeks also marked letters of an ordinary text with tiny dots to indicate which letters, when combined, revealed the secret message. The Greeks even wrote poems in which the first letter of each line of the poetry could be extracted to spell out a message.[1]

By hiding the message on tablets covered with wax or as a tattoo, the Greeks were performing **steganography**, a word from Greek meaning *covered writing*. Steganography hides the existence of information. Today, steganography often hides data in a harmless image, audio, or even video file. It typically takes the data, divides it into small pieces, and hides the pieces among invisible portions of the file. A common scheme is to hide data in the file header fields that describe the file, between sections of the *metadata* (data that is used to describe the content or structure of the actual data), or in the areas of a file that contain the content itself. An example of steganography is shown in Figure 6-1.

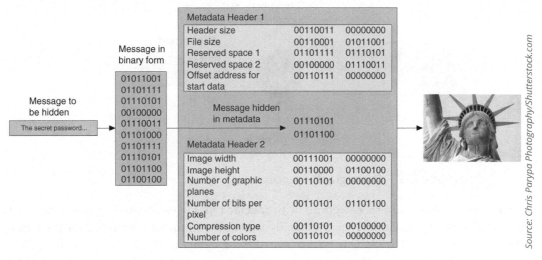

Figure 6-1   Data hidden by steganography

By making the message more difficult to read, such as by substituting letters, the ancient Greeks were also performing one of the early forms of **cryptography**, which is from Greek meaning *hidden writing*. Cryptography is the practice of transforming information so that it cannot be understood by unauthorized parties and, thus, is secure. Cryptography is usually accomplished through "scrambling" the information so that only approved recipients (either human or machine) can understand it.

When using cryptography, the process of changing the original text into a scrambled message is known as **encryption**. (The reverse process is **decryption**, or changing the message back to its original form.) In addition, the following terminology applies to cryptography:

- *Plaintext*. Unencrypted data that is input for encryption or is the output of decryption is called *plaintext*.
- *Ciphertext*. *Ciphertext* is the scrambled and unreadable output of encryption.
- *Cleartext*. Unencrypted data that is not intended to be encrypted is *cleartext* (it is "in the clear").

Plaintext data to be encrypted is input into a cryptographic **algorithm** (also called a *cipher*), which consists of procedures based on a mathematical formula. A *key* is a mathematical value entered into the algorithm to produce the ciphertext. Just as a key is inserted into a door lock to lock the door, in cryptography a unique

NOTE 1

Steganography is sometimes used together with encryption so that the information is doubly protected. First encrypting the data and then hiding it requires someone seeking the information to first find the data and then decrypt it.

NOTE 2

At its essence, cryptography replaces trust with mathematics.

mathematical key is input into the encryption algorithm to "lock" the data by creating the ciphertext. When the ciphertext needs to be returned to plaintext so the recipient can view it, the reverse process occurs with the decryption algorithm and key to "unlock" it. Cryptographic algorithms are public and well known; however, the individualized key for the algorithm that a user possesses must at all costs be kept secret. The cryptographic process is illustrated in Figure 6-2.

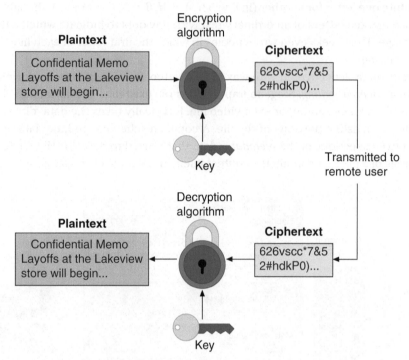

Figure 6-2   Cryptographic process

Ciphers can be separated into several categories, with specific types in each category. One category is a *substitution cipher*, which exchanges one character for another. By substituting *1* for the letter *A, 2* for the letter *B,* etc., the word *security* becomes *1804022017081924*. One type of substitution cipher is *ROT13*, in which the entire alphabet is rotated 13 steps (*A = N, B = O*, etc.) so that the word *security* becomes *frphevgl*. Another cipher is the *XOR cipher*, which is based on the binary operation e*X*clusive *OR* to compare two bits: if the bits are different, a *1* is returned, but if they are identical, then a *0* is returned. For example, to encrypt the word *security* with the word *flapjack* using the XOR cipher, the binary equivalent of the first letter *s (01110011)* is "XOR-ed" with the binary of the letter *f (01100110)* to return *00010101*. The substitution continues for each letter (*e* XOR *l, c* XOR *a,* etc.), so the entire result of *security* XOR *flapjack* is 00010101 00001001 00000010 00000101 00011000 00001000 00010111 00010010.

NOTE 3

The strength of a cryptographic algorithm depends upon several factors, one of which is the quality of *random numbers*, or numbers that do not follow an identifiable pattern or sequence. Software usually relies upon a *pseudorandom number generator (PRNG)*, which is an algorithm for creating a sequence of numbers whose properties approximate those of a random number. PRNGs attempt to create numbers that are as random as possible.

Cryptography Use Cases

Why use cryptography? Several common use cases (situations) for cryptography can provide a range of security protections. These protections include the following:

- *Confidentiality.* Cryptography can protect the confidentiality of information by ensuring that only authorized parties can view it. When private information, such as a list of employees to be laid off, is transmitted across the network or stored on a file server, its contents can be encrypted, which allows only authorized individuals who have the key to read it.

- *Integrity.* Cryptography can protect the integrity of information. Integrity ensures that the information is correct and no unauthorized person or malicious software has altered that data. Because ciphertext requires that a key must be used to open the data before it can be changed, cryptography can ensure its integrity. The list of employees to be laid off, for example, can be protected so that no names can be added or deleted by unauthorized personnel.
- *Authentication.* The authentication of the sender can be verified through cryptography. Specific types of cryptography, for example, can prevent a situation such as circulation of a list of employees to be laid off that appears to come from a manager but, in reality, was sent by an imposter.
- *Nonrepudiation.* Cryptography can enforce nonrepudiation. *Repudiation* is defined as denial; nonrepudiation is the inability to deny. In information technology, nonrepudiation is the process of proving that a user performed an action, such as sending an email message. Nonrepudiation prevents an individual from fraudulently reneging on an action. The nonrepudiation features of cryptography can prevent managers from claiming they never sent lists of employees to be laid off to an unauthorized third party.

NOTE 4

A practical example of nonrepudiation is Astrid taking her car into a repair shop for service and signing an estimate form of the cost of repairs and authorizing the work. If Astrid later returns and claims she never approved a specific repair, the signed form can be used as nonrepudiation.

- *Obfuscation.* Obfuscation is making something obscure or unclear. Cryptography can provide a degree of obfuscation by encrypting a list of employees to be laid off so that an unauthorized user cannot read it.

The security protections afforded by cryptography are summarized in Table 6-1.

Table 6-1   Information protections by cryptography

Characteristic	Description	Protection
Confidentiality	Ensures that only authorized parties can view the information	Encrypted information can only be viewed by those who have been provided the key.
Integrity	Ensures that the information is correct and no unauthorized person or malicious software has altered that data	Encrypted information cannot be changed except by authorized users who have the key.
Authentication	Provides proof of the genuineness of the user	Proof that the sender was legitimate and not an imposter can be obtained.
Nonrepudiation	Proves that a user performed an action	Individuals are prevented from fraudulently denying that they were involved in a transaction.
Obfuscation	Makes something obscure or unclear	By being made obscure, the original information cannot be determined.

Obfuscation is frequently misunderstood and often misapplied. By definition, encrypting data obfuscates that data, and its protection is based on an obfuscated key. However, obfuscation in other areas of cybersecurity cannot provide the same assurance that something is confidential. That is because obfuscation is often used erroneously as an attempt to hide something from outsiders: "If the bad guys don't know about it, that makes it secure." However, this approach (called *security through obscurity*) is flawed since what makes it secure is the fact that it is unknown. Because it is essentially impossible to keep secrets from everyone, eventually the data will be discovered and the security compromised. Thus, obfuscation cannot by itself be used as a general cybersecurity protection.

Unfortunately, some organizations attempt to apply security by obscurity to cryptography. They create proprietary cryptographic algorithms (touted as "military-grade" cryptography) and suggest that because the algorithm is "secret,"

NOTE 5

What makes cryptography secure is the obscurity of the key and not of the algorithm.

it is secure. However, in reality, proprietary algorithms are weak. Modern cryptographic algorithms are based on known mathematical proofs, and the algorithms are selected by competition after having been thoroughly reviewed by the cryptographic community. The algorithms have proven their value over time by their wide adoption and use. Proprietary algorithms, on the other hand, have not been properly vetted and will likely contain flaws and, thus, should not be used.

Cryptography can provide protection to data as that data resides in any of three states:

- *Data in processing.* **Data in processing** (also called *data in use*) is data on which actions are being performed by devices, such as printing a report from a device.
- *Data in transit.* Actions that transmit the data across a network, such as an email sent across the Internet, are called **data in transit** (sometimes called *data in motion*).
- *Data at rest.* **Data at rest** is data stored on electronic media.

Limitations of Cryptography

Despite providing widespread protections, cryptography faces constraints (limitations) that can impact its effectiveness. In recent years, the number of small electronic devices that consume little power (**low-power devices**)
has grown significantly. These devices range from tiny sensors that control office heating and lighting to consumer devices such as thermostats and lightbulbs. Increasingly, low-power devices need to be protected from threat actors who could accumulate their data and use it in nefarious ways. In addition, many applications require extremely fast response times, including communication applications (such as collecting car toll road payments), high-speed optical networking links, and secure storage devices such as solid-state disks. Cryptography is viewed as a necessary feature to add to protect low-power devices and applications that require fast response times to make them secure.

NOTE 6

Compared with the average energy requirements of a laptop computer (60 watts), the typical wireless sensor draws only 0.001 watt.

However, adding cryptography to low-power devices or those that have near instantaneous response times can be difficult. To perform their computations, cryptographic algorithms require time and energy, both of which are typically in short supply for low-power devices and applications needing ultra-fast response times. This results in a **resource vs. security constraint**, or a limitation in providing strong cryptography due to the tug-of-war between the available resources (time and energy) and the security provided by cryptography. Ideally, a cryptographic algorithm should have **low latency**, or a small amount of time that occurs between when a byte is input into a cryptographic algorithm and the time the output is obtained. However, some algorithms require multiple (even 10 or higher) "cycles" on sections of the plaintext, each of which draws power and delays the output. One way to decrease latency is to make the cryptographic algorithm run faster—though doing so increases power consumption, which is not available to low-power devices or would slow the normal operations of the device. The resource vs. security constraint is illustrated in Figure 6-3. Table 6-2 lists additional cryptographic constraints.

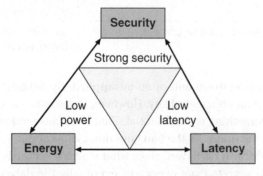

Figure 6-3   Resource vs. security constraint

Table 6-2   Cryptographic constraints

Limitation	Explanation
Speed	The speed at which data can be encrypted or decrypted depends upon several hardware and software factors, and in some instances, a slower speed is unacceptable.
Size	The resulting size of an encrypted file can be as much as one-third larger than the plaintext.
Weak keys	Some ciphers can produce a **weak key** that causes the cipher to behave in unpredictable ways or may compromise overall security.
Key length	Some ciphers have a short **key length**, or the number of bits in a key, which results in weaker security.
Longevity	As computers continue to become more powerful and can "crack" keys, the **longevity** or useful lifetime of service of ciphers may diminish.
Predictability	A weak random number generator or PRNG of the cipher may create predictable output.
Reuse	If someone reuses the same key for each encryption, then it provides a larger data footprint for an attacker to use in attempting to break the encryption.
Entropy	**Entropy** is the measure of randomness of a data-generating function, and ciphers with low entropy give the ability to predict future-generated values.
Computational overhead	Sensors and Internet of Things (IoT) devices often lack the capacity to accommodate the computational overhead for cryptography.

Not all constraints prevent a device from using cryptography; in some instances, encrypting and decrypting may simply slow the device. Therefore, cryptography must have **high resiliency**, or the ability to quickly recover from these constraints. Due to the importance of incorporating cryptography in low-power devices, a new subfield of cryptography called **lightweight cryptography** is being developed. Lightweight cryptography has the goal of providing cryptographic solutions uniquely tailored to low-power devices that need to manage resource vs. security constraints. However, lightweight cryptography is not a weakened cryptography but may simply have fewer features and be less robust than normal cryptography.

NOTE 7

Cryptography tools are also used by threat actors in their attacks. In one recent attack, victims who opened a malicious email attachment triggered a macro that executed a PowerShell script. The script instructed the user's device to visit a legitimate website to download an image. The image contained malicious code that was hidden within the image using steganography and was also encrypted. In a clever move, the script contained an intentional error, and the error code that was returned by the OS was the decryption key for opening the encrypted malware.

TWO RIGHTS & A WRONG

1. Steganography hides the existence of information.
2. Unencrypted data that is input for encryption or is the output of decryption is called cleartext.
3. Entropy is the measure of randomness of a data-generating function.

See Appendix B for the answer.

CRYPTOGRAPHIC ALGORITHMS

2.8 Summarize the basics of cryptographic concepts.

One variation of cryptographic algorithms is based on the device—if any—that is used in the cryptographic process. During the last half of the twentieth century, all cryptography became computer-based, whereas for the first half of that century, people used calculating machines. Before that time, cryptographic algorithms were entirely hand calculated. An example is a *one-time pad (OTP)*, which combines plaintext with a random key. A *pad* is a long sequence of random letters. The letters are combined with the plaintext message to produce the ciphertext. To decipher the message, the recipient must have a copy of the pad to reverse the process.

To encipher a message, the position in the alphabet of the first letter in the plaintext message is added to the position in the alphabet of the first random letter from the pad. For example, to encrypt *SECRET* using the pad *CBYFEA*, the first letter *S* (#19 of the alphabet) is added to the first letter of the pad *C* (#3 of the alphabet), and then 1 is subtracted ($19 + 3 - 1 = 21$). The result is *U* (letter 21 in the alphabet). Each letter is similarly encrypted, with any number larger than 26 wrapping around to the start of the alphabet. To decipher a message, the recipient takes the first letter of the ciphertext and subtracts the first random letter from the pad (any negative numbers are wrapped around to the end of the alphabet). An OTP is illustrated in Table 6-3.

Table 6-3 OTP

Plaintext	Position in alphabet	Pad	Position in alphabet	Calculation	Result
S	19	C	3	$19 + 3 - 1 = 21$	U
E	5	B	2	$5 + 2 - 1 = 6$	F
C	3	Y	25	$3 + 25 - 1 = 1$	A
R	18	F	6	$18 + 6 - 1 = 23$	W
E	5	E	5	$5 + 5 - 1 = 9$	I
T	20	A	1	$20 + 1 - 1 = 20$	T

 **CAUTION** As its name implies, the one-time pad should be used only one time and then destroyed. Because OTP is hand calculated and is the only known encryption method that cannot be broken mathematically, OTPs were used by special operations teams and resistance groups during World War II as well as by intelligence agencies and spies during the Cold War.

Another variation in cryptographic algorithms is the amount of data that is processed at a time. Some algorithms use a **stream cipher** that takes one character and replaces it with one character. Other algorithms make use of a **block cipher**. Whereas a stream cipher works on one character at a time, a block cipher manipulates an entire block of plaintext at one time. The plaintext message is divided into separate blocks of 8 to 16 bytes, and then each block is encrypted independently. For additional security, the blocks can be randomized. Recently, a third type called a *sponge function* has been introduced. A sponge function takes as input a string of any length and returns a string of any requested variable length. This function repeatedly applies a process on the input that has been *padded* with additional characters until all characters are used (*absorbed* in the *sponge*).

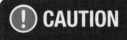 **CAUTION** Stream ciphers are less secure because the engine that generates the stream does not vary; the only change is the plaintext itself. Block ciphers are considered more secure because the output is more random, as the cipher is reset to its original state after each block is processed.

The three broad categories of cryptographic algorithms are hash algorithms, symmetric cryptographic algorithms, and asymmetric cryptographic algorithms.

Hash Algorithms

One type of cryptographic algorithm is a one-way hash algorithm. A **hash** algorithm creates a unique "digital fingerprint" of a set of data. This process is called **hashing**, and the resulting fingerprint is a *digest* (sometimes called a *message digest* or *hash*) that represents the contents. Hashing is used primarily for comparison purposes.

Although hashing is a cryptographic algorithm, its purpose is *not* to create ciphertext that can later be decrypted. Instead, hashing is intended to be one-way in that its digest cannot be reversed to reveal the original set of data. For example, when 12 is multiplied by 34, the result is 408. If a user were asked to determine the two numbers used to create the number 408, it would not be possible to work backward and derive the original numbers with absolute certainty because there are too many mathematical possibilities (1×408, 2×204, 3×136, 4×102, etc.). Hashing is similar in that it is not possible to determine the plaintext from the digest.

NOTE 8

Although hashing and checksums are similar in that they both create a value based on the contents of a file, hashing is not the same as creating a checksum. A checksum is intended to verify (*check*) the integrity of data and identify data-transmission errors, while a hash is designed to create a unique digital fingerprint of the data.

A hashing algorithm is considered secure if it has the following characteristics:

- *Fixed size.* A digest of a short set of data should produce the same size as a digest of a long set of data. For example, a digest of the single letter *a* is 86be7afa339d0fc7cfc785e72f578d33, while a digest of one million occurrences of the letter *a* is 4a7f5723f954eba1216c9d8f6320431f, the same length.
- *Unique.* Two different sets of data cannot produce the same digest. Changing a single letter in one data set should produce an entirely different digest. For example, a digest of *Sunday* is 0d716e73a2a7910bd4ae63407056d79b while a digest of *sunday* (lowercase *s*) is 3464eb71bd7a4377967a30da798a1b54.
- *Original.* It should not be possible to produce a data set that has a desired or predefined hash.
- *Secure.* The resulting hash cannot be reversed to determine the original plaintext.

Hashing is often used as a check to verify that the original contents of an item have not been changed. For example, digests are often calculated and then posted on websites for files that can be downloaded, as seen in Figure 6-4. After downloading the file, users can create their own digest on the file and then compare it with the digest value posted on the website. A match indicates the original file did not change while it was being downloaded.

Image Name	Torrent	Version	Size	SHA256Sum
Kali Linux 64-Bit (Installer)	Torrent	2020.2	3.6G	ae9a3b6a1e016cd464ca31ef5055506cecfc55a10f61bf1acb8313eddbe12ad7
Kali Linux 64-Bit (Live)	Torrent	2020.2	2.9G	e90e0cfb4bc8fc640219dba66c9fe4308c9502164e432c47a30af50ce9cb3ba2
Kali Linux 64-Bit (NetInstaller)	Torrent	2020.2	420M	def160159e12ff52fb5f4991240bd760500d7cd5ee38601a8bf35809a20f9450

Source: Kali Linux

Figure 6-4   Verifying downloads with digests

Common hash algorithms include the following:

- *Message Digest (MD)*. One of the earliest hash algorithms is a "family" of algorithms known as Message Digest (MD). Versions of MD hashes were introduced over almost 20 years, from MD2 (1989) to MD6 (2008). The most widely used of these algorithms is *MD5*. This hash algorithm uses four variables of 32 bits each in a round-robin fashion to create a value that is then compressed. Serious weaknesses have been identified in MD5, and it is no longer considered suitable for use.
- *Secure Hash Algorithm (SHA)*. Another family of hashes is the Secure Hash Algorithm (SHA). *SHA-1* was developed in 1993 but is no longer considered suitable for use. *SHA-2* has six variations, the most common are SHA-256, SHA-384, and SHA-512 (the last number indicates the length in bits of the digest that is generated) and is currently considered a secure hash. In 2015, after eight years of competition between 51 original entries, *SHA-3* was announced as a new standard. One design goal of SHA-3 was to make it dissimilar to previous hash algorithms to prevent threat actors from building on earlier work of compromising the algorithms.
- *RIPEMD*. RIPEMD stands for RACE Integrity Primitives Evaluation Message Digest. The primary design feature of RIPEMD is two different and independent parallel chains of computation, the results of which are then combined at the end of the process. All versions of RIPEMD are based on the length of the digest created, including RIPEMD-128, RIPEMD-256, and RIPEMD-320.

Table 6-4 illustrates the digests generated from several one-way hash algorithms using the word *Cengage*.

Table 6-4   Digests generated from one-time hash algorithms

Hash	Digest
MD2	b365b3f6ca8b35460782a658f2e82009
MD4	4fe043f7a0cde169a5d069b46bcfc0f7
MD5	7e169c6f44088e315c7b1f6513c1b0f7
RipeMD160	dd52a79bce64a1d145b51ce639e0dadda976516d
SHA-1	963ea98f0af1927e02ed0f13786162a5b8e713c0
SHA-256	f6c8a86bf6a5128cbaf2ad251b0beaa3604c11c51587de518737537800098d76
SHA-512	a2221473f8c4737d97f44265b3731a61127cc9521d4e07d18b1be357df4f04f8367a4a5255 cae956611f71b426bf494f2a68f41ca4aa122c2a07b570880e81fd
SHA3-512	3a82d58e17f3991413c5f4e9811930b69513bba02a860eed82070f892ab381f9fd926a88cf68745 565f51a93b97a1317ae8b84e2dfb798e4a2aa331187dc9e34

Symmetric Cryptographic Algorithms

The original cryptographic algorithms for encrypting and decrypting data are symmetric cryptographic algorithms. Symmetric cryptographic algorithms use the same key to encrypt and decrypt the data. Data encrypted by Bob with a key can only be decrypted by Alice using that same key. Because the key must be kept private (confidential), symmetric encryption is also called *private key cryptography*. Symmetric encryption is illustrated in Figure 6-5, where identical keys are used to encrypt and decrypt a document.

Symmetric cryptography can provide strong encryption—if the key is kept secure between the sender and all the recipients. Common symmetric cryptographic algorithms include the following:

- *Data Encryption Standard (DES)*. One of the first widely used symmetric cryptography algorithms was the *Data Encryption Standard (DES)*. The U.S. government officially adopted DES as the standard for encrypting unclassified information. Although DES was once widely implemented, it is no longer considered suitable for use.

NOTE 9

DES effectively catapulted the study of cryptography into the public arena. Until the deployment of DES, cryptography was studied almost exclusively by military personnel. The popularity of DES helped move cryptography implementation and research to academic and commercial organizations.

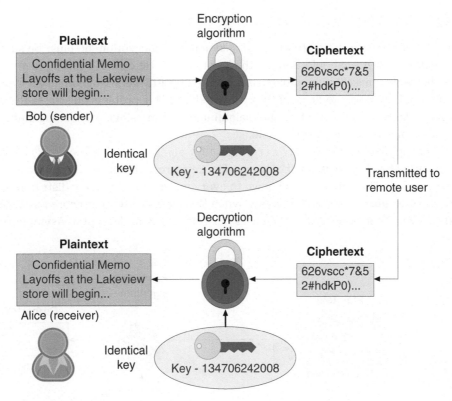

Figure 6-5   Symmetric (private key) cryptography

- *Triple Data Encryption Standard (3DES). Triple Data Encryption Standard (3DES)* was designed to replace DES. As its name implies, 3DES uses three rounds of encryption instead of just one. The ciphertext of one round becomes the entire input for the second iteration. 3DES employs a total of 48 iterations in its encryption (3 iterations × 16 rounds). The most secure versions of 3DES use different keys for each round, as shown in Figure 6-6. Although 3DES addresses several of the key weaknesses of DES, it is no longer considered the most secure symmetric cryptographic algorithm.
- *Advanced Encryption Standard (AES).* The *Advanced Encryption Standard (AES)* is a symmetric algorithm that performs three steps on every block (128 bits) of plaintext. Within step 2, multiple rounds are performed depending upon the key size: a 128-bit key performs nine rounds, a 192-bit key performs 11 rounds, and a 256-bit key, known as AES-256, uses 13 rounds. Within each round, bytes are substituted and rearranged, and then special multiplication is performed based on the new arrangement. To date, no attacks have been successful against AES.
- *Rivest Cipher (RC).* Rivest Cipher (RC) is a family of six algorithms. *RC4*, the most common RC cipher, is a stream cipher that accepts keys up to 128 bits in length.
- *Blowfish. Blowfish* is a block cipher algorithm that operates on 64-bit blocks and can have a key length from 32 to 448 bits.

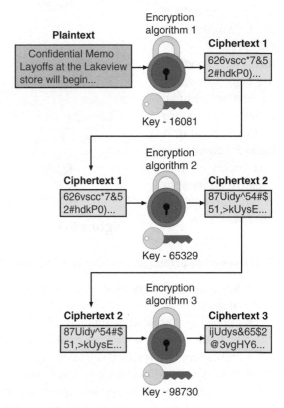

Figure 6-6   3DES

To date, no significant weaknesses have been identified. A later derivation of Blowfish known as Twofish is also considered a strong algorithm, although it has not been used as widely as Blowfish.

Asymmetric Cryptographic Algorithms

If Bob wants to send an encrypted message to Alice using symmetric encryption, he must be sure that she has the key to decrypt the message. Yet how should Bob get the key to Alice? He cannot send it electronically as an email attachment, because that would make it vulnerable to interception by attackers. Nor can he encrypt the key and send it, because Alice would not have a way to decrypt the encrypted key. This problem illustrates the primary weakness of symmetric encryption algorithms: distributing and maintaining a secure single key among multiple users, who are often scattered geographically, poses significant challenges.

A completely different approach is asymmetric cryptographic algorithms, also known as *public key cryptography*. Asymmetric encryption uses two keys instead of only one. The keys are mathematically related and are known as the public key and the private key. The public key is known to everyone and can be freely distributed, while the private key is known only to the individual to whom it belongs. When Bob wants to send a secure message to Alice, he uses Alice's public key to encrypt the message. Alice then uses her private key to decrypt it. Asymmetric cryptography is illustrated in Figure 6-7.

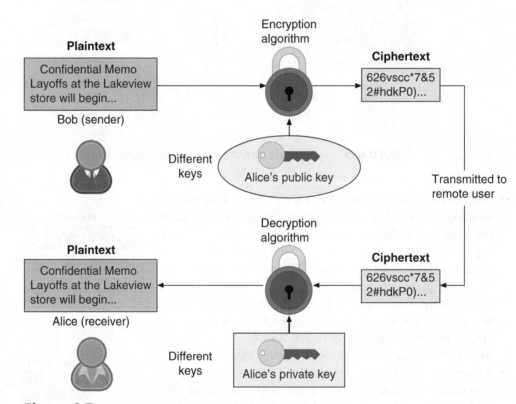

NOTE 10

Although different cryptographers were working on the idea of asymmetric encryption in the early 1970s, the development is often credited to Whitfield Diffie and Martin Hellman, based on a publication of their paper *New Directions in Cryptography* in November 1976.

Figure 6-7   Asymmetric (public key) cryptography

Several important principles regarding asymmetric cryptography are as follows:

- *Key pairs*. Unlike symmetric cryptography that uses only one key, asymmetric cryptography requires a pair of keys.
- *Public key*. Public keys, by their nature, are designed to be public and do not need to be protected. They can be freely given to anyone or even posted on the Internet.
- *Private key*. The private key must be kept confidential and never shared.
- *Both directions*. Asymmetric cryptography keys can work in both directions. A document encrypted with a public key can be decrypted with the corresponding private key. In the same way, a document encrypted with a private key can be decrypted with its public key.

⚠ CAUTION   No user other than the owner must ever have the private key.

There are different asymmetric algorithms and variations as well as issues surrounding key management.

RSA

The asymmetric algorithm *RSA* was published in 1977 and became the basis for several products. The RSA algorithm multiplies two large prime numbers (a prime number is a number divisible only by itself and 1), *p* and *q*, to compute their product ($n = pq$). Next, a number *e* is chosen that is less than *n* and a prime factor to $(p - 1)(q - 1)$. Another number *d* is determined so that $(ed - 1)$ is divisible by $(p - 1)(q - 1)$. The values of *e* and *d* are the public and private exponents. The public key is the pair (n,e) while the private key is (n,d). The numbers *p* and *q* can be discarded.

An illustration of the RSA algorithm using very small numbers is as follows:

1. Select two prime numbers, *p* and *q* (in this example, $p = 7$ and $q = 19$).
2. Multiply *p* and *q* together to create *n* ($7 \times 19 = 133$).
3. Calculate *m* as $p - 1 \times q - 1$ ($[7 - 1] \times [19 - 1]$ or $6 \times 18 = 108$).
4. Find a number *e* so that it and *m* have no common positive divisor other than 1 ($e = 5$).
5. Find a number *d* so that $d = (1 + n \times m)/e$ or ($[1 + 133 \times 108]/5$ or $14{,}364/5 = 2{,}875$).

For this example, the public key *n* is 133 and *e* is 5, while for the private key *n* is 133 and *d* is 2873.

Elliptic Curve Cryptography (ECC)

The basis of RSA asymmetric encryption security is factoring, or the prime numbers that make up a value. As computers become faster and more powerful, the ability to "crack" RSA asymmetric encryption by computing the factoring has grown. Instead of using factoring as the basis, other research looked at an obscure (and esoteric) branch of mathematics called elliptic curves. In short, an elliptic curve is a set of points that satisfy a specific mathematical equation. Elliptic curves paved the way for a different form of asymmetric encryption not based on factoring.

Instead of using large prime numbers as with RSA, **elliptic curve cryptography (ECC)** uses sloping curves. An elliptic curve is a function drawn on an X-Y axis as a gently curved line. By adding the values of two points on the curve, a third point on the curve can be derived, of which the inverse is used, as illustrated in Figure 6-8. With ECC, users share one elliptic curve and one point on the curve. One user chooses a secret random number and computes a public key based on a point on the curve; the other user does the same. They can now exchange messages because the shared public keys can generate a private key on an elliptic curve.

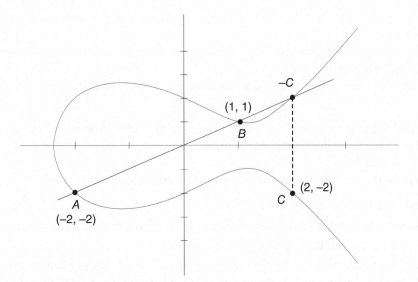

Figure 6-8   Elliptic curve cryptography (ECC)

The difference in size necessary to produce the same level of security between RSA and ECC keys is significant. Table 6-5 compares the key length (in bits) of RSA and ECC keys that have the same level of security. Despite a slow start, ECC has gained wide popularity. It is used by the U.S. government to protect internal communications, by the Tor project to help assure anonymity, and as the mechanism to prove ownership of bitcoins. All modern OSs and web browsers rely on ECC. Because mobile devices are limited in terms of computing power due to their smaller size, ECC offers security that is comparable to other asymmetric cryptography but with smaller key sizes, resulting in faster computations and lower power consumption.

NOTE 11

According to one study to break a 228-bit RSA key, the amount of energy needed would take less energy than what is required to boil a teaspoon of water. However, breaking a 228-bit ECC key would require more energy than it would take to boil all the water on Earth.[2]

Table 6-5   RSA vs. ECC key length for same security level

RSA key length	ECC key length
1,024	160
2,048	224
3,072	256
7,680	384
15,360	521

Digital Signature Algorithm (DSA)

Asymmetric cryptography also can be used to provide proofs. Suppose Alice receives an encrypted document that says it came from Bob. Although Alice can be sure that the encrypted message was not viewed or altered by someone else while being transmitted, how can she know for certain that Bob was the sender? Because Alice's public key is widely available, anyone could use it to encrypt the document. Another individual could have created a fictitious document, encrypted it with Alice's public key, and then sent it to Alice while pretending to be Bob. Alice's key can verify that no one read or changed the document in transport, but it cannot verify the sender.

Proof can be provided with asymmetric cryptography, however, by creating a *digital signature*, which is an electronic verification of the sender. A handwritten signature on a paper document serves as proof that the signer has read and agreed to the document. A digital signature is much the same but can provide additional benefits. A digital signature can

- *Verify the sender.* A digital signature serves to confirm the identity of the person from whom the electronic message originated.
- *Prevent the sender from disowning the message.* The signer cannot later attempt to disown it by claiming the signature was forged (nonrepudiation).
- *Prove the integrity of the message.* A digital signature can prove that the message has not been altered since it was signed.

The basis for a digital signature rests on the ability of asymmetric keys to work in both directions (a public key can encrypt a document that can be decrypted with a private key, and the private key can encrypt a document that can be decrypted by the public key).

The steps for Bob to send a digitally signed message to Alice are as follows:

1. After creating a memo, Bob generates a digest on it.
2. Bob encrypts the digest with his private key. The encrypted digest is the digital signature for the memo.
3. Bob sends both the memo and the digital signature to Alice.
4. When Alice receives them, she decrypts the digital signature using Bob's public key, revealing the digest. If she cannot decrypt the digital signature, then she knows that it did not come from Bob (because only Bob's public key can decrypt the digest generated with his private key).
5. Alice then hashes the memo with the same hash algorithm Bob used and compares the result to the digest she received from Bob. If they are equal, Alice can be confident that the message has not changed since he signed it. If the digests are not equal, Alice will know the message has changed since it was signed.

These steps are illustrated in Figure 6-9.

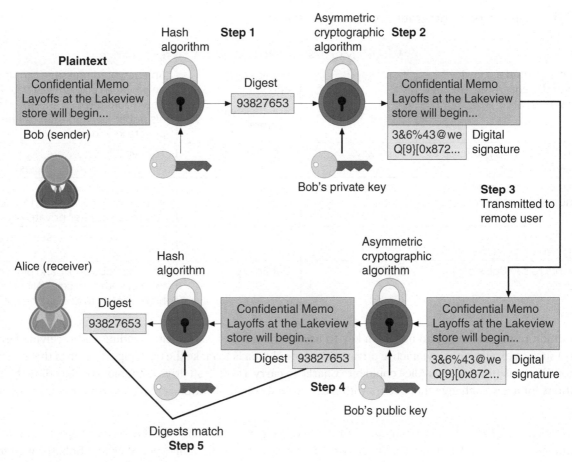

Figure 6-9 Digital signature

> **! CAUTION** Using a digital signature does not encrypt the message itself. In the example, if Bob wanted to ensure the privacy of the message, he also would have to encrypt it using Alice's public key.

The *Digital Signature Algorithm (DSA)* is a U.S. federal government standard for digital signatures. DSA was proposed by NIST in 1991 for use in their Digital Signature Standard (DSS). Although patented, NIST has made the patent available worldwide royalty-free. The standard continues to be revised and updated periodically by NIST.

Key Exchange

Public and private keys may result in confusion regarding whose key to use and which key should be used. Table 6-6 lists the practices to follow when using asymmetric cryptography.

Table 6-6 Asymmetric cryptography practices

Action	Whose key to use	Which key to use	Explanation
Bob wants to send Alice an encrypted message.	Alice's key	Public key	When an encrypted message is to be sent, the recipient's, and not the sender's, key is used.
Alice wants to read an encrypted message sent by Bob.	Alice's key	Private key	An encrypted message can be read only by using the recipient's private key.

(continues)

Table 6-6 Asymmetric cryptography practices *(continued)*

Action	Whose key to use	Which key to use	Explanation
Bob wants to send a copy to himself of the encrypted message that he sent to Alice.	Bob's key	Public key to encrypt Private key to decrypt	An encrypted message can be read only by the recipient's private key. Bob would need to encrypt it with his public key and then use his private key to decrypt it.
Bob receives an encrypted reply message from Alice.	Bob's key	Private key	The recipient's private key is used to decrypt received messages.
Bob wants Susan to read Alice's reply message that he received.	Susan's key	Public key	The message should be encrypted with Susan's key for her to decrypt and read with her private key.
Bob wants to send Alice a message with a digital signature.	Bob's key	Private key	Bob's private key is used to encrypt the hash.
Alice wants to see Bob's digital signature.	Bob's key	Public key	Because Bob's public and private keys work in both directions, Alice can use his public key to decrypt the hash.

In addition to confusion regarding which key to use, there are also issues with sending and receiving keys (**key exchange**) such as exchanging a symmetric private key. One solution is to make the exchange outside of the normal communication channels (for example, Alice could hire Charlie to carry a USB flash drive containing the key directly to Bob).

Solutions for a key exchange that occurs within the normal communications channel of cryptography include the following:

- *Diffie-Hellman (DH).* The Diffie-Hellman (DH) key exchange requires Alice and Bob to each agree upon a large prime number and related integer. Those two numbers can be made public, yet Alice and Bob, through mathematical computations and exchanges of intermediate values, can separately create the same key.
- *Diffie-Hellman Ephemeral (DHE).* Whereas DH uses the same keys each time, Diffie-Hellman Ephemeral (DHE) uses different keys. **Ephemeral keys** are temporary keys that are used only once and then discarded.
- *Elliptic Curve Diffie–Hellman (ECDH).* Elliptic Curve Diffie–Hellman (ECDH) uses elliptic curve cryptography instead of prime numbers in its computation.
- *Perfect forward secrecy.* Public key systems that generate random public keys that are different for each session are called **perfect forward secrecy**. The value of perfect forward secrecy is that if the secret key is compromised, it cannot reveal the contents of more than one message.

TWO RIGHTS & A WRONG

1. A digest of a short set of data should produce the same size as a digest of a long set of data.
2. SHA-1 is considered a secure hash algorithm.
3. Asymmetric cryptography keys can work in both directions.

See Appendix B for the answer.

CRYPTOGRAPHIC ATTACKS AND DEFENSES

 **CERTIFICATION**

1.2 Given a scenario, analyze potential indicators to determine the type of attack.

2.8 Summarize the basics of cryptographic concepts.

Because cryptography provides a high degree of protection, it is a defense that remains under attack by threat actors for any vulnerabilities. However, the new field of quantum cryptography defenses can aid in making cryptography more secure.

Attacks on Cryptography

Two of the most common types of attacks on cryptography include algorithm attacks and collision attacks.

Algorithm Attacks

Modern cryptographic algorithms are reviewed, tested, and vetted by specialists in cryptography over several years before they are released to the public for use. Very few threat actors have the advanced skills needed to even attempt to break an algorithm. However, attackers can use other methods to circumvent strong algorithms—including known ciphertext attacks, downgrade attacks, and taking advantage of improperly implemented algorithms.

Known Ciphertext Attacks   When properly implemented, cryptography prevents threat actors from knowing the plaintext or the key; the only item they can see is the ciphertext itself. Yet they can use sophisticated statistical tools to analyze the ciphertext and discover a pattern in the ciphertexts, which may be useful in revealing the plaintext text or key. This type of attack is called a *known ciphertext attack* or *ciphertext-only attack*, because all that is known is the ciphertext, though it can still reveal clues that may be mined.

Wireless data networks are particularly susceptible to known ciphertext attacks. Threat actors can capture large sets of ciphertexts to analyze and then inject their own frames into the wireless transmissions.

NOTE 12

Two techniques can be added to a cryptographic algorithm to thwart known ciphertext attacks by making the ciphertext more difficult to analyze. *Diffusion* changes a single character of plaintext into multiple characters of ciphertext, while *confusion* makes each character of the ciphertext based upon several parts of the key.

Downgrade Attack   Because new hardware and software are introduced frequently, they often include *backwards compatibility* so that a newer version can still function with the older version. However, in most instances, the newer version must revert to the older and less secure version. In a **downgrade attack**, an attacker forces the system to abandon the current higher security mode of operation and instead "fall back" to implementing an older and less secure mode. The threat actor can then attack the weaker mode.

Attacks Based on Misconfigurations   Most breaches of cryptography are the result of incorrect choices or misconfigurations of the cryptography options, known as misconfiguration implementation. Selecting weak algorithms, such as DES or SHA-1, should be avoided since they are no longer secure. Many cryptographic algorithms have several configuration options, and unless careful consideration is given to the options during setup, the cryptography may be improperly implemented. Careless users can also weaken cryptography if they choose SHA-256, for example, when a much stronger SHA3-512 is available through a simple menu choice.

Collision Attacks

One of the foundations of a hash algorithm is that each digest must be unique. If it were not unique, then a threat actor could trick users into performing an action that was assumed to be safe but in reality was not. For example, digests are calculated and then posted on websites for files that can be downloaded. Suppose an attacker could infiltrate a website and post a malicious file for download, but when the digest was generated for the malicious file, it created the same digest as the one posted for the legitimate file. Two files having the same digest is known as a **collision**. A *collision attack* is an attempt to find two input strings of a hash function that produce the same hash result.

NOTE 13

While for hash algorithms that produce long digests, such as SHA3-512, the odds of such a collision are very low, yet for hash algorithms that produce shorter digests, such as MD5, the odds increase. Table 6-4 compares the length of various digests.

Typically, a threat actor would be forced to try all possible combinations until a collision was found. However, a statistical phenomenon called the **birthday attack** makes it easier. It is based on the *birthday paradox*, which says that for someone in a given room to have a 50 percent chance of sharing your birthday, 253 people would need to be in the room. If, however, you are looking for a greater than 50 percent chance that any two people in the room have the same birthday, you only need 23 people. That's because the matches are based on pairs. If you choose yourself as one side of the pair, then you need 253 people to have 253 pairs (in other words, you combined with 253 other people make up all 253 sets). If you are concerned only with matches and not with matching someone to you specifically, then you need only 23 people in the room, because 23 people can form 253 pairs when cross-matched with each other. The same situation applies to hashing collisions. It is much harder to find something that collides with a specific hash than it is to find two inputs that hash to the same value.

NOTE 14

With the birthday paradox, the question is whether each person must link with every other person. If so, only 23 people are needed; if not, comparing only your single birthday to everyone else's, 253 people are needed.

Quantum Cryptographic Defenses

The foundation of modern technology is the bit (binary digit). A bit can either be off (0) or on (1), much like a light bulb. However, for several years, researchers have been developing a revolutionary type of computer called a **quantum computer**. Quantum computing relies on quantum physics using atomic-scale units (*qubits*) that can be both 0 and 1 at the same time. As a result, one qubit can carry out two separate streams of calculations simultaneously, meaning that quantum computers will be much faster and more efficient than today's computers.

NOTE 15

Businesses today are preparing for the move to quantum computers. Companies in the financial services, automotive, and pharmaceutical sectors have already started experimenting with quantum computing. By 2023, 20 percent of organizations, including businesses and governments, are expected to budget for quantum-computing projects, up from less than 1 percent in 2018.

Although quantum computers are potentially much more powerful than traditional computers, they are also more delicate and prone to faults. Because the technology is still in its early stages, no commercial-grade quantum computer has been built yet. However, online cloud quantum computing platforms are available to provide developers with an online platform to create applications for quantum computers. Developers can also experiment with quantum algorithms on traditional computers.

NOTE 16

Microsoft has eight quantum computing labs around the world. The company is also developing its own quantum computer that relies on topology, a branch of mathematics that studies geometric objects that experience physical changes. Microsoft says the topological approach can help a quantum computer run algorithms more reliably, with fewer risks of temperature or noise impacting the accuracy of a calculation or even preventing the calculation from being completed.

Quantum cryptography takes advantage of quantum computing for increasing cybersecurity. One subcategory of quantum cryptography is **quantum communication** or secure telecommunications. Because eavesdropping changes the physical nature of the information, users in a quantum communication exchange can easily detect eavesdroppers.

NOTE 17

The most well-known and developed application of quantum communication is *quantum key distribution (QKD)*. Bob and Alice are linked together with a quantum channel and a regular channel, such as the Internet. Bob and Alice each use single photons (a type of elementary particle) that are randomly polarized to states representing ones and zeroes, and the photons are used to transmit a series of random number sequences that are then used as keys in cryptographic communications. Alice begins by generating a random stream of qubits that are sent over the quantum channel. Upon reception of the stream, Bob and Alice, using the regular channel, perform operations to check if an attacker has tried to extract information on the qubits stream. The presence of an eavesdropper is revealed by the imperfect correlation between the two lists of bits obtained after the transmission of qubits between them.

Quantum computing also has a drawback for cybersecurity. Asymmetric cryptography begins by multiplying two prime numbers, a strong method because it is difficult for today's computers to determine the prime numbers that make up the value (*factoring*). However, a single quantum computer could perform factoring by using hundreds of atoms in parallel to quickly factor huge numbers, rendering virtually all current asymmetric cryptographic algorithms useless.

While some researchers think that quantum computers will create a "cryptographic apocalypse" soon (10 years from now), most security professionals think it is 30 years or more in the future more. Proposals for new "quantum-safe" encryption that could not be broken by quantum computers are currently being developed. Such encryption is called **post-quantum cryptography**, or cryptographic algorithms that are secure against an attack by a quantum computer.

TWO RIGHTS & A WRONG

1. In a downgrade attack, an attacker forces the system to abandon the current higher security mode of operation and instead "fall back" to implementing an older and less secure mode.
2. Post-quantum cryptography is comprised of algorithms that are secure against an attack by a quantum computer.
3. The basis of a quantum computer is a bit.

See Appendix B for the answer.

USING CRYPTOGRAPHY

 **CERTIFICATION**

2.1 Explain the importance of security concepts in an enterprise environment.

2.8 Summarize the basics of cryptographic concepts.

3.2 Given a scenario, implement host or application security solutions.

Cryptography can be applied through either software or hardware. Also, a relatively new technology known as blockchain uses cryptography as its basis.

Encryption through Software

Cryptography can be implemented through software running on a device. Encryption can also be performed on a larger scale by encrypting the entire disk drive itself.

File and File System Cryptography

Cryptographic software can be used to encrypt or decrypt files one by one. However, this process can be cumbersome. Instead, protecting groups of files, such as all files in a specific folder, can take advantage of the OS's file system. A *file system* is a method used by an OS to store, retrieve, and organize files. Protecting individual files or multiple files through file system cryptography can be performed using third-party software or OS cryptographic features.

Third-Party Software   Third-party software tools available for performing encryption include GNU Privacy Guard (which is abbreviated GNuPG), AxCrypt, Folder Lock, and VeraCrypt, shown in Figure 6-10.

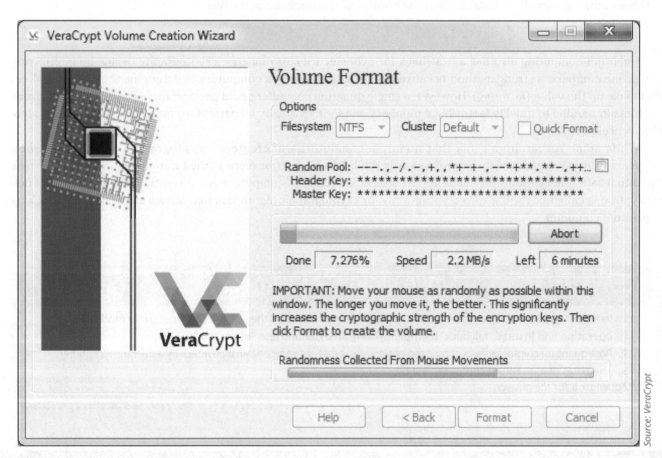

Figure 6-10   VeraCrypt

Operating System Encryption   Modern OSs provide encryption support natively. Microsoft's *Encrypting File System (EFS)* is a cryptography system for Windows releases that use the Windows NT file system (NTFS), while Apple's *FileVault* performs a similar function. Because the technology is tightly integrated with the file system, file encryption and decryption are transparent to the user. Any file created in an encrypted folder or added to an encrypted folder is automatically encrypted. When an authorized user opens a file, it is decrypted as data is read from a disk; when a file is saved, the OS encrypts the data as it is written to a disk.

Full Disk Encryption

Cryptography can also be applied to entire disks instead of individual files or groups of files. This practice is known as *full disk encryption (FDE)* and protects all data on a hard drive. One example of full disk encryption software is that included in Microsoft Windows known as *BitLocker* drive encryption software. BitLocker encrypts the entire system volume, including the Windows Registry and any temporary files that might hold confidential information. BitLocker prevents attackers from accessing data by booting from another OS or placing the hard drive in another computer.

Hardware Encryption

Software encryption suffers from the same fate as any application program: it can be subject to attacks to exploit its vulnerabilities. As a more secure option, cryptography can be embedded in hardware. Hardware encryption cannot be exploited like software encryption. Hardware encryption can be applied to USB devices and standard hard drives. More sophisticated hardware encryption options include self-encrypting drives, the trusted platform module, and the hardware security model.

USB Device Encryption

Many instances of data leakage are the result of USB flash drives being lost or stolen. Although data can be secured with software-based cryptographic application programs, vulnerabilities in the programs can open the door for attackers to access the data.

As an alternative, encrypted hardware-based USB devices such as flash drives can be used to prevent these types of software-based attacks. The drives resemble standard USB flash drives, with the following significant differences:

- Encrypted hardware-based USB drives will not connect to a computer until the correct password has been provided.
- All data copied to the USB flash drive is automatically encrypted.
- The external cases are designed to be tamper-resistant so attackers cannot disassemble the drives.
- Administrators can remotely control and track activity on the devices.
- Compromised or stolen drives can be remotely disabled.

NOTE 18

One hardware-based USB encrypted drive allows administrators to remotely prohibit accessing the data on a device until it can verify its status, to lock out the user completely the next time the device connects, or even to instruct the drive to initiate a self-destruct sequence to destroy all data.

Self-Encrypting Drives (SED)

Just as an encrypted hardware-based USB flash drive will automatically encrypt any data stored on it, **self-encrypting drives (SEDs)** can protect all files stored on them. When the computer or other device with an SED is initially powered up, the drive and the host device perform an authentication process. If the authentication process fails, the drive can be configured to simply deny any access to the drive or even perform a *cryptographic erase* on specified blocks of data. (A cryptographic erase deletes the decryption keys so that no data can be recovered.) It is also impossible to install the drive on another computer to read its contents.

A set of specifications for SEDs developed by the Trusted Computing Group (TCG) is **Opal**. SEDs that support Opal use hardware encryption technology to secure data stored in them. Opal also ensures the interoperability of SEDs among vendors.

Hardware Security Module (HSM)

A **Hardware Security Module (HSM)** is a removable external cryptographic device. An HSM can be a USB device, an expansion card, a device the connects directly to a computer through a port, or a secure network server. An HSM includes an onboard random number generator and key storage facility, as well as accelerated symmetric and asymmetric encryption, and can even back up sensitive material in encrypted form. Because the security is based on hardware and not through software, malware cannot compromise it.

HSMs are popular consumer-level devices. Figure 6-11 shows a USB consumer HSM from Yubico, a provider of authentication and encryption hardware devices. Some financial banking software comes with a specialized HSM hardware key, also called a "security dongle." The device is paired with a specific financial account and cannot be cloned or compromised.

Trusted Platform Module (TPM)

The **Trusted Platform Module (TPM)** is a chip on the motherboard of the computer that provides cryptographic services. For example, TPM includes a true random number generator instead of a PRNG as well as full support for asymmetric encryption. (TPM can also generate public and private keys.) Also, TPM can measure and test key

Source: Yubico

Figure 6-11 USB HSM

NOTE 19

An HSM is external while a TPM is internal.

components as the computer is starting up. It will prevent the computer from booting if system files or data have been altered. With TPM, if the hard drive is moved to another computer, the user must enter a recovery password before gaining access to the system volume.

Blockchain

Consider the company Serious Scooters (SS), which manufactures scooters. Several suppliers sell raw materials to Serious: tires, metal, plastic, seats, nuts, and washers, just to name a few. Serious sells their scooters to many retailers and then deposits the proceeds into their bank so that they can pay their suppliers, employees, and others. In the Accounting Department, a ledger is maintained of all transactions of raw materials that are bought and scooters that are sold. The ledger serves as the central repository of the accounting information for Serious Scooters.

Serious Scooters is not the only entity to keep a ledger: all of its suppliers, the retailers who buy from Serious, the banks, and everyone else also keep ledgers of their transactions with Serious as well as other customers. See Figure 6-12.

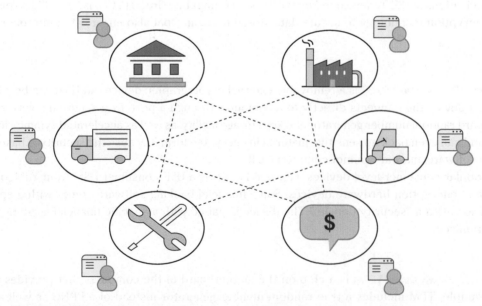

Figure 6-12 Multiple organizations with ledgers

It is inefficient for each entity to maintain its own ledger. Because suppliers, retailers, and banks duplicate parts of transactions, what happens if one supplier to Serious records a transaction in error? It may take a long time to correct the error because the supplier must contact Serious, who may need to contact its bank and even its retailers, to track down the error.

Instead, what if Serious Scooters and everyone else shared a single, tamper-evident ledger? It would eliminate or reduce paper processes, speeding up transaction times and increasing efficiencies. With a shared ledger, any transactions would be recorded only once and could not be altered. All parties must also give consensus before a new transaction is added to the network. Having a single shared ledger is seen in Figure 6-13.

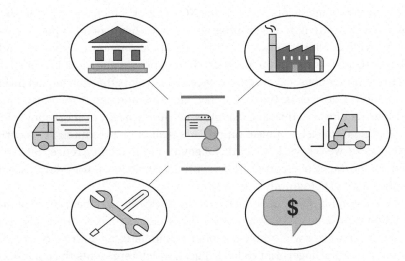

Figure 6-13   Multiple organizations using single ledger

This alternative is a **blockchain**. A blockchain is a shared, immutable ledger that facilitates the process of recording transactions and tracking assets in a business network. At a high level, blockchain technology allows a network of computers to agree at regular intervals on the true state of a distributed ledger. It is a system in which a record of transactions made is maintained across several computers that are linked in a peer-to-peer network.

NOTE 20

Walmart has started using blockchain to manage its supply-chain data for produce. Instead of using bar codes, scanners, paper forms, and individual databases, Walmart uses a digital app to record in blockchain when fruit is picked, packed, and shipped to the store. Before implementing blockchain, it took Walmart 6 days, 18 hours, and 26 minutes to track a single bag of sliced mangoes using the manual system. After implementing blockchain, that same bag was tracked it in 2.2 seconds.

Blockchain relies on cryptographic hash algorithms, most notably the SHA-256, to record its transactions. This makes it computationally infeasible to try to replace a block or insert a new block of information without the approval of all entities involved.

TWO RIGHTS & A WRONG

1. Modern OSs provide encryption support natively.
2. Opal is a standard for FEDs.
3. An HSM is external while a TMP is internal.
See Appendix B for the answer.

 **VM LAB**   You're now ready to complete the live, virtual machine labs for this module. The labs can be found in each module in the MindTap.

SUMMARY

- Cryptography is the practice of transforming information into a secure form so that unauthorized persons cannot access it. Unlike steganography, which hides the existence of data, cryptography masks the content of data so that it cannot be read. The original data, called plaintext, is input into a cryptographic encryption algorithm that has a mathematical value (a key) used to create ciphertext. Of the categories and types of algorithms, a substitution cipher exchanges one character for another, as in ROT13, in which the entire alphabet is rotated 13 steps. Another common algorithm is the XOR cipher, which uses the binary operation e*X*clusive *OR* to compare two bits. The strength of a cryptographic algorithm depends upon several factors.

- Cryptography can provide confidentiality, integrity, authentication, nonrepudiation, and obfuscation. It can also protect data as it resides in any of three states: data in processing, data in transit, and data at rest. Yet despite providing these protections, cryptography faces constraints that can impact its effectiveness. Adding cryptography to low-power devices or those that have near-instantaneous response times can be a problem because the algorithms require both time and energy, which are typically in short supply for low-power devices and applications needing ultra-fast response times. This results in a resource vs. security constraint. Other constraints are speed, size, weak keys, key length, longevity, predictability, reuse, entropy, and computational overhead. Due to the importance of incorporating cryptography in low-power devices, a new subfield of cryptography called lightweight cryptography is being developed.

- One variation of a cryptographic algorithm is based on the device (if any) that is used in the cryptographic process. Another variation is the amount of data that is processed at a time. A stream cipher takes one character and replaces it with one character while a block cipher manipulates an entire block of plaintext at one time.

- Hashing creates a unique digital fingerprint called a digest, which represents the contents of the original material. Hashing is not designed for encrypting material that will be later decrypted. If a hash algorithm produces a unique fixed-size hash and the original contents of the material cannot be determined from the hash, the hash is considered secure. Common hashing algorithms are Message Digest, Secure Hash Algorithm, and RACE Integrity Primitives Evaluation Message Digest.

- Symmetric cryptography, also called private key cryptography, uses a single key to encrypt and decrypt a message. Symmetric cryptography can provide strong protections against attacks if the key is kept secure. Common symmetric cryptographic algorithms include Data Encryption Standard, Triple Data Encryption Standard, Advanced Encryption Standard, Rivest Cipher, and Blowfish.

- Asymmetric cryptography, also known as public key cryptography, uses two keys instead of one. The keys are mathematically related and are known as the public key and the private key. The public key is widely available and can be freely distributed, while the private key is known only to the recipient of the message and must be kept secure. Common asymmetric cryptographic algorithms include RSA, Elliptic Curve Cryptography, Digital Signature Algorithm, and those relating to Key Exchange.

- Because cryptography provides a high degree of protection, it remains under attack. A known ciphertext attack uses statistical tools to attempt to discover a pattern in the ciphertexts, which then may be useful in revealing the plaintext text or key. In a downgrade attack, a threat actor forces the system to abandon the current higher security mode of operation and instead fall back to implementing an older and less secure mode. Many breaches of cryptography are the result not of weak algorithms but instead of incorrect configuration or uses of the cryptography, known as misconfiguration implementation. When two files have the same digest, this is known as a collision. A collision attack is an attempt to find two input strings of a hash function that produce the same hash result.

- Quantum computing relies on quantum physics using atomic-scale units (*qubits*) that can be both 0 and 1 at the same time. As a result, it is possible for one qubit to carry out two separate streams of calculations simultaneously, so that quantum computers will be much faster and more efficient than today's computers. Quantum cryptography takes advantage of quantum computing for increasing cybersecurity. One subcategory of quantum cryptography is quantum communication or secure telecommunications. Because eavesdropping changes the physical nature of the information, users in a quantum communication exchange can easily detect eavesdroppers.

- Cryptography can be applied through either software or hardware. Software-based cryptography can protect large numbers of files on a system or an entire disk. Several third-party software tools are available. Modern OSs provide encryption support natively. Cryptography also can be applied to entire disks, known as full disk encryption (FDE).

- Hardware encryption cannot be exploited like software cryptography. Hardware encryption devices can protect USB devices and standard hard drives. More sophisticated hardware encryption options include self-encrypting drives, the Hardware Security Model, and the Trusted Platform Module.
- A blockchain is a shared, immutable ledger that facilitates the process of recording transactions and tracking assets in a business network. At a high level, blockchain technology allows a network of computers to agree at regular intervals on the true state of a distributed ledger, and it is a system in which a record of transactions made are maintained across several computers that are linked in a peer-to-peer network.

Key Terms

algorithm	encryption	obfuscation
asymmetric cryptographic algorithm	entropy	Opal
	ephemeral key	perfect forward secrecy
birthday attack	Hardware Security Module (HSM)	post-quantum cryptography
block cipher	hash	quantum communication
blockchain	hashing	quantum computer
collision	high resiliency	resource vs. security constraint
cryptography	key exchange	self-encrypting drives (SEDs)
data at rest	key length	steganography
data in processing	lightweight cryptography	stream cipher
data in transit	longevity	symmetric cryptographic algorithm
decryption	low latency	
downgrade attack	low-power devices	Trusted Platform Module (TPM)
elliptic curve cryptography (ECC)	nonrepudiation	weak key

Review Questions

1. Which of the following hides the existence of information?
   a. Encryption
   b. Decryption
   c. Steganography
   d. Ciphering

2. Cryptography can prevent an individual from fraudulently reneging on an action. What is this known as?
   a. Repudiation
   b. Nonrepudiation
   c. Obfuscation
   d. Integrity

3. Brielle is researching substitution ciphers. She came across a cipher in which the entire alphabet was rotated 13 steps. What type of cipher is this?
   a. XOR
   b. XAND13
   c. ROT13
   d. Alphabetic

4. Which of the following is FALSE about "security through obscurity"?
   a. It attempts to hide its existence from outsiders.
   b. It can only provide limited security.
   c. It is essentially impossible.
   d. Proprietary cryptographic algorithms are an example.

5. What is low latency?
   a. A low-power source requirement of a sensor.
   b. The time between when a byte is input into a cryptographic cipher and when the output is obtained.
   c. The requirements for an IoT device that is using a specific network.
   d. The delay between when a substitution cipher decrypts the first block and when it finishes with the last block.

6. What are public key systems that generate different random public keys for each session?
   a. Public Key Exchange (PKE)
   b. perfect forward secrecy
   c. Elliptic Curve Diffie-Hellman (ECDH)
   d. Diffie-Hellman (DH)

7. What is data called that is to be encrypted by inputting it into a cryptographic algorithm?
   a. Plaintext
   b. Byte-text
   c. Cleartext
   d. Ciphertext

8. Which of these is NOT a basic security protection for information that cryptography can provide?
   a. Integrity
   b. Authenticity
   c. Risk
   d. Confidentiality

9. Cicero is researching hash algorithms. Which algorithm would produce the longest and most secure digest?
   a. SHA-256
   b. MD5
   c. SHA3-512
   d. SHA6-6

10. Which of the following is NOT a symmetric cryptographic algorithm?
    a. DES
    b. SHA
    c. Blowfish
    d. 3DES

11. Which of the following is not to be decrypted but is only used for comparison purposes?
    a. Digest
    b. Key
    c. Stream
    d. Algorithm

12. Which of these is NOT a characteristic of a secure hash algorithm?
    a. The results of a hash function should not be reversed.
    b. Collisions should occur no more than 15 percent of the time.
    c. A message cannot be produced from a predefined hash.
    d. The hash should always be the same fixed size.

13. Deo has been asked to explain RSA to his colleague. After his explanation, Deo is asked what, if any, weaknesses RSA has. How would Deo respond?
    a. RSA has no known weaknesses.
    b. As computers become more powerful, the ability to compute factoring has increased.
    c. RSA weaknesses are based on ECC.
    d. The digest produced by the RSA algorithm is too short to be secure.

14. Which of these is the strongest symmetric cryptographic algorithm?
    a. Data Encryption Standard
    b. Advanced Encryption Standard
    c. Triple Data Encryption Standard
    d. RC 1

15. If Bob wants to send a secure message to Alice using an asymmetric cryptographic algorithm, which key does he use to encrypt the message?
    a. Alice's private key
    b. Alice's public key
    c. Bob's public key
    d. Bob's private key

16. Egor wanted to use a digital signature. Which of the following benefits will the digital signature NOT provide?
    a. Verify the sender
    b. Verify the receiver
    c. Prove the integrity of the message
    d. Enforce nonrepudiation

17. Basil was reading about a new attack that forces the system to abandon a higher cryptographic security mode of operation and instead fall back to an older and less secure mode. What type of attack is this?
    a. Deprecation attack
    b. Pullback attack
    c. Downgrade attack
    d. Obfuscation attack

18. What is a collision?
    a. Two files produce the same digest.
    b. Two ciphertexts have the same length.
    c. Two algorithms have the same key.
    d. Two keys are the same length.

19. Which of the following is NOT a characteristic of the Trusted Platform Module (TPM)?
    a. It provides cryptographic services in hardware instead of software.
    b. It can generate asymmetric cryptographic public and private keys.
    c. It can easily be transported to another computer.
    d. It includes a pseudorandom number generator (PRNG).

20. Which of these provides cryptographic services and is external to the device?
    a. Trusted Platform Module (TPM)
    b. Hardware Security Module (HSM)
    c. Self-encrypting hard disk drives (SED)
    d. Encrypted hardware-based USB devices

Hands-On Projects

> **⚠ CAUTION** If you are concerned about installing any of the software in these projects on your regular computer, you can instead install the software in the Windows virtual machine created in the Module 1 Hands-On Projects. Software installed within the virtual machine will not impact the host computer.

Project 6-1: Using OpenPuff Steganography

Time Required: 25 minutes
Objective: Summarize the basics of cryptographic concepts.
Description: Unlike cryptography that scrambles a message so that it cannot be viewed, steganography hides the existence of the data. In this project, you will use OpenPuff to create a hidden message.

1. Use your web browser to go to **embeddedsw.net/OpenPuff_Steganography_Home.html**.

NOTE 21

It is not unusual for websites to change the location of where files are stored. If the URL no longer functions, open a search engine and search for "OpenPuff."

2. Click **Manual** to open the OpenPuff manual. Save this file to your computer. Read through the manual to see the features available. Return to the home page when finished.
3. Click **Download binary for Windows/Linux** to download the program. When a page appears asking for payments, click the **.ZIP** link to download the program for evaluation without submitting a payment.
4. Click **Screenshot** to view a screen capture of OpenPuff. Right-click this image and save it as **OpenPuff_Screenshot.jpg** on your computer. This will be the carrier file that will contain the secret message.

NOTE 22

For added security, OpenPuff allows a message to be spread across several carrier files.

5. Navigate to the location of the download and uncompress the OpenPuff zip file on your computer.
6. Now create the secret message to be hidden. Open Notepad and enter **This is a secret message**.
7. Save this file as **Message.txt** and close Notepad.
8. Create a zip file from the **Message** file. Navigate to the location of this file through File Explorer and right-click it.
9. Click **Send to** and select **Compressed (zipped) folder** to create the zip file.
10. Navigate to the OpenPuff directory and double-click **OpenPuff.exe**.
11. Click **Hide**.

NOTE 23

Under Bit selection options, note the wide variety of file types that can be used to hide a message.

12. Under **(1)**, create three unrelated passwords and enter them into **Cryptography (A)**, **(B)**, and **(C)**. Be sure that the **Scrambling (C)** password is long enough to turn the **Password check** bar from red to green.
13. Under **(2)**, locate the message to be hidden. Click **Browse** and navigate to the file **Message.zip**. Click **Open**.
14. Under **(3)**, select the carrier file. Click **Add** and navigate to **OpenPuff_Screenshot.jpg.**
15. Click **Hide Data!**.
16. Navigate to a different location from that of the carrier files and click **OK**.
17. After the processing has completed, navigate to the location of the carrier file that contains the message, and open the file. Can you detect anything different with the file now that it contains the message?

18. Now uncover the message. Close the OpenPuff Data Hiding screen to return to the main menu.
19. Click **Unhide!**.
20. Enter the three passwords.
21. Click **Add Carriers** and navigate to the location of **Carrier1** that contains the hidden message.
22. Click **Unhide!** and navigate to a location to deposit the hidden message. When it has finished processing, click **OK**.
23. Click **Done** after reading the report.
24. Go to that location and you will see **Message.zip**.
25. Close OpenPuff and close all windows.

Project 6-2: Running an RSA Cipher Demonstration

Time Required: 20 minutes
Objective: Summarize the basics of cryptographic concepts.
Description: The steps for encryption using RSA can be illustrated in a Java applet on a website. In this project, you will observe how RSA encrypts and decrypts.

NOTE 24

It is recommended that you review the section earlier in this module regarding the steps in the RSA function.

1. Use your web browser to go to **people.cs.pitt.edu/~kirk/cs1501/notes/rsademo/**.

NOTE 25

It is not unusual for websites to change the location of where files are stored. If the URL no longer functions, open a search engine and search for "RSA Cipher Demonstration."

2. Read the information about the demonstration.
3. Click **key generation page**.
4. Change the first prime number (P) to **7**.
5. Change the second prime number (Q) to **5**.
6. Click **Proceed**.
7. Read the information in the popup screen and record the necessary numbers. Close the screen when finished.
8. Click **Encryption Page**.
9. Next to **Enter Alice's Exponent key, E:** enter **5** as the key value from the previous screen.
10. Next to **Enter Alice's N Value:** enter **35**.
11. Click **Encrypt**. Read the message and record the values. Close the screen when finished.
12. Click **Decryption Page**.
13. Next to **Enter the encrypted message** enter **1**.
14. Next to **Enter your N value:** enter **35**.
15. Next to **Enter your private key, D:** enter **5**.
16. Click **Proceed**. Note that **1** has been decrypted to **A**.
17. Close all windows.

Project 6-3: Installing GUI Hash Generator and Comparing Digests

Time Required: 20 minutes
Objective: Summarize the basics of cryptographic concepts.
Description: In this project, you will download a GUI hash generator and compare the results of various hash algorithms.

1. Create a Microsoft Word document with the contents **Now is the time for all good men to come to the aid of their country.**
2. Save the document as **Country1.docx** on the desktop or in a directory specified by your instructor.
3. Now make a single change to **Country1.docx** by removing the period at the end of the sentence so it says **Now is the time for all good men to come to the aid of their country** and then save the document as **Country2.docx** in the same directory.

4. Close the document and Microsoft Word.

5. Use your web browser to go to **hashcalc.soft112.com**.

NOTE 26

It is not unusual for websites to change the location of where files are stored. If the URL no longer functions, open a search engine and search for "HashCalc."

6. Scroll down and then click **Download HashCalc**.

7. Click **Download**.

8. Click **Download Link**.

9. Follow the default instructions to install HashCalc.

10. Launch HashCalc to display the HashCalc window.

11. In addition to the hash algorithms selected by default, check the box next to the following hash algorithms to add them: **MD5**, **SHA256**, **SHA384**, **SHA512**, and **MD2**.

12. Click the file explore button next to **Data:**.

13. Navigate to the document **Country1.docx**.

14. Click **Open**.

15. In the HashCalc window, click **Calculate**.

16. Review the digests generated. If necessary, expand the size of the window. What can you say about these digests? Compare MD2 with SHA512. What makes SHA512 better than MD2? Why?

17. Click the file explore button next to **Data:**.

18. Navigate to the document **Country2.docx**.

19. Click **Open**.

20. In the HashCalc window, click **Calculate**.

21. This file is the same as the previous except a single period was removed. Are the digests different? What does this tell you about hashing digests?

22. Close all windows.

Project 6-4: Using Microsoft's Encrypting File System (EFS)

Time Required: 20 minutes

Objective: Given a scenario, implement host or application security solutions.

Description: Microsoft's Encrypting File System (EFS) is a cryptography system for Windows releases that use the Windows NT file system (NTFS). Because EFS is tightly integrated with the file system, file encryption and decryption are transparent to the user. In this project, you will turn on and use EFS.

1. Create a Word document with the contents of the first two paragraphs under **Today's Attacks and Defenses** on the first page of this module.

2. Save the document as **Encrypted.docx**.

3. Save the document again as **Not Encrypted.docx**.

4. Right-click the **Start** button, and then click **File Explorer**.

5. Navigate to the location of **Encrypted.docx**.

6. Right-click **Encrypted.docx**.

7. Click **Properties**.

8. Click the **Advanced** button.

9. Check the box **Encrypt contents to secure data**. This document is now protected with EFS. All actions regarding encrypting and decrypting the file are transparent to the user and should not noticeably affect any computer operations. Click **OK**.

10. Click **OK** to close the Encrypted Properties dialog box.

11. Launch Microsoft Word and then open **Encrypted.docx**. Was there any delay in the operation?

12. Now open **Not Encrypted.docx**. Was it any faster or slower?

13. Retain these two documents for use in the next project. Close Word.

Project 6-5: Using BestCrypt

Time Required: 25 minutes

Objective: Given a scenario, implement host or application security solutions.

Description: Third-party software applications can be downloaded to protect files with cryptography. In this project, you will download and install Jetico BestCrypt.

1. Use your web browser to go to **www.jetico.com**.

NOTE 27

It is not unusual for websites to change the location of where files are stored. If the URL no longer functions, open a search engine and search for "Jetico BestCrypt."

2. Under **ENCRYPT FILES**, click **LEARN MORE**.
3. Click **FREE TRIAL**.
4. Click **DOWNLOAD**.
5. Click **STANDARD EDITION**.
6. Follow the default installation procedures to install BestCrypt. A computer restart may be necessary.

NOTE 28

Note that this is a limited-time evaluation copy. Any files that are encrypted will only be available as read-only after the time limit expires.

7. Launch BestCrypt to display the BestCrypt control panel.
8. Files to be automatically encrypted are placed in a BestCrypt container. To create a container in the left pane, right-click the drive in which you want the container to be created, and then click **Container** and **New**.
9. Note the default file path for this container. Click **Show Advanced Settings**.
10. In the **Security Options** tab, click the arrow next to **Algorithm:** to display the cryptographic algorithms. Change to **Blowfish-448**.
11. Click **Create**.
12. The **Enter password** dialog box opens. Enter a strong password and confirm it. Click **OK**.
13. The **Seed value generation** window opens. Carefully read the instructions. What is the purpose of this window? Follow the instructions by pressing random keys or moving your cursor.
14. The **Format Local Disk** dialog box opens. This is to format the virtual drive that will contain your files. Click **Start** and then **OK**. When completed, click **Close**.
15. Note that you now have a new drive letter added to your computer, which is where you will place the files you want to encrypt. This container is entirely encrypted, including file names and free space, and functions like a real disk. You can copy, save, or move files to this container disk, and they will be encrypted as they are being written.
16. Right-click **Start** and then click **File Explorer**.
17. Click the drive letter of the drive that BestCrypt created.
18. Now drag a file into this drive (BestCrypt container). The file is automatically encrypted.
19. Open the document from your BestCrypt container. Did it take any longer to open now that it is encrypted? Close the document again.
20. Maximize the BestCrypt window and then click **Container** and **Dismount** to stop your container. A container will also be unmounted when you log off.
21. Based on your experiences with BestCrypt and EFS, which do you prefer? Why? What advantages and disadvantages do you see for both applications?
22. Close all windows.

Project 6-6: Blockchain Tutorial

Time Required: 25 minutes

Objective: Summarize the basics of cryptographic concepts.

Description: Understanding how blockchain functions can best be accomplished by performing a hands-on tutorial. In this project, you will use an online tutorial to learn about blockchain.

1. Use your web browser to go to **blockchain.mit.edu/how-blockchain-works**.

NOTE 29

It is not unusual for websites to change the location of where files are stored. If the URL no longer functions, open a search engine and search for "Andersbrown How Blockchain Works."

2. Click **Blockchain 101 – A Visual Demo** and watch the video.
3. When the video has completed click **2. Hash**.
4. In the **Data:** box, enter **This is data set 1** and note how the hash changes as you enter each letter.
5. Now change the **1** to **2**. What happens to the hash?
6. Click **3. Block**.
7. What new fields have been added?
8. Click **4. Blockchain**. Scroll to the right to see all the blocks in the chain. Look at the **Prev:** for **Block #5**. Compare that with the **Hash:** of **Block #4**. Are they identical? Why?
9. Compare the **Prev:** and **Hash:** of each block with the former block.
10. Return to **Block #5**. Enter **This is data set 5**. What happens to the color of the block? Why is this block now nvalid?
11. Go to **Block #4**. Enter **This is data set 4**. What happens to the color of Blocks #4 and #5? Why?
12. Return to **Block #5**. Click **Mine** to correct the information in the block.
13. Return to **Block #3**. Enter **This is data set 3**. What happens to Blocks #3, #4, and #5? Why? How does this illustrate that the blockchain resists change?
14. In **Block #3** click **Mine**. What happens to the color of this block?
15. Go to **Block #4** and click **Mine**.
16. Go to **Block #5** and click **Mine**.
17. If you were to make a change to Block #5, on which block must you click Mine to correct it? If you were to make a change to Block #3, on which blocks must you click Mine? Why the difference?
18. Close all windows.

Case Projects

Case Project 6-1: Broken SHA-1

Since 2004, security researchers theorized that SHA-1 would be vulnerable to a collision attack in which the same digest from two different plaintexts could be created. In early 2017, security researchers decisively demonstrated that SHA-1 could create a collision from two separate documents. However, this attack was limited, and it was estimated it would cost attackers from $110,000 to $560,000 on Amazon's Web Services (AWS) to carry it out. In early 2020, researchers unveiled a new attack on SHA-1 that was even more powerful. The new collision attack gives attackers more options and flexibility to produce the same digest for two or more data sets simply by appending data to each of sets. This attack cost as little as $45,000 to carry out. This compromise of SHA-1 has rendered it no longer suitable for use. How did the researchers do it? Visit the website Shattered (**shattered.io**) to find information about how SHA-1 was breached in 2017. Read the Q&A section and view the infographic. Try dragging one of your files to the File Tester to see if it is part of the collision attack. What did you learn? How serious is a collision? What is the impact? Now do conduct research on the 2020 SHA-1 attack. How was it carried out? Write a one-page paper of what you learned.

Case Project 6-2: Compare Cipher Tools

A variety of online cipher tools demonstrate different cryptographic algorithms. Visit the website Cipher Tools (**http://rumkin .com/tools/cipher/**) and explore the different tools. Select three tools, one of which is mentioned in this module (ROT13, one-time pad, etc.). Experiment with the three tools. Which is easy to use? Which is more difficult? Which tool would you justify as more secure than the others? Why? Write a one-page paper on your analysis of the tools.

Case Project 6-3: Lightweight Cryptography

Due to the importance of incorporating cryptography in low-power devices, a new "subfield" of cryptography called light-weight cryptography is being developed. This has the goal of providing cryptographic solutions that are uniquely tailored for low-power devices that need to manage resource vs. security constraints. Research lightweight cryptography. What are its goals? How will it work? What are its limitations? What are its advantages? Write a one-page paper on your findings.

Case Project 6-4: Twofish and Blowfish

Twofish and Blowfish are considered strong symmetric cryptographic algorithms. For example, Blowfish can accommodate key lengths of up to 448 bits (56 bytes). Use the Internet to research both Twofish and Blowfish. How secure are they? What are their features? What are their strengths and weaknesses? How are they currently being used? How would you compare them? Write a one-page paper on your findings.

Case Project 6-5: SHA-3

The hash algorithms SHA-1 and SHA-2 were not created by publicly sourced contests but instead were created by the National Security Agency (NSA) and then released as public-use patents. Although they are not identical, they share some of the same underlying mathematics, which has been proven to contain some cryptographic flaws. SHA-2 is a safer hash largely because of its increased digest length. SHA-3 is a completely different type of hash algorithm. Research SHA-3. What were its design goals? How is it different from SHA-1 and SHA-2? What are its advantages? How does its performance in hardware and soft-ware compare? When will it be widely implemented? What a one-page paper on your research.

Case Project 6-6: One-Time Pad (OTP) Research

Use the Internet to research OTPs: who was behind the initial idea, when they were first used, in what applications they were found, how they are used today, and other relevant information. Then visit an online OTP creation site such as **www.braingle.com/brainteasers/codes/onetimepad.php** and practice creating your own ciphertext with OTP. If possible, exchange your OTPs with other students to see how you might try to break them. Would it be practical to use OTPs? Why or why not? Write a one-page paper on your findings.

Case Project 6-7: Blockchain

Use the Internet to research how blockchain is currently being used. What are its advantages? What are its disadvantages? How widespread is its acceptance? What are future applications of blockchain? Write a one-page paper on your research.

Case Project 6-8: Information Security Community Site Activity

The Information Security Community Site is an online companion to this textbook. It contains a wide variety of tools, informa-tion, discussion boards, and other features to assist learners. Go to **community.cengage.com/infosec2** and click the *Join or Sign in* icon to login, using your login name and password that you created in Module 1. Click **Forums (Discussion)** and click on **Security+ Case Projects (7ᵗʰ edition)**. Read the following case study.

This is a true story (with minor details changed). Microsoft had uncovered several licensing discrepancies in its software. Clients were using the software while claiming they had purchased it from an authorized software retailer. The sale of one software package to a company in Tampa was traced back to a retailer in Pennsylvania, and yet the retailer had no record of any sales to the Tampa company. A private security consulting agency was called in, and they discovered that the network system administrator "Ed" in Pennsylvania was downloading pirated software from the Internet and selling it to customers as legitimate software behind the company's back. Ed had sold almost a half-million dollars in illegal software. The security firm also noticed a high network bandwidth usage. Upon further investigation, they found that Ed was using one of the company's servers as a pornographic website with more than 50,000 images and 2,500 videos. In addition, a search of Ed's desktop computer uncovered a spreadsheet with hundreds of credit card numbers from the company's e-commerce site. The security firm speculated that Ed was either selling the card numbers to attackers or using them himself.

The situation was complicated by the fact that Ed was the only person who knew certain administrative passwords for the core network router and firewall, network switches, the corporate virtual private network (VPN), the entire human resources system, the email server, and the Windows Active Directory. In addition, the company had recently installed a Hardware Security Module (HSM) to which only Ed had the password. The security consultant and the Pennsylvania company were worried about what Ed might do if he were confronted with the evidence, since he could hold the entire organization hostage or destroy every piece of useful information.

A plan was devised. The company invented a fictitious emergency at one of their offices in California that required Ed to fly there overnight. The long flight gave the security team a window of about five and a half hours during which Ed could not access the system (the flight that was booked for Ed did not have wireless access). Working as fast as they could, the team mapped out the network and reset all the passwords. When Ed landed in California, the chief operating officer was there to meet him and fire Ed on the spot.

Now it's your turn to think outside of the box. What would you have done to keep Ed away so you could reconfigure the network? Or how could you have tricked Ed into giving up the passwords without revealing to him that he was under suspicion? Record your answers on the Community Site discussion board.

Case Project 6-9: North Ridge Security

North Ridge Security provides security consulting and assurance services. You have recently been hired as an intern to assist them.

A new North Ridge client wants to provide encryption for any data that leaves their premises. You are asked to provide an overview of the different ways in which encryption can be used.

1. Create a PowerPoint presentation about encryption through software (third-party software and OS), FDE, SED, HSM, and TPM. Include the advantages and disadvantages of each. Your presentation should contain at least 10 slides.
2. After the presentation, the client asks for your recommendation regarding meeting their needs for encryption when taking data off-site. Create a memo communicating the actions you believe would be best for the company to take.

References

1. Russell, Frank. *Information Gathering in Classical Greece*. Ann Arbor: University of Michigan Press, 1999.
2. Lenstra, Arjen; Kleinjung, Thorsten; Thome, Emmanuel. *Universal Security from Bits and Mips to Pools, Lakes—And Beyond*. Accessed Jun. 3, 2020. https://eprint.iacr.org/2013/635.pdf.

PUBLIC KEY INFRASTRUCTURE AND CRYPTOGRAPHIC PROTOCOLS

After completing this module, you should be able to do the following:

1. Define digital certificates
2. Describe the components of Public Key Infrastructure (PKI)
3. Describe the different cryptographic protocols
4. Explain how to implement cryptography

Front-Page Cybersecurity

With today's super-fast computers and the advancements in cryptography, it would seem that an encrypted message dating back almost 80 years could easily be broken. However, that proved not to be the case in this fascinating incident.

In 1982, David and Anne Martin were renovating a fireplace that had been sealed off for many years in their 17th-century house in the village of Bletchingley, England. In the chimney, the Martins discovered the remains of a carrier pigeon with a small scarlet capsule attached to its leg. The red color of the capsule marked the bird as a military carrier pigeon for the Allied Forces in World War II. Inside the capsule was a message written in code containing 27 groups of five letters or numbers on thin paper the size of a cigarette paper. The message read

AOAKN HVPKD FNFJW YIDDC RQXSR DJHFP GOVFN MIAPX PABUZ WYYNP CMPNW HJRZH NLXKG MEMKK ONOIB AKEEQ WAOTA RBQRH DJOFM TPZEH LKXGH RGGHT JRZCQ FNKTQ KLDTS FQIRW AOAKN 27 1525/6

At the bottom of the coded message were two items that were not in code: "Number of Copies Sent: Two" and "Sender: Serjeant [*sic*] W. Stot." Additional sets of numbers (NURP 40 TW194 and NURP 37 DK 76) probably indicated the military number of the two birds who carried the message.

The Martins contacted several British government authorities about their find but initially there was no interest in the bird's message. However, in 2012, Bletchley Park, which served as the headquarters of British Intelligence codebreakers during World War II and is now a museum, took an interest in the message. It turns out the message may have been top secret. First, although Bletchley Park—only five miles from the Martin's house—used carrier pigeons during World War II, none of its official messages were sent in code; they were all written in longhand. Second, messages were never carried by more than one bird. Evidently the bird's message may have been part of a classified program.

In late 2012, the British Government Communications Headquarters, which is responsible for code breaking, examined the encrypted message. After top government codebreakers spent months using super-fast computers to attempt to break the code, they finally announced that the code could not be cracked. (A few amateur sleuths have claimed to have deciphered the message, but these claims have proved false.)

Why is it so tough to break this code? The code was written using a one-time pad, or OTP. (OTP is covered in Module 6.) As a key, an OTP uses a random set of letters that only the sender and recipient know. If an OTP is truly random, is used only one time, and is kept secret by the sender and receiver, it can be virtually impossible to crack. That seems to be the case in this incident. Thus, it is a matter of "key management": because the key to the code is lost, the message cannot be deciphered.

We may never know what message that pigeon 40TW194 was carrying. Yet, as a Government Communications Headquarters spokesperson said, "It is a tribute to the skills of the wartime code makers that, despite working under severe pressure, they devised a code that was undecipherable both then and now."[1]

Despite the clear benefits of cryptography in protecting data, few users have chosen to use it (other than what occurs by default for them). Yet for enterprises, the encrypting and decrypting of data is not only considered essential, but in many instances, it is required. However, when cryptography is used in the enterprise, a much higher degree of complexity is involved, particularly regarding keys. What happens if an employee has encrypted an important proposal but suddenly falls ill and cannot return to work? Does only the employee know the key? Or could a copy of the key be retrieved? Where is the copy of the key stored? Who can have access to it? How can the keys of hundreds or even thousands of employees be managed?

The issue of managing cryptography, particularly in the enterprise, is the topic of this module. First, you will learn about the authentication and distribution of public keys through digital certificates. Next, you will study the management of keys through public key infrastructure. Finally, you will look at cryptographic protocols to see the role of cryptography on data in transit/motion across a network data and how to implement cryptography.

DIGITAL CERTIFICATES

 CERTIFICATION

3.2 Given a scenario, implement host or application security solutions.

3.9 Given a scenario, implement public key infrastructure.

One of the common applications of public key cryptography is digital certificates. Using digital certificates involves understanding their purpose, knowing how they are managed, and determining which type of digital certificate is appropriate for different situations.

Defining Digital Certificates

Asymmetric cryptography (also called public key cryptography) uses a pair of related keys. The public key can be distributed and shared with anyone, while the corresponding private key must be kept confidential by the owner. Asymmetric cryptography has two uses: it can encrypt or decrypt a set of data, and it can be used as a proof to verify a "signature" of the sender.

Suppose that Alice receives an encrypted document that claims it is from Bob. Because it is encrypted, Alice knows that the document was not viewed by someone else. But how can she know for certain that Bob was the sender? Because Alice's public key is widely available, anyone could use it to encrypt a document. An imposter of Bob could have created a fictitious document, encrypted it with Alice's public key, and then sent it to Alice pretending to be Bob. While Alice can use her private key to decrypt the document to read it, she does not know with absolute certainty who sent it.

A degree of proof can be provided with asymmetric cryptography by creating a *digital signature*, which is an electronic verification of the sender. After creating a document, Bob generates a hash digest on it and then encrypts the digest with his private key, which serves as the digital signature. Bob sends both the encrypted document and the digital signature to Alice, who decrypts the digital signature using Bob's public key, revealing the digest. If she cannot decrypt the digital signature, then she knows that it did not come from Bob (because only Bob's public key can decrypt the digest generated with his private key).

NOTE 1

Digital signatures are covered in Module 6.

However, a digital signature has a weakness: it can only prove the *owner* of the private key and does not necessarily confirm the true identity of the sender. That is, a digital signature only shows that the private key of the sender was used to encrypt the digital signature, but it does not definitively prove *who* was the sender of that key. If Alice receives a message with a digital signature claiming to be from Bob, she cannot know for certain that it is the *real* Bob whose public key she is retrieving.

For example, suppose Bob created a message along with a digital signature and sent it to Alice. However, Mallory intercepted the message. Mallory then created her own set of public and private keys using Bob's identity. Mallory could then create a new message and digital signature (with the imposter private key) and send them to Alice. Upon receiving the message and digital signature, Alice would unknowingly retrieve the imposter public key (thinking it belonged to Bob) and decrypt it. Alice would be tricked into thinking Bob had sent it when, in reality, it came from Mallory. This interception and imposter public key are illustrated in Figure 7-1.

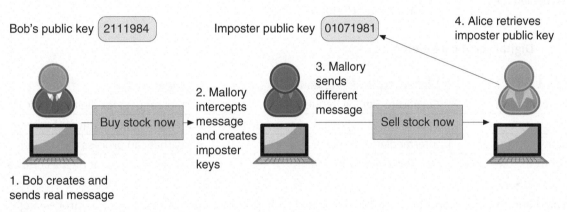

Figure 7-1   Imposter public key

Suppose that Bob wants to ensure that Alice receives his real public key and not an imposter public key. He could travel to Alice's city, knock on her front door, and say, "I'm Bob and here's my key."

Yet how would Alice even know *this* was the real Bob and not Mallory in disguise? For verification, she could ask to see Bob's passport. A passport is a document that is provided by a *trusted third party*. Although Alice may not initially trust Bob because she does not know him, she will trust the government agency that required Bob to provide proof of his identity when he applied for the passport. Using a trusted third party who has verified Bob—and who Alice also trusts—would solve the problem.

This scenario illustrates the concept behind a digital certificate. A **digital certificate** is a technology used to associate a user's identity to a public key and that has been digitally signed by a trusted third party. The third party verifies the owner and that the public key belongs to that owner.

A digital certificate is basically a container for a public key. It can be used to identify objects other than users, such as servers and applications. Typically, a digital certificate contains information such as the owner's name or alias, the owner's public key, the name of the issuer, the digital signature of the issuer, the serial number of the digital certificate, and the expiration date of the public key. It can contain other user-supplied information, such as an email address, postal address, and basic registration information.

When Bob sends a message to Alice, he does not ask her to retrieve his public key from a central site. Instead, Bob attaches the digital certificate to the message. When Alice receives the message with the digital certificate, she can check the signature of the trusted third party on the certificate. If the signature was signed by a party that she trusts, then Alice can safely assume that the public key—contained in the digital certificate—is actually from Bob. Digital certificates make it possible for Alice to verify Bob's claim that the key belongs to him and prevent an attack that impersonates the owner of the public key.

Managing Digital Certificates

Several entities and technologies manage digital certificates, including the certificate authorities and tools for managing certificates.

Certificate Authorities

Alice purchases a new car and visits the local county courthouse to fill out the car title application paperwork to register her car. After signing the application and verifying her identity, the information is forwarded to the state capital, where the state's department of motor vehicles (DMV) issues an official car title that is sent to her as the new owner.

This scenario illustrates some of the entities involved with digital certificates. A user who wants a digital certificate must generate the public and private keys to use and then complete a request with information such as name, address, and email address, known as a **Certificate Signing Request (CSR)**. The user electronically signs the CSR by affixing a public key and then sends it to a **registration authority** responsible for verifying the credentials of the applicant. Once verified, the CSR is transferred to an **intermediate certificate authority (CA)**. The intermediate CA, of which there are many, processes the CSR and issues the digital certificates. The intermediate CAs perform functions on behalf of a **certificate authority (CA)** that is responsible for digital certificates. A comparison between the earlier car title scenario and the elements of a digital certificate are shown in Table 7-1.

NOTE 2

Just as a state has many county courthouses, a CA has many intermediate CAs.

Table 7-1 Digital certificate elements

Car title scenario	Digital certificate element	Explanation
Car title application	Certificate Signing Request (CSR)	Formal request for digital certificate
Sign car title application	Create and affix public key to certificate	Added to digital certificate for security
Visit county courthouse	Intermediate certificate authority	Party that can process CSR on behalf of CA
Title sent from state DMV	Certificate authority (CA)	Party responsible for digital certificates

Intermediate CAs are subordinate entities designed to handle specific CA tasks such as processing certificate requests and verifying the identity of the individual. Depending on the type of digital certificate, the person requesting a digital certificate can be authenticated by:

- *Email.* In the simplest form, the owner might be identified only by an email address. Although this type of digital certificate might be sufficient for basic email communication, it is insufficient for most other activities.
- *Documents.* A registration authority can confirm the authenticity of the person requesting the digital certificate by requiring specific documentation such as a birth certificate or a copy of an employee badge that contains a photograph.
- *In person.* In some instances, the registration authority might require the applicant to apply in person to prove his existence and identity by providing a government-issued passport or driver's license.

NOTE 3

Although the registration function could be implemented directly with the CA, using separate intermediate CAs offers advantages. If many entities require a digital certificate, or if these are spread out across geographical areas, using a single centralized CA could create bottlenecks or inconveniences. Using multiple intermediate CAs, who can "off-load" the registration functions, can create an improved workflow. The process works because the CAs trust the intermediate CAs.

Just as a breach at a state DMV could result in many fraudulent car titles being distributed, so too could the consequences of a compromised CA taint its intermediate CAs and the digital certificates that they issued. CAs must therefore be kept safe from unauthorized access. A common method to ensure the security and integrity of a CA is to keep it in an offline state from the network (**offline CA**). It is only brought online (**online CA**) when needed for specific and infrequent tasks, typically limited to the issuance or reissuance of certificates authorizing intermediate CAs.

Certificate Management

Multiple entities make up strong certificate management, including a certificate repository and a means for certificate revocation.

Certificate Repository (CR) A *certificate repository (CR)* is a publicly accessible centralized directory of digital certificates that can be used to view the status of a digital certificate. The directory can be managed locally by setting it up as a storage area that is connected to the CA server.

Certificate Revocation Digital certificates normally have an expiration date. However, in some circumstances, the certificates are revoked before they expire. Some reasons might be benign, such as when a certificate is no longer used or the details of the certificate—such as the user's address—have changed. Other circumstances could be more dangerous. For example, if attackers steal a user's private key, they could impersonate the victim by using digital certificates without other users being aware of the impersonation. In addition, what would happen if digital certificates were stolen from a CA? The thieves could issue certificates to themselves that would be trusted by unsuspecting users. The CA must publish lists of approved certificates as well as revoked certificates in a timely fashion so that security is not compromised.

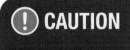 **CAUTION** Digital certificates have been stolen from CAs or intermediate CAs. With a stolen digital certificate, thieves can trick unsuspecting users into connecting with an imposter site, thinking it is a legitimate site. State actors have also been charged with stealing digital certificates to trick their own citizens into connecting with a fraudulent email site to monitor their messages and to locate and crackdown on dissidents.

The status of a certificate can be checked in two ways to see if it has been revoked. The first is to use a **Certificate Revocation List (CRL)**, which is a list of certificate serial numbers that have been revoked. Many CAs maintain an online CRL that can be queried by entering the certificate's serial number. In addition, a local computer receives updates on the status of certificates and maintains a local CRL, as illustrated in Figure 7-2.

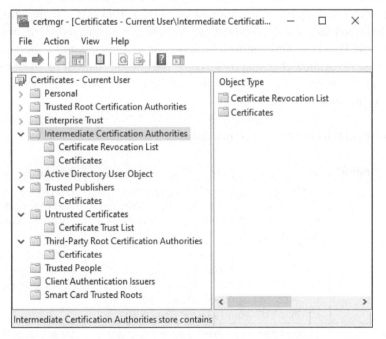

Figure 7-2 Certificate Revocation List (CRL)

The second method is **Online Certificate Status Protocol (OCSP)**, which performs a real-time lookup of a certificate's status. OCSP is called a request-response protocol. The browser sends the certificate's information to a trusted entity like the CA, known as an *OCSP Responder*. The OCSP Responder then provides revocation information on that one specific certificate.

A variation of OCSP is called OCSP *stapling*. OCSP requires the OCSP Responder to provide responses to every web client of a certificate in real time, which may create a high volume of traffic. With OCSP stapling, web servers send queries to the Responder OCSP server at regular intervals to receive a signed time-stamped OCSP response. When a client's web browser attempts to connect to the web server, the server can include (*staple*) in the handshake with the web browser the previously received OCSP response. The browser then can evaluate the OCSP response to determine if it is trustworthy. OCSP stapling is illustrated in Figure 7-3.

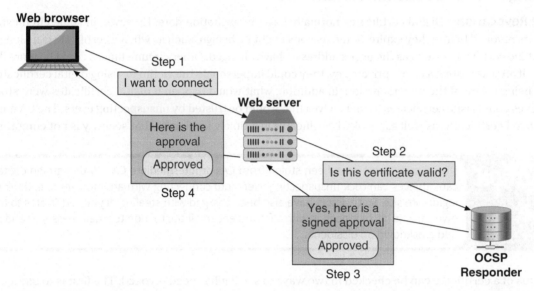

Figure 7-3   OCSP stapling

Determining the revocation status of certificates presented by websites is an ongoing problem in web security. Initially, modern web browsers (Chrome, Firefox, Internet Explorer, Safari, and Opera) used OCSP. However, if the web browser cannot reach the OCSP Responder server, such as when the server is down, then the browser receives a network error message (called a *soft fail*), and the revocation check is simply ignored. Also, online revocation checking by web browsers can be slow. For these reasons, web browsers have implemented a range of solutions to reduce or eliminate the need for online revocation checking by instead "harvesting" lists of revoked certificates from CAs and then pushing them to the user's browser. Table 7-2 lists the solutions used by selected web browsers for determining the revocation status of certificates.

Table 7-2   Web browser certificate revocation procedures

Browser	Procedure name	Description	Resources
Google Chrome	CRLSet	CRLSet is a list of revoked certificates determined by searching CRLs published by CAs that is pushed to the browser as a software update.	Users can view the CRLSet version and manually check for updates at chrome://components.
Mozilla Firefox	OneCRL	OneCRL is a list of intermediate certificates that have been revoked by CAs and then pushed to Firefox in application updates; the browser can also be configured to query OCSP responders.	Lists of OneCRL can be viewed as webpages at https://crt.sh/mozilla-onecrl.
Apple Safari	No name	Collects revoked certificates from CAs that are then periodically retrieved by Apple devices; when revoked certificate request occurs, Safari performs an OCSP check to confirm.	View blocked certificates at https://support.apple.com/en-us/HT209144#blocked.
Microsoft Edge	CRLSet	Windows OS checks for server certificate revocation and Edge relies on this listing.	Can be viewed through Windows OS.

Types of Digital Certificates

Digital certificates can be grouped into the broad categories of root certificates, domain certificates, and hardware and software certificates. In addition there are standardized certificate formats and attributes.

Root Digital Certificates

Suppose that Alice is making a purchase at an online ecommerce site and needs to enter her credit card number. How can she be certain that she is at the authentic website of the retailer and not an imposter's look-alike site that will steal her credit card number? The solution is a digital certificate. The online retailer's web server issues to Alice's web browser a digital certificate that has been signed by a trusted third-party. In this way, Alice can rest assured that she is at the authentic online retailer's site.

However, an estimated 24 million ecommerce sites are in operation.[2] In addition, consider the number of websites for banks, credit card companies, schools, and workplaces, to name a few of the other websites that need to provide protection to its customers and clients. How can each digital certificate be verified as being authentic and not expired or revoked, and how should they be organized?

NOTE 4

In 2016, the nonprofit Internet Security Research Group (ISRG) created *Let's Encrypt*, which is advertised as a free, automated, and open CA run for the public's benefit. Their goal is to provide free digital certificates to any website with the stated reason "because we want to create a more secure and privacy-respecting Web." Let's Encrypt issues up to one million digital certificates daily, and by early 2020, it had issued more than one billion digital certificates.

Grouping and verifying digital certificates relies on **certificate chaining**. Certificate chaining creates a path between the trusted root CAs (of which there are a few) and intermediate CAs (of which there are many) with the digital certificates that have been issued. Every certificate is signed by the entity that is identified by the next-higher certified entity in the chain. In this way, the trust of a certificate can be traced back to the highest level of CA.

The beginning point of the chain is a specific type of digital certificate known as a **root digital certificate**. A root digital certificate is created and verified by a CA. Because a CA has no higher-level authority, root digital certificates are **self-signed** and do not depend upon a higher-level authority for authentication. The next level down from the root digital certificate is one or more *intermediate certificates* that have been issued by intermediate CAs. The root digital certificate (verified by a CA) trusts the intermediate certificate (verified by an intermediate CA), which may in turn validate more lower-level intermediate CAs until it reaches the end of the chain. The endpoint of the chain is the **user digital certificate** itself. Certificate chaining is illustrated in Figure 7-4.

Figure 7-4   Certificate chaining

NOTE 5

How is the Queen of England like a root digital certificate? All British passports are issued in the name of Her Majesty. When the queen travels, she does not need her own passport because there is no higher authority to authorize one. In a similar fashion, a root digital certificate does not depend on any higher-level authority. However, all other members of the queen's royal family must still carry their own passport—even if they are traveling with her.

Approved root digital certificates and intermediate certificates are distributed in one of three ways. First, they can be distributed through updates to the OS. Second, they can be distributed through updates to the web browser. At one time, browsers relied on the underlying OS-approved list, but today they rely on their own browser updates. Web browser certificate chaining and root digital certificates can be seen in the browsers and are illustrated in Figure 7-5. A third option is **pinning**, in which a digital certificate is hard-coded (*pinned*) within the app (program) that is using the certificate. Pinning is common for securing mobile messaging apps and for certain web-based services and browsers.

NOTE 6

As of mid-2020, Microsoft Windows recognized 82 trusted root CAs while Apple recognized 115 for all of its OS versions and one "always ask" root CA, which is untrusted but not blocked.

Figure 7-5   Certificate chaining in web browser

Domain Digital Certificates

Most digital certificates are web server digital certificates that are issued from a web server to an endpoint. Web server digital certificates perform two primary functions: they ensure the authenticity of the web server to the client and the authenticity of the cryptographic connection to the web server. Web servers can set up secure cryptographic connections by providing the server's public key with a digital certificate to the client. The handshake setup between web browser and web server, also called a *key exchange,* is illustrated in Figure 7-6:

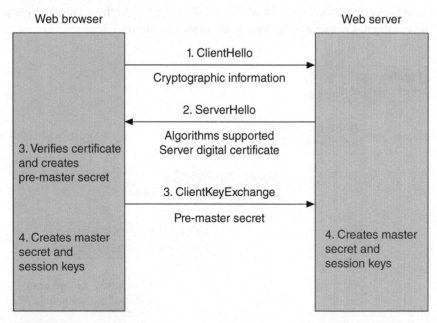

Figure 7-6   Key exchange

1. The web browser sends a message ("ClientHello") to the server that contains information including the list of cryptographic algorithms that the client supports.
2. The web server responds ("ServerHello") by indicating which cryptographic algorithm will be used. It then sends the server digital certificate to the browser.
3. The web browser verifies the server certificate (such as making sure it has not expired) and extracts the server's public key. The browser generates a random value (called the *pre-master secret*), encrypts it with the server's public key, and sends it back to the server ("ClientKeyExchange").
4. The server decrypts the message and obtains the browser's pre-master secret. Because both the browser and server now have the same pre-master secret, they can each create the same *master secret*. The master secret is used to create *session keys*, which are symmetric keys to encrypt and decrypt information exchanged during the session and to verify its integrity.

To address the security of web server digital certificates, there are several types of domain digital certificates. These include domain validation digital certificates, extended validation digital certificates, wildcard digital certificates, and subject alternative names digital certificates.

Domain Validation Some entry-level certificates provide domain-only validation to authenticate that only a specific organization has the right to use a particular domain name. A **domain validation digital certificate** verifies the identity of the entity that has control over the domain name. The certificates indicate nothing regarding the trustworthiness of the individuals behind the site; they simply verify who has control of that domain.

> **NOTE 7**
>
> Because domain validation digital certificates are not verifying the identity of a person but only the control over a site, they often can be generated automatically and are very inexpensive or even free.

Extended Validation (EV) An enhanced type of domain digital certificate is the **Extended Validation (EV) certificate**. This type of certificate requires more extensive verification of the legitimacy of the business. Requirements include the following:

- The intermediate CA must pass an independent audit verifying that it follows the EV standards.
- The existence and identity of the website owner, including its legal existence, physical address, and operational presence, must be verified by the intermediate CA.
- The intermediate CA must verify that the website is the registered holder and has exclusive control of the domain name.
- The authorization of the individual(s) applying for the certificate must be verified by the intermediate CA, and a valid signature from an officer of the company must accompany the application.

Wildcard A **wildcard digital certificate** is used to validate a main domain along with all subdomains. For example, a domain validation digital certificate for *www.example.com* would only cover that specific site. A wildcard digital certificate for **.example.com* would cover *www.example.com*, *mail.example.com*, *ftp.example.com*, and any other subdomains.

Subject Alternative Name (SAN) A **Subject Alternative Name (SAN)** digital certificate, also known as a *Unified Communications Certificate* (*UCC*), is primarily used for Microsoft Exchange servers or unified communications (the integration of different types of electronic communication such as email, SMS text messaging, and fax). The certificate allows multiple server or domain names to use the same secure certificate by associating different values with the certificate.

Hardware and Software Digital Certificates

In addition to root digital certificates and domain digital certificates, more specific digital certificates relate to hardware and software. These include the following:

- *Machine/computer digital certificate*. A **machine/computer digital certificate** is used to verify the identity of a device in a network transaction. For example, a printer may use a machine digital certificate to verify to the endpoint that it is an authentic and authorized device on the network.

> **NOTE 8**
>
> Many network devices can create their own self-signed machine digital certificates.

- *Code signing digital certificate.* Digital certificates are used by software developers to digitally sign a program to prove that the software comes from the entity that signed it and no unauthorized third party has altered or compromised it. This is known as a **code signing digital certificate.** When the installation program is launched that contains a code signing digital certificate, a pop-up window appears that says *Verified publisher,* as shown in Figure 7-7. An installation program that lacks a code digital certificate will display a window with the warning *Publisher:Unknown.*

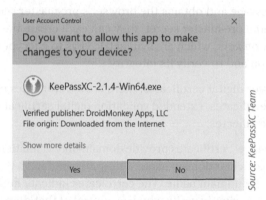

Figure 7-7   Verified publisher message

- *Email digital certificate.* An **email digital certificate** allows a user to digitally sign and encrypt mail messages. Typically, only the user's name and email address are required to receive the certificate.

NOTE 9

In addition to email messages, digital certificates also can be used to authenticate the authors of documents. For example, a user can create a Microsoft Word or Adobe Portable Document Format (PDF) document and then use a digital certificate to create a digital signature.

Digital Certificate Attributes and Formats

Hardware devices require that digital certificates contain specific attributes (fields) and are presented in a specific format. Doing so allows the device to read and process the digital certificate.

The standard format for digital certificates is *X.509.* The format was first introduced more than 20 years ago and was adapted for Internet use. The current version is Version 3. Digital certificates following this standard can be read or written by any hardware device or application that follows the X.509 format.

Several **certificate attributes** make up an X.509 digital certificate; these are used when parties negotiate a secure connection. Attributes that must be included are the certificate validity period, end-host identity information, encryption keys that will be used for secure communications, the signature of the issuing CA, and the **common name (CN).** CN is the name of the device protected by the digital certificate. The CN can reference a single device (*www.example.com*) or multiple devices with a wildcard certificate (**.example.com*) but is not the URL (*https://example.com*). Other optional attributes may also be included. Figure 7-8 illustrates several attributes in a digital certificate.

X.509 certificates can either be contained in a binary file with a **.cer** extension or in a *Base64* file, which is a binary-to-text encoding scheme that presents binary data in ASCII string format. X.509 certificates have three encoding formats (layouts): *Basic Encoding Rules (BER),* **Canonical Encoding Rules (CER),** and **Distinguished Encoding Rules (DER).** The X.509 certificates themselves can be contained within different file formats. Table 7-3 shows several of the formats.

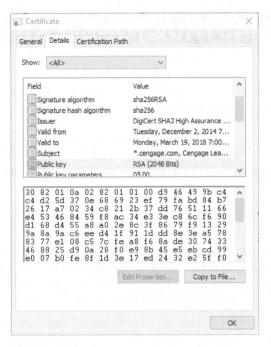

Figure 7-8   Digital certificate attributes

Table 7-3   X.509 file formats

Name	File extension	File type	Comments
Privacy Enhancement Mail (PEM)	.pem	Base64	Designed to provide confidentiality and integrity to emails, it uses DER encoding and can have multiple certificates.
Personal Information Exchange (PFX)	.pfx	Binary	The preferred file format for creating certificates to authenticate applications or websites, PFX is password protected because it contains both private and public keys.
PKCS#7	.P7B	Base64	Cryptographic Message Syntax Standard that defines a generic syntax for defining digital signature and encryption.
PKCS#12	.P12	Binary	Personal Information Exchange Syntax Standard defines the file format for storing and transporting a user's private keys with a public key certificate.

TWO RIGHTS & A WRONG

1. A digital certificate is a technology used to associate a user's identity to a public key and that has been digitally signed by the owner of the private key.
2. A certificate repository (CR) is a publicly accessible centralized directory of digital certificates that can be used to view the status of a digital certificate.
3. Root digital certificates are self-signed.

See Appendix B for the answer.

PUBLIC KEY INFRASTRUCTURE (PKI)

 **CERTIFICATION**

3.9 Given a scenario, implement public key infrastructure.

One of the important management tools for the use of digital certificates and asymmetric cryptography is public key infrastructure. You should understand public key infrastructure, know the PKI trust models, how PKI is managed, and the features of key management.

What Is Public Key Infrastructure (PKI)?

One single digital certificate between Alice and Bob involves multiple entities and technologies. Asymmetric cryptography must be used to create the public and private keys, a registration authority must verify the CSR, an intermediate CA must process the CSR, the digital certificate must be placed in a CR and moved to a CRL when it expires, and so on. In an organization where multiple users have digital certificates (and sometimes multiple digital certificates), it can quickly become overwhelming for someone to manage all of these entities. In short, organizations need a consistent means to manage digital certificates.

Public key infrastructure (PKI) is what you might expect from its name: it is the underlying infrastructure for **key management** of public keys and digital certificates. PKI is a framework for the administration of all the elements involved in digital certificates for digital certificate management—including hardware, software, people, policies, and procedures—to create, store, distribute, and revoke digital certificates. In short, PKI is digital certificate management.

Trust Models

Trust is defined as confidence in or reliance on another person or entity. One of the principal foundations of PKI is that of trust: Alice must trust that the public key in Bob's digital certificate belongs to him.

A **trust model** refers to the type of trust relationship that can exist between individuals or entities. In one type of trust model, *direct trust*, a relationship exists between two individuals because one person knows the other person. Because Alice knows Bob—she has seen him, she can recognize him in a crowd, she has spoken with him—she can trust that the digital certificate that Bob personally gives her contains his public key. A *third-party trust* refers to a situation in which two individuals trust each other because each trusts a common third party. An example of a third-party trust is a courtroom. Although the defendant and prosecutor may not trust one another, they both can trust the judge (a third party) as fair and impartial. In that case, they implicitly trust each other because they share a common relationship with the judge. In terms of PKI, if Alice does not know Bob, it does not mean that she can never trust his digital certificate. Instead, if she trusts a third-party entity who knows Bob, then she can trust that the digital certificate with the public key is Bob's.

A less secure trust model that uses no third party is called the *web of trust* model and is based on direct trust. Each user signs a digital certificate and then exchanges certificates with all other users. Because all users trust each other, each user can sign the certificate of all other users.

Three PKI trust models use a CA: the hierarchical trust model, the distributed trust model, and the bridge trust model.

Hierarchical Trust Model

The *hierarchical trust model* assigns a single hierarchy with one master CA called the *root*. The root signs all digital certificate authorities with a single key. A hierarchical trust model is illustrated in Figure 7-9.

A hierarchical trust model can be used in an organization where one CA is responsible for only the digital certificates for that organization. However, on a larger scale, a hierarchical trust model has several limitations. First, if the CA's single private key were compromised, then all digital certificates would be worthless. Also, having a single CA who must verify and sign all digital certificates may create a significant backlog.

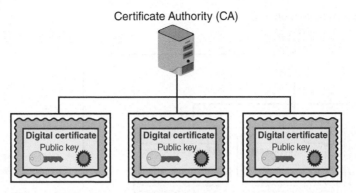

Figure 7-9 Hierarchical trust model

Distributed Trust Model

Instead of having a single CA, as in the hierarchical trust model, the *distributed trust model* has multiple CAs that sign digital certificates. This essentially eliminates the limitations of a hierarchical trust model. The loss of a CA's private key would compromise only those digital certificates it had signed, and the workload of verifying and signing digital certificates can be distributed. In addition, CAs can delegate authority to other intermediate CAs to sign digital certificates. The distributed trust model is the basis for most digital certificates used on the Internet. A distributed trust model is illustrated in Figure 7-10.

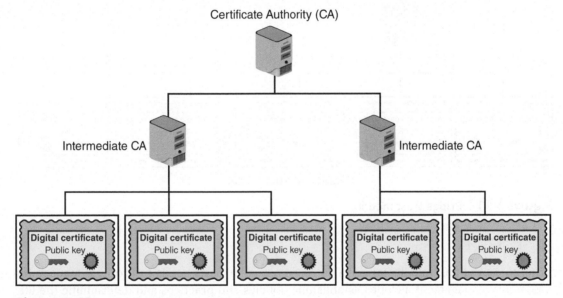

Figure 7-10 Distributed trust model

Bridge Trust Model

The *bridge trust model* is similar to the distributed trust model in that no single CA signs digital certificates. However, with the bridge trust model, one CA acts as a *facilitator* to interconnect all other CAs. The facilitator CA does not issue digital certificates; instead, it acts as the hub between hierarchical trust models and distributed trust models, linking the models together. The bridge trust model is shown in Figure 7-11.

NOTE 10

One application of the bridge trust model involves linking federal and state governments. The U.S. Department of Defense (DOD) has issued millions of identification cards known as Common Access Cards (CACs) to military personnel; these cards are based on the Personal Identity Verification (PIV) standard and are linked to a digital certificate. Some states have begun issuing IDs compatible with the CACs to emergency service personnel, and one state has cross-certified with the federal PKI through a trust bridge for authenticating digital certificates.

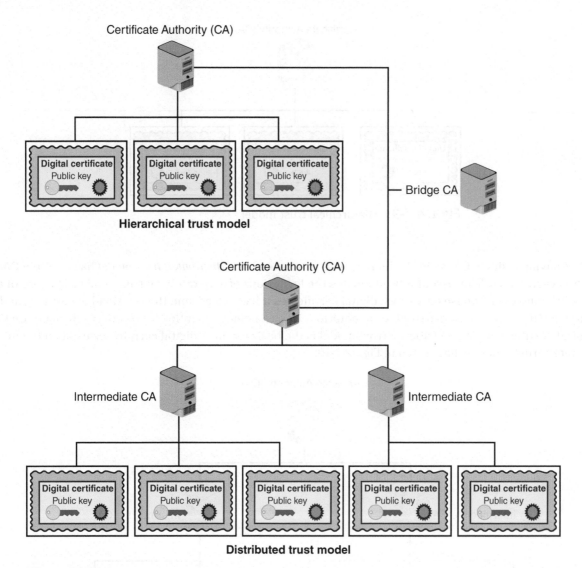

Figure 7-11   Bridge trust model

Managing PKI

An organization that uses multiple digital certificates on a regular basis needs to properly manage those digital certificates. Effective management includes establishing policies and practices and determining the life cycle of a digital certificate.

Certificate Policy (CP)

A *certificate policy* (*CP*) is a published set of rules that govern the operation of a PKI. The CP provides recommended baseline security requirements for the use and operation of CA, intermediate CA, and other PKI components. A CP should cover such topics as CA or intermediate CA obligations, user obligations, confidentiality, operational requirements, and training.

Certificate Practice Statement (CPS)

A *certificate practice statement* (*CPS*) is a more technical document than a CP. A CPS describes in detail how the CA uses and manages certificates. Additional topics for a CPS include how users register for a digital certificate, how to issue digital certificates, when to revoke digital certificates, procedural controls, key pair generation and installation, and private key protection.

X.509 certificates contain a specific field that can link to the associated CP. In addition, extensions may be added to X.509 certificates that indicate how the certificate should be used. One such field, the *Extended Key Usage* field, can contain an *object identifier (OID)*, which names an object or entity. OIDs are made up of a series of numbers separated with a dot, such as *1.2.840.113585*, and correspond to a node in a hierarchy tree structure. OIDs can name every object type in an X.509 certificate, including the CPS. A large standardized set of OIDs exists, or an enterprise can have a root OID assigned to it and then create its own sub-OIDs, much like creating subdomains beneath a domain.

Certificate Life Cycle

Digital certificates do not last forever: employees leave, new hardware is installed, applications are updated, and cryptographic standards evolve. Each change affects the usefulness of a digital certificate. The life cycle of a certificate is typically divided into four parts:

1. *Creation.* At this stage, the certificate is created and issued to the user. Before the digital certificate is generated, the user must be positively identified. The extent to which the user's identification must be confirmed can vary, depending upon the type of certificate and any existing security policies. Once the user's identification has been verified, the request is sent to the CA for a digital certificate. The CA can then apply its appropriate signing key to the certificate, effectively signing the public key. The relevant fields can be updated by the CA, and the certificate is then forwarded to the registration authority. The CA also can keep a local copy of the certificate it generated. A certificate, once issued, can be published to a public directory if necessary.

2. *Suspension.* This stage could occur once or multiple times throughout the life of a digital certificate if the certificate's validity must be temporarily suspended. Suspension may occur, for example, when employees are on a leave of absence and their digital certificates may not be used for any reason until they return. Upon a user's return, the suspension can be withdrawn or the certificate can be revoked.

3. *Revocation.* At this stage, the certificate is no longer valid. Under certain situations, a certificate may be revoked before its normal expiration date, such as when a user's private key is lost or compromised. When a digital certificate is revoked, the CA updates its internal records, and any CRL with the required certificate information and time stamp (a revoked certificate is identified in a CRL by its certificate serial number). The CA signs the CRL and places it in a public repository so that other applications using certificates can access the repository to determine the status of a certificate.

4. *Expiration.* At the expiration stage, the certificate can no longer be used. Every certificate issued by a CA must have an expiration date. Once it has expired, the certificate may not be used for any type of authentication. The user will be required to follow a process to receive a new certificate with a new expiration date.

Key Management

One common vulnerability that allows threat actors to compromise a PKI is improper certificate and key management. Because keys form the foundation of PKI systems, they must be carefully managed. Proper key management includes key storage, key usage, and key handling procedures.

Key Storage

The means of storing keys in a PKI system is important. Public keys can be stored by embedding them within digital certificates, while private keys can be stored on the user's local system. The drawback to software-based storage is that it can leave keys open to attacks: vulnerabilities in the client operating system, for example, can expose keys to attackers.

Storing keys in hardware is an alternative to software-based storage. For storing public keys, special CA root and intermediate CA hardware devices can be used. Private keys can be stored on smart cards or in tokens.

 **CAUTION**   Whether private keys are stored in hardware or software, they must be adequately protected. To ensure basic protection, never share the key in plaintext, always store keys in files or folders that are themselves password protected or encrypted, do not make copies of keys, and destroy expired keys.

Key Usage

If more security is needed than a single set of public and private keys, multiple pairs of dual keys can be created. One pair of keys may be used to encrypt information, and the public key can be backed up to another location. The second pair would be used only for digital signatures, and the public key in that pair would never be backed up.

Key Handling Procedures

Certain procedures can help ensure that keys are properly handled, including the following:

- *Escrow.* **Key escrow** refers to a process in which keys are managed by a third party, such as a trusted CA. In key escrow, the private key is split, and each half is encrypted. The two halves are registered and sent to the third party, which stores each half in a separate location. A user can then retrieve the two halves, combine them, and use the new copy of the private key for decryption. Key escrow relieves users from worrying about losing their private keys. The drawback to this system is that after a user has retrieved the two halves of the key and combined them to create a copy of the key, that copy of the key can be vulnerable to attacks.
- *Expiration.* Keys have an **expiration** date after which they cease to function. This prevents an attacker, who may have stolen a private key, from being able to decrypt messages for an indefinite period. Some systems set keys to expire after a set period by default.
- *Renewal.* Instead of letting a key expire and then creating a new key, an existing key can be renewed. With renewal, the original public and private keys can continue to be used and new keys do not have to be generated. However, continually renewing keys makes them more vulnerable to theft or misuse.
- *Revocation.* Whereas all keys should expire after a set period, a key may need to be revoked prior to its expiration date. For example, the need for revoking a key may be the result of an employee being terminated from his position. Revoked keys cannot be reinstated. The CA should be immediately notified when a key is revoked, and then the status of that key should be entered on the CRL.
- *Recovery.* What happens if employees are hospitalized, and their organization needs to transact business using their keys? Some CA systems have an embedded key recovery system that designates a *key recovery agent (KRA)*, a highly trusted person responsible for recovering lost or damaged digital certificates. Digital certificates can then be archived along with a user's private key. If the user is unavailable or if the certificate is lost, the certificate with the private key can be recovered. Another technique is known as *M-of-N control.* A user's private key is encrypted and divided into a specific number of parts, such as three. The parts are distributed to other individuals with an overlap, so multiple individuals have the same part. For example, the three parts could be distributed to six people, with two people each having the same part. This is known as the N group. If it is necessary to recover the key, a smaller subset of the N group, known as the M group, must meet and agree that the key should be recovered. If a majority of the M group can agree, they can then piece the key together. M-of-N control is illustrated in Figure 7-12.

NOTE 11

The reason for distributing parts of the key to multiple users is that the absence of one member would not prevent the key from being recovered.

- *Suspension.* The revocation of a key is permanent; key suspension is for a set period. For example, if employees are on an extended medical leave, it may be necessary to suspend the use of their keys for security reasons. A suspended key can be later reinstated. As with revocation, the CA should be immediately notified when a key is suspended, and the status of that key should be checked on the CRL to verify that it is no longer valid.
- *Destruction.* Key destruction removes all private and public keys along with the user's identification information in the CA. When a key is revoked or expires, the user's information remains on the CA for audit purposes.

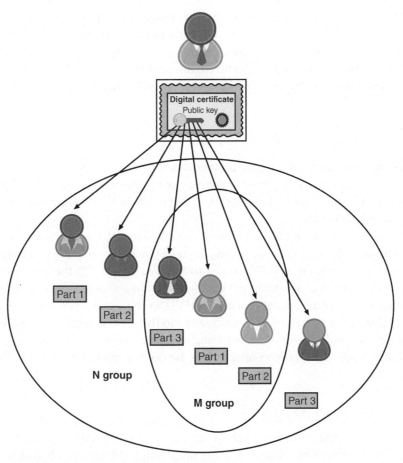

Figure 7-12   M-of-N control

TWO RIGHTS & A WRONG

1. The hierarchical trust model assigns a single hierarchy with one master CA called the root.
2. An OID, which names an object or entity, corresponds to a node in a hierarchy tree structure. OIDs can name every object type in an X.509 certificate.
3. When a digital certificate is revoked, the user must update internal records and any CRL with the required certificate information and timestamp.

See Appendix B for the answer.

CRYPTOGRAPHIC PROTOCOLS

 **CERTIFICATION**

1.3 Given a scenario, analyze potential indicators associated with application attacks.

2.1 Explain the importance of security concepts in an enterprise environment.

2.8 Summarize the basics of cryptographic concepts.

3.1 Given a scenario, implement secure protocols.

In addition to protecting data in processing and at rest, cryptographic algorithms are most often used to protect data in transit or motion across a network. When cryptographic algorithms are used in networks, they are sometimes called *cryptographic protocols*. The most common cryptographic protocols include Secure Sockets Layer, Transport Layer Security, Secure Shell, Hypertext Transport Protocol Secure, Secure/Multipurpose Internet Mail Extensions, Secure Real-time Transport Protocol, and IP security. In addition, cryptographic protocols have weaknesses.

Secure Sockets Layer (SSL)

One of the early and most widespread cryptographic protocols is Secure Sockets Layer (SSL). The protocol was developed by Netscape in 1994 in response to the growing concern over Internet security. The design goal of SSL was to create an encrypted data path between a client and a server that could be used on any platform or operating system. The current version of SSL is Version 3.0.

However, the way SSL functions has left it vulnerable to attack. When the user arrives on a secure webpage via a link from a non-secure site, the following sequence of events take place between a user's browser and a web server: (1) the user's browser sends an unsecured HTTP request to the web server; (2) the server responds via HTTP and redirects the browser (via a *301 redirect* or a temporary *302 redirect*) to a secure page instructing it to use the secure protocol HTTPS; (3) the user's browser then sends a secure HTTPS request, and the secure session begins.

A threat actor can intercept the new request from the user to the server. Attackers can then establish an HTTPS connection between themselves and the server while having an unsecured HTTP connection with the user, giving the threat actors complete control over the secure webpage while the user's responses are sent to the attacker in plaintext. This practice is called SSL stripping.

Transport Layer Security (TLS)

Transport Layer Security (TLS) is a widespread cryptographic protocol that is the replacement for SSL. Although the algorithms SSL and TLS use are sometimes listed as being interchangeable or even linked to each other (*TLS/SSL*), they are not. Although TLS v1.0 was considered marginally more secure than SSL v3.0, subsequent versions of TLS are significantly more secure and address several vulnerabilities in SSL v3.0. The current version of TLS is v1.3.

NOTE 12

TLS v1.3 was a significant upgrade over TLS v1.2. It removes support for MD5 and SHA-224, requires use of Perfect Forward Secrecy in case of public-key-based key exchange, and encrypts handshake messages after the *ServerHello* exchange.

A cipher suite is a named combination of the encryption, authentication, and message authentication code (MAC) algorithms that are used with TLS and SSL. They are negotiated between the web browser and web server during the initial connection handshake. Cipher suites typically use descriptive names to indicate their components. For example, *TLS_ECDHE_ECDSA_WITH_AES_128_GCM_SHA256* specifies that TLS is the protocol, during the handshake keys will be exchanged via the ephemeral Elliptic Curve Diffie Hellman (ECDHE), AES running the Galois Counter Mode with 128-bit key size is the encryption algorithm, and SHA-256 is the hashing algorithm.

Secure Shell (SSH)

Secure Shell (SSH) is an encrypted alternative to the Telnet protocol used to access remote computers. SSH is a Linux/UNIX-based command interface and protocol for securely accessing a remote computer. SSH is actually a suite of the three utilities *slogin* (secure login to a remote computer), *ssh* (execute commands on a remote host without logging in), and *scp* (copy files between remote computers) that are secure versions of the unsecure UNIX counterpart utilities. Both the client and server ends of the connection are authenticated using a digital certificate, and passwords are protected by being encrypted. SSH can even be used as a tool for secure network backups.

Hypertext Transport Protocol Secure (HTTPS)

One common use of TLS and the older SSL is to secure Hypertext Transport Protocol (HTTP) communications between a browser and a web server. The secure version is "plain" HTTP sent over TLS or SSL and is called **Hypertext Transport Protocol Secure (HTTPS)**. HTTPS uses port 443 instead of HTTP's port 80 and users must enter URLs with *https://* instead of *http://*.

NOTE 13

Another cryptographic protocol for HTTP was Secure Hypertext Transport Protocol (SHTTP). However, it was not as secure as HTTPS and is now obsolete.

At one time, web browsers prominently displayed a visual indicator to alert users that the connection between the browser and the web server was using HTTPS. As shown in Figure 7-13, most browsers displayed a green padlock to indicate the connection was encrypted and secure.

Source: Google Chrome web browser

Figure 7-13   Domain validation padlock

However, as more websites transitioned to HTTPS, some web browsers changed from displaying an indicator that the connection *was* secure to only a warning that the connection was *not* secure. In 2018, Google Chrome started displaying a warning if the connection was not secure, as seen in Figure 7-14. Chrome and other browsers, such as Microsoft Edge, still display a padlock, though it is gray, not green.

Source: Google Chrome web browser

Figure 7-14   Google Chrome HTTP warning

NOTE 14

The change away from the green padlock works on the same principle as the lights on a car dashboard. Lights warn drivers of low tire air pressure, low oil pressure, and low gasoline, among other conditions. The lights are designed to turn on only when the vehicle detects a problem, such as the tire air pressure falling below a certain point. The approach of keeping the lights off when "all is OK" and turning on the warning light only when something demands attention is the principle behind migrating away from web browser indicators when a site does not pose a problem.

Secure/Multipurpose Internet Mail Extensions (S/MIME)

Secure/Multipurpose Internet Mail Extensions (S/MIME) is a protocol for securing email messages. MIME is a standard for how an electronic message will be organized, so S/MIME describes how encryption information and a digital certificate can be included as part of the message body. It allows users to send encrypted messages that are also digitally signed.

Secure Real-time Transport Protocol (SRTP)

The **Secure Real-time Transport Protocol (SRTP)** has several similarities to S/MIME. Just as S/MIME is intended to protect MIME communications, SRTP is a secure extension protecting transmissions using the *Real-time Transport Protocol (RTP)*. Also, as S/MIME is designed to protect only email communications, SRTP provides protection for Voice over IP (VoIP) communications. SRTP adds security features, such as message authentication and confidentiality, for VoIP communications.

IP Security (IPsec)

Internet Protocol Security (IPsec) is a protocol suite for securing Internet Protocol (IP) communications. IPsec encrypts and authenticates each IP packet of a session between hosts or networks. IPsec can provide protection to a much wider range of applications than TLS or the older SSL.

IPsec is considered a *transparent* security protocol. It is transparent to the following entities:

- *Applications.* Programs do not have to be modified to run under IPsec.
- *Users.* Unlike some security tools, users do not need to be trained on specific security procedures (such as encrypting with PGP).
- *Software.* Because IPsec is implemented in a device such as a firewall or router, no software changes must be made on the local client.

Unlike TLS, which is implemented as a part of the user application, IPsec is in the operating system or the communication hardware. IPsec is more likely to operate at a faster speed because it can cooperate closely with other system programs and the hardware.

IPsec provides three areas of protection that correspond to three IPsec protocols:

- *Authentication.* IPsec authenticates that packets received were sent from the source. The authentication is identified in the header of the packet to ensure that no specific attacks took place to alter the contents of the packet. This is accomplished by the **Authentication Header (AH)** protocol.
- *Confidentiality.* By encrypting the packets, IPsec ensures that no other parties could view the contents. Confidentiality is achieved through the **Encapsulating Security Payload (ESP)** protocol. ESP supports authentication of the sender and encryption of data.
- *Key management.* IPsec manages the keys to ensure that they are not intercepted or used by unauthorized parties. For IPsec to work, the sending and receiving devices must share a key. This is accomplished through a protocol known as *Internet Security Association and Key Management Protocol/Oakley* (*ISAKMP/Oakley*), which generates the key and authenticates the user using techniques such as digital certificates.

IPsec supports two encryption modes: transport and tunnel. **Transport mode** encrypts only the data portion (payload) of each packet yet leaves the header unencrypted. The more secure **tunnel mode** encrypts both the header and the data portion. IPsec accomplishes transport and tunnel modes by adding new headers to the IP packet. The entire original packet (header and payload) is then treated as the data portion of the new packet.

> **NOTE 15**
>
> Because tunnel mode protects the entire packet, it is generally used in a network-to-network communication, while transport mode is used when a device must see the source and destination addresses to route the packet.

Weaknesses of Cryptographic Protocols

At first glance, it seems cryptographic protocols should have few, if any, weaknesses since they are built upon well-known algorithms. Any security issues with cryptographic protocols would also be equal to those issues within the cryptographic algorithms.

However, that is not the case for the following reasons:

- Due to the inherent complexity of networking, cryptographic protocols are notoriously difficult to design.
- While the mathematics and related security of basic cryptographic algorithms have been extensively studied and are well understood, the same cannot always be said of cryptographic protocols. The critical analysis of these protocols has often not reached the same levels of the cryptographic algorithms. Thus, cryptographic protocol errors and implementation errors in cryptographic protocols that have been in use for decades, are still being uncovered.
- Several older cryptographic protocols still in use today were designed by networking experts and not by cryptographic protocol experts. As a result, cryptographic protocols suffer more from legacy issues than underlying cryptographic algorithm weaknesses.
- The associated security proofs to guarantee the correctness of cryptographic protocols are much more complicated than those for cryptographic algorithms.

TWO RIGHTS & A WRONG

1. SSL is a replacement cryptographic protocol for TLS.
2. A cipher suite is a named combination of the encryption, authentication, and message authentication code (MAC) algorithms that are used with TLS.
3. S/MIME is a protocol for securing email messages.

See Appendix B for the answer.

IMPLEMENTING CRYPTOGRAPHY

 **CERTIFICATION**

2.8 Summarize the basics of cryptographic concepts.

Cryptography that is improperly applied can lead to vulnerabilities that threat actors will exploit. Thus, you should understand the options that relate to cryptography so that it can be implemented correctly. Implementing cryptography includes understanding key strength, secret algorithms, block cipher modes of operation, and cryptographic service providers.

Key Strength

A cryptographic key is a value that serves as input to an algorithm, which then transforms plaintext into ciphertext (and vice versa for decryption). A key, which is essentially a random string of bits, serves as an input parameter for hash, symmetric encryption, and asymmetric cryptographic algorithms.

> **(!) CAUTION**   A key is different from a password. Passwords are designed to have people create and remember them so that the passwords can be reproduced when necessary. A key is used by hardware or software that is running the cryptographic algorithm; as such, human readability is not required.

Three primary characteristics determine the resiliency of the key to attacks (called *key strength*). The first is its randomness. A key is considered strong when it is random with no predictable pattern. A random key thwarts an attacker from attempting to uncover the key.

A second characteristic that determines key strength is its *cryptoperiod*, or the length of time for which a key is authorized for use. Having a limited cryptoperiod helps protect the ciphertext from extended cryptanalysis and limits the exposure time if a key is compromised.

NOTE 16

Different cryptoperiods are recommended for different types of keys.

The final characteristic is the length of the key. Shorter keys can be more easily broken than longer keys. All the possible values for a specific key make up its *key space*. The formula for determining a given key space for symmetric algorithms is *character-set*$^{key\text{-}length}$. For example, suppose a key has a length of 3 and is using a 26-character alphabet. The list of possible keys (*aaa, aab, aac,* etc.) would be 26^3 or 17,576 possible outcomes. Thus, the key length in this example is *3* and the key space is *17,576*.

On average, half the key space must be searched to discover the key. In the example, a key with a length of only 3 that has a key space of 17,576 requires searching only 8,788 keys (on average) until the correct key is discovered. The number of searches is low, creating a risk that threat actors will compromise the key.

However, if the key length of 3 was increased by just one character to 4, the key space increases to *456,976* requiring on average *228,488* attempts. Table 7-4 illustrates the key strength for varying key lengths, the key space, and average attempts necessary to break the key for a 26-character alphabet.

Table 7-4   Key strength

Key length	Key space	Average number of attempts needed to break
3	17,576	8,788
4	456,976	228,488
5	11,881,376	5,940,688
6	308,915,776	154,457,888
7	8,031,810,176	4,015,905,088
8	208,827,064,576	104,413,532,288

Secret Algorithms

Keys must be kept secret (except for public keys). Does the same apply to algorithms? That is, should an enterprise invest in hiring a cryptographer to create a new cryptographic algorithm and then hide the existence of that algorithm from everyone? Wouldn't such a secret algorithm enhance security in the same way as keeping a key or password secret?

The answer is no. In the past, cryptographers have often attempted to keep their algorithms or the workings of devices that encrypted and decrypted documents a secret. However, the approach has always failed. One reason is that cryptography is the most useful when it is widespread: a military force that uses cryptography must by nature allow many users to know of its existence to use it. The more users who know about it, the more difficult it is to keep it a secret. In contrast, a password only requires one person—the user—to keep it confidential.

NOTE 17

In 1883, Auguste Kerckhoffs, a Dutch linguist and cryptographer, published what is known as *Kerckhoffs's principle*, a set of six design principles for military ciphers. One principle stated that systems should not require secrecy so that it should not be a problem if it falls into enemy hands. This principle is still applied today by splitting algorithms from keys: algorithms are public while keys are private.

Block Cipher Modes of Operation

One variation in cryptographic algorithms is the amount of data that is processed at a time. Some algorithms use a *stream cipher*, while other algorithms make use of a *block cipher*. Whereas a stream cipher works on one character at a time, a block cipher manipulates an entire block of plaintext at one time. Because the size of the plaintext is usually larger than the block size itself, the plaintext is divided into separate blocks of specific lengths, and then each block is encrypted independently.

NOTE 18

Stream and block ciphers are covered in Module 6.

A **block cipher mode of operation** specifies how block ciphers should handle the blocks. It uses a symmetric key block cipher algorithm to provide an information service. The service could be **authentication mode of operation** that provides a credentialing service or **unauthentication mode of operation** that provides a service such as confidentiality. The following are some of the most common modes:

- *Electronic Code Book (ECB).* The *Electronic Code Book (ECB)* mode is the most basic approach: the plaintext is divided into blocks, and each block is then encrypted separately. However, this can result in two identical plaintext blocks being encrypted into two identical ciphertext blocks. Attackers can use the repetition to their advantage. They could modify the encrypted message by modifying a block or even reshuffling the order of the blocks of ciphertext. ECB is not considered suitable for use.

NOTE 19

Using ECB is like assigning code words from a codebook to create an encrypted message and was the basis for naming the process Electronic Code Book.

- *Cipher Block Chaining (CBC).* *Cipher Block Chaining (CBC)* is a common cipher mode. After being encrypted, each ciphertext block gets "fed back" into the encryption process to encrypt the next plaintext block. Using CBC, each block of plaintext is XORed with the previous block of ciphertext before being encrypted. Unlike ECB, in which the ciphertext depends only upon the plaintext and the key, CBC is also dependent on the previous ciphertext block, making it much more difficult to break.

NOTE 20

XOR ciphers are covered in Module 6.

- *Counter (CTR).* **Counter (CTR)** mode requires that both the message sender and receiver access a counter, which computes a new value each time a ciphertext block is exchanged. The weakness of CTR is that it requires a synchronous counter for both the sender and receiver.
- *Galois/Counter (GCM).* The *Galois/Counter (GCM)* mode both encrypts plaintext and computes a message authentication code (MAC) to ensure that the message was created by the sender and that it was not tampered with during transmission. Like CTR, GCM uses a counter. It adds a plaintext string called *additional authentication data (AAD)* to the transmission. The AAD may contain the addresses and parameters of a network protocol that is being used.

NOTE 21

Block cipher modes can specialize in encryption, data integrity, privacy and integrity, and hard drive encryption. Some specialized modes can even gracefully recover from errors in transmission, while other modes are designed to stop upon encountering transmission errors.

Crypto Service Providers

A *crypto service provider* allows an application to implement an encryption algorithm for execution. Typically, crypto service providers implement cryptographic algorithms, generate keys, provide key storage, and authenticate users by calling various crypto modules to perform the specific tasks. Crypto service providers can be implemented in software, hardware, or both and are often part of the operating system. OSs have cryptographic services enabled and providers may also be created and distributed by third parties, allowing for a broader algorithm selection.

NOTE 22

Applications cannot manipulate the keys created by crypto service providers or alter the cryptographic algorithm itself.

TWO RIGHTS & A WRONG

1. Three primary characteristics determine the resiliency of the key to attacks (called key strength).
2. Counter (CTR) mode requires that both the message sender and receiver access a counter, which computes a new value each time a ciphertext block is exchanged.
3. A block cipher mode of operation specifies how block ciphers should handle streams.

See Appendix B for the answer.

⬈ VM LAB   You're now ready to complete the live, virtual machine labs for this module. The labs can be found in each module in the MindTap.

SUMMARY

- A digital certificate is the user's public key that has been digitally signed by a trusted third party who verifies the owner and that the public key belongs to that owner. It also binds the public key to the certificate. A user who wants a digital certificate must generate the public and private keys to use and then complete a request known as a Certificate Signing Request (CSR). The user electronically signs the CSR by affixing the public key and then sending it to a registration authority, who verifies the authenticity of the user. The CSR is then sent to an intermediate certificate authority (CA), who processes the CSR. The intermediate CAs perform functions on behalf of a certificate authority (CA) that is responsible for digital certificates. A common method to ensure the security and integrity of a root CA is to keep it in an offline state from the network (offline CA) rather than having it directly connected to a network (online CA).

- A Certificate Repository (CR) is a list of approved digital certificates. Revoked digital certificates are listed in a Certificate Revocation List (CRL), which can be accessed to check the certificate status of other users. The status also can be checked through the Online Certificate Status Protocol (OCSP). When using OCSP stapling, web servers send queries to the Responder OCSP server at regular intervals to receive a signed time-stamped OCSP response. Because digital certificates are used extensively on the Internet, all modern web browsers are configured with a default list of CAs and the ability to automatically update certificate information.

- The process of verifying that a digital certificate is genuine depends upon certificate chaining, or linking several certificates together to establish trust between all the certificates involved. The beginning point of the chain is a specific type of digital certificate known as a root digital certificate, which is created and verified by a CA and also self-signed. Between the root digital certificate and the user certificate can be one or more intermediate certificates that have been issued by intermediate CAs. Root digital certificates and intermediate certificates can be packaged as part of modern OSs, part of web browser software, or hard coded within the app (program) that is using the certificate. The endpoint of the chain is the user digital certificate itself.

- Domain validation digital certificates verify the identity of the entity that has control over the domain name but indicate nothing regarding the trustworthiness of the individuals behind the site. Extended Validation (EV) certificates require more extensive verification of the legitimacy of the business. A wildcard digital certificate is used to validate a main domain along with all subdomains. A Subject Alternative Name (SAN) digital certificate, also known as a Unified Communications Certificate (UCC), is primarily used for Microsoft Exchange servers or unified communications. A machine/computer digital certificate is used to verify the identity of a device in a network transaction. Code signing digital certificates are used by software developers to digitally sign a program and prove that the software comes from the entity that signed it and no unauthorized third party has altered or compromised it. The most widely accepted format for digital certificates is the X.509 standard. Several certificate attributes make up an X.509 digital certificate.

- A public key infrastructure (PKI) is the underlying infrastructure for key management of public keys and digital certificates. It is a framework for all the entities involved in digital certificates—including hardware, software, people, policies, and procedures—to create, store, distribute, and revoke digital certificates. One of the principal foundations of PKI is that of trust. Three basic PKI trust models use a CA. The hierarchical trust model assigns a single hierarchy with one master CA called the root, who signs all digital certificate authorities with a single key. The bridge trust model is similar to the distributed trust model. No single CA signs digital certificates, and yet the CA acts as a facilitator to interconnect all other CAs. The distributed trust model has multiple CAs that sign digital certificates.

- An organization that uses multiple digital certificates on a regular basis needs to properly manage those digital certificates. Such management includes establishing policies and practices and determining the life cycle of a digital certificate. Because keys form the very foundation of PKI systems, they must be carefully stored and handled.

- Cryptography is commonly used to protect data in transit/motion. When cryptographic algorithms are used in networks, they are sometimes called cryptographic protocols. Secure Sockets Layer (SSL) was an early cryptographic transport protocol but was replaced with the more secure Transport Layer Security (TLS). Secure Shell (SSH) is a Linux/UNIX-based command interface and protocol for securely accessing a remote computer communicating over the Internet. Hypertext Transport Protocol Secure (HTTPS), a secure version for web communications, is HTTP sent over TLS or SSL. Secure/Multipurpose Internet Mail Extensions (S/MIME) is a protocol for securing email messages. The Secure Real-time Transport Protocol (SRTP) provides protection for Voice over IP (VoIP) communications. IP security (IPsec) is a set of protocols developed to support the secure exchange of packets. Security weaknesses are associated with cryptographic protocols.

- Cryptography that is improperly applied can lead to vulnerabilities that will be exploited; thus, it is necessary to understand the options that relate to cryptography so that it can be implemented correctly. A key must be strong to resist attacks. A strong key must be random with no predictable pattern. Keys should also be long, and the length of time for which a key is authorized for use should be limited. Any attempt to keep an algorithm secret will not result in strong security. A block cipher mode of operation specifies how block ciphers should handle blocks of plaintext. A crypto service provider allows an application to implement an encryption algorithm for execution.

Key Terms

.cer
.P12
.P7B
Authentication Header (AH)
authentication mode of operation
block cipher mode of operation
Canonical Encoding Rules (CER)
certificate attributes
certificate authority (CA)
certificate chaining
Certificate Revocation List (CRL)
Certificate Signing Request (CSR)
cipher suite
code signing digital certificate
common name (CN)
counter (CTR)
digital certificate
Distinguished Encoding Rules (DER)
domain validation digital
  certificate
email digital certificate

Encapsulating Security
  Payload (ESP)
expiration
Extended Validation (EV) certificate
Hypertext Transport Protocol
  Secure (HTTPS)
intermediate certificate
  authority (CA)
Internet Protocol Security (IPsec)
key escrow
key management
machine/computer digital
  certificate
offline CA
online CA
Online Certificate Status
  Protocol (OCSP)
Personal Information
  Exchange (PFX)
pinning
Privacy Enhancement Mail (PEM)

public key infrastructure (PKI)
registration authority
root digital certificate
Secure Real-time Transport
  Protocol (SRTP)
Secure Shell (SSH)
Secure Sockets Layer (SSL)
Secure/Multipurpose Internet Mail
  Extensions (S/MIME)
self-signed
SSL stripping
stapling
Subject Alternative Name (SAN)
Transport Layer Security (TLS)
Transport mode
trust model
tunnel mode
unauthentication mode of
  operation
user digital certificate
wildcard digital certificate

Review Questions

1. Which is an IPsec protocol that authenticates that packets received were sent from the source?
   a. PXP
   b. DER
   c. CER
   d. AH

2. What is the name of the fields in an X.509 digital certificate that are used when the parties negotiate a secure connection?
   a. Electronic Code Book (ECB) repositories
   b. Certificate attributes
   c. CTR
   d. PFX

3. What entity calls in crypto modules to perform cryptographic tasks?
   a. Certificate Authority (CA)
   b. Crypto service provider
   c. Intermediate CA
   d. OCSP

4. _____ are symmetric keys to encrypt and decrypt information exchanged during the session and to verify its integrity.
   a. Digital digests
   b. Encrypted signatures
   c. Session keys
   d. Digital certificates

5. What is the name of the device protected by a digital certificate?
   a. CN
   b. TLXS
   c. RCR
   d. V2X2

6. What is the strongest technology that would assure Alice that Bob is the sender of a message?
   a. Digital signature
   b. Encrypted signature
   c. Digest
   d. Digital certificate

7. Olivia is explaining to a friend about digital certificates. Her friend asks what two entities a digital certificate associates or binds together. What would Olivia say?
   a. The users' symmetric key with the public key
   b. The users' public key with their private key
   c. The users' identity with their public key
   d. A private key with a digital signature

8. Which of the following can a digital certificate NOT be used for?
   a. To encrypt messages for secure email communications
   b. To encrypt channels to provide secure communication between clients and servers
   c. To verify the authenticity of the CA
   d. To verify the identity of clients and servers on the web

9. Who verifies the authenticity of a CSR?
   a. Certificate signatory
   b. Registration authority
   c. Certificate authority
   d. Signature authority

10. A centralized directory of digital certificates is called a(n) _____.
    a. Digital signature permitted authorization (DSPA)
    b. Authorized digital signature (ADS)
    c. Digital signature approval list (DSAP)
    d. Certificate repository (CR)

11. Elton needs his application to perform a real-time lookup of a digital certificate's status. Which technology would he use?
    a. Certificate Revocation List (CRL)
    b. Real-Time CA Verification (RTCAV)
    c. Online Certificate Status Protocol (OCSP)
    d. Staple

12. What is the purpose of certificate chaining?
    a. To ensure that a web browser has the latest root certificate updates
    b. To look up the name of intermediate RA
    c. To group and verify digital certificates
    d. To hash the private key

13. Which of the following is NOT a means by which a newly approved root digital certificate is distributed?
    a. Pinning
    b. OS updates
    c. Application updates
    d. Web browser updates

14. Which block cipher mode of operating requires that both the message sender and receiver access a counter that computes a new value whenever a ciphertext block is exchanged?
    a. CTR
    b. CN
    c. CD
    d. CXL

15. Which is the first step in a key exchange?
   a. The browser generates a random value ("pre-master secret").
   b. The web server sends a message ("ServerHello") to the client.
   c. The web browser verifies the server certificate.
   d. The web browser sends a message ("ClientHello") to the server.

16. What is the file extension for a Cryptographic Message Syntax Standard based on PKCS#7 that defines a generic syntax for defining digital signature and encryption?
   a. .P7B
   b. .cer
   c. .P12
   d. .xdr

17. Juan needs a certificate that must only authenticate that a specific organization has the right to use a particular domain name. What type of certificate does he need?
   a. Website validation
   b. Root
   c. Extended validation
   d. Domain validation

18. How is confidentiality achieved through IPsec?
   a. ESP
   b. AHA
   c. ISAKMP
   d. AuthX

19. Which refers to a situation in which keys are managed by a third party, such as a trusted CA?
   a. Key authorization
   b. Key escrow
   c. Remote key administration
   d. Trusted key authority

20. Which is a protocol for securely accessing a remote computer in order to issue a command?
   a. Transport Layer Security (TLS)
   b. Secure Shell (SSH)
   c. Secure Sockets Layer (SSL)
   d. Secure Hypertext Transport Protocol (SHTTP)

Hands-On Projects

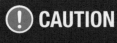 **CAUTION**   If you are concerned about installing any of the software in these projects on your regular computer, you can instead install the software in the Windows virtual machine created in the Module 1 Hands-On Projects. Software installed within a sandbox or the virtual machine will not impact the host computer.

Project 7-1: SSL Server and Client Tests

Time Required: 20 minutes
Objective: Explain the importance of security concepts in an enterprise environment.
Description: In this project, you will use online tests to determine the security of web servers and your local web browser.

NOTE 23

It is not unusual for websites to change the location of their stored files. If the URL no longer works, open a search engine and search for "Qualys SSL Server Test."

1. Go to **www.ssllabs.com**.
2. Click **Test your server >>**.
3. Click the first website listed under **Recent Best**.
4. Note the grade given for this site. Under **Summary**, note the **Overall Rating** along with the scores for **Certificate**, **Protocol Support**, **Key Exchange**, and **Cipher Strength**, which make up the cipher suite.
5. If this site did not receive an Overall Rating of *A* under **Summary**, you will see the reasons listed. Read through these. Would you agree? Why?
6. Scroll through the document and read through the **Certificate #1** information. Note the information supplied regarding the digital certificates. Under **Certification Paths**, click **Click here to expand**, if necessary, to view the certificate chaining. What can you tell about it?
7. Scroll down to **Configuration**. Note the list of protocols supported and not supported. If this site were to increase its security, which protocols should it no longer support? Why?

8. Under **Cipher Suites**, interpret the suites listed. Notice that they are given in server-preferred order. To increase its security, which cipher suite should be listed first? Why?

9. Under **Handshake Simulation**, select the web browser and operating system that you are using or that are similar to what you are using. Read through the capabilities of this client interacting with this web server. Note particularly the order of preference of the cipher suites. Click the browser's back button when finished.

10. Scroll to the top of the page, and then click **Scan Another >>**.

11. Select one of the **Recent Worst** sites. Review the **Summary, Authentication, Configuration, Cipher Suites**, and **Handshake Simulation**. Would you agree with this site's score?

12. If necessary, return to the **SSL Report** page, and then click **Scan Another >>**.

13. Enter the name of your school or work URL and generate a report. What score did it receive?

14. Review the **Summary, Authentication, Configuration, Cipher Suites**, and **Handshake Simulation**. Would you agree with this site's score?

15. Make a list of the top five vulnerabilities that you believe should be addressed in order of priority. If possible, share this list with any IT personnel who may be able to take action.

16. Click **Projects**.

17. Now test the capabilities of your web browser. Click **SSL Client Test**. Review the capabilities of your web browser. Print or take a screen capture of this page.

18. Close this web browser.

19. Open a different web browser on this computer or on another computer.

20. Return to **www.ssllabs.com**, click **Projects**, and then click **SSL Client Test** to compare the two scores. From a security perspective, which browser is better? Why?

21. Close all windows.

Project 7-2: Viewing Digital Certificates

Time Required: 20 minutes

Objective: Given a scenario, implement public key infrastructure.

Description: In this project, you will view digital certificate information using the Google Chrome web browser.

1. Use the Google Chrome web browser to go to **www.google.com**.

2. Note the padlock in the address bar. Although you did not enter *https://*, Google created a secure HTTPS connection. Why would it do that?

3. Click the three vertical buttons at the far edge of the address bar.

4. Click **More tools**.

5. Click **Developer tools**.

6. Click the **Security** tab, if necessary. (If the tab does not appear, click the **>>** button to display more tabs.)

7. Read the information under **Security Overview**.

8. Click **View certificate**.

9. Note the general information displayed on the **General** tab.

10. Now click the **Details** tab. The fields are displayed for this X.509 digital certificate.

11. Click **Valid to** to view the expiration date of this certificate.

12. Click **Public key** to view the public key associated with this digital certificate. Why is this site not concerned with distributing this key? How does embedding the public key in a digital certificate protect it from impersonators?

13. Click the **Certification Path** tab. Because web certificates are based on the distributed trust model, there is a *path* to the root certificate. Click the root certificate, and then click the **View Certificate** button. Click the **Details tab**, and then click **Valid to**. Why is the expiration date of this root certificate longer than that of the website certificate? Click **OK** and then click **OK** again to close the Certificate window.

14. Click **Copy to File**.

15. Click **Next**.

16. Note the different file formats that are available. What do you know about each of these formats?

17. Click **Cancel** to close this window.

18. Close all windows.

Project 7-3: Viewing Digital Certificate Revocation Lists (CRL) and Untrusted Certificates

Time Required: 20 minutes

Objective: Given a scenario, implement public key infrastructure.

Description: Revoked digital certificates are listed in a Certificate Revocation List (CRL), which can be accessed to check the certificate status of other users. In this project, you will view the CRL and any untrusted certificates on your Microsoft Windows computer.

1. Press the **Windows+X** keys.
2. Click **Windows PowerShell (Admin)**.
3. Type **certmgr.msc** and then press **Enter**.
4. In the left pane, expand **Trusted Root Certification Authorities**.
5. In the right pane, double-click **Certificates** to display the CAs approved for this computer. Scroll through this list. How many of these CAs have your heard of before?
6. In the left pane, expand **Intermediate Certification Authorities**.
7. Double-click **Certificates** to view the intermediate CAs. Scroll through this list.
8. In the left pane, click **Certificate Revocation List**. The right pane displays all revoked certificates.
9. In the right pane, select a revoked certificate and double-click it.
10. Read the information about the revoked certificate, and click fields for more detail, if necessary. Why do you think this certificate has been revoked? Close the Certificate Revocation List by clicking the **OK** button.
11. In the left pane, expand **Untrusted Certificates**.
12. Click **Certificate Trust List**. The right pane displays certificates that are no longer trusted.
13. In the right pane, double-click an untrusted certificate. Read the information about it, and click fields for more detail, if necessary. Why do you think this certificate is no longer trusted?
14. Click **OK** to close the Certificate dialog box.
15. Close all windows.

Project 4-4: Downloading and Installing a Digital Certificate

Time Required: 25 minutes

Objective: Given a scenario, implement public key infrastructure.

Description: In this project, you will download and install a digital certificate within the Adobe Acrobat Reader DC.

1. Check to determine if Adobe Acrobat Reader DC or Adobe Acrobat Professional is installed on your computer. If so, you may skip these download and installation steps and go directly to Step 5.

NOTE 24

It is not unusual for websites to change the location of stored files. If the URL no longer works, open a search engine and search for "Adobe Acrobat Reader DC Download."

2. Go to **get.adobe.com/reader/**.
3. Click **Download Acrobat Reader**.
4. Follow the instructions to install Reader.
5. Launch Reader.
6. Click **Edit**.
7. Click **Preferences**.
8. Click **Signatures**.
9. Under **Identities & Trusted Certificates**, click **More**.
10. In the left pane, click **Digital IDs** to display the menu choices, if necessary.
11. At the menu at the top of the main pane, click the **Add ID** icon (it is the first icon and has a plus sign).
12. Click **A new digital ID I want to create now**. Click **Next**.
13. If necessary, click **New PKCS#12 digital ID file**. What is a PKCS#12? What type of file extension will it have? Click **Next**.

14. Enter the requested information. Under **Key Algorithm**, click the down arrow to display two options. The default is **2048-bit RSA**, which provides more security, while 1024-bit RSA provides less security but is more universally compatible. Accept the 2048-bit RSA.

15. Under **Use digital ID for**, click the down arrow to display three options. Select the default **Digital Signatures and Data Encryption**. Click **Next**.

16. Create and enter a strong password, and then confirm that password. Click **Finish**.

17. Your file is now created. Click **Export**.

18. If necessary, click **Save the data to a file** and then click **Next**.

19. Save the file to your computer.

20. Close the windows associated with configuring your certificate. You can use this certificate by sending it to anyone who needs to validate your identity.

21. Close all windows.

Case Projects

Case Project 7-1: Transport Layer Security (TLS)

Use the Internet to research TLS. Who was responsible for developing it? When was the first version released? What was the relationship between TLS and SSL? What are its strengths? What are its weaknesses? When will the next version be released? What improvements are projected? Write a one-page paper on your research.

Case Project 7-2: Recommended Cryptoperiods

How long should a key be used before it is replaced? Search the Internet for information regarding cryptoperiods for hash, symmetric, and asymmetric algorithms. Find at least three sources for each of the algorithms. Draw a table that lists the algorithms and the recommended time, and then calculate the average for each. Do you agree or disagree? What would be your recommendation on cryptoperiods for each? Why?

Case Project 7-3: Certificate Authorities (CAs)

OSs come packaged with many digital certificates from certificate authorities (CAs). Use the Internet to determine how to view the CAs for the type and version of OS that you are using and view the list. How many have you heard of? How many are unknown? Select three of the publishers and research their organizations on the Internet. Write a one-paragraph summary of each CA.

Case Project 7-4: Root Certificate Breaches

Use the Internet to research breaches of CAs. What CAs were involved? Were they root or intermediate CAs? Who was behind the theft? How did the thefts occur? How were the stolen certificates then used? Are certificates from these CAs still accepted? Write a one-page paper of your research.

Case Project 7-5: Block Cipher Modes of Operation

Research block cipher modes of operation. Find information regarding how ECB can be compromised and write a detailed description of that. Then research one of the other modes (CBC, CTR, or GCM) in detail. Draw a picture of how this mode functions by turning plaintext into ciphertext. Write a detailed description of your research.

Case Project 7-6: Digital Certificate Costs

Use the Internet to research the costs of the different types of digital certificates: domain validation, EV, wildcard, SAN, machine/computer, code signing, and email. Look up at least three providers of each, and create a table listing the type of certificate, the costs, and the length of time the certificate is valid.

Case Project 7-7: Community Site Activity

The Information Security Community Site is an online companion to this textbook. It contains a wide variety of tools, information, discussion boards, and other features to assist learners. Go to **community.cengage.com/infosec2** and click the *Join or Sign in* icon to login, using your login name and password that you created in Module 1. Click **Forums (Discussion)** and click on **Security+ Case Projects (7th edition)**. Read the following case study.

Read again the section in the module on *Weaknesses of Cryptographic Protocols.* A weak cryptographic protocol can have serious implications for tens or even hundreds of millions of Internet users in a single day. What protections should be implemented over the development and deployment of cryptographic protocols to prevent this? What type of testing should be used? Should there be penalties for vulnerabilities that are uncovered in cryptographic protocols? Record your answers on the Community Site discussion board.

Case Project 7-8: North Ridge Security

North Ridge Security provides security consulting and assurance services. You have recently been hired as an intern to assist them.

Family Spas and Pools (FS&P) is a new North Ridge client that had been the recent victim of different security breaches. A vice president has recently heard about digital certificates for the first time and now wants all users to have and use digital certificates for every function related to FS&P. You are asked to provide information about digital certificates to help FS&P create and use digital certificates in the most meaningful way.

1. Create a PowerPoint presentation about digital certificates, including what they are, what they can protect, how they should be used, and the various types of certificates. Include the advantages and disadvantages of each. Your presentation should contain at least 10 slides.
2. After the presentation, the vice president of FS&P asks which certificates they should use and how they should be managed. Create a memo communicating the actions you believe would be best for the company to take.

References

1. Cowell, Alan, "Code found on pigeon baffles British cryptographers," *New York Times,* Nov. 24, 2012, accessed Feb. 5, 2014, www.nytimes.com/2012/11/24/world/europe/code-found-on-pigeon-baffles-british-cryptographers.html?_r=0.
2. Gennaro, Lisa, "68 useful ecommerce statistics you must know in 2020," *Wpforms*, Feb. 15, 2020, accessed Jun. 9, 2020, https://wpforms.com/ecommerce-statistics/.

NETWORK SECURITY

The modules in Part 4 deal with securing an enterprise computer network. In Module 8, you learn about the attacks that target networks and how to assess vulnerabilities and create physical defenses. Module 9 demonstrates how to protect a network through network security appliances and technologies. In Module 10, you will explore the concepts and tools for protecting cloud and virtual environments. Finally, in Module 11, you learn how to manage wireless network security.

PART 4

NETWORKING THREATS, ASSESSMENTS, AND DEFENSES

After completing this module, you should be able to do the following:

1. Describe the different types of networking-based attacks
2. List the different network assessment tools
3. Explain how physical security defenses can be used

Front-Page Cybersecurity

What would you think if the CEO of Apple said, "Nobody really wants to hack us."? Or if Google posted on its website, "Attackers aren't interested in targeting us." Or the president of Amazon said, "We're not on any attacker's radar screen."

In today's cybersecurity environment, it would be surprising—probably shocking—to hear people say that attackers are not interested in them. But that's exactly what happened recently. Could it be true that attackers are not interested in a particular company? Or does the CEO of the company not understand cybersecurity?

A new startup called View manufactures and installs "smart windows" that automatically adjust to sunlight and glare. The blue-tinted windows are expensive: they cost about five times as much as traditional glass windows. However, View windows have several advantages. They reduce cooling costs by blocking heat from sunlight and they can eliminate the need for blinds or window treatments. If a criminal breaks one of the windows, police can immediately be notified. Finally, View windows allow more people to fit into a building. Because View windows reduce glare and heat from the sun, employees can be seated in areas that they could not normally use. One organization installing View windows will be able to place the same number of employees in one-third of the space.

All View windows are interconnected. They are attached to the organization's local area network (LAN), allowing them to be accessed over the Internet. In fact, each View window has its own IP address. Users can control the windows via a smartphone app.

The View CEO recently said about the company's windows, "The good news is the window's not that interesting to hack."

Most security professionals would strongly disagree with the View CEO. In fact, View windows are interesting to attackers for three reasons.

1. *Entry point into the owner's corporate network.* Internet of Things (IoT) devices, such as View windows, are the target of attackers because the devices lack security. The same week the View CEO made his bold statement, the Microsoft Threat Intelligence Center said state actors working for the Russian government were using printers, video decoders, and similar IoT devices as a beachhead or entry point to penetrate targeted computer networks. "These devices became points of ingress from which the actor established a presence on the network and continued looking for further access," Microsoft

said. In other words, IoT devices with little or no security allowed an attacker an entry point into the network. Attackers could then pivot to move through the network in search of higher-privileged accounts that would grant access to higher-value data. In the latest attack referenced by Microsoft, after gaining access to the IoT devices, the threat actors ran Tcp-dump, a program often used by security personnel to assess network security by sniffing network traffic on local subnets. They also dropped a simple shell script that allowed them to stay on the network for an extended period of time. An analysis of network traffic showed the IoT devices were communicating with an external command and control (C&C) server.

2. *Attack point against other networks.* For several years, threat actors have compromised unprotected IoT devices and then gathered them into a botnet. The botnets attacked other devices or networks. Most notably, IoT-based botnets have been used to launch distributed denial of service or DDoS attacks. A company with View windows installed could find that the windows are a launching point for other attacks.

3. *Backflow into View's own network.* View requires that all its windows have remote connectivity to the company's headquarters so that View can "commission, configure, monitor, and maintain the system." The product documentation lists options for allowing remote access, ranging from "Firewall via DMZ" and "Firewall via Port Mapping" to "Firewall with VPN Access" and other options. However, an attacker who can circumvent these protections can "backflow" into the View network. Because the windows are remotely connected to View's own network, an attacker could compromise a View window belonging to another company and then sneak into the View network. In this way, View windows could allow an attacker entry into View's network.

Despite the statement from the CEO of View that "The good news is the window's not that interesting to hack," the bad news is that View windows are very interesting to hack. The worse news may be that the View CEO is evidently not taking these risks seriously.

Whereas technology devices—including smartphones, tablets, and laptop computers—usually receive all the praise for ushering the world into a new and exciting era, in reality, the invisible network that is connecting the devices should be receiving an equal share of adoration. Imagine a smartphone that cannot connect to a network to receive messages or link to websites but instead can use only what is contained on the smartphone. Most users would quickly dump an unconnected smartphone in the nearest trash bin. The connectivity through networks is what has made today's devices revolutionary.

Invisible networks can link a device to a virtually unlimited volume of information for research. They can also support relationships between people who are separated by hundreds of feet or thousands of miles. E-commerce through networks makes it possible to perform nearly any real-world task online, including retail shopping, banking, real estate transactions, airline bookings, and movie streaming. Networks have empowered today's technology devices to create our digital revolution.

However, networks have also introduced new issues surrounding privacy, trust, and reliability and are responsible for the explosive growth of cybersecurity attacks. They have opened the door for threat actors to reach across the world to invisibly and instantaneously launch attacks on any device connected to the network. Just as users can surf the web without openly identifying themselves, attackers can use this anonymity to cloak their identity and prevent authorities from finding and prosecuting them.

This module begins a study of network attacks and defenses. First, the module explores common attacks that are launched against networks today. Then it looks at tools for assessing and defending networks. Finally, it examines physical security defenses for protecting network technology devices.

ATTACKS ON NETWORKS

 **CERTIFICATION**

1.3 Given a scenario, analyze potential indicators associated with application attacks.

1.4 Given a scenario, analyze potential indicators associated with network attacks.

3.1 Given a scenario, implement secure protocols.

Threat actors place a high priority on targeting networks in their attacks. Exploiting a single network vulnerability can expose hundreds or thousands of devices. Several types of attacks target a network or a process that relies on a network, including interception attacks, Layer 2 attacks, DNS attacks, distributed denial of service attacks, and malicious coding and scripting attacks.

Interception Attacks

Some attacks are designed to intercept network communications. Three of the most common interception attacks are man-in-the-middle, session replay, and man-in-the-browser attacks.

Man-in-the-Middle (MITM)

Suppose that Angie, a high school student, is in danger of receiving a poor grade in math. Her teacher, Mr. Ferguson, mails a letter to Angie's parents requesting a conference regarding her performance. However, Angie waits for the mail and retrieves the letter from the mailbox before her parents come home. She forges her parent's signature on the original letter declining a conference and mails it to her teacher. Angie also replaces the real letter with a counterfeit pretending to be from Mr. Ferguson that compliments Angie on her math work. The parents read the fake letter and tell Angie they are proud of her, while Mr. Ferguson is puzzled that Angie's parents are not concerned about her grades.

Angie has conducted a type of **man-in-the-middle (MITM)** attack. In an MITM, a threat actor is positioned in a communication between two parties, as shown in Figure 8-1. Neither of the legitimate parties is aware of the presence of the threat actor and communicate freely, thinking they are talking only to the authentic party. The goal of an MITM attack is to eavesdrop on the conversation or impersonate one of the parties.

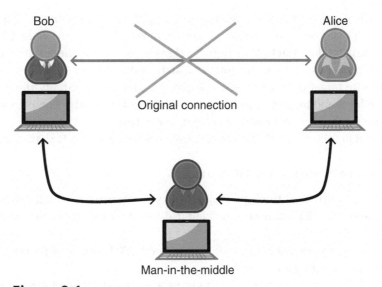

Figure 8-1 MITM attack

A typical MITM attack has two phases. The first phase is intercepting the traffic. A common form of interception is for the threat actor to pretend to be an approved web application by altering packet headers in an IP address. When users attempt to access a URL connected to the application, they are instead sent to the attacker's website.

The second phase is to decrypt the transmissions. An attacker could send a fake digital certificate associated with a compromised application to the victim's computer to trick the computer into verifying the authenticity of the application. The attacker can then access any data entered by the victim.

Session Replay

A *replay* attack is a variation of an MITM attack. Whereas an MITM attack alters and then sends the transmission immediately, a replay attack makes a copy of the legitimate transmission before sending it to the recipient. This copy is used later when the MITM "replays" the transmission.

NOTE 1

Each time a user visits a website, the web server issues a new session ID that usually remains active as long as the browser is open. In some instances, after several minutes of inactivity, the server may generate a new session ID. Closing the browser terminates the active session ID, and it should not be used again.

A specific type of replay attack is a **session replay** attack, which involves intercepting and using a *session ID* to impersonate a user. A session ID is a unique number that a web server assigns a specific user for the duration of the user's visit (session). Most servers create complex session IDs by using the date, time of the visit, and other variables such as the device IP address, email address, username, user ID, role, privilege level, access rights, language preferences, account ID, current state, last login, session timeouts, and other internal session details. Session IDs are usually least 128 bits in length and hashed using a secure hash function such as SHA-256.

Session IDs can be contained as part of a URL extension, by using hidden form fields in which the state is sent to the client as part of the response and returned to the server as part of a form's hidden data, or through cookies. A sample session ID is *fa2e76d49a0475910504cb3ab7a1f626d174d2d*.

Threat actors use several techniques for stealing an active session ID. These include network attacks (hijacks and altered communication between two users) and endpoint attacks (cross-site scripting, Trojans, and malicious JavaScript coding). Once a session ID has been successfully stolen, a threat actor can impersonate the user.

Man-in-the-Browser (MITB)

Like an MITM attack, a **man-in-the-browser (MITB)** attack intercepts communication between parties to steal or manipulate the data. Whereas an MITM attack occurs between two endpoints—such as between two laptops or a user's computer and a web server—an MITB attack occurs between a browser and the underlying computer. Specifically, an MITB attack seeks to intercept and then manipulate the communication between the web browser and the security mechanisms of the computer.

An MITB attack usually begins with a Trojan infecting the computer and installing an "extension" into the browser configuration so that opening the browser activates the extension. When a user enters the URL of a site, the extension checks whether the site is targeted for attack. After the user signs in to the site, the extension waits for a specific webpage to be displayed in which the user enters information, such as the account number and password for an online financial institution (a favorite target of MITB attacks). When the user clicks Submit, the extension captures all the data from the fields on the form and may even modify some of the entered data. The browser sends the data to the server, which performs the transaction, generates a receipt, and returns it to the browser. The malicious extension captures the receipt data and modifies it (with the data the user originally entered) so that it appears that a legitimate transaction has occurred.

Threat actors gain several advantages in an MITB attack:

- Most MITB attacks are distributed through Trojan browser extensions, which provide a valid function to the user but also install the MITB malware, making it difficult to recognize that malicious code has been installed.
- Because MITB malware selects websites to target, an infected MITB browser might remain dormant for months until triggered by the user visiting a targeted site.
- MITB software resides exclusively within the web browser, making it difficult for standard antimalware software to detect it.

Layer 2 Attacks

In 1978, the International Organization for Standardization (ISO) released a set of specifications to describe how dissimilar computers could be connected together on a network. The ISO demonstrated that what happens on a network device when sending or receiving traffic can be best understood by portraying this transfer as a series of related steps. The ISO called its work the *Open Systems Interconnection (OSI)* reference model. After a revision in 1983, the OSI reference model is still used today.

The key to the OSI reference model is *layers*. The model separates networking steps into a series of seven layers. Within each layer, different networking tasks are performed that cooperate with the tasks in the layers immediately above and below it. Each layer in the sending device corresponds to the same layer in the receiving device. The OSI model is shown in Figure 8-2.

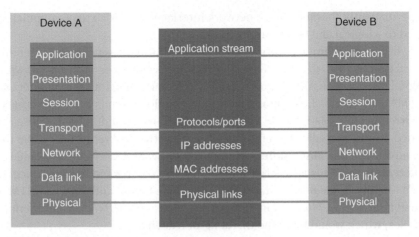

Figure 8-2 OSI model

However, the OSI model was designed so that each layer is compartmentalized: different layers work without the knowledge and approval of the other layers. This means that if one layer is compromised, the other layers are unaware of any problem, which results in the entire communication being compromised.

Layer 2 of the OSI model is particularly weak in this regard and is a frequent target of threat actors. Layer 2, the Data Link Layer, is responsible for dividing the data into packets along with error detection and correction, and performs physical addressing, data framing, and error detection and handling. A compromise at Layer 2 can affect the entire communication, as shown in Figure 8-3.

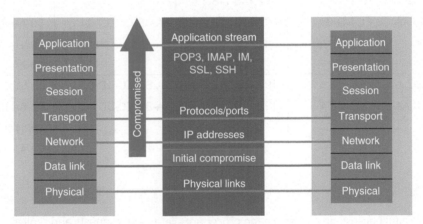

Figure 8-3 Layer 2 compromise

NOTE 2

There is not universal agreement on the usage of the terms *frame*, *packet*, *datagram*, and *segment*. The OSI uses the terms *protocol data unit (PDU)* and *service data unit (SDU)*. Usually, an Ethernet frame is used for Data Link Layer (Layer 2) functions, an IP packet or datagram is at the Network Layer (Layer 3), and a segment is at the Transport Layer (Layer 4). However, the terms are not used consistently. Although some network certification exams do require specific terminology when referring to these data units, the Security+ certification does not. To minimize confusion, the term *packet* is used in the text in a generic sense of a unit of data.

Two common Layer 2 attacks are address resolution protocol poisoning and media access control attacks.

Address Resolution Protocol Poisoning

The TCP/IP protocol suite requires that logical Internet Protocol (IP) addresses be assigned to each device on a network. These addresses can be changed as necessary. However, an Ethernet LAN uses the physical media access control

(MAC) address that is permanently "burned" into a network interface card (NIC) to communicate. How can a physical MAC address be mapped to a logical and temporary IP address?

A device using TCP/IP on an Ethernet network can find the MAC address of another endpoint based on the IP address with the **Address Resolution Protocol (ARP)**. If the IP address for an endpoint is known, but the MAC address is not, the sending endpoint delivers an ARP packet to all devices on the network that in effect says, "If this is your IP address, send me your MAC address." The endpoint with that IP address sends back a packet with the MAC address so the packet can be correctly addressed. The IP address and the corresponding MAC address are stored in an ARP cache for future reference. In addition, all other endpoints that hear the ARP reply also cache that data.

Threat actors take advantage of a MAC address stored in a software ARP cache to change the data so that an IP address points to a different device. This attack is known as **ARP poisoning** and uses *spoofing*, which is deceiving by impersonating another's identity. Table 8-1 illustrates the ARP cache before and after an MITM attack using ARP poisoning. Notice that the IP address *192.146.118.4* in Victim 1's device and *192.146.118.3* in Victim 2's device now point to different MAC addresses, which would be to the threat actor's device.

Table 8-1   ARP poisoning attack

Device	IP and MAC address	ARP cache before attack	ARP cache after attack
Threat actor	192.146.118.2	192.146.118.3=>00-AA-BB-CC-DD-03	192.146.118.3=>
	00-AA-BB-CC-DD-02	192.146.118.4=>00-AA-BB-CC-DD-04	00-AA-BB-CC-DD-03
			192.146.118.4=>
			00-AA-BB-CC-DD-04
Victim 1	192.146.118.3	192.146.118.2=>00-AA-BB-CC-DD-02	192.146.118.2=>
	00-AA-BB-CC-DD-03	192.146.118.4=>00-AA-BB-CC-DD-04	00-AA-BB-CC-DD-02
			192.146.118.4=>
			00-AA-BB-CC-DD-02
Victim 2	192.146.118.4	192.146.118.2=>00-AA-BB-CC-DD-02	192.146.118.2=>
	00-AA-BB-CC-DD-04	192.146.118.3=>00-AA-BB-CC-DD-03	00-AA-BB-CC-DD-02
			192.146.118.3=>
			00-AA-BB-CC-DD-02

NOTE 3

ARP poisoning is successful because no authentication procedures verify ARP requests and replies.

Media Access Control Attacks

Besides ARP poisoning, other attacks manipulate MAC addresses through spoofing. The target for these attacks is a network switch.

A network *switch* is a device that connects network devices and, unlike some other network devices, has a degree of "intelligence." Operating at the Layer 2 Data Link layer, a switch can learn which device is connected to each of its ports. It does so by examining the MAC address of packets it receives and observing at which of the switch's port that packet arrived. It associates the port with the MAC address of the device connected to the port, storing the information in a *MAC address table*. The switch then knows on which port to forward packets intended for that specific device.

NOTE 4

A switch not only improves network performance by limiting the number of packets distributed but also provides better security. A threat actor who installs software to capture packets on a computer attached to a switch sees only packets that are directed to that device and not those intended for any other network device.

Two common attacks involving spoofing MAC addresses on a switch are MAC cloning and MAC flooding.

MAC Cloning   In a MAC cloning attack, threat actors discover a valid MAC address of a device connected to a switch. They spoof the MAC address on their device and send a packet onto the network. The switch changes its MAC address table to reflect the new association of the MAC address with the port to which the attackers' device is connected. All packets intended for the victim's device will now be sent to the attackers' device.

MAC Flooding   A MAC flooding attack is another attack based on spoofing, MAC cloning, and the MAC address table of a switch. A threat actor overflows the switch with Ethernet packets that have been spoofed so that every packet contains a different source MAC address, each appearing to come from a different endpoint. This can quickly consume all the memory (called the *content addressable memory* or *CAM*) for the MAC address table.

Once the MAC address table is full and cannot store any additional MAC addresses, the switch enters a *fail-open* mode and broadcasts frames to all ports. A threat actor can then install software or a hardware device that captures and decodes packets on one client connected to the switch to view all traffic.

> **NOTE 5**
>
> A MAC flooding attack that consumes all the CAM on one switch will ultimately fill the CAM tables of adjacent switches.

DNS Attacks

The predecessor to today's Internet was the network ARPAnet. This network was completed in 1969 and used a 50 Kbps connection to link together single computers located at four sites (the University of California at Los Angeles, the Stanford Research Institute, the University of California at Santa Barbara, and the University of Utah). To reference the computers, each was assigned an identification number. (IP addresses were not introduced until later.) However, as computers were added to the network, it became more difficult for people to accurately recall the identification number of each computer.

The network needed a naming system that would assign computers both numeric addresses and friendlier human-readable names composed of letters, numbers, and special symbols (called a symbolic name). In the early 1970s, each computer site began to assign simple names to network devices and to manage its own *host table* that mapped names to computer numbers. However, because each site attempted to maintain its own local host table, inconsistencies developed between the sites. A standard master host table that could be downloaded to each site was then created. When TCP/IP was developed, the host table concept was expanded to a hierarchical name system for matching computer names and numbers known as the *Domain Name System (DNS)*, which is the basis for domain name resolution of names-to-IP addresses used today.

Because of the important role it plays, DNS is the focus of attacks. Like ARP poisoning, a DNS-based attack substitutes a DNS address so that the computer is silently redirected to a different device. A successful DNS attack has two consequences:

- *URL redirection.* The goal of DNS attacks is usually a URL redirection: instead of users reaching their intended site, they instead are redirected to another site. The site is often fictitious, one that looks identical to a bank or e-commerce site so that users enter their username, password, and credit card number. The threat actors at the fictitious site capture and use the confidential information.
- *Domain reputation.* Online algorithms are continually evaluating the reputation of webpages, domains, and email services. Consider email reputation: because every email message can be traced to an IP address, and IP addresses gain an IP reputation based on past incidents, an email service that has sent spam or unwanted bulk email earns a low reputation score. An email service might reject email messages with low reputation scores or deliver them more slowly than other email. Similar to an IP reputation, a domain reputation can identify a domain used for a distributing malware or launching attacks. A company's competitor could hire a threat actor to use a DNS attack that earns the company a low domain reputation score, thus affecting sales.

> **NOTE 6**
>
> On Labor Day in 1969, the first test of ARPAnet was conducted. A switch was turned on, and to almost everyone's surprise, the network worked. Researchers in Los Angeles attempted to type the word *login* on the computer hundreds of miles away at Stanford University. When a user in Los Angeles pressed the letter *L*, it appeared on the screen at Stanford. Next, the letter *O* was pressed, and it too appeared. However, when the third letter, *G*, was typed, the network crashed.

Attacks using DNS include DNS poisoning and DNS hijacking.

DNS Poisoning

Similar to ARP poisoning, **DNS poisoning** modifies a local lookup table on a device to point to a different domain. Usually, the alternative domain points to a malicious DNS server controlled by a threat actor. The DNS server redirects traffic to a website designed to steal user information or infect the device with malware.

DNS poisoning on the local device involves modifying the local host table. TCP/IP still uses host tables stored on the local device. When a user enters a symbolic name, TCP/IP first checks the local host table to find an entry; if no entry exists, it uses the external DNS system. Attackers can target a local HOSTS file to create new entries that redirect users to a fraudulent site. A sample local host table is shown in Figure 8-4.

```
127.0.0.1        localhost
161.6.18.20      www.wku.edu        # Western Kentucky University
74.125.47.99     www.google.com     # My favorite search engine
216.77.188.41    www.att.net        # Internet service provider
```

Figure 8-4   Sample HOSTS file

NOTE 7

Host tables are stored in the */etc/* directory in UNIX, Linux, and macOS, and they are located in the *Windows\System32\drivers\etc* directory in Windows.

In a DNS poisoning attack, the local HOSTS file contains an entry to a malicious DNS server. This allows the threat actor to control *all* websites that a user attempts to visit. In addition, since most users are unaware of the HOSTS file on their device, DNS poisoning infections can remain undetected for extended periods of time.

NOTE 8

Some governments use DNS poisoning to restrict their citizens from reading what they consider as unfavorable Internet content.

DNS Hijacking

Whereas DNS poisoning attempts to modify the local device HOSTS file, **DNS hijacking** is intended to infect an external DNS server with IP addresses that point to malicious sites. DNS hijacking has the advantage of redirecting *all* users accessing the server.

Instead of attempting to break into a DNS server to change its contents, attackers use a more basic approach. Because DNS servers exchange information among themselves (known as *zone transfers*), attackers attempt to exploit a protocol flaw and convince the authentic DNS server to accept fraudulent DNS entries sent from the attackers' DNS server. If the DNS server does not correctly validate DNS responses to ensure they have come from an authoritative source, it stores the fraudulent entries locally and serves them to users, spreading them to other DNS servers.

The steps in a DNS poisoning attack from attackers who have a domain name of *www.evil.net* with their own DNS server *ns.evil.net* are shown in Figure 8-5:

1. The attackers send a request to a valid DNS server asking it to resolve the name *www.evil.net*.
2. Because the valid DNS server does not know the address, it asks the responsible name server, which is the attackers' *ns.evil.net*, for the address.
3. The name server *ns.evil.net* sends the address of not only *www.evil.net* but also all of its records (a zone transfer) to the valid DNS server, which then accepts them.
4. Any requests to the valid DNS server will now respond with the fraudulent addresses entered by the attackers.

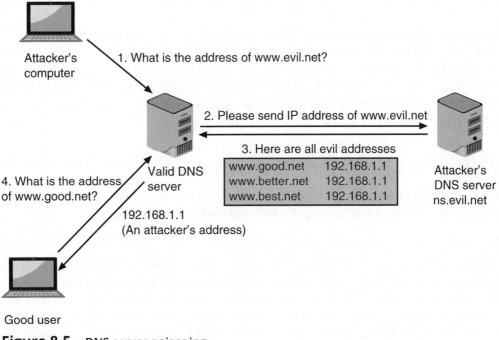

Figure 8-5   DNS server poisoning

NOTE 9

The advantage of a DNS poisoning attack is that all domains one victim uses can be controlled by a threat actor. In contrast, the advantage of a DNS hijacking attack is that although fewer domains are controlled, all users accessing the DNS server are redirected.

Distributed Denial of Service Attack

Suppose Gabe is having a conversation with Cora in a coffee shop when a "flash mob" of friends descends upon them and all talk to Gabe at the same time. He could not continue his conversation with Cora because he is overwhelmed by the number of people talking to him.

In a similar fashion, a technology-based *denial of service (DoS)* attack bombards a system with "bogus" requests, overwhelming the system so that it cannot respond to legitimate requests. DoS attacks today are **distributed denial of service (DDoS)** attacks: instead of only one source making a bogus request, a DDoS involves hundreds, thousands, or even millions of sources producing a torrent of fake requests.

The devices participating in a DDoS attack are infected and controlled by threat actors so that users are completely unaware that their endpoints are part of a DDoS attack. The sources used in DDoS attacks are listed in Table 8-2.

Table 8-2   Sources of DDoS attacks

Name	Source	Example	Target
Network	Computer	Desktop, laptop, tablet	Using Layer 3, it is designed to overwhelm web servers and networks
Application	IoT devices	Baby camera monitors, garage door openers	Focuses on cloud-based resources
Operational Technology (OT)	Endpoints that can be programmed and have an IP address	Automobiles, drones, robots	Using Layer 7, it targets infrastructures like an electrical power grid

NOTE 10

The volume of data directed at a target in a DDoS attack has continued to rise in recent years. The first massive DDoS attack occurred in 2016, when threat actors used 145,607 compromised IoT video cameras and digital video recorders (DVRs) against a French web hosting service, flooding it with 1.1 terabits per second (Tbps) of data. That record was eclipsed in 2018 with an attack of 1.7 Tbps, and again in early 2020, when a DDoS attack registered 2.3 Tbps. It is estimated that a botnet of only one million compromised IoT devices could easily send 4 Tbps in a DDoS attack, which is the equivalent of streaming 800,000 high-definition movies simultaneously.

Malicious Coding and Scripting Attacks

Several successful network attacks come from malicious software code and scripts. These attacks use PowerShell, Visual Basic for Applications, the coding language Python, and the Linux/UNIX Bash.

PowerShell

PowerShell is a task automation and configuration management framework from Microsoft. Initially, PowerShell was a Microsoft Windows component known as Windows PowerShell and was built on the Windows.NET framework (a developer platform that can be used to write apps in specific programming languages). In 2016, it was updated and released both as an open-source and a cross-platform product running on Windows, macOS, and Linux platforms.

Administrative tasks in PowerShell are performed by *cmdlets* ("command-lets"), which are specialized .NET classes that implement a specific operation. PowerShell *providers* give access to data in a data repository, such as the file system or Windows registry. Users and developers can create and add their own cmdlets to PowerShell. PowerShell also provides a hosting application program interface (API) so the PowerShell runtime can even be embedded inside other applications. On the Microsoft Windows platform, PowerShell has full access to a range of OS components and APIs. It can run locally on an endpoint or across a network accessing other endpoint devices.

The power and reach of PowerShell make it a prime target for threat actors. PowerShell allows attackers to inject code from the PowerShell environment into other processes without first storing any malicious code on the hard disk. Commands can then be executed while bypassing security protections and leave no evidence behind. PowerShell can also be configured so that its commands are not detected by antimalware running on the computer. Because most applications flag PowerShell as a "trusted" application, its actions are rarely scrutinized.

 **CAUTION**   These are not vulnerabilities but rather are features of PowerShell as a result of its tight integration with the .NET Framework. PowerShell provides a powerful and easy means to access sensitive elements of an OS and is frequently used by developers and system administrators.

One recent attack illustrates how threat actors can use PowerShell. The attack started with a phishing email containing the subject line "URGENT!" and an Excel attachment with a malicious embedded script. Once the user opened the attachment and approved the script to run its active content, it decrypted and executed a PowerShell script. The script ran with the PowerShell parameters *ExecutionPolicyByPass* (allow the PowerShell script to run despite any system restrictions), *WindowStyleHidden* (run the script quietly without any notification to the user), and *NoProfile* (do not load the system's custom PowerShell environment).

Visual Basic for Applications (VBA)

Visual Basic for Applications (VBA) is an event-driven Microsoft programming language. VBA allows developers and users to automate processes that normally would take multiple steps or levels of steps. It can be used to control many tasks of the host application, including manipulating user interface features such as toolbars, menus, forms, and dialog boxes.

VBA is built into most Microsoft Office applications (Word, Excel, and PowerPoint, for example) for Windows and Apple macOS platforms. It is also included in select non-Microsoft products, such as AutoCAD, CorelDraw, and LibreOffice. VBA can even control one application from another application using Object Linking and Embedding (OLE) automation. For example, VBA can automatically create a Microsoft Word report from data in a Microsoft Excel spreadsheet. The VBA development environment is shown in Figure 8-6.

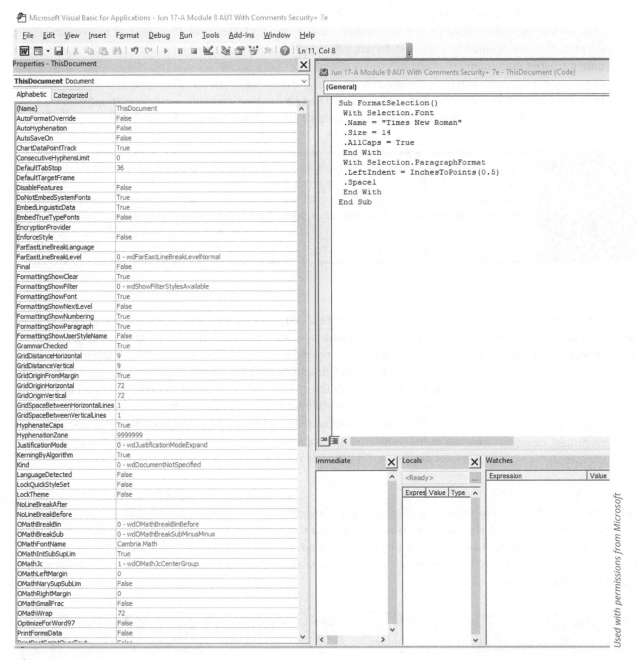

Figure 8-6   VBA development environment

VBA is most often used to create **macros**. A macro is a series of instructions that can be grouped together as a single command. Macros are used to automate a complex task or a repeated series of tasks. Macros are generally written using VBA, are stored within the user document (such as in an Excel .xlsx worksheet or Word .docx file), and can be launched automatically when the document is opened.

Although macros date back to the late 1990s, they continue to be a key attack vector. Microsoft has reported that 98 percent of all Office-targeted threats are a result of macro-based malware, and it has warned users that Office macros, particularly in Excel, are still used to compromise Windows systems.[1] Due to the impact of macro malware, Microsoft has implemented several protections:

- *Protected View. Protected View* is a read-only mode for an Office file in which most editing functions are disabled and macros cannot run. When opened, files will display a Protected View warning message if they are from an Internet site, potentially unsafe location, or another user's OneDrive storage; received as an email attachment; or have active content (macros or data connections).

- *Trusted Documents*. A *trusted document* is a file that contains active content that can open without a warning. Users can access the Office Trust Center to designate files as trusted. However, files opened from an unsafe location cannot be designated as a trusted document. A system administrator can also turn off the ability to designate a trusted document.
- *Trusted Location*. Files retrieved from a *trusted location* can be designated as safe and open in standard rather than Protected View. It is recommended that if a user trusts a file that contains active content, it should be moved to a trusted location instead of changing the default Trust Center settings to allow macros.

>  **CAUTION** Unless there is a business requirement for macros, support for their use should be disabled across the Microsoft Office suite. If macros are required, only those that have been digitally signed by a trusted publisher should be allowed to run. To prevent users or an adversary from bypassing macro security controls, all support for trusted documents and trusted locations should be disabled. Organizations can disable Trust Center settings and apply macro security controls using Group Policy settings.

Python

Python is a popular programming language that can run on several OS platforms. Python's syntax allows programmers to write code that takes fewer lines than in other programming languages such as Java and C++. Python also supports object-oriented programming. It has a large standard library in which developers can use routines created by other developers.

NOTE 11

Python was created in the late 1980s by a Dutch programmer as a side project during his Christmas vacation.

There are several best practices to follow when using Python so that the code does not contain vulnerabilities. These include using the latest version of Python, staying current on vulnerabilities within Python, being careful when formatting strings in Python, and downloading only vetted Python libraries. (A library is a collection of functions and methods that can perform actions so that the programmer does not have to write the code for it.)

Bash

Bash is the command language interpreter (called the "shell") for the Linux/UNIX OS. *Bash scripting* is using Bash to create a *script* (a script is essentially the same as a program, but it is *interpreted* and executed without the need for it to be first *compiled* into machine language). Exploits have taken advantage of vulnerabilities in Bash. For example, one vulnerability allowed attackers to remotely attach a malicious executable file to a *variable* (a value that changes) that is executed when Bash is invoked.

TWO RIGHTS & A WRONG

1. The goal of an MITM attack is to either eavesdrop on the conversation or impersonate one or both of the parties.
2. A session ID is a unique number that a web browser assigns for the duration of that user's visit.
3. In a MAC cloning attack, a threat actor will discover a valid MAC address of a device connected to a switch, spoof that MAC address on his device, and send a packet onto the network.

See Appendix B for the answer.

TOOLS FOR ASSESSMENT AND DEFENSE

 **CERTIFICATION**

4.1 Given a scenario, use the appropriate tool to assess organizational security.

Several assessment tools determine the strength of a network. Other tools can be used to create a stronger network defense. Both types of tools can be categorized into network reconnaissance and discovery tools, Linux file manipulation tools, scripting tools, and packet capture and replay tools.

Network Reconnaissance and Discovery Tools

Some network reconnaissance and discovery tools are command-line utilities that are part of multiple OSs (sometimes with slight variations in their names or different switches or parameters), while others function under only a single OS. These tools are listed in Table 8-3.

Table 8-3 OS network reconnaissance and discovery tools

Name and OS	Description	Important switches or parameters
tracert (Windows) traceroute (Linux)	Shows the details about the path a packet takes from a computer or device to a destination	-d (Displays the route using numeric addresses and prevents tracert from resolving IP addresses to hostnames for a faster display) -h hops (Specifies the maximum number of hops while searching for the target)
nslookup (Windows) dig (Linux)	A DNS diagnostic utility; can be used in interactive mode but the non-interactive version of nslookup is easier and therefore is used more often	host (Look up the host using the default server) host [server] (Look up the host using the specified server) -server (Launch interactive mode using the server)
ipconfig (Windows) ifconfig (Linux)	Displays network configuration information such as the IP address, network mask, and gateway for all physical and virtual network adapters	-all (Displays detailed configuration information about all network interfaces) -release [adapter] (Terminates the DHCP lease on the specified adapter or on all interfaces) -displaydns (Displays the contents of the DNS resolver cache)
ping (Windows, Linux)	Tests the ability of the source computer to reach a specified destination computer; commonly used to verify that a computer can communicate over a network with another computer or network device	-t (Force the target to respond until pressing Ctrl+C) -a (Resolve the hostname of an IP address target) -i TTL (Set the Time to Live (TTL) value up to 255) -R (Trace the round-trip path) -r count (Specify number of hops between computer and the target computer)
netstat (Windows, Linux)	Provides detailed information about current network connections as well as network connections for the Transmission Control Protocol (TCP), network interfaces, and routing tables	-a (All active connections and the ports that the computer is listening on) -e (Ethernet data such as number of bytes and packets sent and received) -g (Multicast group membership data) -n (Active TCP connections with addresses and port numbers displayed numerically)
pathping (Windows)	A combination of ping and tracert that will test the connection to each hop.	-q (Limit number of queries) -n (Prevents resolving hostnames)
route (Linux)	Displays and manipulates IP routing table to create static routes to specific hosts	-n (Display numerical addresses) gw gateway (Route packets via gateway)
curl (Linux)	Transfers data to or from a server	-o filename (Save downloaded file with filename) -C – (Resume interrupted download)
hping (Linux)	Sends custom TCP/IP packets	-i interval (Wait interval seconds between sending packets)

Network reconnaissance and discovery tools from third parties are listed in Table 8-4.

Table 8-4 Third-party OS network reconnaissance and discovery tools

Name	Source	Description
theHarvester	Kali Linux	Provides information about email accounts, user names, and hostnames/subdomains from different public sources
dnsenum	Kali Linux	List DNS information of a domain
sn1per	XeroSecurity	Penetration testing tool
Cuckoo	Cuckoo	Automated malware analysis system
Nessus	Tenable	Vulnerability assessment tool
scanless	Vesche	Tool for using websites to perform port scan
nmap	Nmap	Network discovery and security auditing

Linux File Manipulation Tools

Text files are a fundamental element in the Linux OS. Because virtually all configuration files in Linux are text files, changing the configuration of a security application involves modifying the text configuration file. Thus, managing Linux security, applications, and the OS itself demands excellent text manipulation skills. Table 8-5 lists several Linux text file manipulation tools that are part of the Linux OS.

Table 8-5 Linux text file manipulation tools

Tool name	Description	Example
head	Display the first 10 lines of a file	*head etc/snort/snort.conf*
tail	Display the last 10 lines of a file	*tail etc/snort/snort.conf*
cat	Display an entire file	*cat etc/snort/snort.conf*
grep	Search for keyword	*grep apache1*
chmod	Change file permissions	*chmod 774 rules*
logger	Add content to syslog file	*logger comment*

Scripting Tools

Scripting tools are used to create scripts that facilitate tasks. PowerShell is one of the most powerful scripting tools, and Python can also be used to create scripts. Scripts can also be created when using Secure Shell (SSH), which is used to access remote computers.

NOTE 12

SSH is covered in Module 7.

Another tool that supports scripting is **OpenSSL**, a cryptography library that offers open source applications of the TLS protocol. It was first released in 1998 and is available for Linux, Windows, and macOS platforms. OpenSSL allows users to perform various SSL-related tasks, including CSR (Certificate Signing Request), private key generation, and SSL certificate installation.

Packet Capture and Replay Tools

Collecting and analyzing data packets that cross a network can provide valuable information. Packet analysis typically examines the entire contents of the packet, which consists of the header information and the payload. However, because all the information needed is rarely contained in a single packet, packet analysis examines multiple packets— often hundreds and even thousands of them— to piece together the information.

NOTE 13

Some common uses of packet analysis include troubleshooting network connectivity (determine packet loss, review TCP retransmission, and create graphs of high latency packet responses), examining Application Layer sessions (captured packets can be used to view a full HTTP session for both requests and responses, view Telnet session commands and responses, and even read email traffic), and solving DHCP issues (examine DHCP client broadcasts, view DHCP offers with addresses and options, observe client requests for an address, and see the server's acknowledgment of the request).

Packet analysis can also be used extensively for security. It can detect unusual behavior (such as a high number of DNS responses) that could indicate the presence of malware, search for unusual domains or IP address endpoints, and discover regular connections (beacons) to a threat actor's command and control (C&C) server.

Wireshark is a popular GUI packet capture and analysis tool and is shown in Figure 8-7. **Tcpdump** is a command-line packet analyzer. It displays TCP/IP packets and other packets being transmitted or received over a network. It runs on UNIX and Linux operating systems, and various forks of it are available for Windows computers. However, the output from Tcpdump can be voluminous and difficult to parse. **Tcpreplay** is a tool for editing packets and then "replaying" the packets back onto the network to observe their behavior.

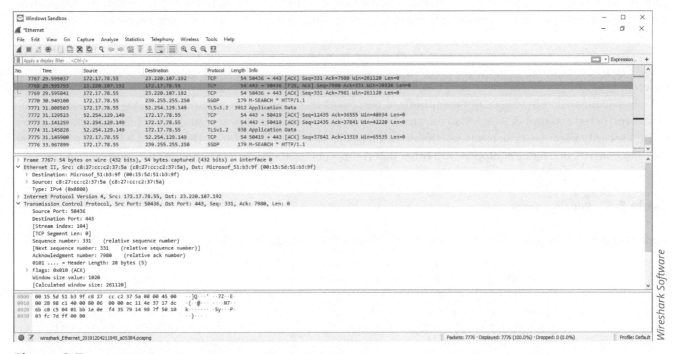

Figure 8-7   Wireshark packet capture and analysis tool

NOTE 14

Several switches are available for Tcpdump. A complete list of Tcpdump switches is available at *www.tcpdump.org/manpages/tcpdump.1.html*.

TWO RIGHTS & A WRONG

1. The tools tracert (Windows) and traceroute (Linux) show the details about the path a packet takes from a computer or device to a destination.
2. Nessus is from Kali Linux.
3. The Linux text file manipulation tool logger adds content to the syslog file.

See Appendix B for the answer.

PHYSICAL SECURITY CONTROLS

 **CERTIFICATION**

2.7 Explain the importance of physical security controls.

An obvious but often-overlooked consideration when defending a network is physical security: preventing a threat actor from physically accessing the network is as important as preventing the attacker from accessing it remotely. Physical security controls include external perimeter defenses, internal physical security controls, and computer hardware security.

External Perimeter Defenses

Some organizations use **industrial camouflage** in an attempt to make the physical presence of a building as non-descript as possible so that to a casual viewer, the building does not look like it houses anything important. When camouflage is not possible, external perimeter defenses must be used. External perimeter defenses are designed to restrict access to the areas in which equipment is located. This type of defense includes barriers, personnel, and sensors.

Barriers

Different types of passive barriers can restrict people or vehicles from entering a secure area. **Fencing** is usually a tall, permanent structure to keep out unauthorized personnel. It is usually accompanied by **signage** that explains the area is restricted and proper **lighting** so the area can be viewed after dark. However, standard chain link fencing offers limited security because it can easily be circumvented by climbing over it or cutting the links. Most modern perimeter security consists of a fence equipped with other deterrents such as those listed in Table 8-6.

Table 8-6 Fencing deterrents

Technology	Description	Comments
Anticlimb paint	A nontoxic petroleum gel-based paint that is thickly applied and does not harden, making any coated surface very difficult to climb.	Typically used on poles, downpipes, wall tops, and railings above head height (8 feet or 2.4 meters).
Anticlimb collar	Spiked collar that extends horizontally for up to 3 feet (1 meter) from the pole to prevent anyone from climbing it; serves as both a practical and visual deterrent.	Used for protecting equipment mounted on poles like cameras or in areas where climbing a pole can be an easy point of access over a security fence.
Roller barrier	Independently rotating large cups (diameter of 5 inches or 115 millimeters) affixed to the top of a fence prevents the hands of intruders from gripping the top of a fence to climb over it.	Often found around public grounds and schools where a nonaggressive barrier is important.
Rotating spikes	Installed at the top of walls, gates, or fences; the tri-wing spike collars rotate around a central spindle.	Designed for high-security areas; can be painted to blend into fencing.

Like fencing, a **barricade** is generally designed to block the passage of traffic. However, barricades are most often used for directing large crowds and are generally not designed to keep out individuals. This is because barricades are usually not as tall as fences and can easily be circumvented by climbing over them. A **bollard** is a short but sturdy vertical post that is used as a vehicular traffic barricade to prevent a car from ramming into a secured area. A pair of bollards is pictured in Figure 8-8.

MartineDF/Shutterstock.com

Figure 8-8 Bollards

Personnel

Whereas barriers act as passive devices to restrict access, personnel are considered active security elements. Unlike passive devices, personnel can differentiate between an intruder and someone looking for a lost pet and then decide when it is necessary to take appropriate action.

Human **security guards** who patrol and monitor restricted areas are most often used as an active security defense. In settings that require a higher level of protection, two security guards may be required. This prevents one security guard who has been compromised (through bribery, threats, or other coercion) from participating in an attack, such as allowing malicious actors entrance through a locked door. Using two security guards is called **two-person integrity/control**.

NOTE 15

Most of the major heists involving the theft of large amounts of cash or precious jewels have been the result of an inside employee of a bank, airport warehouse, or other facility participating in the theft.

Some guards are responsible for monitoring activity captured by video surveillance cameras that transmit a signal to a specific and limited set of receivers called **closed circuit television (CCTV)**. Some CCTV cameras are fixed in a single position pointed at a door or a hallway, while other cameras resemble a small dome and allow guards to move the camera 360 degrees for a full panoramic view. High-end video surveillance cameras only record when they detect movement (**motion recognition**), while others can identify a suspicious object such as a backpack left in a chair and sound an alert (**object detection**). Increasingly, drones, also called unmanned aerial vehicles (UAVs), include cameras for monitoring activity.

NOTE 16

When guards actively monitor a CCTV, it is a preventive measure: any unauthorized activity seen on video surveillance results in the guard taking immediate action by going to the scene or calling for assistance. When a guard does not actively monitor a CCTV, the video is recorded and, if a security event occurs, the recording is examined later to identify the culprit.

Robot sentries that patrol and use CCTV with object detection are increasingly being used in public areas. Figure 8-9 shows a robot sentry. Armed robberies, burglaries, and hit-and-run incidents have been solved by data recorded by a robot sentry.

Figure 8-9   Robot sentry

A receptionist who staffs a public reception area can also provide a level of active security. Public reception areas are an often-overlooked risk: once visitors are in the reception area, they are already inside the facility beyond external barriers. The receptionist's duty should be to observe and interact appropriately with the public so that potential malicious actors feel they are always being observed. This means receptionists should not have additional clerical duties beyond maintaining a visitor log or record (either paper or electronic) of those individuals granted access; otherwise, the receptionists will be distracted from their primary duty.

NOTE 17

Other precautions that should be taken in a public reception area include anchoring furnishings and wall hangings so they cannot be picked up and thrown or used as weapons. The reception room should not be used for mail deliveries, as an employee entrance, or a designated escape route. Receptionists should be able to observe visitors before they enter the reception room and electrically lock out suspicious persons. Receptionists should not be expected to physically intercept or impede a real or perceived attacker but, instead, call for help.

Sensors

With human personnel, an incident may occur during a lapse of attention by a security guard. To supplement the work of security guards, sensors can be placed in strategic locations to alert guards by generating an audible alarm of an unexpected or unusual action. Table 8-7 lists different types of sensors.

Table 8-7   Sensors

Name	Usage	Description
Motion detection	Can determine an object's change in position in relation to its surroundings.	Passive and active infrared light sensors; can be accurately placed by using sensor cards that can safely locate optical beams invisible to human eye.
Noise detection	Can detect a suspicious noise.	Microphones that turn on when the sensor is using noise-activated technology.
Temperature detection	Will detect a sudden increase or decrease in temperature or the temperature of an object in relation to its surroundings.	A thermal camera can be used to determine if a person is lurking in a dark room.
Moisture detection	Can detect water leaks, dampness, or increased moisture levels.	Often used to detect location of a leak from a water pipe.
Proximity	A sensor that detects the presence of an object ("target") when the target enters the sensor's field.	Depending on the type of proximity sensor, sound, light, infrared radiation (IR), or electromagnetic fields may be utilized by the sensor to detect a target.

Internal Physical Security Controls

External perimeter defenses are designed to keep an intruder from entering a campus, building, or other area. If unauthorized personnel defeat external perimeter defenses, they should next face internal physical access security, such as locks, secure areas, and protected cable distribution. In addition, fire suppression is considered an internal physical control.

Locks

A variety of locks can restrict access. **Physical locks** that require a key or other device to open doors or cabinets are the most common types of physical locks.

NOTE 18

The categories of commercial door locks include storeroom (the outside is always locked, entry is by key only, and the inside lever is always unlocked), classroom (the outside can be locked or unlocked, and the inside lever is always unlocked), store entry double cylinder (includes a keyed cylinder in both the outside and inside knobs so that a key in either knob locks or unlocks both at the same time), and communicating double cylinder lock (includes a keyed cylinder in both outside and inside knobs, and the key unlocks its own knob independently).

However, physical locks that use keys can be compromised if the keys are lost, stolen, or duplicated. Keys distributed to multiple users to access a single locked door increases the risk of a key being compromised. A more secure option is to use an **electronic lock**, as shown in Figure 8-10. Electronic locks use buttons that must be pushed in the proper sequence to open the door. An electronic lock can also be programmed to maintain a record of when the door was opened and by which code and to allow someone's code to be valid only at specific times. Growing in popularity are *smart locks* that use a smartphone that sends a code via wireless Bluetooth to open the door, and *fingerprint locks* that have a pad that scans a user's fingerprint.

myboys.me/Shutterstock.com

Figure 8-10   Electronic lock

A problem with an electronic lock is that someone can watch a user enter the code on a physical keypad by shoulder surfing or even detect fingerprint "smudges" on keys to uncover the code. One brand of electronic lock mitigates this weakness by using a virtual screen that substitutes physical buttons with four circles. Each circle displays the numbers associated with that circle (for example, Circle A may display the digits 1, 2, and 3, while Circle B displays the digits 4, 5, and 6) and the digits are randomly assigned to different circles: Circle A now may be 4, 7, and 0 while later it is 2, 5, and 9. This prevents a shoulder surfer from pressing the same circles to unlock the door.

Secure Areas

In a combat area, a **demilitarized zone (DMZ)** separates two warring nations. In cybersecurity, a DMZ is likewise an area that separates threat actors from defenders (also called a physical **air gap**). Enterprises often have DMZs or **secure areas** in a building or office to separate the secure facilities from unknown and potentially hostile outsiders.

Before electronic security was available, vestibules with two locked doors controlled access to sensitive areas. Individuals would give their credentials to a security officer, who opened the first door to a small room (a vestibule) and asked the individuals to enter and wait while their credentials (usually a **badge** or other token that indicates they have been approved) were checked. If the credentials were approved, the second door would be unlocked; if the credentials were fraudulent, the person would be trapped in the vestibule (a *mantrap*).

A modern **mantrap** is designed as an air gap to separate a nonsecure area from a secured area. A mantrap device monitors and controls two interlocking doors to a vestibule, as shown in Figure 8-11. When in operation, only one door can be open at any time. Creating a physical air gap, or the absence of any type of connection between the areas, can improve security. Mantraps are used in high-security areas where only authorized persons can enter, such as cash-handling areas and research laboratories.

Another area that must be secured is the *data center* that houses the on-prem network, server, and storage equipment. Because network equipment and servers in a data center generate large amounts of heat, a **hot aisle/cold aisle** layout can reduce the heat by managing air flow. In a data center using a hot aisle/cold aisle layout, the server racks are arranged in alternating rows, with cold air intakes facing one direction and hot air exhausts facing the other direction. The rows composed of the rack fronts are the cold aisles and face air conditioner output ducts. The rows with the backs of the racks where the heated exhausts exit are the hot aisles and generally face the air conditioner return ducts.

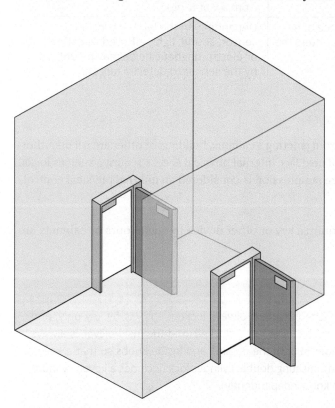

Figure 8-11 Mantrap

Protected Cable Distribution

Cable conduits are hollow tubes that carry copper wire or fiber-optic cables, as shown in Figure 8-12. A **protected cable distribution** is a system of cable conduits used to protect classified information that is being transmitted between two secure areas. PDS is a standard created by the U.S. Department of Defense (DOD).

Two types of PDS are commonly used. In a *hardened carrier PDS*, the data cables are installed in a conduit constructed of special electrical metallic tubing or similar

Peter Sobolev/Shutterstock.com

Figure 8-12 Cable conduits

material. All the connections between segments are permanently sealed with welds or special sealants. If the hardened carrier PDS is buried underground, such as running between buildings, the carrier containing the cables must be encased in concrete, and any manhole covers that give access to the PDS must be locked down. A hardened carrier PDS must be visually inspected on a regular basis.

An alternative to a hardened carrier PDS is an *alarmed carrier PDS*. In this type of PDS, the carrier system is deployed with specialized optical fibers in the conduit that can sense acoustic vibrations that occur when an intruder attempts to gain access to the cables, which triggers an alarm. The advantages of an alarmed carrier PDS are that it provides continuous monitoring, eliminates the need for periodic visual inspections, allows the carrier to be hidden above the ceiling or below the floor, and eliminates the need for welding or sealing connections.

Fire Suppression

Damage inflicted as a result of a fire is a constant threat to persons as well as property. **Fire suppression** includes the attempts to reduce the impact of a fire.

In a data center that contains electronic equipment, using water or a handheld fire extinguisher is not recommended because it can contaminate the equipment. Instead, stationary fire suppression systems are integrated into the building's infrastructure and release fire suppressant. The systems can be classified as dry chemical systems that disperse a fine, dry powder over the fire or clean agent systems that do not harm people, documents, or electrical equipment in the room. Clean agents can extinguish a fire by reducing heat, removing or isolating oxygen, or inhibiting the chemical reaction.

Computer Hardware Security

Computer hardware security is the physical security that specifically involves protecting endpoint hardware, such as laptops that can easily be stolen. Most portable devices (as well as many expensive computer monitors) have a special steel bracket security slot built into the case. A **cable lock** can be inserted into the security slot of a portable device and rotated so that the cable lock is secured to the device, as illustrated in Figure 8-13. The cable can then be connected to an immovable object.

For storage, a laptop can be placed in a **safe** or a **vault**, which is a ruggedized steel box with a lock. Some offices have safes in employee cubicles for the users to lock up important papers when away from their desks, even for a short period of time. The sizes typically range from small (to accommodate one laptop) to large (for multiple devices). Safes and cabinets also can be prewired for electrical power as well as wired network connections. This allows the laptops stored in the locking cabinet to charge their batteries and receive software updates while not in use.

Figure 8-13 Cable lock

O.Bellini/Shutterstock.com

Computer systems, printers, and similar digital electronic devices emit electromagnetic fields, which can result in interference, called *electromagnetic interference (EMI)*. Electromagnetic spying, or picking up electromagnetic fields and reading the data that is producing them, is a risk.

NOTE 20

In mid-2020, researchers revealed a new technique for long-distance eavesdropping they call "lamphone." Anyone with a computer, telescope, and a $400 electrooptical sensor can listen to any sounds in a room hundreds of feet away in real time simply by observing the minuscule vibrations those sounds create on the glass surface of a light bulb inside the room. By measuring the tiny changes in light output from the bulb that those vibrations cause, the researchers show that a spy can pick up sound clearly enough to discern the contents of conversations or even recognize a piece of music.

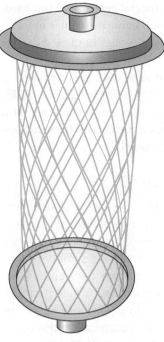

One means of protecting against EMI is a **Faraday cage**, a metallic enclosure that prevents the entry or escape of an electromagnetic field. A Faraday cage, consisting of a grounded, fine-mesh copper screening, as shown in Figure 8-14, is often used for testing in electronic labs. In addition, lightweight and portable *Faraday bags* made of special materials can shield cell phones and portable computing devices such as tablets and notebook computers. Faraday bags are often used in crime scene investigations. Phones, tablets, or laptops found on scene are placed in Faraday bags, thus eliminating inbound and outbound signals and preventing the devices from being remotely wiped of evidence.

TWO RIGHTS & A WRONG

1. A barricade is a short but sturdy vertical post that is used as a vehicular traffic barricade to prevent a car from ramming into a secured area.
2. An electronic lock is a combination lock that uses buttons that must be pushed in the proper sequence to open the door.
3. A DMZ is also called a physical air gap.

See Appendix B for the answer.

Figure 8-14   Faraday cage

☐ VM LAB   You're now ready to complete the live, virtual machine labs for this module. The labs can be found in the Practice It folder in each MindTap module.

SUMMARY

- Some attacks are designed to intercept network communications. A man-in-the-middle (MITM) attack intercepts legitimate communication and forges a fictitious response to the sender or eavesdrops on the conversation. A session replay attack intercepts and uses a session ID to impersonate a user. A man-in-the-browser (MITB) attack occurs between a browser and the underlying computer. An MITB attack seeks to intercept and then manipulate the communication between the web browser and the security mechanisms of the computer.

- Layer 2 of the OSI model is particularly weak and is a frequent target of threat actors. ARP poisoning changes the ARP cache so the corresponding IP address is pointing to a different computer. In a MAC cloning attack, threat actors will discover a valid MAC address of a device connected to a switch and then spoof that MAC address on their device and send a packet onto the network. The switch will change its MAC address table to reflect this new association of that MAC address with the port to which the attackers' device is connected. In a MAC flooding attack, threat actors will overflow the switch with Ethernet packets that have been spoofed so that every packet contains a different source MAC address, each appearing to come from a different endpoint. This can quickly consume all the memory for the MAC address table and will enter a fail-open mode and function like a network hub, broadcasting frames to all ports. Threat actors could then install software or a hardware device that captures and decodes packets on one client connected to the switch to view all traffic.

- DNS poisoning modifies a local lookup table on a device to point to a different domain, which is usually a malicious DNS server controlled by a threat actor that will redirect traffic to a website designed to steal user information or infect the device with malware. DNS hijacking is intended to infect an external DNS server with IP addresses that point to malicious sites. A distributed denial of service (DDoS) attack involves a device being overwhelmed by a torrent of fake requests so that it cannot respond to legitimate requests for service.

- Several successful network attacks come from malicious software code and scripts. PowerShell is a task automation and configuration management framework from Microsoft. The power and reach of PowerShell make it a prime target for threat actors who use it to inject malware. Visual Basic for Applications (VBA) is an "event-driven" Microsoft programming language that is used to automate processes that normally would take multiple steps or levels of steps. VBA is most often used to create macros. A macro is a series of instructions that can be grouped together as a single command. Macros are still used to distribute malware. Python is a popular programming language that can run on several different OS platforms. There are several "best prac-tices" to follow when using Python so that the code does not contain vulnerabilities. Bash is the command language interpreter (called the "shell") for the Linux/UNIX OS. Bash scripting is using Bash to create a script (a script is essentially the same as a program, but it is interpreted and executed without the need for it to be first compiled into machine language). Exploits have taken advantage of vulnerabilities in Bash.

- There are several different assessment tools for determining the strength of a network. Text files are a funda-mental element when using the Linux OS. Because virtually all configuration files in Linux are text files, chang-ing the configuration of a security application involves modifying the text configuration file. Thus, being able to manipulate text is an important skill in managing Linux security, as well as other applications and even the OS itself. There are a variety of different tools that can be used to create scripts that facilitate tasks. One tool that supports scripting is OpenSSL, a cryptography library that offers open source applications of the TLS protocol.

- Collecting and analyzing data packets that cross a network can provide a wealth of valuable information. Packet analysis can also be used extensively for security. Wireshark is a popular GUI packet capture and analysis tool. Tcpdump is a command-line packet analyzer. Tcpreplay is a tool for editing packets and then "replaying" the packets back onto the network to observe their behavior.

- An often-overlooked consideration when defending a network is physical security: preventing a threat actor from physically accessing the network is as important as preventing the attacker from accessing it remotely. External perimeter defenses are designed to restrict access to the areas in which equipment is located. Fencing is usually a tall, permanent structure to keep out unauthorized personnel. It is usually accompanied by signage that explains the area is restricted and proper lighting so the area can be viewed after dark. A barricade is generally designed to block the passage of traffic. A bollard is a short but sturdy vertical post that is used to as a vehicular traffic barricade to prevent a car from ramming into a secured area.

- While barriers act as passive devices to restrict access, personnel are considered active security elements. Human security guards who patrol and monitor restricted areas are most often used as an active security defense. Using two security guards is called two-person integrity/control. Some guards are responsible for monitoring activity captured by video surveillance cameras that transmit a signal to a specific and limited set of receivers called closed circuit television (CCTV). High-end video surveillance cameras only record when they detect movement (motion recognition) while others can identify a suspicious objective and sound an alert. Increasingly, drones/unmanned aerial vehicles (UAV) with cameras are also being used for monitoring activity. Robot sentries that patrol and use CCTV with object detection are increasingly being used in public areas. A receptionist who staffs a public reception area can also provide a level of active security. To supple-ment the work of security guards, sensors can be placed in strategic locations to alert guards by generating an audible alarm of an unexpected or unusual action.

- In the event that unauthorized personnel defeat external perimeter defenses, they should then face internal physical access security. A variety of types of locks can be used to restrict access. Physical locks that require a key or other device to open doors or cabinets are the most common types of physical locks. However, physical locks that use keys can be compromised if the keys are lost, stolen, or duplicated. A more secure option is to use an electronic lock. These locks use buttons that must be pushed in the proper sequence to open the door.

- A demilitarized zone (DMZ) is an area that separates threat actors from defenders (also called a physical air gap). A mantrap is designed as an air gap to separate a nonsecure area from a secured area. A mantrap device monitors and controls two interlocking doors to a vestibule. A protected cable distribution is a system of cable conduits used to protect classified information that is being transmitted between two secure areas. Damage inflicted as a result of a fire is a constant threat to persons as well as property. Fire suppression includes the attempts to reduce the impact of a fire. In a data center that contains electronic equipment, using a handheld fire extinguisher is not recommended because the chemical contents can contaminate the equipment. Instead, stationary fire suppression systems are integrated into the building's infrastructure and release fire suppressant in the room.

- A cable lock can be inserted into the security slot of a portable device and rotated so that the cable lock is secured to the device. When storing a laptop, it can be placed in a safe or a vault, which is a ruggedized steel box with a lock. Some offices have safes in employee cubicles for the users to lock up important papers when away from their desks, even for a short period of time. A Faraday cage is a metallic enclosure that prevents the entry or escape of an electromagnetic field.

Key Terms

Address Resolution Protocol (ARP)	hot aisle/cold aisle	protected cable distribution
air gap	hping	proximity
alarm	ifconfig	Python
ARP poisoning	industrial camouflage	receptionist
badge	ipconfig	robot sentries
barricade	lighting	route
Bash	logger	safe
bollard	MAC cloning attack	scanless
cable lock	MAC flooding attack	secure areas
cat	macro	security guards
chmod	man-in-the-browser (MITB)	sensors
closed circuit television (CCTV)	man-in-the-middle (MITM)	session replay
Cuckoo	mantrap	signage
curl	moisture detection	sn1per
demilitarized zone (DMZ)	motion detection	tail
dig	motion recognition	Tcpdump
distributed denial of service (DDoS)	Nessus	Tcpreplay
DNS hijacking	netstat	temperature detection
DNS poisoning	nmap	theHarvester
dnsenum	noise detection	traceroute
domain name resolution	nslookup	tracert
domain reputation	object detection	two-person integrity/control
electronic lock	OpenSSL	URL redirection
Faraday cage	Operational Technology (OT)	vault
fencing	pathping	visitor log
fire suppression	physical locks	Visual Basic for
grep	ping	Applications (VBA)
head	PowerShell	Wireshark

Review Questions

1. Which attack intercepts communications between a web browser and the underlying OS?
   a. Interception
   b. Man-in-the-browser (MITB)
   c. DIG
   d. ARP poisoning

2. Calix was asked to protect a system from a potential attack on DNS. What are the locations he would need to protect?
   a. Web server buffer and host DNS server
   b. Reply referrer and domain buffer

   c. Web browser and browser add-on
   d. Host table and external DNS server

3. What is the result of an ARP poisoning attack?
   a. The ARP cache is compromised.
   b. Users cannot reach a DNS server.
   c. MAC addresses are altered.
   d. An internal DNS must be used instead of an external DNS.

4. Deacon has observed that the switch is broadcasting all packets to all devices. He suspects

it is the result of an attack that has overflowed the switch MAC address table. Which type of attack is this?

a. MAC spoofing attack
b. MAC cloning attack
c. MAC flooding attack
d. MAC overflow attack

5. Tomaso is explaining to a colleague the different types of DNS attacks. Which DNS attack would only impact a single user?

a. DNS hijack attack
b. DNS poisoning attack
c. DNS overflow attack
d. DNS resource attack

6. Proteus has been asked to secure endpoints that can be programmed and have an IP address so that they cannot be used in a DDoS attack. What is the name for this source of DDoS attack?

a. Network
b. Application
c. IoT
d. Operational Technology

7. Which of the following is NOT a reason that threat actors use PowerShell for attacks?

a. It cannot be detected by antimalware running on the computer.
b. It leaves behind no evidence on a hard drive.
c. It can be invoked prior to system boot.
d. Most applications flag it as a trusted application.

8. What is the difference between a DoS and a DDoS attack?

a. DoS attacks are faster than DDoS attacks.
b. DoS attacks use fewer computers than DDoS attacks.
c. DoS attacks do not use DNS servers as DDoS attacks do.
d. DoS attacks use more memory than DDoS attacks.

9. Which of the following is NOT true about VBA?

a. It is commonly used to create macros.
b. It is built into most Microsoft Office applications.
c. It is included in select non-Microsoft products.
d. It is being phased out and replaced by PowerShell.

10. Which of the following is NOT a Microsoft defense against macros?

a. Protected View
b. Trusted documents
c. Trusted domain
d. Trusted location

11. Theo uses the Python programming language and does not want his code to contain vulnerabilities. Which of the following best practices would Theo NOT use?

a. Only use compiled and not interpreted Python code.
b. Use the latest version of Python.
c. Use caution when formatting strings.
d. Download only vetted libraries.

12. What is Bash?

a. The command-language interpreter for Linux/UNIX OSs
b. The open source scripting language that contains many vulnerabilities
c. A substitute for SSH
d. The underlying platform on which macOS is built

13. Gregory wants to look at the details about the patch a packet takes from his Linux computer to another device. Which Linux command-line utility will he use?

a. tracepacket
b. trace
c. tracert
d. traceroute

14. Which utility sends custom TCP/IP packets?

a. curl
b. hping
c. shape
d. pingpacket

15. Which of the following is a third-party OS penetration testing tool?

a. theHarvester
b. scanless
c. Nessus
d. sn1per

16. Eros wants to change a configuration file on his Linux computer. He first wants to display the entire file contents. Which tool would he use?

a. head
b. show
c. display
d. cat

17. Which of the following is a tool for editing packets and then putting the packets back onto the network to observe their behavior?

a. Tcpreplay
b. Tcpdump
c. Wireshark
d. Packetdump

18. Estevan has recommended that the organization hire and deploy two security guards in the control room to limit the effect if one of the guards has been compromised. What is Estevan proposing?
    a. Dual observation protocol (DOP)
    b. Compromise mitigation assessment (CMA)
    c. Two-person integrity/control
    d. Multiplayer recognition

19. Which of the following sensors can detect an object that enters the sensor's field?
    a. Proximity
    b. Field detection
    c. IR verification
    d. Object recognition

20. Which of the following does NOT describe an area that separates threat actors from defenders?
    a. DMZ
    b. Air gap
    c. Secure area
    d. Containment space

Hands-On Projects

 CAUTION   If you are concerned about installing any of the software in these projects on your regular computer, you can instead use the Windows Sandbox or install the software in the Windows virtual machine created in the Module 1 Hands-On Projects. Software installed within the virtual machine will not impact the host computer.

Project 8-1: DNS Poisoning

Time Required: 20 minutes

Objective: Given a scenario, analyze potential indicators associated with network attacks.

Description: Substituting a fraudulent IP address can be done by either attacking the Domain Name System (DNS) server or the local host table. Attackers can target a local hosts file to create new entries that will redirect users to their fraudulent site. In this project, you add a fraudulent entry to the local hosts file.

1. Go to the Western Kentucky University website at **www.wku.wku**.
2. Go to the Ivy Tech Community College website at **www.ivytech.edu**.
3. Now find the IP address of the website of the two schools. Open a command line and enter **ping** *name_of_website* or go to **ipaddress.com/ip_lookup/** and enter the domain name to receive the correct IP address.

 **CAUTION**   You will likely receive a message that says "Request timed out" indicating the web server is rejecting any ping request. However, it will resolve the name of the web site by displaying the IP address in square brackets.

4. Click **Start** and then **Windows Accessories**.
5. Right-click **Notepad** and then **More** and select **Run as administrator**. If you receive the message **Do you want to allow this app to make changes to the device?** click **Yes**.
6. Click **File** and then **Open**. Click the **File Type** drop-down arrow to change from **Text Documents (*.txt)** to **All Files (*.*)**.

7. Navigate to the file **C:\Windows\System32\drivers\etc\hosts** and open it.

8. At the end of the file following all hashtags (#) in the first column enter the IP address you recorded of Western Kentucky University.

9. Press **Tab** and enter *www.ivytech.edu*. In this hosts table, the domain name of Ivy Tech Community College is now resolved to the IP address of Western Kentucky University.

10. Click **File** and then **Save**.

11. Open your web browser and then enter the URL of Ivy Tech Community College (**www.ivytech.edu**). What website appears?

12. Return to the hosts file and remove this entry.

13. Click **File** and then **Save**.

14. Close all windows.

Project 8-2: ARP Poisoning

Time Required: 25 minutes
Objective: Given a scenario, analyze potential indicators associated with network attacks.
Description: Attackers frequently modify the Address Resolution Protocol (ARP) table to redirect communications away from a valid device to an attacker's computer. In this project, you view the ARP table on your computer and modify it. You will need to have another "victim's" computer running on your network (and know the IP address), as well as a default gateway that serves as the switch to the network.

1. Open a Command Prompt window by right-clicking **Start** and selecting **Windows PowerShell (Admin)**.

2. To view your current ARP table, type **arp -a** and then press **Enter**. The Internet Address is the IP address of another device on the network while the Physical Address is the MAC address of that device.

3. To determine network addresses, type **ipconfig/all** and then press **Enter**.

4. Record the IP address of the default gateway.

5. Delete the ARP table entry of the default gateway by typing **arp -d** followed by the IP address of the gateway, such as **arp -d 192.168.1.1**, and then press **Enter**.

6. Create an automatic entry in the ARP table of the victim's computer by typing **ping** followed by that computer's IP address, such as **ping 192.168.1.100**, and then press **Enter**.

7. Verify that this new entry is now listed in the ARP table by typing **arp -a** and then press **Enter**. Record the physical address of that computer.

8. Add that entry to the ARP table by entering **arp -s** followed by the IP address and then the MAC address.

9. Delete all entries from the ARP table by typing **arp -d**.

10. Close all windows.

Project 8-3: MAC Spoofing

Time Required: 25 minutes
Objective: Given a scenario, analyze potential indicators associated with network attacks.
Description: In a MAC cloning attack, threat actors discover a valid MAC address of a device connected to a switch. They spoof the MAC address on their device and send a packet onto the network. In this activity, you will spoof a MAC address.

1. Go to the Technitium website at **technitium.com/tmac/**. (If you are no longer able to access the program through this URL, use a search engine to search for "Technitium MAC address changer.")

2. Click **Download Now**.

3. Click **Direct Download**.

4. Save the file to your computer, install the application, and then start it.

5. If necessary, click **Yes** to respond to the dialog box.

6. Scroll through the list of network connections on your computer, and then select your Internet connection.

7. Read the information on the **Information** tab.
8. Click **Random MAC Address** to display another MAC address that can be assigned to this device.
9. Click the down arrow in the box below the new random MAC address. Note the long list of different NIC vendors from which a MAC address can be chosen.
10. Click **(2C-30-33) Netgear**.
11. Look at the new MAC address under **Change MAC Address** and note the first three pairs of numbers. What does this correspond to?
12. Click **Why?** next to **Use '02' as first octet of MAC address**.
13. Read the explanation about why 02 should be used as the first octet.
14. If you want to change your MAC address, click **Change Now!** or close the application if you do not want to change the address.
15. How easy was it to spoof a MAC address? How can a threat actor use this in a MAC cloning attack?
16. Close all windows.

Case Projects

Case Project 8-1: DDoS Mitigation

How do organizations attempt to mitigate a sudden DDoS attack directed at their web servers? Use the Internet to research DDoS mitigation techniques, technologies, and third-party entities that provide mitigation services. Write a one-page paper on your research.

Case Project 8-2: DNS Services

Many organizations offer a free domain name resolution service that resolves DNS requests through a worldwide network of redundant DNS servers. The claim is that this is faster and more reliable than using the DNS servers provided by Internet service providers (ISPs). These DNS servers are supposed to improve security by maintaining a real-time blacklist of harmful websites and warning users when they attempt to access a site containing potentially threatening content. The providers also say that using their services can reduce exposure to types of DNS poisoning attacks. Research free DNS services. Identify at least three providers and create a table comparing their features. Are the claims of providing improved security valid? How do they compare with your ISP's DNS service? Write a one-page paper on your research.

Case Project 8-3: DNS-over-HTTPS (DoH)

To protect DNS, some providers are using DNS-over-HTTPS, also called DoH. As its name implies, DoH uses HTTPS instead of HTTP to send DNS queries via an encrypted HTTPS connection (Port 443) rather than sending them in cleartext (Port 53). The encrypted DoH query is sent to a special DoH-resolving server that aggregates all user's DoH queries and then translates them into regular unencrypted DNS queries for processing by DNS servers. However, DoH has become controversial. Why? What are the advantages of DoH? What are its disadvantages? How does it compare with DNS-over-TLS (DoT)? Write a one-page paper on your research.

Case Project 8-4: CCTV Technologies

Research new technologies for CCTV, including motion recognition and object detection. How accurate are the technologies? What are the advantages? What are the disadvantages? Write a one-page paper on your research.

Case Project 8-5: Robot Sentries

Research the Internet regarding robot sentries. Where are they being used? What is the purpose of a robot sentry? What are the risks? What is your projection on the future for robot sentries? Write a one-page paper on your research.

Case Project 8-6: Locks

Lock technology is changing rapidly. Use the Internet to research physical locks, electronic locks, smart locks, and fingerprint locks. Create a table of these types of locks and list their strengths, weaknesses, and costs. Which would you recommend? Why?

Case Project 8-7: Community Site Activity

The Information Security Community Site is an online companion to this textbook. It contains a wide variety of tools, information, discussion boards, and other features to assist learners. Go to **community.cengage.com/infosec2** and click the *Join or Sign in* icon to login, using your login name and password that you created in Module 1. Click **Forums (Discussion)** and click on **Security+ Case Projects (7ᵗʰ edition)**. Read the following case study.

Read again the Front-Page Cybersecurity at the beginning of this module. In addition to the three reasons listed why View windows would be interesting to attackers, can you think of two or more other reasons how attackers (either cybersecurity attackers or physical criminals) could manipulate these windows? Now pretend that you are a security consultant and View is one of your clients. What would you say to the View CEO about his public statement that "The good news is the window's not that interesting to hack." Should CEOs first talk with employees before making those statements? Or have the security employees done a poor job in educating the View CEO about cybersecurity risks? Record your answers on the Community Site discussion board.

Case Project 8-8: North Ridge Security

North Ridge Security provides security consulting and assurance services. You have recently been hired as an intern to assist this company.

It's Your Birthday (IYB)! is a new North Ridge client that creates fun and innovative birthday experiences for clients of all ages. Recently, IYB! decided that the security at its corporate office needed to be addressed after several incidences of unauthorized personnel entering the offices. You are asked to provide information about internal physical security controls as a starting point in the discussion.

1. Create a PowerPoint presentation about internal physical security controls, including what they are, what they can protect, how they should be used, and the various types of controls. Include the advantages and disadvantages of each. Your presentation should contain at least 10 slides.
2. After the presentation, you were asked to follow up about reception areas and mantraps, especially how to configure each. Create a memo communicating which you would recommend and why.

References

1. Thompson, Mia, "How to stay safe from Office macro-based malware with email security," *Solarwinds MSP*, Feb. 10, 2020, accessed Jun. 17, 2020, www.solarwindsmsp.com/blog/how-stay-safe-office-macro-based-malware-email-security.

NETWORK SECURITY APPLIANCES AND TECHNOLOGIES

After completing this module, you should be able to do the following:

1 List the different types of network security appliances and how they can be used

2 Describe network security technologies

Front-Page Cybersecurity

One constant across all of the Star Wars films is the use of weapons: lightsabers, blasters, ion cannons, and planetary turbolasers are just a few that are used by both the Rebellion and the Evil Empire. An additional weapon in the Star Wars arsenal did not appear in any film but was extremely important. The weapon kept cyber threat actors from stealing the script as it was developed. As with most Star Wars weapons, it worked.

Protecting new Star Wars scripts is a high-stakes effort. The Star Wars franchise is estimated to have grossed more than $10 billion since the first movie came out in 1977. The success of the movies shows no signs of diminishing. The latest movie, *Star Wars: The Rise of Skywalker*, has already grossed more than $1 billion since its release in December 2019. Those involved with the Star Wars films have every incentive to make sure that scripts for future releases are kept secure and are not stolen. A leaked script would spoil the impact of the storyline and affect ticket sales for the movie.

In recent years, attackers have stolen scripts or entire movies from movie studios or their affiliates. In 2017, a group of attackers stole and then leaked the entire fifth season of Netflix's *Orange Is the New Black* videos along with several other productions from Larson Studios, a Hollywood-based audio post-production company. In late 2004, attackers breached Sony security and posted online several unreleased movies, including *Annie*, *Mr. Turner*, *To Write Love on Her Arms*, and *The Interview*.

What weapons has Star Wars used to protect itself from attackers?

Consider the weapon that the writer and director, Rian Johnson, used to protect his script while he was developing *Star Wars: The Last Jedi* from theft.

He used an air gap.

One of the best means of providing security is to completely disconnect a device from any and all networks. Sometimes called an air gap, this method simply means that the device is not connected to a network or anything else. In today's world, it can be cumbersome and inconvenient to have an unconnected device, but it provides a high level of security.

That's exactly what Rian Johnson did. While writing the script, Rian never connected his MacBook Air to any network (either a LAN or the Internet) and never used it for email, online research, or anything else. In fact, his MacBook Air was only used for one purpose: to write the script. Isolating the laptop meant that no outsiders could get to his script through a network vulnerability. While he was not using it, the MacBook Air was locked securely in a safe at the studios. Rian's air gap weapon worked as expected and the script was never stolen.

    Rian did say that his producer had a constant worry. He was terrified that Rian would walk off and leave the MacBook at a coffee shop.

At one time, *information security* and *network security* were virtually synonymous. That was because the network was viewed as the "moat" around which endpoint computers could be kept safe. A secure network was seen as the key to keeping attackers away.

    This approach, however, proved to be untenable. Too many entry points allow attackers to circumvent the network and introduce malware. For example, users could insert an infected USB flash drive into their computer, thus installing malware while bypassing the secure network. With computers connected to the unsecure Internet, malware could take advantage of common network protocols, such as Hypertext Transfer Protocol (HTTP), without being detected or blocked by network security appliances.

    This is not to say that network security is unimportant. Having a secure network is still essential. Even today, not all applications are designed and written with security in mind, so it falls on the network to provide protection. Network-delivered services can also scale better for larger environments and can complement server and application functionality. Because an attacker who successfully penetrates a computer network can access hundreds or even thousands of endpoints, servers, and storage devices, a secure network defense remains a critical element in any enterprise's overall security plan.

    This module explores network security. It investigates how to build a secure network through network security appliances and technologies.

SECURITY APPLIANCES

 **CERTIFICATION**

2.1 Explain the importance of security concepts in an enterprise environment.

3.3 Given a scenario, implement secure network designs.

All modern networks have both standard networking devices (such as switches and routers) and specialized security appliances. Security can be achieved through the appliances that directly address security and by using the security features in standard networking devices. Using both standard networking devices and security appliances can result in a layered security approach, which can significantly improve security. To breach a network with layered security, an attacker must have the tools, knowledge, and skills to break through the various layers.

    While it is worthwhile to take advantage of the security features of standard networking devices, several security appliances can be dedicated to protecting a network. These appliances include firewalls, proxy servers, deception instruments, intrusion detection and prevention systems, and network hardware security modules. In addition, these appliances must be properly configured.

NOTE 1

Security appliances are only one element in network security and should not be exclusively relied upon for protection. This can be illustrated through a successful attack on NASA's Jet Propulsion Laboratory (JPL) that resulted in 500 MB of stolen data related to a Mars mission. A 49-page report by the NASA Office of Inspector General (OIG) revealed that although the NASA JPL network had security appliances installed, the point of entry into the network by attackers was a $35 Raspberry Pi, small enough to fit in your hand, that a JPL employee connected to the JPL network without authorization.

Firewalls

Probably the most misunderstood security appliance is a firewall. Due to the nature of its name (*It's an impenetrable wall!*) and aided by inaccurate portrayals in movies and television, the general public often perceives a firewall as the ultimate security device that blocks anything and everything malicious from entering a network. Unfortunately, this is a wildly inaccurate perception. Firewalls are an important element in network security, but they fall far short of being the ultimate defense. To use them effectively, you should understand the function of firewalls and know the different types of firewalls and specialized firewall appliances.

Firewall Functions

Both national and local building codes require commercial buildings, apartments, and other similar structures to have a *firewall*. In building construction, a firewall is usually a brick, concrete, or masonry wall positioned vertically through all stories of the building. Its purpose is to contain a fire and prevent it from spreading. A computer **firewall** serves a similar purpose: it is designed to limit the spread of malware.

A firewall uses bidirectional inspection to examine both outgoing and incoming network packets. It allows approved packets to pass through but can take different actions when it detects a suspicious packet. The actions are based on specific criteria or rules; these types of firewalls are called *rule-based firewalls*. Firewall rules can contain parameters such as the following:

- *Source address*. The source address is the location of the origination of the packet (where the packet is *from*). Addresses generally can be indicated by a specific IP address or range of addresses, an IP mask, the MAC address, or host name.
- *Destination address*. This is the address the connection is attempting to reach (where the packet is going *to*). Destination addresses can be indicated in the same way as the source address.
- *Source port*. The source port is the TCP/IP port number used to send packets of data. Options for setting the source port often include a specific port number or a range of numbers.
- *Destination port*. This setting gives the port on the remote computer or device that the packets will use. Options are the same as for the source port.
- *Protocol*. The protocol defines the network protocol (such as *TCP, UDP, TCP or UDP, ICMP, or IP*) used when sending or receiving packets of data.
- *Direction*. This is the direction of traffic for the data packet (*Incoming, Outgoing, or Both*).
- *Priority*. The priority determines the order in which the rule is applied.
- *Time*. Rules can be set so they are active only during a scheduled time.
- *Context*. A rule can be created that is unique for specific circumstances (contexts). For example, different rules may be in effect depending on whether a laptop is on-site or is remote (sometimes called **geographical consideration**).
- *Action*. The action setting indicates what the firewall should do when the conditions of the rule are met. Typical firewall rule actions are listed in Table 9-1.

Table 9-1 Typical firewall rule actions

Action	Description	Example	Comments
Allow	Explicitly allows traffic that matches the rule to pass	Permit incoming Address Resolution Protocol (ARP) traffic	Allow implicitly denies all other traffic unless explicitly allowed
Bypass	Allows traffic to bypass the firewall	Bypass based on IP, port, traffic direction, and protocol	Designed for media-intensive protocols or traffic from a trusted source
Deny	Explicitly blocks all traffic that matches the rule	Deny traffic from IP address	Deny generally drops the packet with no return message to the sender
Force Allow	Forcibly allows traffic that would normally be denied by other rules	Useful for determining if essential network services are able to communicate	Traffic will still be subject to inspection by other security appliances
Log Only	Traffic is logged but no other action is taken	Bypass rules do not generate log files but Log Only will	Log Only occurs if the packet is not stopped by a Deny rule or an Allow rule that excludes it

Older firewalls often listed each rule as a separate instruction that was processed in sequence so that firewall rules were essentially *IF-THEN-ELSE* constructions: *IF* these rule conditions are met, *THEN* the action occurs, *ELSE* go on to the next rule. This construction made administrators consider the rules themselves and their sequencing. For example, if Rule #13 allowed an FTP connection to a specific address, but later Rule #27 was added to deny all FTP traffic, then FTP packets meeting Rule #13 would be allowed because it occurred first. More modern firewalls allow a priority order to be created to eliminate the confusion that often surrounded conflicting rules.

A more flexible type of firewall than a rule-based firewall is a *policy-based firewall*. This type of firewall allows more generic statements instead of specific rules. For example, the policy statement *Allow management traffic from trusted networks* could translate into specific rules that allow traffic from *192.2.0.0/24* to *TCP Port 22* and *192.2.100.0/24* to *TCP Port 3389*.

In addition to filtering based on packets, firewalls can also apply content/URL filtering. The firewall can monitor websites accessed through HTTP to create custom filtering profiles. The filtering can be performed by assessing webpages by their content category and then creating whitelists and blacklists of specific URLs. This type of filtering is often available with consumer-oriented firewalls and advertised as a parental control feature that is easily configurable, as shown in Figure 9-1.

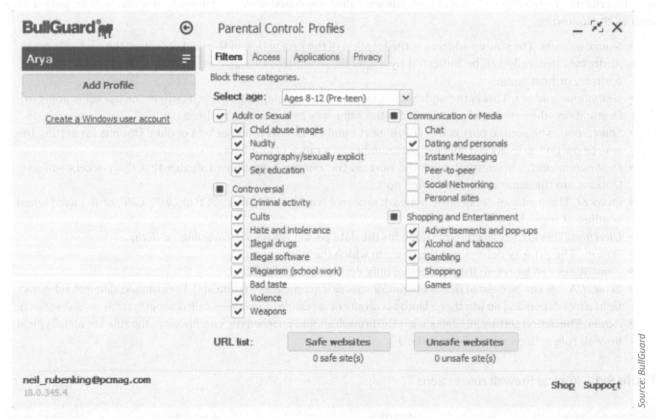

Figure 9-1   Content/URL filtering

Firewall Categories

The categories of firewalls can be compared as opposites and include the following:

- *Stateful vs. stateless.* Stateless packet filtering looks at a packet and permits or denies it based solely on the firewall rules. Stateful packet filtering uses both the firewall rules and the state of the connection: that is, did the internal device request this packet? A stateful packet filtering firewall keeps a record of the state of a connection between an internal endpoint and an external device. While a stateless packet filter firewall might allow a packet to pass through because it met all the necessary criteria (rules), a stateful packet filter would not let the packet pass if that internal endpoint did not first request the information from the external server.

- *Open source vs. proprietary.* Some firewalls are freely available (**open source firewalls**) while other firewalls are owned by an entity that has an exclusive right to them (**proprietary firewalls**). Open source firewalls have been gaining wider acceptance as they incorporate more features and are built on a secure foundation. For example, pfSense is built on the same underlying OS as many commercial products. See Figure 9-2.

	Floating	LocalNetworks	WAN	LAN	DMZ	WAN2	L2TP VPN	IPsec	OpenVPN				

Rules (Drag to Change Order)

	States	Protocol	Source	Port	Destination	Port	Gateway	Queue	Schedule	Description	Actions
Remote Administration											🗑
☐ ✓	6/803 KiB	IPv4 TCP	RemoteAdmin	*	This Firewall	admin ports	*	none		Allow firewall admin	⚓✎📋⊘🗑
VPN Rules											🗑
☐ ✓	0/0 B	IPv4 UDP	203.0.113.5	*	WAN address	1195	*	none		OpenVPN from Remote Site 2	⚓✎📋⊘🗑
☐ ✓	0/0 B	IPv4 UDP	203.0.113.5	*	WAN address	1194 (OpenVPN)	*	none		OpenVPN from Remote Site B	⚓✎📋⊘🗑
☐ ✓	0/0 B	IPv4 UDP	*	*	WAN address	1194 (OpenVPN)	*	none		Allow traffic to OpenVPN server	⚓✎📋⊘🗑
Public Services											🗑
☐ ✓	0/0 B	IPv4 TCP	*	*	10.3.0.15	80 (HTTP)	*	none		NAT HTTP to web server	⚓✎📋⊘🗑
☐ ✓	0/0 B	IPv4 TCP	bob	*	10.3.0.5	22 (SSH)	*	none		NAT Bob - SSH	⚓✎📋⊘🗑
☐ ✓	0/0 B	IPv4 TCP	sue	*	10.3.0.15	22 (SSH)	*	none		NAT Sue - SSH	⚓✎📋⊘🗑
Misc											🗑
☐ ✓	0/0 B	IPv4 TCP/UDP	WAN net	*	*	1812 - 1813	*	none		RADIUS from other test firewalls	⚓✎📋⊘🗑

Source: pfSense

Figure 9-2   pfSense open source firewall

- *Hardware vs. software.* A **software firewall** runs as a program or service on a device, such as a computer or router. **Hardware firewalls** are specialized separate devices that inspect traffic. Because they are specialized devices, hardware firewalls tend to have more features but are more expensive and can require more effort to configure and manage. However, a disadvantage of a software firewall is that a malware infection on the device on which it is running, such as a computer, could also compromise the software firewall. Whereas a hardware firewall also has underlying software, typically that footprint is smaller (to provide less of a target for attackers) or specialized.

- *Host vs. appliance vs. virtual.* A **host-based firewall** is a software firewall that runs on and protects a single endpoint device (a host). All modern OSs include a host-based firewall. The settings for the Microsoft Windows Defender host-based firewall are shown in Figure 9-3. A closer look at the configuration settings reveals that these firewalls tend to be application-centric: users can create an opening in the firewall for each specific application. This approach is more secure than permanently opening a port in the firewall that always remains open as opposed to a port that is only opened when the application requires it and is then closed. An **appliance firewall** is typically a separate hardware device designed to protect an entire network, as shown in Figure 9-4. A **virtual firewall** is one that runs in the cloud. Virtual firewalls are designed for settings, such as public cloud environments, in which deploying an appliance firewall would be difficult or even impossible.

Figure 9-3   Windows host-based firewall

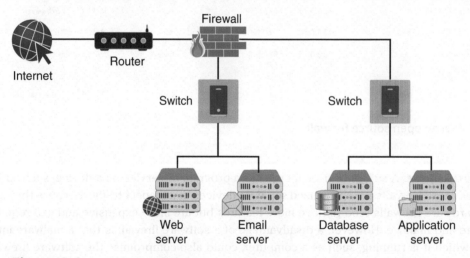

Figure 9-4   Appliance firewall

Specialized Firewall Appliances

Specialized firewall appliances include the following:

- *Web application firewall.* One specialized firewall is a **web application firewall (WAF)** that looks at the applications using HTTP. A web application firewall, which can be a separate hardware appliance or a software plug-in, can block specific websites or attacks that attempt to exploit known vulnerabilities in specific client software and can even block cross-site scripting and SQL injection attacks.

- *Network address translation gateway.* Network address translation (NAT) is a technique that allows private IP addresses to be used on the public Internet. It does this by replacing a private IP address with a public IP address. As a packet leaves a network, NAT removes the private IP address from the sender's packet and replaces it with an alias IP public address, and then maintains a record of the substitution. When a packet is returned, the process is reversed. A **network address translation gateway** is a cloud-based technology that performs NAT translations for cloud services. It can also provide a degree of security by masking the IP addresses of internal devices.

- *Next generation firewall*. A **next generation firewall (NGFW)** has additional functionality beyond a traditional firewall. NGFW can filter packets based on applications. NGFWs can detect applications by using *deep packet inspection* and thus can examine the payloads of packets and determine if they are carrying malware. In addition to basic firewall protections, filtering by applications, and deep packet inspection, NGFWs can also perform URL filtering and intrusion prevention services.
- *Unified threat management*. **Unified threat management (UTM)** is a device that combines several security functions. These include packet filtering, antispam, antiphishing, antispyware, encryption, intrusion protection, and web filtering.

NOTE 2

Often a device that performs services beyond that of a NGFW is called a UTM.

Proxy Servers

In general terms, a *proxy* is a person who is authorized to act as the substitute or agent on behalf of another person. For example, a family member who has been granted the power of attorney for a sick relative can make decisions and take actions on behalf of that person as a proxy.

Proxies are also devices used in computer networking. These devices act as substitutes on behalf of the primary device. A **forward proxy** is a computer or an application that intercepts user requests from the internal secure network and then processes the requests on behalf of the user. When an internal endpoint requests a service such as a file or a webpage from an external web server, it normally connects directly to the remote server. In a network using a forward proxy server, the endpoint first connects to the proxy server, which checks its memory to see if a previous request already has been fulfilled and if a copy of that file or page is residing on the proxy server in its temporary storage area (*cache*). If not, the proxy server connects to the external web server using its own IP address (instead of the internal endpoint's address) and requests the service. When the proxy server receives the requested item from the web server, the item is forwarded to the requester.

A **reverse proxy** routes requests coming from an external network to the correct internal server. To the outside user, the IP address of the reverse proxy is the final IP address for requesting services; however, only the reverse proxy can access the internal servers. Forward proxy and reverse proxy servers are illustrated in Figure 9-5.

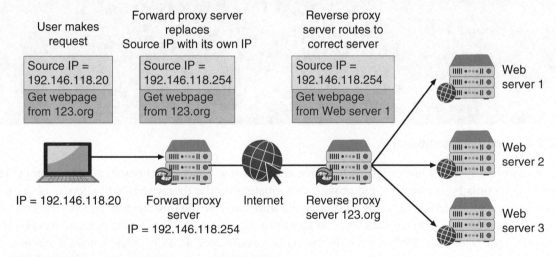

Figure 9-5 Forward and reverse proxy servers

Acting as the intermediary, a proxy server can provide a degree of protection. First, it can look for malware by intercepting it before it reaches the internal endpoint. Second, a proxy server can hide the IP address of endpoints inside the secure network so that only the proxy server's IP address is used on the open Internet.

Deception Instruments

Deception is the act of causing someone to accept as true that is false. Deception can be used as a security defense: by directing threat actors away from a valuable asset to something that has little or no value, threat actors can be tricked into thinking what they are attacking is valuable when it is not, or that their attack is successful when it is not. Creating network deception can involve creating and using honeypots and sinkholes.

NOTE 3

Niccolo Machiavelli, an Italian Renaissance diplomat and philosopher who is often called the father of modern political science, once said, "Never attempt to win by force what can be won by deception."

Honeypots

A **honeypot** is a computer located in an area with limited security that serves as "bait" to threat actors. The honeypot is intentionally configured with security vulnerabilities so that it is open to attacks. Security personnel generally have two goals when using a honeypot:

- *Deflect.* A honeypot can deflect or redirect threat actors' attention away from legitimate servers by encouraging them to spend their time and energy on the decoy server, distracting their attention from the data on the actual server.
- *Discover.* A honeypot can trick threat actors into revealing their attack techniques. Security experts can then determine if actual production systems could thwart such an attack.

Figure 9-6 shows the results from a honeypot dashboard; it lists attacker probes by time and country.

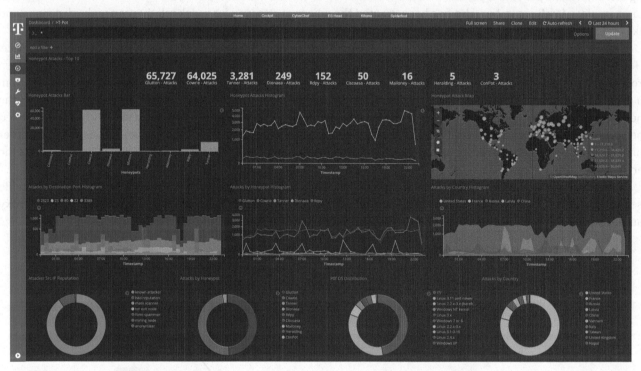

Figure 9-6   Honeypot dashboard

There are different types of honeypots. A *low-interaction honeypot* may only contain a login prompt. This type of honeypot only records login attempts and provides information on the threat actor's IP address of origin. A *high-interaction honeypot* is designed for capturing much more information from the threat actor. Usually it is configured with a default login and loaded with software, data files that appear to be authentic but are actually imitations of real data files (**honeyfiles**), and **fake telemetry**. (*Telemetry* is the collection of data such as how certain software features are used, application crashes, and general usage statics and behavior.) A high-interaction honeypot can collect valuable information from threat actors about attack techniques or the particular information they are seeking from the organization.

NOTE 4

The number of attempts against a honeypot is staggering. In one study, 10 honeypots around the world were created to simulate the Secure Shell (SSH) service. One honeypot started receiving login attempts just *52 seconds* after it went online. When all 10 of the honeypots were discovered, a login attempt was made about every *15 seconds on each one*. At the end of one month, over five million attacks had been attempted on the honeypots.[1]

Similar to a honeypot, a **honeynet** is a network set up with intentional vulnerabilities. Its purpose is also to invite attacks so that the attacker's methods can be studied; that information can then be used to increase network security. A honeynet typically contains one or more honeypots.

CAUTION Setting up a honeypot to attract threat actors can be dangerous. There must be no connection between the honeypot and the production network. A safer approach is to use a cloud service provider for setting up a honeypot.

Sinkholes

Another deception technique is to use *sinkholes*. A sinkhole is essentially a "bottomless pit" designed to steer unwanted traffic away from its intended destination to another device, deceiving the threat actor into thinking the attack is successful when the sinkhole is actually providing information about the attack. One type of sinkhole is a **DNS sinkhole**. A DNS sinkhole changes a normal DNS request to a pre-configured IP address that points to a firewall with a rule of *Deny* set for all packets so that every packet is dropped with no return information provided to the sender.

NOTE 5

DNS sinkholes are commonly used to counteract DDoS attacks. Many enterprises contract with a DDoS mitigation service to help identify DDoS traffic and send it to a sinkhole while allowing legitimate traffic to reach its destination. Law enforcement also uses sinkholes to stop a widespread ongoing attack by redirecting traffic away from the attacker's command and control (C&C) server to a sinkhole. As an added step, the sinkhole can save these packets for further examination in an to attempt to identify the threat actors.

Intrusion Detection and Prevention Systems

An *intrusion detection system (IDS)* can detect an attack as it occurs, while an *intrusion prevention system (IPS)* attempts to block the attack. An **inline** system is connected directly to the network and monitors the flow of data as it occurs. A **passive** system is connected to a port on a switch, which receives a copy of network traffic. Table 9-2 lists the differences between inline and passive systems.

Table 9-2 Inline vs. passive IDS

Function	Inline	Passive
Connection	Directly to network	Connected to port on switch
Traffic flow	Routed through the device	Receives copy of traffic
Blocking	Can block attacks	Cannot block attacks
Detection error	May disrupt service	May cause false alarm

In addition, IDS systems can be managed in different ways. *In-band* management is through the network itself by using network protocols and tools, while **out-of-band management** is using an independent and dedicated channel to reach the device.

IDS systems can use different methodologies for monitoring for attacks. In addition, IDS and IPS can be installed on networks as they can on local endpoints.

Monitoring Methodologies

Monitoring involves examining network traffic, activity, transactions, or behavior to detect security-related anomalies. The four monitoring methodologies are anomaly-based monitoring, signature-based monitoring, behavior-based monitoring, and heuristic monitoring.

Anomaly monitoring is designed for detecting statistical anomalies. First, a baseline of normal activities is compiled over time. (A *baseline* is a reference set of data against which operational data is compared.) Whenever activity deviates significantly from the baseline, an alarm is raised. An advantage of this approach is that it can detect the anomalies quickly without trying to first understand the underlying cause. However, normal behavior can change easily and even quickly, so anomaly-based monitoring is subject to false positives. In addition, anomaly-based monitoring can impose heavy processing loads on the systems where they are being used. Finally, because anomaly-based monitoring takes time to create statistical baselines, it can fail to detect events before the baseline is completed.

A second method for auditing usage is to examine network traffic, activity, transactions, or behavior and look for well-known patterns, much like antivirus scanning. This is known as signature-based monitoring because it compares activities against a predefined signature. Signature-based monitoring requires access to an updated database of signatures along with a means to actively compare and match current behavior against a collection of signatures. One of the weaknesses of signature-based monitoring is that the signature databases must be constantly updated, and as the number of signatures grows, the behaviors must be compared against an increasingly large number of signatures. Also, if the signature definitions are too specific, signature-based monitoring can miss variations.

Behavioral monitoring attempts to overcome the limitations of both anomaly-based monitoring and signature-based monitoring by being adaptive and proactive instead of reactive. Rather than using statistics or signatures as the standard by which comparisons are made, behavior-based monitoring uses the "normal" processes and actions as the standard. Behavior-based monitoring continuously analyzes the behavior of processes and programs on a system and alerts the user if it detects any abnormal actions, at which point the user can decide whether to allow or block the activity. One advantage of behavior-based monitoring is that it is not necessary to update signature files or compile a baseline of statistical behavior before monitoring can take place. In addition, behavior-based monitoring can more quickly stop new attacks.

The final method takes a completely different approach and does not try to compare actions against previously determined standards (like anomaly-based monitoring and signature-based monitoring) or behavior (like behavior-based monitoring). Instead, it is founded on *experience-based techniques*. Known as heuristic monitoring, it attempts to answer the question, *Will this do something harmful if it is allowed to execute?* Heuristic (from the Greek word for *find* or *discover*) monitoring is like heuristic antivirus detection. However, instead of creating a virtual environment in which to test a threat, IDS heuristic monitoring uses an algorithm to determine if a threat exists. Table 9-3 illustrates how heuristic monitoring could trap an application that attempts to scan ports that the other methods might not catch.

Table 9-3 Methodology comparisons to trap port scanning application

Monitoring methodology	Trap application scanning ports?	Comments
Anomaly-based monitoring	Depends	Only if this application has tried to scan previously and a baseline has been established
Signature-based monitoring	Depends	Only if a signature of scanning by this application has been previously created
Behavior-based monitoring	Depends	Only if this action by the application is different from other applications
Heuristic monitoring	Yes	IDS is triggered if any application tries to scan multiple ports

NOTE 6

A major difference between a NIDS and a NIPS is its location. A NIDS has sensors that monitor the traffic entering and leaving a firewall, and reports back to the central device for analysis. A NIPS, on the other hand, would be located inline on the firewall itself. This allows the NIPS to act more quickly to block an attack.

Network Detection and Prevention Systems IDS and IPS can be applied to networks as well as hosts (endpoints). These network-based systems include the following:

- *Network intrusion detection systems.* A network intrusion detection system (NIDS), similar to a software-based host intrusion detection system (HIDS), watches for attacks on the network. As network traffic moves through the network, NIDS sensors—usually installed on network devices such as firewalls and routers—gather information and report back to a central device.
- *Network intrusion prevention system.* A network intrusion prevention system (NIPS) not only monitors to detect malicious activities but also attempts to stop them, much like a host intrusion detection system (HIPS).

Network Hardware Security Modules

NOTE 7

HSMs are covered in Module 6.

A *hardware security module (HSM)* is a removable external cryptographic device. For endpoints, an HSM is typically a USB device, an expansion card, or a device the connects directly to a computer through a port.

However, if many endpoints use an HSM, having a centralized device can improve processing times and increase security. A **network hardware security module** is a special trusted network computer that performs cryptographic operations such as key management, key exchange, onboard random number generation, key storage facility, and accelerated symmetric and asymmetric encryption. Due to the risks associated with a compromised network hardware security module, these are usually built on specialized hardware running a security-focused OS and have limited external access.

Configuration Management

It is essential that these security appliances be properly configured. Not only does a misconfigured device allow threat actors an opening into the network; it also provides a false sense of security that makes it difficult to realize a problem exists (*we've got our NIPS running; that will give us protection*). Basic configuration management tools include the following:

- *Secure baseline configurations.* The purpose of a *baseline* is twofold: it is the initial starting point and the minimum that can be used for comparisons. A secure **baseline configuration** for security appliances likewise has two purposes. First, it is the starting point for configuring a device. While many security appliance configurations go beyond the baseline, the baseline sets the core fundamentals of how the device should be initially configured before the specific configurations are applied. Second, the baseline configuration can be considered the bare minimum: no configuration should be less than the secure baseline configuration.

NOTE 8

Secure baseline configuration documents can be purchased to help organizations define and document what constitutes a hardened and secure system. These configurations can also ensure that the organization is meeting all statutory, regulatory, and contractual requirements.

- *Standard naming conventions.* Using the same conventions for assigning names to appliances (**standard naming conventions**) can eliminate confusion regarding the various appliances. These conventions will vary by organization, but an example is: *"Device names are limited to 15 characters by technical necessity. To ensure interoperability with other systems, only letters and numbers shall be used. Each device name shall have the following minimum structure: the first three characters are the appropriate unit identifier (mandatory); the next six numbers are the device's inventory control tag number (mandatory); the remaining six characters may be used at the discretion of the department, or not used at all (optional)."*
- *Defined Internet Protocol schema.* An **Internet Protocol schema** is a standard guide for assigning IP addresses to devices. This makes it easier to set up and troubleshoot devices and helps to eliminate overlapping or duplicate subnets and IP address device assignments, avoid unnecessary complexity, and not waste IP address space.
- *Diagrams.* Creating a visual mapping (**diagram**) of security appliances can likewise be valuable when new appliances are added or when troubleshooting is required.

TWO RIGHTS & A WRONG

1. The bypass firewall rule action is designed for media-intensive protocols or traffic from a trusted source.
2. A stateful packet filter looks at packets and permits or denies it based solely on the firewall rules.
3. A forward proxy is a computer or an application program that intercepts user requests from the internal secure network and then processes these requests on behalf of the user.

See Appendix B for the answer.

SECURITY TECHNOLOGIES

 CERTIFICATION

2.1 Explain the importance of security concepts in an enterprise environment.

3.3 Given a scenario, implement secure network designs.

In addition to security appliances are general security technologies that can provide a defense. Some of these security technologies can be found in both standard networking devices (such as switches and routers) and specialized security appliances. The categories of these security technologies are access technologies, monitoring and managing technologies, and design technologies.

Access Technologies

Some security technologies are designed to grant or deny access. The access may be to the network or to specific data. These technologies include access control list, virtual private network, network access control, and data loss prevention.

NOTE 9

While a separate security device can provide in-depth protection, it can also slow the flow of data as the data must be sent through the device. A router using an ACL, on the other hand, can operate at the higher speed of the router and not delay network traffic.

Access Control List (ACL)

As its name implies, an **access control list (ACL)** contains rules that administer the availability of digital assets by granting or denying access to the assets. The two types of ACLs include *filesystem ACLs*, which filter access to files and directories on an endpoint by telling the OS who can access the device and what privileges they are allowed. *Networking ACLs* filter access to a network. Network ACLs are often found on routers.

On external routers that face the Internet, router ACLs can restrict known vulnerable protocols from entering the network. They can also be used to limit traffic entering the network from unapproved networks. ACLs can also protect against IP spoofing that imitates another computer's IP address. Because IP spoofing attacks often use known unused and untrusted addresses, an external router ACL can help block these addresses (usually by designating a range of IP addresses) and thus minimize IP spoofing attacks.

 **CAUTION**   Antispoofing ACLs on external routers require frequent monitoring because the address ranges that are denied can frequently change.

NOTE 10

Software-based VPNs are often used on mobile devices and offer the most flexibility in how network traffic is managed. However, hardware-based VPNs, typically used for site-to-site connections, are more secure, have better performance, and can offer more flexibility.

Router ACLs can also be used on internal routers that process interior network traffic. Internal router ACLs usually are less restrictive but more specific than those on external routers ACLs since the devices on the internal network are generally considered to be friendly. Internal router ACLs are often configured with explicit *allow* and *deny* statements for specific addresses and protocol services. Internal router ACLs can also limit devices on the network from performing IP spoofing by applying outbound ACLs that limit the traffic to known valid local IP addresses.

Virtual Private Network (VPN)

A **virtual private network (VPN)** is a security technology that enables authorized users to use an unsecured public network, such as the Internet, as if it were a secure private network. It does this by encrypting all data transmitted between the remote endpoint and the network, not just specific documents or files. There are two common types of VPNs. A **remote access VPN** is a user-to-LAN connection for remote users. The second type is a **site-to-site VPN**, in which multiple sites can connect to other sites over the Internet. Some VPNs allow the user to always stay connected instead of connecting and disconnecting from it. These are called **always-on VPNs**.

The two options for using a VPN depend on which traffic needs to be protected. A **full tunnel** sends all traffic to the VPN concentrator and protects it. However, not all traffic—such as web surfing or reading personal email—may need to be protected through a VPN. In this case, a **split tunnel**, or routing only some traffic over the secure VPN while other traffic directly accesses the Internet, may be used instead. Using a split tunnel can help to preserve bandwidth and reduce the load on the VPN concentrator.

Many protocols can be used for VPNs. The most common are IPsec and SSL or the weaker TLS. The **Layer 2 Tunneling Protocol (L2TP)** is a VPN protocol that does not offer encryption or protection, so it is usually paired with IPsec (L2TP/IPsec). The current version of HTML, **HTML 5**, can be used as a "clientless" VPN on an endpoint so that no additional software must be installed. Other popular VPN protocols include OpenVPN, SoftEther, WireGuard, SSTP, and IKEv2/IPsec.

Network Access Control (NAC)

The waiting room at a doctor's office is an ideal location for the spread of germs. Waiting patients are in a confined space, feel ill, and typically have weakened immune systems. A sick patient in the waiting room could easily infect all other waiting patients. It is not uncommon for a physician to post a nurse at the door of the waiting room to screen patients. Anyone who comes to the waiting room with certain symptoms is denied access (and rescheduled to a special after-hours appointment), given a prescription by the nurse for general medication, or directed to a separate quarantine room away from other patients.

> **NOTE 11**
>
> NAC also can be used to ensure that systems not owned by the organization—such as those owned by customers, visitors, and contractors—can be granted access without compromising security.

This is the logic behind **network access control (NAC)**. NAC examines the current state of an endpoint before it can connect to the network. Any device that does not meet a specified set of criteria, such as having the most current antivirus signature or the software firewall properly enabled, is denied access to the network, given restricted access to computing resources, or connected to a "quarantine" network where the security deficiencies are corrected, after which the endpoint is connected to the normal network. The goal of NAC is to prevent computers with suboptimal security from potentially infecting other computers through the network.

Some NAC systems use software installed on endpoints (**agents**) to gather information (called a host agent health check). An agent may be a *permanent NAC agent* and reside on end devices until uninstalled, or it may be a *dissolvable NAC agent* that disappears after reporting information to the NAC. Instead of installing agents on each device, the NAC technology can be embedded within a Microsoft Windows Active Directory domain controller. When a device joins the domain and a user logs in, NAC uses Active Directory to scan the device to verify that it complies with the necessary criteria. This is an **agentless** NAC because no additional software is required.

An example of the NAC process is illustrated in Figure 9-7:

1. The client performs a self-assessment using a System Health Agent (SHA) to determine its current security posture.

2. The assessment, known as a Statement of Health (SoH), is sent to a server called the Health Registration Authority (HRA). This server enforces the security policies of the network. It also integrates with other external authorities such as antivirus and patch management servers to retrieve current configuration information.

3. If the client is approved by the HRA, it is issued a Health Certificate.

4. The Health Certificate is then presented to the network servers to verify that the client's security condition has been approved.

5. If the client is not approved, it is connected to a quarantine network where the deficiencies are corrected, and then the computer is allowed to connect to the network.

> **NOTE 12**
>
> NAC uses two methods to direct an infected endpoint away from the normal production network. Interestingly, threat actors also use each method in their attacks. The first method is ARP poisoning and the second is DNS poisoning, each of which is covered in Module 8.

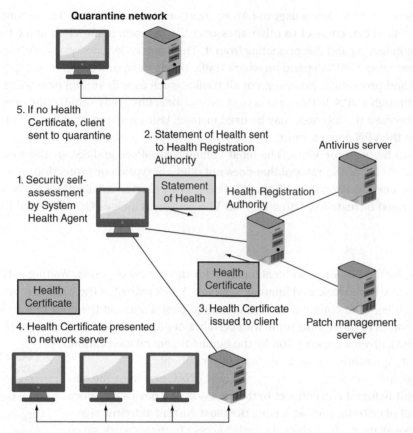

Figure 9-7   Network access control (NAC) process

Data Loss Prevention (DLP)

Keeping corporate data secure is a challenge for all organizations. While the threat of data theft from outside threat actors remains high, increasingly inside employees are careless or make mistakes when handling confidential corporate data. Employee carelessness with data has been identified in two primary areas. First, against company policy, many employees routinely send confidential data to their private email accounts so they can easily access it when needed. About one-third of employees admit to sending corporate data to their personal email accounts up to three times each month. Second, sensitive data is often sent to an approved third-party as an email attachment—but to the wrong recipient. Almost three-fourths of employees admit to sending data to the wrong recipient once per month.[2]

NOTE 13

Surprisingly, research has shown that security awareness training has not had an impact on employee mishandling of sensitive data. The percentage of employees who admit to sending misdirected emails is the highest in organizations that provide security awareness training most frequently. These same employees are almost twice as likely to send company data to their personal email accounts.

One means of securing internal corporate data is through **data loss prevention (DLP)**. DLP is considered as **rights management**, or the authority of the owner of the data to impose restrictions on its use. DLP is a system of security tools used to recognize and identify data critical to the organization and ensure it is protected. This protection involves monitoring who is using the data and how it is being accessed. Critical or confidential data can be tagged as such. A user who attempts to access the data to disclose it to an unauthorized user will be prevented from doing so.

Most DLP systems use *content inspection*. Content inspection is a security analysis of the transaction within its approved context. Content inspection looks at the security level of the data, who is requesting it, where the data is stored, when it was requested, and where it is going. DLP systems also can use *index matching*. Documents that have been identified as needing protection, such as the program source code for a new software application, are analyzed by the DLP system and complex computations are conducted based on the analysis. Thereafter, if even a small part of that document is leaked, the DLP system can recognize the snippet as being from a protected document.

DLP begins with an administrator creating DLP rules based on the data (what is to be examined) and the policy (what to check for). DLPs can be configured to look for specific data (such as Social Security and credit card numbers), lines of computer software source code, words in a sequence (to prevent a report from leaving the network), maximum file sizes, and file types. In addition, whitelists and blacklists can be created to prevent specific files from being scanned. These rules are then loaded into a DLP server.

When a policy violation is detected by the DLP agent, it is reported back to the DLP server. Different actions can then be taken. These could include blocking the data, redirecting it to an individual who can examine the request, quarantining the data until later, or alerting a supervisor of the request.

In addition to using DLP to protect data, organizations use other techniques as well. Applying encryption can naturally protect the data but may pose barriers for the recipient to decrypt it. When the data is used only for testing purposes, such as determining if a new app functions properly, masking may be used. Data masking involves creating a copy of the original data but obfuscating (making unintelligible) any sensitive elements such as a user's name or Social Security number. By replacing the actual information with fictitious information, testing can still be carried out. Similar to masking, tokenization obfuscates sensitive data elements, such as an account number, into a random string of characters (*token*). The original sensitive data element and the corresponding token are then stored in a database called a *token vault* so that if the actual data element is needed, it can be retrieved as needed. Unlike encryption, which requires using an algorithm and a key, tokenization can hide the data while making the retrieval process more seamless. Tokenization is illustrated in Figure 9-8.

> **NOTE 14**
>
> One of the drawbacks of DLP is that rules must be continually created and maintained as new employees, third-party agent contractors, and customers are added and new data sets are created. Increasingly, machine learning (ML) is used by DLP to continually create and modify the criteria for protecting data.

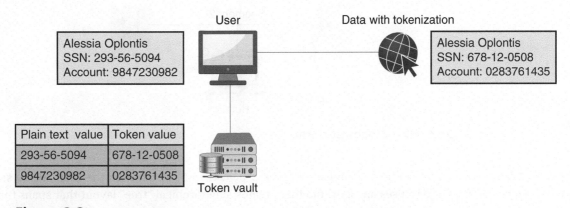

Figure 9-8 Tokenization

> ⊘ **CAUTION** Data masking may not always provide strong protection from identifying individuals, even if the user's name or Social Security Number is obfuscated. According to a study of census data, 87 percent of the American population has a unique combination of sex, birth date, and zip code. This means that the combination of these three pieces of information is sufficient to identify a huge portion of the population.

Technologies for Monitoring and Managing

Several security technologies relate to monitoring and managing network resources. These technologies include port security, packet capture and analysis, monitoring services, file integrity monitors, and quality of service.

Port Security

Securing the ports on a network device like a switch or router is essential to securing a network. Threat actors who access a network device through an unprotected port can reconfigure the device to their advantage. This introduces a number of vulnerabilities, one of which is the compromise of route security or the trust of packets sent through a router. False route information can be injected or altered by weak port security that would enable the insertion of individual false route updates or the installation of bogus routers into the routing infrastructure.

In Figure 9-9, computer Alpha, which is connected to Switch A, wants to send frames to computer Beta on Segment 2. Because Switch A does not know where Beta is located, it "floods" the network with the packet (sends it to all destinations). The packet then travels down Segment 1 to Switch B and down Segment 3 to Switch C. Switch B then adds Alpha to its lookup table that it maintains for Segment 1, and Switch C also adds it to its lookup table for

> **NOTE 15**
>
> Because the headers that a Layer 2 switch examines do not have a time to live (TTL) value, a packet could loop through the network indefinitely.

Segment 3. Yet if Switch B or C has not yet learned the address for Alpha, they will both flood Segment 2 looking for Beta; that is, each switch will take the packet sent by the other switch and flood it back out again because they still do not know where Beta is located. Switch A then will receive the packet from each segment and flood it back out on the other segment. This *switching loop* causes a *broadcast storm* as the frames are broadcast, received, and rebroadcast by each switch. Broadcast storms can cripple a network in a matter of seconds to the point that no legitimate traffic can occur.

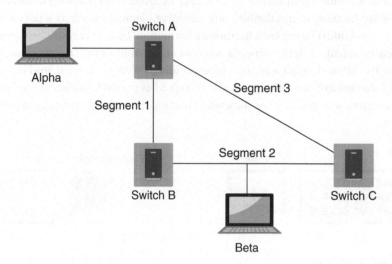

Figure 9-9   Broadcast storm

Broadcast storm prevention can be accomplished by **loop prevention**, which uses the IEEE 802.1d standard *spanning-tree protocol (STP)*. The STP uses an algorithm that creates a hierarchical "tree" layout that spans the entire network. It determines all the redundant paths that a switch has to communicate, recognizes the best path, and then blocks out all other paths. STP does this by sending out *bridge protocol data units (BPDU)* that give information about the switch port (such as MAC address and priority). This enables switches in the STP to share information with other switches. BPDUs are also periodically sent to inform other switches of port changes.

However, threat actors can try to take advantage of the STP by sending out their own malicious BPDUs to the switch to change its configuration. Because BPDUs should only be exchanged between switches, a defense is to enable **BPDU guard**, which is a feature on the switch that creates an alert when a BPDU is received from an endpoint and not a switch. In such an instance, the port on the switch is disabled and no traffic is sent or received by that port.

> **NOTE 16**
>
> DHCP snooping can also prevent users from connecting a consumer-grade router at their desk that also provides DHCP addresses.

A BPDU guard in a switch has similar port security protections. *Dynamic Host Configuration Protocol (DHCP)* is a network management protocol that automates the process of configuring an endpoint on IP networks by dynamically assigning an IP address and other network configuration parameters to endpoints. Threat actors may attempt to connect a DHCP server to the network to offer their own IP address to DHCP clients. A switch with **DHCP snooping** drops any DHCP traffic that the switch determines is unacceptable. It also stores information about the incident for further investigation.

Other port security steps to thwart an attack directed at network devices are summarized in Table 9-4.

Table 9-4   Thwarting attacks through port security

Type of attack	Description	Port security defense
MAC flooding	An attacker can overflow the switch's address table with fake MAC addresses, forcing it to act like a hub, sending packets to all devices.	Use a switch that can close ports with too many MAC addresses.
MAC address spoofing	If two devices have the same MAC address, a switch may send frames to each device. An attacker can change the MAC address on her device to match the target device's MAC address.	Configure the switch so that only one port can be assigned per MAC address.
ARP poisoning	The attacker sends a forged ARP packet to the source device, substituting the attacker's computer MAC address.	Use an ARP detection appliance.
Unauthorized packet capturing	Attackers connect their device to the switch's port.	Secure the switch in a locked room and close all unused ports on the switch.

Packet Capture and Analysis

Capturing packets and performing an analysis are critical for understanding the current state of the network. Analyzing packets helps to monitor network performance and reveal cybersecurity incidents.

Monitoring traffic on switches generally can be done in two ways. A separate **port TAP (test access point)** can be installed. A port TAP transmits the send and receive data streams simultaneously on separate dedicated channels so that all data arrives at the monitoring tool in real time. A port TAP is shown in Figure 9-10.

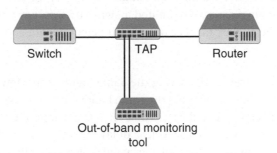

Switch   TAP   Router

Out-of-band monitoring
tool

Figure 9-10   Port TAP

A managed switch on an Ethernet network supports **port mirroring**. Port mirroring is also called **port spanning** because it uses a *Switch Port Analyzer (SPAN)*. Port mirroring allows the administrator to configure the switch to copy (mirror) traffic on some or all ports to a designated monitoring port on the switch. Port mirroring is illustrated in Figure 9-11, where the monitoring tool is connected to the mirror port and can view all network traffic moving through the switch. Port mirroring is designed for "spot checking," while a TAP is best for high-speed networks that have a large volume of traffic.

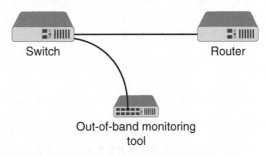

Switch   Router

Out-of-band monitoring
tool

Figure 9-11   Port mirroring

NOTE 17

A TAP device is completely passive: it has no power source or IP or MAC address so that it cannot be attacked. Also, TAPs are "court approved" so that all data captured can be used as evidence in an investigation or trial.

A network TAP is one example of a device that can be placed on a network to gather information. Other devices include **network sensors** to monitor traffic (for network intrusion detection and prevention devices), **collectors** to gather traffic (for SIEM devices), and **aggregators** to combine multiple network connections into a single link.

Monitoring Services

As a supplement to the internal data gathering and analysis of security data, an external third-party **monitoring service** can also be used. These services can provide additional resources to assist an organization in its cybersecurity defenses, such as processing cybersecurity data on managed SIEM platforms and continuously updating and applying rules to detect attacks.

File Integrity Monitors

File integrity monitors are based on a technology designed to "keep an eye on" files to detect any changes within the files that may indicate a cyberattack. After establishing a baseline for "clean" files, a file integrity monitor examines files to see if they have changed, when the change occurred, how they changed, who changed them, and what can be done to restore those files if the changes are unauthorized.

File integrity monitors are used for detecting malware as well as maintaining compliance with industry-specific regulations. The Payment Card Industry Data Security Standard (PCI DSS) has no less than four requirements related to file integrity monitors. The PCI DSS Requirement 10.5.5 states that organizations in compliance will "Use file integrity monitoring or change detection software on logs to ensure that existing log data cannot be changed without generating alerts (although new data being added should not cause an alert)."

NOTE 18

PCI DSS is covered in Module 2.

The problem with file integrity monitors is the high volume of "noise," or too much unhelpful information. Files may change frequently for many benign reasons with limited insight into whether a change poses a security risk. While file integrity monitors can be beneficial, they need to provide sufficient insight so that proper actions can be taken.

Quality of Service (QoS)

Modern networks have many types of traffic, all sharing the same bandwidth. However, not all network traffic is the same: a critical video conference call could be sharing the same bandwidth as someone downloading a huge movie file on the same network (in violation of company policy) so that each are competing for the same bandwidth. This often results in packet loss for the video conference call as well as delay and jitter, all of which affects the quality of the call.

Quality of Service (QoS) is a set of network technologies used to guarantee its ability to dependably serve network resources and high-priority applications to endpoints. QoS technologies provide "differentiated" handling and capacity allocation to specific network traffic. A network administrator can assign the order in which packets are handled and the amount of bandwidth given to an application or traffic flow (called traffic shaping).

The first step in QoS is that traffic must be classified or differentiated using QoS tools. Classifying traffic according to the corporate policy allows organizations to ensure the consistency and adequacy of network resources for the most important applications. While traffic can be prioritized by port or IP address, doing so has obvious limitations. (It is unlikely that a specific IP address should always have high network capacity, no matter what activity is being performed.) Instead, traffic should be viewed by the application or user, which can then result in a more meaningful classification of the data.

Almost all firewalls today recognize QoS settings. (They do so through configuring the "Type of Service" eight-bit field within an IP packet that is reserved for QoS markings.) However, some firewalls do not have this level of granularity but still provide QoS by defining "Low," "Medium," "High," and "Guaranteed" ratings to different types of traffic.

Design Technologies

Technologies that relate to the secure design of the network include network segmentation and load balancing.

Network Segmentation

Understanding network segmentation involves first knowing the principle of zero trust. Examples of network segmentation include virtual LANs and a demilitarized zone.

Zero Trust   Several principles govern network segmentation. One principle is zero trust. Zero trust is a strategic initiative about networks that is designed to prevent successful attacks. As its name implies, zero trust attempts to eliminate the concept of trust from an organization's network architecture.

Many networks are based on a traditional security model that operates on the assumption that everything inside an organization's network should be trusted. This is now considered an outdated and broken trust model because it is assumed that a user's identity has not been compromised and that all users will act responsibly and thus can be trusted.

The zero-trust model recognizes instead that trust is a vulnerability. Once on the network, users can freely move laterally to access or exfiltrate data. Because most networks have already been compromised and threat actors are "lurking in the shadows," malicious attackers likewise can freely move through the network.

There are several steps in creating a zero-trust network architecture:

1. Identify a "protect surface" that is made up of the network's most critical and valuable data, assets, applications, and services. Because it contains only data most critical to an organization's operations, the protect surface is much smaller than the network itself.

2. Determine the entities that interact with the protect surface. This includes determining how traffic moves across the organization in relation to it. East-west traffic is the movement of data from one server to another server within a data center. (In contrast, *north-south traffic* describes endpoint-to-server traffic that moves between the data center and an unsecured location outside of the data center network.) Besides understanding traffic across the protect surface, this step involves knowing who the users are that access it, which applications they are using, and how they are connecting to it.

3. Put controls in place as close to the protect surface as possible. This is seen as creating a "microperimeter" around it that "moves" with the protect surface as it grows. A microperimeter is often created by deploying a NGFW to ensure only known and allowed traffic or legitimate applications have access to the protect surface.

Virtual LANs (VLANs)   Zero trust requires that networks be segmented. This can be accomplished by using switches to divide the network into a hierarchy. *Core switches* reside at the top of the hierarchy and carry traffic between switches, while *workgroup switches* are connected directly to the devices on the network. It is often beneficial to group similar users together, such as all the members of the Accounting Department. However, grouping by user can be difficult because all users might not be in the same location and served by the same switch.

It is possible to segment a network by separating devices into logical groups. This is known as creating a virtual LAN (VLAN). A VLAN allows scattered users to be logically grouped together even though they are physically attached to different switches. This can reduce network traffic and provide a degree of security. VLANs can be isolated so that sensitive data is transported only to members of the VLAN.

VLAN communication can take place in two ways. If multiple devices in the same VLAN are connected to the same switch, the switch itself can handle the transfer of packets to the members of the VLAN group. However, if VLAN members on one switch need to communicate with members connected to another switch, a special "tagging" protocol must be used, either a proprietary protocol or the vendor-neutral IEEE 802.1Q. These special protocols add a field to the packet that "tags" it as belonging to the VLAN.

NOTE 19

Zero trust is not designed to make a system trusted but, instead, to eliminate trust. The motto of zero trust is "Never trust; always verify."

NOTE 20

Core switches must work faster than workgroup switches because core switches must handle the traffic of several workgroup switches.

NOTE 21

Although network subnetting and VLANs are often considered to be similar, they do have differences. Subnets are subdivisions of IP address classes (Class A, B, or C) and allow a single Class A, B, or C network to be used instead of multiple networks. VLANs are devices that are connected logically rather than physically, either through the port they are connected to or by their MAC address.

NOTE 22

Another security advantage of VLANs is that they can be used to prevent direct communication between servers, which can bypass firewall or IDS inspection. Servers that are placed in separate VLANs will require that any traffic headed toward the default gateway for inter-VLAN routing be inspected.

Demilitarized Zone (DMZ)   Imagine a bank that located its automated teller machine (ATM) in the middle of their vault. This would be an open invitation for disaster by inviting every outside user to enter the secure vault to access the ATM. Instead, the ATM and the vault should be separated so that the ATM is in a public area that anyone can access, while the vault is restricted to trusted individuals. In a similar fashion, locating public-facing servers such as web and email servers inside the secure network is also unwise. An attacker must only break out of the security of the server to access the secure network.

NOTE 23

DMZs were first introduced in Module 8 concerning physical security controls.

To allow untrusted outside users access to resources such as web servers, most networks employ a *demilitarized zone (DMZ)*. The DMZ functions as a separate network that rests outside the secure network perimeter: untrusted outside users can access the DMZ but cannot enter the secure network.

Consider Figure 9-4 (shown earlier), which illustrates a DMZ containing a web server and an email server that are accessed by outside users. In this configuration, a single firewall with three network interfaces is used: the link to the Internet is on the first network interface, the DMZ is formed from the second network interface, and the secure internal LAN is based on the third network interface. However, this makes the firewall device a single point of failure for the network. It also must take care of all the traffic to the DMZ and internal network. A more secure approach is to have two firewalls, as seen in Figure 9-12. In this configuration, an attacker would have to breach two separate firewalls to reach the secure internal LAN.

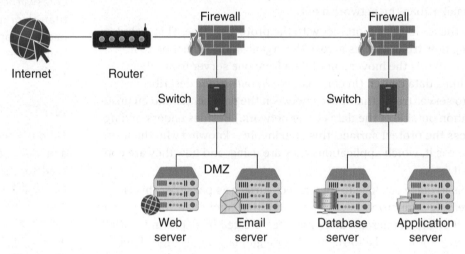

Figure 9-12   DMZ with two firewalls

 **CAUTION**   Some consumer routers advertise support to configure a DMZ. However, this is not a DMZ. Rather, the feature allows only one local device to be exposed to the Internet for Internet gaming or videoconferencing by forwarding all the ports at the same time to that one device.

How should a DMZ be configured so that trusted administrators can still access the hardware and software in a DMZ? If a pathway is enabled for administrators to enter the zone, that same pathway, if compromised, can provide access to threat actors back to the secure network.

A common approach is to use a **jump box** (sometimes called a *jump server* or *jump host*), as shown in Figure 9-13. A jump box is a minimally configured administrator server (either physical or virtual) within the DMZ. Running only essential protocols and ports, it connects two dissimilar security zones while providing tightly restricted access between them. An administrator accesses the jump box, which is connected to the administrative interface of the devices within the DMZ.

CAUTION   To further limit the vulnerabilities of a jump box, administrators should ensure that all jump box software is regularly updated, limit the programs that can run on a jump box, implement multifactor authentication for logins, do not allow outbound access or severely restrict access from the jump box, and use ACLs to restrict access to specific authorized users.

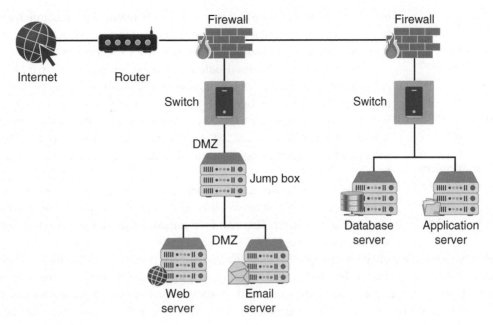

Figure 9-13   Jump box

In recent years, an additional security configuration has been used to limit risks when administering a DMZ. Instead of an administrator connecting to a jump box from any computer, only a dedicated *secure admin workstation (SAW)* can be used to connect to the jump box. Using a SAW prevents an administrator's infected computer from compromising the jump box.

Other zones can also be used for security. These are listed in Table 9-5.

Table 9-5   Other network zones

Name	Description	Security benefits
Intranet	A private network that belongs to an organization that can only be accessed by approved internal users	Closed to the outside public, thus data is less vulnerable to external threat actors
Extranet	A private network that can also be accessed by authorized external customers, vendors, and partners	Can provide enhanced security for outside users compared to a publicly accessible website
Guest network	A separate open network that anyone can access without prior authorization	Permits access to general network resources like web surfing without using the secure network

Load Balancing

Load balancing is a technology that can help to evenly distribute work across a network. Requests that are received can be allocated across multiple devices such as servers. To the user, this distribution is transparent and appears as if a single server is providing the resources. Load-balancing technology reduces the probability of overloading a single server and ensures that each networked server benefits from having optimized bandwidth. Load balancing can be performed either through software running on a computer or as a dedicated hardware device known as a *load balancer*.

Different **scheduling** protocols are used in load balancers. In a *round-robin* scheduling protocol, the rotation applies to all devices equally. A scheduling protocol that distributes the load based on which devices can handle the load more efficiently is known as *affinity* scheduling. Affinity scheduling may be based on which load balancers have the least number of connections at a given point in time.

When multiple load balancers are used together to achieve *high efficiency (H/A)*, they can be placed in different configurations. In an **active-passive** configuration, the primary load balancer distributes the network traffic to the most suitable server, while the secondary load balancer operates in a "listening mode." This second load balancer constantly monitors the performance of the primary load balancer and will step in and take over the load-balancing duties should the primary load balancer start to experience difficulties or fail. The active-passive configuration allows for uninterrupted service and can also handle planned or unplanned service outages. In an **active-active** configuration, all load balancers are always active. Network traffic is combined, and the load balancers then work together as a team.

The servers behind load balancers are often given a **virtual IP (VIP)** address. As its name suggests, this is not an actual IP address. Instead, it is an IP address and a specific port number that can be used to reference physical servers. A VIP with the address and port *172.32.250.1:80* can be configured to accept one type of traffic, while the VIP *172.32.250.1:443* can accept another type of traffic. Multiple VIPs can be created using the same IP address as long as a different port number is used.

Load balancing can also support session **persistence**, a process in which a load balancer creates a link between an endpoint and a specific network server for the duration of a session. This can help improve the user experience and optimize network resource usage.

Using a load balancer has security advantages. Because load balancers generally are located between routers and servers, they can detect and stop attacks directed at a server or application. A load balancer can also detect and prevent protocol attacks that could cripple a single server. Some load balancers can hide HTTP error pages or remove server identification headers from HTTP responses, denying attackers additional information about the internal network.

TWO RIGHTS & A WRONG

1. There are two types of ACLs: filesystem ACLs filter access to files and directories on an endpoint, and networking ACLs filter access to a network. Network ACLs are often found on routers.
2. The Layer 2 Tunneling Protocol (L2TP) is a VPN protocol that does not offer any encryption or protection, so it is usually paired with IPsec.
3. Tokenization is used for creating test data.

See Appendix B for the answer.

⤴ VM LAB You're now ready to complete the live, virtual machine labs for this module. The labs can be found in the Practice It folder in each MindTap module.

SUMMARY

- Today, networks have both standard networking devices and specialized security appliances. Security can be achieved by using security appliances that directly address security and by using the security features found in standard networking devices. Using both standard networking devices and security appliances can result in a layered security approach, which can significantly improve security.
- A computer firewall is designed to limit the spread of malware. A firewall uses bidirectional inspection to examine outgoing and incoming network packets, allowing approved packets to pass through but taking different actions when it detects a suspicious packet. The actions are based on specific criteria or rules. Older firewalls often processed each rule as a separate instruction in sequence, while modern firewalls allow a priority order. In addition to filtering based on packets, firewalls can also apply content/URL filtering.
- Stateless packet filtering on a firewall looks at a packet and permits or denies it based solely on the firewall rules. Stateful packet filtering uses both the firewall rules and the state of the connection. Open source firewalls are freely available; other firewalls are owned by an entity that has an exclusive right to them and are called proprietary firewalls. A software firewall runs as a program or service on a device, such as a computer or router. Hardware firewalls are specialized separate devices that inspect traffic. A host-based firewall is a

software firewall that runs on and protects a single endpoint device (a host). An appliance firewall is typically a separate hardware device designed to protect an entire network. A virtual firewall is one that runs in the cloud.

- There are several specialized firewall appliances. A web application firewall (WAF) looks at applications using HTTP. A network address translation gateway is a cloud-based technology that performs NAT translations for cloud services. A next generation firewall (NGFW) has additional functionality beyond a traditional firewall. Unified threat management (UTM) is a device that combines several security functions. These include packet filtering, antispam, antiphishing, antispyware, encryption, intrusion protection, and web filtering.

- A forward proxy is a computer or an application program that intercepts user requests from the internal secure network and then processes these requests on behalf of the user. A reverse proxy routes requests coming from an external network to the correct internal server. Acting as the intermediary, a proxy server can provide a degree of protection.

- A honeypot is a computer located in an area with limited security that serves as "bait" to threat actors. The honeypot is intentionally configured with security vulnerabilities so that it is open to attacks. A high-interaction honeypot is usually configured with a default login and loaded with software, data files that appear to be authentic but are actually imitations of real data files called honeyfiles, and fake telemetry data. A honeynet is a network set up with intentional vulnerabilities. A sinkhole is essentially a "bottomless pit" designed to steer unwanted traffic away from its intended destination to another device. One type of sinkhole is a DNS sinkhole.

- An intrusion detection system (IDS) can detect an attack as it occurs, while an intrusion prevention system (IPS) attempts to block the attack. An inline system is connected directly to the network and monitors the flow of data as it occurs. A passive system is connected to a port on a switch, which receives a copy of network traffic. Monitoring involves examining network traffic, activity, transactions, or behavior to detect security-related anomalies. The four monitoring methodologies are anomaly-based monitoring, signature-based monitoring, behavior-based monitoring, and heuristic monitoring. A network intrusion detection system (NIDS), similar to a software-based host intrusion detection system (HIDS), watches for attacks on the network. A network intrusion prevention system (NIPS) not only monitors to detect malicious activities but also attempts to stop them.

- A network hardware security module is a special trusted network computer that performs cryptographic operations such as key management, key exchange, onboard random number generation, key storage facility, and accelerated symmetric and asymmetric encryption. These security appliances must be properly configured. Not only does a misconfigured device allow threat actors an opening into the network, it also provides a false sense of security that makes it difficult to realize the problem.

- An access control list (ACL) contains rules that administer the availability of digital assets by granting or denying access to the assets. On external routers that face the Internet, router ACLs can restrict known vulnerable protocols from entering the network. Router ACLs can also be used on internal routers that process interior network traffic. These router ACLs usually are less restrictive but more specific than those on external routers ACLs since the devices on the internal network are generally considered to be friendly. A virtual private network (VPN) is a security technology that enables authorized users to use an unsecured public network, such as the Internet, as if it were a secure private network. It does this by encrypting all data that is transmitted between the remote endpoint and the network.

- Network access control (NAC) examines the current state of an endpoint before it can connect to the network. Any device that does not meet a specified set of criteria, such as having the most current antivirus signature or the software firewall properly enabled, is denied access to the network, given restricted access to computing resources, or connected to a "quarantine" network where the security deficiencies are corrected. Some NAC systems use software installed on endpoints (agents), while other systems are agentless and do not require additional software to be installed.

- Data loss prevention (DLP) is a system of security tools used to recognize and identify data critical to the organization and ensure that it is protected. This protection involves monitoring who is using the data and how it is being accessed. Data that is considered critical to the organization or is confidential can be tagged as such. A user who attempts to access the data to disclose it to an unauthorized user will be prevented from doing so. In addition to using DLP to protect data, masking may be used. Data masking involves creating a copy of the original data but obfuscates (makes unintelligible) any sensitive elements such as a user's name or Social Security number. By replacing the actual information with fictitious information, the testing can still be carried out. Similar to masking, tokenization obfuscates sensitive data elements, such as an account number, into a random string of characters (token). The original sensitive data element and the corresponding token are then stored in a database called a token vault so that if the actual data element is needed, it can be retired as needed.

- Broadcast storm prevention can be accomplished by loop prevention, which uses the IEEE 802.1d standard spanning-tree protocol (STP). The STP uses an algorithm that creates a hierarchical "tree" layout that "spans" the entire network. It determines all the redundant paths that a switch has to communicate, recognizes the best path, and then blocks all other paths. STP sends out bridge protocol data units (BPDUs) that give information about the switch port to enable switches in the STP to share information with other switches. A threat actor can try to take advantage of the STP by sending out their own malicious BPDUs to the switch to change its configuration. Such an attack can be thwarted by a BPDU guard, which is a feature on the switch that creates an alert when a BPDU is received from an endpoint and not a switch.

- Monitoring traffic on switches generally can be done in two ways. A separate port TAP (test access point) can be installed. A TAP transmits the send and receive data streams simultaneously on separate dedicated channels so that all data arrives at the monitoring tool in real time. A managed switch on an Ethernet network supports port mirroring, also called port spanning. Port mirroring allows the administrator to configure the switch to copy (mirror) traffic that occurs on some or all ports to a designated monitoring port on the switch. As a supplement to the internal data gathering and analysis of security data, an external third-party monitoring service can also be used. File integrity monitors are based on a technology designed to "keep an eye on" files to detect any changes within the files that may indicate a cyberattack. After establishing a baseline for "clean" files, a file integrity monitor examines files to see if they have changed, when the change occurred, how they changed, who changed them, and what can be done to restore those files if the changes are unauthorized. Quality of Service (QoS) is a set of network technologies used to guarantee a network's ability to dependably serve resources and high-priority applications to endpoints. Almost all firewalls today recognize QoS settings. Load balancing is a technology that can help to evenly distribute work across a network.

Key Terms

access control list (ACL)	hardware firewall	out-of-band management
active-active	heuristic monitoring	passive
active-passive	honeyfiles	persistence
agentless	honeynet	port mirroring (port spanning)
agents	honeypot	port TAP (test access point)
aggregators	host-based firewall	proprietary firewall
always-on VPN	HTML 5	Quality of Service (QoS)
anomaly monitoring	inline	remote access VPN
appliance firewall	Internet Protocol schema	reverse proxy
baseline configuration	intranet	rights management
behavioral monitoring	jump box	route security
BPDU guard	Layer 2 Tunneling Protocol (L2TP)	scheduling
broadcast storm prevention	load balancing	signature-based monitoring
collectors	loop prevention	site-to-site VPN
content/URL filtering	masking	software firewall
data loss prevention (DLP)	monitoring service	split tunneling
DHCP snooping	network access control (NAC)	standard naming conventions
diagram	network address translation	stateful packet filtering
DNS sinkhole	gateway	stateless packet filtering
east-west traffic	network hardware security module	tokenization
extranet	network intrusion detection	unified threat management (UTM)
fake telemetry	system (NIDS)	virtual firewall
file integrity monitors	network intrusion prevention	virtual IP (VIP)
firewall	system (NIPS)	virtual LAN (VLAN)
forward proxy	network sensors	virtual private network (VPN)
full tunnel	next generation firewall (NGFW)	web application firewall
geographical consideration	open source firewall	zero trust

Review Questions

1. Which of the following is NOT a firewall rule parameter?
   a. Visibility
   b. Time
   c. Context
   d. Action

2. Which firewall rule action implicitly denies all other traffic unless explicitly allowed?
   a. Force Allow
   b. Force Deny
   c. Bypass
   d. Allow

3. Leah is researching information on firewalls. She needs a firewall that allows for more generic statements instead of creating specific rules. What type of firewall should Leah consider purchasing that supports her need?
   a. Content/URL filtering firewall
   b. Policy-based firewall
   c. Hardware firewall
   d. Proprietary firewall

4. Emilie is reviewing a log file of a new firewall. She notes that the log indicates packets are being dropped for incoming packets for which the internal endpoint did not initially create the request. What kind of firewall is this?
   a. Stateful packet filtering
   b. Connection-aware firewall
   c. Proxy firewall
   d. Packet filtering firewall

5. What is a virtual firewall?
   a. A firewall that runs in the cloud
   b. A firewall that runs in an endpoint virtual machine
   c. A firewall that blocks only incoming traffic
   d. A firewall appliance that runs on a LAN

6. Which of these appliances provides the broadest protection by combining several security functions?
   a. NAT
   b. WAF
   c. UTM
   d. NGFW

7. Which of the following contains honeyfiles and fake telemetry?
   a. High-interaction honeypot
   b. Attacker-interaction honeypot
   c. Honeypotnet
   d. Honeyserver

8. Maja has been asked to investigate DDoS mitigations. Which of the following should Maja consider?
   a. DDoS Prevention System (DPS)
   b. DNS sinkhole
   c. MAC pit
   d. IP denier

9. Which type of monitoring methodology looks for statistical deviations from a baseline?
   a. Behavioral monitoring
   b. Signature-based monitoring
   c. Anomaly monitoring
   d. Heuristic monitoring

10. Which statement regarding a demilitarized zone (DMZ) is NOT true?
    a. It can be configured to have one or two firewalls.
    b. It typically includes an email or web server.
    c. It provides an extra degree of security.
    d. It contains servers that are used only by internal network users.

11. Which of the following functions does a network hardware security module NOT perform?
    a. Fingerprint authentication
    b. Key management
    c. Key exchange
    d. Random number generator

12. Which of these is NOT used in scheduling a load balancer?
    a. The IP address of the destination packet
    b. Data within the application message itself
    c. Round-robin
    d. Affinity

13. In which of the following configurations are all the load balancers always active?
    a. Active-active
    b. Active-passive
    c. Passive-active-passive
    d. Active-load-passive-load

14. Which device intercepts internal user requests and then processes those requests on behalf of the users?
    a. Forward proxy server
    b. Reverse proxy server
    c. Host detection server
    d. Intrusion prevention device

15. Sofie needs to configure the VPN to preserve bandwidth. Which configuration would she choose?
    a. Narrow tunnel
    b. Split tunnel
    c. Full tunnel
    d. Wide tunnel

16. Which of the following is not a basic configuration management tool?
    a. Baseline configuration
    b. Standard naming convention
    c. Diagrams
    d. MAC address schema

17. Which of the following is NOT correct about L2TP?
    a. It is used as a VPN protocol.
    b. It must be used on HTML 5 compliant devices.
    c. It does not offer encryption.
    d. It is paired with IPsec.

18. Which of the following is NOT a NAC option when it detects a vulnerable endpoint?
    a. Deny access to the network.
    b. Give restricted access to the network.

c. Update Active Directory to indicate the device is vulnerable.
d. Connect to a quarantine network.

19. Hanna has received a request for a data set of actual data for testing a new app that is being developed. She does not want the sensitive elements of the data to be exposed. What technology should she use?
    a. Masking
    b. Tokenization
    c. Data Object Obfuscation (DOO)
    d. PII Hiding

20. How does BPDU guard provide protection?
    a. It detects when a BPDU is received from an endpoint.
    b. It sends BPDU updates to all routers.
    c. BPDUs are encrypted so that attackers cannot see their contents.
    d. All firewalls are configured to let BPDUs pass to the external network.

Hands-On Projects

 **CAUTION** If you are concerned about installing any of the software in these projects on your regular computer, you can instead use the Windows Sandbox or install the software in the Windows virtual machine created in the Module 1 Hands-On Projects. Software installed within the virtual machine will not impact the host computer.

Project 9-1: Using GlassWire Firewall

Time Required: 25 minutes
Objective: Given a scenario, implement secure network designs.
Description: GlassWire is a firewall and Security and Information Event Management (SIEM) product. In this activity, you will download and install GlassWire.

1. Use your web browser to go to **www.glasswire.com**. (If you are no longer able to access the site through the URL, use a search engine to search for "GlassWire.")
2. Click **Features** and scroll through the page to read about the different features and configuration options in this product.
3. Click **FREE DOWNLOAD** and then click **DOWNLOAD GLASSWIRE** to download the file.
4. Navigate to the location of the downloaded file **GlassWireSetup.exe** and launch this program to install GlassWire by accepting the default settings.
5. Click **Finish** to run GlassWire.
6. Note that the information scrolls horizontally to the left regarding events that are occurring. Open a web browser and surf the Internet for several minutes.
7. Return to GlassWire.
8. Slide the scroller at the bottom of the screen to consolidate the views.
9. Click **Apps**. What information is given in the left pane? How can this be useful?
10. Click **Traffic** to view an analysis of the different traffic types.

11. Open a web browser, and then arrange the GlassWire window and the browser window side by side on your computer screen.
12. Use your web browser to surf the web, and watch the GlassWire screen as well. What can you learn from this?
13. Close the browser window and maximize GlassWire.
14. Click the **Firewall** button. What apps or services have recently gone through your firewall?
15. Click the **Usage** button to see a summary of the local Apps utilized, the Hosts accessed, and the Traffic Type.
16. Click **Alerts**. Scroll through any alerts that have been issued. What can you tell about them?
17. How valuable is this information from GlassWire?
18. Close all windows.

Project 9-2: Configuring Microsoft Windows Defender Firewall—Apps

Time Required: 20 minutes
Objective: Given a scenario, implement secure network designs.
Description: In this project, you explore configuration settings on Windows Firewall for allowing an app to penetrate the firewall.

NOTE 25

Windows Firewall uses three different profiles: domain (when the computer is connected to a Windows domain), private (when connected to a private network, such as a work or home network), and public (used when connected to a public network, such as a public Wi-Fi). A computer may use multiple profiles so that a business laptop computer may use the domain profile at work, the private profile when connected to the home network, and the public profile when connected to a public Wi-Fi network. Windows asks whether a network is public or private when you first connect to it.

1. Click **Start** and then **Settings**.
2. Click **Update & Security**.
3. Click **Windows Security**.
4. Click **Firewall & network protection**.
5. Click **Allow an app through firewall**. Depending upon your network configuration, click the type of network that says **(active)**.
6. The Microsoft Windows Defender host-based firewall is application-centric: users can create an opening in the firewall for each specific application. This is more secure than permanently opening a port in the firewall that will always remain open as opposed to a port that is only opened when the application requires it and is then closed. However, there is an issue with these types of firewalls in that installed apps routinely give themselves permissions through the firewall without making that clear to the user. Scroll down through the apps that have access through the firewall. Does this lengthy list surprise you? What are the security risks?
7. Click **Microsoft Lync**.
8. Click **Details**.
9. Click **Network Types** and read through the options. Why would an app be approved for one type but not the other?
10. Click **Cancel**.
11. Click **What are the risks of unblocking an app?** What type of information is provided? How helpful is this information? How could it be improved?
12. Close the browser window.
13. Click **Cancel**.
14. Now add an app that can penetrate the firewall. Click **Allow another app**.
15. See the apps that have been installed on this computer by clicking **Browse**.
16. Scroll down and select an app and click **Open**.
17. Click **Network Types**. For this app, which network type would you select? Why?
18. Click **Cancel**.
19. Click **Cancel** on the **Add an app** window.
20. Click **Cancel** on the **Allow apps to communicate through Windows Defender Firewall**.
21. Close all windows.

Project 9-3: Configuring Microsoft Windows Defender Firewall—Ports

Time Required: 20 minutes

Objective: Given a scenario, implement secure network designs.

Description: In this project, you explore configuration settings on Windows Firewall for opening a port on the firewall.

1. Click **Start** and then **Settings**.
2. Click **Update & Security**.
3. Click **Windows Security**.
4. Click **Firewall & network protection**.
5. Click **Advanced settings**.
6. In the **Windows Defender Firewall with Advanced Security** window, click **Inbound Rules** in the left pane. Expand the screen so you can see all of the columns.
7. Why do some apps have **Any** for **Protocol**, **Local Port**, and **Remote Port** while other apps are more restrictive for these parameters?
8. Click **Outbound Rules** and view the same parameters.
9. Create a specific rule to open a firewall port. Click **Outbound Rules** in the left pane.
10. In the right pane, notice the different ways in which a firewall filter can be created. What is the advantage of **Filter by Profile**?
11. Click **New Rule**.
12. Note that there are four types of rules that can be created. Click **Custom** and then **Next**.
13. A custom rule can apply to all programs, a specific program, or a Windows service. Click **Customize** next to **Services**.
14. Click **Apply to this service** and scroll through the list of available services.
15. Click **Cancel**.
16. Be sure that **All programs** is selected, and click **Next**.
17. Specific ports and protocols can be selected for this rule. Under **Protocol type**, select **TCP**. Note the **Protocol number** is automatically selected.
18. In **Local port**, select **Specific Ports**.
19. Enter **80**.
20. In **Remote port**, select **All ports**, if necessary.
21. Click **Next**.
22. Under **Which local IP addresses does this rule apply to?** click **These IP addresses**.
23. Click **Add**.
24. Click **This IP address range**.
25. In **From**, enter **192.168.0.0**.
26. In **To**, enter **192.168.0.255** and click **OK**.
27. Click **Next**.
28. Read through the three options for actions. Be sure that **Block the connection** is selected. Click **Next**.
29. Read through the three options for when this rule applies. Click **Next**.
30. A name can be given to this rule. However, click the back button and review each of the settings that were created for this rule. What type of rule have you just created? What will it block? Why?
31. Click **Cancel** and close all windows.

Case Projects

Case Project 9-1: Data Loss Prevention Comparison

Research at least four different data loss prevention (DLP) products from four different vendors. Create a table that compares at least six different functions and options. Based on your research, which would you choose? What features make this product the optimum? Why? Write a short paragraph that summarizes your research.

Case Project 9-2: Cloud-Based Honeypots

Research cloud-based honeypots. What are their advantages? What are their disadvantages? When should they not be used? How could one be set up? Create a one-page paper of your research.

Case Project 9-3: Hardening a Jump Box

How should a jump box be configured? Create a list of configurations that you would use to set up a jump box that had the fewest risks.

Case Project 9-4: Researching Network Access Control

Use the Internet to research the network access control products from Microsoft and Cisco. How are they different? How are they similar? What are some of the options for each product? Which would you choose, and why? Write a one-page paper on your research.

Case Project 9-5: UTM Comparison

Create a table of four UTM devices available today. Include the vendor name, pricing, a list of features, the type of protections it provides, etc. Based on your research, assign a value of 1–5 (from lowest to highest ranking) that you would give that UTM. Include a short explanation of why you gave it that ranking.

Case Project 9-6: Zero Trust

Use the Internet to research zero trust. What is it? What are its advantages? What are its disadvantages? What technologies does it require? Is it a long-term security solution? Is it widely accepted? What do you think about it? Write a one-page paper on your research.

Case Project 9-7: Network Firewall Comparison

Use the Internet to identify three network firewalls and create a chart that compares their features. Note if they are rule based or policy based, perform stateless or stateful packet filtering, what additional features they include (IDS, content filtering, etc.), their costs, etc. Which would you recommend? Why?

Case Project 9-8: Community Site Activity

The Information Security Community Site is an online companion to this textbook. It contains a wide variety of tools, information, discussion boards, and other features to assist learners. Go to **community.cengage.com/infosec2** and click the *Join or Sign in* icon to log in, using your login name and password that you created in Module 1. Click **Forums (Discussion)** and click on **Security+ Case Projects (7ᵗʰ edition)**. Read the following case study.

Some schools and libraries use Internet content filters to prohibit users from accessing undesirable websites. These filters are designed to protect individuals, but some claim it is a violation of their freedom. What are your opinions about Internet content filters? Do they provide protection for users or are they a hindrance? Who should be responsible for determining which sites are appropriate and which are inappropriate? And what punishments should be enacted against individuals who circumvent these filters? Visit the Community Site discussion board and post how you feel about Internet content filters.

Case Project 9-9: North Ridge Security

North Ridge Security provides security consulting and assurance services. You have recently been hired as an intern to assist them.

Believe It's Magic (BIM) is a regional hair salon with retail outlets in major cities. Because the company was the victim of several recent attacks, BIM wants to completely change its network infrastructure. Currently, the company has a small IT staff, so they have contracted with North Ridge to make recommendations and install the new equipment. First, however, they have asked North Ridge to give a presentation to their executive staff about the current state of network security defenses.

1. Create a PowerPoint presentation for the executive staff about network security appliances. Include firewalls, proxy servers, IDS and IPS, and network hardware security modules. Your presentation should contain at least 10 slides.
2. One of the BIM's executives has heard about honeypots and has decided BIM should install it to, in his words, "punish those attackers." North Ridge has advised BIM that the purpose of a honeypot is not retaliation, but the executive has been difficult to persuade. However, he saw your presentation and was impressed with your knowledge. North Ridge has asked you to create a memo about deception instruments and why it could be risky and unnecessary for BIM to install those devices. Create a memo that outlines the advantages and disadvantages of deception instruments, and give your recommendation.

References

1. Boddy, Matt, "Exposed: Cyberattacks on cloud honeypots," *Sophos*, Apr. 9, 2019, accessed Jun. 5, 2019, *www.sophos.com/en-us/press-office/press-releases/2019/04/cybercriminals-attack-cloud-server-honeypot-within-52-seconds.aspx*.
2. "The state of data loss prevention 2020: What you need to know," *Tessian*, May 28, 2020, accessed Jun. 26, 2020, *www.tessian.com/blog/the-state-of-data-loss-prevention-2020-what-you-need-to-know/*.

CLOUD AND VIRTUALIZATION SECURITY

After completing this module, you should be able to do the following:

1. Define the cloud and explain how it is used and managed
2. Explain virtualization
3. Describe cloud and virtualization security controls
4. List different secure network protocols

Front-Page Cybersecurity

"Our data center is underwater." Any system administrator who received this message would immediately go into panic mode, thinking that a flash flood or burst water pipe had ruined the enterprise's networking equipment and servers. Yet an underwater data center is exactly what Microsoft created in support of cloud computing—and all for good reason.

In 2018, Microsoft announced that it had intentionally sunk its first waterproof and self-sustaining data center. The data center, which now rests more than 100 feet (30.4 meters) beneath the ocean's surface near the Orkney Islands in Scotland, is about the size of a shipping container but shaped like a tube. It is loaded with 12 racks that contain 864 servers and is anchored to the seabed by a large triangular weight. Called Project Natick, the data center is the culmination of four years of research.

Why would anybody sink a data center to the bottom of the ocean? There are several reasons:

Time. The amount of time to build a data center on land usually takes about two years. However, a submersible data center can be fitted and sunk in only 90 days.

Temperature. One of the biggest costs of running a land-based data center is cooling: hundreds of servers generate large amounts of heat. Data centers or rooms that house this equipment typically have special cooling requirements: not only do they need additional cooling; they also need more precise cooling. This requires expensive heating, ventilation, and air conditioning (HVAC) systems. However, the floor of the ocean is naturally cool, so no additional cooling equipment is needed.

Protection. A data center on the bottom of the ocean is protected from any number of natural and man-made disasters: fires, floods, hurricanes, and wars, just to name a few. The risk of theft is decreased as well.

Energy. The naturally occurring ocean waves have been used to harvest renewable "tidal energy." The Orkney Islands are home to the European Marine Energy Center (EMEC), which uses tidal energy and wind energy to generate enough power for the 10,000 inhabitants of the islands, also powers Project Natick.

Location. More than half of the world's population lives within about 120 miles of a coastline. By putting data centers in bodies of water near coastal cities, data has a shorter distance to travel to reach users, leading to fast and smooth web surfing, video streaming, and game playing.

Project Natick may be the start of the next generation of cloud data centers. Microsoft, which has more than 160 cloud data centers around the world for its Azure cloud computing platform, could much more quickly and easily add submarine centers as needed. For now, Microsoft says that data from its first underwater data center continues to be evaluated to determine if this is the wave (pun intended) of the future.

Consider how we give input to a device. The original terminals to computer systems had integrated keyboards so that the terminal and monitor were a single unit. Moving the keyboard to make it easier to type required moving the entire terminal, often resulting in the keyboard being in the right place but not the monitor. Over time, keyboards were separated as detached units connected by a cable. Today keyboards are usually wireless devices that can be freely moved with no restrictions.

Another means by which we give input to a device today is through speech. Instead of typing, we simply speak the command. It is both faster and easier than typing on a keyboard.

Comparing these two input technologies—keyboards and speech—helps to illustrate how some changes to technology are *evolutionary* while others are *revolutionary*. The changes to keyboards from being integrated into a terminal to a wireless device show a technological evolution. But going from typing a command on a keyboard to speaking it is a revolution because it is an entirely radical and completely different way to input data.

Many technology changes are gradual and evolutionary. However, fewer changes are considered as monumental and revolutionary. In computer networking, the move to virtualization, in which hardware is created as software, is often considered as an evolutionary technology that first began in the 1960s. The move to cloud computing is considered revolutionary because it is a completely different way of providing and paying for computing and network resources.

In this module, you will explore cloud computing and virtualization. You will examine these technologies, how they function, and how they can be secured. Because cloud computing relies on secure network connections, you will also look at secure network protocols.

CLOUD SECURITY

 CERTIFICATION

2.2 Summarize virtualization and cloud computing concepts.

3.6 Given a scenario, apply cybersecurity solutions to the cloud.

Understanding cloud security involves an overall introduction to cloud computing. It also means taking specific steps to secure the cloud computing environment.

Introduction to Cloud Computing

Understanding cloud computing involves knowing what cloud computing is; identifying the types of clouds, cloud locations, architectures, and cloud models; and knowing how cloud computing is managed.

What Is Cloud Computing?

Forty years ago, as computing technology became widespread, enterprises employed an on-premises model, in which they purchased all the hardware and software necessary to run their organizations. As more resources were needed, more purchases were made, and more personnel were hired to manage the technology.

Because this resulted in spiraling costs, some enterprises turned to *hosted services*. In a hosted services environment, servers, storage, and the supporting networking infrastructure were shared by multiple enterprises over a remote network connection that had been contracted for a specific period. As more resources were needed (such as additional storage space or computing power), the enterprise contacted the hosted service and negotiated a fee as well as signed a contract for those new services.

Today an entirely new approach for computing has gained widespread use. This approach is known as **cloud computing**. Although various definitions of cloud computing have been proposed, the definition from the National Institute of Standards and Technology (NIST) may be the most comprehensive: "Cloud computing is a model for enabling convenient, on-demand network access to a shared pool of configurable computing resources (e.g., networks, servers, storage, applications, and services) that can be rapidly provisioned and released with minimal management effort or service provider interaction."[1] In some ways, cloud computing is similar to a corporate data center but at a different scale because it supports multiple tenants online while providing rapid and even automatic scalability and elasticity. Entities that offer cloud computing are called **cloud service providers**.

Cloud computing takes a much more flexible approach to computing resources. All cloud resources are available online so that users from virtually anywhere around the world can access them. Access is achieved simply through opening a web browser without needing to install additional software. Cloud computing allows an almost endless array of servers, software, and network appliances to be quickly and easily configured as needed. It is also a pay-per-use computing model in which customers pay only for the online computing resources they need. As computing needs increase or decrease, cloud computing resources can be quickly scaled up or scaled back. Cloud computing is illustrated in Figure 10-1. Table 10-1 lists the advantages of cloud computing.

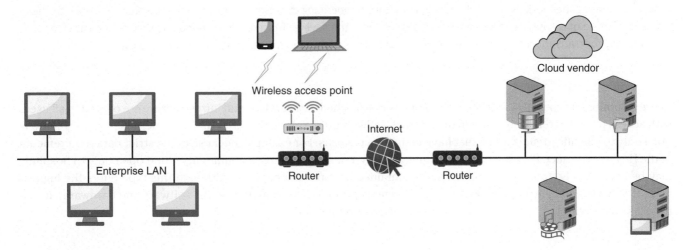

Figure 10-1   Cloud computing

Table 10-1   Cloud computing advantages

Characteristic	Explanation
On-demand self-service	The consumer can make changes, such as increasing or decreasing computing resources, without requiring human interaction from the service provider.
Universal client support	Virtually any networked device (desktop, laptop, smartphone, or tablet, for example) can access the cloud computing resources.
Invisible resource pooling	Physical and virtual computing resources are pooled together to serve multiple, simultaneous consumers that are dynamically assigned or reassigned based on the consumers' needs; the customer has little or no control or knowledge of the physical location of the resources.
Immediate elasticity	Computing resources can be increased or decreased quickly to meet demands.
Metered services	Fees are based on the computing resources used.

One of the attractive features of cloud computing is cost savings. The savings available through cloud computing are due to the following factors:

- *Elasticity and scalability.* Cloud computing gives organizations the ability to expand and reduce resources according to specific service requirements. Users can create an ongoing infrastructure or provision any number of resources only for a specific task. For example, an e-commerce site may provision multiple servers to accommodate a large number of orders during the holiday season and then drop those resources after the holidays, when they are no longer needed.
- *Pay-per-use.* Organizations pay for cloud services when they are used, either for the short term (for computing power for one day or several months) or for a longer duration (for using cloud-based storage).
- *On demand.* Because cloud services are only activated when needed, they are not permanent parts of an IT infrastructure. This means that hardware and software do not need to be purchased and installed, and IT staffing needs are also reduced.
- *Resiliency.* The resiliency of cloud services can completely isolate the failure of a server and storage resources from cloud users. If an issue occurs, the cloud provider will migrate the hardware and software to a different resource in the cloud without the user's knowledge. This relieves the organization from needing to have excess capacity sitting idle that can only to be used in an emergency.

NOTE 1

Cloud computing involves shifting the bulk of the costs from *capital expenditures* (CapEx)—or purchasing and installing servers, storage, networking, and related infrastructure to *operating expenses* (OpEx) in which the costs are only for the usage of these of resources. In some ways, this is similar to the savings from using a ride-hailing service such as Uber or Lyft to pay for transportation only when needed instead of purchasing, maintaining, and insuring a car.

Types of Clouds

There are different types of clouds. A **public cloud** is one in which the services and infrastructure are offered to all users with access provided remotely through the Internet. Unlike a public cloud that is open to anyone, a **community cloud** is open only to specific organizations that have common concerns. For example, because of the strict data requirements of the Health Insurance Portability and Accountability Act of 1996 (HIPAA), a community cloud open only to hospitals may be used. A **private cloud** is created and maintained on a private network. Although this type offers the highest level of security and control (because the company must purchase and maintain all the software and hardware), it also reduces cost savings. A **hybrid cloud** is a combination of public and private clouds.

Locations

The introduction of cloud computing has redefined the location of computing resources. Computing now takes place in several locations. These are listed in Table 10-2 and illustrated in Figure 10-2.

Table 10-2   Computing locations

Location	Description	Example
On-premises	Computing resources located on the campus of the organization	Desktop computer, local area network, data center
Off-premises	A computing resource hosted and supported by a third party	Remote backup facility
Fog	A decentralized computing infrastructure in which data, compute capabilities, storage, and applications are located between the data source and the cloud	Automated guided vehicles on an industrial shop floor
Edge	Computing that is performed at or very near to the source of data instead of relying on the cloud or on-prem for processing	IoT device
Cloud	A remote facility for computing	Artificial intelligence processing engine

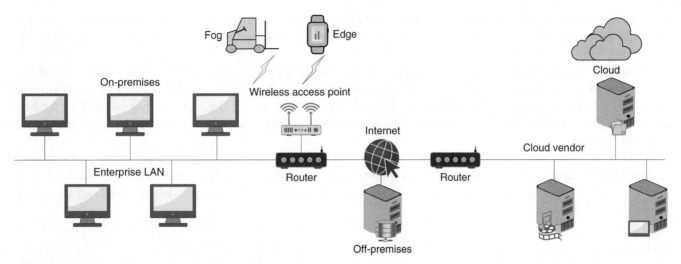

Figure 10-2   Computing locations

Cloud Architecture

Many elements make up a cloud architecture. A sampling of these elements include the following:

- *Thin client.* A **thin client** is a computer that runs from resources stored on a central cloud server instead of a localized hard drive. Thin clients connect remotely to the cloud computing environment where applications and data are stored and processing takes place.
- *Transit gateway.* A **transit gateway** is an Amazon Web Services (AWS) technology that allows organizations to connect all existing virtual private clouds (VPCs), physical data centers, remote offices, and remote gateways into a single managed source. The transit gateway gives full control over all resources—including network routing and security, VPCs, shared services, and other resources that may even span multiple AWS accounts. Transit gateways can consolidate edge connectivity and route it through a single cloud entry point.

NOTE 2

A transit gateway is considered a "hub-and-spoke" network topology that enables the user to monitor all activity.

- *Serverless infrastructure.* Although the term "serverless" is used occasionally, it is actually a misnomer. While using servers (somewhere) to perform a critical function, a **serverless infrastructure** is one in which the capacity planning, installation, setup, and management are all invisible to the user because they are handled by the cloud provider. Because the server resources of the cloud are inconspicuous to the user, this type of infrastructure is called "serverless."

NOTE 3

Serverless essentially means that provisioning, deploying, and managing a physical server disappears from a list of concerns.

Cloud Models

There are several service models in cloud computing. These are software as a service, platform as a service, infrastructure as a service, and anything as a service.

Software as a Service (SaaS)   A typical enterprise must manage many sets of software licenses for the software applications it uses. These applications typically include human resources, finance, and customer relationship management (CRM), along with OSs, productivity software, utilities, and many others. Significant costs are associated with purchasing desktop or service licenses, installing and upgrading the software, distributing patches, and managing them.

What if, as an alternative, enterprises paid a low monthly or annual fee per user for an external service to host the software on their own hardware? What if the service was made available through a web browser to users? Not only would the enterprise be relieved of the burden of purchasing and maintaining the software, but because it could be accessed via a browser, all authorized users could access the software from any number of endpoints without needing to install specialized software.

This is the definition of Software as a Service (SaaS). SaaS is a cloud computing hosted software environment. SaaS eliminates software purchases, installation, maintenance, upgrades, and patches; instead, the cloud computing provider centrally manages the software on a per-user basis. SaaS usually includes provisions for a fixed amount of bandwidth and storage.

NOTE 4

SaaS offers commercial and well-known software to users, without any technical intervention from the IT staff. The software is offered as a complete *service* to users.

Platform as a Service (PaaS)   Platform as a Service (PaaS) provides a software *platform* on which the enterprise or users can build their own applications and then host them on the PaaS provider's infrastructure. The software platform can be used as a development framework to build and debug the app and then deploy it.

NOTE 5

PaaS can also provide "middleware" services such as database and component services for use by the applications.

Unlike SaaS, in which everything is transparent to the enterprise, PaaS provides a moderate degree of control for the enterprise over the cloud computing environment. However, the enterprise does not always need to monitor usage and manually add resources; rather, the cloud provider can guarantee elasticity and scalability.

 **CAUTION**   Not all applications developed for a traditional enterprise network may seamlessly migrate to PaaS. Often the most success is from new applications developed specifically on and for the cloud.

Infrastructure as a Service (IaaS)   Infrastructure as a Service (IaaS) provides unlimited "raw" computing, storage, and network resources that the enterprise can use to build its own virtual infrastructure in the cloud. The number of CPU processors and their speed, the amount of memory, the volume of storage, and the desired virtual networking resources such as routers and switches can be arranged to create the necessary virtual infrastructure. Enterprises can then load their own OSs (or "rent" them from the cloud provider) and software, web services, and database applications. Scaling and elasticity are not always automatically provided as with PaaS but, instead, are the enterprises' responsibility to monitor and request additional services.

How much of an enterprise's network architecture should be migrated to the cloud—and how much should remain on-prem? A traditional three-tier on-prem architecture is illustrated in Figure 10-3. (Note that for simplicity, no security appliances are illustrated.) This multitiered design helps control connections, provide scaling, and increase security. An enterprise could migrate Tier 1—Web servers and Tier 2—Application servers to a cloud computing provider but keep Tier 3—Database servers on-prem for security. However, it could just as easily migrate all three tiers to the cloud computing provider. Such a decision is based on several different factors.

Another question with IaaS involves using Layer 2 (switching) or Layer 3 (routing) when connecting to the virtual cloud network. Whereas Layer 2 is the simpler mode, in which the Ethernet MAC address and Virtual LAN (VLAN) information is used for forwarding, the disadvantage of Layer 2 networks is scalability. Using Layer 2 addressing and

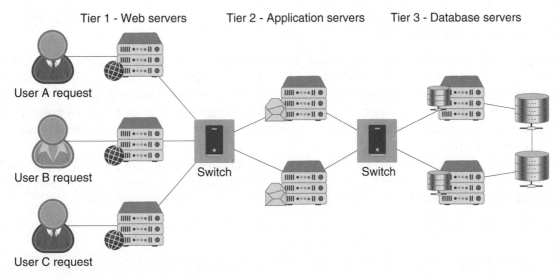

Figure 10-3   Three-tier architecture

connectivity can result in a "flat" topology, which is unrealistic with a large number of endpoints. Instead, using routing and subnets to provide segmentation for the appropriate functions provides greater flexibility but at a cost of forwarding performance and network complexity.

Anything as a Service (XaaS)   Anything as a Service (XaaS) describes a broad category of subscription services related to cloud computing. XaaS is any IT function or digital component that can be transformed into a service for enterprise or user consumption. Today a vast number of products, tools, and technologies are delivered as a service over the Internet. For example, *Security as a Service (SECaaS)* provides security services—such as intrusion detection and SIEM—all delivered from the cloud to the enterprise. This relieves the enterprise from purchasing and managing security hardware and software.

NOTE 6

Examples of IT-based services include Communication as a Service (CaaS), Desktop as a Service (DaaS), and Healthcare as a Service (HaaS). One example of a non-IT service is ridesharing like Uber and Lyft and is called Transportation as a Service (TaaS).

A comparison of the IT responsibilities in the different cloud computing models is shown in Table 10-3.

Table 10-3   Cloud computing comparisons

Model	IT responsibilities	Explanation
SaaS	Low	The organization contracts with the cloud computing provider for access to software, relieving the IT staff of any responsibilities.
PaaS	Medium	The IT staff has moderate duties of creating the platform, but once completed, the duties diminish.
IaaS	High	Designing, building, and monitoring the virtual environment rely on IT staff.
XaaS	Varies	The role of IT depends on the service.

Management

After implementing a cloud computing solution, an organization must provide ongoing management. Managing cloud resources can be more challenging than managing on-prem resources. Typically, a cloud computing infrastructure, consisting of a virtual network and related servers, encompasses many cloud elements. It is not uncommon for a large organization to contract with several cloud computing providers. Properly managing multiple services from multiple providers can be cumbersome.

Cloud management can be conducted by the local organization performing the work itself or by contracting with a third-party management service provider.

Local Management   One of the questions when locally managing cloud computing is how best to perform services integration, or the combined management function of multiple services into a single entity. Services integration attempts to achieve a "boundary-less" approach, which involves integrating all users across the enterprise who are using cloud computing. Services integration includes integrating SaaS and PaaS, on-prem applications, third-party gateways, and social media services. The goal is being able to monitor a seamless flow of data and transactions across systems.

When locally managing cloud computing, an enterprise should have written resource policies in place. These policies must clearly outline who is responsible for cloud computing, what are their duties and responsibilities, how cloud computing can be used (and not used), and the processes for acquiring these resources.

NOTE 7

Because a cloud environment can be set up by virtually all employees using their own credit card, these unauthorized or shadow IT cloud environments are a serious threat. One survey revealed that 93 percent of respondents said they continue to deal with shadow IT cloud computing, 82 percent have experienced security events as a result, and 71 percent said that employees are violating formal policies regarding cloud use by using cloud computing without authorization.[2]

Service Providers   Instead of relying on local effort to manage a cloud environment, many organizations turn to external third-party service providers. A managed service provider (MSP) delivers services—such as network, application, infrastructure, and security—through ongoing and regular support as well as active administration of those resources. In short, an MSP assumes the role of a traditional on-prem IT organization.

An MSP can manage on the customers' premises, in the MSP's own data center (*hosting*), in a third-party data center, or in a cloud computing environment. "Pure-play" MSPs focus on a single vendor or technology, which is usually their own core offerings, while other MSPs include services from other types of providers.

A specialized type of MSP is a managed security service provider (MSSP). An MSSP can assist with or even fully assume the cybersecurity defenses by providing an organization with a negotiated amount of cybersecurity monitoring and management on the organization's premises. These services typically include installing and monitoring antivirus and spam blocking, intrusion detection systems, firewalls, and virtual private networks (VPNs). An MSSP can also handle system changes, modifications, and upgrades.

Securing Cloud Computing

Cloud computing has several potential security issues. These are listed in Table 10-4.

Table 10-4   Cloud security issues

Security issue	Description
Unauthorized access to data	Improper cloud security configurations can result in data being left exposed.
Lack of visibility	Organizations have limited or no visibility into the security mechanisms of the cloud provider and thus cannot verify the effectiveness of security controls.
Insecure application program interfaces (APIs)	While APIs help cloud customers customize their PaaS by providing data recognition, access, and effective encryption, a vulnerable API can be exploited by threat actors.
Compliance regulations	Maintaining compliance requires that an organization know where its data is, who can access it, and how it is protected, but this can be difficult in an opaque cloud system, which lacks transparency.
System vulnerabilities	A cloud infrastructure is prone to system vulnerabilities due to complex networks and multiple third-party platforms.

The cloud provider should guarantee that the means are in place by which authorized users are given access while threat actors are denied. Also, the customer's data must be isolated from the data of other customers, and the highest level of application availability and security must be maintained. Finally, all transmissions to and from the cloud must be adequately protected. Securing cloud computing involves using cloud security controls, managing application security, and applying security to virtual devices.

Cloud Security Controls

A *security control* exists to reduce or mitigate the risk to assets. A control can be a policy, procedure, technique, method, solution, plan, action, or device designed to help accomplish that goal. Some controls are inherent to the cloud computing platforms and offered by the cloud computing providers to their customers (cloud native controls), while other security controls are available from external sources (third-party solutions).

Securing cloud computing involves using controls such as conducting audits, using regions and zones, implementing secrets management, and enforcing mitigations on the three function areas of cloud computing: storage, network, and compute.

Conduct Audits   A cloud security audit is an independent examination of cloud service controls. Once completed, the auditor renders an objective assessment of the security. A cloud auditor can evaluate the services from a cloud provider in terms of security controls, privacy impact, availability, and performance. An auditor can also review the *integration* of the elements used in the overall infrastructure, such as VPCs, physical data centers, remote offices, and remote gateways.

Audits are typically performed to verify the conformance to established standards so that the organization can be authenticated as being in compliance. Auditing is particularly important for federal agencies because they are required to include a contractual clause enabling third parties to assess security controls of cloud providers. The organization itself can also benefit from the independent audit by being made aware of any deficiencies that must be addressed.

Use Regions and Zones   Highly available systems are reliable because they can continue operating even when critical components fail. These systems are also resilient, meaning that they can simply handle failure without service disruption or data loss and seamlessly recover from such a failure. In a cloud computing environment, reliability and resiliency are achieved through duplicating processes across one or more geographical areas. This is called high availability across zones.

The cloud provider Amazon Web Services (AWS) maintains multiple geographic *Regions*—including Regions in North America, South America, Europe, China, Asia Pacific, South Africa, and the Middle East. An *Availability Zone (AZ)* is one or more data centers within an AWS Region, each with redundant power, networking, and connectivity. By spreading their cloud infrastructure across several AZs, AWS clients can create systems that are more highly available, fault tolerant, and scalable than would be possible from using a single data center. If an application is partitioned across multiple AZs, then organizations are better isolated and protected from problems such as power outages, lightning strikes, tornadoes, and earthquakes.

NOTE 8

All AZs in an AWS Region are interconnected with high-bandwidth, low-latency networking, over fully redundant, dedicated fiber connections. All AZs are physically separated from each other by a "meaningful distance" from any other AZ, although all are within 60 miles (100 km) of each other.

Implement Secrets Management   Traditional application design is often called *monolithic* because the entire program is developed as a single entity. While monolithic code writing and deploying was originally done for convenience because it all occurred at a single location in the organization's office, these applications soon became larger and more complex as more features were added and requirements were expanded. This made managing the applications difficult for the following reasons:

- As the applications became larger, deployment times likewise became longer.
- Due to the complexity, any modifications often affected other parts of the code so that the application became unstable, unsecure, or failed to function as designed.
- The codebase became too large for any single developer or development team to fully understand.

The solution to monolithic application design is to divide it into smaller entities. These were not divided by *technical* processes but rather designed to make each entity a specialized part of the code. This is known as **microservices architecture** and is illustrated in Figure 10-4. A microservices architecture has smaller and more specialized elements—each of which manages its own database, generates its own logs, and handles user authentication by using **microservices APIs** and specialized APIs called RESTful APIs.

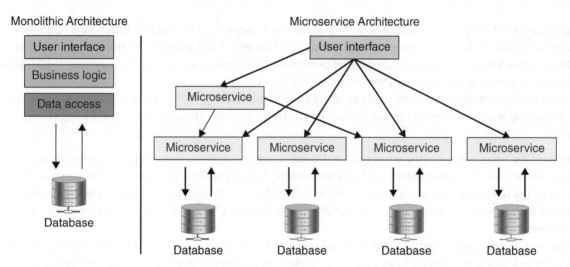

Figure 10-4 Monolithic versus microservices architecture

NOTE 9

When the British Broadcasting Corporation (BBC) moved its monolithic on-demand video platform to a cloud computing environment using a microservices architecture, the final product comprised 30 separate microservices.

The microservices need to communicate among themselves. However, cloud-based microservices must have keys to access the other microservices—such as API keys, passwords, certificates, encryption keys, and tokens. How should these "secrets" be passed or accessed securely? Embedding the keys as part of the software code (*hard coding*) is not a secure option.

The answer is to use **secrets management**. Secrets management enables strong security and improved management of a microservices-based architecture. It allows the entire cloud infrastructure to remain flexible and scalable without sacrificing security. A secrets manager provides a central repository and single source to manage, access, and audit secrets across a cloud infrastructure. Typical features of a secrets management system are listed in Table 10-5.

Table 10-5 Secrets management features

Feature	Description
Limited and automated replication	While secret data and secret names are "project-global" resources, the secret data is stored in regions, which the user can specify or the cloud provider can designate.
Secret-specific versioning	A secret can be pinned to a specific version of the code (like "v3.2").
Audit logging	Every interaction generates an audit entry in a log file that can be used to find abnormal access patterns that may indicate possible security breaches.
Default encryption	Data is encrypted in transit and at rest with AES-256-bit encryption keys.
Extensibility	One system is able to extend and integrate into other existing secrets management systems.

Cloud computing providers typically offer their own proprietary secrets management systems. Several third-party systems are also available.

Enforce Functional Area Mitigations   Cloud computing has three functional areas: storage, network, and compute. Each of these has its own set of security mitigations and is listed in Table 10-6.

Table 10-6   Functional area controls

Functional area	Control	Description
Storage	Permissions	Enforce what actions can be taken on stored data (such as edit, delete, and copy).
Storage	Encryption	Encrypt data at rest in the cloud.
Storage	Replication for high availability	Store multiple copies of critical data across regions and zones to protect against loss.
Network	Virtual networks	Create a **virtual network** that connects services and resources such as virtual machines and database applications with each other via a secure, encrypted, and private network, as seen in Figure 10-5.
Network	Public and private subnets	Configure a VPC with a **public subnet** for public-facing web server applications and a different **private subnet** for backend servers that are not publicly accessible.
Network	Segmentation	Create network segments to enforce rules for which services are permitted between accessible zones so that only designated endpoints belonging to other approved zones can reach them.
Network	API inspection and integration	Use automated **API inspection and integration** services for authentication, authorization, encryption, availability, and policy compliance of APIs.
Compute	Security groups	Use **security groups** to segment computing resources into logical groupings that form network perimeters.
Compute	Dynamic resource allocation	**Dynamic resource allocation** is deprovisioning computing resources when they are no longer needed.
Compute	Instance awareness	Implement **instance awareness** or the ability for security appliances to differentiate between instances of cloud apps.
Compute	VPC endpoint	When creating a VPC endpoint, attach an endpoint policy that controls access to the service.

Application Security

While securing the functional areas of the cloud (storage, networking, and compute) is universally considered as important, an area often overlooked is **application security** or protecting applications. There are several common misperceptions, ranging from application security being entirely the cloud computing provider's responsibility to the native "out of the box" security of the applications providing adequate security. However, misconfigurations of the application setup and insecure APIs or interfaces can provide vulnerabilities for threat actors to exploit.

One of an organization's security protections for cloud computing application security is to use a **cloud access security broker (CASB)**. A CASB is a set of software tools or services that resides between an enterprise's on-prem infrastructure and the cloud provider's infrastructure. Acting as the gatekeeper, a CASB ensures that the security policies of the enterprise extend to its data in the cloud. For example, if the enterprise has a policy for encrypting data, a CASB can enforce that control and ensure that data is encrypted when it is copied from the cloud to a local device. Another security protection is to use cloud-based data loss prevention (DLP) to extend the enterprise's policies to data stored in the cloud.

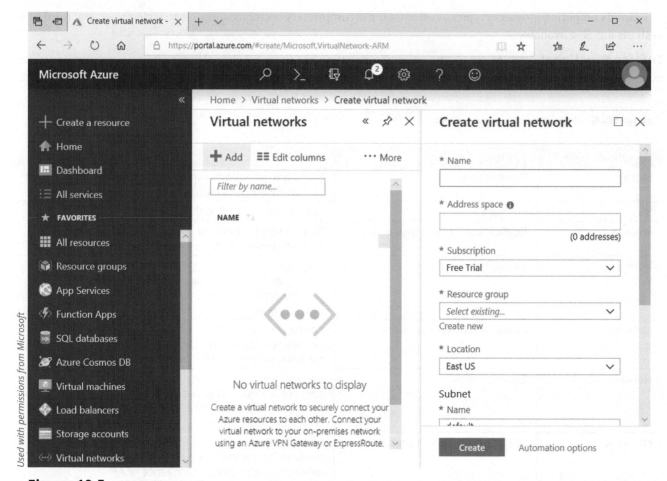

Figure 10-5 Virtual network

Security Virtual Device Solutions

Just as security appliances are needed in a physical network, so too are security virtual devices in a cloud computing environment. Next generation secure web gateways and virtual firewalls are considered important. However, determining which security appliances to implement in a cloud computing infrastructure is more challenging due to a lack of a cloud conceptual model.

Next Generation Secure Web Gateway (SWG) A next generation secure web gateway (SWG) combines several features into a single product. It examines both incoming and outgoing traffic and performs basic URL and monitoring in web applications. A next generation SWG also analyzes received traffic (even traffic encrypted by SSL), performs DLP, and provides alerts to a monitoring device such as a security information and event management (SIEM) appliance. An SWG can be placed on endpoints, at the edge, or in the cloud.

Cloud Firewall A cloud firewall is virtual software that functions in a similar manner to a physical security appliance by examining traffic into and out of the cloud. Sometimes called a *public cloud firewall, next gen firewall,* or *virtual firewall*, these devices are deployed in the public cloud. However, they have several advantages over a physical appliance such as the ability to scale quickly as the need arises.

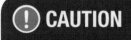 **CAUTION** When deploying a cloud firewall, the costs should be considered. Like cloud providers, third-party cloud firewall providers charge an hourly rate for the service. This is especially the case if the network has been "microsegmented" with each segment requiring its own cloud firewall.

Lack of Cloud Conceptual Model   Determining the correct security virtual device for the cloud can be challenging. A primary reason for this challenge is that physical networks neatly map to the Open Systems Interconnection (OSI) seven-layer model that illustrates network functionality, as seen in Figure 10-6. When managing an on-prem infrastructure, it is relatively straightforward for a network administrator to understand what is being done at each layer, who is responsible for physical connectivity, who manages Layer 3 routing and control, and who has access to the upper layers. When "Layer 3" is used to describe IP-based routing or when "Layer 7" is used to describe functions interacting at a software level, these terms are universally and uniformly applied. Security professionals can then more easily identify the security appliances needed and understand how they interact with the other layers and appliances.

Layer	Application/Example
Application (7) Serves as the window for users and application processes to access the network services.	**End user layer** Program that opens what was sent or creates what is to be sent
	Resource sharing • Remote file access • Remote printer access • Directory services • Network management
Presentation (6) Formats the data to be presented in the Application layer. It can be viewed as the "translator" for the network.	**Syntax layer** Encrypt and decrypt (if needed)
	Character code translation • Data conversion • Data compression • Data encryption • Character set translation
Session (5) Allows session establishment between processes running on different stations.	**Synch and send to ports** (logical ports)
	Session establishment, maintenance, and termination • Session support • Perform security, name recognition, logging, etc.
Transport (4) Ensures that messages are delivered error-free, in sequence, and with no losses or duplications.	**TCP** Host to host, flow control
	Message segmentation • Message acknowledgement • Message traffic control • Session multiplexing
Network (3) Controls the operations of the subnet, deciding which physical path the data takes	**Packets** ("letter," contains IP address)
	Routing • Subnet traffic control • Frame fragmentation • Logical-physical address mapping • Subnet usage accounting
Data Link (2) Provides error-free transfer of data frames from one node to another over the Physical layer.	**Frames** ("envelopes," contains MAC address) (NIC card—Switch—NIC card) (End to end)
	Establishes and terminates the logical link between nodes • Frame traffic control • Frame sequencing • Frame acknowledgement • Frame delimiting Frame error checking • Media access control
Physical (1) Concerned with the transmission and reception of the unstructured raw bit stream over the physical medium.	**Physical structure** Cables, hubs, etc.
	Data encoding • Physical medium attachment • Transmission technique • Baseband or broadband • Physical medium transmission bits and volts

Figure 10-6   OSI seven-layer model

However, with cloud computing, the OSI model no longer is as useful—if it is useful at all. First, the cloud provider manages cabling, Internet connections, power, cooling, disks, redundancy, and physical security instead of the customer. Second, everything the cloud customer "sees" is abstract and virtual, and essentially exists only as code. Third, there is a higher level of interaction: an organization may create multiple cloud computing accounts with multiple cloud providers in order to separate environments from each other, each with different VPCs for different applications, multiple subnets for different functions, and a variety of storage, network, and compute configurations. The lack of a conceptual model like the OSI model makes selecting and managing security virtual devices more challenging.

Different cloud-based conceptual models are starting to be proposed. One model is shown in Table 10-7. However, no single model has been widely adapted, and it appears that there is no model that will become the standard in the near future.

Table 10-7 Proposed cloud-based conceptual model

Layer and name	Description	Party responsible
5—Application Experience	End-user facing interface	Customer
4—Native Service	Create, store, process	Customer
3—Software-Defined Datacenter	Create infrastructure	SaaS—Cloud computing provider
		PaaS and IaaS—Customer
2—Virtualization Software	Software that virtualizes the hardware	Cloud computing provider
1—Physical Infrastructure	Buildings, power, cables, hardware, utilities	Cloud computing provider

TWO RIGHTS & A WRONG

1. A community cloud is a cloud that is open only to specific organizations that have common concerns.
2. The fog computing location is performed at or very near the source of the data instead of relying on the cloud or on-prem for processing.
3. A serverless infrastructure is one in which the capacity planning, installation, setup, and management are all invisible to the user because they are handled by the cloud provider.

See Appendix B for the answer.

VIRTUALIZATION SECURITY

 **CERTIFICATION**

2.2 Summarize virtualization and cloud computing concepts.

Like cloud security, virtualization security also involves first an understanding of the topic along with specific examples. It includes specific steps to be taken to secure a virtualized environment.

Defining Virtualization

Understanding virtualization includes knowing what it is and how it can be used along with its advantages.

What Is Virtualization?

Virtualization is a means of managing and presenting computer resources by function without regard to their physical layout or location. One type of virtualization in which an entire operating system environment is simulated is known as *host virtualization*. Instead of using a physical computer, a *virtual machine (VM)*, which is a simulated software-based emulation of a computer, is created instead. The *host system* (the operating system installed on the computer's hardware) runs a VM monitor program that supports one or more *guest systems* (a foreign virtual operating system) that run applications. For example, a computer that boots to Windows 10 (host) could support a VM of Linux (guest) as well as another Windows 10 (guest) system.

Virtualization is used to consolidate multiple physical servers into VMs that can run on a single physical computer. Because a typical server utilizes only about 10–15 percent of its capacity, multiple VMs can run on a single physical server.

NOTE 10

Virtualization is not new. It was first developed by IBM in the 1960s for running multiple software "contexts" on its mainframe computers. It has gained popularity over the last 20 years as on-prem data centers used it for migrating away from physical servers to more economical VMs.

In addition, virtualization is used extensively in cloud computing environments. It gives the flexibility necessary for rapid deployments. In fact, the adoption and popularity of cloud computing can be directly attributed to the widespread use of on-prem server virtualization.

The VM monitor program is called a *hypervisor*, which manages the VM operating systems. Hypervisors use a small "layer" of computer code in software or firmware to allocate resources in real time as needed, such as input/output functions and memory allocations. There are two types of hypervisors:

- *Type I.* *Type I hypervisors* run directly on the computer's hardware instead of the underlying operating system. Type I hypervisors are sometimes called "native" or "bare metal" hypervisors.
- *Type II.* Instead of running directly on the computer hardware, *Type II hypervisors* run on the host operating system, much like a regular application. Type I and Type II hypervisors are illustrated in Figure 10-7.

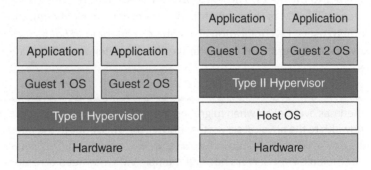

Figure 10-7   Type I and Type II hypervisors

An even more reduced instance of virtualization is a **container**. With both Type I and Type II hypervisors, the entire guest operating system must be started and fully functioning before an application can be launched. A container, on the other hand, holds only the necessary OS components (such as binary files and libraries) that are needed for that specific application to run. And in some instances, containers can even share binary files and libraries. This not only reduces the necessary hard drive storage space and random access memory (RAM) needed but also allows for containers to start more quickly because the entire operating system does not have to be started. Containers can be easily moved from one computer to another. A container is illustrated in Figure 10-8.

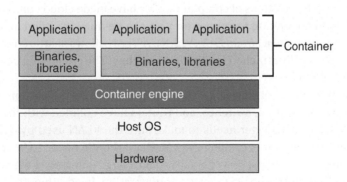

Figure 10-8   Container

NOTE 11

Another application of VMs is known as *Virtual Desktop Infrastructure (VDI)*. VDI is the process of running a user desktop inside a VM that resides on a server. This enables personalized desktops for each user to be available on any computer or device that can access the server so that their personalized desktop and files can be accessed as if they were sitting at their own computer. VDI allows centralized management as opposed to the need for technical support personnel to access a system remotely or even visit a user's desk to troubleshoot, saving substantial time and money.

Advantages of Virtualization

Virtualization has several advantages. First, new virtual server machines can be quickly made available (*host availability*), and resources such as the amount of RAM or hard drive space can easily be expanded or contracted as needed (*host elasticity*). Also, virtualization can reduce costs. Instead of purchasing one physical server to run one network operating system and its applications, a single physical server can run multiple VMs and host multiple operating systems. This results in a significant cost savings in that fewer physical computers must be purchased and maintained. In addition, the cost of electricity to run these servers as well as keep data center server rooms cool is also reduced.

Another advantage of server virtualization is that it can be beneficial in providing uninterrupted server access to users. Data centers must schedule planned "downtime" for servers to perform maintenance on the hardware or software. However, it is often difficult to find a time when users will not be inconvenienced by the downtime. This can be addressed by virtualization that supports *live migration*; this technology enables a VM to be moved to a different physical computer with no impact to the users. The VM stores its current state onto a shared storage device immediately before the migration occurs. The VM is then reinstalled on another physical computer and accesses its storage with no noticeable interruption to users. Live migration also can be used for *load balancing*; if the demand for a service or application increases, network managers can quickly move this high-demand VM to another physical server with more RAM or CPU resources.

 **CAUTION**   Sometimes overlooked when migrating multiple physical servers to VMs is the need for increased bandwidth to the physical server that houses the VMs. Prior to the migration, each physical server had its own network connection; now, however, a single physical server must handle all the traffic for multiple VMs. Servers housing multiple VMs may need a 10 Gbps Ethernet card to handle the increase in traffic.

Infrastructure as Code

Instances of virtualization is sometimes referred to as *infrastructure as code*. Two examples are software-defined networks and software-defined visibility.

Software-Defined Network (SDN)

Virtualization has been an essential technology in changing the face of computing over the last decade. Racks of individual physical servers running a single application have been replaced by only a few hardware devices running multiple VMs, simulated software-based emulations of computers. VMs have made cloud computing possible; as computing needs increase or decrease, cloud computing resources on VMs can be quickly scaled up or back. Networks can also be configured into logical groups to create a *virtual LAN* (VLAN). A VLAN allows scattered users to be logically grouped together even though they are physically attached to different switches. The computing landscape today would simply not be possible without virtualization.

Yet VMs and virtual LANs run into a bottleneck: the physical network. Dating back more than 40 years, networks comprised of physical hardware like bridges, switches, and routers have collided with the world of VMs and VLANs.

Consider this problem. A network manager needs to make sure the VLAN used by a VM is assigned to the same port on a switch as the physical server that is running the VM. But if the VM needs to be migrated, the manager must reconfigure the VLAN every time that a virtual server is moved. In a large enterprise, whenever a new VM is installed, it can take hours for managers to perform the necessary reconfiguration. In addition, these managers must configure each vendor's equipment separately, tweaking performance and security configurations for each session and application. This process is difficult to do with conventional network switches because the *control logic* for each switch is bundled together with the *switching logic*.

What is needed is for the flexibility of the virtual world to be applied to the network. This would allow the network manager to add, drop, and change network resources quickly and dynamically on the fly.

The solution is a **software-defined network (SDN)**. An SDN virtualizes parts of the physical network so that it can be more quickly and easily reconfigured. This is accomplished by separating the *control plane* from the *data plane*, as illustrated in Figure 10-9. The control plane consists of one or more SDN servers and performs the complex functions such as routing and security checks. It also defines the data flows through the data plane.

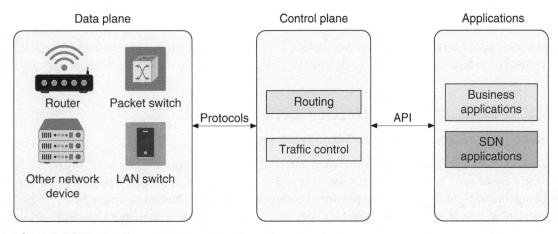

Figure 10-9   Software-defined network

NOTE 12

In an SDN, the control plane is essentially an application running on a computer that can manage the physical plane.

If traffic needs to flow through the network, it first receives permission from the SDN controller, which verifies that the communication is permitted by the network policy of the enterprise. Once approved, the SDN controller computes a route for the flow to take and adds an entry for that flow in each of the switches along the path. Because all the complex networking functions are handled by the SDN controller, the switches simply manage "flow tables" whose entries are created by the controller. The communication between the SDN controller and the SDN switches uses a standardized protocol and API.

NOTE 13

The architecture of SDN is very flexible, using different types of switches from different vendors at different protocol layers. SDN controllers and switches can be implemented for Ethernet switches (Layer 2), Internet routers (Layer 3), Transport (Layer 4) switching, or Application layer switching and routing.

With the decoupling of the control and data planes, SDN enables applications to deal with one "abstracted" network device without any care for the details of how the device operates. This is because the network applications see only a single API to the controller. This makes it possible to quickly create and deploy new applications to orchestrate network traffic flow to meet specific enterprise requirements for performance or security.

NOTE 14

From a security perspective, SDNs can provide stronger protection. SDN technology can simplify extending VLANs beyond just the perimeter of a building, which can help secure data. Also, an SDN can ensure that all network traffic is routed through a firewall. And because all network traffic flows through a single point, it can help capture data for NIDS and NIPS.

Software-Defined Visibility (SDV)

Software-defined visibility (SDV) is a framework that allows users to create programs in which critical security functions that previously required manual intervention can now be automated. As technology moves from a user interacting with a machine to a machine interacting with multiple machines, it is necessary to improve this interaction. SDV allows network administrators to automate multiple functions in a network infrastructure—including dynamic response to detected threat patterns, adjustments to traffic mode configurations for in-line security tools, and additional IT operations-management functions and capabilities.

NOTE 15

SDV relies upon a set of APIs known as *RESTful APIs*. These RESTful APIs use existing HTTP methods of GET, PUT, POST, and DELETE. RESTful APIs have become so foundational that they are sometimes called the "backbone of the Internet."

Security Concerns for Virtual Environments

Host virtualization also has several security-related advantages:

- The latest security updates can be downloaded and run in a VM to determine compatibility or the impact on other software or even hardware. This is used instead of installing the update on a production computer and then being forced to "roll back" to the previous configuration if it does not work properly.
- A *snapshot* of a state of a VM can be saved for later use. A user can make a snapshot before performing extensive modifications or alterations to the VM, and then the snapshot can be reloaded so that the VM is at the beginning state before the changes were made. Multiple snapshots can be made, all at different states, and loaded as needed.
- Testing the existing security configuration, known as *security control testing*, can be performed using a simulated network environment on a computer using multiple VMs. For example, one VM can virtually attack another VM on the same host system to determine vulnerabilities and security settings. This is possible because all the VMs can be connected through a virtual network.
- VMs can promote security segregation and isolation. Separating VMs from other machines can reduce the risk of infections transferring from one device to another.
- A VM can be used to test for potential malware. A suspicious program can be loaded into an isolated VM and executed (*sandboxing*). If the program is malware, it will impact only the VM, and it can easily be erased and a snapshot reinstalled. This is how antivirus software using heuristic detection can spot the characteristics of a virus.

NOTE 16

Threat actors have learned that when their malware is run in a sandbox, it most likely is being examined by a security professional. Many modern instances of malware will refuse to function or even self-destruct if it detects that it is being run in a sandbox.

However, there are security concerns for virtualized environments:

- Not all hypervisors have the necessary security controls to keep out determined attackers. If a single hypervisor is compromised, multiple virtual servers are at risk.
- Traditional security tools—such as antivirus, firewalls, and IDS—were designed for single physical servers and do not always adapt well to multiple VMs. Instead, "virtualized" versions can be used instead, such as a *firewall virtual appliance* that is optimized for VMs.
- VMs must be protected from both outside networks and other VMs on the same physical computer. In a network without VMs, external devices such as firewalls and IDS that reside between physical servers can help prevent one physical server from infecting another physical server, but no such physical devices exist between VMs.
- VMs may be able to "escape" from the contained environment and directly interact with the host operating system. It is important to have virtual machine escape protection so that a VM cannot directly interact with the host operating system and potentially infect it, which could then be transmitted to all other VMs running on the host operating system.

Because VMs can easily and quickly be created and launched, this has led to *virtual machine sprawl*, or the widespread proliferation of VMs without proper oversight or management. It is often easy for a VM to be created and then forgotten. A guest operating system that has remained dormant for a period may not contain the latest security updates, even though the underlying host operating system has been updated. When the guest is launched, it will be vulnerable until properly updated.

Combating VM sprawl is called virtual machine sprawl avoidance. Suggestions for limiting VM sprawl include performing regular audits to identify VMs that are no longer needed, using good naming conventions to be able to more easily identify the purpose of a VM, and periodically cleaning up VMs so that new processes can be easily added to an existing VM. Another option is to install a virtual machine manager, which can provide a dashboard of the status of the VMs. A virtual machine manager is seen in Figure 10-10.

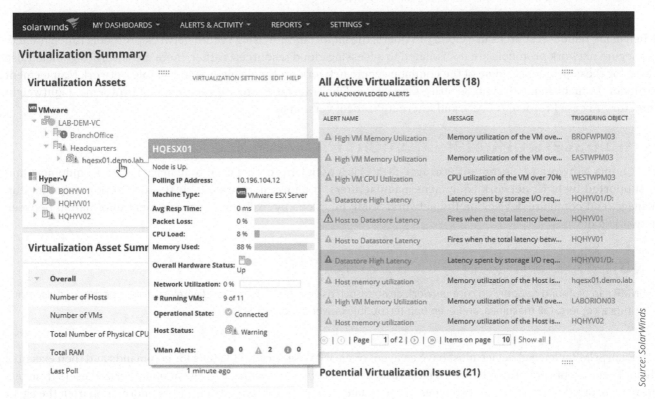

Figure 10-10   Virtual machine manager

In addition to protecting VMs, container security or protecting containers from attacks is also important. Best practices for securing a container include the following:

- Always manage container-based processes using non-privileged user accounts.
- Use trusted images to create a container because a compromised image can more easily circumvent existing security measures.
- Use tools such as Security-Enhanced Linux (SELinux) to harden the hosts.

TWO RIGHTS & A WRONG

1. A host system runs a VM monitor program that supports one or more guest systems that run applications.
2. SDV allows network administrators to automate multiple functions in a network infrastructure.
3. Type II hypervisors run directly on the computer's hardware instead of the underlying operating system.

See Appendix B for the answer.

SECURE NETWORK PROTOCOLS

 **CERTIFICATION**

1.3 Given a scenario, analyze potential indicators associated with application attacks.

3.1 Given a scenario, implement secure protocols.

3.3 Given a scenario, implement secure network designs.

When using remote resources like cloud providers, the importance of using secure network protocols is heightened. Yet secure network protocols are not isolated to accessing cloud resources; rather, there are several significant use cases for these protocols. Some of the common secure network protocols include the Simple Network Management Protocol, Domain Name System Security Extensions, File Transfer Protocol, secure email protocols, Lightweight Directory Access Protocol (LDAP), and Internet Protocol version 6.

Simple Network Management Protocol (SNMP)

The **Simple Network Management Protocol (SNMP)** is a popular protocol used to manage network equipment and is supported by most network equipment manufacturers. It allows network administrators to remotely monitor, manage, and configure devices on the network. SNMP functions by exchanging management information between networked devices.

NOTE 17

SNMP can be found not only on core network devices such as switches, routers, and wireless access points, but also on printers, copiers, fax machines, and even uninterruptible power supplies (UPSs).

Each SNMP-managed device must have an agent or an SNMP service that listens for commands and then executes them. These agents are protected with a password, called a *community string*, to prevent unauthorized users from taking control of a device. There are two types of community strings: a *read-only* string allows information from the agent to be viewed, and a *read-write* string allows settings on the device to be changed.

There were several security vulnerabilities with the use of community strings in the first two versions of SNMP, known as SNMPv1 and SNMPv2. Because of the security vulnerabilities of SNMPv1 and SNMPv2, significant security enhancements were made to the next (and now current) version known as **SNMPv3**. SNMPv3 supports authentication and encryption. Authentication is used to ensure that SNMPv3 information is available only to the intended recipient, while encryption ensures that any messages cannot be read by threat actors.

NOTE 18

Cloud computing virtual network equipment can also be managed by using SNMP.

Domain Name System Security Extensions (DNSSEC)

The Domain Name System (DNS), which is the basis for domain name resolution of names to IP addresses, is often the focus of attacks. These attacks using DNS include DNS poisoning and DNS hijacking.

NOTE 19

DNS, DNS poisoning, and DNS hijacking are covered in Module 8.

These DNS attacks can be thwarted by using Domain Name System Security Extensions (DNSSEC). DNSSEC adds additional *resource records* (these records define the data types being used) and message header information, which can be used to verify that the requested data has not been altered in transmission. Using asymmetric cryptography, a private key that is specific to a zone is used in encrypting a hash of a set of resource records, which is then used to create the digital signature to be stored in the resource record (along with the corresponding public key).

NOTE 20

DNSSEC essentially adds two important features to the DNS protocol: data origin authentication allows a resolver to verify that the data it received actually came from the zone from which it claims to have originated, and data integrity protection proves the data has not been modified in transit since it was originally signed by the zone owner with the zone's private key.

File Transfer Protocol (FTP)

In its early days, prior to the development of the World Wide Web and Hypertext Transfer Protocol (HTTP), the Internet was primarily a medium for transferring files from one device to another. Today transferring files is still an important task. Transferring files can be performed using the File Transfer Protocol (FTP), which is an unsecure TCP/IP protocol. FTP is used to connect to an FTP server, much in the same way that HTTP links to a web server.

NOTE 21

A "light" version of FTP known as *Trivial File Transfer Protocol (TFTP)* uses a small amount of memory but has limited functionality. It is often used for the automated transfer of configuration files between devices.

There are several different methods for using FTP on a local computer. These include using an FTP client application that displays files on the local endpoint as well as the remote server so files can be dragged and dropped between devices, using a web browser by prefacing a URL with the protocol ftp:// instead of the http://, or even from an OS command prompt using *get* (retrieve a file from the server), and *put* (transfer a file to the server).

FTP typically uses two ports: TCP port 21 is the FTP control port used for passing FTP commands, and TCP port 20 is the FTP data port through which data is sent and received. Using *FTP active mode,* an FTP client initiates a session to a server by opening a *command channel* connection to the server's TCP port number 21. A file transfer is requested by the client by sending a *PORT* command to the server, which then attempts to initiate a *data channel* connection back to the client on TCP port 20. In *FTP passive mode*, the client initiates the data channel connection, yet instead of using the *PORT* command, the client sends a *PASV* command on the command channel. The server responds with the TCP port number to which the client should connect to establish the data channel (typically port 1025 to 5000).

NOTE 22

Increased security can be established by restricting the port range used by the FTP service and then creating a firewall rule that allows FTP traffic only on those allowed port numbers.

Several security vulnerabilities are associated with using FTP. First, FTP does not use encryption, so any usernames, passwords, and files being transferred are in cleartext and could be accessed by using a protocol analyzer. Also, files being transferred by FTP are vulnerable to man-in-the-middle attacks.

There are two options for secure transmissions over FTP. FTP Secure (FTPS) uses Secure Sockets Layer (SSL) or Transport Layer Security (TLS) to encrypt commands sent over the control port (port 21) in an FTP session. FTPS is a file transport layer resting on top of SSL or TLS, meaning that it uses the FTP protocol to transfer files to and from SSL- or TLS-enabled FTP servers. However, a weakness of FTPS is that although the control port commands are encrypted, the data port (port 20) may or may not be encrypted. This is because a file that has already been encrypted by the user would not need to be encrypted again by FTPS and incur the additional overhead.

The second option is to use Secure FTP (SFTP). There are several differences between SFTP and FTPS. First, FTPS is a combination of two technologies (FTP and SSL or TLS), whereas SFTP is an entire protocol itself and is not pieced together with multiple parts. Second, SFTP uses only a single TCP port instead of two ports like FTPS. Finally, SFTP encrypts and compresses all data and commands (FTPS might not encrypt data).

Secure Email Protocols

Since developer Ray Tomlinson sent the first email message in 1971, email has become an essential part of everyday life. It is estimated that more than 400 billion emails are sent daily. However, only 15 percent of this total (60 billion) are legitimate; the remaining 85 percent or 340 billion daily emails are spam.[3]

Two different electronic email systems are in use today. An earlier email system uses two TCP/IP protocols to send and receive messages: the Simple Mail Transfer Protocol (SMTP) handles outgoing mail, while the Post Office Protocol (POP), more commonly known as *POP3* for the current version, is responsible for incoming mail. POP3 is a basic protocol that allows users to retrieve messages sent to an email server by using a local program running on their computer called an *email client*. The email client connects to the POP3 server and downloads the messages onto the local computer. After the messages are downloaded, they may be erased from the POP3 server. The SMTP server listens on port 25 while POP3 listens on port 110.

 **CAUTION** SMTP servers can forward email sent from an email client to a remote domain, known as *SMTP relay*. However, if SMTP relay is not controlled, an attacker can use it to forward spam and disguise his identity to make himself untraceable. An uncontrolled SMTP relay is known as an *SMTP open relay*. It is important to defend against SMTP open relays. The mail relay should be turned off altogether so that all users send and receive email from the local SMTP server or limit relays to only local users.

IMAP (Internet Mail Access Protocol) is a more recent and advanced electronic email system for incoming mail. While POP3 is a "store-and-forward" service, IMAP is a "remote" email storage. With IMAP, the email remains on the email server and is not downloaded to the user's computer. Mail can be organized into folders on the mail server and read from any device: desktop computer, tablet, smartphone, etc. IMAP users can even work with email while offline. This is accomplished by downloading email onto the local device without erasing the email on the IMAP server. A user can read and reply to email offline. The next time a connection is established, the new messages are sent, and any new email is downloaded. The current version of IMAP is IMAP4.

As a means of security, a *mail gateway* monitors emails for unwanted content and prevents these messages from being delivered. Many mail gateways also have monitoring capabilities for outbound emails. For inbound emails, a mail gateway can search the content in email messages for various types of malware, spam, and phishing attacks. For outbound email, a mail gateway can detect and block the transmission of sensitive data, such as Social Security numbers or healthcare records. In addition, a mail gateway can automatically and transparently encrypt outbound email messages.

Lightweight Directory Access Protocol (LDAP)

A directory service is a database stored on the network itself that contains information about users and network devices. It contains information such as the user's name, telephone extension, email address, login name, and other facts. The directory service also keeps track of all the resources on the network and a user's privileges to those resources and grants or denies access based on the directory service information. Directory services make it much easier to grant privileges or permissions to network users.

The International Organization for Standardization (ISO) created a standard for directory services known as *X.500*. The purpose of the X.500 standard was to standardize how the data was stored so that any computer system could access these directories. The X.500 standard also defines a protocol for a client application to access an X.500 directory called the *Directory Access Protocol (DAP)*. However, the DAP is too large to run on a personal computer. The Lightweight Directory Access Protocol (LDAP), sometimes called X.500 Lite, is a simpler subset of DAP.

LDAP makes it possible for almost any application running on virtually any computer platform to obtain directory information. Because LDAP is an open protocol, applications need not worry about the type of server hosting the directory. Today many LDAP servers are implemented using standard relational database management systems as the engine and communicate via Extensible Markup Language (XML) documents served over the Hypertext Transport Protocol (HTTP).

> **⚠ CAUTION** By default, LDAP traffic is transmitted in cleartext. LDAP traffic can be made secure by using Secure Sockets Layer (SSL), which is known as LDAP over SSL (LDAPS).

However, a weakness of LDAP is that it can be subject to LDAP injection attacks. These attacks, similar to SQL injection attacks, can occur when user input is not properly filtered. This may allow an attacker to construct LDAP statements based on user input statements. The attacker could then retrieve information from the LDAP database or modify its content. The defense against LDAP injection attacks is to examine all user input before processing.

NOTE 23

Injection attacks are covered in Module 3.

Internet Protocol Version 6 (IPv6)

The current version of the IP protocol is version 4 and is called *IPv4*. Developed in 1981, long before the Internet was universally popular, IPv4 has several weaknesses. One of the weaknesses is the number of available IP addresses: an IP address is 32 bits in length, providing about 4.3 billion possible IP address combinations, which is no longer is sufficient for the number of devices that are being connected to the Internet. Another weakness is that of security: due to its structure, IPv4 can be subject to several types of attacks.

NOTE 24

Prior to the release of IPv4 in 1981, the total number of IP addresses available was only 255.

The solution to these weaknesses is the next generation of the IP protocol called Internet Protocol version 6 (IPv6). IPv6 addresses the weaknesses of IPv4 and also provides several other significant improvements. First, IPv6 increases the number of available addresses. The number of IPv6 addresses is 340,282,366,920,463,463,374,607,431,768, 211,456 or 340 trillion, trillion, trillion addresses. This translates to 665 million billion IP addresses per square meter on earth.

IPv6 also has several enhanced security features. IPv6 can implement end-to-end encryption, making man-in-the-middle attacks significantly more difficult. IPv6 also supports more secure name resolution. The Secure Neighbor Discovery (SEND) protocol can send cryptographic confirmation that an endpoint is who it claims to be at the time of connection. This effectively renders Address Resolution Protocol (ARP) poisoning more difficult.

Use Cases

Different applications or "use cases" require different secure network protocols. Several of the recommended protocols for specific applications or technologies are summarized in Table 10-8.

Table 10-8 Secure network protocol recommendations

Application or technology	Recommended secure protocol
Voice and video	Secure Real-time Transport Protocol (SRTP)
Time synchronization	Network Time Protocol (NTP)
Email	Secure/Multipurpose Internet Mail Extensions (S/MIME)
Web browsing	Hypertext Transport Protocol Secure (HTTPS)
File transfer	Secure FTP (SFTP)
Directory services	Secure Sockets Layer (SSL)
Remote access	Virtual Private Network (VPN)
Domain name resolution	DNS Security Extensions (DNSSEC)
Routing and switching	IP Security (IPsec)
Network address translation	IP Security (IPsec)
Subscription services	IP Security (IPsec)

TWO RIGHTS & A WRONG

1. The current version of SNMP is SNMPv2.
2. SFTP is considered more secure than FTPS.
3. A mail gateway can automatically and transparently encrypt outbound email messages.

See Appendix B for the answer.

 **VM LAB** You're now ready to complete the live, virtual machine labs for this module. The labs can be found in the Practice It folder in each MindTap module.

SUMMARY

- Cloud computing is a popular and flexible approach to computing resources. All cloud resources are available online from virtually anywhere, and access is achieved through a web browser without the need for installing additional software. Cloud computing allows an almost endless array of servers, software, and network appliances to be quickly and easily configured as needed, and then as computing needs increase or decrease, these resources can be quickly scaled up or scaled back. As a pay-per-use computing model, customers pay only for the online computing resources they need.
- A public cloud is one in which the services and infrastructure are offered to all users with access provided remotely through the Internet. A community cloud is a cloud that is open only to specific organizations that have common concerns. A private cloud is created and maintained on a private network. Although this type offers the highest level of security and control (because the company must purchase and maintain all the software and hardware), it also reduces cost savings. A hybrid cloud is a combination of public and private clouds.
- Computing now takes place in several different locations. On-premises is computing resources located on the campus of the organization while off-premises is a computing resource hosted and supported by a third party. Fog is a decentralized computing infrastructure in which data, compute capabilities, storage, and applications are located between the data source and the cloud. Edge is computing that is performed

at or very near to the source of data instead of relying on the cloud or on-prem for processing. Cloud is a remote facility for computing.

- There are many elements that make up a cloud architecture. A thin client is a computer that runs from resources stored on a central cloud server instead of a localized hard drive. A transit gateway is a technology that allows organizations to connect all existing virtual private clouds (VPC), physical data centers, remote offices, and remote gateways into a single managed source. A serverless infrastructure is one in which the capacity planning, installation, setup, and management are all invisible to the user because they are handled by the cloud provider.

- There are several services models in cloud computing. Software as a Service (SaaS) is a cloud computing hosted software environment. Platform as a Service (PaaS) provides a software platform on which the enterprise or users can build their own applications and then host them on the PaaS provider's infrastructure. Infrastructure as a Service (IaaS) provides unlimited "raw" computing, storage, and network resources that the enterprise can use to build its own virtual infrastructure in the cloud. Anything as a Service (XaaS) describes a broad category of subscription services related to cloud computing. XaaS is any IT function or digital component that can be transformed into a service for enterprise or user consumption. Cloud management can be conducted by the local organization performing the work itself or by contracting with a third-party management service provider.

- Cloud computing has several potential security issues. Mitigating these issues involves using security controls. Some controls are inherent to the cloud computing platforms and offered by the cloud computing providers to their customers (cloud native controls) while other security controls are available from external sources (third-party solutions). One control is a cloud security audit conducted by as an independent examination of cloud service controls. Once completed, the auditor renders an objective assessment of the security. Another control uses regions and zones. In a cloud computing environment, reliability and resiliency is achieved through duplicating processes across one or more geographical areas. This is called high availability across zones. Secrets management enables strong security and improved management of a microservices-based architecture. It allows the entire cloud infrastructure to remain flexible and scalable without sacrificing security. Cloud computing has three functional areas: storage, network, and compute. Each of these has its own set of security mitigations.

- While securing the functional areas of the cloud (storage, networking, and compute) is universally considered as important, an area often overlooked is application security or protecting applications. A cloud access security broker (CASB) is a set of software tools or services that resides between an enterprise's on-prem infrastructure and the cloud provider's infrastructure. Acting as the gatekeeper, a CASB ensures that the security policies of the enterprise extend to its data in the cloud. Just as security appliances in a physical network are important, so too are security virtual devices in a cloud computing environment. Next generation secure web gateways and virtual firewalls are considered important. However, determining which security appliances to implement in a cloud computing infrastructure is more challenging due to a lack of a cloud conceptual model.

- Virtualization is a means of managing and presenting computer resources by function without regard to their physical layout or location. One type of virtualization in which an entire operating system environment is simulated is known as host virtualization. Instead of using a physical computer, a VM, which is a simulated software-based emulation of a computer, is created instead. Virtualization is used to consolidate multiple physical servers into VMs that can run on a single physical computer. Virtualization is used extensively in cloud computing environments. The VM monitor program is called a hypervisor, which manages the VM operating systems. A reduced instance of virtualization is a container. A container holds only the necessary OS components such as binary files and libraries that are needed for that specific application to run.

- Instances of virtualization are sometimes referred to as infrastructure as code. A software-defined network (SDN) virtualizes parts of the physical network so that it can be more quickly and easily reconfigured by separating the control plane from the data plane. Software-defined visibility (SDV) is a framework that allows users to create programs in which critical security functions that previously required manual intervention can now be automated. There are security concerns for virtualized environments. One concern is that VMs may be able to "escape" from the contained environment and directly interact with the host operating system. It is important to have virtual machine escape protection so that a VM cannot directly interact with the host operating system and potentially infect it, which could then be transmitted to all other VMs running on the host operating system. Another concern is that VMs can easily and quickly be created and launched, leading to virtual machine sprawl, or the widespread proliferation of VMs without proper oversight or management, increasing security vulnerabilities. Combating VM sprawl is called virtual machine sprawl avoidance.

- There are several secure network protocols that are used today. The Simple Network Management Protocol (SNMP) is a popular protocol used to manage network equipment and is supported by most network equipment manufacturers. It allows network administrators to remotely monitor, manage, and configure devices on the network. DNS attacks can be thwarted by using Domain Name System Security Extensions (DNSSEC), which adds resource records and message header information to verify that the requested data has not been altered in transmission. Transferring files can be performed using the File Transfer Protocol (FTP), which is an unsecure TCP/IP protocol. FTP Secure (FTPS) uses SSL or TLS to encrypt commands sent over the control port in an FTP session. Another option is to use Secure FTP (SFTP), which uses only a single TCP port instead of two ports like FTPS and encrypts and compresses all data and commands.

- There are two different electronic email systems that are in use today. An earlier email system uses two TCP/IP protocols to send and receive messages: the Simple Mail Transfer Protocol (SMTP) handles outgoing mail, while the Post Office Protocol (POP), more commonly known as POP3 for the current version) is responsible for incoming mail. IMAP (Internet Mail Access Protocol) is a more recent and advanced electronic email system for incoming mail. The Lightweight Directory Access Protocol (LDAP) is a directory service database stored on the network itself that contains information about users and network devices. A weakness of LDAP is that it can be subject to LDAP injection attacks. Internet Protocol version 6 (IPv6) addresses the weaknesses of the older version IPv4 and also provides several other significant improvements, including stronger security.

Key Terms

Anything as a Service (XaaS)
API inspection and integration
application security
cloud
cloud access security
  broker (CASB)
cloud computing
cloud native controls
cloud security audit
cloud service providers
community cloud
container
container security
directory service
Domain Name System Security
  Extensions (DNSSEC)
dynamic resource allocation
edge
File Transfer Protocol (FTP)
fog
FTP Secure (FTPS)
high availability across zones
hybrid cloud

IMAP (Internet Mail Access
  Protocol)
Infrastructure as a Service (IaaS)
instance awareness
Internet Protocol version 6 (IPv6)
LDAP injection attacks
Lightweight Directory Access
  Protocol (LDAP)
managed security service provider
  (MSSP)
managed service provider (MSP)
microservices APIs
microservices architecture
next generation secure web
  gateway (SWG)
off-premises
on-premises
Open Source Interconnection (OSI)
  seven-layer model
Platform as a Service (PaaS)
Post Office Protocol (POP)
private cloud
private subnet

public cloud
public subnet
resource policies
secrets management
Secure FTP (SFTP)
security groups
serverless infrastructure
services integration
Simple Mail Transfer Protocol
  (SMTP)
Simple Network Management
  Protocol (SNMP)
SNMPv3
Software as a Service (SaaS)
software-defined network (SDN)
software-defined visibility (SDV)
thin client
third-party solutions
transit gateway
virtual machine escape protection
virtual machine sprawl avoidance
virtual network
virtualization

Review Questions

1. Which of the following is NOT a characteristic of cloud computing?
   a. Metered services
   b. Immediate elasticity
   c. Universal client support
   d. Invisible resource pooling

2. Zuzana is creating a report for her supervisor about the cost savings associated with cloud computing. Which of the following would she NOT include on her report on the cost savings?
   a. Reduction in broadband costs
   b. Resiliency
   c. Scalability
   d. Pay-per-use

3. Aleksandra, the company HR manager, is completing a requisition form for the IT staff to create a type of cloud that would only be accessible to other HR managers like Aleksandra who are employed at manufacturing plants. The form asks for the type of cloud that is needed. Which type of cloud would best fit Aleksandra's need?
   a. Public cloud
   b. Group cloud
   c. Hybrid cloud
   d. Community cloud

4. Alicja is working on a project to deploy automated guided vehicles on the industrial shop floor of the manufacturing plant in which she works. What location of computing would be best for this project?
   a. Fog
   b. Edge
   c. Off-premises
   d. Remote

5. Wiktoria is frustrated that her company is using so many different cloud services that span multiple cloud provider accounts and even different cloud providers. She wants to implement a technology to give full control and visibility over all the cloud resources, including network routing and security. What product does Wiktoria need?
   a. Thin virtual visibility appliance (TVVA)
   b. SWG
   c. CASB
   d. Transit gateway

6. What does the term "serverless" mean in cloud computing?
   a. The cloud network configuration does not require any servers.
   b. Server resources of the cloud are inconspicuous to the end user.
   c. Servers are run as VMs.
   d. All appliances are virtual and do not interact with physical servers.

7. Oliwia has been given a project to manage the development of a new company app. She wants to use a cloud model to facilitate the development and deployment. Which cloud model will she choose?
   a. SaaS
   b. XaaS
   c. IaaS
   d. PaaS

8. Which cloud model requires the highest level of IT responsibilities?
   a. IaaS
   b. SaaS
   c. PaaS
   d. Hybrid cloud

9. The CEO is frustrated by the high costs associated with security at the organization and wants to look at a third party assuming part of their cybersecurity defenses. Nikola has been asked to look into acquiring requests for proposal (RFPs) from different third parties. What are these third-party organizations called?
   a. MSSPs
   b. MPSs
   c. MSecs
   d. MHerrs

10. Which of the following is NOT a cloud computing security issue?
    a. System vulnerabilities
    b. Insecure APIs
    c. Compliance regulations
    d. Bandwidth utilization

11. Which of the following is NOT correct about high availability across zones?
    a. In a cloud computing environment, reliability and resiliency are achieved through duplicating processes across one or more geographical areas.

b. An Availability Zone (AZ) is one or more data centers within a Region, each with redundant power, networking, and connectivity.

c. They are more highly available, fault tolerant, and scalable than would be possible with a single data center.

d. They require that specific security appliances be located on-prem so that the local data center can be considered as a qualified Zone.

12. Which of these is NOT created and managed by a microservices API?
   a. User experience (UX)
   b. Database
   c. Logs
   d. Authentication

13. Which of the following is true about secrets management?
   a. It provides a central repository.
   b. It can only be used on-prem for security but has a connection to the cloud.
   c. It requires AES-512.
   d. It cannot be audited for security purposes.

14. Nadia has been asked to perform dynamic resource allocation on specific cloud computing resources. What action is Nadia taking?
   a. Creating security groups to segment computing resources into logical groupings that form network perimeters
   b. Decreasing the network bandwidth to the cloud
   c. Deprovisioning resources that are no longer necessary
   d. Expanding the visibility of intrusion prevention devices

15. Which of the following is NOT a feature of a next generation SWG?
   a. DLP
   b. Send alerts to virtual firewalls

c. Analyze traffic encrypted by SSL
d. Can be placed on endpoints, at the edge, or in the cloud

16. Which type of hypervisor runs directly on the computer's hardware?
   a. Type I
   b. Type II
   c. Type III
   d. Type IV

17. Which of the following is NOT correct about containers?
   a. Containers start more quickly.
   b. Containers reduce the necessary hard drive storage space to function.
   c. Containers require a full OS whenever APIs cannot be used.
   d. Containers include components like binary files and libraries.

18. Which of the following virtualizes parts of a physical network?
   a. SDN
   b. SDV
   c. SDX
   d. SDA

19. Which of the following will NOT protect containers?
   a. Using a hardened OS
   b. Using reduced-visibility images to limit the risk of a compromise
   c. Only using containers in a protected cloud environment
   d. Eliminating APIs

20. Which of the following provides the highest level of security?
   a. FTP
   b. XFTP
   c. FTPS
   d. SFTP

Hands-On Projects

 **CAUTION**   If you are concerned about installing any of the software in these projects on your regular computer, you can instead use the Windows Sandbox or install the software in the Windows virtual machine created in the Module 1 Hands-On Projects. Software installed within the virtual machine will not impact the host computer.

Project 10-1: Viewing SNMP Management Information Base (MIB) Elements

Time Required: 20 minutes
Objective: Given a scenario, implement secure protocols.
Description: SNMP information is stored in a management information base (MIB), which is a database for different objects. In this project, you view MIBs.

1. Use your web browser to go to **www.mibdepot.com**. (The location of content on the Internet may change without warning. If you are no longer able to access the program through this URL, use a search engine to search for "MIB Depot.")
2. In the left pane, click **Single MIB View**.
3. Scroll down and click **Linksys** in the right pane. This will display the Linksys MIBs summary information.
4. In the left pane, click **v1 & 2 MIBs** to select the SNMP Version 1 and Version 2 MIBs.
5. In the right pane, click **LINKSYS-MIB** under **MIB Name (File Name)**. This will display a list of the Linksys MIBs.
6. Click **Tree** under **Viewing Mode** in the left pane. The MIBs are now categorized by Object Identifier (OID). Each object in a MIB file has an OID associated with it, which is a series of numbers separated by dots that represent where on the MIB "tree" the object is located.
7. Click **Text** in the left pane to display textual information about the Linksys MIBs. Scroll through the Linksys MIBs and read several of the descriptions. How could this information be useful in troubleshooting?
8. Now look at the Cisco MIBs. Click **Vendors** in the left pane to return to a vendor list.
9. Scroll down and click **Cisco Systems** in the right pane. How many total Cisco MIB objects are listed? Why is there a difference?
10. In the right pane, click the link **Traps**.
11. Scroll down to **Trap 74**, which begins the list of Cisco wireless traps. Notice the descriptive names assigned to the wireless traps.
12. Close all windows.

Project 10-2: Using a Secure Email Feature

Time Required: 25 minutes

Objective: Given a scenario, implement secure protocols.

Description: Basic email lacks many privacy features. However, settings are available that allow users to encrypt and control emails. In this project, you will configure Google Gmail to send and open confidential emails.

1. Launch your Gmail email account.
2. Click **Compose** to open the **New Message** screen to create a new email message.
3. In the **To** field enter the address of someone who also has a Gmail account.
4. In the row of icons at the bottom of the **New Message** screen, click the icon that represents **Turn confidential mode on/off** (you can hover your mouse over the icons to display their functions).
5. The **Confidential mode** dialog box will open. Click **Learn more** and read about sending and opening confidential emails.
6. Return to the **Confidential mode** dialog box.
7. Under **Set Expiration**, click the down arrow and change the expiration to **Expires in 1 day**.
8. Under **Require Passcode**, click **SMS passcode**.
9. Click **Save**.
10. Note at the bottom of the **New Message** screen it tells when the email content will expire and that recipients cannot forward, copy, print, or download this email message.
11. Compose a brief message and click **Send**.
12. The **Confirm phone numbers** dialog box appears. This is required for the recipient of the email to receive a passcode through a text message. Enter the phone number of the email recipient and click **Send**.
13. The recipient of the email message will receive a text message with a passcode, which is used to open the email message that you sent.
14. The options to copy, paste, download, print, and forward the email message text will be disabled. The recipient can view the message and attachments until the expiration date or until the sender removes access.
15. How valuable is this feature? Is it easy to use? What are its limitations?
16. Close all windows.

Project 10-3: Creating a Virtual Machine from a Physical Computer

Time Required: 25 minutes

Objective: Summarize virtualization and cloud computing concepts.

Description: The VMware vCenter Converter creates a virtual machine from an existing physical computer. In this project, you download and install vCenter to create a virtual machine.

1. Use your web browser to go to **www.vmware.com**. (The location of content on the Internet may change without warning. If you are no longer able to access the program through this URL, use a search engine to search for "VMware.")
2. Click **Downloads**.
3. Click **Free Products Downloads**.
4. Click **vCenter Converter**.
5. If necessary, click **Create an account**, enter the requested information, and log into VMware.
6. If necessary, accept the terms of use and click **I agree**.
7. Click **Manually Download**.
8. When the download completes, run the installation program to install vCenter by accepting the default settings.
9. Launch vCenter to display the VMware vCenter Converter Standalone menu.
10. Click **Convert machine**.
11. Under **Select source type**, choose **This local machine**. Click **Next**.
12. Next to **Select destination type**, choose **VMware Workstation or other VMware virtual machine**.
13. Under **Select a location for the virtual machine**, click **Browse**.
14. Navigate to a location to store the new virtual machine. Click **Next** and then click **Next** again.
15. Click **Finish** to create the virtual machine from the physical machine.

NOTE 25

Note that depending upon the computer configuration, it could take up to 60 minutes to create the virtual machine.

16. When the vCenter has finished, note the location of the image, which will be one or more *.vmx and *.vmdk files in the destination folder. It will be used in the next project.
17. Close all windows.

Project 10-4: Loading the Virtual Machine

Time Required: 25 minutes
Objective: Summarize virtualization and cloud computing concepts.
Description: In this project, you download a program to load the virtual machine created in Project 10-3.

1. Use your web browser to go to **my.vmware.com**. (The location of content on the Internet may change without warning. If you are no longer able to access the program through this URL, use a search engine to search for "VMware Workstation.")
2. Click **Downloads**.
3. Click **Free Products Downloads**.
4. Click **Workstation Player**.
5. Select the Workstation Player for your computer's operating system. Click **Download**.
6. When the download completes, launch the installation program to install VMware Workstation Player.
7. Start VMware Workstation Player after the installation completes.
8. Click **Open a Virtual Machine**.
9. Navigate to the location of the virtual machine that you created in Project 10-3. Click **Open**.
10. Click **Edit virtual machine settings**. Note the different options for configuring the hardware of the virtual machine. Click through these options and, if desired, change any of the settings. Click **Close**.

NOTE 26

Note that to run this virtual machine, a previously unlicensed version of the operating system must first be installed.

11. How easy was it to create a virtual machine from a physical machine?
12. Close all windows.

Case Projects

Case Project 10-1: Trustworthy Email Protocols and Standards

In addition to S/MIME, there are several protocols and standards that protect email. These include STARTTLS, DNS-Based Authentication of Named Entities (DANE), Sender Policy Framework (SPF), DomainKeys Identified Mail (DKIM), and Domain-based Message Authentication, Reporting, and Conformance (DMARC). Use the Internet to research each of these. Create a summary of each along with the respective strengths and weaknesses. Which would you recommend? Why?

Case Project 10-2: Secrets Management Systems

Cloud computing providers typically offer their own proprietary secrets management systems, and there are several third-party systems available. Identify two proprietary secrets management systems from cloud providers and two third-party systems. Research each and then create a document outlining how they are used, their strengths, and their weaknesses.

Case Project 10-3: Comparing MSSPs

Identify three MSSPs and research the services that they provide. Create a document that outlines the services provided by each MSSP. Would you support contracting with an MSSP for part of an organization's security functions? Would you support using an MSSP for all security functions? Write a one-page paper arguing both the pros and cons of using MSSPs.

Case Project 10-4: Create a Cloud Conceptual Model

Use the Internet to research different cloud conceptual models and identify at least three. Then create your own model. Draw the different layers and label each along with how each layer would function.

Case Project 10-5: IPv6

Use the Internet to research the security enhancements of IPv6. Write a one-page paper on how IPv6 is more secure than IPv4.

Case Project 10-6: Community Site Activity

The Information Security Community Site is an online companion to this textbook. It contains a wide variety of tools, information, discussion boards, and other features to assist learners. Go to **community.cengage.com/infosec2** and click the *Join or Sign in* icon to log in, using your login name and password that you created in Module 1. Click **Forums (Discussion)** and click on **Security+ Case Projects (7ᵗʰ edition)**. Read the following case study.

Suppose you were working as part of a cybersecurity defense team at an organization and you were told that the company is considering hiring a managed security service provider (MSSP) to handle the cybersecurity functions. What arguments would you give to support this proposal? What reasons would you give for not supporting this proposal? Visit the Community Site discussion board and post how you would feel about MSSPs.

Case Project 10-7: North Ridge Security

North Ridge Security provides security consulting and assurance services. You have recently been hired as an intern to assist them.

The new CEO of Premier Landscape Services (PLS) wants to migrate all IT functions to the cloud. He argues that PLS could then downsize the IT staff as well as eliminate the need to purchase hardware and software on a regular cycle. The CEO also wants to outsource all security functions to MSSPs. The current CIO supports a migration to the cloud but only for selected services, and is opposed to using MSSPs for security. North Ridge has been brought in to help PLS.

1. Create a PowerPoint presentation for the executive staff about cloud computing. Include types of clouds, locations, architectures, models, and management. Your presentation should contain at least 10 slides.
2. The CEO of PLS was impressed with your knowledge of cloud computing and has asked for your opinion of moving all IT resources to the cloud and contracting with MSSPs for security. Create a memo that outlines the advantages and disadvantages of each side of the argument, and then give your recommendation.

References

1. Mell, Peter, and Grance, Tim, "The NIST definition of cloud computing," NIST Computer Security Division Computer Security Resource Center. Oct. 7, 2009, accessed Apr. 2, 2011, http://csrc.nist.gov/groups/SNS/cloud-computing/.
2. Donovan, Fred, "Shadow IT plagues organizations, undermining cloud security", *HIT Infrastructure*, Feb. 21, 2019, accessed Jul. 3, 2020, https://hitinfrastructure.com/news/shadow-it-plagues-organizations-undermining-cloud-security.
3. "Email & spam data," *Cisco Talos,* accessed Jul. 7, 2020, https://talosintelligence.com/reputation_center/email_rep.

WIRELESS NETWORK SECURITY

After completing this module, you should be able to do the following:

1. Describe the different types of wireless network attacks
2. List the vulnerabilities of WLAN security
3. Explain the solutions for securing a wireless network

Front-Page Cybersecurity

Attacks on wireless systems are certainly not uncommon. But it may be surprising to learn that the first recorded attack on a wireless system occurred more than 100 years ago and involved the person credited as the inventor of the radio.

Guglielmo Marconi was an Italian electrical engineer and inventor who pioneered work on long-distance radio transmission. In 1895, Marconi could transmit and receive a signal for only less than one mile (1.6 kilometers or km), but through persistence and applying new techniques, he was able to increase that distance the following year to 3.7 miles (6 km). Over the next several years, the distances gradually became longer, so that by 1900, Marconi was experimenting with transmissions across the Atlantic Ocean, which he achieved the following year. However, skeptics challenged this experiment because it was not independently verified. One of Marconi's skeptics was Nevil Maskelyne, who likewise was an inventor interested in wireless systems. Maskelyne was the manager of a rival wireless company that had been involved in several disputes with Marconi over patents for wireless telegraphy systems.

In 1903, Marconi decided to put on a public demonstration of his wireless system. He wanted to show that it could indeed transmit over long distances. But he also wanted to demonstrate that his wireless system was secure. Marconi had often claimed that other signals would not interfere with his wireless transmissions. Maskelyne, on the other hand, was not convinced that Marconi's signal was secure. So Maskelyne decided to "hack" Marconi's public demonstration.

The demonstration was on June 4, 1903, at the lecture theater of the Royal Institution in London. Marconi was in Cornwall, more than 300 miles (482 km) away. The plan was for Marconi's colleague Professor Fleming to be in the theater to receive Marconi's Morse code message sent wirelessly and to be printed on an attached printer. But Maskelyne had his own ideas. He set up a wireless transmitter not far from the lecture theater. He later claimed that he did not run it at full power because he did not want to block Marconi's signal; instead, he wanted to send his own signal to show that Marconi's signal was not secure.

Toward the end of Fleming's lecture, signals started coming in—but they were not from Marconi. First a brass slide projector arc lamp in the theater, used to display Fleming's presentation, made a rhythmic ticking noise. The audience assumed that the projector was malfunctioning. But Arthur Blok, Fleming's assistant, quickly recognized it as the "tap-tap" of a human hand keying a message in Morse code. Blok realized that someone was sending powerful wireless pulses into the theater, strong enough to interfere with the electric arc lamp. The wireless receiver came to life, and the Morse code printer started printing—but the message was from Maskelyne instead of from Marconi. One word was repeated over and over on the printer: "Rats." Then the printer spelled out an insulting limerick. Marconi's supposedly secure wireless system had been hacked.

Fleming later complained to the *London Times* of "scientific hooliganism." Fleming and Maskelyne exchanged letters, many of which were printed in the *Times*, arguing over the source of the interference. (Fleming argued that it was caused by electrical lighting in the theater.) It was also discovered that the receiver Fleming used was not tuned to the specific frequency on which Marconi was transmitting but was a receiver that could pick up signals across the frequency spectrum. Because this fact was not disclosed to the audience, the public felt that Marconi had been deceptive in his demonstration. When Maskelyne later wrote about the incident, he ended his account with a Latin legal phrase translated as, "Let him be deceived who wishes to be deceived."

Maskelyne's attack had little impact on Marconi's work or reputation. After sending the first wireless signal across the Atlantic in 1901, Marconi started a commercial transatlantic wireless service 1907. In 1909, he shared the Nobel Prize in Physics in recognition of his contributions to the development of wireless telegraphy. When Marconi died in 1937, the British Broadcasting Company (BBC) observed two minutes of radio silence in respect.

What Maskelyne's attack did do, however, was to make the scientific community question Marconi's claim that wireless signals were secure and could not be interfered with. Researchers examined how wireless signals could be monitored, jammed, or manipulated. Eventually, the research led to the development of wireless security measures that were first used in World War I and continue today.

Ubiquitous means *being everywhere*. Perhaps that is the best word to describe wireless data networks. They are *everywhere*. When was the last time you were at a coffee shop that did not have Wi-Fi? Or a library? Or a hotel? Or even a sports stadium? Not only do we expect wireless networks everywhere, but we demand it: a coffee shop that does not have Wi-Fi has more than its share of empty seats.

Statistics confirm how widespread wireless data technology has become. Almost 70 percent of the global population, about 5.7 billion users, will have wireless data connectivity by 2023 and will be using 13.1 billion devices (an increase from 8.8 billion devices in 2018). The number of public Wi-Fi hotspots will increase fourfold from 169 million in 2018 to 628 million by 2023, and the speeds at which they transmit will be even faster: Wi-Fi speeds will triple by 2023. Retail establishments will have the highest number of hotspots globally by 2023, while the fastest growth is in healthcare facilities such as hospitals, where Wi-Fi hotspots will triple.[1]

NOTE 1

The impact of those who consume the most wireless data is now inverted: in 2010, the top 1 percent of mobile users accounted for more than half of all mobile data usage; by 2019, the top 1 percent only accounted for 5 percent of wireless data usage.

Just as users are drawn to wireless data networks, so too are attackers. Wi-Fi and other wireless data networks are tempting and often too-easy targets for attackers to compromise, despite the wide range of security protections available to modern devices. However, these protections are often overlooked or misconfigured, or users are not aware of their importance.

This module explores wireless network security. You will first investigate the attacks on wireless devices that are common today. Next, you will explore vulnerabilities in wireless security. Finally, you will examine several secure wireless protections.

WIRELESS ATTACKS

✔ CERTIFICATION

1.4 Given a scenario, analyze potential indicators associated with network attacks.

3.4 Given a scenario, install and configure wireless security settings.

3.5 Given a scenario, implement secure mobile solutions.

Several attacks can be directed against wireless data systems. These are attacks against Bluetooth systems, near field communication devices, radio frequency identification systems, and wireless local area networks.

Bluetooth Attacks

Bluetooth is the name given to a wireless technology that uses short-range radio frequency (RF) transmissions and provides rapid device pairings. Named after the tenth-century Danish King Harald "Bluetooth" Gormsson, who was responsible for unifying Scandinavia, Bluetooth was originally designed in 1994 by the cellular telephone company Ericsson to replace personal computer cables. However, Bluetooth has moved well beyond its original design.

Bluetooth is a *personal area network (PAN)* technology designed for data communication over short distances and enables users to connect wirelessly to a wide range of computing and telecommunications devices. It provides for virtually instantaneous connections with little user intervention between a Bluetooth-enabled device and receiver. Several Bluetooth-enabled products are listed in Table 11-1.

Table 11-1   Bluetooth Products

Category	Bluetooth pairing	Usage
Automobile	Hands-free car system with cell phone	Drivers can speak commands to browse the cell phone's contact list, make and receive hands-free phone calls, or use its navigation system.
Home entertainment	Stereo headphones with portable music player	Users can create a playlist on a portable music player and listen through a set of wireless headphones or speakers.
Photographs	Digital camera with printer	Digital photos can be sent directly to a photo printer or from pictures taken on one cell phone to another phone.
Computer accessories	Computer with keyboard and mouse	Small travel mouse can be linked to a laptop or a full-size mouse and keyboard that can be connected to a desktop computer.
Sports and fitness	Heart rate monitor with wristwatch	Exercisers can track heart rates and blood oxygen levels.
Medical and health	Blood pressure monitors with smartphones	Patient information can be sent to a smartphone, which can then send an emergency phone message if necessary.

NOTE 2

Bluetooth is also finding its way into some unlikely devices. A Victorinox Swiss Army pocketknife model has Bluetooth technology that can be used to remotely control a computer when projecting a PowerPoint presentation. Other unusual devices include Bluetooth-enabled toothbrushes, keychain breathalyzers, stethoscopes, and even trash cans that send reminders to take out the garbage.

The current version, Bluetooth 5.2, was introduced in early 2020. (All Bluetooth devices are backward compatible with previous versions.) There are two implementations of Bluetooth 5.2. Bluetooth *Classic*, also called *Bluetooth Basic Rate/Enhanced Data Rate (BR/EDR)*, is designed for devices needing short-range continuous connectivity (such as streaming music to a Bluetooth headset), while Bluetooth *low energy (LE)* is for devices that require short bursts of data over longer distances (such as inventory control devices at a retail store). The number of *bits per second (bps)* that Bluetooth LE can transmit is between 125 Kbps and 2 Mbps, while Bluetooth Classic supports data rates from 1 Mbps to 3 Mbps. Bluetooth devices are categorized by their *class*; currently, there are three classes of Bluetooth devices. The advertised ranges for Class 1 devices are up to 328 feet (100 meters), Class 2 devices have a maximum range of 98 feet (30 meters), and Class 3 devices can send and receive up to 33 feet (10 meters).

> **① CAUTION**   A number of factors can affect the range of transmission. For Bluetooth, this includes the physical layer of the protocol, the receiver sensitivity, the device's transmit power, antenna gain, and path loss. Advertised ranges are generalizations of the range of transmission.

The primary type of Bluetooth network topology is a *piconet*. When two Bluetooth devices come within range of each other, after an initial pairing confirmation, they automatically connect whenever they meet. One device is the leader, which controls all the wireless traffic. The other device is a follower that takes commands from the leader. Follower devices that are connected to the piconet and are sending transmissions are active followers; devices that are connected but not actively participating are parked followers. Devices can also switch roles so that a follower temporarily becomes a leader but then switches back to a follower role or vice versa. An example of two piconets with multiple followers is illustrated in Figure 11-1.

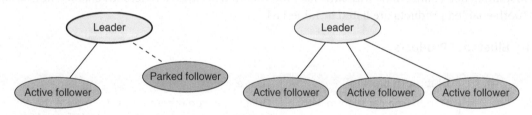

Figure 11-1   Bluetooth piconets

NOTE 3

The Bluetooth specification also allows for a device to be a member in two or more overlaying piconets that cover the same area. This group of piconets in which connections exist between different piconets is called a *scatternet*. However, scatternets are rarely used.

The *network topology* (the arrangement of the nodes of a communication network) of Bluetooth is usually **point-to-point** (one device connected one device—or, in the case of Bluetooth, one follower connected to one leader) or **point-to-multipoint** (one device connected to multiple devices), as seen in Figure 11-1. The point-to-multipoint Bluetooth topology allows, for example, a single Bluetooth-enabled smartphone to control multiple Bluetooth devices (such as a speaker and fitness tracker). Bluetooth LE also supports a *many-to-many* topology, known as a *mesh*. Mesh topologies are often used to extend the range of a Bluetooth network: instead of being limited to the range a follower can communicate with its leader, a follower can send packets to another follower closer to the leader, who can then send it on to yet another follower still closer to the leader, until the packet reaches the leader.

One of the primary features of Bluetooth is its ability for followers to connect to a leader dynamically and automatically "on the fly" as needed whenever Bluetooth devices enter and leave the coverage area. However, this also opens the door for attacks on Bluetooth. Two common Bluetooth attacks are bluejacking and bluesnarfing.

NOTE 4

Bluejacking has been used for advertising purposes by vendors.

Bluejacking

Bluejacking is an attack that sends unsolicited messages to Bluetooth-enabled devices. Usually, bluejacking involves sending text messages, though images and sounds also can be transmitted. Bluejacking is usually considered more annoying than harmful because no data is stolen; however, many Bluetooth users resent receiving unsolicited messages.

Bluesnarfing

Bluesnarfing is an attack that accesses unauthorized information from a wireless device through a Bluetooth connection. In a bluesnarfing attack, the attacker copies emails, calendars, contact lists, cell phone pictures, or videos by connecting to the Bluetooth device without the owner's knowledge or permission.

Near Field Communication (NFC) Attacks

Near field communication (NFC) is a set of standards used to establish communication between devices in very close proximity. Once the devices are brought within four centimeters of each other or tapped together, two-way communication is established. Devices using NFC can be active or passive. A *passive NFC* device, such as an NFC tag, contains information that other devices can read. The tag does not read or receive any information. *Active NFC* devices can read information as well as transmit data.

The NFC communication between a smartphone and an NFC tag functions as follows:

1. The smartphone (*interrogator*) sends a signal to the tag, which becomes powered by the energy in the interrogator's wireless signal.

2. The interrogator and tag each create a high-frequency magnetic field from an internal antenna. Once the fields are created, a connection can be formed between the devices (known as *magnetic induction*). This is illustrated in Figure 11-2. (In this figure, the antennas are shown outside of the interrogator and tag for clarity.)

3. The interrogator sends a message to the tag to find out what type of communication the tag uses. When the tag responds, the interrogator sends its first commands based on that type.

4. When the tag receives the instruction, it checks to determine if the instruction is valid. If it is not, the tag ignores the communication. If it is a valid request, the tag responds with the requested information. For sensitive transactions, such as credit card payments, a secure communication channel is established and all transmitted information is encrypted.

Examples of NFC use include the following:

- *Entertainment.* NFC devices can be used as a ticket to a stadium or concert, for purchasing food and beverages, and downloading upcoming events by tapping a smart poster.
- *Office.* An NFC-enabled device can be used to enter an office, clock in and out on a factory floor, or purchase snacks from a vending machine.
- *Retail stores.* Coupons or customer reward cards can be provided by tapping the point-of-sale (PoS) terminal.
- *Transportation.* On a bus or train, NFC can be used to quickly pass through turnstiles and receive updated schedules by tapping the device on a kiosk.

Consumer NFC devices are most often used as an alternative to cash or a credit card as a **payment method** and are called *contactless payment systems*. Users store payment card numbers in a "virtual wallet" on a watch or smartphone to pay for purchases at an NFC-enabled PoS checkout device. Figure 11-3 shows one such contactless payment system.

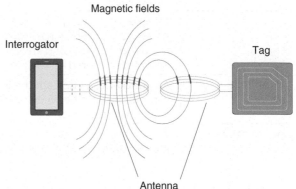

Figure 11-2 NFC magnetic induction

NOTE 5

Bluejacking and bluesnarfing can be mitigated by turning off Bluetooth when not needed, making the device non-discoverable, or rejecting pairing requests from an unknown device.

NOTE 6

The ability of an NFC tag to be powered by the interrogator's signal allows tags to be very small. It also does not require a tag to have its own battery or another power source.

NOTE 7

There are five types of NFC tags, Type 1 through Type 5, which are used in different settings. For example, Type 2 tags are often used for event tickets and transit passes, while Type 5 is used to tag library books.

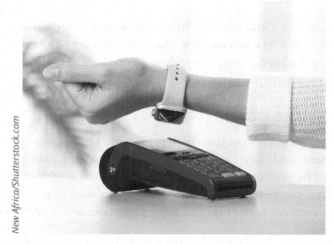

New Africa/Shutterstock.com

Figure 11-3   Contactless payment system

The use of NFC has risks because of the nature of this technology. The risks and defenses of using NFC are listed in Table 11-2.

Table 11-2   NFC Risks and Defenses

Vulnerability	Explanation	Defense
Eavesdropping	Unencrypted NFC communication between the device and terminal can be intercepted and viewed.	Because an attacker must be extremely close to pick up the signal, users should remain aware of their surroundings while making a payment.
Data theft	Attackers can "bump" a portable reader to a user's smartphone in a crowd to make an NFC connection and steal payment information stored on the phone.	This can be prevented by turning off NFC while in a large crowd.
Man-in-the-middle attack	An attacker can intercept the NFC communications between devices and forge a fictitious response.	Devices can be configured in pairing so one device can only send while the other can only receive.
Device theft	The theft of a smartphone could allow an attacker to use that phone for purchases.	Smartphones should be protected with passwords or strong PINs.

NOTE 8

COVID-19 generated a spike in the use of contactless payment systems. About 31 million Americans used these systems in March 2020, when the pandemic began, which was an increase of 150 percent over March 2019.[2]

Radio Frequency Identification (RFID) Attacks

Another wireless technology similar to NFC is radio frequency identification (RFID). RFID is commonly used to transmit information between employee identification badges, inventory tags, book labels, and other paper-based tags that can be detected by a proximity reader. For example, an RFID tag can easily be affixed to the inside of an ID badge and can be read by an RFID reader as the user walks through the turnstile with the badge in a pocket.

Most RFID tags are passive and do not have their own power supply; instead, the electrical current induced in the antenna by the incoming signal from the transceiver provides enough power for the tag to send a response. Because it does not require a power supply, passive RFID tags can be very small, only 0.4 mm × 0.4 mm and thinner than a sheet of paper, as illustrated in Figure 11-4. The amount of data transmitted typically is limited to an ID number. Passive tags have ranges from about one-third inch to 19 feet (10 millimeters to 6 meters). Active RFID tags must have their own power source.

Figure 11-4   RFID tag

RFID tags are susceptible to attack. Table 11-3 lists several attacks that could occur in a retail store that uses RFID inventory tags.

Table 11-3   RFID Attacks in Retail Store

RFID attack type	Description of attack	Implications of RFID attack
Unauthorized tag access	A rogue RFID reader can determine the inventory on a store shelf to track the sales of specific items.	Sales information could be used by a rival product manufacturer to negotiate additional shelf space or better product placement.
Fake tags	Authentic RFID tags are replaced with fake tags that contain fictitious data about products that are not in inventory.	Fake tags undermine the integrity of the store's inventory system by showing data for items that do not exist.
Eavesdropping	Unauthorized users could listen in on communications between RFID tags and readers.	Confidential data, such as a politician's purchase of antidepressants, could be sold to a rival candidate in a "smear" campaign.

Wireless Local Area Network Attacks

A *wireless local area network (WLAN)*, commonly called Wi-Fi, is designed to replace or supplement a wired local area network (LAN). Devices such as tablets, laptop computers, and smartphones that are within range of a centrally located connection device can send and receive information at varying transmission speeds.

The following sections provide a brief history and the specifications of WLAN versions, identify the hardware necessary for a wireless network, and describe the types of WLAN attacks directed at both the enterprise and consumers.

NOTE 9

One of the most well-known IEEE standards is 802.3, which set specifications for Ethernet local area network technology.

WLAN Versions

For computer networking and wireless communications, the most widely known and influential organization is the *Institute of Electrical and Electronics Engineers (IEEE)*, which dates to 1884. In the early 1980s, the IEEE began work on developing computer network architecture standards. This work was called Project 802 and quickly expanded into several categories of network technology.

In 1990, the IEEE started work to develop a standard for WLANs operating at 1 and 2 Mbps. Several proposals were recommended before a draft was developed. This draft, which went through seven revisions, took seven years to complete. In 1997, the IEEE approved the final draft known as *IEEE 802.11*.

Although bandwidth of 2 Mbps was acceptable in 1990 for wireless networks, by 1997, it was no longer sufficient for network applications. The IEEE body revisited the 802.11 standard shortly after it was released to determine what changes could be made to increase the speed. In 1999, a new *IEEE 802.11b* amendment was created, which added two higher speeds (5.5 Mbps and 11 Mbps) to the original 802.11 standard. At the same time, the IEEE also issued another standard with even higher speeds, the *IEEE 802.11a* standard with a speed of 54 Mbps.

The success of the IEEE 802.11b standard prompted the IEEE to reexamine the 802.11b and 802.11a standards to determine if a third intermediate standard could be developed. This "best of both worlds" approach would preserve the stable and widely accepted features of 802.11b but increase the data transfer rates to those similar to 802.11a. The *IEEE 802.11g* standard was formally ratified in 2003 and can support devices transmitting at 54 Mbps.

NOTE 10

Opening the 1–6 GHz spectrum was ratified by the Federal Communications Commission (FCC) for Wi-Fi usage in April 2020. That same month, the Telecom Advisory Service published a report, cited by the FCC, claiming that by allowing usage of this spectrum, the total economic value would be $183 billion between 2020 and 2025, of which $23 billion would be as a result of faster Wi-Fi download speeds.[3]

In 2004, the IEEE began work on a new WLAN standard that would significantly increase the speed, range, and reliability of wireless local area networks. This standard, known as *IEEE 802.11n*, was ratified in 2009. The 802.11n standard has four significant improvements over previous standards: speed (600 Mbps), coverage area (doubles the indoor range and triples the outdoor range of coverage), increased resistance to interference, and stronger security.

Work on an updated standard to support the demand for wireless video delivery, called *IEEE 802.11ac*, was started in 2011. Building on many of the enhancements introduced in 802.11n, this standard, ratified in early 2014, has data rates greater than 7 Gbps. Another update known as *IEEE 802.11ax* is designed to operate in the unlicensed spectrum between 1 and 6 GHz.

To reduce confusion, in 2018, the Wi-Fi Alliance adopted "consumer-friendly" version numbers instead of using "IEEE 802.11" followed by one or two letters. Table 11-4 compares several WLAN standards.

Table 11-4 WLAN Standards

IEEE name	Wi-Fi Alliance version	Ratification date	Frequency used	Maximum data rate
802.11	None	1997	2.4 GHz	2 Mbps
802.11b	Wi-Fi 1	1999	2.4 GHz	11 Mbps
802.11a	Wi-Fi 2	1999	5 GHz	54 Mbps
802.11g	Wi-Fi 3	2003	2.4 GHz	54 Mbps
802.11n	Wi-Fi 4	2009	2.4 GHz & 5 GHz	600 Mbps
802.11ac	Wi-Fi 5	2014	5 GHz	7.2 Gbps
802.11ax	Wi-Fi 6	2019	2.4 GHz & 5 GHz & 1–6 GHz	9.6 Gbps

NOTE 11

Other WLAN standards that are not as widely used include IEEE 802.11ah (HaLow) designed for low-data-rate long-range sensors and controllers, IEEE 802.11af, which uses portions of unused television spectrums instead of 2.4 GHz or 5 GHz bands for transmission, and IEEE 802.11ad, created for very short range but very high speeds.

WLAN Hardware

For all of its functionality, the number of hardware elements needed to operate a WLAN is surprisingly small. Endpoints must have a *wireless client network interface card* or *wireless adapter* that performs the same functions as a wired adapter with one major exception: it has no external cable RJ-45 connection. In its place is an antenna (embedded into the adapter or the device) to send and receive signals through the airwaves.

The second hardware device needed is a wireless *access point (AP)*, which is a centrally located WLAN connection device that can send and receive information. It primarily consists of an antenna and a radio transmitter/receiver to send and receive wireless signals, special bridging software to interface wireless devices to other devices, and a wired network interface that allows it to connect by cable to a standard wired network.

An AP has two basic functions. First, it acts as the "base station" for the wireless network. All wireless devices with a wireless NIC transmit to the AP, which in turn redirects the signal—if necessary—to other wireless devices. The second function of an AP is to act as a bridge between the wireless and wired networks. The AP can be connected to the wired network by a cable, allowing all the wireless devices to access the wired network through the AP (and vice versa), as shown in Figure 11-5.

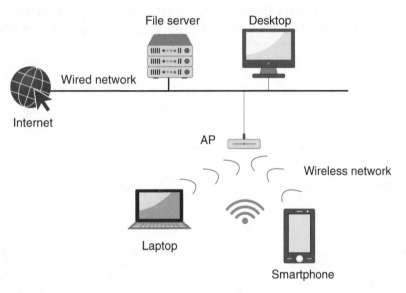

Figure 11-5   Access point (AP) in WLAN

A WLAN using an AP is operating in *infrastructure mode*. The IEEE specifications also define networks that are not using an AP. This mode is called an *Independent Basic Service Set (IBSS)* or, more commonly, **ad hoc mode**. In ad hoc mode, devices can only communicate between themselves and cannot connect to another network. The Wi-Fi Alliance has also created a similar technical specification called **Wi-Fi Direct**.

Instead of using an enterprise-grade AP, a small office or home commonly uses another device that combines multiple features into a single hardware unit. These features often include those of an AP, firewall, router, and dynamic host configuration protocol (DHCP) server, along with other features. Strictly speaking these devices are *residential WLAN gateways* as they are the entry point from the Internet into the wireless network. However, most vendors instead choose to label their products as simply *wireless routers*.

There are different types of enterprise APs. These include fat vs. thin APs, controller vs. standalone, and captive portal APs.

Fat vs. Thin APs   Standard APs are *autonomous*, or independent, because they are separate from other network devices and even other autonomous APs. Autonomous

NOTE 12

Ad hoc mode is useful for quickly and easily setting up a wireless network anywhere that users need to share data between themselves but do not need a connection to the Internet or an external network. An example might be when a wireless user needs to quickly send a last-minute document to an associate across the table in a meeting room. However, this mode is rarely used.

APs have the intelligence required to manage wireless authentication, encryption, and other functions for the wireless client devices that they serve. Because everything is self-contained in these single devices, they are sometimes called *fat APs*.

Although fat APs are functional for a small office setting with a handful of APs, what happens in a large enterprise or college campus with hundreds or even thousands of APs? In this case, fat APs are not a viable option. Because each AP is autonomous, a single wireless network configuration change would require reconfiguring each AP individually, which could take an extended period and manpower to complete.

When multiple APs are widely deployed, a *thin AP* can be a better solution. These "lightweight" APs do not contain all the management and configuration functions found in fat APs. Much of the configuration is centralized in the wireless switch so that the network administrator can work directly with the switch from the wired network. This can also improve security because managing from a central location instead of visiting and configuring each fat AP reduces the risk of a security setting being overlooked.

Standalone vs. Controller APs   Although thin APs can be managed from a switch, a further improvement can be made by managing from a device dedicated to configuring APs. Instead of installing *standalone APs* like fat or thin APs, controller APs can be managed through a dedicated *wireless LAN controller (WLC)*. The WLC is a single device that can be configured and then used to distribute the settings automatically to all controller APs. (A remote office WLAN controller is used to manage multiple WLCs at remote sites from a central location.) Controller APs with a WLC are shown in Figure 11-6.

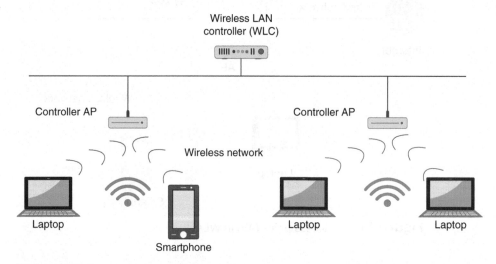

Figure 11-6   Controller APs with WLC

NOTE 13

Controller APs handle only the real-time medium access control (MAC) layer functionality within themselves; all other (non-real-time) MAC functionality is processed by the WLC. This type of division is referred to as a *split MAC architecture*.

Besides centralized management, controller APs provide other advantages over standalone APs. As wireless client devices move through a WLAN, a lengthy handoff procedure occurs during which one standalone AP transfers authentication information to another. Slow handoffs can be unacceptable on WLAN systems using time-dependent communication, such as voice or video. With controller APs, however, this handoff procedure is eliminated because all authentications are performed in the WLC. Another advantage of WLCs is the tools that many provide for monitoring the environment and providing information regarding the best locations for APs, wireless configuration settings, and power settings.

CAUTION   There are disadvantages to controller APs. WLCs still do not provide true convergence (integration) of the wired and wireless networks but only ease some of the management burdens of WLANs. In addition, these devices are proprietary, which means all the thin APs and WLCs on a network must be from the same vendor to function cohesively.

Captive Portal APs   In a public area that is served by a WLAN, opening a web browser rarely gives immediate Internet access because the owner of the WLAN usually wants to advertise itself as providing this service, or wants the user to read and accept an acceptable use policy (AUP) before using the WLAN. Sometimes a general authentication, such as a password given to all current hotel guests, must be entered before users gain access to the network. This type of information, approval, or authentication can be supported through a *captive portal AP*. A captive portal AP uses a standard web browser to present information and gives the wireless user the opportunity to agree to a policy or enter valid login credentials, providing a higher degree of security.

CAUTION   When accessing a public WLAN, users should consider using a virtual private network (VPN) to encrypt all transmissions.

WLAN Enterprise Attacks

In a traditional wired network, a well-defined boundary or "hard edge" protects data and resources. There are two types of hard edges. The first is a network hard edge. A wired network typically has one point (or a limited number of points) through which data must pass from an external network to the secure internal network. This single data entry point makes it easier to defend the network because any attack must pass through the single point. Security appliances can be used to block attacks from entering the network. The combination of a single-entry point plus security appliances that can defend it make up a network's hard edge, which protects important data and resources. This is illustrated in Figure 11-7.

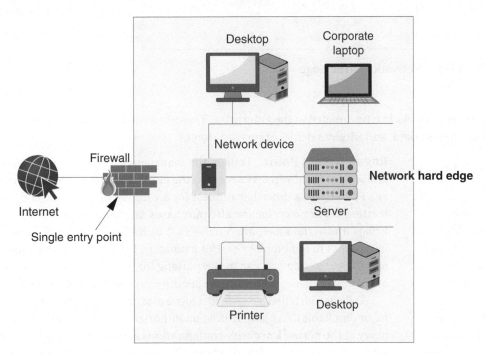

Figure 11-7   Network hard edge

The second hard edge is made up of the walls of the building that houses the enterprise. Because the walls keep out unauthorized personnel, attackers cannot access the network. In other words, the walls serve to physically separate computing resources from attackers.

The introduction of WLANs in enterprises, however, has changed hard edges to "blurred edges." Instead of a network hard edge with a single data entry point, a WLAN can contain multiple entry points. As shown in Figure 11-8, the RF signals from APs create several data entry points into the network through which attackers can inject attacks or steal data. Multiple entry points make it difficult to create a hard network edge. In addition, because RF signals extend beyond the boundaries of the building, the walls cannot be considered as a physical hard edge to keep away attackers. A threat actor in a car well outside of the building's security perimeter can still easily pick up a wireless RF signal to eavesdrop on data transmissions or inject malware behind the firewall. An AP whose security settings have not been set or have been improperly configured can allow attackers access to the network.

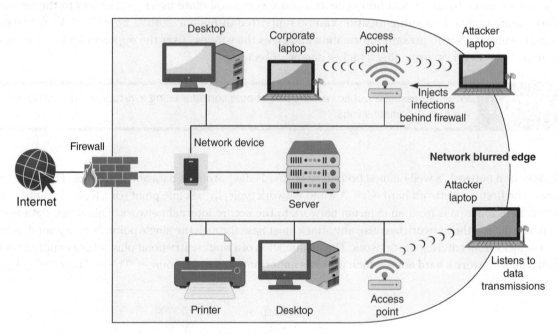

Figure 11-8 Network blurred edge

Several types of wireless attacks can be directed at the enterprise. These include rogue access points (rogue APs), evil twins, intercepting wireless data, and wireless denial of service attacks.

NOTE 14

Rogue APs do not even have to be separate network devices. The wireless Hosted Network function in Microsoft Windows makes it possible to virtualize the physical wireless network interface card (NIC) into multiple virtual wireless NICs (Virtual Wi-Fi) that can be accessed by a software-based wireless AP (SoftAP). This means any computer can easily be turned into a rogue AP. Some smartphone apps also allow these devices to function as APs.

Rogue Access Point Lejla is the manager of a recently opened retail storefront and wants to add wireless access in the employee break room. However, her employer's IT staff turns down her request for a wireless network. Lejla decides to take the matter into her own hands: she purchases an inexpensive wireless router, secretly brings it into the store, and connects it to the wired network, thus providing wireless access to her employees. Unfortunately, Lejla also has provided open access to an attacker sitting in a car in the parking lot who picks up the wireless signal. The attacker can then circumvent the security protections of the company's network.

Lejla has installed a rogue AP (rogue means someone or something that is deceitful or unreliable). A rogue AP is an unauthorized AP that allows an attacker to bypass many of the network security configurations and opens the network and its users to attacks. For example, although firewalls are typically used to restrict specific attacks from entering a network, an attacker who can access the network through a rogue AP is behind the firewall.

Evil Twin While a rogue AP is set up by an internal user, an evil twin is an AP that is set up by an attacker. This AP is designed to mimic an authorized AP, so a user's mobile device such as a laptop or tablet unknowingly connects to the evil twin instead. Attackers can then capture the transmissions from users to the evil twin AP.

Figure 11-9 illustrates rogue AP and evil twin attacks on an enterprise network, which further create a "blurred edge" to a corporate network.

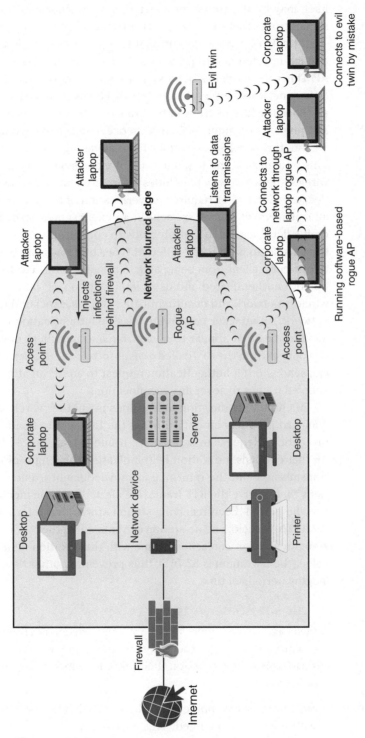

Figure 11-9   Rogue access point and evil twin attacks

Intercepting Wireless Data   One of the most common wireless attacks is intercepting and reading transmitted data. An attacker can pick up the RF signal from an open or misconfigured AP and read confidential wireless transmissions. To make matters worse, if attackers manage to connect to the enterprise wired network through a rogue AP, they also could read broadcast and multicast wired network traffic that leaks from the wired network to the wireless network. Using a WLAN to read this data could yield significant information to an attacker regarding the wired enterprise network.

NOTE 15

Several types of devices transmit a radio signal that can cause incidental interference with a WLAN. These devices include microwave ovens, elevator motors, photocopying machines, and certain types of outdoor lighting systems, to name a few. These may cause errors or completely prevent transmission between a wireless device and an AP.

NOTE 16

Jamming attacks generally are rare because sophisticated and expensive equipment is necessary to flood the RF spectrum with enough interference to impact the network. In addition, because a very powerful transmitter must be used at a relatively close range to execute the attack, it is possible to identify the location of the transmitter and therefore identify the source of the attack.

NOTE 17

The amendment IEEE 802.11w was designed to protect against wireless DoS attacks. However, it only protects specific management frames instead of all management frames, requires updates to both the AP and the wireless clients, and might interfere with other security devices. For these reasons, it has not been widely implemented.

Wireless Denial of Service Attacks   Because wireless devices operate using RF signals, there is the potential for signal interference. Although the wireless device itself may be the source of interference for other devices, attackers can leverage signals from other devices to disrupt valid wireless transmissions.

Attackers can use intentional RF interference to flood the RF spectrum with enough interference to prevent a device from effectively communicating with the AP. This wireless denial of service (DoS) attack prevents the transmission of data to or from network devices. In one type of wireless DoS attack, an attacker can intentionally flood the RF spectrum with extraneous RF signal "noise" that creates interference and prevents communications from occurring. This is called jamming.

Another wireless DoS attack takes advantage of an IEEE 802.11 design weakness. This weakness is the implicit trust of management frames transmitted across the wireless network, which includes information such as the sender's source address. Because IEEE 802.11 requires no verification of the source device's identity (and so all management frames are sent in an unencrypted format), an attacker can easily craft a fictitious frame that pretends to come from a trusted client when it is in fact from a malicious attacker. Different types of frames can be "spoofed" by an attacker to prevent a client from being able to remain connected to the WLAN. A client must be both authenticated and associated with an AP before being accepted into the wireless network and deauthenticated and disassociated when the client leaves the network. An attacker can create false deauthentication or disassociation management frames that appear to come from another client device, causing the client to disconnect from the AP (called a disassociation attack). Although the client device can send another authentication request to an AP, an attacker can continue to send spoofed frames to sever any reconnections.

Manipulating duration field values is another wireless DoS attack. The 802.11 standard provides an option using the Request to Send/Clear to Send (RTS/CTS) protocol. A Request to Send (RTS) frame is transmitted by a mobile device to an AP that contains a duration field indicating the length of time needed for both the transmission and the returning acknowledgment frame. The AP, as well as all stations that receive the RTS frame, are alerted that the medium will be reserved for a specific period. Each receiving station stores that information in its net allocation vector (NAV) field, and no station can transmit if the NAV contains a value other than zero. An attacker can send a frame with the duration field set to an arbitrarily high value (the maximum is 32,767), thus preventing other devices from transmitting for lengthy periods of time.

WLAN Consumer Attacks

Attacks against consumers' home WLANs are considered easy because many users fail to properly configure security on their home wireless networks. Consumers face several risks from attacks on their insecure wireless networks. Among other things, attackers can

- *Steal data*. On a computer in the home WLAN, an attacker could access any folder with file sharing enabled. This essentially provides an attacker full access to steal sensitive data from the computer.
- *Read wireless transmissions*. Usernames, passwords, credit card numbers, and other information sent over the WLAN could be captured by an attacker.
- *Inject malware*. Because attackers could access the network behind a firewall, they could inject viruses and other malware onto the computer.

- *Download harmful content.* In several instances, attackers have accessed a home computer through an unprotected WLAN, downloaded child pornography to the computer, and then turned that computer into a file server to distribute the content. When authorities have traced the files to that computer, the unsuspecting owner has been arrested and the equipment confiscated.

TWO RIGHTS & A WRONG

1. Bluetooth LE also supports a many-to-many topology, known as a mesh.

2. Most RFID tags are active and require their own power supply.

3. An AP primarily consists of an antenna and a radio transmitter/receiver to send and receive wireless signals, special bridging software to interface wireless devices to other devices, and a wired network interface that allows it to connect by cable to a standard wired network.

See Appendix B for the answer.

VULNERABILITIES OF WLAN SECURITY

 CERTIFICATION

1.4 Given a scenario, analyze potential indicators associated with network attacks.

3.3 Given a scenario, implement secure network designs.

3.4 Given a scenario, install and configure wireless security settings.

The original IEEE 802.11 committee recognized that wireless transmissions could be vulnerable. Because of this, they implemented several wireless security protections in the 802.11 standard while leaving other protections to be applied at the WLAN vendor's discretion. Several of these protections, though well intended, were vulnerable and led to multiple attacks. These vulnerabilities can be divided into those based on Wired Equivalent Privacy (WEP), Wi-Fi Protected Setup (WPS), MAC address filtering, and Wi-Fi Protected Access (WPA).

Wired Equivalent Privacy

Wired Equivalent Privacy (WEP) is an IEEE 802.11 security protocol designed to ensure that only authorized parties can view transmitted wireless information. WEP accomplishes this confidentiality by encrypting the transmissions. WEP relies on a shared secret key that is known only by the wireless client and the AP. The same secret key must be entered on the AP and on all devices before any transmissions can occur because the key is used to encrypt any packets to be transmitted as well as decrypt packets that are received. IEEE 802.11 WEP shared secret keys must be a minimum of 64 bits in length. Most vendors add an option to use a longer 128-bit shared secret key for higher security.

The shared secret key is combined with an initialization vector (IV), which is a 24-bit value that changes each time a packet is encrypted. The IV and the key are combined and used as a seed for generating a random number necessary in the encryption process. The IV and encrypted ciphertext are both transmitted to the receiving device. Upon arrival, the receiving device first separates the IV from the encrypted text and then combines the IV with its own shared secret key to decrypt the data.

WEP has several security vulnerabilities. First, to encrypt packets, WEP can use only a 64-bit or 128-bit number, which is made up of a 24-bit IV and either a 40-bit or 104-bit default key. Even if a longer 128-bit number is used, the length of the IV remains at 24 bits. The relatively short length of the IV limits its strength, since shorter keys are easier to break than longer keys.

Second, WEP implementation violates the cardinal rule of cryptography: anything that creates a detectable pattern must be avoided at all costs. This is because patterns provide an attacker with valuable information to break the encryption. The implementation of WEP creates a detectable pattern for attackers. Because IVs are 24-bit numbers, there are only 16,777,216 possible values. An AP transmitting at 11 Mbps can send and receive 700 packets each second. If a different IV were used for each packet, then the IVs would start repeating in less than seven hours. (A "busy" AP can produce duplicates in fewer than five hours.) An attacker who captures packets for this length of time can see the duplication and use it to crack the code.

Wi-Fi Protected Setup

Wi-Fi Protected Setup (WPS) is an optional means of configuring security on WLANs. It is designed to help users who have little or no knowledge of security to implement security quickly and easily on their WLANs.

There are two common WPS methods. The PIN method uses a personal identification number (PIN) printed on a sticker of the wireless router or displayed through a software setup wizard. The user types the PIN into the wireless device (such as a wireless tablet, laptop computer, or smartphone), and the security configuration automatically occurs. This is the mandatory model, and all devices certified for WPS must support it. The second method is the push-button method: the user pushes a button (usually an actual button on the wireless router and a virtual one displayed through a software setup wizard on the wireless device) and the security configuration takes place. Support for this model is mandatory for wireless routers and optional for connecting devices.

However, WPS using the PIN method has significant design and implementation flaws:

- There is no lockout limit for entering PINs, so an attacker can make an unlimited number of PIN attempts.
- The last PIN character is only a checksum.
- The wireless router reports the validity of the first and second halves of the PIN separately, so essentially an attacker must break only two short PIN values (a four-character PIN and a three-character PIN).

Due to the PIN being divided into two shorter values, only 11,000 different PINs must be attempted before determining the correct value. If the attacker's computer can generate 1.3 PIN attempts per second (or 46 attempts per minute), the attacker can crack the PIN in less than four hours and become connected to the WLAN. This effectively defeats security restrictions that allow only authorized users to connect to the wireless network.

>  **CAUTION**   Some wireless vendors are implementing additional security measures for WPS, such as limiting the number and frequency of PIN guesses. However, unless it can be verified that WPS supports these higher levels of security, it is recommended that WPS be disabled through the wireless router's configuration settings.

MAC Address Filtering

One means of protecting a WLAN is to control which devices are permitted to join the network. Wireless access control is intended to limit a user's admission to the AP: only those who are authorized can connect to the AP and thus become part of the wireless LAN.

The most common type of wireless access control is Media Access Control (MAC) address filtering. The MAC address is a hardware address that uniquely identifies each node of a network. It is a unique 48-bit number "burned" into the network interface card adapter when it is manufactured. The IEEE 802.11 standard permits controlling which devices can connect to the WLAN but does not specify how the control is to be implemented. Since a wireless device can be identified by its MAC address, however, virtually all wireless AP vendors implement MAC address filtering as the means of access control. A wireless client device's MAC address is entered into software running on the AP, which then is used to permit or deny a device from connecting to the network. As shown in Figure 11-10, restrictions can be implemented by either whitelisting (a specific device can be allowed access into the network) or blacklisting (a device can be blocked).

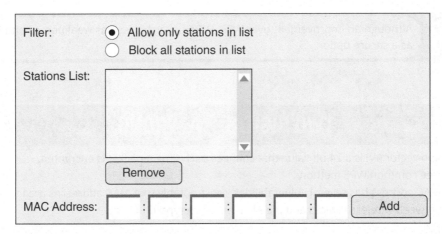

Figure 11-10   MAC address filtering

NOTE 18

MAC address filtering is usually implemented by permitting instead of preventing, because it is not possible to know the MAC addresses of all the devices that are to be excluded.

Filtering by MAC address has several vulnerabilities. First, MAC addresses are initially exchanged between wireless devices and the AP in an unencrypted format. Attackers monitoring the airwaves could easily see the MAC address of an approved device and then substitute it on their own device. Another weakness of MAC address filtering is that managing several MAC addresses can pose significant challenges. The sheer number of users often makes it difficult to manage all the MAC addresses. As new users are added to the network and old users leave, keeping track of MAC address filtering demands almost constant attention. For this reason, MAC address filtering is not always practical in a large and dynamic wireless network.

 **CAUTION** It is not uncommon to read of controlling access to the WLAN by hiding the *Service Set Identifier (SSID)* of the wireless network, which is the user-supplied network name of a wireless network and generally can be any alphanumeric string up to 32 characters. Although normally the SSID is broadcast so that any device can see it, the broadcast can be restricted so that only those users that know the "secret" SSID in advance would be allowed to access the network. However, the SSID can be easily discovered even when it is not contained in beacon frames because it is transmitted in other management frames sent by the AP. Hiding the SSID is not recommended as a security protection.

Wi-Fi Protected Access (WPA)

The Wi-Fi Alliance introduced *Wi-Fi Protected Access (WPA)* to fit into the existing WEP engine without requiring extensive hardware upgrades or replacements. There were two modes of WPA. *WPA Personal* was designed for individuals or small office/home office (SOHO) settings, which typically have up to 10 employees. A more robust *WPA Enterprise* was intended for larger enterprises, schools, and government agencies. WPA addresses both encryption and authentication.

A wireless network in which no authentication is required, such as at a local coffee shop, is using an **open method**. However, most WLANs need to restrict who can access the network through authentication. Authentication for WPA Personal is accomplished by using a **preshared key (PSK)**. In cryptography, a PSK is a value that has been previously shared using a secure communication channel between two parties. In a WLAN, a PSK is slightly different. It is a secret value that is manually entered on both the AP and each wireless device, making it essentially identical to the "shared secret" used in WEP. Because this secret key is not widely known, it can be assumed that only approved devices have the key value. Devices that have the secret key are then automatically authenticated by the AP.

 **CAUTION**   Although an improvement over WEP, WPA nevertheless has weaknesses and is not considered as a secure option.

TWO RIGHTS & A WRONG

1. An initialization vector (IV) is a 24-bit value that changes each time a packet is encrypted.
2. There are three common WPS methods.
3. Filtering by MAC address has several vulnerabilities, most notably that MAC addresses are initially exchanged between wireless devices and the AP in an unencrypted format.

See Appendix B for the answer.

WIRELESS SECURITY SOLUTIONS

 **CERTIFICATION**

3.4 Given a scenario, install and configure wireless security settings.

Despite the vulnerabilities in some early wireless security protections, it is generally recognized that modern wireless security solutions are much more secure. Wi-Fi Protected Access 2 (WPA2) and Wi-Fi Protected Access 3 (WPA3) form the foundation of today's wireless security solutions.

Wi-Fi Protected Access 2 (WPA2)

Due to the shortcomings of WPA, a more robust wireless security standard was introduced by the IEEE known as *IEEE 802.11i*. Shortly thereafter, the Wi-Fi Alliance introduced Wi-Fi Protected Access 2 (WPA2), which is based on the final IEEE 802.11i standard and is almost identical to it. As with WPA, there are two modes of WPA2, *WPA2 Personal* for individuals or small offices and *WPA2 Enterprise* for larger enterprises, schools, and government agencies. WPA2 addresses the two major security areas of WLANs—namely, encryption and authentication.

NOTE 19

CCM itself does not require that a specific block cipher be used, but the most secure cipher AES is mandated by the WPA2 standard. For this reason, CCMP for WLANs is sometimes designated as *AES-CCMP*.

AES-CCMP Encryption

The encryption protocol used for WPA2 is the Counter Mode with Cipher Block Chaining Message Authentication Code Protocol (CCMP) and specifies the use of CCM (a general-purpose cipher mode algorithm providing data privacy) with AES. The Cipher Block Chaining Message Authentication Code (CBC-MAC) component of CCMP provides data integrity and authentication.

IEEE 802.1x Authentication

Authentication for the WPA2 Enterprise model (called the enterprise method) uses the IEEE 802.1x standard. This standard, originally developed for wired networks, provides a greater degree of security by implementing port-based authentication. IEEE 802.1x blocks all traffic on a port-by-port basis until the client is authenticated using credentials stored on an authentication server. This prevents an unauthenticated device from receiving any network traffic until its identity can be verified. It also strictly limits access to the device that provides the authentication to prevent attackers from reaching it. Figure 11-11 illustrates the steps in an 802.1x authentication procedure.

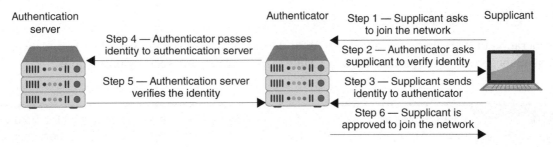

Figure 11-11   IEEE 802.1x process

1. The device (called a *supplicant*) requests permission from the *authenticator* to join the network.
2. The authenticator asks the supplicant to verify its identity.
3. The supplicant sends identity information to the authenticator.
4. The authenticator passes the identity credentials to an *authentication server*, whose only job is to verify the authentication of devices. The identity information is sent in an encrypted form.
5. The authentication server verifies or rejects the supplicant's identity and returns the information to the authenticator.
6. If approved, the supplicant can join the network and transmit data.

The communication between the supplicant, authenticator, and authentication server in an IEEE 802.1x configuration must be secure. A framework for transporting the authentication protocols is known as the **Extensible Authentication Protocol (EAP)**. Despite its name, EAP is a *framework* for transporting authentication protocols instead of the authentication protocol itself. EAP essentially defines the format of the messages and uses four types of packets: *request*, *response*, *success*, and *failure*. Request packets are issued by the authenticator and ask for a response packet from the supplicant. Any number of request-response exchanges may be used to complete the authentication. If the authentication is successful, a success packet is sent to the supplicant; if not, a failure packet is sent.

NOTE 20

Although IEEE 802.1x is commonly used on wireless networks, it can be used for wired networks as well. For example, in a public conference room, an RJ-45 network connection may be accessible to both trusted employees and untrusted public users. IEEE 802.1x permits the trusted employees to access both the secure internal corporate network and the Internet while restricting public users to Internet access only from the same network connection.

NOTE 21

An EAP packet contains a field that indicates the function of the packet (such as response or request) and an identifier field used to match requests and responses. Response and request packets also have a field that indicates the type of data being transported (such as an authentication protocol) along with the data itself.

A common EAP protocol is **Protected EAP (PEAP)**. PEAP is designed to simplify the deployment of 802.1x by using Microsoft Windows logins and passwords. PEAP is considered a more flexible EAP scheme because it creates an encrypted channel between the client and the authentication server, and the channel then protects the subsequent user authentication exchange. To create the channel, the PEAP client first authenticates the PEAP authentication server using enhanced authentication.

Several EAP protocols are supported in WPA2 Enterprise; the most common are listed in Table 11-5.

Table 11-5   Common EAP Protocols Supported by WPA2 Enterprise

EAP name	Description
EAP-TLS	This protocol uses digital certificates for authentication.
EAP-TTLS	This protocol securely tunnels client password authentication within Transport Layer Security (TLS) records.
EAP-FAST	This protocol securely tunnels any credential form for authentication (such as a password or a token) using TLS.

Wi-Fi Protected Access 3 (WPA3)

The next generation of Wi-Fi Protected Access (WPA) is known as **WPA3**. The goal of WPA3 is to deliver a suite of features to simplify security configuration for users while enhancing network security protections.

 **CAUTION** WPA3, as well as WPA2, is not officially a standard nor is it a protocol. WPA3 is a hardware certification program that specifies what existing standards a product must support in order to be labeled as "Wi-Fi CERTIFIED WPA3." This means that the device will be interoperable with other similar devices that have also obtained the WPA3 certified label.

The following four security improvements are part of WPA3:

- WPA3 includes **Simultaneous Authentication of Equals (SAE)**. SAE is designed to increase security at the time of the handshake when keys are being exchanged. The result is that WPA3 can give stronger security even if short or weak passwords are used.
- WPA3 supports a longer 192-bit encryption.
- When using open or public Wi-Fi networks in airports and coffee shops, WPA3 applies individualized data encryption so that every connection between a client and an AP/wireless router is encrypted with a unique key. Known as *Opportunistic Wireless Encryption (OWE)*, it can mitigate against man-in-the-middle (MITM) attacks.
- WPA3 has improved interaction capabilities with Internet of Things (IoT) devices. The older WPA2 was primarily designed to work with traditional mobile devices that had screens (such as smartphones and laptops) in which the user could enter a password and configure the wireless settings. However, most IoT devices have no screens. WPA3 contains new ways to configure security for these types of devices.

TWO RIGHTS & A WRONG

1. There are two modes of WPA2, WPA2 Professional and WPA2 Enterprise.
2. The encryption protocol used for WPA2 is the Counter Mode with Cipher Block Chaining Message Authentication Code Protocol (CCMP) and specifies the use of CCM (a general-purpose cipher mode algorithm providing data privacy) with AES.
3. EAP-TLS uses digital certificates for authentication.

See Appendix B for the answer.

ADDITIONAL WIRELESS SECURITY PROTECTIONS

 **CERTIFICATION**

2.6 Explain the security implications of embedded and specialized systems.

3.4 Given a scenario, install and configure wireless security settings.

Other security steps can be taken to protect a wireless network. These include installation and configuration, specialized systems communications, and rogue AP system detection.

Installation

When installing a wireless LAN in a home or apartment, most users do not give much time to determining the optimum location for the wireless router so that its RF signal coverage is uniform throughout the house but extends outside it as little as possible. Instead, the devices are typically placed wherever it is convenient, such as next to the Internet connection, near a desktop computer, or even tucked away on a bookcase. If the wireless signal does not to reach into the far corners of the house or outside onto an outdoors deck, then those areas are simply recognized as being "dead space" and are avoided when using the network.

However, when installing a WLAN for an organization, areas of dead space cannot be so easily tolerated. Whereas at home a user may simply move to another room for better reception, that may not always be possible in a building with multiple offices, locked doors, and private cubicles. This means important considerations must be taken into account when installing a new WLAN for an organization: all areas of a building should have adequate wireless coverage; all employees must have a reasonable amount of bandwidth; and, for security reasons, a minimum amount of wireless signal should "bleed" outside the walls of the building.

Assuring that a WLAN can provide its intended functionality and meet its required design goals can best be achieved through a **site survey**. A site survey is an in-depth examination and analysis of a WLAN site. A site survey mainly addresses placing the AP in the optimum location, known as **wireless access point placement**.

Several tools can be used in a site survey for installation:

- *Heat maps*. A Wi-Fi **heat map** is a visual representation of the wireless signal coverage and strength. Wi-Fi heat maps are generally overlaid on top of a building or facility floor plan to help clearly indicate where problem areas are located in relation to the collected site survey data. Figure 11-12 illustrates a heat map.

Map

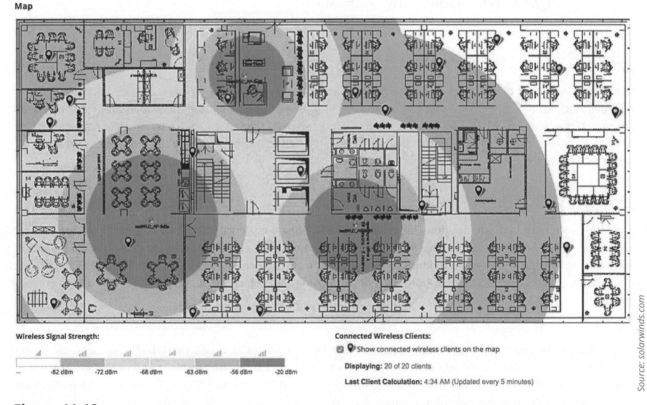

Wireless Signal Strength:

-82 dBm   -72 dBm   -68 dBm   -63 dBm   -56 dBm   -20 dBm

Connected Wireless Clients:
☑ 📍 Show connected wireless clients on the map
Displaying: 20 of 20 clients
Last Client Calculation: 4:34 AM (Updated every 5 minutes)

Source: solarwinds.com

Figure 11-12   Wi-Fi heat map

- *Wi-Fi analyzers*. A **Wi-Fi analyzer** tool helps to visualize the essential details of the wireless network. An analyzer can provide information such as signal strength, network health, channel bandwidth, channel coverage, data rate, and interference (noise).

- *Channel overlays.* It is not uncommon for multiple APs to attempt to use the same frequency (*channel*), causing interference. Software that illustrates these **channel overlays** can help visualize conflicting overlaps. Channel overlay software is seen in Figure 11-13.

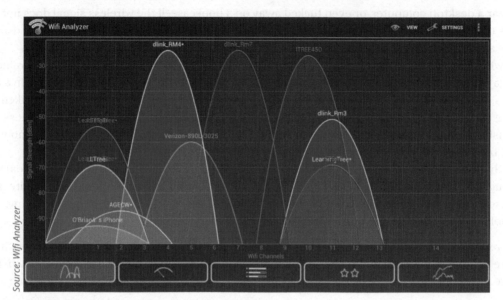

Figure 11-13   Channel overlay software

Source: Wifi Analyzer

NOTE 22

Although the placement of a wireless router in a home or apartment may not have as many options as an office, there are some principles to keep in mind that can improve Wi-Fi service. If possible, place the wireless router in a central location so the wireless signal does not have to penetrate more than two rooms and two interior walls. Also, the higher the wireless router can be placed above the heads of people, the better: one human body can block the signal about as much as one interior wall.

Configuration

Selecting the proper configuration options for the AP can also enhance security. Some of these settings are designed to limit the spread of the wireless RF signal so that a minimum amount of signal extends past the physical boundaries of the enterprise to be accessible to outsiders. AP configuration and device options include setting the signal strength and choosing the correct RF spectrum options. One device option is to select the best type of antenna and to correctly locate it.

Signal Strength Settings

A security feature on some APs is the ability to adjust the level of power at which the WLAN transmits. On devices with that feature, the power can be adjusted so that less of the signal leaves the premises and reaches outsiders. For IEEE WLANs, the maximum transmit power is 200 milliwatts (mW). APs that can adjust the power level usually permit the level to be adjusted in predefined increments—such as 1, 5, 20, 30, 40, 100, or 200 mW.

Spectrum Selection

Some APs provide the ability to adjust frequency spectrum settings. These include the following:

- *Frequency band.* An increasing number of APs support dual bands of spectrum. If one band is not being used, it should be disabled. If both bands are used, it is recommended that both have the same configuration settings.

- *Channel selection.* Some APs have an *Auto* mode in which the AP selects the optimum channel within the frequency band. On those devices in which this mode is not supported, it is important to choose a channel that is different from that of other nearby APs or sources of interference.
- *Channel width.* Channel width controls how much of the spectrum is available to transfer data. However, larger channels are more subject to interference and more likely to interfere with other devices.

Antenna Placement and Type

APs use antennas that radiate a signal in all directions. Because these devices are generally positioned to provide the broadest area of coverage, APs should be located near the middle of the coverage area. Generally, the AP can be secured to the ceiling or high on a wall. It is recommended that APs be mounted as high as possible for two reasons: to minimize obstructions for the RF signal and to prevent thieves from stealing the device. For security purposes, the AP and its antenna should be positioned so that, when possible, a minimal amount of signal reaches beyond the security perimeter of the building or campus. Another option is to use a type of antenna that focuses its signal in a concentrated direction toward authorized users instead of broadcasting it over a wide area.

Specialized Systems Communications

Several wireless technologies relate to communications for specialized and embedded systems. These include the following:

- *Zigbee.* Zigbee is a low-power, short-range, and low-data rate specification. It is based on the IEEE 802.15.4 standard but includes network configuration, security, and other higher-level features that are not covered by IEEE standard. Zigbee's data rate is 250 kbps and is designed for occasional data or signal transmission from a sensor or IoT device.
- *5G.* Unlike Wi-Fi transmitting over a localized geographical area, 5G is the fifth-generation cellular wireless standard. Compared to 4G, 5G supports faster speeds, is more responsive, and can connect to more devices simultaneously.
- *Narrowband IoT.* Narrowband Internet of Things (NB-IoT) is a low-power wide area network (LPWAN) radio technology standard. NB-IoT is a wide-range cellular service that focuses on indoor coverage, low cost, long battery life, and high connection density.
- *Cellular IoT baseband.* One cellular-based network for IoT devices that is optimized for these transmissions uses a baseband radio. (Baseband refers to the original frequency range of a transmission signal before it is converted to a different frequency range.) *Cellular IoT baseband* can transmit using standard 4G transmissions or NB-IoT.
- *Subscriber identity module (SIM) card.* Some IoT devices use a SIM card (subscriber identity module card) for data transmissions. A SIM card is an integrated circuit that securely stores information used to identify and authenticate the IoT device on a cellular network like 5G.

> **NOTE 23**
>
> The Zigbee name comes from the peculiar behavior of bees. After zigging and zagging through fields when collecting nectar, bees return to the hive and perform a waggle dance to communicate the distance, direction, and type of food to other bees in the hive. Once they receive this information, the other bees fly off directly to the source of food.

Rogue AP System Detection

As the cost of consumer wireless routers has fallen, the problem of rogue APs has risen. Identifying these devices in an enterprise is known as *rogue AP system detection*. Several methods can be used to detect a rogue AP by continuously monitoring the RF airspace. This requires a special sensor called a *wireless probe*, a device that can monitor the airwaves for traffic. There are four types of wireless probes:

- *Wireless device probe.* A standard wireless device, such as a portable laptop computer, can be configured to act as a wireless probe. At regular intervals during the normal course of operation, the device can scan and record wireless signals within its range and report this information to a centralized database. The scanning is performed when the device is idle and not receiving any transmissions. Using several mobile devices as wireless device probes can provide a high degree of accuracy in identifying rogue access points.

- *Desktop probe*. Instead of using a mobile wireless device as a probe, a desktop probe uses a standard desktop PC. A universal serial bus (USB) wireless adapter is plugged into the desktop computer to monitor the RF in the area for transmissions.
- *Access point probe*. Some AP vendors have included in their APs the functionality of detecting neighboring APs, friendly as well as rogue. However, this approach is not widely used. The range for a single AP to recognize other APs is limited because APs are typically located so that their signals overlap only to provide roaming to wireless users.
- *Dedicated probe*. A dedicated probe is designed to exclusively monitor the RF for transmissions. Unlike access point probes that serve as both an AP and a probe, dedicated probes only monitor the airwaves. Dedicated probes look much like standard access points.

Once a suspicious wireless signal is detected by a wireless probe, the information is sent to a centralized database where WLAN management system software compares it to a list of approved APs. Any device not on the list is considered a rogue AP. The WLAN management system can instruct the switch to disable the port to which the rogue AP is connected, thus severing its connection to the wired network.

SUMMARY

- Bluetooth is a wireless technology that uses short-range RF transmissions. It enables users to connect wirelessly to a wide range of computing and telecommunications devices by providing for rapid "on-the-fly" connections between Bluetooth-enabled devices. The primary type of Bluetooth network topology is a piconet. Two of the common attacks on wireless Bluetooth technology are bluejacking, which is sending unsolicited messages, and bluesnarfing, or accessing unauthorized information from a wireless device through a Bluetooth connection.
- Near field communication (NFC) is a set of standards that can be used to establish communication between devices in close proximity. Once the devices are either tapped together or brought very close to each other, a two-way communication is established. NFC devices are increasingly used in contactless payment systems so that consumers can pay for a purchase by simply tapping a store's payment terminal with their smartphone. There are risks with using NFC contactless payment systems because of the nature of this technology.
- A wireless technology similar to NFC is radio frequency identification (RFID). RFID is commonly used to transmit information between paper-based tags that can be detected by a proximity reader. Because RFID tags do not require a power supply, they can be very small and thinner than a sheet of paper. RFID tags are susceptible to some types of attacks.
- A wireless local area network (WLAN), commonly called Wi-Fi, is designed to replace or supplement a wired LAN. The IEEE has developed standards for WLANs. An enterprise WLAN requires a wireless client adapter and an AP for communications, whereas a home network uses a wireless router instead of an AP. There are different types of enterprise APs. A thin AP is a lightweight AP that does not contain all the management and configuration functions found in fat APs. Much of the configuration is centralized in the wireless switch. Instead of installing standalone APs like fat or thin APs, controller APs can be managed through a dedicated wireless LAN controller (WLC). The WLC is a single device that can be configured and then used to automatically distribute the settings to all controller APs. A captive portal AP uses a standard web browser to present information and give the wireless user the opportunity to agree to a policy or enter valid login credentials, providing a higher degree of security.
- In a traditional wired network, the security of the network itself along with the walls and doors of the secured building protect the data and resources. Because an RF signal can easily extend past the protective perimeter of a building and because an AP can provide unauthorized entry points into the network, WLANs are frequently the target of attackers.

- A rogue AP is an unauthorized AP that allows an attacker to bypass network security and opens the network and its users to attacks. An evil twin is an AP that is set up by an attacker to mimic an authorized AP and capture the transmissions from users. One of the most common wireless attacks is intercepting and reading transmitted data. In addition, if attackers manage to connect to the enterprise wired network through a rogue AP, they could also read broadcast and multicast wired network traffic. Attackers likewise can use intentional RF interference to flood the RF spectrum with enough radio interference or manipulate Wi-Fi standards to prevent a device from effectively communicating with the AP, performing a wireless DoS attack that prevents the transmission of data to or from network devices. Consumer wireless networks that are not protected are subject to attackers stealing data, reading transmissions, or injecting malware behind the firewall.

- The original IEEE 802.11 committee recognized that wireless transmissions could be vulnerable and implemented several wireless security protections in the 802.11 standard while leaving other protections to be applied at the WLAN vendor's discretion. Despite their intended design, several of these protections were vulnerable to attacks. Wired Equivalent Privacy (WEP) was designed to ensure that only authorized parties can view transmitted wireless information by encrypting transmissions. WEP relies on a secret key shared between the wireless client device and the AP that is combined with an initialization vector (IV). However, WEP has several security vulnerabilities. Wi-Fi Protected Setup (WPS) is an optional means of configuring security on WLANs and is designed to help users who have little or no knowledge of security to implement security quickly and easily. However, there are significant design and implementation flaws in WPS.

- One method of controlling access to the WLAN so that only approved users can be accepted is to limit a device's access to the AP. Virtually all wireless AP vendors offer Media Access Control (MAC) address filtering. Filtering by MAC address, however, has several vulnerabilities. One weakness is that MAC addresses are initially exchanged between wireless devices and the AP in an unencrypted format. Wi-Fi Protected Access (WPA) was designed to fit into the existing WEP engine without requiring extensive hardware upgrades or replacements. WPA replaces WEP with the Temporal Key Integrity Protocol (TKIP), which uses a longer key and dynamically generates a new key for each packet that is created. WPA authentication for WPA Personal is accomplished by using preshared key (PSK) technology. A key must be created and entered in both the access point and all wireless devices ("shared") prior to ("pre") the devices communicating with the AP. Security vulnerabilities can be found in WPA.

- Wi-Fi Protected Access 2 (WPA2) is the second generation of WPA security. Encryption under WPA2 is accomplished by using AES-CCMP. The Cipher Block Chaining Message Authentication Code (CBC-MAC) component of CCMP provides data integrity and authentication. WPA2 authentication is accomplished by the IEEE 802.1x standard. Because the communication between the supplicant, authenticator, and authentication server in an IEEE 802.1x configuration must be secure, it uses a framework for transporting the authentication protocols known as the Extensible Authentication Protocol (EAP). EAP is a framework for transporting authentication protocols by defining the format of the messages. The next generation of Wi-Fi Protected Access (WPA) is known as WPA3. The goal of WPA3 is to deliver a suite of features to simplify security configuration for users while enhancing network security protections.

- Other steps can be taken to protect a wireless network. Important considerations must be taken into account when installing a new WLAN for an organization: all areas of a building should have adequate wireless coverage; all employees must have a reasonable amount of bandwidth; and, for security reasons, a minimum amount of wireless signal should "bleed" outside the walls of the building. Assuring that a WLAN can provide its intended functionality and meet its required design goals can best be achieved through a site survey. A site survey is an in-depth examination and analysis of a WLAN site. A site survey mainly addresses placing the AP in the optimum location, known as wireless access point placement.

- Selecting the proper configuration options for the AP can also enhance security. Some of these settings are designed to limit the spread of the wireless RF signal so that a minimum amount of signal extends past the physical boundaries of the enterprise to be accessible to outsiders. AP configuration and device options include setting the signal strength and choosing the correct RF spectrum options. One device option is to select the best type of antenna and to correctly locate it.

- Several wireless technologies relate to communications for specialized and embedded systems. Zigbee is a low-power, short-range, and low-data rate specification. It is best designed for occasional data or signal transmission from a sensor or IoT device. Unlike Wi-Fi transmitting over a localized geographical area, 5G is the fifth-generation cellular wireless standard. Compared to 4G, 5G supports faster speeds, is more responsive, and can connect to more devices simultaneously. Narrowband Internet of Things (NB-IoT) is a low-power wide area network (LPWAN) radio technology standard. NB-IoT is a wide range cellular service that focuses on indoor coverage, low cost, long battery life, and high connection density. One cellular-based network for IoT devices that is optimized for these transmissions uses a baseband radio. Cellular IoT baseband can transmit using standard 4G transmissions or NB-IoT. Some IoT devices use a SIM card (subscriber identity module card) for data transmissions. A SIM card is an integrated circuit that securely stores information used to identify and authenticate the IoT device on a cellular network like 5G.
- The problem of rogue APs is of increasing concern to organizations. Several methods can be used to detect a rogue AP by continuously monitoring the RF airspace. This requires a special sensor called a wireless probe, a device that can monitor the airwaves for traffic.

Key Terms

5G	enterprise method	Protected EAP (PEAP)
ad hoc mode	evil twin	radio frequency identification
baseband	Extensible Authentication	(RFID)
bluejacking	Protocol (EAP)	rogue AP
bluesnarfing	heat map	Simultaneous Authentication of
Bluetooth	IEEE 802.1x	Equals (SAE)
captive portal AP	initialization vector (IV)	site survey
channel overlays	jamming	subscriber identity module (SIM)
Cipher Block Chaining Message	Media Access Control (MAC)	card
Authentication Code (CBC-MAC)	address filtering	Wi-Fi
controller AP	Narrowband Internet of Things	Wi-Fi analyzer
Counter Mode with Cipher Block	(NB-IoT)	Wi-Fi Direct
Chaining Message Authentication	near field communication (NFC)	Wi-Fi Protected Access 2
Code Protocol (CCMP)	open method	(WPA2)
disassociation attack	payment method	Wi-Fi Protected Setup (WPS)
EAP-FAST	point-to-multipoint	wireless access point placement
EAP-TLS	point-to-point	WPA3
EAP-TTLS	preshared key (PSK)	Zigbee

Review Questions

1. Aaliyah has been asked to do research in a new payment system for the retail stores that her company owns. Which technology is predominately used for contactless payment systems that she will investigate?

   a. Bluetooth

   b. Near field communication (NFC)

   c. Wi-Fi

   d. Radio frequency ID (RFID)

2. Nyla is investigating a security incident in which the smartphone of the CEO was compromised and confidential data was stolen. She suspects that it was an attack that used Bluetooth. Which attack would this be?

   a. Blueswiping

   b. Bluesnarfing

   c. Bluejacking

   d. Bluestealing

3. What is a difference between NFC and RFID?

   a. NFC is based on wireless technology while RFID is not.

   b. RFID is faster than NFC.

   c. RFID is designed for paper-based tags while NFC is not.

   d. NFC devices cannot pair as quickly as RFID devices.

4. Which technical specification of the Wi-Fi Alliance is the same as ad hoc mode in a Wi-Fi network?
   a. Ad hoc II
   b. Dynamic ad hoc
   c. Alliance IBSS
   d. Wi-Fi Direct

5. Fatima has just learned that employees have tried to install their own wireless router in the employee lounge. Why is installing this rogue AP a security vulnerability?
   a. It uses the weaker IEEE 80211i protocol.
   b. It allows an attacker to bypass network security configurations.
   c. It conflicts with other network firewalls and can cause them to become disabled.
   d. It requires the use of vulnerable wireless probes on all mobile devices.

6. Which of these is NOT a risk when a home wireless router is not securely configured?
   a. An attacker can steal data from any folder with file sharing enabled.
   b. Wireless endpoints must be manually approved to connect to the WLAN.
   c. Usernames, passwords, credit card numbers, and other information sent over the WLAN could be captured by an attacker.
   d. Malware can be injected into a computer connected to the WLAN.

7. Which of these Wi-Fi Protected Setup (WPS) methods is vulnerable?
   a. Push-button method
   b. Piconet method
   c. PIN method
   d. Click-to-connect method

8. Flavio visits a local coffee shop on his way to school and accesses its free Wi-Fi. When he first connects, a screen appears that requires him to agree to an acceptable use policy (AUP) before continuing. What type of AP has he encountered?
   a. Authenticated portal
   b. Captive portal
   c. Control portal
   d. Rogue portal

9. Which of the following is NOT a means by which a threat actor can perform a wireless denial of service attack?
   a. Jamming
   b. Disassociation
   c. IEEE 802.11iw separate
   d. Manipulate duration field values

10. Zariah is writing an email to an employee about a wireless attack that is designed to capture the wireless transmissions from legitimate users. Which type of attack is Zariah describing?
    a. Rogue access point
    b. Bluetooth grabber
    c. WEP-II
    d. Evil twin

11. Which of these is a vulnerability of MAC address filtering in a WLAN?
    a. Not all operating systems support MACs.
    b. APs use IP addresses instead of MACs.
    c. The user must enter the MAC.
    d. MAC addresses are initially exchanged unencrypted.

12. Which of these is a 24-bit value that changes each time a packet is encrypted and then is combined with a shared secret key?
    a. RC
    b. IV
    c. SL
    d. SSD

13. Which of these does not require authentication?
    a. Open method
    b. PSK
    c. Enterprise method
    d. Initialization method

14. Which of these is the encryption protocol for WPA2?
    a. CMAC-RSTS
    b. CPB
    c. CBD-MAC
    d. CCMP

15. Adabella was asked by her supervisor to adjust the frequency spectrum settings on a new AP. She brought up the configuration page and looked through the different options. Which of the following frequency spectrum settings would she NOT be able to adjust?
    a. Frequency band
    b. Channel selection
    c. RFID spectrum
    d. Channel width

16. Imani has been asked to purchase wireless LAN controllers (WLCs) for the office. What type of APs must she also purchase that can be managed by a WLC?
    a. Standalone AP
    b. Controller AP
    c. Fat AP
    d. Any type of AP can be managed by a WLC.

17. Which WPA3 security feature is designed to increase security at the time of the handshake?
    a. WEP
    b. MIT
    c. OWE
    d. SAE

18. Maryam is explaining the Extensible Authentication Protocol (EAP). What would be the best explanation of EAP?
    a. It is the transport protocol used in TCP/IP for authentication.
    b. It is a framework for transporting authentication protocols.

c. It is a subset of WPA2.
d. It is a technology used by IEEE 802.11 for encryption.

19. Minh has been asked to recommend an EAP for a system that uses both passwords and tokens with TLS. Which should she recommend?
    a. EAP-FAST
    b. EAP-TLS
    c. EAP-TTLS
    d. EAP-SSL

20. Which of these is NOT a type of wireless AP probe?
    a. Wireless device probe
    b. WNIC probe
    c. Dedicated probe
    d. AP probe

Hands-On Projects

 **CAUTION**   If you are concerned about installing any of the software in these projects on your regular computer, you can instead use the Windows Sandbox or install the software in the Windows virtual machine created in the Module 1 Hands-On Projects. Software installed within the virtual machine will not impact the host computer.

Project 11-1: Using a Wireless Monitor Tool

Time Required: 25 minutes
Objective: Given a scenario, install and configure wireless security settings.
Description: Most Wi-Fi users are surprised to see how far their wireless signal will reach, and if the network is unprotected, a long reach makes it easy for an attacker hiding several hundred feet away to break into the network. Several tools can show the different wireless signals that can be detected from Wi-Fi networks. In this project, you download and install the NirSoft WifiInfoView tool. You will need a computer with a wireless adapter, such as a laptop, to complete this project.

1. Use your web browser to go to **www.nirsoft.net/utils/wifi_information_view.html**. (If you are no longer able to access the site through the web address, use a search engine to search for "NirSoft WifiInfoView.")
2. Scroll down and click **Download WifiInfoView**.
3. Download the tool and when finished, extract the files and then launch the program.
4. Wait until WiFiInfoView displays all Wi-Fi networks that it detects.
5. Scan through the information that is displayed. Does the amount of available information from Wi-Fi networks to which you are not connected surprise you?
6. Scroll back to the first column of information.
7. Under **SSID**, is there a service set identifier for each network? Why would an SSID not appear? Does disabling the broadcast of the SSID name give any enhanced level of security? Why not?
8. Note the value under the column **MAC Address**. How could a threat actor use this information?
9. Under **RSSI**, the signal strength is displayed. (Lower numbers indicate a stronger signal.)
10. The **Frequency** column displays the frequency on which the network is transmitting, and the **Channel** column gives the corresponding channel. Click **Channel** to sort the channels. Is there any channel overlap? How could this be a problem?
11. Double-click the Wi-Fi network to which you are currently connected. A window is displayed showing the available information that is being transmitted through the Wi-Fi. This is information regarding your Wi-Fi network that anyone can see. Close this window.

12. Now select a network other than the one to which you are connected and double-click it to display information. After reading the information, close the window.
13. Scroll to the **Security** and **Cipher** columns. What security are the networks using?
14. Scroll to **WPS Support**. How many networks have WPS turned on? Is this secure?
15. What additional information do you find useful? What information would a threat actor find useful?
16. Close all windows.

Project 11-2: Viewing WLAN Security Information with Vistumbler

Time Required: 25 minutes
Objective: Given a scenario, install and configure wireless security settings.
Description: Vistumbler can be used to display the security information that is beaconed out from WLANs. Note that Vistumbler does not allow you to "crack" any WLANs but instead only displays information. In this project, you use Vistumbler to view this information. This project works best when you are in an area in which you can pick up multiple WLAN signals.

1. Use your web browser to go to **www.vistumbler.net**. (The location of content on the Internet may change without warning. If you are no longer able to access the program through this URL, use a search engine and search for "Vistumbler.")
2. Click **EXE Installer (Mirror)**.
3. Follow the prompts to download and install Vistumbler using the default settings.
4. If the program does not start after the installation is complete, launch Vistumbler.

> **(!) CAUTION** Some AV software may indicate that Vistumbler is a virus. It might be necessary to temporarily turn off your AV software for this project. Be sure to turn AV back on when the project is completed.

5. If necessary, expand the window to full screen.
6. Click **Scan APs**. If no networks appear, click **Interface** and then select the appropriate wireless NIC interface.
7. Note the columns **Signal** and **High Signal**. How could they be used in a site survey?
8. Click **Graph 1**.
9. Click one of the APs displayed at the bottom of the screen. Allow Vistumbler to accumulate data over several minutes. What information is displayed on this graph?
10. Click **Graph 2**.
11. Click another one of the APs displayed at the bottom of the screen. Allow Vistumbler to accumulate data over several minutes. What information is displayed on this graph? How is this different from the previous graph?
12. Click **No Graph** to return to the previous screen.
13. Use the horizontal scroll bar to move to the right. Note the columns **Authentication**, **Encryption**, **Manufacturer**, and **Radio Type**. How would this information be useful to an attacker?
14. Use the horizontal scroll bar to move back to the far left.
15. In the left pane, expand the information under **Authentication**. What types are listed?
16. Expand the information under these types and note the information given for the wireless LAN signals.
17. In the left pane, expand the information under **Encryption**. What types are listed? Which types are most secure? Which types are least secure?
18. Expand the information under these types and note the information given for each WLAN.
19. Record the total number of different WLANs that you can detect, along with the number of encryption types. Which type is most common?
20. One of the features of Vistumbler is its ability to use audio and text-to-speech information so that the location and strength of WLANs can be detected without the need to constantly monitor the screen. Be sure that the speakers on the laptop computer are turned on.
21. Click **Options**.
22. Click **Speak Signals**. Vistumbler will "speak" the percentage of signal strength.
23. Now carry the laptop away from the AP and note the changes. How would this be helpful to an attacker?
24. Close Vistumbler.

25. Close all windows and do not save any data. If necessary, restart your AV software.
26. How does Vistumbler compare with WiFiInfoView? Which is easier to use? Which tool gives more information?

Project 11-3: Configuring Access Points

Time Required: 25 minutes
Objective: Given a scenario, install and configure wireless security settings.
Description: The ability to properly configure an AP is an important skill for any wireless network professional as well as, to a lesser degree, for users. In this project, you use an online emulator from TRENDnet to configure an AP.

1. Use your web browser to go to **www.trendnet.com/emulators/TEW-818DRU_v1/login.htm**. (The location of content on the Internet may change without warning; if you are no longer able to access the program through this URL, use a search engine and search for "Trendnet Emulators.")
2. The emulated login screen will appear. Click **Login** without entering a username or password.
3. An emulated Setup screen is displayed, showing what a user would see when configuring an actual TRENDnet.
4. Be sure that the **BASIC** tab is selected in the left pane. Note the simulated **Network Status** information.
5. Click **Wireless** in the left pane and read the information displayed.
6. Under **Broadcast Network Name (SSID)**, click the down arrow next to **Enabled**. What other option is available? Would it be an advantage to change this setting? Why or why not?
7. Under **Frequency (Channel)**, note that the default is **Auto**. What does this mean?
8. Click the down arrow on **Auto**. When would you want to change the channel on which the wireless signal is broadcast?
9. Under **Channel BandWidth**, click the down arrow on **20 MHz**. What is the other option? Why would you choose this option? What are the advantages and disadvantages of changing the channel bandwidth?
10. Under **Security Policy** is a single configuration option, **Security Mode**. Note the default setting. Is this a good option default option? What does **WPA2-PSK** mean?
11. Click the down arrow on **WPA2-PSK**. What are the other options? What do they mean?
12. Under **WPA**, note the option **WPA Encryption**. Click the down arrow on **AES**. What are the other options available and what do they mean?
13. Under **WPA passphrase**, note the length of the default passphrase. Is that sufficient?
14. In the left pane, click **Guest Network**. A guest network allows you to have an additional open network for occasional guests that does not affect the main wireless network. How could this be an advantage?
15. Note the option under **Internet Access Only**. When would you select this option?
16. Note the option under **Wireless Client Isolation**. Why is this not enabled by default?
17. Under **Security Policy**, note that the **Security Mode** is set to **Disable** by default. Why would a guest network's security be turned off by default? (Hint: If it were turned on, what would the guests need before they could use the network?)
18. In the left pane, click **Advanced**.
19. Click **Security**.
20. Under **Access Control**, what is the **LAN Client Filter Function**? Does it provide strong security if it were enabled?
21. How easy is this user interface to navigate? Does it provide enough information for a user to set up the security settings on this system?
22. Close all windows.

Project 11-4: Using Microsoft Windows Netsh Commands

Time Required: 25 minutes
Objective: Given a scenario, install and configure wireless security settings.
Description: The Windows *netsh* commands for a wireless local area network (WLAN) provide the means to configure wireless connectivity and security settings using the command line instead of a graphical user interface (GUI). Benefits of the wireless *netsh* interface include easier wireless deployment as an alternative to Group Policy, ability to configure clients to support multiple security options, and even the ability to block undesirable networks. In this project, you will explore some of the *netsh* commands.

NOTE 24

For this project, you need a computer running Microsoft Windows that has a wireless NIC and can access a wireless LAN.

1. In Microsoft Windows, right-click the **Start** button.
2. Select **Windows PowerShell (Admin)**. The Windows command window opens in elevated privilege mode.
3. Type **netsh** and then press **Enter**. The command prompt changes to *netsh>*.
4. Type **wlan** and then press **Enter**. The command prompt changes to *netsh wlan>*.
5. Type **show drivers** and then press **Enter** to display the wireless NIC driver information. It may be necessary to scroll toward the top to see all the information.
6. Next, view the WLAN interfaces for this computer. Type **show interfaces** and then press **Enter**. Record the SSID value and the name of the profile.
7. View the global wireless settings for this computer. Type **show settings** and then press **Enter**.
8. Display all the available networks to this computer. Type **show networks** and then press **Enter**.
9. Windows creates a profile for each network that you connect to. To display those profiles, type **show profiles** and then press **Enter**. If there is a profile of a network that you no longer use, type **delete profile name**=*profile-name*.
10. Disconnect from your current WLAN by typing **disconnect** and then pressing **Enter**. Note the message you receive, and observe the status in your system tray.
11. Reconnect to your network by typing **connect name**=*profile-name* **ssid**=*ssid-name* as previously recorded and then press **Enter**.
12. Netsh allows you to block specific networks. Select another network name that you are not currently connected to. Type **show networks**, press **Enter**, and then record the SSID of the network you want to block. Type **add filter permission = block ssid**=*ssid-name* **networktype = infrastructure** and then press **Enter**.
13. Type **show networks** and then press **Enter**. Does the network that you previously blocked appear in the list?
14. Display the blocked network (but do not allow access to it). Type **set blockednetworks display=show** and then press **Enter.**
15. Type **show networks** and then press **Enter**. Does the network that you previously blocked appear in the list?
16. Click the wireless icon in your system tray. Does the network appear in this list?
17. If necessary, click the wireless icon in your system tray again. What appears next to the name of this blocked network? Click the name of the network. What does it say?
18. Now re-enable access to the blocked network by typing **delete filter permission = block ssid**=*ssid-name* **networktype = infrastructure** and then press **Enter**.
19. Type **Exit** and then press **Enter**.
20. Type **Exit** again and then press **Enter** to close the command window.

Case Projects

Case Project 11-1: Comparisons of Contactless Payment Systems

Three of the most popular contactless payment systems are Apple Pay, Google Pay, and Samsung Pay. Each has advantages and disadvantages. Using the Internet, research these three different systems. Create a table that lists each system and its features, strengths and weaknesses, ease of use, security, etc. Which of them would you recommend? In your opinion, what can be done to make these more popular? Write a one-paragraph summary to accompany your table.

Case Project 11-2: Bluetooth Range Estimator

The range at which a Bluetooth device can transmit depends on several factors. Understanding the ranges helps you be aware of whether a Bluetooth-enabled device could be the victim of a bluejacking or bluesnarfing attack. Go to **www.bluetooth.com/learn-about-bluetooth/bluetooth-technology/range/** to explore the Bluetooth Range

Estimator tool. First, watch the video and then read the details of each of the key factors. Then use the range estimator tool, changing the different parameters (receiver sensitivity, path loss, transmit power, transmitter antenna gain, and receiver antenna gain) to determine the estimated range. What does this tell you about Bluetooth ranges? How could this tool be used? Write a one-page paper on what you have learned.

Case Project 11-3: EAP

Use the Internet to research information on the EAP protocols that are supported in WPA2 Enterprise (see Table 11-5). Write a brief description of each, and indicate the relative strength of its security. Write a one-page paper on your research.

Case Project 11-4: WPA3 Features

Use the Internet to research WPA3 features, particularly SAE and OWE. What are the primary advantages and disadvantages of each of these features? How do they enhance Wi-Fi security? Write a one-page paper on your research.

Case Project 11-5: Antennas

To many users, antennas are just one of life's great mysteries. They know from experience that any antenna is better than having no antenna and that the higher the antenna is located, the better the reception will be. Yet the antenna is arguably one of the most important parts of a wireless network. Antennas play a vital role in both sending and receiving signals, and a properly positioned and functioning antenna can make all the difference between a WLAN operating at peak efficiency or a network that nobody can use. Use the Internet to research antennas for APs. What different types of antennas are used? What are their strengths? What are their weaknesses? Which types would be used to concentrate a signal to a more confined area? Write a one-page paper on what you find.

Case Project 11-6: Your Personal Wireless Security

Is the wireless network you own as secure as it should be? Examine your wireless network or that of a friend or neighbor, and determine which security model it uses. Next, outline the steps it would take to move it to the next highest level. Estimate how much it would cost and how much time it would take to increase the level. Finally, estimate how long it would take you to replace all the data on your computer and what you might lose if the data were corrupted by an attacker. Would this be motivation to increase your current wireless security model? Write a one-page paper on your work.

Case Project 11-7: Community Site Activity

The Information Security Community Site is an online companion to this textbook. It contains a wide variety of tools, information, discussion boards, and other features to assist learners. Go to **community.cengage.com/infosec2** and click the *Join or Sign in* icon to log in, using your login name and password that you created in Module 1. Click **Forums (Discussion)** and then click **Security+ Case Projects (7th edition)**. Read the following case study.

Comcast is a nationwide ISP offering its Xfinity product to consumers. The device from Comcast that consumers use to connect to the Internet also includes a Wi-Fi wireless gateway. However, this gateway broadcasts two Wi-Fi signals: one for the consumer and a second network signal that any Xfinity Internet customer can use without the customer's permission by simply signing on. This means that any Xfinity customer can use another customer's Wi-Fi service without first receiving approval. There is not a means to disable this free service. How do you feel about Xfinity offering this service without the customer's express approval for others to access this second Wi-Fi signal? Would you want strangers accessing your Wi-Fi service without your knowledge or approval? What are the advantages? What are the risks? Visit the Community Site discussion board and post how you feel about Internet content filters.

Case Project 11-8: North Ridge Security

North Ridge Security provides security consulting and assurance services. You have recently been hired as an intern to assist them.

Pomodoro Fresco is a regional Italian pizza chain that provides free open wireless access to its customers and secure wireless access for its staff. However, Pomodoro Fresco is concerned about the security of the WLAN. They have asked North Ridge to make a presentation about wireless attacks and their options for security. North Ridge has asked you to help them in the presentation.

1. Create a PowerPoint presentation for the staff about the threats against WLANs and the weaknesses of Wi-Fi. Also, include information about the more secure WPA3. Your presentation should contain at least 10 slides.
2. After the presentation, Pomodoro Fresco is trying to decide if they should install a captive portal for their customer WLAN. Create a memo to their management outlining the advantages and disadvantages, along with your recommendation.

References

1. "Cisco annual internet report (2018–2023) white paper," *Cisco*, Mar. 9, 2020, accessed Jul. 9, 2020, www.cisco.com/c/en/us/solutions/collateral/executive-perspectives/annual-internet-report/white-paper-c11-741490.html.
2. Tepper, Taylor, "Contactless credit cards and payments: The good, the bad, and the ugly," *Wirecutter*, May 7, 2020, accessed Jul. 10, 2020, www.nytimes.com/wirecutter/money/credit-cards/contactless-payment/.
3. "Assessing the economic value of unlicensed use in the 5.9 GHz & 6 GHz bands," Telecom Advisory Service, Apr. 2020, accessed Jul. 10, 2020, http://wififorward.org/wp-content/uploads/2020/04/5.9-6.0-FINAL-for-distribution.pdf.

ENTERPRISE SECURITY

The modules in Part 5 deal with issues primarily pertaining to enterprise security. In Module 12, you learn about authentication credentials. Module 13 covers incident preparation, response, and investigation, while Module 14 looks at cybersecurity resilience. Finally, in Module 15, you learn about risk management and data privacy protections.

PART 5

AUTHENTICATION

After completing this module, you should be able to do the following:

1. Describe the different types of authentication credentials
2. Explain the different attacks on authentication
3. Describe how to implement authentication security solutions

Front-Page Cybersecurity

What would happen if a massive security breach at a financial institution involving the theft of user identifiers such as passwords? Most likely, all users would be required to change their passwords to prevent attackers from accessing the accounts. But what would happen if there was a similar security breach—a theft not of passwords but of biometric user identifiers such as facial scans or fingerprints? What could users do? Obviously, they cannot change their face or fingerprint as they can change a password.

Security researchers have worried over such a scenario since biometrics have become commonplace. Recently, such a breach occurred. The implications of millions of users having their biometric data stolen may affect them for the rest of their lives.

BioStar 2 is a web-based security platform that allows customers to control access to secure areas of facilities, record activity logs, and manage user permissions. The BioStar 2 system is currently in use by more than 5,700 organizations in 83 countries with 1.5 million installations—including large multinational businesses, small local businesses, governments, banks, and even the United Kingdom Metropolitan Police. As is common today with controlling access in facilities, BioStar 2 employs facial recognition and fingerprinting technology to identify users.

Security researchers from vpnMentor discovered in 2019 that BioStar 2's online database of was unprotected. Once vpnMentor uncovered the vulnerabilities, the security researchers tried to privately contact BioStar to make the company aware of the problem. However, they had difficulty getting anyone to talk to them. (In one instance, a BioStar employee in Germany even hung up on them.) The security researchers finally managed to have BioStar in France take them seriously, and the vulnerabilities were closed—but too late.

The unprotected BioStar 2 data included almost 28 million records (23 gigabytes of data) that contained the personal employee information of customers who were using BioStar 2. This included employee home addresses and emails, their security levels and clearances, work start dates, usernames and passwords, biometric data such as fingerprint information and facial scans, along with other data. The online database itself that contained this information was never designed for this type of usage, and was unprotected to the point that records could be added, deleted, or modified by anyone with a web browser. In addition, the passwords and biometric data were stored in plaintext.

Attackers could take over an account on the BioStar 2 online database to access security settings and change user permissions and lock approved employees out of a secure facility. They could also create new user accounts, add their own facial recognition and fingerprint information, and give themselves access to secure areas within a building or facility. Attackers could even create libraries of fingerprints and facial scans to be used any time they wanted to enter a secure location without being detected. Because they also had access to activity logs, attackers could delete or alter the data to hide their activities. In the words of the researchers, "A hacked building's entire security infrastructure becomes useless. Anybody with this data will have free movement to go anywhere they choose, undetected."

BioStar 2 was the first publicized wide-scale biometric breach. While the full potential danger of this theft is still unknown, what is known is that once your fingerprint or facial scan is stolen, unlike a password, it cannot be changed. When attackers develop technology to replicate your fingerprint from stolen data, they will gain access to all the private information on any device that uses biometrics or any door that unlocks based on your biometrics. For example, attackers could manipulate your biometric data to allow them to enter a nuclear power plant in which you were authorized to enter based on your biometrics, and then lock you and everyone else out—while they melt it down.

Users are urged to think twice about using biometrics until there are regulations in place. While it may be inconvenient to type a password to access a device instead of using a fingerprint, remember that once your biometric data is stolen, it potentially affects you for the rest of your life—and by then, there's nothing you can do about it.

Authentication in information security is the process of ensuring that the person or system desiring access to resources is *authentic* and not an imposter. In this module, you study authentication and the secure management techniques that enforce authentication. First, you will look at the different types of authentication credentials that can be used to verify a user's identity. Then you will look into the techniques and technology used to manage user accounts in a secure fashion.

TYPES OF AUTHENTICATION CREDENTIALS

✅ CERTIFICATION

1.2 Given a scenario, analyze potential indicators to determine the type of attack.

1.3 Given a scenario, analyze potential indicators associated with application attacks.

2.4 Summarize authentication and authorization design concepts.

3.5 Given a scenario, implement secure mobile solutions.

3.8 Given a scenario, implement authentication and authorization solutions.

4.1 Given a scenario, use the appropriate tool to assess organizational security.

Consider this scenario: Riker, Peyton, and Paolo work on a local military base, and each afternoon, they go to the gym on the base to exercise. As they reach the entrance to the building, each must press a finger to the fingerprint reader to enter the building. (A "no tailgating" policy is strictly enforced.) As they walk to the receptionist's desk, Riker holds up his ID card to the RFID reader so the door to the locker room opens for him. As Peyton searches for his card, the receptionist, Li, waves him through to the locker room because she knows him. Riker laughs and says to Li, "It's only because of Peyton's flaming red hair that you recognize him, and it runs in his family!" Paolo, however, is new to the base and must sign in. After Li compares his signature to his membership application on file, she allows him to enter. In the locker room, each of them opens his locker using a combination lock with a series of memorized numbers.

In this scenario, the three men have been demonstrated to be *genuine* or *authentic* and not an imposter, by the seven separate elements listed in Table 12.1.

Table 12-1 Elements that prove authenticity

Element	Description	Scenario example
Somewhere you are	Restricted location	Restricted military base
Something you are	Unique biological characteristic that cannot be changed	Fingerprint reader to enter building
Something you have	Possession of an item that nobody else has	Riker's RFID card
Someone you know	Validated by another person	Li knows Peyton
Something you exhibit	Genetically determined characteristic	Peyton's flaming red hair
Something you can do	Perform an activity that cannot be exactly copied	Paolo's signature
Something you know	Knowledge that nobody else possesses	Combination to unlock locker

Because only the real or "authentic" person possesses one or more of these elements, they can be considered as types of authentication, which is proof of genuineness. These types of authentications can confirm a person's identity and thus give access to restricted areas or materials while also denying access by an imposter. In information technology (IT), these types of elements are known as *authentication credentials* and are presented to an IT system to verify the genuineness of the user.

NOTE 1

Three of these elements (something you know, something you have, and something you are) are called *factors* while the remaining four (somewhere you are, something you can do, something you exhibit, and someone you know) are called *attributes*. The element *something you exhibit* is often linked to more specialized attributes than the color of hair in the scenario and may even include neurological traits that can be identified by specialized medical equipment.

Although any of these elements can be used as an authentication credential, the most common in IT are something you know, something you have, something you are, and something you can do.

NOTE 2

Although many authentication credentials can be presented to an IT system to verify the genuineness of the user, all credentials can be classified into one of these seven categories.

Something You Know: Passwords

The most common IT authentication credential is providing information that only the user would know. A **password** is a secret combination of letters, numbers, and/or characters. Despite their widespread use, passwords provide weak protection and are constantly under attack.

NOTE 3

The person credited with inventing the computer password, Fernando "Corby" Corbato, who passed away in late 2019, was a researcher for MIT and worked on the Compatible Time-Sharing System (CTSS), which allowed multiple users to share computer time. He devised a way to isolate users from each other with password-protected user accounts. In his later years, Corbato lamented that passwords had become problematic. He said that the Internet made logins with passwords a "kind of a nightmare."

Password Weaknesses

The weakness of passwords centers on human memory. Human beings can memorize only a limited number of items. Passwords place heavy loads on human memory in multiple ways:

- The most effective passwords are long and complex. However, these are difficult for users to memorize and then accurately recall when needed.
- Users must remember multiple passwords for many accounts. Most users have accounts for different computers and mobile devices at work, school, and home; multiple email accounts; online banking; Internet site accounts; and so on. According to one study, in the United States, the average number of online accounts registered to a single email address is 130. The average number of accounts per Internet user is estimated to be 207.
- For the highest level of security, each account password should be unique, which further strains human memory.
- Many security policies mandate that passwords expire after a set period of time, such as every 45–60 days, when a new one must be created. Some security policies even prevent a previously used password from being recycled and used again, forcing users to repeatedly memorize new passwords.

NOTE 4

In recognition of the difficulties surrounding expired passwords, a growing trend has been to drop this requirement. In 2019, Microsoft changed its long-held policy and recommended that password expiration be dropped, and in 2017, guidelines released by the National Institute of Standards and Technology (NIST) also recommended that password expiration should no longer be used. However, the Payment Card Industry (PCI) still requires that merchants and other providers change their passwords every 90 days. Some security professionals are calling for a modified password expiration so that the length of the password dictates its expiration. For example, a user who creates a 30-character password would not have to change that password for two years, while a password that is 15-25 characters in length would expire annually, and one of fewer than 15 characters would have to be reset every 90 days. One company that tried this approach found that calls to its help desk for password resets declined by 70 percent.

Because of the burdens that passwords place on human memory, users take shortcuts to help them memorize and recall their passwords. One shortcut is to create and use a *weak password*. Weak passwords use a common word as a password (*princess*), a short word (*desk*), a predictable sequence of characters (*abc123*), or personal information (*Hannah*) in a password. Another common shortcut that dramatically weakens passwords is to reuse the same password (or a slight derivation of it) for multiple accounts: although this makes it easier for the user, it also makes it easier for an attacker who compromises one account to access all other accounts.

Even when users attempt to create stronger passwords, they generally follow predictable patterns:

- *Appending.* When users combine letters, numbers, and punctuation (*character sets*), they do it in a pattern. Most often they only add a number after letters (*caitlin1* or *cheer99*). If they add all three character sets, it is in the sequence *letters+punctuation+number* (*braden.8* or *chris#6*).
- *Replacing.* Users also use replacements in predictable patterns. Generally, a zero is used instead of the letter *o* (*passw0rd*), the digit *1* for the letter *i* (*denn1s*), or a dollar sign for an *s* (*be$tfriend*).

 **CAUTION** | Attackers are aware of these patterns in passwords and can search for them, making it faster and easier to crack the password.

The widespread use of weak passwords can be illustrated easily. An analysis of more than 562 million stolen passwords revealed that the most common length of a password was only nine characters, while fewer than 1 percent of the passwords were more than 14 characters. In addition, the percentage of passwords that used characters other than lowercase letters was remarkably low: uppercase characters were found in only 6 percent of passwords while special symbols were in just 4 percent. The 10 most common passwords in the 562 million stolen passwords are very weak and are listed in Table 12-2.[1]

Table 12-2   Ten most common passwords

Rank	Password
1	123456
2	123456789
3	abc123
4	password
5	password1
6	12345678
7	111111
8	1234567
9	12345
10	1234567890

A noted security expert summarized the password problem well by stating the following:

> *The problem is that the average user can't and won't even try to remember complex enough passwords to prevent attacks. As bad as passwords are, users will go out of the way to make it worse. If you ask them to choose a password, they'll choose a lousy one. If you force them to choose a good one, they'll write it [down] and change it back to the password they changed it from the last month. And they'll choose the same password for multiple applications.*[2]

NOTE 5

A recent study looked at users who had been told that the password to their account had been stolen in a data breach. Only one-third of the users then changed their passwords. And the users were in no rush to change their passwords: only 3 percent changed their password within 30 days after the breach, while 12 percent waited between 60 and 90 days. Incredibly, only 14 percent of users changed their password to a *stronger* password; all others created passwords that were actually weaker or the same strength as the stolen password by reusing character sequences from their previous password or creating a new password that was similar to other weak passwords they use.

Attacks on Passwords

While some attacks on passwords involve the attacker entering a password "guess" at a login prompt, these attacks have a low rate of success. Instead, attackers use a different technique that generates a high success rate.

When a user creates a password, it is not stored (or it should not be stored) in an unencrypted plaintext format; this would make it too easy for attackers to use stolen passwords. Instead, a one-way hash algorithm creates a message digest (or hash) of the password. This digest is then stored instead of the original plaintext password. When a user later enters a password to log in, a digest is created from the entered password. This digest is compared against the stored digest, and if they match, the user is authenticated.

NOTE 6

Hash algorithms are covered in Module 6.

Attackers work to steal the file of password digests. Once that file is in the hands of threat actors, it can be used in one of two ways. One method is to use a stolen hash to impersonate the user. This has been used to take advantage of a vulnerability in the Microsoft Windows NTLM (New Technology LAN Manager) hash for storing passwords on a Windows endpoint computer. An attacker who can steal the digest of an NTLM password could pretend to be the user by sending that hash to the remote system to then be authenticated. This is known as a **pass the hash** attack.

A more common use of a stolen file of password digests is for the threat actors to load that file onto their own computers and then use a sophisticated password cracker, which is software designed to break passwords. Password crackers create known digests (called *candidates*) and then compare them against the stolen digests. When a match occurs, the attacker knows the underlying password. Password crackers differ as to *how* the candidates are created. These different means of creating candidates include brute force, rule, dictionary, rainbow tables, and password collections.

NOTE 7

Password crackers do not "unravel" a digest to determine the underlying password; rather, they compare a digest created by a known word to a password digest created by an unknown word; when the digests match, the password has been "cracked." For example, using a password cracker, an attacker might create the digest *2602ab347f0ba5c63a0c936e-ba832ec5* from the word *Sunday* and then search the stolen digest file for that specific digest. If a match of digests occurs, then the attacker knows the password is *Sunday*.

NOTE 8

When cracking passwords using a brute force attack, attackers often use computers with multiple graphics processing units (GPUs). Whereas the central processing unit (CPU) of a computer can do a wide variety of tasks, a GPU, which is separate from the CPU, is used to render screen displays on computers. GPUs are very good at performing video processing, which involves the repetitive work of performing the same function over and over on large groups of pixels on the screen. This makes GPUs superior to CPUs at repetitive tasks like breaking passwords.

Password Spraying   One password attack that does not attempt to steal a file of password digests instead uses a type of "targeted guessing." A password spraying attack selects one or a few common passwords (*Password1* or *123456*) and then enters the same password when trying to login to several user accounts. Because this targeted guess is spread across many accounts, instead of attempting multiple password variations on a single account, it is much less likely to raise any alarms or lock out the user account from too many failed password attempts. Although password spraying may result in occasional success, it is not considered the optimal means for breaking into accounts.

Brute Force Attack   In an automated brute force attack, every possible combination of letters, numbers, and characters is attempted to determine the user's password. The attack is not done in a random fashion but instead uses a meticulous approach to create the passwords.

Unlike a password spraying attack, in which one password is used on multiple accounts, in an online brute force attack, the same account is continuously attacked (called *pounded*) by entering different passwords. However, an online brute force attack is rarely used by attackers because it is impractical. Even at two or three tries per second, it could take thousands of years to guess the right password. In addition, most accounts can be set to disable all logins after a limited number of incorrect attempts (such as five), thus putting an end to the threat.

An offline brute force attack begins with a stolen digest file. An attacker loads this file onto a computer and then uses password cracking software to create candidate digests of every possible combination of letters, numbers, and characters. The candidates are matched against those in a stolen digest file to find a match. This is the slowest yet most thorough method.

Rule Attack   A *rule attack* conducts a statistical analysis on the stolen passwords. The results of this analysis is then used to create a *mask* of the format of the candidate password. A mask of *?u ?l ?l ?l ?l ?d ?d ?d ?d* (u = uppercase, l = lowercase, and d = digit) would tell the password cracking program, *Use an uppercase letter for the first position, a lowercase letter for the next four positions, and digits for the remaining four positions.* Using a mask will significantly reduce the time needed to crack a password. There are three basic steps in a rule attack:

1. A small sample of the stolen password plaintext file is obtained.
2. Statistical analysis is performed on the sample to determine the length and character sets of the passwords, as seen in Figure 12-1.

```
[*] Length Statistics...
[+]                              8: 62% (612522)
[+]                              6: 18% (183307)
[+]                              7: 14% (146152)
[+]                              5: 02% (26438)
[+]                              4: 01% (15088)
[+]                              3: 00% (2497)
[+]                              2: 00% (308)
[+]                              1: 00% (113)

[*] Charset statistics...
[+]                loweralphanum: 47% (470580)
[+]                   loweralpha: 46% (459208)
[+]                      numeric: 05% (56637)
```

Figure 12-1   Rule attack statistical analysis

3. A series of masks is generated that will be most successful in cracking the highest percentage of passwords. This is illustrated in Figure 12-2.

```
[*] Advanced Mask statistics...
[+]         ?l?l?l?l?l?l?l?l: 04% (688053)
[+]           ?l?l?l?l?l?l: 04% (601257)
[+]         ?l?l?l?l?l?l?l: 04% (585093)
[+]     ?l?l?l?l?l?l?l?l?l: 03% (516862)
[+]           ?d?d?d?d?d?d?d: 03% (487437)
[+]     ?d?d?d?d?d?d?d?d?d?d: 03% (478224)
[+]         ?d?d?d?d?d?d?d?d: 02% (428306)
[+]         ?l?l?l?l?l?l?d?d: 02% (420326)
[+]   ?l?l?l?l?l?l?l?l?l?l: 02% (416961)
[+]             ?d?d?d?d?d?d: 02% (390546)
[+]       ?d?d?d?d?d?d?d?d?d: 02% (307540)
[+]         ?l?l?l?l?l?l?d?d: 02% (292318)
[+]         ?l?l?l?l?l?l?d?d: 01% (273640)
```

Figure 12-2   Rule attack generated masks

NOTE 9

A rule attack is not intended to crack every password but instead gives the highest probability of the largest number of passwords that can be broken.

Dictionary Attack   Another common password attack is a **dictionary attack**. A dictionary attack begins with the attacker creating digests of common dictionary words as candidates and then comparing them against those in a stolen digest file. A dictionary attack is shown in Figure 12-3. Dictionary attacks are successful because users often create passwords from simple dictionary words.

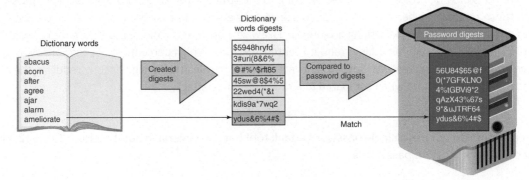

Figure 12-3   Dictionary attack

A dictionary attack that uses a set of dictionary words and compares it with the stolen digests is known as a *pre-image attack*, in that one known digest (dictionary word) is compared to an unknown digest (stolen digest). A *birthday attack* is slightly different, in that the search is for *any* two digests that are the same. A password attack that is a combination of a dictionary attack and a mask attack is called a *hybrid attack*.

NOTE 10

Birthday attacks are covered in Module 6.

Rainbow Tables   Rainbow tables make password attacks easier by creating a large pregenerated data set of candidate digests. A rainbow table is a compressed representation of passwords that are related and organized in a sequence (called a *chain*).

Although generating a rainbow table requires a significant amount of time, once it is created, it has three significant advantages over other password attack methods. A rainbow table can be used repeatedly for attacks on other passwords; rainbow tables are much faster than dictionary attacks; and the amount of memory needed on the attacking machine is greatly reduced.

NOTE 11

Although once popular, rainbow tables are not used as extensively today due to advances in other password attack tools.

Password Collections   A watershed moment in password attacks occurred in late 2009. An attacker using an SQL injection attack broke into a server belonging to a developer of several popular social media applications. This server contained more than 32 million user passwords, all in cleartext. These passwords were later posted on the Internet.

Attackers quickly seized upon this opportunity. This "treasure trove" collection of passwords gave attackers, for the first time, a large corpus of real-world passwords. Because users repeat their passwords on multiple accounts, attackers could now use these passwords as candidate passwords in their attacks with a high probability of success.

Using stolen password collections as candidate passwords is the foundation of password cracking today, and almost all password cracking software tools accept these stolen "wordlists" as input. Websites host lists of these leaked passwords that attackers can download along with important statistics and masks for a rule attack. These sites also attempt to crack submitted password collections. One website boasts more than 1.45 *trillion* cracked hashes.

NOTE 12

Password collections provide attackers advanced insight into the strategic thinking of how users create passwords. For example, on those occasions when users mix uppercase and lowercase in passwords, users tend to capitalize at the beginning of the password, much like writing a sentence. Likewise, punctuation and numbers are more likely to appear at the end of the password, again mimicking standard sentence writing. A high percentage of passwords was comprised of a name and date, such as *Braden2008*. Such insights are valuable in rule attacks, significantly reducing the amount of time needed to break a password when compared to a raw brute force attack.

Most threat actors do not use a single password attack tool but use several in combination. Table 12-3 lists a common sequence of attack tools on passwords.

Table 12-3   Common sequence of password attack tools

Order	Password attack	Explanation
1	Custom wordlist	Download a stolen password collection
2	Custom wordlist using rule attack	Generate password statistics using a rule attack to create specialized masks
3	Dictionary attack	Perform a dictionary attack on passwords
4	Dictionary attack using rules	Conduct a refined dictionary attack using results from a rule attack
5	Updated custom wordlist using rules	Input any cracked passwords from previous steps to create more refined rules
6	Hybrid attack	Perform a focused dictionary attack with a mask attack
7	Mask attack	Conduct a mask attack on harder passwords that have not already been cracked
8	Brute force attack	Last-resort effort on any remaining passwords

NOTE 13

Note that Table 12-3 assumes that a sample of the passwords in plaintext can be examined; if this is not available, then most attacks will skip to Step 3, which results in enough cracked passwords so that rules can be developed for the next step.

Something You Have: Smartphone and Security Keys

Another type of authentication credential is based on the approved user having a specific item in his possession (something you have). Such items are often used along with passwords. Because this involves more than one type of authentication credential—both what a user knows (the password) and what the user has—this type of authentication credential is called **multifactor authentication (MFA)**. Using just one type of authentication is called *single-factor authentication*, and using two types is called *two-factor authentication (2FA)*. The most common items that are used for this type of authentication are specialized devices, smartphones, and security keys.

Specialized Devices

Two specialized devices provide authentication based on something you have. These are smart cards and windowed tokens.

Smart Cards   A smart card is a credit-card-sized plastic card that can hold information to be used as part of the authentication process. Smart cards used for authentication generally require that the card be inserted into a card reader that is connected to the computer, although some cards are contactless cards that only require it to be in close proximity to the reader.

Smart cards are used in specialized settings. For example, one type of smart card is currently being distributed by the U.S. government. A *common access card (CAC)* is a U.S. Department of Defense (DoD) smart card that is used for identification of active-duty and reserve military personnel along with civilian employees and special contractors. In addition to an integrated circuit chip, it has a bar code and magnetic stripe along with the bearer's picture and printed information. This card can be used to authenticate the owner as well as for encryption.

NOTE 14

The smart card standard covering all U.S. government employees is the Personal Identity Verification (PIV) standard.

There are several disadvantages to smart cards. Each device that uses smart card authentication must have a specialized hardware reader and device driver software installed. Also, smart cards that have a magnetic strip (called *magnetic stripe cards*) are subject to unauthorized duplication called card cloning. Stealing this information is often done by a process called skimming, in which a threat actor attaches a small device that fits just inside the card readers so that when the card is inserted and removed, both the actual reader and the skimming device capture the information from the magnetic strip.

Windowed Tokens   A hardware windowed token is typically a small device (usually one that can be affixed to a keychain called a *key fob*) with a window display. A windowed token is shown in Figure 12-4. A windowed token does not display a value that never changes (static code); instead, the value dynamically changes. This value is a *one-time password (OTP)*, which is an authentication code that can be used only once or for a limited period of time.

Figure 12-4   Windowed token

There are two types of OTPs. A time-based one-time password (TOTP) changes after a set period of time. As illustrated in Figure 12-5, the windowed token and a corresponding authentication server share an algorithm (each user's token has a different algorithm), and the token generates a code from the algorithm once every 30 to 60 seconds. (This code is valid for only the brief period that it is displayed on the token.) The user logs in by entering a username along with the code currently being displayed on the token. When the authentication server receives it, the server looks up the algorithm associated with that specific user, generates its own code, and then compares it with what the user entered. If they are identical, the user is authenticated.

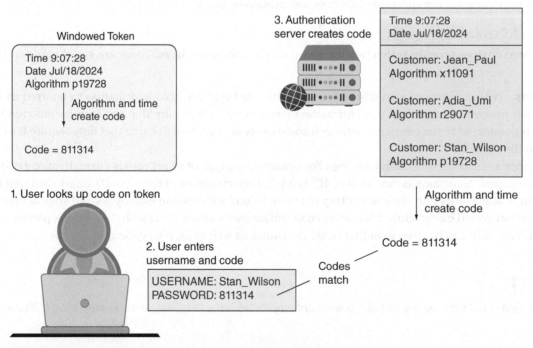

Figure 12-5   Time-based one-time password (TOTP)

NOTE 15

The TOTP is not transmitted to the token; instead, both the token and authentication server have the same algorithm and time setting.

Instead of changing after a set number of seconds, an **HMAC-based one-time password (HOTP)** password is "event driven" and changes when a specific event occurs, such as when a user enters a personal identification number (PIN) on the token's keypad, which triggers the token to create a random code. For example, after entering the PIN *1729*, the code *833854* is displayed.

While windowed tokens have some advantages, such as creating dynamic OTPs, they are considered cumbersome to use. Once an OTP is received, it must then be manually entered on the endpoint device. Because the OTP is valid for only a short time, the user must enter it quickly.

Smartphones

Whereas smart cards and windowed tokens are specialized devices, using a smartphone for authentication is considered a more practical approach. Because smartphones are ubiquitous and carried by users virtually everywhere, they can be used for authentication by a wide range of users without the need for an additional device.

Once users enter their username and password on the endpoint, their smartphone (something they have) is then used for the second authentication factor. Authentication through using a smartphone can be accomplished by the following:

- *Phone call.* An automated **phone call** to the user's smartphone asks if the user has requested to log in and, if so, to press a digit on the keypad for approval or to decline if the user has not just tried to log in.
- *SMS text message.* Another option is for the user to receive an OTP in an SMS text message. The user must then manually enter the OTP.
- *Authentication app.* An **authentication app** can be installed on the smartphone to authenticate the user. When the app is first installed, the user goes through a verification process. Whenever a user attempts to log in to an account by entering a username and password, a message is displayed on a specified phone (called a **push notification**) through the authentication app that asks the user to approve or deny the request. Using an authentication app is seen in Figure 12-6.

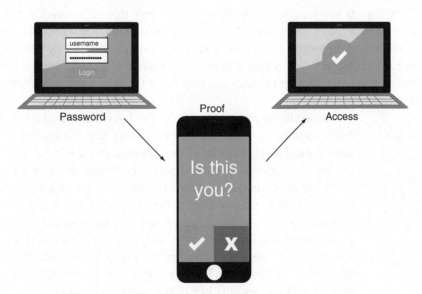

Figure 12-6   Authentication app

Despite its convenience and ability to reach a wide range of users, using a smartphone for authentication is not considered to be a secure option. An OTP received through an SMS text message can be "phished" (when a user is tricked into providing it to an attacker through a phishing attack), SMS text messages can be intercepted, and a malware infection on the phone can target the authentication app.

NOTE 16

Another authentication method involves certificate-based authentication, which is using digital certificates to authenticate a user before granting access. For example, when users go to a website that requires authentication, the web browser will prompt users for their client certificate. However, a user must select the correct certificate and the user's identity is then transmitted through the browser. Certificate-based authentication is not considered to be a viable option.

Security Keys

A secure option that is gaining acceptance is using a dedicated token key, more commonly called a security key. As seen in Figure 12-7, a security key is a dongle that is inserted into the USB port (Windows and Apple) or Lightning port (Apple) or held near the endpoint (such as a smartphone using near field communication, or NFC). It contains all the necessary cryptographic information to authenticate the user.

Source: Google LLC

Figure 12-7   Security keys

One feature of security keys is attestation. Attestation is a key pair that is "burned" into the security key during manufacturing time and is specific to a device model. It can be used to cryptographically prove that a user has a specific model of device when it is registered. When a user creates a new credential key pair (that links to a specific service like Facebook or PayPal), the public key that is sent to the service is signed with the attestation private key. The service that is creating the new account for the user can verify that the attestation signature on the newly created public key came from the device.

NOTE 17

Security keys do not transmit OTPs that can be intercepted or phished and are considered easier to use. Many security professionals recommend that users consider security keys as alternatives to other types of MFA.

Generally speaking, attestation keys have associated attestation certificates, and those certificates chain to a root certificate that the service trusts. This is how the service establishes its trust in the authenticator's attestation key.

Security keys can be used when logging in to an endpoint device and when accessing online accounts. Some security key systems require that users must initially enroll *two* security keys in the event that one is lost or destroyed. Once the keys are enrolled, all devices that may be logged in to the user's account are then automatically logged out and can only be logged back in using one of the keys as a second factor. Users must also use the keys when logging in from any new endpoint devices for the first time. However, once a device is authenticated, by default, it no longer needs the security key during subsequent logins.

Something You Are: Biometrics

In addition to authentication based on what a person knows or has, another category rests on the features and characteristics of the individual. This type of authentication, something you are, involves physiological biometrics and cognitive biometrics.

Physiological Biometrics

Physiological means *relating to the way in which a body part functions*. For authentication, physiological biometrics uses the way in which a body part uniquely functions in an individual. Several unique characteristics of a person's body can be used to authenticate a user. These can be divided into those that require specialized biometric scanners and those that use standard technology input devices for recognition. However, there are several issues regarding using biometrics.

Specialized Biometric Scanners   Some types of biometric authentication require specialized and dedicated biometric scanners that are inspect a person's features. A retinal scanner uses the human **retina** as a biometric identifier. The retina is a layer at the back (posterior) portion of the eyeball that contains cells sensitive to light, which trigger nerve impulses that pass these through the optic nerve to the brain, where a visual image is formed. Due to the complex structure of the capillaries that supply the retina with blood, each person's retina is unique.

A retinal scanner maps the unique patterns of a retina by directing a beam of low-energy infrared light (IR) into people's eyes as they look in the scanner's eyepiece (the beam cannot be detected by a user). Because retinal blood vessels are more absorbent of IR than the rest of the eye, the amount of reflection varies during the scan. This pattern of variations is recorded and used for comparison when the user attempts to authenticate.

> **NOTE 18**
>
> The network of blood vessels in the retina is so complex that even identical twins do not share a similar pattern. Even though retinal patterns may be altered in cases of diabetes, glaucoma, or retinal degenerative disorders, the retina generally remains unchanged through a person's lifetime.

Using a **fingerprint** as a biometric identifier has become the most common type of biometric authentication. Every user's fingerprint consists of several ridges and valleys, with ridges being the upper skin layer segments of the finger and valleys the lower segments. In one method of fingerprint scanning, the scanner locates the point where these ridges end and split, converts them into a unique series of numbers, and then stores the information as a template. A second method creates a template from selected locations on the finger.

There are two basic types of fingerprint scanners. A *static fingerprint scanner* requires the user to place the entire thumb or finger on a small oval window on the scanner. The scanner takes an optical "picture" of the fingerprint and compares it with the fingerprint image on file. The other type of scanner is known as a *dynamic fingerprint scanner*. A dynamic fingerprint scanner has a small slit or opening, as shown in Figure 12-8.

Figure 12-8   Dynamic fingerprint scanner

> **NOTE 19**
>
> Dynamic fingerprint scanners work on the same principle as stud finders that carpenters use to locate wood studs behind drywall. This is known as capacitive technology.

Another human characteristic that can be used for authentication is a person's **vein** (one of the "tubes" that form part of the blood circulation system in the human body that carries oxygen-depleted blood back toward the heart). Typically vein images in a user's palm or finger for authentication can be identified through a vein-scanning tablet.

A person's **gait**, or manner of walking, can also uniquely authenticate an individual. Research has shown that gait recognition can achieve greater than 99 percent accuracy. Typically, small sensors less than an inch in height can be placed on a floor at intervals of about 65 feet (20 meters) to measure gait.

NOTE 20

The payment provider Mastercard is working on developing a system that would uniquely identify mass transit passengers so that they do not need to swipe a transit card.

Standard Input Devices   Unlike some biometric identifiers that require specialized scanners, other types of biometrics can use standard computer input devices for recognition, such as a microphone or camera.

Because all users' voices are different, **voice** recognition, using a standard computer microphone, can be used to authenticate users based on the unique characteristics of a person's voice. Several characteristics make each person's voice unique, from the size of the head to age. These differences can be quantified to create a user voice template.

> **⊘ CAUTION**   Voice recognition is not to be confused with speech recognition, which accepts spoken words for input as if they had been typed on the keyboard.

NOTE 21

To protect against even the remote possibility of an attacker attempting to mimic a user's voice, identification phrases can be selected that would rarely (if ever) come up in normal speech.

One of the concerns regarding voice recognition is that an attacker could record the user's voice and then create a recording to use for authentication. However, this would be difficult to do. Humans speak in phrases and sentences instead of isolated words. The *phonetic cadence*, or speaking two words together in a way that one word "bleeds" into the next word, becomes part of each user's speech pattern. It would be difficult to capture several hours of someone's voice, parse it into separate words, and then combine the words in real time to defeat voice recognition security.

An iris scanner, which can use a standard computer webcam, uses the unique characteristic of the **iris**, which is a thin, circular structure in the eye. A human iris is seen in Figure 12-9. The iris is responsible for controlling the diameter and size of the pupils to regulate the amount of light reaching the retina. Iris recognition identifies the unique random patterns in an iris for authentication.

Figure 12-9   Iris

creativemarc/Shutterstock.com

NOTE 22

A person's eye color is actually the color of the iris, which is most often brown, blue, or green. In some cases, it can be hazel, grey, violet, or even pink.

A biometric authentication that is becoming increasingly popular—but also controversial—is facial recognition. Every person's face has several distinguishable "landmarks" that make up their facial features. These landmarks are called *nodal points*. Each human face has approximately 80 nodal points, such as the width of the nose, the depth of the eye sockets, the shape of the cheekbones, and the length of the jaw line. Using a standard computer webcam, facial recognition software can measure the nodal points and create a numerical code (*faceprint*) that represents the face.

NOTE 23

Facial recognition is frequently used by law enforcement agencies to scan crowds for missing children, fugitive criminals, or even terrorists. This type of recognition is much less precise than personal facial recognition using a smartphone or computer for authentication. This is because variations in the lighting in a large crowd make recognition difficult, a cap or hat can obscure the subject's face, or the subject might not look directly into the camera. These limitations can partially be overcome by using a 3-D camera to compare against 3-D images.

Biometric Disadvantages Using biometrics has four disadvantages. The first is the cost for specialized biometric scanners. These scanners must be installed at each location where authentication is required.

The second disadvantage is that biometric authentication is not foolproof: genuine users may be rejected while imposters are accepted. The false acceptance rate (FAR) or *false positive* is the frequency at which imposters are accepted as genuine, while the false rejection rate (FRR) or *false negative* is the frequency that legitimate users are rejected. Biometric systems are tuned so that the FAR and FRR are equal over the size of the population (called the crossover error rate (CER)). Ideally, the CER should be as low as possible to produce the lowest number of accepted imposters and rejected legitimate users.

Not only do biometric sensors provide false positives and false negatives; often biometric systems can be "tricked." Security researchers have demonstrated that fingerprints can be collected from water glasses and used to trick fingerprint readers on smartphones. Tricking an iris recognition system requires taking a picture of the authentic user's eye with a digital camera in "night" mode or with the infrared filter removed. The iris picture is then printed by a color laser printer. To emulate the curvature of the eye, a normal contact lens is placed on top of the print. This can successfully trick the iris recognition system into thinking the user's real eye is in front of the camera.

A final concern with biometrics is the efficacy rate. *Efficacy* may be defined as the benefit achieved. While biometrics can aid in authentication, some experts question the sacrifice of user privacy: as individuals provide their biometric characteristics, how can this data be kept secure? Who can have access to it? How can it be used? The trade-offs continue to be weighed across society.

NOTE 24

Currently, six states have biometric privacy laws in place. The first and oldest regulation dating back to 2008 is the Illinois Biometric Information Privacy Act (BIPA). It regulates the collection and storage of biometric information including retina scans, iris scans, fingerprints, palm prints, voice recognition, facial-geometry recognition, DNA recognition, gait recognition, and even scent recognition. A 2019 court ruling held that people do not have to prove they were actually harmed by the use of their biometric data in order to file a case.

Cognitive Biometrics

Whereas most biometrics considers a person's physical characteristics, the field of *cognitive biometrics* is related to the perception, thought process, and understanding of the user. Cognitive biometrics is considered to be much easier for the user to remember because it is based on the user's life experiences. This also makes it more difficult for an attacker to imitate. Cognitive biometrics is also called knowledge-based authentication.

One type of cognitive biometrics introduced by Microsoft is called Windows Picture Password for Windows 10 touch-enabled devices. Users select a picture that has at least 10 "points of interest" that can serve as "landmarks" or places to touch, connect with a line, or draw a circle around. Specific gestures—tap, line, or circle—are then used to highlight any parts of the picture while these gestures are recorded. When logging in, a user reproduces those same gestures on the photograph, as illustrated in Figure 12-10. For attackers to replicate these actions, they would need to know the parts of the image that were highlighted, the order of the gestures, the direction, and the starting and ending points of the circles and lines. However, security researchers have found that one of the most common methods used in Picture Password was using a photo of a person and triple tapping on the face, with the most common face tap is the eyes, followed by nose and jaw.

Figure 12-10 Picture password authentication

NOTE 25

Other examples of cognitive biometrics include requiring someone to identify specific faces or recall "memorable events," such as taking a special vacation, celebrating a personal achievement, or attending a specific family dinner. The user is asked specific questions about that memorable event, such as what type of food was served, how old the person was when the event occurred, where the event was located, who was in attendance, and the reason for the event. The user authenticates by answering the same series of questions when logging in.

Something You Do: Behavioral Biometrics

Another type of authentication is based on actions that the user is uniquely qualified to perform, or something you do. This is sometimes called *behavioral biometrics*.

One type of behavioral biometrics is *keystroke dynamics*, which recognizes a user's unique typing rhythm. Keystroke dynamics uses two unique typing variables. The first is known as *dwell time*, which is the time it takes for a key to be pressed and then released. The second characteristic is *flight time*, or the time between keystrokes (both "down" when the key is pressed and "up" when the key is released are measured). After collecting multiple typing samples, a user template can be formed so that when the user enters a username and password to log in, the typing rhythm is compared to the template. If both what was entered (the password) and how it was entered (the typing rhythm) are correct, then the user is authenticated; otherwise, the user is rejected. This is shown in Figure 12-11.

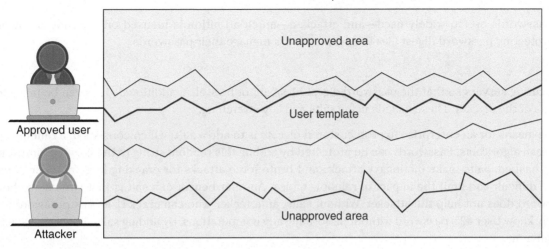

Username password

Figure 12-11   Authentication by keystroke dynamics

Keystroke dynamics holds a great deal of potential. Because it requires no specialized hardware and because the user does not have to take any additional steps beyond entering a username and password, some security experts predict that keystroke dynamics will become more widespread in the near future.

TWO RIGHTS & A WRONG

1. Password crackers differ as to when candidate digests are created.
2. Online brute force attacks are considered impractical.
3. An HMAC-based one-time password (HOTP) password is "event driven."

See Appendix B for the answer.

AUTHENTICATION SOLUTIONS

✔ CERTIFICATION

2.4 Summarize authentication and authorization design concepts.

2.8 Summarize the basics of cryptographic concepts.

3.2 Given a scenario, implement host or application security solutions.

3.5 Given a scenario, implement secure mobile solutions.

3.7 Given a scenario, implement identity and account management controls.

3.8 Given a scenario, implement authentication and authorization solutions.

There are several solutions for securing authentication. These include security surrounding passwords and secure authentication technologies.

NOTE 26

Solutions for protecting authentication services in the cloud are similar to protecting other cloud services and are covered in Module 10. The solutions here are primarily on-prem protections.

Password Security

Because passwords are so widely used—and attacked—much attention is focused on securing passwords. This includes protecting password digest files and helping users manage their passwords.

Protecting Password Digests

Besides securing servers so that the password digest files cannot be stolen, additional steps can be taken to protect the contents of the digests. These include using salts and key stretching.

Salts   One means for an enterprise to protect stored digests is to add a salt, which consists of a random string that is used in hash algorithms. Passwords can be protected by adding this random string to the user's plaintext password before it is hashed. Salts make dictionary attacks and brute force attacks for cracking large number of passwords much more difficult and limit the impact of rainbow tables. Another benefit of a salt is that two users choosing the same password does not help the attacker. Without salts, an attacker who can crack User #1's password would also immediately know User #2's password without performing any computations. By adding salts, however, each password digest is different.

 **CAUTION**   Salts should be random (never sequential like *0001*, *0002*, etc.) and unique for each user.

Applying salts is not just limited to protected stored password digests. Salts can also be applied to sensitive information contained in a database. Database data can be further protected by hashing data and using tokenization.

NOTE 27

Tokenization is covered in Module 9.

Key Stretching   Using general-purpose hash algorithms such as MD5 and SHA is not considered secure for creating digests because these hashing algorithms are designed to create a digest as quickly as possible. The speed of general-purpose hash algorithms works in an attacker's favor. When an attacker is creating candidate digests, a general-purpose hashing algorithm can rapidly create a large number of passwords for matching purposes.

A more secure approach for creating password digests is to use a specialized password hash algorithm that is intentionally designed to be slower. This would then limit the ability of an attacker to crack passwords because it requires significantly more time to create each candidate digest, thus slowing down the entire cracking process. This is called key stretching. Two popular key stretching password hash algorithms are bcrypt and PBKDF2. These can be configured to require more time to create a digest. A network administrator can specify the number of iterations (*rounds*), which sets how "expensive" (in terms of computer time and/or resources) the password hash function will be. Whereas the increased time is a minor inconvenience when one user logs in and waits for the password digest to be generated, it can significantly reduce attackers' speed of generating candidates.

NOTE 28

Using a general password algorithm, an attacker could generate about 95^8 candidate passwords in 5.5 hours. However, using bcrypt, only 71,000 candidate passwords could be generated in that same amount of time.

However, the problem with key stretching is that CPUs continue to process faster and faster, so yesterday's key stretching algorithms may become too fast with tomorrow's processors. The original standards written in 2000 for key stretching recommended at least 1,000 iterations. Today, iterations of 100,000 are not uncommon. To address this, a competition was initiated to develop an even stronger key stretching algorithm. After working through 24 proposals, a winner was announced: *Argon2*. Argon2 can be configured based on several different parameters: adding a salt (which must be between 8 and 16 characters), the number of iterations (default of three), and the memory usage (default parameter of 12).

Managing Passwords

While password digest files must be secured, it is likewise important that individual user passwords be kept safe. The most critical factor in a strong password is not complexity but length: a longer password is always more secure than a shorter password. This is because the longer a password is, the more attempts an attacker must make to break it. The formula for determining the number of possible passwords requires knowing only two items: the character set being used and the password length. Since the character set of most passwords is equal to the number of keys on a keyboard that can be used, the formula is *Number of Keyboard Keys ^ Password Length = Total Number of Possible Passwords*. Table 12-4 illustrates the number of possible passwords for different password lengths using a standard 95-key keyboard, along with the average attempts needed to break a password. Obviously, a longer password takes significantly more time to attempt to break than a short password.

Table 12-4   Number of possible passwords

Keyboard keys	Password length	Number of possible passwords	Average attempts to break password
95	2	9,025	4,513
95	3	857,375	428,688
95	4	81,450,625	40,725,313
95	5	7,737,809,375	3,868,904,688
95	6	735,091,890,625	367,545,945,313

NOTE 29

The average attempts to break a password is calculated as one-half of the total number of possible passwords. That is because an attack could break the password on the first attempt or on the very last attempt.

However, due to the limitations of human memory, it is virtually impossible for users to memorize long, complex, and unique passwords for all accounts. Instead of relying on human memory for passwords, security experts universally recommend using technology to store and manage passwords. The technology used for securing passwords includes using password vaults, password keys, and hardware modules.

Password Vaults   As its name implies, a **password vault** is a secure repository in which users can store their passwords. Also known as a *password manager*, there are three basic types:

- *Password generators.* These are web browser extensions that generate passwords. The user enters a master password and the password generator creates a password based on the master password and the website's URL "on the fly." The disadvantage of password generators is that the browser extension must be installed on each computer and web browser.
- *Online vaults.* An online vault also uses a web browser extension, but instead of creating the user's password each time, it retrieves the password from a central online repository. The disadvantage is that online sites storing the passwords are vulnerable to attackers.
- *Password management applications.* A password management application is a program installed on a computer through which the user can create and store multiple strong passwords in a single user "vault" file that is protected by one strong master password. Users can retrieve individual passwords as needed by opening the user file, thus freeing the user from need to memorize multiple passwords. The disadvantage is that the program must be carried with the user or installed on multiple computers.

NOTE 30

A password management application is recognized as having the highest level of security. However, these applications are more than a password-protected list of passwords: they typically include drag-and-drop capabilities, enhanced encryption, in-memory protection that prevents the OS cache from being exposed to reveal retrieved passwords, and timed clipboard clearing. Some password management applications can even require that a secret key file be present when entering the master password to open the vault so that even if the vault file was stolen, it still could not be opened. The value of using a password management application is that long, complex, and unique strong passwords can be easily created and used for all accounts.

Password Keys   A weakness of vaults is that they are software-based, making them susceptible to malware. More secure hardware-based solutions are also available in which to store passwords. They are called **password keys**. Just as a security key can be used by itself for MFA, a password key can also be used as a separate storage facility for passwords. Figure 12-12 illustrates a password key. Password keys often serve as a hardware-based password manager, two-factor security key, and file encryption device.

Source: OnlyKey

Figure 12-12   Password key

Hardware Modules   Comprehensive cryptographic hardware modules can also facilitate password management. A hardware security module (HSM) is a removable external cryptographic device. An HSM can be a USB device, an expansion card, a device that connects directly to a computer through a port, or a secure network server. An HSM includes an onboard random number generator and key storage facility, as well as accelerated symmetric and asymmetric encryption, and can even back up sensitive material in encrypted form.

An example of an HSM in a small consumer-oriented form factor is a **MicroSD HSM**. A *Secure Digital (SD)* card is a small form factor storage media and has evolved from its inception in 1999 from a single card type and size to a variety of different types and sizes. The SD format includes four card "families" available in three form factors with different speed ratings. Currently, there are three sizes of SD cards: *full SD*, *miniSD*, and *microSD*. Full SD memory cards are typically used in personal computers, video cameras, digital cameras, and other large consumer electronics devices. MicroSD and miniSD cards are commonly used in smaller electronic devices like smartphones and tablets.

NOTE 31

HSM and TPM are covered in Module 6.

In addition to the HSM, the Trusted Platform Module (TPM) is a chip on the motherboard of the computer that provides cryptographic services. For example, TPM includes a true random number generator instead of a PRNG as well as full support for asymmetric encryption and can even generate public and private keys.

Secure Authentication Technologies

Several technologies can enhance secure authentication. These include single sign-on and authentication services.

Single Sign-On

One of the problems facing users today is the fact that they have many accounts across multiple platforms that each should use a unique username and password. Because managing different authentication credentials is difficult, users frequently compromise by selecting the least burdensome password and then use it for all accounts. A solution to this problem is to have one username and password to gain access to all accounts so that the user has only one username and password to remember.

This is the idea behind *identity management*, which is using a single authentication credential that is shared across multiple networks. When those networks are owned by different organizations, it is called federation (sometimes called *federated identity management* or *FIM*). One application of federation is single sign-on (SSO) or using one authentication credential to access multiple accounts or applications. SSO holds the promise of reducing the number of usernames and passwords that users must memorize (potentially, to just one).

NOTE 32

Several large Internet providers support SSO, but only for their own suite of services and applications. For example, a Google user can access all of Google's features—such as Gmail, Google Docs and Spreadsheets, Calendar, and Photos—by entering a single Google account username and password. Microsoft offers a similar service through its Microsoft Account. An advantage besides only using a single username and password is that settings made on one device are automatically synced with all other devices. However, these SSOs are proprietary and restricted to Google or Microsoft applications and are not "federated" with other organizations.

There are several current technologies for federation systems. These are listed in Table 12-5.

Table 12-5   Federation systems technologies

Name	Description	Explanation
OAuth (Open Authorization)	Open source federation framework	OAuth 2.0 is a framework to support the development of authorization protocols.
Open ID	Open standard decentralized authentication protocol	Authentication protocol that can be used in OAuth 2.0 as a standard means to obtain user identity.
Shibboleth	Open source software package for designing SSO	Uses federation standards to provide SSO and exchanging attributes.

NOTE 33

OAuth relies upon token credentials. Users send their authentication credentials to a server (such as a web application server) and authorize the server to issue token credentials to a third-party server. These token credentials are used in place of transferring the user's username and password. The tokens are not generic but are for specific resources on a site for a limited period.

Authentication Services

A user accessing a computer system must present authentication credentials or identification when logging in to the system. Different services can be used to provide authentication. These include RADIUS, Kerberos, Terminal Access Control Access Control Systems, directory services, Security Assertion Markup Language, and authentication framework protocols.

RADIUS   RADIUS, or Remote Authentication Dial-In User Service, was developed in 1992 and quickly became the industry standard with widespread support across nearly all vendors of networking equipment. RADIUS was originally designed for remote dial-in access to a corporate network. However, the word *remote* in the name RADIUS is now almost a misnomer because RADIUS authentication is used for more than connecting to remote networks. With the development of IEEE 802.1x port security for both wired and wireless LANs, RADIUS has seen even greater usage.

NOTE 34

IEEE 802.1x is covered in Module 11.

A RADIUS client is not the device requesting authentication, such as a desktop system or wireless laptop computer. Instead, a RADIUS client is typically a device such as a wireless access point (AP) or dial-up server that is responsible for sending user credentials and connection parameters in the form of a RADIUS message to a RADIUS server. The RADIUS server authenticates and authorizes the RADIUS client request and sends back a RADIUS message response. RADIUS clients also send RADIUS accounting messages to RADIUS servers. The strength of RADIUS is that messages are never sent directly between the wireless device and the RADIUS server. This prevents an attacker from penetrating the RADIUS server and compromising security.

The detailed steps for RADIUS authentication with a wireless device in an IEEE 802.1x network, which are illustrated in Figure 12-13, are as follows:

1. A wireless device, called the *supplicant* (it makes an "appeal" for access), sends a request to an access point (AP) requesting permission to join the wireless LAN (WLAN). The AP prompts the user for the user ID and password.

2. The AP, serving as the *authenticator* that will accept or reject the wireless device, creates a data packet from this information called the *authentication request*. This packet includes information such as identification of the specific AP that is sending the authentication request and the user name and password. For protection from eavesdropping, the AP (acting as a RADIUS client) encrypts the password before it is sent to the RADIUS server. The authentication request is sent over the network from the AP to the RADIUS server. This communication can be done over either a local area network or a wide area network. This allows the RADIUS clients to be remotely located from the RADIUS server. If the RADIUS server cannot be reached, the AP can usually route the request to an alternate server.

3. When an authentication request is received, the RADIUS server validates that the request is from an approved AP and then decrypts the data packet to access the username and password information. This information is passed on to the appropriate security user database. This could be a text file, UNIX password file, a commercially available security system, or a custom database.

4. If the username and password are correct, the RADIUS server sends an authentication acknowledgment that includes information on the user's network system and service requirements. For example, the RADIUS server may tell the AP that the user needs TCP/IP. The acknowledgment can even contain filtering information to limit a user's access to specific resources on the network. If the username and password are not correct, the RADIUS server sends an authentication reject message to the AP and the user is denied access to the network. To ensure that requests are not responded to by unauthorized persons or devices on the network, the RADIUS server sends an authentication key, or signature, identifying itself to the RADIUS client.

5. If accounting is also supported by the RADIUS server, an entry is started in the accounting database.

6. Once the server information is received and verified by the AP, it enables the necessary configuration to deliver the wireless services to the user.

RADIUS allows an organization to maintain user profiles in a central database that all remote servers can share. Doing so increases security, allowing a company to set up a policy that can be applied at a single administered network point. Having a central service also means that it is easier to track usage for billing and for keeping network statistics.

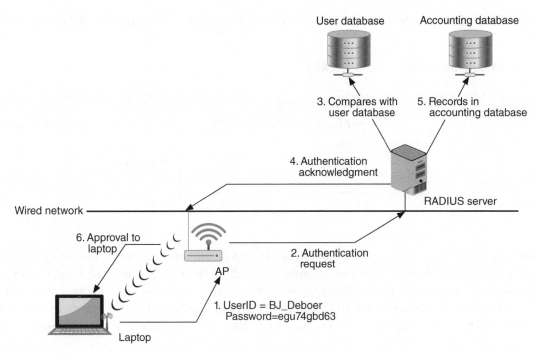

Figure 12-13 RADIUS authentication

Kerberos **Kerberos** is an authentication system developed by the Massachusetts Institute of Technology (MIT) in the 1980s and used to verify the identity of networked users. Named after a three-headed dog in Greek mythology that guarded the gates of Hades, Kerberos uses encryption and authentication for security. Kerberos will function under Windows, macOS, and Linux.

Kerberos has often been compared to using a driver's license to cash a check. A state agency, such as the Department of Motor Vehicles (DMV), issues a driver's license that has these characteristics:

- It is difficult to copy.
- It contains specific information (name, address, weight, height, etc.).
- It lists restrictions (must wear corrective lenses, etc.).
- It will expire at some future date.

Kerberos, which works in a similar fashion, is typically used when a user attempts to access a network service and that service requires authentication. The user is provided a ticket that is issued by the Kerberos authentication server, much as a driver's license is issued by the DMV. This ticket contains information linking it to the user. The user presents this ticket to the network for a service. The service then examines the ticket to verify the identity of the user. If the user is verified, he is then accepted. Kerberos tickets share some of the same characteristics as a driver's license: tickets are difficult to copy (because they are encrypted), they contain specific user information, they restrict what a user can do, and they expire after a few hours or a day. Issuing and submitting tickets in a Kerberos system is handled internally and is transparent to the user.

Terminal Access Control Access Control System+ (TACACS+) Similar to RADIUS, *Terminal Access Control Access Control System (TACACS)* is an authentication service commonly used on UNIX devices that communicates by forwarding user authentication information to a centralized server. The centralized server can be either a TACACS database or a database such as a Linux or UNIX password file with TACACS protocol support. The first version was simply called TACACS, while a later version introduced in 1990 was known as *Extended TACACS (XTACACS)*. The current version is **TACACS+**.

NOTE 35

TACACS is a proprietary system developed by Cisco Systems.

There are several differences between TACACS+ and RADIUS. These are summarized in Table 12-6.

Table 12-6 Comparison of RADIUS and TACACS+

Feature	RADIUS	TACACS+
Transport protocol	User Datagram Protocol (UDP)	Transmission Control Protocol (TCP)
Authentication and authorization	Combined	Separate
Communication	Unencrypted	Encrypted
Interacts with Kerberos	No	Yes
Can authenticate network devices	No	Yes

Directory Service A directory service is a database stored on the network itself that contains information about users and network devices. It contains information such as the user's name, telephone extension, email address, login name, and other facts. The directory service also keeps track of all the resources on the network and a user's privileges to those resources and grants or denies access based on the directory service information. Directory services make it much easier to grant privileges or permissions to network users and provide authentication.

Security Assertion Markup Language (SAML) Security Assertion Markup Language (SAML) is an XML standard that allows secure web domains to exchange user authentication and authorization data. This allows a user's login credentials to be stored with a single identity provider instead of being stored on each web service provider's server. SAML is used extensively for online e-commerce business-to-business (B2B) and business-to-consumer (B2C) transactions. The steps of a SAML transaction, which are illustrated in Figure 12-14, are as follows:

1. The user attempts to reach a website of a service provider that requires a username and password.
2. The service provider generates a SAML authentication request that is then encoded and embedded into a URL.
3. The service provider sends a redirect URL to the user's browser that includes the encoded SAML authentication request, which is then sent to the identity provider.

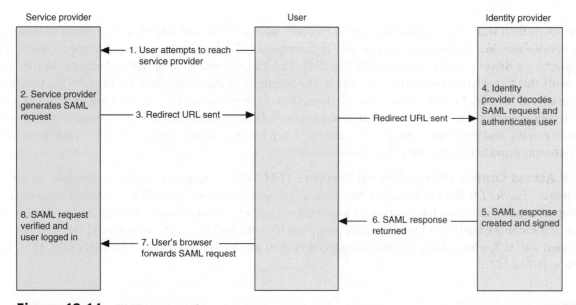

Figure 12-14 SAML transaction

4. The identity provider decodes the SAML request and extracts the embedded URL. The identity provider then attempts to authenticate the user either by asking for login credentials or by checking for valid session cookies.

5. The identity provider generates a SAML response that contains the authenticated user's username, which is then digitally signed using asymmetric cryptography.

6. The identity partner encodes the SAML response and returns that information to the user's browser.

7. Within the SAML response, there is a mechanism so that the user's browser can forward that information back to the service provider, either by displaying a form that requires the user to click a *Submit* button or by automatically sending to the service provider.

8. The service provider verifies the SAML response by using the identity provider's public key. If the response is successfully verified, the user is logged in.

NOTE 36

SAML works with multiple protocols including Hypertext Transfer Protocol (HTTP), Simple Mail Transfer Protocol (SMTP), and File Transfer Protocol (FTP).

Authentication Framework Protocols In an IEEE 802.1x configuration, communication between the supplicant, authenticator, and authentication server must be secure. A framework for transporting the authentication protocols is known as the *Extensible Authentication Protocol (EAP)*. EAP was created as a more secure alternative than the weak **Challenge-Handshake Authentication Protocol (CHAP)**, the Microsoft version of CHAP (**MS-CHAP**), and **Password Authentication Protocol (PAP)**. Despite its name, EAP is a *framework* for transporting authentication protocols instead of the authentication protocol itself. EAP essentially defines the format of the messages and uses four types of packets: *request*, *response*, *success*, and *failure*. Request packets are issued by the authenticator and ask for a response packet from the supplicant. Any number of request-response exchanges may be used to complete the authentication. If the authentication is successful, a success packet is sent to the supplicant; if not, a failure packet is sent.

NOTE 37

An EAP packet contains a field that indicates the function of the packet (such as response or request) and an identifier field used to match requests and responses. Response and request packets also have a field that indicates the type of data being transported (such as an authentication protocol) along with the data itself.

TWO RIGHTS & A WRONG

1. A salt is a random string that is used in hash algorithms.
2. Two popular key stretching password hash algorithms are bcrypt and PBKDF2.
3. A complex password (*xi8s7$t#6%*) is more secure than a long password (*thisisalongpassword*).

See Appendix B for the answer.

> ⤢ **VM LAB** You're now ready to complete the live, virtual machine labs for this module. The labs can be found in the Practice It folder in each MindTap module.

SUMMARY

- Authentication is proof of genuineness. Three authentication elements (something you know, something you have, and something you are) are called factors while the remaining four (somewhere you are, something you can do, something you exhibit, and someone you know) are called attributes. In information technology (IT), these types of elements are known as authentication credentials and are presented to an IT system to verify the genuineness of the user. Although any of these elements can be used as an authentication credential, the most common in IT are something you know, something you have, something you are, and something you can do.

- The most common "something you know" type of authentication (and any type of authentication) is a password. A password is a secret combination of letters, numbers, and/or characters that only the user should have knowledge of. Passwords provide a weak degree of protection because they rely on human memory. Human beings have a finite limit to the number of items that they can memorize. Because of the burdens that passwords place on human memory, users often take shortcuts to help them recall their passwords.

- While some attacks on passwords involve the attacker entering a password "guess" at a login prompt, these have a low rate of success. Instead, attackers use a different technique that generates a high success rate. Attackers steal the file of password digests and then load that file onto their own computers so they can attempt to discover the passwords through password cracking software. These programs create known digests (called candidates) and then compare them against the stolen digests. When a match occurs, then the attacker knows the underlying password. Password crackers differ as to how these candidates are created.

- One password attack that does not attempt to steal a file of password digests instead uses a type of "targeted guessing." A password spraying attack uses one or a small number of commonly used passwords and then uses this same password when trying to login to several different user accounts. Unlike a password spraying attack in which one password is used on multiple accounts, in an online brute force attack, the attacker continuously attacks the same account by entering different passwords. However, a password spraying attack is not considered to be practical.

- An offline brute force attack begins with a stolen digest file. An attacker loads this file onto their computer and then uses password cracking software to create candidate digests of every possible combination of letters, numbers, and characters. These are then matched against those in a stolen digest file looking for a match. A rule attack conducts a statistical analysis on the stolen passwords. The result of this analysis is then used to create a mask of the format of the candidate password. A dictionary attack begins with the attacker creating digests of common dictionary words as candidates and then comparing them against those in a stolen digest file. Dictionary attacks are successful because users often create passwords from simple dictionary words. Rainbow tables make password attacks easier by creating a large pregenerated data set of candidate digests. A rainbow table is a compressed representation of passwords that are related and organized in a sequence (called a chain). Using stolen password collections as candidate passwords is the foundation of password cracking today. Websites host lists of these leaked passwords that attackers can download along with important statistics and masks for a rule attack.

- Another type of authentication credential is based on approved users having a specific item in their possession (something you have). Such items are often used along with passwords, and because this involves more than one type of authentication credential, this is called multifactor authentication (MFA). Two specialized devices provide authentication based on something you have. A smart card is a credit-card-sized plastic card that can hold information to be used as part of the authentication process. Smart cards used for authentication generally require that the card be inserted into a card reader that is connected to the computer, although some cards are contactless cards that only require it to be in very close proximity to the reader. A hardware windowed token is typically a small device with a window display. A windowed token does not display a value that never changes (static code); instead, the value dynamically changes. This value is a one-time password (OTP), which is an authentication code that can be used only once or for a limited period of time.

- Whereas smart cards and windowed tokens are specialized devices, using a smartphone for authentication is considered a more practical approach. Authentication through using a smartphone can be accomplished by an automated phone call, an SMS text message, or through an authentication app using push notification. A more secure option that is gaining acceptance is using a dedicated token key, more commonly called a security key. A security key is a dongle that is inserted into the computer's port or held near the endpoint (such as a smartphone using near field communication or NFC). It contains all the necessary cryptographic information to authenticate the user.

- The features and characteristics of the individual (something you are) can serve as authentication. Physiological biometrics uses a person's unique physical characteristics for authentication. This includes fingerprints, retinas, voice, iris, facial recognition, veins, and gait. There are disadvantages to biometrics. Cognitive biometrics is related to the perception, thought process, and understanding of the user. Cognitive biometrics is considered to be much easier for the user because it is based on the user's life experiences, which also makes it difficult for an attacker to imitate. Behavioral biometrics, or something you do, authenticates by normal actions that the user performs. Behavioral biometric technologies include keystroke dynamics.

- There are several solutions for securing authentication. One means for an enterprise to protect stored digests is to add a salt, which consists of a random string that is used in hash algorithms. Passwords can be protected by adding this random string to the user's plaintext password before it is hashed. Using general-purpose hash algorithms is not considered secure for creating digests because these hashing algorithms are designed to create a digest as quickly as possible. The speed of general-purpose hash algorithms works in an attacker's favor. A more secure approach for creating password digests is to use a specialized password hash algorithm that is intentionally designed to be slower. This would then limit the ability of an attacker to crack passwords because it requires significantly more time to create each candidate digest, thus slowing down the entire cracking process. This is called key stretching.

- While password digest files must be secured, it is likewise important that individual user passwords be kept safe. The most critical factor in a strong password is not complexity but length: a longer password is always more secure than a shorter password. This is because the longer a password is, the more attempts an attacker must make to break it. A password vault, also known as a password manager, is a secure repository in which users can store their passwords. A hardware-based password key can also be used as a separate storage facility for passwords. Comprehensive cryptographic hardware modules can also facilitate password management.

- Identity management is using a single authentication credential that is shared across multiple networks. When those networks are owned by different organizations, it is called federation. One application of federation is single sign-on (SSO), or using one authentication credential to access multiple accounts or applications. A user accessing a computer system must present authentication credentials or identification when logging in to the system. Different services can be used to provide authentication. RADIUS authentication is used for both wired and wireless LANs. Kerberos is an authentication system used to verify the identity of networked users. Terminal Access Control Access Control System (TACACS) is an authentication service commonly used on UNIX devices that communicates by forwarding user authentication information to a centralized server. A directory service is a database stored on the network itself that contains information about users and network devices. Directory services make it much easier to grant privileges or permissions to network users and provide authentication. A framework for transporting the authentication protocols is known as the Extensible Authentication Protocol (EAP). EAP was created as a more secure alternative than the weak Challenge-Handshake Authentication Protocol (CHAP), the Microsoft version of CHAP (MS-CHAP), and Password Authentication Protocol (PAP).

Key Terms

attestation
authentication
authentication app
brute force attack
card cloning
Challenge-Handshake
  Authentication Protocol (CHAP)
crossover error rate (CER)
dictionary attack
directory service

efficacy rate
facial recognition
false acceptance rate (FAR)
false rejection rate (FRR)
federation
fingerprint
gait
HMAC-based one-time password
  (HOTP)
iris

Kerberos
key stretching
knowledge-based authentication
MicroSD HSM
MS-CHAP
multifactor authentication (MFA)
OAuth (Open Authorization)
offline brute force attack
online brute force attack
Open ID

pass the hash
password
Password Authentication Protocol
  (PAP)
password crackers
password keys
password spraying
password vault
phone call
push notification
RADIUS (Remote Authentication
  Dial-In User Service)

rainbow tables
retina
salt
Security Assertion Markup
  Language (SAML)
security key
single sign-on (SSO)
skimming
smart card
someone you know
something you are
something you can do

something you exhibit
something you have
something you know
somewhere you are
static code
TACACS+
time-based one-time password
  (TOTP)
token
token key
vein
voice

Review Questions

1. How is the Security Assertion Markup Language (SAML) used?
   a. It serves as a backup to a RADIUS server.
   b. It allows secure web domains to exchange user authentication and authorization data.
   c. It is an authenticator in IEEE 802.1x.
   d. It is no longer used because it has been replaced by LDAP.

2. Which of the following is the Microsoft version of EAP?
   a. EAP-MS
   b. AD-EAP
   c. PAP-Microsoft
   d. MS-CHAP

3. Which of the following is NOT used for authentication?
   a. Somewhere you are
   b. Something you exhibit
   c. Something you can do
   d. Something you can find

4. Ilya has been asked to recommend a federation system technology that is an open source federation framework that can support the development of authorization protocols. Which of these technologies would he recommend?
   a. OAuth
   b. Open ID
   c. Shibboleth
   d. NTLM

5. How is key stretching effective in resisting password attacks?
   a. It takes more time to generate candidate password digests.
   b. It requires the use of GPUs.
   c. It does not require the use of salts.
   d. The license fees are very expensive to purchase and use it.

6. Which of these is NOT a reason that users create weak passwords?
   a. A lengthy and complex password can be difficult to memorize.
   b. A security policy requires a password to be changed regularly.
   c. Having multiple passwords makes it hard to remember all of them.
   d. The length and complexity required force users to circumvent creating strong passwords.

7. Fernando is explaining to a colleague how a password cracker works. Which of the following is a valid statement about password crackers?
   a. Most states prohibit password crackers unless they are used to retrieve a lost password.
   b. Due to their advanced capabilities, they require only a small amount of computing power.
   c. A password cracker attempts to uncover the type of hash algorithm that created the digest because once it is known, the password is broken.
   d. Password crackers differ as to how candidates are created.

8. Which attack uses one or a small number of commonly used passwords to attempt to log in to several different user accounts?
   a. Online brute force attack
   b. Offline brute force attack
   c. Password spraying attack
   d. Role attack

9. Why are dictionary attacks successful?
   a. Password crackers using a dictionary attack require less RAM than other types of password crackers.
   b. They link known words together in a "string" for faster processing.
   c. Users often create passwords from dictionary words.
   d. They use pregenerated rules to speed up the processing.

10. Which of these attacks is the last-resort effort in cracking a stolen password digest file?
   a. Hybrid
   b. Mask
   c. Rule list
   d. Brute force

11. Which of the following should NOT be stored in a secure password database?
   a. Iterations
   b. Password digest
   c. Salt
   d. Plaintext password

12. Which of the following is NOT an MFA using a smartphone?
   a. Authentication app
   b. Biometric gait analysis
   c. SMS text message
   d. Automated phone call

13. Timur was making a presentation regarding how attackers break passwords. His presentation demonstrated the attack technique that is the slowest yet most thorough attack that is used against passwords. Which of these password attacks did he demonstrate?
   a. Dictionary attack
   b. Hybrid attack
   c. Custom attack
   d. Brute force attack

14. Which human characteristic is NOT used for biometric identification?
   a. Retina
   b. Iris
   c. Height
   d. Fingerprint

15. _____ biometrics is related to the perception, thought processes, and understanding of the user.
   a. Cognitive
   b. Standard
   c. Intelligent
   d. Behavioral

16. Which of the following is an authentication credential used to access multiple accounts or applications?
   a. Single sign-on
   b. Credentialization
   c. Identification authentication
   d. Federal login

17. What is a disadvantage of biometric readers?
   a. Speed
   b. Cost
   c. Weight
   d. Standards

18. Which of these creates a format of the candidate password to significantly reduce the time needed to crack a password?
   a. Rainbow
   b. Mask
   c. Rule
   d. Pass the hash

19. Pablo has been asked to look into security keys that have a feature of a key pair that is "burned" into the security key during manufacturing time and is specific to a device model. What feature is this?
   a. Authorization
   b. Authentication
   c. Attestation
   d. Accountability

20. Which one-time password is event driven?
   a. HOTP
   b. TOTP
   c. ROTP
   d. POTP

Hands-On Projects

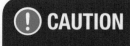 **CAUTION** If you are concerned about installing any of the software in these projects on your regular computer, you can instead use the Windows Sandbox or install the software in the Windows virtual machine created in the Module 1 Hands-On Projects. Software installed within the virtual machine will not impact the host computer.

Project 12-1: Using an Online Password Cracker

Time Required: 20 minutes

Objective: 4.1 Given a scenario, use the appropriate tool to assess organizational security.
- Password crackers

Description: In this project, you create a hash on a password and then crack it through an online dictionary attack to demonstrate the speed of cracking passwords that use dictionary words.

1. The first step is to use a general-purpose hash algorithm to create a password hash. Use your web browser to go to **www.fileformat.info/tool/hash.htm**. (The location of content on the Internet may change without warning; if you are no longer able to access the program through this URL, use a search engine and search for "Fileformat.info.")
2. Under **String hash**, enter the simple password **apple123** in the **Text** box.
3. Click **Hash**.
4. Scroll down the page and copy the MD5 hash of this password to your Clipboard by selecting the text, right-clicking it, and choosing **Copy**.
5. Open a new tab on your web browser.
6. Go to **https://crackstation.net/**.
7. Paste the MD5 hash of *apple123* into the text box below **Enter up to 20 non-salted hashes, one per line**.
8. Follow the directions to affirm that you are not an automated device.
9. Click **Crack Hashes**.
10. How long did it take to crack this hash?
11. Click the browser tab to return to FileFormat.Info.
12. Under **String hash**, enter the longer password **applesauce1234** in the **Text** box.
13. Click **Hash**.
14. Scroll down the page and copy the MD5 hash of this password to your Clipboard.
15. Click the browser tab to return to the CrackStation site.
16. Paste the MD5 hash of *applesauce1234* into the text box below **Enter up to 20 non-salted hashes, one per line**.
17. Follow the directions to affirm that you are not an automated device, and then click **Crack Hashes**.
18. How long did it take this online rainbow table to crack the stronger password hash?
19. Click the browser tab to return to FileFormat.Info and experiment by entering new passwords, computing their hash, and testing them in the CrackStation site. If you are bold, enter a string hash that is similar to a real password that you use.
20. What does this tell you about the speed of password cracking tools? What does it tell you about how easy it is for attackers to crack weak passwords?
21. Close all windows.

Project 12-2: Using Facial Recognition Software with Federation Technology

Time Required: 25 minutes

Objective: 2.4 Summarize authentication and authorization design concepts.
- Biometrics

Description: Facial recognition is a biometric authentication that is becoming increasingly popular on smartphones. In this project, you download and use a facial recognition app that supports the federation technologies OAuth running on OpenID Connect and uses multifactor authentication. You need either an Apple iOS or Android device for this project.

1. On your mobile device, launch either the Apple App Store or Android Play Store app.
2. Search for **BioID Facial Recognition Authenticator**.

3. Download and install this app on your mobile device.
4. Click **Open**.
5. Use your web browser to go to **mobile.bioid.com**. (If you are no longer able to access the program through this URL, use a search engine and search for "BioID Facial Recognition.")
6. Follow the instructions to create an account.
7. Return to your mobile device, sign in to BioID, and then click **Register**.
8. Click **Yes**.
9. Click **Allow**.
10. Follow the instructions to take four sets of pictures.
11. Click **Verify**. You are now logged in using BioID. Close this app and log in again using different positions of your face. How easy is this to use? How accurate is it?
12. Open a web browser and enter the URL **playground.bioid.com**.
13. Click **Sign in or register**.
14. Click your user name to view your account information.
15. Click **Biometrics** in the left pane.
16. Under **Biometric template**, click **Examine** and then **Face** to display the photos. Read through the information and delete any photos that would not be helpful in recognizing your face. Be sure to keep at least four photos.
17. Return to the **My BioID profile** page.
18. Under **Challenge-response**, click **Enable** and read through the information. What additional degree of protection would this give you? Close the pop-up window.
19. Click **Multi-factor** in the left pane.
20. Under **Time-based one-time password (TOTP)**, click **Synchronize**. Read this information. What additional degree of protection would this give you? Click the browser's back button.
21. Under **Multi-factor authentication**, click **Configure**. Read this information. What additional degree of protection would this give you? Click the browser's back button.
22. How much would you trust this application for your authentication? Would you use it to replace your passwords? Why or why not?
23. Close all windows.

Project 12-3: Practicing Keystroke Dynamics

Time Required: 25 minutes
Objective: 2.4 Summarize authentication and authorization design concepts.
- Biometrics

Description: One type of behavioral biometrics is keystroke dynamics, which attempts to recognize a user's unique typing rhythm. In this project, you will use an online site that illustrates keystroke dynamics.

1. Use your web browser to go to **typingdna.com**. (If you are no longer able to access the program through this URL, use a search engine and search for "Typingdna.")
2. Click **Quick demo**.
3. Under **Login authentication**, click **Start demo**.
4. Enter your email and a fictitious password. Note that as you type, your information is being recorded.
5. Click **Start demo**.
6. Review and accept the terms.
7. Click **Start demo**.
8. Click **Try authentication**.
9. Enter your email and password again and log in. What percentage did you achieve?
10. Click **Try again** and this time try to alter your typing cadence. Were you able to make the program think that you are not authentic?
11. Now ask a friend to enter your email and password information. What was the result?
12. Under **Try other demos**, select one or two different demos, and determine the results. If possible, have your friend register and try to imitate their typing cadence.
13. How reliable would you consider this technology to be? How useful could it be?
14. Close all windows.

Project 12-4: Installing a Password Vault

Time Required: 25 minutes

Objective: 3.8 Given a scenario, implement authentication and authorization solutions.
- Password vaults

Description: The drawback to using strong passwords is that they can be very difficult to remember, particularly when a unique password is used for each account that a user has. As another option, password management programs allow users to store account information such as a username and password. These programs are themselves protected by a single strong password. One example of a password storage program is KeePass Password Safe, which is an open source product. In this project, you download and install KeePass.

1. Use your web browser to go to **keepass.info** and then click **Downloads**. (If you are no longer able to access the program through this URL, use a search engine and search for "KeePass.")
2. Locate the most recent portable version of KeePass and click it to download the application. Save this file in a location such as your desktop, a folder designated by your instructor, or your portable USB flash drive. When the file finishes downloading, extract and then install the program. Accept the installation defaults.

NOTE 38

Because this is the portable version of KeePass, it does not install under Windows. To use it after installation, you must double-click the filename KeePass.exe.

3. Launch KeePass to display the opening screen.
4. Click **File** and then **New** to start a password database. Enter a strong master password for the database to protect all the passwords in it.
5. Click **Entry** and then **Add Entry**. You will enter information about an online account that has a password that you already use.
6. Create a group by clicking **Group** and then **Add Group**. Enter **Websites** and then click **OK**.
7. Select the **Websites** group in the left pane, click **Entry**, and then click **Add Entry**.
8. Enter a title for your website (such as *Google Gmail*) under **Title**.
9. Under **User name**, enter the username that you use to log in to this account.
10. Delete the entries under **Password** and **Repeat** and enter the password that you use for this account and confirm it.
11. Enter the URL for this account under **URL**.
12. Click **OK**.
13. Click **File** and then **Save**. Enter your last name as the file name and then click **Save**.
14. Exit KeePass.
15. If necessary, navigate to the location of KeePass and double-click the file **KeePass.exe** to launch the application.
16. Enter your master password to open your password file.
17. If necessary, click the group to locate the account you just entered; it will be displayed in the right pane.
18. Click under **URL** to go to that website.
19. Click KeePass in the taskbar so that the window is now on top of your browser window.
20. Drag and drop your username from KeePass into the login username box for this account in your web browser.
21. Drag and drop your password from KeePass for this account.
22. Click the button on your browser to log in to this account.
23. Because you can drag and drop your account information from KeePass, you do not have to memorize any account passwords and can instead create strong passwords for each account. Is this an application that would help users create and use strong passwords? What are the strengths of such password programs? What are the weaknesses? Would you use KeePass?
24. Close all windows.

Project 12-5: Using Cognitive Biometrics

Time Required: 20 minutes

Objective: 2.4 Summarize authentication and authorization design concepts.
- Biometrics

Description: Cognitive biometrics holds great promise for adding two-factor authentication without placing a tremendous burden on the user. In this project, you participate in a demonstration of Passfaces.

1. Use your web browser to go to **www.passfaces.com/demo**. (If you are no longer able to access the program through this URL, use a search engine and search for "Passfaces demo.")
2. Under **First Time Users**, enter the requested information and then click **START THE DEMO**.
3. Click **Start the Demo**.
4. If you are prompted, accept **demo** as the name, and then click **OK**.
5. When asked, click **NEXT** to enroll now.
6. When the **Enroll in Passfaces** dialog box is displayed, click **NEXT**.
7. Look closely at the three faces you are presented with. After you are familiar with the faces, click **NEXT**.
8. You will then be asked to think of associations with the first face (who it looks like or who it reminds you of). Follow each step with the faces and then click **NEXT** after each face.
9. When the **STEP 2 Practice Using Passfaces** dialog box is displayed, click **NEXT**.
10. You will then select your faces from three separate screens, each of which has nine total faces. Click the face (which is also moving as a hint).
11. You can practice one more time. Click **NEXT**.
12. When the **STEP 3 Try Logging On with Passfaces** dialog box is displayed, click **NEXT**. Identify your faces, and click **NEXT**.
13. Click **DONE** and click **OK**.
14. Click **Try Passfaces** and then click **Logon**.
15. Click **OK** under the username and identify your faces.
16. Is this type of cognitive biometrics effective? If you came back to this site tomorrow, would you remember the three faces?
17. Close all windows.

Project 12-6: Using Windows Picture Password

Time Required: 25 minutes
Objective: 2.4 Summarize authentication and authorization design concepts.
- Biometrics

Description: In this project, you use another cognitive biometrics tool, Windows Picture Password.

1. Select a photo or other image that you want to use as a picture password. Be sure the image is clear enough so that you can create lines, dots, or circles easily and distinctively.
2. Click **Start**, then **Settings**, then **Accounts**, and finally **Sign-in options**.
3. In the right pane, scroll down and click **Picture Password**.
4. Click **Add**.
5. Enter your password when requested, and click **OK**.
6. Windows displays a generic image along with details. Click **Choose Picture**.
7. Navigate to the location of the picture that you want to use.
8. Double-click that picture.
9. Click **Use this picture**.
10. You will now create three gestures for this photo. They can be any combinations of circles, lines, and taps. On the initial screen use your mouse, stylus, or finger to draw a circle, line, or dot on the screen.
11. Windows will then prompt you to add two more gestures.
12. Windows displays an outline of the gestures for your review. You can either click **Start over** or accept these gestures.
13. Be sure to remember each gesture in sequence and where they occur on the photo. When requested, draw them again for confirmation.
14. Close all windows.
15. Now try your picture password. Click **Start** and **Sign out**.
16. Press any key when the lock screen appears to display the sign-in options along with your picture.
17. Draw the gestures to sign in. If you are unable to recreate them, click **Sign-in options** to enter your password.
18. How easy is picture password to use? How difficult? Would you consider it more or less secure than a password? Why?

Case Projects

Case Project 12-1: Testing Password Strength

How strong are your passwords? Various online tools can provide information on password strength, but not all feedback is the same. First, assign the numbers 1 through 3 to three passwords that are very similar (but not identical) to passwords you are currently using, and write down the number (not the password) on a piece of paper. Then, enter those passwords into these three online password testing services:

- How Secure Is My Password (*howsecureismypassword.net/*)
- Password Checker Online (*password-checker.online-domain-tools.com*)
- Password Meter (*www.passwordmeter.com/*)

Record next to each number the strength of that password as indicated by these three online tools. Then use each online password tester to modify the password by adding more random numbers or letters to increase its strength. How secure are your passwords? Would any of these tools encourage someone to create a stronger password? Which provided the best information? Create a one-paragraph summary of your findings.

Case Project 12-2: Password Management Applications

Research at least four password vaults, more commonly known as password management applications, one of which is a stand-alone application and another of which is a browser-based application. Create a table that lists and compares their features. Which would you recommend? Why? Create a report on your findings.

Case Project 12-3: Create Your Own Cognitive Biometric Memorable Event

What type of cognitive biometric "memorable event" do you think would be effective? Design your own example that is different from those given in the module. There should be five steps, and each step should have at least seven options. The final step should be a fill-in-the-blank user response. Compare your steps with those of other learners. Which do you think would be the easiest for users?

Case Project 12-4: Biometric Analysis

Use the Internet and other sources to research the two disadvantages of standard biometrics: cost and error rates. Select one biometric technique (fingerprint, palm print, iris, facial features, etc.) and research the costs for having biometric readers for that technique located at two separate entrances into a building. Next, research ways in which attackers attempt to defeat this particular standard biometric technique. Finally, how often will this technique reject authorized users while accepting unauthorized users compared to other standard biometric techniques? Based on your research, would you recommend this technique? Why or why not? Write a one-page paper on your findings.

Case Project 12-5: Password Requirements

Visit the website Passwords Requirements Shaming (**password-shaming.tumblr.com**), which is a list of password requirements for different websites that are considered weak. Read through several of the submissions. Select three that you consider the most egregious. Why are they the worst? Next, indicate what you would suggest to make the requirement stronger, while maintaining a requirement that most users could meet. Write a one-paragraph summary.

Case Project 12-6: Security Assertion Markup Language (SAML)

Use the Internet to research SAML. What are its features? How is it being used? What are its advantages and disadvantages? Write a one-page paper on your research.

Case Project 12-7: Log In With Other Sites

When logging in to an online account sometimes the option is provided for the user to log in using a different set of authentication credentials, such as "Log in With Facebook" in which the user's Facebook username and password is used instead. Research the rewards and risks of logging in using authentication credentials from other sites. Is this like SSO? What are the advantages? What are the disadvantages? Is this safe? Would you recommend it? Write a one-page paper on your research.

Case Project 12-8: Biometric Laws

Several states now have biometric laws, and others are considering similar legislation. Research these laws that are currently in place from three states. Compare the laws. Are they sufficient? What are their weaknesses? Finally, create your own law that you believe would protect the biometric data of users. Write a one-page paper on your research.

Case Project 12-9: North Ridge Security

North Ridge Security provides security consulting and assurance services. You have recently been hired as an intern to assist them.

You have been asked to make a presentation for a local community group about password security.

1. Create a PowerPoint presentation for the group about the risks of weak passwords and how to create strong passwords. Include information about security keys and how smartphones can be used for MFA. Your presentation should contain at least 10 slides.
2. After the presentation, the community group has asked for your recommendation on security vaults and keys. Use the Internet to identify two of each type that you would recommend and create a memo to the group that includes why you see these as being strong choices.

Case Project 12-10: Community Site Activity

The Information Security Community Site is an online companion to this textbook. It contains a wide variety of tools, information, discussion boards, and other features to assist learners. Go to **community.cengage.com/infosec2** and click the *Join or Sign in* icon to log in, using your login name and password that you created in Module 1. Click **Forums (Discussion)** and click on **Security+ Case Projects (7ᵗʰ edition)**. Read the following case study.

Should facial recognition be limited for identification? What are the risks of having public cameras attempt to identify known criminals? Does that outweigh the potential benefits of being able to find a kidnapped child? Should there be restrictions on facial recognition? If so, what should they be? Record your thoughts on the Community Site discussion board.

References

1. Lady, Kyle, "A security analysis of over 500 million usernames and passwords," *Duo Labs*, May 11, 2017, retrieved Jul. 27, 2020, https://duo.com/blog/a-security-analysis-of-over-500-million-usernames-and-passwords.
2. Schneier, Bruce, *Secrets and Lies: Digital Security in a Networked World* (New York: Wiley Computer Publishing), 2004.

INCIDENT PREPARATION, RESPONSE, AND INVESTIGATION

After completing this module, you should be able to do the following:

1. Explain the steps in preparing for a cybersecurity incident
2. Describe how to respond in an incident
3. List the steps in an incident investigation

Front-Page Cybersecurity

Suppose that in your house or apartment you have something very valuable (a rare gemstone, a roll of cash, or a famous painting, for example). Unfortunately, a burglar finds out about it and wants to steal it. He waits until you are away from home one night and decides that now is his chance. He tries to open the front door and finds that it is securely locked. Would he then just walk away?

Probably not. Instead, he would look for a different entry point. He might check the windows in the garage, and if he finds that one of them is easy to force open, he enters the garage. He then works on the door in the garage that leads to the kitchen and opens it. He moves through the house until he finally arrives at the room where your valuable is hidden. He grabs it and disappears.

How this fictitious burglar works is how a cybersecurity attacker works. All the efforts focus on a single word: pivot. Synonyms of pivot are rotate, turn, revolve, spin, swivel, twirl, whirl, and wheel about. That's how burglars and cybersecurity attackers work today; they swiftly move from the initial entry point to other locations until they find what they are seeking.

Security researchers spend long hours analyzing how a successful cybersecurity incident occurs. This analysis helps to provide information about how threat actors can successfully compromise a system, information the victim can use to strengthen the system from future attacks. It also helps security personnel at other organizations understand how attacks take place and shore up their systems, too.

Analyzing successful cybersecurity incidents has resulted in a recipe that attackers generally follow in an attack. The steps are as follows:

1. The attackers first conduct reconnaissance against the systems, looking for vulnerabilities.
2. When a path to a vulnerability is exposed, they gain access to the system through the vulnerability.
3. Once access is gained, the attackers escalate that access to acquire more advanced privileges.
4. With the advanced privileges, they tunnel through the network looking for additional systems they can access from their elevated position.
5. Attackers install tools on the compromised systems to gain even deeper access to the network.

6. Attackers may install a backdoor that allows them repeated and long-term access to the system. The backdoors are not related to the initial vulnerability, so access remains even if the initial vulnerability is corrected.

7. Once the backdoor is installed, the attackers continue to probe until they find their ultimate target and perform their intended malicious action.

What lesson can be learned about pivoting? Think back to the burglar. Would a homeowner spend huge amounts of money on having a super-strong front door to prevent the burglar from entering the house—but not bother to even lock the garage windows? Of course not.

Yet that's what often happens when it comes to the thinking on cybersecurity. Many users, for example, decide that an email account does not need to have a strong password. Because almost all online accounts allow users to reset their password by sending a reset link to their email account, what would happen if an attacker could gain access to that email account? He could have password resets for all of the user's accounts sent to that single compromised email account, where he could then reset the password on these accounts to whatever he wanted. He could use those new passwords to enter these accounts and perform malicious actions like wiping out a bank account or gathering sensitive data.

Because cybersecurity attackers pivot like a burglar, there are no garage windows on our computers that can be left unlocked. Everything needs to be secured.

It is highly unlikely that any organization today would consider itself immune from a successful cybersecurity attack. Rather, virtually all organizations clearly understand that successful attacks are inevitable. That means that the sole focus of cybersecurity cannot be on trying to prevent an attack; rather, plans must be made for when a cybersecurity incident occurs.

The plans for preparing for an incident can be divided into three areas: incident preparation, incident response, and then a follow-up investigation as to how the incident occurred and how similar future events can be mitigated. In this module, you will study the three areas of incident preparation, response, and investigation.

INCIDENT PREPARATION

⊘ CERTIFICATION

2.1 Explain the importance of security concepts in an enterprise environment.

2.4 Summarize authentication and authorization design concepts.

3.5 Given a scenario, implement secure mobile solutions.

3.7 Given a scenario, implement identity and account management controls.

3.8 Given a scenario, implement authentication and authorization solutions.

4.2 Summarize the importance of policies, processes, and procedures for incident response.

4.1 Given a scenario, use the appropriate tool to assess organizational security.

5.5 Explain privacy and sensitive data concepts in relation to security.

Consider these two classical aphorisms: *Don't bury your head in the sand* and *An ounce of prevention is worth a pound of cure*. These pithy observations can directly apply to cybersecurity incident preparation. It is a major mistake to think that no attack could penetrate cybersecurity defenses, and being prepared for an incident significantly offsets the resources needed to recover from one if no preparations have been made. These **response and recovery controls**, or measures for identifying and counteracting security attacks, are essential.

Preparing for an incident first involves understanding the reasons such incidents are successful. This understanding can be useful in preparing for an incident.

Reasons for Cybersecurity Incidents

While there are any number of reasons a cybersecurity incident can occur, many can be classified into two broad areas. The first area is weak account types and the second is poor access control.

Weak Account Types

As outlined in the *Front-Page Cybersecurity* introduction to this module, once access is gained by threat actors, their next step is to pivot and then escalate that access to gain more advanced privileges. This is often achieved by looking for a **user account** (an approved identity between a user and an endpoint, network, or service) that has weak security and is associated with a high level of privileges. If this account can be compromised, the threat actors can imitate the owner of the account and use those privileges to access other protected systems, steal confidential data, or perform any number of nefarious activities.

Besides requiring strong authentication on user accounts, the accounts themselves should be routinely reviewed for security and, if necessary, be deleted or strengthened. For example, any **shared account** (an account used by more than one user), **generic account** (an account not tied to a specific person, such as *HelpDesk_1*), or **guest account** (given to temporary users) should be prohibited. These types of accounts that cannot be linked to a single authorized individual are common entry points threat actors compromise. In addition, a **service account**, which is a user account that is created explicitly to provide a security context for services running on a server, should be carefully configured so as not to provide more privileges than are absolutely necessary.

 **CAUTION** Suspicious accounts that are identified should be disabled (made inactive) instead of immediately deleted. Disabling an account serves to create an audit trail to conform with compliance regulations and makes the reestablishment of an account easier if further investigation reveals that the account is valid.

Poor Access Control

As its name implies, *access control* is granting or denying approval to use specific resources; it is controlling access. While physical access control consists of fencing, hardware door locks, and mantraps to limit contact with devices, technical access control consists of technology restrictions that limit users on digital devices from accessing resources and data. Access control has a set of associated concepts and terminology used to describe its actions. Standard access control schemes and access control lists are also used to help enforce access control, though these have their own weaknesses.

NOTE 1

Most home users have full privileges on their personal computers so they can install programs, access files, or delete folders at will and give no thought to access control. In the enterprise, however, where multiple individuals could potentially have access to sensitive information, access control is essential.

Access Control Concepts   Suppose that Gabe is babysitting his sister Mia one afternoon. Before leaving the house, his mother tells Gabe that a package delivery service is coming to pick up a box, which is inside the front door. Soon there is a knock at the door, and as Gabe looks out, he sees the delivery person standing on the porch. Gabe asks her to display her employee credentials, which the delivery person is pleased to do, and then he opens the door and allows her inside, but only to the area by the front door, to pick up the box. Gabe then signs the delivery person's tablet device so there is a confirmation record that the package was picked up.

This scenario illustrates the basic steps in limiting access. The package delivery person first presents an ID to Gabe to be reviewed. A user accessing a computer system would likewise present credentials or *identification*, such as a username, when logging in to the system. Identification is the process of recognizing and distinguishing the user from any other user. Checking the delivery person's credentials to be sure that they are authentic and not fabricated is *authentication*. Computer users, likewise, must have their credentials authenticated to ensure that they are who they claim to be, often by entering a password, fingerprint scan, or other means of authentication. Authorization, granting permission to take an action, is the next step. Gabe allowed the package delivery person to enter the house because she had been preapproved by Gabe's mother and her credentials were authentic. Likewise, once users have presented their identification and been authenticated, they can be authorized to log in to the system and access resources.

Gabe only allowed the package delivery person access to the area by the front door to retrieve the box; he did not allow her to go upstairs or into the kitchen. Likewise, computer users are granted access only to the specific services, devices, applications, and files needed to perform their job duties. Gabe signing on the tablet is akin to accounting, which is a record that is preserved of who accessed the network, what resources they accessed, and when they disconnected from the network. Accounting data can be used to provide an audit trail, and for billing, determining trends, identifying resource utilization, and future capacity planning. The basic steps in this access control process are summarized in Table 13-1.

NOTE 2

Authentication, authorization, and accounting are sometimes called AAA ("triple-A"), providing a framework for controlling access to computer resources.

Table 13-1 Basic steps in access control

Action	Description	Scenario example	Computer process
Identification	Review of credentials	Delivery person shows employee badge	User enters username
Authentication	Validate credentials as genuine	Gabe reads badge to determine it is real	User provides password
Authorization	Permission granted for admittance	Gabe opens door to allow delivery person in	User authorized to log in
Access	Right given to access specific resources	Delivery person can only retrieve box by door	User allowed to access only specific data
Accounting	Record of user actions	Gabe signs to confirm the package was picked up	Information recorded in log file

Other terminology describes how computer systems impose this technical access control:

- *Object*. An object is a specific resource, such as a file or a hardware device.
- *Subject*. A subject is a user or a process functioning on behalf of the user that attempts to access an object.
- *Operation*. The action that is taken by the subject over the object is called an operation. For example, a user (subject) may attempt to delete (operation) a file (object).

Individuals are given different roles in relationship to access control objects or resources. These roles are summarized in Table 13-2.

Figure 13-1 illustrates selected technical access control roles and terminology.

Access Control Schemes Consider a system administrator who needs to act as an access control data custodian/steward. One afternoon she must give a new employee access to specific servers and files. With hundreds of thousands of files scattered across a multitude of different servers, and with the new employee being given different access privileges to each file (for example, he can view one file but not edit it, but for a different file he can edit but not delete), controlling access could prove to be a daunting task.

Table 13-2   Roles in access control

Role	Description	Duties	Example
Data privacy officer (DPO)	Manager who oversees data privacy compliance and manages data risk	Ensures the enterprise complies with data privacy laws and its own privacy policies	Decides that users can have permission to access SALARY.XLSX
Data custodian/ steward	Individual to whom day-to-day actions have been assigned by the owner	Periodically reviews security settings and maintains records of access by end-users	Sets and reviews security settings on SALARY.XLSX
Data owner	Person responsible for the data	Determines the level of security needed for the data and delegates security duties as required	Determines that the file SALARY.XLSX can be read only by department managers
Data controller	Principal party for collecting the data	Acquire user's consent, store the data, and manage consent or revoking access	Gathers data for SALARY.XLSX and identifies where it is stored
Data processor	Proxy who acts on behalf of data controller	Person or agency that holds and processes personal data for a third party but does not make decisions about using the data and is not responsible for the data	Manages SALARY.XLSX file on behalf of data controller

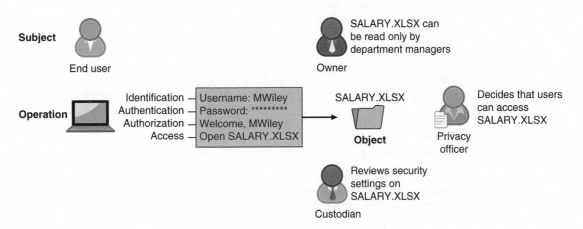

Figure 13-1   Technical access control roles and terminology

However, this job is made easier by the fact that the hardware and software have a predefined framework that the custodian can use for controlling access. This framework, called an **access control scheme**, is embedded in the software and hardware. The custodian/steward can use the appropriate scheme to configure the necessary level of control. Using these schemes is part of **privileged access management**, which is the technologies and strategies for controlling elevated (privileged) access and permissions.

NOTE 3

Access control schemes are variously referred to as access control models, methods, modes, techniques, or types. They are used by data custodians/stewards for access control but are neither created nor installed by them. Instead, these schemes are already part of the software and hardware.

There are five major access control schemes: Discretionary Access Control, Mandatory Access Control, Role-Based Access Control, Rule-Based Access Control, and Attribute-Based Access Control. Although the schemes can be used to help mitigate a threat actor's attempts at privilege elevation, they still have weaknesses and often result in cybersecurity incidences.

Discretionary Access Control (DAC)   The Discretionary Access Control (DAC) scheme is the least restrictive. With the DAC scheme, every object has an owner, who has total control over that object. Most importantly, the owner has discretion (the choice) as to who can access the owner's objects and can grant permissions to other subjects over these objects. DAC is used on major operating systems (OSs). Figure 13-2 illustrates the DAC that a Microsoft Windows owner has over an object. These controls can be configured so that another user can have full or limited access over a file, printer, or other object.

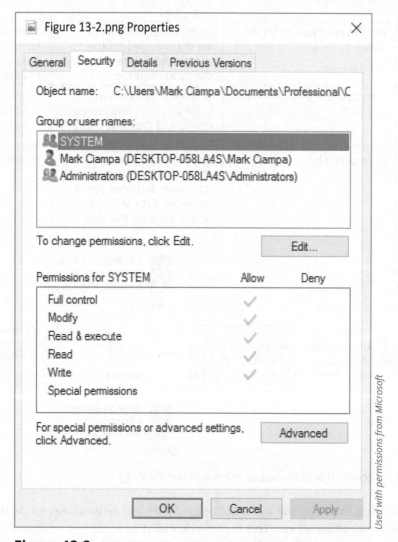

Figure 13-2   Windows Discretionary Access Control (DAC)

DAC has two significant weaknesses. First, although it gives a degree of freedom to the subject, DAC poses risks in that it relies on decisions made by the user to set the proper level of security. As a result, incorrect permissions might be granted to a subject or permissions might be given to an unauthorized subject. A second weakness is that a subject's permissions will be "inherited" by any programs that the subject executes. Threat actors often take advantage of this inheritance because users frequently have a high level of privileges. Malware downloaded onto a user's computer that uses the DAC scheme would then run at the same high level as the user's privileges.

Mandatory Access Control (MAC)   The opposite of DAC is the most restrictive access control scheme, Mandatory Access Control (MAC). MAC assigns users' access controls strictly according to the custodian's desires. This is considered the most restrictive access control scheme because the user has no freedom to set any controls or distribute access to other subjects. SEAndroid, which is a security-enhanced version of the Android operating system, uses MAC.

There are two key elements to MAC:

- *Labels.* In a system using MAC, every entity is an object (laptops, files, projects, and so on) and is assigned a classification label. These labels represent the relative importance of the object, such as *confidential, secret,* and *top secret.* Subjects (users, processes, and so on) are assigned a privilege label (sometimes called a *clearance*).
- *Levels.* A hierarchy based on the labels is also used, both for objects and subjects. *Top secret* has a higher level than *secret,* which has a higher level than *confidential.*

MAC grants permissions by matching object labels with subject labels based on their respective levels. To determine if a file can be opened by a user, the object and subject labels are compared. The subject must have an equal or greater level than the object in order to be granted access. For example, if the object label is *top secret,* yet the subject has only a lower *secret* clearance, access is denied. Subjects cannot change the labels of objects or other subjects to modify the security settings.

NOTE 4

In the original MAC scheme, all objects and subjects were assigned a numeric access level and the access level of the subject had to be higher than that of the object for access to be granted. For example, if EMPLOYEES.XLSX was assigned Level 500 while SALARIES.XLSX was assigned level 700, then a user with an assigned level of 600 could access EMPLOYEES.XLSX (Level 500) but not SALARIES.XLSX (Level 700). This scheme was later modified to use labels instead of numbers.

Microsoft Windows uses a MAC implementation called *Mandatory Integrity Control (MIC)* that ensures data integrity by controlling access to securable objects. A *security identifier (SID)* is a unique number issued to the user, group, or session. Each time a user logs in, the system retrieves the SID for that user from the database and then uses that SID to identify the user in all subsequent interactions with Windows security. Windows links the SID to an *integrity level.* Objects such as files, processes, services, and devices are assigned integrity levels—*low, medium, high,* and *system—* that determine their levels of protection or access. To write to or delete an object, the integrity level of the subject must be equal to or greater than the object's level. This ensures that processes running with a low integrity level cannot write to an object with a medium integrity level. MIC works in addition to Windows DAC: Windows first checks any requests against MIC, and if they pass, it checks DAC.

This can be seen in practice through a Windows feature known as *User Account Control (UAC).* The standard user (lower level) who attempts to install software (higher level) is first required by UAC to enter the higher-level administrative password before being allowed to proceed (which elevates the action to the higher level). As an additional check, an administrative user also must confirm the action (yet does not need to enter the administrative password). In this way, UAC attempts to match the subject's privilege level with that of the object.

NOTE 5

By default, Windows switches to "Secure Desktop mode" when the UAC prompt appears. Secure Desktop mode allows only trusted processes with the integrity level *System* to run, which prevents malware from "spoofing" what appears on the screen to trick users. Secure Desktop mode is similar to what appears when a Windows login screen appears or the keystroke combination Ctrl+Alt+Delete is pressed. In Secure Desktop mode, users cannot click any icon other than the Windows prompt.

Role-Based Access Control   The third access control scheme is Role-Based Access Control (RBAC), sometimes called *Non-Discretionary Access Control.* RBAC is considered a more "real-world" access control than the other schemes because the access under RBAC is based on a user's job function within an organization. Instead of setting permissions for each user or group, the RBAC scheme assigns permissions to particular roles in the organization and then assigns users to those roles. Objects are set to be a certain type, to which subjects with that particular role have access. For example, instead of creating a user account for Ahmed and assigning specific privileges to that account, the role

Business_Manager can be created based on the privileges an individual in that job function should have. Ahmed and all other business managers in the organization can then be assigned to that role. The users and objects inherit all the permissions for the role.

Rule-Based Access Control   The Rule-Based Access Control scheme, also called the *Rule-Based Role-Based Access Control (RB-RBAC)* scheme or *automated provisioning*, can dynamically assign roles to subjects based on a set of rules defined by a custodian (called conditional access). Each resource object contains a set of access properties based on the rules. When a user attempts to access that resource, the system checks the rules contained in that object to determine if the access is permissible.

Rule-Based Access Control is often used for managing user access to one or more systems, where business changes may trigger the application of the rules that specify access changes. For example, a subject on Network A wants to access objects on Network B, which is located on the other side of a router. This router contains the set of access control rules and can assign a certain role to the user, based on the network address or protocol, which will then determine whether the user will be granted access. Similar to MAC, Rule-Based Access Control cannot be changed by users. All access permissions are controlled based on rules established by the custodian or system administrator.

Attribute-Based Access Control   While the Rule-Based Access Control scheme uses predefined rules, Attribute-Based Access Control (ABAC) uses more flexible policies that can combine attributes. These policies can take advantage of many types of attributes, such as object attributes, subject attributes, and environment attributes. ABAC rules can be formatted using an *If-Then-Else* structure, so that a policy can be created such as *If this subject has the role of manager, then grant access; else deny access.*

NOTE 6

ABAC systems can also enforce both DAC and MAC schemes.

Table 13-3 summarizes the features of the five access control schemes.

Table 13-3   Access control schemes

Name	Explanation	Description
Mandatory Access Control (MAC)	End-user cannot set controls	Most restrictive scheme
Discretionary Access Control (DAC)	Subject has total control over objects	Least restrictive scheme
Role-Based Access Control (RBAC)	Assigns permissions to particular roles in the organization and then users are assigned to roles	Considered a more "real-world" approach
Rule-Based Access Control	Dynamically assigns roles to subjects based on a set of rules defined by a custodian	Used for managing user access to one or more systems
Attribute-Based Access Control (ABAC)	Uses policies that can combine attributes	Most flexible scheme

Access Control Lists (ACLs)   An access control list (ACL) is a set of permissions that is attached to an object. This list specifies which subjects are allowed to access the object and what operations they can perform on it. When a subject requests permission to perform an operation on an object, the system checks the ACL for an approved entry in order to decide if the operation is allowed.

Although ACLs can be associated with any type of object, these lists are most often viewed in relation to files maintained by the OS. All OSs use a *filesystem*, which is a method for storing and organizing computer files to facilitate access. ACLs provide filesystem permissions for protecting files managed by the OS. ACLs have also been ported to SQL and relational database systems so that ACLs can provide database security as well.

NOTE 7

ACLs are the oldest and most basic form of access control. These became popular in the 1970s with the growth of multiuser systems, particularly UNIX systems, when it became necessary to limit access to files and data on shared systems. Later, as multiuser operating systems for personal use became popular, the concept of ACLs was added to them. Today all major OS make use of ACLs at some level.

Although widely used, ACLs have limitations. First, using ACLs is not efficient. The ACL for each file, process, or resource must be checked every time the resource is accessed. ACLs control not only user access to system resources but also application and system access. This means that in a typical computing session, ACLs are checked whenever a user accesses files, when applications are opened (along with the files and applications those applications open and modify), when the operating system performs certain functions, and so on. A second limitation to ACLs is that they can be difficult to manage in an enterprise setting where many users need to have different levels of access to many different resources. Selectively adding, deleting, and changing ACLs on individual files, or even groups of files, can be time consuming and open to errors, particularly if changes must be made frequently.

Preparing for an Incident

Due to weak account types, poor access control, and other vulnerabilities that lead to successful attacks, it is important to prepare in advance for an incident. The steps to take in preparation are creating an incident response plan, performing exercises, and studying attack frameworks.

Creating an Incident Response Plan

System weaknesses that lead to successful attacks mean that a formal plan of action is essential. An **incident response plan** is a set of written instructions for reacting to a security incident. Without such a plan, enterprises are at risk of being unable to quickly identify the attack, contain its spread, recover, and learn from the attack to improve defenses.

The six action steps to be taken when an incident occurs, called the **incident response process**, also make up the six elements of an incident response plan. These are listed in Table 13-4.

Table 13-4   Incident response process

Action step	Description
Preparation	Equipping IT staff, management, and users to handle potential incidents when they arise
Identification	Determining whether an event is actually a security incident
Containment	Limiting the damage of the incident and isolating those systems that are impacted to prevent further damage
Eradication	Finding the cause of the incident and temporarily removing any systems that may be causing damage
Recovery	After ensuring no threat remains, permitting affected systems to return to normal operation
Lessons learned	Completing incident documentation, performing detailed analysis to increase security and improve future response efforts

At a minimum, an incident response plan should contain the following information:

- *Documented incident definitions*. The plan should provide clear descriptions of the types and categories of documented incident definitions, which outline in detail what is—and is not—an incident that requires a response.
- *Incident response teams*. An **incident response team** is responsible for responding to security incidents. In addition to technical specialists who can address specific threats, it should also include members who are public relations employees and managers who can guide enterprise executives on appropriate communication. Each member should have clearly designated duties, roles, and responsibilities in the team.

- *Reporting requirements/escalation.* The reporting requirements/escalation indicates to whom information should be distributed and at what point the security event has escalated to the degree that specific actions should be implemented.
- *Retention policy.* A **retention policy** as part of an incident response plan outlines how long the evidence of the incident should be retained. This policy should also consider the costs associated with the retention.
- *Stakeholder management.* An incident response plan must identify the relevant stakeholders within the organization who need to be initially informed of an incident and then kept up to date. Known as **stakeholder management**, it includes areas such as operations, legal, technical, finance, and even human resources.
- *Communication plan.* A **communication plan** outlines the internal and external constituents who need to be informed of an incident, how they should be informed, and when communication should take place. Depending upon the size of the organization, the communications staff may be charged with this task, but the details should be contained in the communication plan. Because the communications staff are professionals in this area, using the staff instead of members of the incident response team helps to ensure consistent messaging that complies with business requirements, including with respect to the public, investors, affected individuals or customers, and employee communications within the organization.

NOTE 8

A communication plan will usually require coordination with the legal team to ensure that the communications comply with all applicable legal requirements.

Performing Exercises

An incident response plan must be tested by conducting simulated **exercises** to make necessary adjustments. The types of exercises are summarized in Table 13-5.

Table 13-5 Incident response exercises

Exercise Name	Description	Example
Tabletop	A monthly 30-minute discussion of a scenario conducted in an informal and stress-free environment.	This scenario is presented: An employee casually remarks about how generous it is of a vendor to provide the box of USB drives on the conference room table, embossed with the company logo. After making some inquiries, you find the vendor did not provide USB drives to employees. What do we now do?
Walkthrough	A review by IT personnel of the steps of the plan by paying particular attention to the IT systems and services that may be targeted in an attack.	A technician with knowledge of the current system will walk through the proposed recovery procedures to determine if there are omissions, gaps, errors, or false assumptions.
Simulation	A hands-on simulation exercise using a realistic scenario to thoroughly test each step of the plan.	A simulation of a senior vice president who opens a malicious attachment and introduces malware into the network is presented.

NOTE 9

During the first few months of the COVID-19 pandemic, many medical professionals around the world who were active in combating the disease participated online in a tabletop game called Pandemic. The players collaborated (not competed) to contain outbreaks around the world and search for cures. Each player chose a role like scientist, researcher, or medic, each with unique abilities, and had to work together to develop cures before the diseases overwhelmed them. Many medical professions reported that playing the game was therapeutic and a boost to morale.

Studying Attack Frameworks

Just as a cybersecurity framework, or series of documented processes, can be used to define policies and procedures for implementing and managing security controls in an enterprise environment, frameworks about how attacks occur can also be studied. These **exploitation frameworks** serve as models of the thinking and actions of today's threat actors.

Three common attack frameworks include the following:

- *MITRE ATT&CK.* **MITRE ATT&CK** is a knowledge base of attacker techniques that have been broken down and classified in detail. The attacks are offensively oriented actions that can be used against particular platforms. The focus of ATT&CK is not on the tools and malware that attackers use but on how they interact with systems during an operation. These techniques are arranged into a set of tactics to help explain and provide context for the technique. Figure 13-3 displays a sample of the ATT&CK framework.

NOTE 10

Frameworks are covered in Module 2.

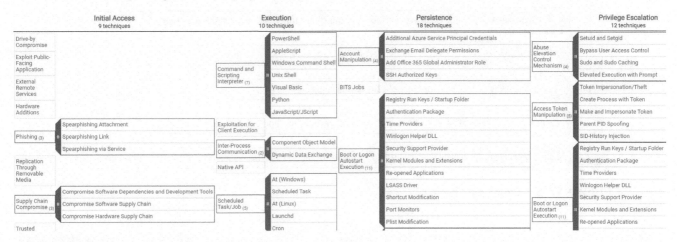

Figure 13-3   MITRE ATT&CK framework

Source: The MITRE Corporation. MITRE ATT&CK and ATT&CK are registered trademarks of The MITRE Corporation

- *The Diamond Model of Intrusion Analysis.* The **Diamond Model of Intrusion Analysis** is a framework for examining network intrusion events. This framework derives its name and shape from the four core interconnected elements that comprise any event: adversary, infrastructure, capability, and victim. Analyzing security incidents involves piecing together the Diamond using information collected about these four facets to understand the threat in its full context. Figure 13-4 illustrates the Diamond Model.

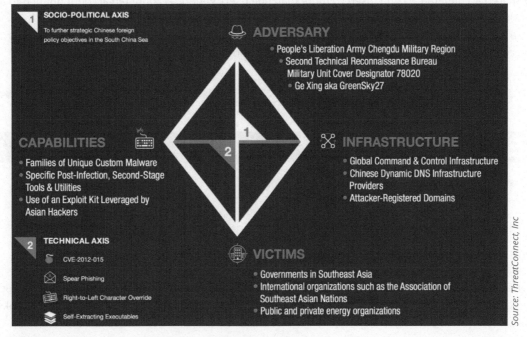

Figure 13-4   Diamond Model of Intrusion Analysis

- *Cyber Kill Chain.* A *kill chain* is a military term used to describe the systematic process to target and engage an enemy. An attacker who attempts to break into a web server or computer network actually follows these same steps. Known as the Cyber Kill Chain, it outlines the steps of an attack. Figure 13-5 shows the Cyber Kill Chain. The underlying purpose of the Cyber Kill Chain is to illustrate that attacks are an integrated and end-to-end process like a "chain." Disrupting any one of the steps will interrupt the entire attack process, but the ability to disrupt the early steps of the chain is the most effective and least costly.

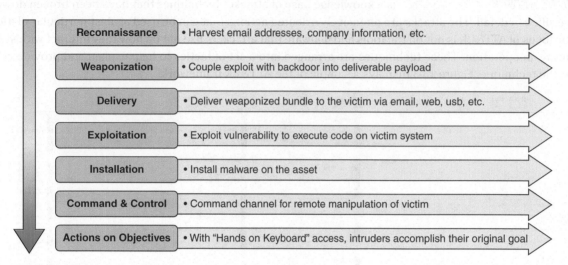

Reconnaissance	• Harvest email addresses, company information, etc.
Weaponization	• Couple exploit with backdoor into deliverable payload
Delivery	• Deliver weaponized bundle to the victim via email, web, usb, etc.
Exploitation	• Exploit vulnerability to execute code on victim system
Installation	• Install malware on the asset
Command & Control	• Command channel for remote manipulation of victim
Actions on Objectives	• With "Hands on Keyboard" access, intruders accomplish their original goal

Figure 13-5   Cyber Kill Chain

NOTE 11

The Cyber Kill Chain was first introduced by researchers at Lockheed Martin in 2011, which later trademarked the term, "Cyber Kill Chain."

TWO RIGHTS & A WRONG

1. Any shared account (an account used by more than one user), generic account (an account not tied to a specific person), or guest account (given to temporary users) should be prohibited.
2. A data privacy officer (DPO) is someone to whom day-to-day actions have been assigned by the owner.
3. An access control scheme is embedded in the software and hardware.

See Appendix B for the answer.

INCIDENT RESPONSE

 CERTIFICATION

2.1 Explain the importance of security concepts in an enterprise environment.

4.4 Given an incident, apply mitigation techniques or controls to secure an environment.

Several important steps should be taken when responding to an incident in order to recover from it (called response and recovery controls). In general, these steps include taking advantage of SOAR runbooks and playbooks, performing containment, and making configuration changes.

Use SOAR Runbooks and Playbooks

A Security Orchestration, Automation, and Response (SOAR) product can help security teams manage and respond to security warnings and alarms. By combining more comprehensive data gathering and analytics to automate incident response, a SOAR allows a security team to automate incident responses.

NOTE 12

SOARs are covered in Module 2.

Two elements that are closely associated with using SOARs are a SOAR playbook and a runbook. A **playbook** is a linear-style checklist of required steps and actions needed to successfully respond to specific incident types and threats. These playbooks give a top-down step-by-step approach to incident response by establishing formalized incident response processes and procedures. A playbook can help ensure that required steps are systematically followed, particularly when it is necessary to comply with regulatory frameworks. Although playbooks support both human tasks and automated actions, most organizations use playbooks to document processes and procedures that rely heavily on manual tasks, such as breach notification or malware reverse engineering.

A **runbook** is a series of automated conditional steps (like threat containment) that are part of an incident response procedure. Whereas a playbook focuses more on manual steps to be performed, a runbook is usually actions that are performed automatically. These automated responses can help to speed up the assessment and containment of incidences. While runbooks can also include human decision making as required, generally, however, most runbooks are automated action-based steps.

 **CAUTION**   Playbooks are not exclusively manual procedures, nor are runbooks exclusively automated procedures. However, playbooks are predominantly manual while runbooks are mostly automated.

Most SOAR platforms have different pre-configured "out-of-the-box" playbooks that are based on industry best practices and recognized standards. These playbooks identify and automate responses to frequent enterprise incidents, including phishing, compromised accounts, and malware. Organizations can craft their own customized playbooks, which are more simplified or advanced than pre-configured playbooks. This gives the organization freedom to react to an incident that is in accordance with regulations or compliance measures that more directly apply to them.

NOTE 13

Playbooks can be customized to enforce role-based security requirements that require authorization for containment.

Used together, runbooks and playbooks provide organizations with streamlined methods for orchestrating incident response and to document different security processes. Multiple runbooks and playbooks can even be assigned to a single incident so that the correct type and level of automation and orchestration can be delivered.

Perform Containment

One of the most critical steps in incident response is limiting the spread of the attack (containment). However, containment can be most effective when the network has been properly designed. A secure network design takes advantage of network *segmentation* based upon the principle of zero trust, which is a strategic initiative about secure network design. Network segments (sometimes called IP ranges, security groups, subnets, or network zones) can be created based on business units, locations, or the level of sensitivity of the network data. Network administrators can use access controls to configure services that are allowed between different zones.

NOTE 14

Network segmentation and zero trust are covered in Module 9.

Although important, network segmentation only restricts attackers by limiting access to other parts of the network. When an incident occurs, **isolation** is then used to segregate both the attacker and the infected systems from reaching other devices. During isolation, the compromised systems are either disconnected or disabled until the incident is resolved.

Make Configuration Changes

To neutralize the attacker, limit the spread of the attack, and prevent additional successful incidents, it may be necessary to make configuration changes to devices and processes. Configuration changes may need to be applied to the following:

- Firewall rules
- Content/URL filters
- Digital certificates
- Data loss prevention settings
- Mobile device management settings

TWO RIGHTS & A WRONG

1. A runbook is a linear-style checklist of required steps and actions required to successfully respond to specific incident types and threats.
2. SOAR platforms have different pre-configured playbooks that are based on industry best practices and recognized standards.
3. When an incident occurs, isolation is then used to segregate both the attacker and the infected systems from reaching other devices.

See Appendix B for the answer.

INCIDENT INVESTIGATION

 **CERTIFICATION**

4.1 Given a scenario, use the appropriate tool to assess organizational security.

4.3 Given an incident, utilize appropriate data sources to support an investigation.

4.5 Explain the key aspects of digital forensics.

Following a cybersecurity incident, it must be fully investigated. The investigation is to not only pinpoint how it occurred so that future incidents can be prevented but also for regulatory compliance reporting. Incident investigation involves analyzing data sources and performing a digital forensics investigation.

Data Sources

Several sources of data can provide helpful clues in uncovering how an incident occurred. These data sources include log files and data from other sources.

Log Files

Using data from log files involves identifying log file sources, collecting data, and analyzing data.

Types of Logs A log is a record of events that occur. Security logs are particularly important for an incident investigation because they can reveal the type of attack that was directed at the network and how it successfully circumvented existing security defenses. Network-based device logs that provide the most beneficial security data for an investigation, in order of importance, are listed in Table 13-6.

Table 13-6 Network device log sources

Device	Explanation
Firewalls	Firewall logs can be used to determine whether new IP addresses are attempting to probe the network and if stronger firewall rules are necessary to block them. Outgoing connections, incoming connections, denied traffic, and permitted traffic should all be recorded.
Network intrusion detection systems (NIDS) and network intrusion prevention systems (NIPS)	Intrusion detection and intrusion prevention systems record detailed security log information on suspicious behavior as well as any attacks that are detected. In addition, these logs also record any actions NIPS used to stop the attacks.
Web servers	Web servers are usually the primary target of attackers. These logs can provide valuable information about the type of attack that can help in configuring good security on the server.
DHCP servers	DHCP server logs can identify new systems that mysteriously appear and then disappear as part of the network. They can also show what hardware device had which IP address at a specific time.
VPN concentrators	VPN logs can be monitored for attempted unauthorized access to the network.
Proxies	As intermediate hosts access websites, these devices keep a log of all URLs that are accessed through them. This information can be useful when determining if a zombie is "calling home."
Domain Name System (DNS)	A DNS log can create entries in a log for all queries that are received. Some DNS servers also can create logs for error and alert messages.
Email servers	Email servers can show the latest malware attacks that are being launched through the use of attachments.
Routers and switches	Router and switch logs provide general information about network traffic.

Different system log files should also be investigated. Particular interest should be directed at authentication servers that facilitate authentication of an entity that attempts to access a network, such as a user or another server. Authentication servers provide valuable information about failed authentication attempts and brute force attacks.

In addition, application log files can give information about attacks focused on different applications. If an application log identifies an app that has been the source of a compromise, software can be used to create a dump file, which is a snapshot of the process that was executing and any modules that were loaded for an app at a specific point in time. Dump file output is seen in Figure 13-6.

Log files that relate to voice and video communication should not be overlooked. Vulnerabilities in these services are often compromised to allow attackers to pivot to other resources. Session Initiation Protocol (SIP) is a signaling protocol used to create "sessions" between multiple participants and is widely found in voice telephony products. A call manager is a platform used to provide telephony, video, and web conferences. Voice over IP (VoIP) is the convergence of voice and data traffic over a single Internet Protocol (IP) network. Each of these produces valuable log files.

NOTE 15

VoIP is covered in Module 5.

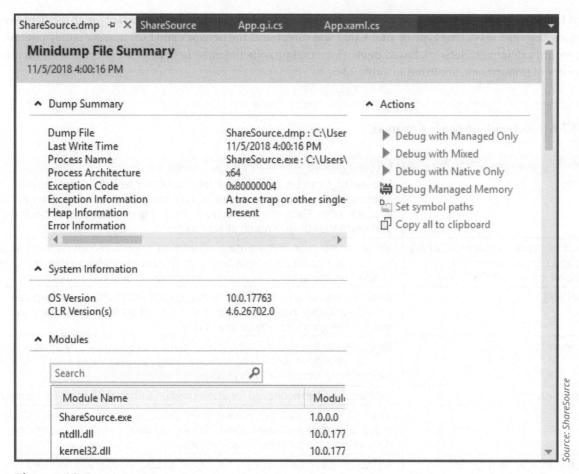

Figure 13-6   Dump file output

Collection and Analysis   Several problems are associated with *log management*—or transmitting, collecting, analyzing, and disposing of log data. This is due to the following:

- *Multiple devices generating logs.* As noted, virtually every network device, both standard network devices and network security devices, can create logs. Each device may interpret an event in a different context, so that a router looks at a single event differently than a firewall does. This can create a confusing mix of log data.
- *Very large volume of data.* Because each device generates its own data, a very large amount of data can accumulate in a very short period of time. In addition, many devices record all events, even those that are not security related, which increases the amount of data that is generated. Filtering through this large volume of data can be overwhelming.
- *Different log formats.* Perhaps the biggest obstacle to log management is that different devices record log information in different formats and even capture different data. Combining multiple logs, each with a different format, can be a major challenge.

There are different solutions to these problems. These are listed in Table 13-7.

Table 13-7   Log management tools

Solution	Description
syslog	syslog (system logging protocol) is a standard to send system log or event messages to a server.
nxlog	nxlog is a multi-platform log management tool and supports various platforms, log sources, and formats.
rsyslog	rsyslog (rocket-fast system for log processing) is an open source utility for forwarding log messages in an IP network on UNIX devices.
syslog-ng	syslog-ng is an open source utility for UNIX devices that includes content filtering.
journalctl	journalctl is a Linux utility for querying and displaying log files.

NOTE 16

The question of how long a log file should be retained depends on several different factors, including regulatory compliance and organizational policy. Generally, logs that provide evidence of an incident should be retained for at least one year.

Other Data Sources

Data accumulated from various other sources can also provide useful information. These include the following:

- *IP monitors.* Various IP software monitors can provide insight into an incident. NetFlow is a session sampling protocol feature on Cisco routers that collects IP network traffic as it enters or exits an interface and uses TCP/IP Internet Control Message Protocol (ICMP) Echo request packets, while sFlow is a packet sampling protocol that gives a statistical sampling instead of the actual flow of packets. IPFIX (IP Flow Information Export) is similar to NetFlow but with additional capabilities, such as integrating Simple Network Management Protocol (SNMP) information directly into the IPFIX information so that all the information is available instead of requiring separate queries to the SNMP server.
- *Metadata.* Metadata is "data about data," or data that describes information about other data. Analyzing file, web, mobile, and email metadata can give clues regarding an attack.
- *Analyzers.* Other types of monitors and analyzers that provide useful information are bandwidth monitors and protocol analyzers.
- *Vulnerability scans.* Data from a vulnerability scan and Security Information and Event Management (SIEM) products that consolidate real-time security monitoring and management of security information with analysis and reporting of security events is useful. A SIEM dashboard can provide information collected from its sensors. This information includes alerts, trends, sensitivity, and correlation data.

NOTE 17

Vulnerability scans and SIEMs are covered in Module 2.

Digital Forensics

Digital forensics is an important element in incident investigation. In fact, many users equate incident investigation with digital forensics, although they are not exactly the same: forensics is one important part of incident investigation. Understanding digital forensics involves knowing what it is, the procedures for forensics, tools that are used, and the difference between on-prem and cloud forensics.

What Is Forensics?

Forensics, also known as *forensic science*, is the application of science to questions that are of interest to the legal profession. While most users associate forensics with analyzing evidence from a murder scene, it also can be applied to technology. Digital forensics uses technology to search for evidence pertaining to a cybercrime or damage that occurred during a cyber incident. Digital evidence can be retrieved from computers, mobile devices, cell phones, digital cameras, and virtually any device that has a processor, memory, or storage.

Forensics Procedures

When responding to an incident that requires an examination using computer forensics, five basic steps are followed, which are similar to those of standard forensics. The steps are secure the crime scene, preserve the evidence, document the chain of custody, examine the evidence, and enable recovery.

Secure the Scene   When an on-prem illegal or unauthorized incident occurs that involves technology, action must be taken immediately. A delay of even a few minutes can allow digital evidence to be overwritten in the normal function of the device, become contaminated by other users, or give the perpetrator time to destroy the evidence.

When an incident occurs, those individuals in the immediate vicinity should perform *damage control*, which is the effort to minimize any loss of evidence. The steps in damage control include contacting the incident response team, securing and then quarantining the electronic equipment involved, and, if necessary, reporting the incident to the appropriate external authorities.

Once the incident response team arrives, its first job is to secure the scene, which includes the following actions:

- The physical surroundings of the device computer should be clearly documented. Many forensics experts use a video camera to capture video of all the work performed by the incident response team to demonstrate that proper procedures were followed.
- Photographs of the area should be taken before anything is touched to help document that the computer was working prior to the attack. (Some defense attorneys have argued that a computer was not functioning properly, and, thus, the attacker could not be held responsible for any damages.) The device should be photographed from several angles, including the images displayed on the screen. Because digital pictures can be altered, some security professionals recommend that photographs be taken with a standard camera using film.
- Any cables connected to a device should be labeled to document the hardware components and how they are connected.
- The team should take custody of the device along with any peripherals. In addition, USB flash drives and any other media must be secured.
- The team must speak with those present to perform witness interviews and everyone who had access to the system and document their findings, including what those people were doing with the system, what its intended functions were, and how it has been affected by the unauthorized actions.

Preserve the Evidence   The next task is preservation of the evidence, or ensuring that important proof is not corrupted or even destroyed. Preserving evidence can also help mitigate *nonrepudiation*, or a denial by the perpetrators that they were involved or did anything wrong.

Evidence from a suspected device should be placed in bags that have tags or identifying labels that have a description of the item, a numeric identifier, date, collection location, and other relevant information. These bags should then be sealed to serve as protection against evidence being altered. Two types of seals are commonly used. A tamper-evident seal is a seal or tape that cannot be removed and reapplied without leaving obvious visual evidence. If the seal or tape is lifted or removed, a clearly visible *OPENED* message appears on the packaging. For additional traceability and security, the tape is often labeled with a unique sequential number every 9 inches (22 centimeters). Tamper-evident tape is shown in Figure 13-7. A tamper-resistant seal is designed to deter tampering with the bag. However, it does not necessarily produce visual evidence if tampering has occurred: If the sticker is removed carefully, it can be reapplied with no visual evidence of tampering.

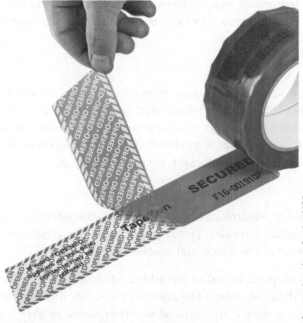

Source: American Casting MFG

Figure 13-7   Tamper-evident tape

Depending upon the type and severity of the incident, it may be necessary to immediately involve the judicial system to help collect and preserve the digital evidence. This ensures that the integrity of the evidence is maintained and can hold up in a court of law (**admissibility**). One of the first steps is **e-discovery**, which is identifying, collecting, and producing electronically stored information (ESI) in response to a request in an investigation or lawsuit. Once data has been identified, it can be placed under a **legal hold**, meaning that it cannot be modified, deleted, erased, or otherwise destroyed.

There is a tendency to issue legal holds that are too broad in scope. For example, to place a legal hold on all email correspondence may result in retaining thousands or millions of unneeded messages and associated attachments, while placing a legal hold on all portable devices requiring them to be locked away makes them useless to the organization. Instead, appropriate filters should be used to capture only data that is relevant.

Document Chain of Custody   As soon as the team begins its work, it must start and maintain a strict chain of custody. Documenting the evidence from the very beginning is called **provenance**. The **chain of custody** documents that the evidence was always under strict control and no unauthorized person was given the opportunity to corrupt the evidence. A chain of custody includes documenting all the serial numbers of the systems involved, who handled and had custody of the systems and for what length of time, how the computer was shipped, and any other steps in the process. In short, a chain of custody is a detailed document describing where the evidence was at all times from the beginning of the investigation.

Gaps in a chain of custody can result in severe legal consequences. Courts have dismissed cases involving computer forensics because a secure chain of custody could not be verified.

A chain of custody form helps to document that evidence was under strict control at all times and no unauthorized person was given the opportunity to corrupt it, as shown in Figure 13-8.

Examine for Evidence   When examining technology devices that may contain evidence, called **artifacts**, it is critical to follow a specific order. This is because different data sources have different degrees of preservation. An **order of volatility** must be followed to preserve the most fragile data first. Table 13-8 lists the order of volatility.

Table 13-8   Order of volatility

Order	Examples	Description
1	Registers and CPU cache	Registers and the CPU cache are extremely volatile and change constantly.
2	Routing tables, ARP cache, process table, kernel statistics, RAM	The network routing and process tables have data located on network devices that can change quickly while the system is in operation, and kernel statistics are moving between cache and main memory, which make them highly volatile. RAM information can be lost if power is lost.
3	Temporary filesystems	Temporary filesystems are not subject to the degree of rapid changes as the prior elements.
4	Hard drive	Hard drive data is relatively stable.
5	Remote logging and monitoring data	Although remote logging and monitoring is more volatile than hard drive data, the data on a hard drive is considered more valuable and should be preserved first.
6	Physical configuration and network topology	These items are not considered volatile and do not have a significant impact on an investigation.
7	Archival media	Data that has been preserved in archival form is not volatile.

Property Record Number: _____

EVIDENCE CHAIN OF CUSTODY TRACKING FORM

Case Number: _____ Offense: _____
Submitting Official: (Name/ID#) _____
Date/Time Seized: _____ Location of Seizure: _____

Description of Evidence		
Item #	Quantity	Description of Item (Model, Serial #, Condition, Marks, Scratches)

Chain of Custody				
Item #	Date/Time	Released by (Signature & ID#)	Received by (Signature & ID#)	Comments/Location

Final Disposal Authority

Item(s) #: _____ on this document pertaining to (suspect): _____
is(are) no longer needed as evidence and is/are authorized for disposal by (check appropriate disposal method)
☐ Return to Owner   ☐ Auction/Destroy/Divert
Name & ID# of Authorizing Official: _____ Signature: _____ Date: _____

Witness to Destruction of Evidence

Item(s) #: _____ on this document were destroyed by Evidence Custodian _____ ID#: _____
in my presence on (date) _____.
Name & ID# of Witness to destruction: _____ Signature: _____ Date: _____

Release to Lawful Owner

Item(s) #: _____ on this document was/were released by Evidence Custodian
_____ ID#: _____ to
Name _____
Address: _____ City: _____ State: _____ Zip Code: _____

Telephone Number: (____) _____
Under penalty of law, I certify that I am the lawful owner of the above item(s).

Signature: _____ Date: _____

Copy of Government-issued photo identification is attached. ☐ Yes ☐ No

This Evidence Chain-of-Custody form is to be retained as a permanent record.

Figure 13-8   Chain of custody form

The first two levels are considered the most volatile because they can change very quickly. A **cache** is a type of high-speed memory that stores recently used information so that it can be quickly accessed again at a later time. Both the CPU and ARP caches can easily change and should be captured immediately. To facilitate this, there are tools that allow capturing the system image, or a **snapshot** of the current state of these elements that contains all current settings and data. On the other hand, data that is stored in a less volatile state, such as **OS event logs** that document incorrect login attempts, system setting modifications, application or system failures, and other events can be retrieved after the most volatile data is secured.

After retrieving the volatile data, the team next focuses on the hard drive. A *mirror image backup*, also called a *bit-stream backup*, is an evidence-grade backup because its accuracy meets evidence standards. A mirror image backup is not the same as a normal copy of the data. Standard file copies or backups include only files. Mirror image backups replicate all sectors of a computer hard drive, including all files and any hidden data storage areas. Using a standard copy procedure can miss significant data and can taint the evidence. For example, copying a file may change file date information on the source drive, which is information that is often critical in a computer forensic investigation.

To guarantee the integrity of the data, mirror image backup programs rely upon *hashing algorithms* as part of the validation process. The digest of the original source data is compared against the digest of the copied data to help create a snapshot of the current system based on the contents of the drives. This is done to document that any retrieved evidence came from the system and was not "planted" there.

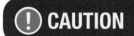 **CAUTION**   Many resources that describe forensic hashing call it "creating a checksum." A hash and a checksum are very different and have different purposes, as explained in Module 6.

Two elements are frequently overlooked when performing a forensics investigation. A mirror image backup will capture the swap file or pagefile that contains data that has been moved from RAM to the hard drive due to a lack of RAM space, and this should be examined for evidence. A second element is firmware, or software in hardware. It is not uncommon for a threat actor to infect unprotected firmware as an entry point into a system.

Often clues are not obvious and must be mined and exposed. One source of hidden data is called *slack*. Windows computers use two types of slack. The first is RAM slack. Windows stores files on a hard drive in 512-byte blocks called sectors, and multiple sectors are used to make up a cluster. Clusters are made up of blocks of sectors. When a file that is being saved is not large enough to fill up the last sector on a disk (a common occurrence because a file size only rarely matches the sector size), Windows pads the remaining cluster space with data that is currently stored in RAM. This padding creates *RAM slack*, which can contain any information that has been created, viewed, modified, downloaded, or copied since the computer was last booted. Thus, if the computer has not been shut down for several days, the data stored in RAM slack can come from activity that occurred during that time. RAM slack is illustrated in Figure 13-9.

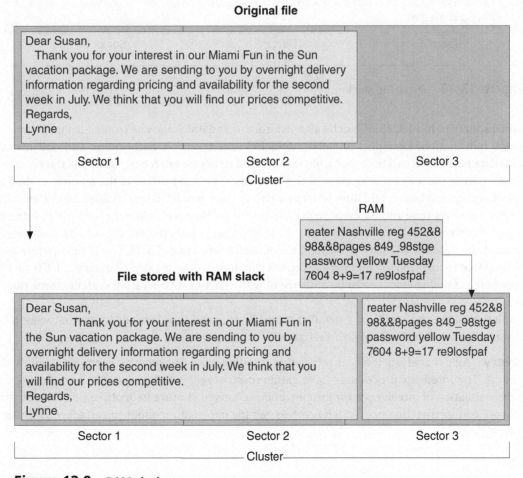

Figure 13-9   RAM slack

RAM slack pertains only to the last sector of a file. If additional sectors are needed to round out the block size for the last cluster assigned to the file, then a different type of slack is created. This is known as *drive file slack* (sometimes called *drive slack*) because the padded data that Windows uses comes from data stored on the hard drive. Such data could contain remnants of previously deleted files or data from the format pattern associated with disk storage space that has yet to be used by the computer. Drive file slack is illustrated in Figure 13-10. Both RAM slack and drive slack can hold valuable evidence.

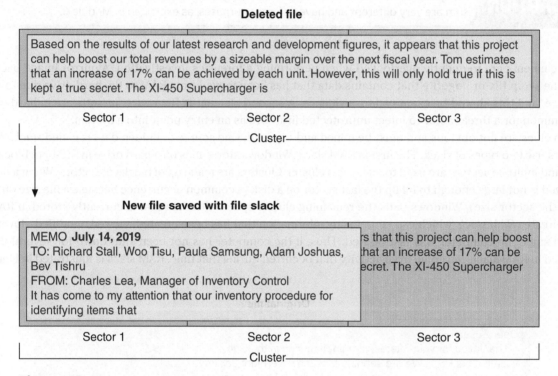

Figure 13-10   Drive file slack

An additional source of hidden clues can be gleaned from metadata. Some electronic files may contain hundreds of pieces of such information. Examples of metadata include the file type, authorship, and edit history. Another example of metadata is the date and time that a file was created or accessed. A **time stamp** is the recorded time that an event took place irrespective of the location of the endpoint. The **time offset** is the amount of time added to or subtracted from Coordinated Universal Time (UTC) to arrive at the current "actual" (called *civil*) time, which may be affected by daylight savings time and different regional time zones. However, different operating systems store time values differently. Microsoft Windows uses a 64-bit time stamp that counts the number of 100 nanosecond intervals that have occurred since January 1, 1601, at 00:00:00 Greenwich Mean Time (GMT). The Linux operating system uses a 32-bit time stamp that recognizes the number of seconds that have occurred since January 1, 1970, at 00:00:00 GMT. It is important when examining evidence to be aware of how the particular operating system stores time and record its time offset.

Upon completion of the examination, a detailed report is required that lists the steps that were taken and any evidence that was uncovered in the forensic investigation.

Enable Recovery   A final analysis looks at recovering the data from the security event and the lessons that can be learned from it. The forensics procedures have gathered **strategic intelligence**, or the collection, processing, analysis, and dissemination of intelligence for forming policy changes. A more in-depth application of strategic intelligence is **strategic counterintelligence**, which involves gaining information about the attacker's intelligence collection capabilities.

Forensics Tools

There are different software and hardware forensics tools available for analysis.

Forensics Software Tools   An *imaging utility* is used for generating a physical copy. A utility named dd, sometimes called GNU dd, is the oldest imaging tool still in use, primarily because it requires only minimal resources to run and generates raw image files that can be read by many other programs. However, dd is a command-line program and lacks some of the useful features found in more modern imagers, such as metadata gathering, error correction, and a user-friendly interface.

 **CAUTION**   Because dd is a command-line program, it requires several ambiguous command-line arguments (*switches* or *flags*) to tailor the imaging command. Some of these arguments are similar and easily confused and can even result in destroying the source media being duplicated. Users should exercise extreme caution when using the dd utility.

Other popular forensics software tools are **memdump**, a Linux utility that "dumps" system memory; **WinHex**, a hexadecimal editor that can be used for forensics; and **Autopsy**, a digital forensics platform.

Products are available that package multiple tools into a single *suite* that has a common user interface and can more easily exchange information among the different tools. Two of the most common forensic suites are EnCase (shown in Figure 13–11) and **FTK Imager**.

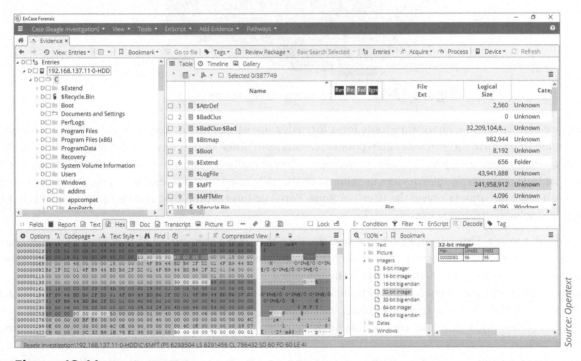

Figure 13-11   EnCase software

Forensics Hardware Tools   Instead of gathering different forensics software tools, a digital forensic workstation, which is a computer that is specially configured to perform forensics activities, can be used instead. A digital forensic workstation is shown in Figure 13-12.

Digital forensic workstations are typically configured with the latest computer hardware, such as multiple gigabit network ports and USB ports, along with up to 10 drive "hot swap" bays to hold as many as eight drives. The two additional empty bays can be used for backups or additional processing, such as copying data directly to a network attached storage (NAS) device. These workstations also are configured with eight or more 6 TB hard drives configured in RAID 5 for redundancy, and they have 1000-watt power supply units, multiple fans for cooling, and the latest high-end CPUs.

NOTE 18

Digital forensic workstations are expensive. Depending on the options installed, such a workstation might cost more than $20,000.

Source: Teel Technologies

Figure 13-12   Digital forensics workstation

There are also specialized hardware tools for a forensics investigation. For example, a mobile device forensics tool is designed to perform forensics on smartphones, tablets, and other similar devices. Although mobile devices are sometimes characterized merely as "portable computers," they actually contain a broader wealth of information than a desktop or laptop computer. Mobile devices are almost continually in a user's possession, unlike a standard computer, and, thus, can more accurately reveal the user's actions. Forensic information that can be uniquely extracted from a mobile device includes the following:

- *Call detail records.* This information can reveal the date and time a telephone call was started and ended, the terminating and originating cell phone towers that were used, whether the call was outgoing or incoming, the call's duration, who was called, and who made the call.
- *Global Positioning System (GPS) data.* GPS data can accurately pinpoint the location of a user and what activities he was performing in a specific location.
- *App data.* Many apps store and access data such as media files, contact lists, and a gallery of all the photos on the device.
- *Short Message Service (SMS) texts.* Text messaging is a popular means of communication. It leaves electronic records of dialogue that can be used as evidence.
- *Photos and videos.* Media recorded as photos and videos on a mobile device can often contain incriminating evidence.

Cloud Forensics

If the incident is the result of a breach of cloud-based resources, it is not possible to secure the scene as in an on-prem incident. When dealing with a cloud incident, the following should be considered:

- A primary concern is to ensure that the digital evidence has not been tampered with by third parties so it can be admissible in a court of law. In Software as a Service (SaaS) and Platform as a Service (PaaS) models, because customers do not have control of the hardware, they must depend on the cloud service providers to accumulate log data. A **right to audit clause** in a cloud contract gives the customer the legal right to review the logs, and these should also be negotiated in advance.
- When a cloud customer is notified by its cloud service provider that an incident occurred, the immediate response from the customer's in-house legal and IT teams will be to ask for details about the scope of the

impact. However, unless they are contractually obligated, the cloud provider may take weeks or even months to provide its client with details as they perform an investigation. However, once the cloud customer has been notified, the "clock has started ticking" regarding **data breach notification law** deadlines. This can place the cloud customer in an awkward situation.

- The legal **regulatory/jurisdiction** laws that govern the site in which the cloud data resides may present difficulties. For example, a court order issued in a jurisdiction where the cloud data center is located will likely not be applicable to another jurisdiction in another country.

> **⚠ CAUTION** When creating a cloud platform, the customer can often choose the region in which the data will reside. It is at this time that issues regarding jurisdiction should be considered and the region chosen carefully.

TWO RIGHTS & A WRONG

1. A DNS service is the most important network-based device log to examine.
2. A multi-platform log management tool that supports various platforms, log sources, and formats is nxlog.
3. IPFIX (IP Flow Information Export) is similar to NetFlow but with additional capabilities, such as integrating Simple Network Management Protocol (SNMP) information directly into the IPFIX information.

See Appendix B for the answer.

>  **VM LAB** You're now ready to complete the live, virtual machine labs for this module. The labs can be found in the Practice It folder in each MindTap module.

SUMMARY

- Access control is granting or denying approval to use specific resources; it is controlling access. Authentication, authorization, and accounting, sometimes called AAA, provide a framework for controlling access to computer resources. Individuals are given different roles in relationship to access control objects or resources. These include data privacy officer, data custodian/steward, data owner, data controller, and data processor. Hardware and software have a predefined framework that the custodian can use for controlling access. This framework, called an access control scheme, can be used by a custodian/steward to configure the necessary level of control. Using these schemes is part of privileged access management, which is the technologies and strategies for controlling elevated (privileged) access. There are five major access control schemes: Discretionary Access Control, Mandatory Access Control, Role-Based Access Control, Rule-Based Access Control, and Attribute-Based Access Control.

- An access control list (ACL) is a set of permissions that is attached to an object. This list specifies which subjects are allowed to access the object and what operations they can perform on it. Although ACLs can be associated with any type of object, these lists are most often viewed in relation to files maintained by the OS. Although widely used, ACLs have limitations. First, using ACLs is not efficient. A second limitation to ACLs is that they can be difficult to manage in an enterprise setting where many users need to have different levels of access to many different resources.

- An incident response plan is a set of written instructions for reacting to a security incident. An incident response team is responsible for responding to security incidents. In addition to technical specialists who can address specific threats, it should also include members who are public relations employees and managers who can guide enterprise executives on appropriate communication. It is important for an incident response plan to identify the relevant stakeholders within the organization who need to be initially informed of an incident and then kept up to date. Known as stakeholder management, it includes areas such as operations, legal, technical, finance, and human resources.

- It is important to test an incident response plan by conducting simulated exercises to make necessary adjustments. The different types of exercises are tabletop, walkthrough, and simulation. Just as a cybersecurity framework, or series of documented processes, can be used to define policies and procedures for implementing and managing security controls in an enterprise environment, frameworks about how attacks occur can also be studied. These exploitation frameworks serve as models of the thinking and actions of threat actors. Common attack frameworks are MITRE ATT&CK, the Diamond Model of Intrusion Analysis, and Cyber Kill Chain.

- Two elements that are closely associated with using SOARs are a SOAR playbook and a runbook. A playbook is a linear-style checklist of required steps and actions needed to successfully respond to specific incident types and threats. A runbook is a series of automated conditional steps (like threat containment) that are part of an incident response procedure. Whereas a playbook focuses more on manual steps to be performed, a runbook is usually actions that are performed automatically. One of the most critical steps in incident response is limiting the spread of the attack (containment). However, containment can be most effective when the network has been properly designed. In order to neutralize the attacker, limit the spread of the attack, and prevent additional successful incidents, it may be necessary to make configuration changes to devices and processes.

- Following a cybersecurity incident, it must be fully investigated. This is to not only pinpoint how it occurred so that future incidents can be prevented but also for regulatory compliance reporting. There are several sources of data that can provide helpful clues in uncovering how an incident occurred. A log is a record of events that occur. Security logs are particularly important as they relate to incident investigation because they can reveal the type of attack that was directed at the network and how it successfully circumvented existing security defenses. Application log files can give information about attacks focused on different applications. If an application log identifies an app that has been the source of a compromise, software can be used to create a dump file, which is a snapshot of the process that was executing and any modules that were loaded for an app at a specific point in time. There are several problems associated with log management—or transmitting, collecting, analyzing, and disposing of log data. There are different solutions to these problems, such as syslog, nxlog, rsyslog, syslog-ng, and journalctl.

- IP software monitors can provide insight into an incident. NetFlow is a session sampling protocol feature on Cisco routers that collects IP network traffic as it enters or exits an interface and uses ICMP Echo request packets. The tool sFlow is a packet sampling protocol that gives a statistical sampling instead of the actual flow of packets. IPFIX (IP Flow Information Export) is similar to NetFlow but adds additional capabilities, such as integrating SNMP information directly into the IPFIX information. Metadata is data that describes information about other data. Analyzing file, web, mobile, and email metadata can give clues regarding an attack. Data from a vulnerability scan and SIEM products that consolidate real-time security monitoring and management of security information with analysis and reporting of security events is useful.

- Forensics is the application of science to questions that are of interest to the legal profession. Digital forensics uses technology to search for evidence pertaining to a cybercrime or damage that occurred during a cyber incident. When an on-prem illegal or unauthorized incident occurs that involves technology, action must be taken immediately. A delay of even a few minutes can allow digital evidence to be overwritten in the normal function of the device, become contaminated by other users, or give the perpetrator time to destroy the evidence. Preservation of evidence, or ensuring that important proof is not corrupted or even destroyed, is also critical. Preserving evidence can also help mitigate nonrepudiation, or a denial by the perpetrators that they were involved or did anything wrong.

- As soon as the incident response team begins its work, it must start and maintain a strict chain of custody. The chain of custody documents that the evidence was always under strict control and no unauthorized person was given the opportunity to corrupt the evidence. When examining technology devices that may contain evidence, called artifacts, it is critical to follow a specific order. This is because different data sources have different degrees of preservation. An order of volatility must be followed to preserve the most fragile data first. A final analysis looks at recovering the data from the security event and what lessons can be learned from it. The forensics procedures have gathered strategic intelligence—or the collection, processing, analysis, and dissemination of intelligence for forming policy changes. A more in-depth application of strategic intelligence is strategic counterintelligence, which involves gaining information about the attacker's intelligence collection capabilities.

- There are different software and hardware forensics tools available for analysis. Instead of using individual software tools for a forensics investigation, products are available that package multiple tools into a single suite that has a common user interface and can more easily exchange information among the different tools. A digital forensic workstation is a computer that is specially configured to perform forensics activities. If an incident is the result of a breach of cloud-based resources, it is not possible to secure the scene as in an on-prem incident. When dealing with a cloud incident, there are different procedures that must be followed.

Key Terms

access control list (ACL)

access control scheme

accounting

admissibility

artifacts

Attribute-Based Access Control (ABAC)

authentication servers

authorization

Autopsy

cache

call manager

chain of custody

communication plan

conditional access

containment

Cyber Kill Chain

data breach notification law

data controller

data custodian/steward

data owner

data privacy officer (DPO)

data processor

dd

Diamond Model of Intrusion Analysis

Discretionary Access Control (DAC)

dump file

Echo

e-discovery

eradication

exercises

exploitation frameworks

filesystem permissions

firmware

forensics

FTK Imager

generic account

guest account

identification

incident response plan

incident response process

incident response team

IPFIX (IP Flow Information Export)

isolation

journalctl

legal hold

lessons learned

log

Mandatory Access Control (MAC)

memdump

metadata

MITRE ATT&CK

NetFlow

nxlog

order of volatility

OS event logs

pagefile

playbook

preparation

preservation of the evidence

privileged access management

provenance

recovery

regulatory/jurisdiction

response and recovery controls

retention policy

right to audit clause

Role-Based Access Control

rsyslog

Rule-Based Access Control

runbook

SEAndroid

service account

Session Initiation Protocol (SIP)

sFlow

shared account

simulation

snapshot

stakeholder management

strategic counterintelligence

strategic intelligence

swap file

syslog

syslog-ng

tabletop

tags

time offset

time stamp

user account

walkthrough

WinHex

Review Questions

1. Which of the following is NOT part of the AAA framework?
   a. Authentication
   b. Access
   c. Authorization
   d. Accounting

2. Raul has been asked to serve as the individual to whom day-to-day actions have been assigned by the owner. What role is Raul taking?
   a. Data custodian/steward
   b. Data privacy officer
   c. Data controller
   d. Data processor

3. Which access control scheme is the most restrictive?
   a. Role-Based Access Control
   b. DAC
   c. Rule-Based Access Control
   d. MAC

4. Which type of access control scheme uses predefined rules that makes it the most flexible scheme?
   a. ABAC
   b. DAC
   c. MAC
   d. NAC

5. Which statement about Rule-Based Access Control is true?
   a. It requires that a custodian set all rules.
   b. It is no longer considered secure.
   c. It dynamically assigns roles to subjects based on rules.
   d. It is considered a real-world approach by linking a user's job function with security.

6. Which of these is a set of permissions that is attached to an object?
   a. ACL
   b. SRE
   c. Object modifier
   d. Entity attribute (EnATT)

7. What can be used to provide both filesystem security and database security?
   a. RBASEs
   b. LDAPs
   c. CHAPs
   d. ACLs

8. What is the amount of time added to or subtracted from Coordinated Universal Time to determine local time?
   a. Greenwich Mean Time (GMT)
   b. Civil time
   c. Daylight savings time
   d. Time offset

9. Cheryl has been asked to set up a user account explicitly to provide a security context for services running on a server. What type of account will she create?
   a. Generic account
   b. Service account
   c. User account
   d. Privilege account

10. Which of these is NOT an incident response process step?
    a. Recovery
    b. Reporting
    c. Eradication
    d. Lessons learned

11. Which of the following is typically a monthly discussion of a scenario conducted in an informal and stress-free environment to evaluate an incident response plan?
    a. Walkthrough
    b. Simulation
    c. Tabletop
    d. Incident Response Plan Evaluation (IRP-E)

12. Ella wants to research an attack framework that incorporates adversary, infrastructure, capability, and victim. Which of the following would she choose?
    a. Diamond Model of Intrusion Analysis
    b. Cyber Kill Chain
    c. Mitre ATT&CK
    d. Basic-Advanced Incident (BAI) Framework

13. Blaise needs to create a document that is a linear-style checklist of required manual steps and actions needed to successfully respond to a specific type of incident. What does she need to create?
    a. Playbook
    b. Runbook
    c. SIEM-book
    d. ARC Codebook

14. Which of the following should be performed in advance of an incident?
    a. Containment
    b. Segmentation
    c. Isolation
    d. Capture

15. What is a platform used to provide telephony, video, and web conferences that can serve as an entry point to a threat actor?
    a. SIP
    b. VoIP
    c. Call manager
    d. IP voice

16. Which of the following is NOT a problem associated with log management?
    a. Multiple devices generating logs
    b. Large volume of log data
    c. Different log formats
    d. Time-stamped log data

17. Which tool is an open source utility for UNIX devices that includes content filtering?
    a. syslog
    b. nxlog
    c. rsyslog
    d. syslog-ng

18. Which of the following is a packet sampling protocol that gives a statistical sample instead of the actual flow of packets?
    a. NetFlow
    b. sFlow
    c. IPFIX
    d. journalctl

19. Which of the following is the most fragile and should be captured first in a forensics investigation?
    a. ARP cache
    b. Kernel statistics
    c. CPU cache
    d. RAM

20. Which of the following is a Linux utility that displays the contents of system memory?
    a. Autopsy
    b. WinHex
    c. dd
    d. memdump

Hands-On Projects

 **CAUTION** If you are concerned about installing any of the software in these projects on your regular computer, you can instead use the Windows Sandbox or install the software in the Windows virtual machine created in the Module 1 Hands-On Projects. Software installed within the virtual machine will not impact the host computer.

Project 13-1: Entering and Viewing Metadata

Time Required: 25 minutes
Objective: 4.5 Explain the key aspects of digital forensics.
   • Data recovery
Description: Although most file metadata is not accessible to users, they can enter and change some types of metadata. In this project, you view and enter metadata in a Microsoft Word document.

1. Use Microsoft Word to create a document containing your name. Save the document as **Metadata1.docx**.
2. Click the **File** tab on the Ribbon, and then click **Info**.
3. Click the **Properties** arrow and then click **Advanced Properties**.
4. Enter the following information in the Advanced Properties dialog box:
   • Title—**Project 13-1**
   • Author—Your name
   • Category—**Computer Forensics**
   • Comments—**Viewing metadata in Microsoft Word**
5. Click **OK**.
6. Save **Metadata1.docx**.
7. Click the **File** tab on the Ribbon, and then click **Info**.
8. Click the **Properties** arrow and then click **Advanced Properties**.
9. Click the **Statistics** tab in the Properties dialog box and view the information it contains. How could a computer forensics specialist use this metadata when examining this file?
10. Click the **Custom** tab. Notice that it includes several predefined fields that can contain metadata.
11. In the Name box, enter **Editor**.
12. Be sure the Type is set to **Text**.
13. Enter your name in the **Value** field, and then press **Enter**.
14. Select three predefined fields and enter values for each field. Click **OK**. Save your document when you are finished.
15. Click the **Back** button to return to **Metadata1.docx.**
16. Delete your name from **Metadata1.docx** so you have a blank document. However, this file still has the metadata. Enter today's date and save this as **Metadata2.docx**.
17. Close **Metadata2.docx**.
18. Reopen **Metadata2.docx**.
19. Click the **File** tab on the Ribbon, and then click **Info**.
20. Click to **Properties** arrow and then click **Advanced Properties**.
21. What properties carried over to **Metadata2.docx** from **Metadata1.docx**, even though the content of the file was erased? Why did this happen? Could a computer forensics specialist use this technique to examine metadata, even if the contents of the document were deleted?
22. Close all windows.

Project 13-2: Viewing Windows Slack and Hidden Data

Time Required: 20 minutes

Objective: 4.5 Explain the key aspects of digital forensics.
- Data recovery

Description: RAM slack, drive slack, and other hidden data can be helpful to a computer forensics investigator. In this project, you download and use a program to search for hidden data.

1. Use your web browser to go to **www.briggsoft.com**. (The location of content on the Internet may change without warning. If you are no longer able to access the program through the above URL, use a search engine and search for "Directory Snoop.")
2. Scroll down to the current version of **Directory Snoop** and click **Download** above **Free Trial**.
3. Follow the default installation procedures to install Directory Snoop.
4. Launch Directory Snoop.
5. Depending on the filesystem on your computer, click **FAT Module** or **NTFS Module**.
6. Under Select Drive, click **C:** or the drive letter of your hard drive. If the RawDisk Driver dialog box appears, click **Install Driver**, click **OK**, and then select the appropriate drive again.
7. Click to select a file and display its contents, preferably a user-created document (such as a Microsoft Word file). Scroll down under **Text data** to view the contents that you can read.
8. Select other files to look for hidden data. Did you discover anything that might be useful to a computer forensics specialist?
9. To create a text document using Notepad, click the **Start** button, enter **Notepad** in the Search box, and then click the app.
10. Enter the text **Now is the time for all good men to come to the aid of their country.**
11. Save the document on your desktop as **Country.txt**.
12. Exit Notepad.
13. Right-click **Start**, click **File Explorer**, and then navigate to **Country.txt**.
14. Right-click **Country.txt** and then click **Delete** to delete the file.
15. Search for information contained in the file you just deleted. Return to **Directory Snoop**, click the top-level node for the **C:** drive, and then click the **Search** icon.
16. Click **Files**.
17. Enter **country** as the item that you are searching for.
18. Click **Search in slack area also**.
19. Click **OK**. Did the program find this data? Why or why not?
20. Close all windows.

Project 13-3: Using Discretionary Access Control to Share Files in Windows

NOTE 19

You should have a standard user named "Abby Lomax" created in Windows and a Notepad document Sample.txt created by an administrative user to complete this assignment.

Time Required: 25 minutes

Objective: 3.8 Given a scenario, implement authentication and authorization solutions.
- Access control schemes

Description: Discretionary Access Control can be applied in Microsoft Windows. In this project, you set up file sharing with other users.

1. Right-click the file **Sample.txt**.
2. To see the current permissions on this file, click **Properties**, and then click the **Security** tab.
3. Click your username and then click **Edit**.
4. Click your username again (if necessary), and then, under **Permissions for [user]**, click **Deny** for the **Read** attribute.
5. Click **Apply** and then click **Yes** at the warning dialog box.
6. Click **OK** in the Properties dialog box and then click **OK** in the Sample.txt dialog box.
7. Double-click the file **Sample.txt** to open it. What happens?

8. Give permission to Abby Lomax to open the file. Click the file **Sample.txt**.

9. Click the **Share** tab and then click **Specific people**.

10. Click the arrow and select **Abby Lomax**. Click **Add**.

11. Click **Share**.

12. Click **Done** when the sharing process is completed.

13. Click **Start**, click your account name or picture, and then click **Switch User**.

14. Log in as Abby Lomax.

15. Right-click **Start** and then click **File Explorer**.

16. Navigate to your account name and locate the file Sample.txt.

17. Double-click **Sample.txt** to open the file. Using DAC, permissions have been granted to another user.

18. Close all windows.

Project 13-4: Exploring User Account Control (UAC)

Time Required: 20 minutes

Objective: 3.8 Given a scenario, implement authentication and authorization solutions.

- Access control schemes

Description: Microsoft Windows provides several options with user account control (UAC). In this project, you configure and test UAC settings. Note that during this project, the UAC dialog box may appear after specific steps. Be sure to always confirm the selection by clicking **OK** or **Yes**.

1. First ensure that UAC is set at its highest level. Enter **UAC** in the search box, and then press **Enter**.

2. The User Account Control Settings dialog box is displayed. If necessary, move the slider up to the higher level of **Always notify**.

3. Click **OK**.

4. Type **mmc** in the search box, and then press **Enter**.

5. The UAC confirmation box is displayed. Click **No**.

6. Enter **UAC** in the search box, and then press **Enter**.

7. The User Account Control settings dialog box is displayed. Move the slider down to the lowest level of **Never notify me when**.

8. Click **OK**.

9. Type **mmc** in the search box, and then press **Enter**. What happens?

10. Enter **UAC** in the search box, and then press **Enter**.

11. Change the account settings to **Notify me only when apps try to make changes to my computer (default)** and click **OK**.

12. Type **mmc** in the search box, and then press **Enter**. What happens? Close the Console1 dialog box.

13. Enter **UAC** in the search box, and then press **Enter**.

14. Change the account settings to **Notify me only when apps try to make changes to my computer (do not dim my desktop)** and click **OK**.

15. Type **mmc** in the search box, and then press **Enter**. What happens?

16. Enter **UAC** in the search box, and then press **Enter**.

17. The User Account Control Settings dialog box is displayed. Move the slider up to the higher level of **Always notify**.

18. Click **OK**.

19. Next, change the settings to disable secure desktop mode in UAC. Enter **gpedit.msc** in the search box, and then press **Enter**.

20. If necessary, click **Computer Configuration**.

21. Expand **Windows Settings**.

22. Expand **Security Settings**.

23. Expand **Local Policies**.

24. Expand **Security Options**.

25. Navigate to **User Account Control: Switch to the secure desktop when prompting for elevation** and double-click it.

26. Change **Enabled** to **Disabled**.

27. Click **Apply** and then click **OK**.

28. Enter **UAC** in the search box, and then press **Enter**.
29. What is different about your desktop now?
30. Return to the Security Options in gpedit.msc.
31. Review the other UAC options available.
32. Navigate to **User Account Control: Switch to the secure desktop when prompting for elevation** and double-click it.
33. Change **Disabled** to **Enabled**.
34. Click **Apply** and then **OK**.
35. Close all windows.

Case Projects

Case Project 13-1: Forensics Tools

Search the Internet for websites that advertise computer forensic tools. Locate reviews of four tools. Create a chart that lists the tool, the type of data that it searches for, its features, the cost, etc. Which would you recommend if you could purchase only one tool and budget were not a concern?

Case Project 13-2: Diamond Model of Intrusion Analysis

The Diamond Model of Intrusion Analysis is a framework for examining network intrusion events. Use the Internet to research this model. Identify how it is used, its strengths and weaknesses, and how widely implemented it is. What is your conclusion about this framework? How useful does it appear to be to you? Write a one-page analysis of your research.

Case Project 13-3: SOAR Runbooks and Playbooks

Research SOAR runbooks and playbooks. If possible, locate an example and read through each type. What are their advantages? What are their disadvantages? How are they used? Write a one-page paper on your research.

Case Project 13-4: Sources of Forensics Data

IP software monitors can provide insight into an incident for a forensics evaluation. Use the Internet to research NetFlow, sFlow, and IPFIX. How are they used? What are their differences? What are their similarities? Create a table that lists the strengths and weaknesses of each.

Case Project 13-5: Log Collection and Analysis Tools

Research the log tools syslog, nxlog, rsyslog, syslog-ng, and journalctl. Create a table that compares each of them, and list how they are used. Include a detailed description of the strengths and weaknesses of each tool. Write a one-page paper on your research.

Case Project 13-6: Cloud Forensics

Use the Internet to research cloud forensics. What can a cloud provider customer do when they are alerted to a cloud security breach? What are the responsibilities of the cloud provider when this occurs? What are the responsibilities of the customer? How can customers insulate themselves from damages? If you were a cloud customer, what would you require of the cloud provider? Write a one-page paper on your research.

Case Project 13-7: North Ridge Security

North Ridge Security provides security consulting and assurance services. You have recently been hired as an intern to assist them.

Impact Industries is a new client of North Ridge and wants an update on forensics investigations. You have been asked to make a presentation to them.

1. Create a PowerPoint presentation for Impact Industries about forensics, including the procedures for conducting an investigation and the tools that can be used. Your presentation should contain at least 10 slides.
2. After the presentation, Impact Industries has asked about how a forensic examination would be performed on the data stored by their cloud provider. Use the Internet to research cloud forensics and then create a memo about your findings and recommendations.

Case Project 13-8: Community Site Activity

The Information Security Community Site is an online companion to this textbook. It contains a wide variety of tools, information, discussion boards, and other features to assist learners. Go to **community.cengage.com/infosec2** and click the *Join or Sign in* icon to log in, using your login name and password that you created in Module 1. Click **Forums (Discussion)** and click on **Security+ Case Projects (7ᵗʰ edition)**. Read the following case study.

Although a data breach may require that an organization contact the affected parties, it is often less clear whether law enforcement agencies should be contacted after a cyber incident has occurred. One study revealed that only 28 percent of businesses in the United Kingdom (UK) reported a cybercrime to law enforcement agencies.[1] In the United States, the FBI estimates that only 15 percent of victims report cybercrimes against them.[2] The following reasons are often cited for the reluctance to report cyber incidents to law enforcement agencies:

- Identifying threat actors, especially when attacks come from abroad, is notoriously difficult for domestic law enforcement agencies and often leads to no arrests or convictions.
- While the interest of the organization is to resume operations as quickly as possible, the interest of law enforcement is to identify, track down, and prosecute the perpetrator. This may result in competing interests and could impede the organization from resuming normal operations as law enforcement seeks to retain evidence and launch its own investigation.
- Reporting an incident may make it public knowledge and harm the organization's reputation unnecessarily.

   However, there are advantages to reporting a cyber incident:

- Law enforcement agencies can work with foreign counterparts to stop organized cybercrime gangs, which can help reduce the number of overall attacks on a business.
- Large federal law enforcement agencies have extensive resources and experience and can even make the company's own internal investigation easier by having experts at hand.
- Companies that report incidents to law enforcement can help provide information toward intelligence-sharing efforts.
- Many law enforcement agencies emphasize that a business might have the missing piece of a puzzle that can help capture repeat cyber criminals.

   Would you contact law enforcement if there were a breach at your place of business? Take your side of this argument and post your opinions to on the Community Site discussion board.

References

1. "Cyber security underpinning the digital economy," *IoD*, March 3, 2016, retrieved Aug. 16, 2019, www.iod.com/cyber-security-for-your-business/articles/cyber-security-underpinning-the-digital-economy.
2. "2016 internet crime report," *IC3*, retrieved Aug. 16, 2019, https://pdf.ic3.gov/2016_IC3Report.pdf.

CYBERSECURITY RESILIENCE

After completing this module, you should be able to do the following:

1. Define business continuity
2. Describe how to achieve resilience through redundancy
3. Explain what a policy is
4. Describe different types of security policies

Front-Page Cybersecurity

Ransomware continues to plague users and organizations of all types and sizes. However, the threat actors behind ransomware have not stood still. The most effective tool to combat ransomware—backups—is now under attack.

When ransomware first became widespread, users were reminded that their key defense was to make regular backups of their data. If ransomware locked a computer, the data backups could be used to restore a computer to its preransomware state. While it still essentially remains true that up-to-date backups are a good defense, threat actors have expanded their targets to include backups, too. Instead of ransomware encrypting only files on the user's local computer, the "next level" of ransomware will encrypt all files on any network or device connected to the local computer. This includes secondary hard disk drives, USB hard drives, network attached storage (NAS) devices, network servers, and even cloud-based data repositories.

How can users defend themselves against ransomware that may infect their data backups? How can users protect their files stored on a networked or attached device connected to the computer or even cloud storage repositories? If an endpoint becomes infected with ransomware, is there a way to protect remote backup files as well?

Users can apply two tests to determine if files other than those stored on the local hard drive are at risk from ransomware. First, if a remote storage device is "mounted" on the local computer and displays a drive letter (such as "D:"), then those files are at risk from a ransomware attack. Second, if a cloud storage repository is configured so that files automatically placed in a local folder are synchronized to the cloud storage, they too are at risk. This is because the ransomware can move encrypted files into the folder, where they will be replicated onto the cloud.

The defense against this next level of ransomware involves a different approach to storage devices and the cloud. Users should first think about having an "air gap," or physically isolating (putting distance between) the computer and the remote backup files. "Manual authentication" that requires the user to enter a username and password, not automatically applied authentication, can also mitigate this next level of ransomware. Some suggestions for devices include the following:

External USB storage device. Unplug the storage device from the computer when not using it.

Secondary hard disk drive. Unmount the drive when it is not needed and then mount it again when needed. (Unmounting the drive hides it from the computer but retains the data.) The command "mountvol D: /p" at the command line will unmount the drive, as will using the Windows Disk Management utility.

Network attached storage (NAS). Create a new share ("admin") and then create a new user account that is the only account with access to the share. Give this user account a strong username and password, and then log in to (and out of) that share as needed.

Cloud storage. Consider turning off automatic synchronization so that files placed in a local folder are not immediately synced to cloud storage. Instead, users should log in to their cloud storage provider through a web browser that requires entering a username and password to sync the files. If this is not feasible, users should check with their cloud storage provider. Many cloud providers have some type of short-term "versioning," meaning that older versions are retained online for a limited period of time (perhaps seven days but sometimes up to a month). If cloud storage files become locked with ransomware, it is possible to roll back to a previous version of unencrypted files.

Earthquakes, tsunamis, tornados, hurricanes, floods, wildfires—these and other natural disasters have a major impact on businesses around the world. The worldwide global economic loss due to natural disasters for 2019 was $232 billion dollars. Although this is a very high amount, it actually is the lowest over the last four years. (The amount fluctuates each year due to the number, type, and duration of natural disasters.) In 2017, this loss was more than double, at $475 billion dollars. Flooding generates the highest loss of both property and lives each year.[1] Natural disasters are virtually impossible to predict in time to make quick preparations.

Not all disasters, however, are acts of nature. Sabotage, terrorism, cyberattacks, and pandemics also can quickly bring a business to its knees—or put it out of operation entirely. The ability of an organization to maintain its operations and services in the face of catastrophe is crucial if it is to survive.

Although preparation for disasters is an essential task for organizations both large and small, it remains sadly lacking in practice. Many organizations are completely unprepared. It is estimated that four out of every 10 businesses do not reopen following a disaster, and another 25 percent fail within one year. Nine out of 10 businesses fail within two years of being struck by a disaster.[2] Of those organizations that do have plans on paper, most have never tested the plans to determine whether they would successfully bring the business through an unforeseen event.

One of the keys for an organization to continue to function following any type of disaster is *resilience*, which is defined as the capacity to recovery quickly from difficulties and spring back into shape. But resilience does not happen by accident: it requires planning and preparation.

In this module, you learn about applying resilience to keep an organization operational during and after a disaster. You first learn what business continuity is and why it is important. Next, you investigate how to prevent disruptions through redundancy. Finally, you see how business policies can help provide resilience to an organization.

BUSINESS CONTINUITY

2.5 Given a scenario, implement cybersecurity resilience.

4.2 Summarize the importance of policies, processes, and procedures for incident response.

5.4 Summarize risk management processes and concepts.

This section explains what business continuity is and how it can be achieved through redundancy.

Introduction to Business Continuity

Defining business continuity can best be done by comparing similar but different types of processes and plans. A business impact analysis and a disaster recovery plan are closely associated with business continuity.

What Is Business Continuity?

Business continuity can be defined as the ability of an organization to maintain its operations and services in the face of a disruptive event or a major disaster. These disasters may be environmental disasters such as floods, hurricanes, and tornados, or man-made disasters such as industrial accidents, oil spills, terrorist attacks, and transportation accidents. Although most disasters to an organization are external disasters (such as environmental disasters), some are internal disasters (such as a fire in a data center).

A business continuity plan (BCP) is a strategic document that provides alternative modes of operation for business activities that, if interrupted, could result in a significant loss to the enterprise. Creating a BCP involves identifying exposure to threats, creating preventive and recovery procedures, and then testing them to determine if they are sufficient. In short, a BCP is designed to ensure that an organization can continue to function (*continuity of operations*) in the event of an environmental disaster or man-made disaster; it is *recovery planning*.

NOTE 1

BCP may also include succession planning, which is determining in advance who will be authorized to take over in the event of the incapacitation or death of key employees.

A BCP generally has three goals:

- *Business recovery planning*. This involves resuming critical business functions and processes that relate to and support the delivery of the core products or services to a customer.
- *Crisis management and communications*. Crisis management and communications is the process of giving an effective response to an event. It is intended to stabilize the situation through effective leadership communication.
- *Disaster recovery*. This element addresses the recovery of critical information technology (IT) assets, including systems, applications, databases, storage, and network assets.

A BCP may sometimes be confusing due to conflicting terminology. Because BCPs are used across a wide range of industries and by different regulatory groups and agencies, many of these use their own unique terminology that is similar to BCP but slightly different. Table 14-1 lists several of the terms that are similar to or related to a BCP but have different meanings.

Table 14-1   BCP terminology

Terminology	Definition	How it compares to BCP
Resumption planning	Used for the recovery of critical business functions separate from IT, such as resuming a critical manufacturing process	Part of the BCP process
Contingency actions	Tactical solutions addressing a core business resource or process, such as how to handle the loss of a specific vendor	Contingency planning is usually considered an isolated action and not part of an overall BCP
Emergency response	The immediate actions taken to preserve lives and safeguard property and assets, such as an evacuation plan	Emergency response is a subset of a BCP
Disaster recovery	The recovery and resumption of critical technology assets in the event of a disaster	Disaster recovery is a component of an overall BCP program

A BCP should include the following elements:

- *High availability*. A BCP should address high availability, which is the ability to withstand all outages—planned and unplanned outages, and environmental and internal disasters—while providing continuous processing for critical applications. For example, a high availability solution for critical e-commerce servers and databases would require a fully automated failover to a backup system so that sales can continue functioning without any disruption.

- *Scalability.* Organizations continue to grow and expand on a regular basis. A BCP that only looks at the organization as it stands today will find that the plan is out of date tomorrow. Instead, a BCP must have the capability to cover increased capacity; in other words, a BCP must have scalability.
- *Diversity.* Just as a BCP must have scalability as capacity increases, it must also include diversity as different technologies, third-party vendors, controls, and even cryptographic solutions are added.
- *On-prem and cloud.* As more and more resources are moved from on-premises to the cloud, a BCP should have the flexibility to address this movement without needing to continually rewrite the plan.

Similar to creating a BCP is continuity of operation planning (COOP). This is a federal initiative that is intended to encourage organizations (and departments with an organization) to address how critical operations will continue under a broad range of negative circumstances. A COOP plan addresses emergencies from an "all-hazards approach" instead of focusing more narrowly on a specific event. It is designed to establish requirements for ensuring that critical functions continue and even includes how personnel and resources can be relocated in case of emergencies.

Business Impact Analysis (BIA)

One important tool for creating a BCP is a business impact analysis (BIA). A BIA identifies business processes and functions and then quantifies the impact a loss of these functions may have on business operations. These impacts include the impact on property (tangible assets), impact on finance (monetary funding), impact on safety (physical protection), impact on reputation (status), and even the impact on life (well-being). By identifying the critical processes and functions through a site risk assessment (a detailed evaluation of the processes performed at a site and how they can be impacted), a BIA can then be the foundation for a functional recovery plan that addresses the steps to take to restore those processes, if necessary.

 **CAUTION** An organization with remote sites sometimes assumes that all sites perform essentially the same functions as the main headquarters. However, that is not always true. In one case, a third-party vendor was hired to perform a BIA but was told to only look at the headquarters. The vendor convinced the organization to examine all the sites. They found that the headquarters performed more than 80 functions, of which half were centrally managed and implemented. The other 40 functions could be performed at the satellite offices in various combinations, which would have been overlooked if the BIA were not conducted at each site.

A BIA is designed to identify those processes that are critically important to an enterprise. A BIA will help determine the mission-essential function, or the activity that serves as the core purpose of the enterprise. For example, a mission-essential function for a hospital could be to *deliver healthcare services to individuals and their families*, while a nonessential function is to *generate and distribute a monthly online newsletter*. In addition, a BIA can also help in the identification of critical systems that in turn support the mission-essential function. In a hospital setting, a critical system could be to *maintain an emergency room facility for the community*. Whereas this is a critical system, is not the core purpose of the hospital.

Identifying the single point of failure, which is a component or entity in a system that if it no longer functions will disable the entire system, is also a goal of a BIA. A patient information database in a hospital could be considered a single point of failure. Minimizing these single failure points results in a system that can function for an extended period with little downtime. This availability is often expressed as a percentage of uptime in a year. Table 14-2 lists the percentage availability and the corresponding downtimes.

Table 14-2 Percentage availability and downtimes

Percentage availability	Name	Weekly downtime	Monthly downtime	Yearly downtime
90%	One Nine	16.8 hours	72 hours	36.5 days
99%	Two Nines	1.68 hours	7.20 hours	3.65 days
99.9%	Three Nines	10.1 minutes	43.2 minutes	8.76 hours
99.99%	Four Nines	1.01 minutes	4.32 minutes	52.56 minutes
99.999%	Five Nines	6.05 seconds	25.9 seconds	5.26 minutes
99.9999%	Six Nines	0.605 second	2.59 seconds	31.5 seconds

NOTE 2

Because privacy of data is of high importance today, many BIAs also contain a privacy impact assessment, which is used to identify and mitigate privacy risks. This includes an examination of what personally identifiable information (PII) is being collected, the reasons it is collected, and the safeguards regarding how the data will be accessed, shared, and stored. A privacy threshold assessment can determine if a system contains PII, whether a privacy impact assessment is required, and if any other privacy requirements apply to the IT system.

Disaster Recovery Plan (DRP)

Whereas a BCP considers the needs of the business as a whole in recovering from a catastrophe, a subset of it focuses on continuity in the context of IT. This is called a **disaster recovery plan (DRP)**, which is involved with restoring IT functions and services. A DRP is a written document that details the process for restoring IT resources following an event that causes a significant disruption in service. Comprehensive in scope, a DRP is intended to be a detailed document that is updated regularly.

Most DRPs cover a standard set of topics. One common topic is the sequence in restoring systems. After a disaster has occurred, in what sequence should systems be reinstated (**restoration order**)? That is, which systems should have priority and be restored before other systems? Several factors may be considered. One factor is obvious dependencies: that is, the network must be restored before applications that rely on the network are restored. A second factor is the processes that are of fundamental importance to an enterprise: critical systems that support the mission-essential function and those systems that require high availability need to be restored before other systems. Another factor is the alternative business practices, or those "workaround" activities that can temporarily substitute for normal business activities. That is, how long can a manual workaround process meet the temporary needs without causing bigger problems such as unmanageable backlogs?

Resilience Through Redundancy

Adding cybersecurity resilience to promote business continuity is important to prevent certain events from crippling an enterprise. This is sometimes known as incorporating "fault tolerance" into IT systems. A "fault" is a malfunction or deviation from the systems' normal expected behavior, while "tolerance" is the capacity for enduring. Fault tolerance refers to a system's ability to deal with malfunctions.

NOTE 3

Fault tolerance is a realization that systems will always have faults or the potential for faults, so they must be designed in such a way that the system will be tolerant of those faults. The system should compensate for the faults yet continue to function.

Because no IT system can ever be completely free of faults, the solution to fault tolerance is to build in **redundancy**, or the use of duplicated equipment to improve the availability of the system. The goal of redundancy is to reduce a variable known as the **mean time to recovery (MTTR)**. Some systems are designed to have a MTTR of zero, which means they have redundant components that can take over the instant the primary component fails.

Redundancy planning can involve redundancy for endpoints, servers, disks, networks, power, sites, and data.

Endpoints

Although resilience through redundancy is critical for business continuity, not all systems may require it. For example, the downtime from a user's endpoint, such as a desktop computer, is not as critical as that for servers, disks, and networks. Also, a desktop or laptop computer is a ubiquitous commodity item today that, if necessary, can be quickly replaced in the event of a hardware component failure, and thus would not require hardware redundancy (such as two identical hard disks, two identical keyboards, and so on).

In the event of a software issue, such as a malware infection, many OSs have a feature known as **revert to known state** in which it is possible to "roll back the clock" on the OS and restore it to an earlier point prior to the problem. Versions of Microsoft Windows through Windows 7 had a **last known good configuration** option in which the OS could be rolled back to the last time the device properly booted. If the problem persisted, then live boot media (such as a USB device that contained a complete bootable OS) could be used as a recovery mechanism. Newer versions of Windows have comparable options.

To protect an endpoint from malware infections, programs are available that can "freeze" a computer to prevent it from accepting any changes from malware. This makes the computer nonpersistent. *Persistent* is to continue to exist, so a computer that is nonpersistent means that any changes or additions are not saved when the computer is rebooted and thus returns to its original state.

Servers

Because servers play such a key role in a network infrastructure, the loss of one or more servers that supports a critical application can have a significant impact. In the past, some organizations stockpiled spare parts to replace a part that failed (such as a server's power supply) or even had entire redundant servers as standbys. However, the time it takes to install a new part or add a new server to the network and then load software and backup data was sometimes longer than an organization could tolerate.

Another approach that some organizations take is to design the network infrastructure so that multiple servers are incorporated into the network yet appear to users and applications as a single computing resource. One method to do this is by *clustering* or combining two or more devices to appear as a single unit. A *server cluster* is the combination of two or more servers that are interconnected to appear as one, as shown in Figure 14-1. These servers are connected through both a *public cluster connection* so that clients see them as a single unit as well as a *private cluster connection* so that the servers can exchange data when necessary. There are two types of server clusters. In an *asymmetric server cluster*, a standby server exists only to take over for another server in the event of its failure. The standby server performs no useful work other than to be ready if it is needed. In a *symmetric server cluster*, every server in the cluster performs useful work. If one server fails, the remaining servers continue to perform their normal work as well as that of the failed server.

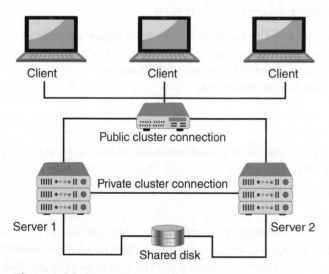

Figure 14-1   Server cluster

Today, however, just as virtualization has reduced the number of physical servers that are needed in a data center, so too has virtualization impacted the number of server clusters that are needed for server redundancy in disaster recovery. Because a virtualized image can be quickly moved to another physical server, the need for server clusters supporting large numbers of physical servers for disaster recovery has diminished. Tools are available so that as one virtual machine is shut down, a copy of that virtual machine is automatically launched (replication).

Disks

There are two hardware redundancies for disks that store data. These are RAID and SAN multipath.

RAID   A trend in data storage technologies for computers today is to use solid state drives (SSDs), which essentially store data on chips instead of magnetic platters. Because SSDs lack spinning platters, actuator arms with read/write heads, and motors, they are more resistant to failure and are considered more reliable than traditional hard disk drives (HDDs). However, due primarily to lower cost, HDDs still serve as the backbone of data storage for servers.

Because HDDs are mechanical devices, they often are the first component of a system to fail. Some organizations maintain a stockpile of hard drives as spare parts to replace those that fail. Yet how many spare hard drives should an organization keep on hand?

A statistical value that is used to answer this question is **mean time between failures (MTBF)**. MTBF refers to the average (*mean*) amount of time until a component fails, cannot be repaired, and must be replaced. Calculating the MTBF involves taking the total time measured divided by the total number of failures observed. For example, if 15,400 hard drive units were run for 1,000 hours each and that resulted in 11 failures, the MTBF would be $(15,400 \times 1,000)$ hours/11, or 1.4 million hours. This MTBF rating can be used to determine the number of spare hard drives that should be available for a quick replacement. If an organization had 1,000 hard drives operating continuously with an MTBF rating of 1.4 million hours, it could be expected that one drive would fail every 58 days, or 19 failures over three years. This data can help an organization know how many spare hard drives are needed.

 **CAUTION**   The MTBF certainly does not mean that a single hard drive is expected to last 1.4 million hours (159 years)! MTBF is a statistical measure and, as such, cannot predict anything for a single unit.

Instead of waiting for a hard drive to fail, a more proactive approach can be used. A system of hard drives based on redundancy can be achieved through using a technology known as **RAID (Redundant Array of Independent Drives** or **Redundant Array of Inexpensive Disks)**, which uses multiple hard disk drives for increased reliability and performance. RAID can be implemented through either software or hardware. Software-based RAID is implemented at the operating system level, while hardware-based RAID requires a specialized hardware controller either on the client computer or on the array that holds the RAID drives.

 **CAUTION**   Although some motherboards have built-in RAID, this is simply BIOS-assisted software RAID and is usually proprietary and nonstandard. It is commonly known as "Fake RAID."

There are several standard RAID configurations (called *levels*). Additional levels include "nested" levels that often combine two other RAID levels. For example, RAID Level 10 is a combination of RAID Level 0 and Level 1. With nested RAID, the elements can be either individual disks or entire RAIDs.

The most common levels of RAID are Level 0, 1, 5, 6, and 10. Descriptions of several of these common levels include the following:

- *RAID Level 0 (striped disk array without fault tolerance).* RAID 0 technology is based on *striping*. Striping partitions divides the storage space of each hard drive into smaller sections (*stripes*), which can be as small as 512 bytes or as large as several megabytes. Data written to the stripes is alternated across the drives, as shown in Figure 14-2. Although RAID Level 0 uses multiple drives, it is not fault tolerant; if one of the drives fails, all the data on that drive is lost.

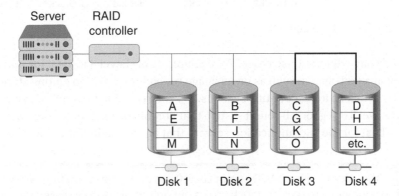

Figure 14-2   RAID Level 0

- *RAID Level 1 (mirroring)*. RAID Level 1 uses *disk mirroring*. Disk mirroring involves connecting multiple drives in the server to the same disk controller card. When a request is made to write data to the drive, the controller sends that request to each drive; when a read action is required, the data is read twice, once from each drive. By "mirroring" the action on the primary drive, the other drives become exact duplicates. In case the primary drive fails, the other drives take over with no loss of data. This is shown in Figure 14-3. A variation of RAID Level 1 is to include *disk duplexing*. Instead of having a single disk controller card that is attached to all hard drives, disk duplexing has separate cards for each disk. A single controller card failure affects only one drive. This additional redundancy protects against controller card failures.

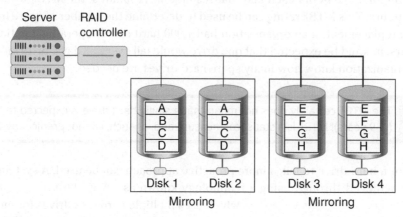

Figure 14-3   RAID Level 1

- *RAID 5 (independent disks with distributed parity)*. RAID Level 5 distributes *parity* data (a type of error checking) across all drives instead of using a separate drive to hold the parity error checking information. Data is always stored on one drive while its parity information is stored on another drive, as shown in Figure 14-4. Distributing parity across other disks provides an additional degree of protection.

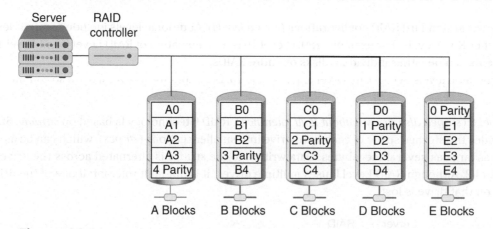

Figure 14-4   RAID Level 5

Different levels of RAID have different use cases. For example, RAID Level 0 is ideal for non-critical storage of data that must be read/written at a high speed, such as on an image retouching or video editing station. RAID Level 1 is best for mission-critical storage, such as for accounting systems. It is also suitable for small servers in which only two data drives will be used. RAID Level 5 is a good all-round system that combines efficient storage with excellent security and decent performance. It is best for file and application servers that have a limited number of data drives.

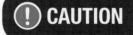 **CAUTION**   Although all levels of RAID except Level 0 can offer protection from a single drive failure, RAID is not intended to replace data backups but only to provide increased reliability and performance.

SAN Multipath In the enterprise, the standard data storage facilities and networking protocols cannot always cope with the need to store and transmit large volumes of data. Most organizations have turned to using a storage area network (SAN), which is a dedicated network storage facility that provides access to data storage over a high-speed network. SANs consolidate different storage facilities—disk arrays, tape libraries, and even "optical jukeboxes" that can load thousands of discs by robotic arms—so they are accessible to servers. The different storage facilities actually appear as a single pool of locally attached devices.

NOTE 4

SANs can also support SAN-to-SAN replication: a SAN at Site A can update a duplicate SAN at Site B to serve as a backup copy. This type of replication does not impact the performance of normal servers and thus is very efficient.

Multipath is a technique for creating more than one physical path between devices and a SAN. If one path is interrupted (due to a cable break or a technician unplugging the wrong cable) multipath would simply redirect the broken connection to another path. Multipath can also assist with increasing the speed of a SAN by spreading connections across multiple paths so that a "bottleneck" is not created.

Networks

Due to the critical nature of connectivity today, redundant networks also may be necessary. A redundant network waits in the background during normal operations and uses a replication scheme to keep its copy of the live network information current. If a disaster occurs, the redundant network automatically launches so that it is transparent to users. A redundant network ensures that network services are always accessible.

NOTE 5

Some enterprises contract with more than one Internet service provider (ISP) for remote site network connectivity. In case the primary ISP is no longer available, the secondary ISP will be used. Enterprises can elect to use redundant fiber-optic lines to the different ISPs, each of which takes a diverse path through an area.

Virtually all network hardware components can be duplicated to provide a redundant network. Some manufacturers offer switches and routers that have a primary active port as well as a standby failover network port for physical redundancy. If a special packet is not detected in a specific time frame on the primary port, the failover port automatically takes over. Load balancers can provide a degree of network redundancy by blocking traffic to servers that are not functioning. Also, multiple redundant switches and routers can be integrated into the network infrastructure. Virtual software-defined network (SDN) controllers can increase network reliability and may lessen the need for redundant equipment. One technique that an SDN controller can use to increase network reliability is to set up multiple paths between the origin and the destination so that the network is not impacted by the outage of a single link.

NOTE 6

Load balancers are covered in Module 9, and SDNs are covered in Module 10.

Another network hardware element that can be configured for redundancy is the network interface card (NIC) adapters. A server that performs a critical function can have up to 32 physical adapters installed and then configured into one or more software-based virtual network adapters. This is called NIC teaming and provides redundancy as well as faster performance.

Power

Maintaining electrical power is essential when planning for redundancy. Critical devices such as servers can be fitted with a dual power supply so that if one power supply fails, the other can take over. A dual power supply from Athena Power is shown in Figure 14-5. A managed power distribution unit (PDU) is a device fitted with multiple electrical outputs and is designed to distribute electric power, especially to racks of computers and networking equipment located within a data center.

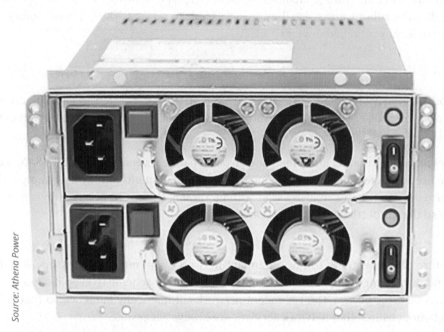

Figure 14-5   Dual power supply

An **uninterruptible power supply (UPS)** is a device that maintains power to equipment in case of an interruption in the primary electrical power source. A UPS is more than just a big battery, however. UPS systems also can communicate with the network operating system on a server to ensure that an orderly shutdown occurs. Specifically, if the power goes down, a UPS can complete the following tasks:

- Send a message to the network administrator's computer, or page or telephone the network manager, to indicate that the power has failed.
- Notify all users that they must finish their work immediately and log off.
- Prevent any new users from logging on.
- Disconnect users and shut down the server.

There are two primary types of UPSs. An *offline UPS* is considered the least expensive and simplest solution. During normal operation, the equipment being protected is served by the standard primary power source. The offline UPS battery charger is also connected to the primary power source to charge its battery. If power is interrupted, the UPS quickly (usually within a few milliseconds) begins supplying power to the equipment. When the primary power is restored, the UPS automatically switches back into standby mode. An *online UPS* is always running off its battery while the main power runs the battery charger. An advantage of an online UPS is that it is not affected by dips or sags in voltage. An online UPS can clean the electrical power before it reaches the server to ensure that a correct and constant level of power is delivered to the server. The online UPS also can serve as a surge protector, which keeps intense spikes of electrical current, common during thunderstorms, from reaching systems.

Because a UPS can supply power for a limited amount of time, some organizations turn to a backup **generator** to create power. Backup generators can be powered by diesel, natural gas, or propane gas to generate electricity. Unlike portable residential backup generators, commercial backup generators are permanently installed as part of the building's power infrastructure. They include automatic transfer switches that can, in less than one second, detect the loss of a building's primary power and switch to the backup generator.

Sites

Just as redundancy can be planned for servers, storage, networks, and power, it also can be planned for the entire site. A major disaster such as a flood or hurricane can inflict such extensive damage to a building that the organization must temporarily move to another location. Many organizations maintain redundant recovery sites in case this occurs. Three basic types of redundant sites are used: hot sites, cold sites, and warm sites.

- *Hot site.* A **hot site** is generally run by a commercial disaster recovery service that allows a business to continue computer and network operations to maintain business continuity. A hot site is essentially a duplicate of the production site and has all the equipment needed for an organization to continue running, including office space and furniture, telephone jacks, computer equipment, and a live telecommunications link. Data backups of information can be quickly moved to the hot site, and in some instances the production site automatically synchronizes all its data with the hot site so that all data is immediately accessible. If the organization's data processing center becomes inoperable, typically all data processing operations can be moved to a hot site within an hour.
- *Cold site.* A **cold site** provides office space, but the customer must provide and install all the equipment needed to continue operations. In addition, there are no backups of data immediately available at this site. A cold site is less expensive but requires more time to get an enterprise in full operation after a disaster.
- *Warm site.* A **warm site** has all the equipment installed but does not have active Internet or telecommunications facilities and does not have current backups of data. This type of site is much less expensive than constantly maintaining those connections as required for a hot site; however, the amount of time needed to turn on the connections and install the backups can be as much as half a day or more.

NOTE 7

Businesses usually have an annual contract with a company that offers hot and cold site services with a monthly service charge. Some services also offer data backup services so that all company data is available regardless of whether a hot site or cold site is used.

However, it is important when creating alternate sites to consider **geographic dispersal**. Instead of all sites being clustered in a limited geographic area, they should be distributed across a larger area to mitigate the impact of an environmental disasters (such as hurricanes and tornados) and man-made disasters (such as terrorist attacks and transport accidents). Geographic dispersal should also be considered when using cloud computing in conjunction with sites. Some organizations back up their applications and data to the cloud and then, if a disaster occurs, restore it to hardware in a hot, cold, or warm site. Other organizations also back up to the cloud but, instead of restoring to hardware at a site, they restore to virtual machines in the cloud, which then can be accessed from almost any location. This approach reduces or even eliminates the need for maintaining sites. When creating a cloud platform, the customer can often choose the region in which the data will reside.

Data

A **data backup** is copying information to a different medium and storing it so that it can be used in the event of a disaster. Backing up data involves data backup calculations, creating different types of data backups, and storing the backups.

Data Backup Calculations   Two elements are used in the calculation of when backups should be performed. The first is known as the **recovery point objective (RPO)**, which is defined as the maximum length of time that an organization can tolerate between backups. Simply put, RPO is the "age" of the data that an organization wants the ability to restore in the event of a disaster. For example, if an RPO is six hours, this means that an organization wants to be able to restore systems back to the state they were in no longer than six hours ago. To achieve this, it is necessary to make backups at least every six hours; any data created or modified between backups will be lost.

Related to the RPO is the **recovery time objective (RTO)**. The RTO is the length of time it will take to recover the data that has been backed up. An RTO of two hours means that data can be restored within that time frame.

Types of Data Backups   One of the keys to backing up files is knowing which files need to be backed up. Software that is used to create backups of files can internally designate which files have already been backed up by setting an archive bit in the properties of the file. A file with the archive bit cleared (set to 0) indicates that the file has been backed up. Any time the contents of that file are changed, the archive bit is set (to 1), meaning that this modified file now needs to be backed up. The archive bit is illustrated in Figure 14-6.

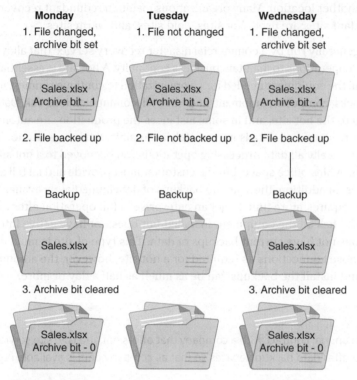

Figure 14-6   Archive bit

There are different types of backups, and three of the most common are summarized in Table 14-3. The archive bit is not always cleared after each type of backup; this provides additional flexibility regarding which files should be backed up.

Table 14-3   Types of data backups

Type of backup	How used	Archive bit after backup	Files needed for recovery
Full backup	Starting point for all backups	Cleared (set to 0)	The full backup is needed.
Differential backup	Backs up any data that has changed since last full backup	Not cleared (set to 1)	The full backup and only last differential backup are needed.
Incremental backup	Backs up any data that has changed since last full backup or last incremental backup	Cleared (set to 0)	The full backup and all incremental backups are needed.

The drawback to backing up only files (called a *file backup*) is that it does not provide the means to restore the apps that created the files or the operating system. An alternative is to perform an image backup that captures the entire contents of the disk. This enables an entire restoration of the contents of the disk to a new hard disk or computer. Image backups can also restore a single file or directory and can create an incremental image based on the previous image created.

A more comprehensive backup technology than file backups or image backups is known as *continuous data protection (CDP)*. As its name implies, CDP performs continuous data backups that can be restored immediately, thus providing excellent RPO and RTO times. CDP maintains a historical record of all changes made to data by constantly monitoring all writes to the hard drive. It does this by creating a snapshot of the data, which is essentially a series of "reference markers" of the data at a specific point in time.

NOTE 8

Many CDP products even let users restore their own documents. A user who accidentally deletes a file can search the CDP system by entering the name of the document and then view the results through an interface that looks like a web search engine. Clicking the desired file then restores it. For security purposes, users may search only for documents for which they have permissions.

Storing Backups   A key consideration with backups is where they should be stored. It is not required that only the original backup be stored; instead, a **backup copy** (a copy of the original backup) can—and should—be made and stored in more than one location for additional protection. The options for storing backups are onsite, offsite, and the cloud.

Onsite   Once a backup has been created, it is then stored locally onsite on media (local magnetic disk, optical disk, or magnetic tape) that is accessible. It can also be stored on a SAN or a **network-attached storage (NAS)** device. (A NAS is a single storage device that serves files over the network and is relatively inexpensive.) The advantage of storing the backup onsite is that it allows quick access to data (for example, to retrieve a file that was erroneously deleted by a user). Even if the backup is stored offline, it can quickly be made available. The disadvantages of storing a backup onsite are security (it may be vulnerable to theft) and damage (an environmental disaster or man-made disaster that impacts the data center will likewise impact the data backup).

Offsite   In the past, offsite backups were typically stored in a secure location such as a local bank vault. Later services became available in which a courier would routinely visit the enterprise and pick up magnetic tapes or hard drives that contained the most recent backups and transport them to the vendor's secure site. However, the location selection of where the media should be stored was often an issue (called **distance considerations**) due to security concerns (transporting media over long distances increased the risk of accident or theft) or a delay in accessing the media in the event the data backup had to be quickly restored. This is because at offsite locations it was stored offline instead of online.

NOTE 9

One of the most secure offsite backup facilities is in a former salt mine facility in Kansas. It is 650 feet (198 meters) or about 45 stories beneath the surface. The facility is encased in solid stone and covers the equivalent of 35 football fields with more than 1.7 million square feet (0.52 million square meters) of storage space. The temperature and humidity levels remain constant year round. The site protects against natural disasters (tornado, hurricane, flooding, etc.) as well as man-made disasters (explosion, fire, civil unrest, etc.). It serves as the largest single storage facility for the movie and television film industry worldwide.

Cloud   Today many organizations store their offsite backups using an online cloud repository. These online sites often use CDP to continually back up data and provide the highest degree of protection today to users. There are several Internet services available that provide similar features:

- *Automatic continuous backup*. Once the initial backup is completed, any new or modified files are also backed up. Usually the backup software "sleeps" while the computer is being used and performs backups only when there is no user activity. This helps to lessen any impact on the computer's performance or Internet speed.
- *Universal access*. Files backed up through online services can be made available to another computer.
- *Delayed deletion*. Files that are copied to the online server will remain accessible for up to 30 days before they are deleted. This allows a user to have a longer window of opportunity to restore a deleted file.
- *Online or media-based restore*. If a file or the entire computer must be restored, then this can be done online. Some services also provide the option of shipping backup files on a new media device such as an SSD or on optical media.

Most security experts recommend that at minimum, a *3-2-1 backup* plan should be used. This plan says that there should always be *three* different copies of backups (that does not count the original data itself) on at least *two* different types of storage media, and *one* of the backups should be stored at a different location such as the cloud or in a remote site.

NOTE 10

Home users should likewise follow the 3-2-1 backup plan by always maintaining *three* different copies of backups (that does not count the original data itself) by using at least *two* different types of media on which to store these backups (a separate hard drive, an external hard drive, a USB device, etc.) and storing *one* of the backups offsite.

TWO RIGHTS & A WRONG

1. A business continuity plan (BCP) is the development of a strategic document that provides alternative modes of operation for business activities that, if interrupted, could result in a significant loss to the enterprise.
2. Mean time to recovery (MTTR) is the average amount of time that it will take a device to recover from a failure that is not a terminal failure.
3. RAID can be implemented only through hardware.

See Appendix B for the answer.

POLICIES

 **CERTIFICATION**

3.7 Given a scenario, implement identity and account management controls.

5.3 Explain the importance of policies to organizational security.

Another means of cybersecurity resilience is through a security policy. It is important to know the definition of a policy and the different types of policies that are used.

Definition of a Policy

Several terms describe the "rules" that a user follows in an organization. A *standard* is a collection of requirements specific to the system or a procedure that must be met by everyone. For example, a standard might describe how to secure a computer at home that remotely connects to the organization's network. Users must follow this standard if they want to be able to connect. A *guideline* is a collection of suggestions that should be implemented. These are not requirements to be met but are strongly recommended. A **policy** is a document that outlines specific requirements or rules that must be met. A policy is considered the correct tool for an organization to use when establishing security because a policy applies to a wide range of hardware or software (it is not a standard) and is required (it is not just a guideline).

NOTE 11

If the question "What is a security policy?" were posed to both a manager and a security technician, the answers would likely be different. A manager might say that a security policy is a set of management statements that defines an organization's philosophy of how to safeguard its information. A security technician might respond that a security policy is the cybersecurity configuration settings in a system. These two responses are not conflicting but are complementary: a written policy dictates what technology configuration settings should be used.

A policy generally has these characteristics:

- Communicates a consensus of judgment
- Defines appropriate behavior for users
- Identifies what tools and procedures are needed
- Provides directives for human resources action in response to inappropriate behavior
- May be helpful if it is necessary to prosecute violators

NOTE 12

The purpose of security policies is not to serve as a motivational tool to force users to practice safe security techniques. The results from research have indicated that the specific elements of a security policy do not have an impact on user behavior. Relying on a security policy as the exclusive defense mechanism will not provide adequate security for an organization.

Types of Security Policies

There are several types of security policies. These include account management policies, mobile device location-based policies, personnel policies, organizational policies, and data policies.

Account Management Policies

Account management involves the restrictions regarding user accounts. This includes not only who is authorized to access resources, but when, how, and from what location they can do so. Common account management "sub-policies" are **credential policies** that address requirements for authentication credentials, such as the length and complexity of passwords. Credential policies apply to all personnel (users, administrators, and third parties) but to also devices and service accounts.

Unlike most other written policies that an organization may have written, account management policies can be enforced through technology. There are different technologies that can be used to enforce these policies. In a Microsoft environment, these can be enforced through Windows Group Policy, Active Directory, and Cloud App Security.

Group Policy   Managing login credentials such as passwords in user accounts (credential management) can be accomplished by setting technology restrictions regarding the creation and use of passwords. Although these restrictions can be performed on a user-by-user basis, this quickly becomes cumbersome and is a security risk: it is too easy to overlook one setting in one user account and create a security vulnerability.

A preferred approach is to assign privileges to a group of common users. In a Microsoft Windows environment, controls over user and computer accounts can be set through a feature known as Group Policy. Group Policy settings can be made on an individual computer (*Local Group Policy*) but will only apply to that computer, while settings applied to users in a domain will apply to all users (*Domain Group Policy*).

NOTE 13

If a Local Group Policy setting is different from a Domain Group Policy setting, the Domain Group Policy takes precedence.

Establishing controls on authentication credentials such as passwords and on the accounts can be configured by using Group Policy. Several of the common domain policy settings called Microsoft setting objects are listed in Table 14-4.

NOTE 14

Other common password parameters, such as length and expiration, can also be set through Group Policy.

Active Directory   Microsoft's directory service manager, Active Directory, can also be used to enforce account management policies. An **access policy** allows a network administrator to create **account permissions** (the privileges that the user is given) and restrictions based on a role-based access control scheme.

Table 14-4 Windows Group Policy password settings

Setting name	Microsoft setting object	Description	Recommended setting
Password reuse	Enforce password history	Determines the number of unique new passwords a user must use before an old password can be reused (from 0 to 24).	24 new passwords
Password history	Minimum password age	Determines how many days a new password must be kept before the user can change it (from 0 to 999). This setting is designed to work with the Enforce password history setting so that users cannot quickly reset their passwords the required number of times and then change back to their old passwords.	1 day
Password complexity	Passwords must meet complexity requirements	Determines whether the following are used in creating a password: Passwords cannot contain the user's account name or parts of the user's full name that exceed two consecutive characters; must contain characters from three of the following four categories—English uppercase characters (A through Z), English lowercase characters (a through z), digits (0 through 9), and nonalphabetic characters (!, $, #, %).	Enabled
Network Location	Network List Manager policies	Network type can be set as Not Configured, Public, or Private.	Private
Account Audits	Audit Logon Events and Audit Account Logon Events	Logon Events audits every user attempt to log on and off a computer, while Audit Accounts Logon Events logs every event generated on a computer.	Enabled

NOTE 15

Role-based access control is covered in Module 13.

Another setting is a **time-based login** based on **time of day** restrictions can be used to limit when a user can log in to their account to access resources. When setting these restrictions, a network administrator would typically indicate the times a user is restricted from accessing the system or resources. Figure 14-7 illustrates time-based login implemented by indicating the specific days and times.

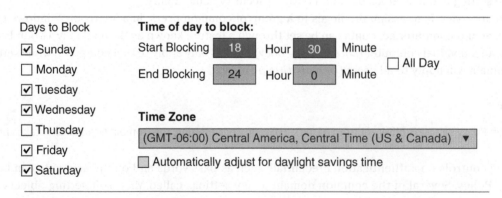

Figure 14-7 Time-based login

Cloud App Security A growing set of enforcement technologies is based on the accumulation and analysis of real-time data that is processed in the cloud. These give a higher level of protection over setting static policies found in Group Policy and Active Directory.

Suppose users access their online account from Nashville. However, 10 minutes later someone tries to access that same user account from Tampa or even Beijing. The Microsoft Cloud App Security feature Impossible Travel would deny the second login and generate a security alert because it is not possible for someone to travel that distance within that time. Another feature is Risky IP address, which examines the IP address that was used to attempt a login and compares it against a list of IP addresses involved in malicious activities.

NOTE 16

Other Cloud App Security features include Activity from Infrequent Country, Activity from Anonymous IP Address, Activity Performed by Terminated User, Suspicious Inbox Forwarding, Unusual Multiple File Download Activities, and Unusual File Share Activities.

If a suspicious login is trapped by Cloud App Security, generally an automatic and immediate lockout is placed on the account, meaning that the account cannot be accessed until a security administrator reviews the incident and removes the lockout. This is different from a disablement in which the account requires an administrator to suspend the account. A lockout occurs automatically while a disablement requires manual intervention.

NOTE 17

System administrators cannot perform a lockout but only a disablement.

Mobile Device Location-Based Policies

Policies can also enforce what mobile devices can access or perform based on the location of the device. The technologies for identification and enforcement include the following:

- *Geolocation*. Mobile devices typically support geolocation, or identifying the geographical location of the device. When finding a person carrying a mobile device, geolocation also identifies the location of a close friend or displays the address of the nearest coffee shop. Location services are used extensively by social media, navigation systems, weather systems, and other mobile-aware applications.
- *Geo-tagging*. Geo-tagging is adding geographical identification data to media such as digital photos taken on a mobile device. A user who, for example, posts a photo on a social networking site may inadvertently identify a private location to anyone who can access the photo.
- *Geofencing*. Geofencing is using the device's GPS to define geographical boundaries where an app can be used.

NOTE 18

Geofencing is commonly used in law enforcement. An individual under house arrest is fitted with an ankle bracelet that alerts authorities if the individual leaves the house.

These technologies can be used for identification and enforcement of how a mobile device can be used based on its location. These are enforced automatically as the device moves into and out of a specific network zone. For example, a tablet containing patient information that leaves the hospital grounds or an employee who attempts to enter a restricted area with a device can result in an alert sent to an administrator. Policies can also include such actions as disabling the camera to prevent users from taking unauthorized pictures in specific geographic locations, disabling automatic screen lock so that users do not have to unlock their device repeatedly while at work, or disabling apps and browsers entirely.

NOTE 19

Geolocation, geo-tagging, and geofencing are all covered in Module 5.

Personnel Policies

Several policies relate to matters of personnel. While these policies cannot be enforced through technology as with account management policies and mobile device location, nevertheless, they are important for creating cybersecurity resiliency. The personnel policies include separation of duties, job rotation, mandatory vacations, clean desk space, least privilege, onboarding and offboarding, and acceptable use.

Separation of Duties   News headlines such as "County Official Charged with Embezzlement" appear all too frequently. Often this fraud results from a single user being trusted with a set of responsibilities that place the person in complete control of the process. For example, one person may be given total control over the collection, distribution, and reconciliation of money. If no other person is involved, it might be too tempting for that person to steal, knowing that nobody else is watching and that there is a good chance the fraud will go undetected. To counteract this possibility, most organizations require that more than one person be involved with functions that relate to handling money, because it would require a conspiracy of all the individuals for fraud to occur.

Likewise, a foundational principle of computer access control is not to give one person total control. Known as separation of duties, this practice requires that if the fraudulent application of a process could potentially result in a breach of security, the process should be divided between two or more individuals. For example, if the duties of the owner and the custodian are performed by a single individual, it could provide that person with total control over all security configurations. It is recommended that these responsibilities be divided so that the system is not vulnerable to the actions performed by a single person.

Job Rotation   Another way to prevent one individual from having too much control is to use job rotation. Instead of one person having sole responsibility for a function, individuals are periodically moved from one job responsibility to another. Employees can rotate either within their home department or across positions in other departments. The best rotation procedure involves multiple employees rotating across many positions for different lengths of time to gain exposure to different roles and functions.

Job rotation has several security advantages. It limits the amount of time that individuals are in a position to manipulate security configurations. It also helps to expose any potential avenues for fraud by having multiple individuals with different perspectives learn about the job and uncover vulnerabilities that someone else may have overlooked.

NOTE 20

Job rotation also has disadvantages. In some cases, employees may not be in a specific job long enough to develop proficiency, and productivity may be lost in the time it takes to train employees in new tasks. Also, job rotation is often limited to less specialized positions. For these reasons, job rotation might not always be practical.

Mandatory Vacation   In many fraud schemes, the perpetrator must be present every day to continue the fraud or keep it from being exposed. Many organizations require mandatory vacations for all employees to counteract this. For sensitive positions within an organization, an audit of the employees' activities is usually scheduled while they are away on vacation.

Clean Desk Space   A clean desk space policy is designed to ensure that all confidential or sensitive materials, either in paper form or electronic, are removed from a user's workspace and secured when the items not in use or employees leaves their workspace. This not only reduces the risk of theft or "prying eyes" reading confidential information, but it can also increase the employee's awareness about the need to protect sensitive information. A clean desk space policy may include such statements as the following:

- Computer workstations must be locked when the workspace is unoccupied and turned off at the end of the business day.
- Confidential or sensitive information must be removed from the desk and locked in a drawer or safe when the desk is unoccupied and at the end of the work day.
- File cabinets must be kept closed and locked when not in use or not attended, and keys may not be left at an unattended desk.
- Laptops must be either locked with a locking cable or locked in a drawer or filing cabinet.
- Mass storage devices such as USB flash drives or portable external hard drives must be locked in a drawer or filing cabinet.
- Paper documents no longer needed must be shredded using the official shredder bins.
- Printouts should be immediately removed from the printer.
- Whiteboards containing confidential or sensitive information should be erased.

Least Privilege   As its name implies, the cybersecurity principle of least privilege means that only the minimum amount of privileges necessary to perform a job or function should be allocated. This helps reduce the attack surface by eliminating unnecessary privileges that could provide an avenue for an attacker. Least privilege should apply both to user accounts and to processes running on the system.

NOTE 21

One of the reasons home computers are so frequently and easily compromised is that they use an account with administrative rights. A more secure option is to use an account with lower privileges and then invoke administrative privileges only when necessary.

Onboarding and Offboarding   Employee onboarding refers to the tasks associated with hiring a new employee. Background checks are now considered essential when hiring a new employee. In addition, viewing the social media posts of potential candidates (social media analysis) can also reveal important insights into applicants.

 **CAUTION**   Many serious issues surround social media analysis of posts made by applicants and employees. For example, while looking at social media posts, employers could easily learn other details such as religion, disability, or pregnancy of an applicant. By law, hiring decisions cannot take these into account, but just knowing them could introduce bias in hiring decisions. Yet if an employer ignores a history of inflammatory social media posts, it could expose that employer to liability. One solution is to use artificial intelligence (AI) software to perform social media analysis.

Once an employee is "onboard," several steps should be taken. Most new hires are required to sign an employee nondisclosure agreement (NDA) to make clear to employees that they may not disclose trade secrets and confidential information without permission. In addition, the setup and account configuration of new employees must be performed. In a common Microsoft Windows environment using Active Directory, the steps may include provisioning the new computer (the new computer can be added to the Active Directory domain and then moved into a specific organizational unit (OU), or the computer account can be set up inside the correct OU before it is joined), creating email mailboxes, adding user accounts to groups, and creating a home folder. It is also important to review the security settings of the different accounts to ensure that they fit within the policy guidelines of the enterprise.

Employee offboarding entails actions to be taken when an employee leaves an enterprise. The necessary steps should include backing up all employee files from the local computer and file server, archiving email, forwarding email to a manager or coworker, hiding the name from the email address book, etc. In addition, when an employee leaves an organization, that employee's accounts should be immediately disabled.

NOTE 22

Orphaned accounts are user accounts that remain active after an employee has left an organization and are a serious security risk. For example, an employee who left under unfavorable circumstances might be tempted to "get even" with the organization by stealing or erasing sensitive information through her account. To assist with controlling dormant accounts, *account expiration* can be used. Account expiration is the process of setting a user's account to expire. Account expiration can be explicit, in that the account expires on a set date, or it can be based on a specific number of days of inactivity.

Acceptable Use Policy (AUP)   An acceptable use policy (AUP) is a written policy that defines the actions users may perform while accessing systems and networking equipment. The users are not limited to employees but should also include vendors, contractors, and visitors, each with different privileges. AUPs typically cover all computer use, including mobile devices.

An AUP may have an overview regarding what is covered by the policy, as in the following sample:

Internet/intranet/extranet-related systems, including but not limited to computer equipment, software, operating systems, storage media, network accounts providing electronic mail, and web browsing, are the property of the Company. These systems are to be used for business purposes in serving the interests of the company, and of our clients and customers, in the course of normal operations. Personal use is strictly prohibited.

The AUP usually provides explicit prohibitions regarding security and proprietary information:

Keep passwords secure and do not share accounts. Authorized users are responsible for the security of their passwords and accounts.

All computers and laptops should be secured with a password-protected screensaver with the automatic activation feature set at 10 minutes or less, or by logging off when the host is unattended.

Postings by employees from a Company device or using a Company email address to personal blogs or personal social media accounts is prohibited.

Unacceptable use may also be outlined by the AUP, as in the following sample:

The following actions are not acceptable ways to use the system:

- *Introduction of malicious programs into the network or server*
- *Revealing your account password to others or allowing use of your account by others, including family and other household members when work is being done at home*
- *Using the Company's computing asset to actively engage in procuring or transmitting material that is in violation of sexual harassment or hostile workplace laws in the user's local jurisdiction*
- *Any form of harassment via email, telephone, text, or social media, whether through language, frequency, or size of messages*
- *Unauthorized use, or forging, of email header information*

Organizational Policies   Several policies relate to the management and functioning of the organization as a whole (**organizational policies**). These include the following:

- *Change management.* Change management refers to a formal process for making modifications to a system and keeping track of those changes. A **change management policy** is a written document that defines the types of changes that can be made and under what circumstances.
- *Change control.* A **change control policy** stipulates the processes to be followed for implementing system changes. It involves communicating the changes to relevant stakeholders and reviewing the processes for validating a change. Change control should be made following the standards set in the change management policy.
- *Asset management.* An **asset management policy** provides the guidelines and practices that govern decisions about how assets should be acquired, maintained, and disposed.

Data Policies   Organizations also need policies to address data. This includes how it should be classified, governed, and retained.

Data classification policy   Not all data is the same: Some is critical and must be protected at all costs (such as research and development data), while other data is of lesser importance (such as marketing data). Labels can be assigned to similar data elements based on their importance (sometimes called their *sensitivity level*), a process known as data classification. A written policy that addresses assigning labels is a **data classification policy**.

NOTE 23

The measure of the importance of data can often be gauged by asking the basic question, *what would an unexpected loss or disclosure of this information mean to us?*

In a commercial (corporate) environment, no standards exist for data classification. Some organizations simply use *Public* and *Confidential* as their only classifications. However, using multiple data classification levels can help clarify the data's importance and prevent data that is "mostly public but a little confidential" from being mislabeled. Table 14-5 lists a typical commercial data classification from the lowest level of sensitivity to the highest.

Table 14-5 Commercial data classification levels (lowest to highest)

Classification level	Description	Example
Public	Data that is the least sensitive and would cause only a small amount of harm if disclosed	Number of current employees
Proprietary	Data disclosed outside the company on only a limited basis to trusted third parties; an unexpected disclosure could reduce the company's competitive advantage	Nontechnical specifications for a new product
Private	Data that might not harm the company itself but could cause damage to others	Human resources data of employees
Confidential	Data used internally within the company; a public disclosure would cause significant harm to the organization	News of an impending merger or acquisition
Sensitive	Data that could cause catastrophic harm to the company if disclosed	Technical specifications for a new product

NOTE 24

When considering which classification a data element should be assigned, the confidentiality of the data should be considered along with its integrity and availability.

Government data classifications have continued to evolve. At one time, the classification levels were *top secret*, *secret*, *confidential*, *sensitive but unclassified (SBU)*, and *unclassified*, but now only the first three levels are used (*top secret*, *secret*, and *confidential*). The level of sensitivity is based on a calculation of the damage to national security that the information's disclosure would cause.

Data governance policy   A **data governance policy** is a series of formal guidelines regarding the data itself. This includes who is responsible for the data, how it can be accessed, how it should be used, and how its integrity can be maintained.

Data retention policy   A **data retention policy** (also called a *records retention policy*) specifies how long data should be retained after it has fulfilled its initial purpose. This policy should outline the business reasons or regulatory requirements for retaining the data, how it can be accessed and by whom while it is in retention, how it should be disposed, and how that disposal is documented.

TWO RIGHTS & A WRONG

1. A policy is a collection of suggestions that should be implemented.
2. Risky IP address examines the IP address that was used to attempt a login and compares it against a list of IP addresses involved in malicious activities.
3. Employee offboarding entails actions to be taken when an employee leaves an enterprise.

See Appendix B for the answer.

⧉ VM LAB   You're now ready to complete the live, virtual machine labs for this module. The labs can be found in the Practice It folder in each MindTap module.

SUMMARY

- Business continuity, which is the ability of an organization to maintain its operations and services in the face of a disruptive event, involves identifying exposure to threats, creating preventive and recovery procedures, and then testing the procedures to determine if they are sufficient. A business continuity plan (BCP) is a document that provides alternative modes of operation for business activities. One important tool in BCP is a business impact analysis (BIA), which analyzes the most mission-essential business functions and identifies critical systems and single points of failure.

- While business continuity planning and testing look at the needs of the business as a whole in recovering from a catastrophe, a subset of BCP focuses on continuity in the context of IT. IT contingency planning involves developing an outline of procedures to follow in the event of a major IT incident or an incident that directly impacts IT. This outline is called a disaster recovery plan (DRP), which is the plan for restoring IT functions and services to their former state. Disaster recovery planning involves creating, implementing, and testing DRPs. Most DRPs also cover a standard set of topics. One common topic is the sequence of reinstating different systems.

- One way to prevent certain issues from crippling an enterprise is to incorporate resilience, also called fault tolerance, into IT systems. Because no IT system can ever be completely free of faults, the solution to fault tolerance is to build in redundancy, or the use of duplicated equipment to improve the availability of the system. Due to how they are used, endpoints rarely require hardware redundancy. Because servers play such a key role in a network infrastructure, the loss of a single server that supports a critical application can have a significant impact. A common approach is for the organization to design the network infrastructure so that multiple servers are incorporated into the network yet appear to users and applications as a single computing resource. One method of doing this is by using a server cluster, which is the combination of two or more servers that are interconnected to appear as one. A system of hard drives based on redundancy can be achieved through using a technology known as RAID, which uses multiple hard disk drives for increased reliability and performance. SAN multipath, a technique for creating more than one physical path between devices and a SAN, can also be used to protect disks.

- Most network hardware components can be duplicated to provide a redundant network. Maintaining electrical power is also essential when planning for redundancy. An uninterruptible power supply (UPS) is a device that maintains power to equipment in the event of an interruption in the primary electrical power source. Because a UPS can supply power for a limited amount of time, some organizations turn to a backup generator to create power. Just as redundancy can be planned for servers, storage, networks, and power, it also can be planned for the entire site. A major disaster such as a flood or hurricane can inflict such extensive damage to a building that the organization may have to temporarily move to another location. Many organizations maintain redundant sites in case this occurs. Three basic types of redundant sites are hot sites, cold sites, and warm sites.

- The most important redundancy is that of the data itself, which is accomplished through data backups. A data backup is copying information to a different medium and storing it so that it can be used in the event of a disaster. The storage location is preferably at an offsite facility. The recovery point objective (RPO) is the maximum length of time that an organization can tolerate between backups. The recovery time objective (RTO) is the length of time it will take to recover data that has been backed up. The three common types of backups are full backup, differential backup, and incremental backup. Another newer backup technology is continuous data protection (CDP), which performs continuous data backups that can be restored immediately, thus providing excellent RPO and RTO times. A key consideration with backups is where they should be stored. Today most organizations store their offsite backups using an online cloud repository.

- A policy is a document that outlines specific requirements or rules that must be met. A security policy is a written document that states how an organization plans to protect the company's information technology assets. There are several types of security policies. Account management involves the restrictions regarding user accounts. This includes not only who is authorized to access resources, but when, how, and from what location they can do so. Unlike most other written policies that an organization may have, written account management policies can be enforced through technology. Different technologies can be used to enforce these policies. In a Microsoft environment, these can be enforced through Windows Group Policy, Active Directory, and Cloud App Security. Policies can also enforce what mobile devices can access or perform based on the location of the device.

- Several policies relate to matters of personnel. These include separation of duties (dividing a process between two or more individuals), job rotation (periodically moving employees from one job responsibility to another), mandatory vacation (requiring that employees take periodic vacations), clean desk space (ensuring that all confidential or sensitive materials, either in paper form or electronic, are removed from a user's workspace and secured), least privilege (assigning permissions only relative to the user's necessary job functions), onboarding and offboarding (tasks associated with when a new employee is hired and when that employee leaves), and acceptable use policy (defines the actions users may perform while accessing systems and networking equipment).
- Several policies relate to the management and functioning of the organization as a whole (organizational policies). Change management refers to a formal process for making modifications to a system and keeping track of those changes. A change management policy is a written document that defines the types of changes that can be made and under what circumstances. A change control policy stipulates the processes to be followed for implementing system changes. It involves communicating the changes to relevant stakeholders and reviewing the processes for validating a change. An asset management policy provides the guidelines and practices that govern decisions about how assets should be acquired, maintained, and disposed.
- A data classification policy identifies types of data. A data governance policy is a series of formal guidelines regarding the data itself. This includes who is responsible for the data, how it can be accessed, how it should be used, and how its integrity can be maintained. A data retention policy (also called a records retention policy) specifies how long data should retained after it has fulfilled its initial purpose. This policy should outline the business reasons or regulatory requirements for retaining the data, how it can be accessed and by whom while it is in retention, and how it should be disposed and how that disposal is documented.

Key Terms

acceptable use policy (AUP)	full backup	onboarding
access policy	functional recovery plan	organizational policies
Account Audits	generator	password complexity
account permissions	geographic dispersal	password history
asset management policy	high availability	password reuse
background checks	hot site	policy
backup copy	identification of critical systems	power distribution unit (PDU)
business continuity plan (BCP)	image backup	RAID (Redundant Array of
business impact analysis (BIA)	Impossible Travel	Independent Drives or Redundant
change control policy	incremental backup	Array of Inexpensive Disks)
change management policy	internal disasters	recovery point objective (RPO)
clean desk space	job rotation	recovery time objective (RTO)
cold site	last known good configuration	redundancy
continuity of operation planning	least privilege	replication
(COOP)	live boot media	restoration order
credential policies	lockout	revert to known state
data backup	mandatory vacations	Risky IP address
data classification policy	man-made disasters	scalability
data governance policy	mean time between failures (MTBF)	separation of duties
data retention policy	mean time to recovery (MTTR)	single point of failure
differential backup	mission-essential function	site risk assessment
disablement	multipath	snapshot
disaster recovery plan (DRP)	network-attached storage (NAS)	social media analysis
distance considerations	Network Location	storage area network (SAN)
diversity	NIC teaming	time of day
dual power supply	nondisclosure agreement (NDA)	time-based login
environmental disasters	nonpersistent	uninterruptible power supply (UPS)
external disasters	offboarding	warm site

Review Questions

1. Mary Alice has been asked to help develop an outline of procedures to be followed in the event of a major IT incident or an incident that directly impacts IT. What type of planning is this?
   a. Business impact analysis planning
   b. IT contingency planning
   c. Disaster recovery planning
   d. Risk IT planning

2. Which of the following is NOT an element that should be part of a BCP?
   a. High availability
   b. Robustness
   c. Diversity
   d. Scalability

3. Which of the following is a federal initiative that is designed to encourage organizations to address how critical operations will continue under a broad range of negative circumstances?
   a. DPPR
   b. BIA
   c. MTBF
   d. COOP

4. A BIA can be a foundation for which of the following?
   a. Functional recovery plan
   b. Site risk assessment
   c. Contingency reaction plan
   d. Resumption assessment plan

5. Which of the following will a BIA NOT help determine?
   a. Mission-essential functions
   b. Identification of critical systems
   c. Single point of failure
   d. Percentage availability of systems

6. Which of these is NOT a factor in determining restoration order?
   a. Dependencies
   b. Speed of implementation
   c. Process of fundamental importance
   d. Alternative business practices

7. What is the average amount of time that it will take a device to recover from a failure that is not a terminal failure?
   a. MTTR
   b. RTO
   c. RPO
   d. MTBF

8. Which of the following is NOT true about RAID?
   a. It can be implemented in hardware or software.
   b. Nested levels can combine other RAID levels.
   c. It is designed primarily to backup data.
   d. The most common levels of RAID are Level 0, 1, 5, 6, and 10.

9. Linnea is researching a type of storage that uses a single storage device to serve files over a network and is relatively inexpensive. What type of storage is Linnea researching?
   a. SAN
   b. NAS
   c. RAID
   d. ARI

10. Which of the following is a document that outlines specific requirements or rules that must be met?
    a. Guideline
    b. Policy
    c. Framework
    d. Specification

11. What device is always running off its battery while the main power runs the battery charger?
    a. Secure UPS
    b. Backup UPS
    c. Offline UPS
    d. Online UPS

12. Which type of site is essentially a duplicate of the production site and has all the equipment needed for an organization to continue running?
    a. Cold site
    b. Warm site
    c. Hot site
    d. Replicated site

13. Which of the following can a UPS NOT perform?
    a. Prevent certain applications from launching that will consume too much power
    b. Disconnect users and shut down the server
    c. Prevent any new users from logging on
    d. Notify all users that they must finish their work immediately and log off

14. What is a definition of RPO?
    a. The maximum length of time that can be tolerated between backups
    b. Length of time it will take to recover data that has been backed up
    c. The frequency that data should be backed up
    d. How a backup utility reads an archive bit

15. What does an incremental backup do?
    a. Copies all files changed since the last full or incremental backup
    b. Copies only user-selected files
    c. Copies all files
    d. Copies all files since the last full backup

16. Molly needs to access a setting in Microsoft Windows Group Policy to change the type of a network to which a computer is attached. Which setting must Molly change?
    a. Wi-Fi/Wired Network Policy
    b. Network Config
    c. Network Type
    d. Network Location

17. Thea has received a security alert that someone in London attempted to access the email account of Sigrid, who had accessed it in Los Angeles one hour before. What feature determined an issue and send this alert to Thea?
    a. Impossible Travel
    b. Incompatible Location
    c. Remote IP address
    d. Risky IP address

18. Which of the following is NOT used to identify or enforce what mobile devices can do based on the location of the device?
    a. Geo-spatial
    b. Geolocation
    c. Geo-tagging
    d. Geofencing

19. Margaux is reviewing the corporate policy that stipulates the processes to be followed for implementing system changes. Which policy is she reviewing?
    a. Change management policy
    b. Change format policy
    c. Change modification policy
    d. Change control policy

20. Which commercial data classification level would be applied to a data set of the number of current employees at an organization and would only cause a small amount of harm if disclosed?
    a. Public
    b. Open
    c. Private
    d. Confidential

Hands-On Projects

 **CAUTION** If you are concerned about installing any of the software in these projects on your regular computer, you can instead use the Windows Sandbox or install the software in the Windows virtual machine created in the Module 1 Hands-On Projects. Software installed within the virtual machine will not impact the host computer.

Project 14-1: Using Windows File History to Perform Data Backups

Time Required: 25 minutes

Objective: 2.5 Given a scenario, implement cybersecurity resilience.
- Backup types

Description: The software backup utility File History is the Microsoft Windows 10 primary tool for backing up user files. Once configured, File History will automatically back up files to a storage device on a schedule. Note that File History is designed to back up user files and does not create a system image of the drive. In this project, you configure and use File History.

1. Connect an external storage device such as a large-capacity USB flash drive or external hard drive to the computer as a repository for the backups. (You cannot back up files to the same drive that contains the user files.)
2. Click **Start** and then click **Settings**.
3. Click **Update & Security**.
4. Click **Backup**.
5. Click **More options**.
6. Click **See advanced settings**.
7. Click **Turn on**.

8. Click **Advanced settings**.

9. Click the down arrow under **Save copies of files**. Note the default setting is **Every hour (default)**. Scroll through the other options. Which would you consider the best option for you? Why?

10. Click the down arrow under **Keep saved versions**. Note the default setting is **Forever (default)**. Scroll through the other options. What is the advantage to having backups kept indefinitely? What is the disadvantage? Which would you consider the best option for you? Why?

11. Click the **Back** arrow and look at the list of items that File History automatically backs up under **Copy files from**. By default, File History is set to back up important folders in the user account's home folder, such as Desktop, Libraries (Documents, Downloads, Music, Pictures, Videos, and so on), and Favorites. Do these folders include all your important data?

12. Click **Exclude folders**.

13. Click **Add** and select a folder that does not contain your important data such as **Downloads**. Click **Select folder**.

14. Click the **Back** arrow to return to the File History window.

15. Click **Advanced settings** again.

16. Under **Event logs**, click **Open File History event logs to view recent events or errors**. This allows you to see the log of any errors that may have occurred during the backup. Why is this important? How often should this log be viewed?

17. How easy is File History to use? Would you recommend it as a basic file backup software utility? Why or why not?

18. Close all windows.

Project 14-2: Viewing and Changing the Backup Archive Bit

Time Required: 20 minutes

Objective: 2.5 Given a scenario, implement cybersecurity resilience.
- Backup types

Description: One of the keys to backing up files is to know which files need to be backed up. Backup software can internally designate which files have already been backed up by setting an archive bit in the properties of the file. A file with the archive bit cleared (set to 0) indicates that the file has been backed up. However, when the contents of that file are changed, the archive bit is set (to 1), meaning that this modified file now needs to be backed up. In this project, you view and change the backup archive bit.

1. Start Microsoft Word and create a document that contains your name and today's date.

2. Save this document as **Bittest.docx**, and then close Microsoft Word.

3. Click **Start**, enter **cmd**, and then press **Enter**. The Command Prompt window opens.

4. Navigate to the folder that contains **Bittest.docx**.

5. Type **attrib/?** and then press **Enter** to display the options for this command.

6. Type **attrib Bittest.docx** and then press **Enter**. The attributes for this file are displayed. The A indicates that the bit is set and the file should be backed up.

7. You can clear the archive bit like the backup software does after it copies the file. Type **attrib –a Bittest.docx** and then press **Enter**.

8. Now look at the setting of the archive bit. Type **attrib Bittest.docx** and then press **Enter**. Has it been cleared?

9. Close the Command Prompt window.

Project 14-3: Creating and Using a Nonpersistent Live Boot Media

Time Required: 25 minutes

Objective: 2.5 Given a scenario, implement cybersecurity resilience.
- Nonpersistence

Description: Another nonpersistence tool is a live boot media, which is an operating system that boots from a USB flash drive or optical disc but retains no information. In this project, you will create a Linux live boot media USB flash drive using UNetbootin. Note that you will need a flash drive of at least 32 GB formatted as FAT32.

1. Use your web browser to go to **unetbootin.github.io**. (If you are no longer able to access the program through the above URL, use a search engine and search for "unetbootin.")

2. Read through the features of UNetbootin.
3. Under **Supported Distributions**, note that UNetbootin has built-in support for several different Linux distributions.
4. Click **Linux Mint**.
5. On the Linux Mint website, click **About** to see more information on Linux Mint. It is a graphical user interface distribution that has many similarities to Microsoft Windows and Apple macOS.
6. Click your browser's **Back** button to return to UNetbootin.
7. Scroll up to select the operating system of your computer and then click **Download**.
8. When the download is complete, launch UNetbootin. Note that no installation is required. The UNetbootin screen is shown in Figure 14-8.

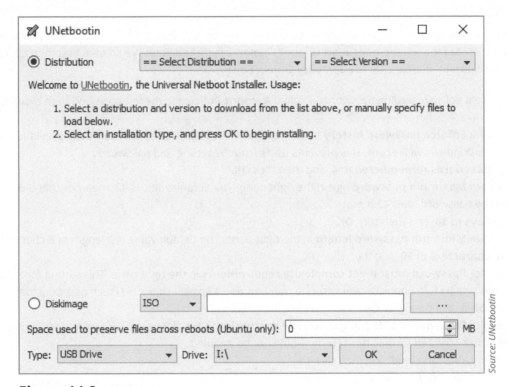

Figure 14-8   UNetbootin screen

9. Click the down arrow under **Select Distribution**. Scroll through the list of natively supported distributions from which a live boot media can be created.
10. Click **Linux Mint**.
11. Under **Type**, be sure that **USB Drive** is selected and that is the correct flash drive on which to install it is selected under **Drive**.
12. Click **OK**. UNetbootin will download the Linux Mint files and then create the bootable USB flash drive. Note that this may take several minutes to complete depending upon your network bandwidth.
13. After the installation is complete, reboot the computer to boot from the USB flash drive. (Many systems require pressing the **F12** key when rebooting to choose an alternative booting device.)
14. Boot from the USB flash drive to load the live boot media Linux Mint.
15. Reboot your computer again to access the operating system on the hard drive.

Project 14-4: Using Windows Local Security Policy

Time Required: 25 minutes
Objective: 3.7 Given a scenario, implement identity and account management controls.
   • Account policies
Description: The Local Group Policy Editor is a Microsoft Management Console (MMC) snap-in that gives a single user interface through which all the Computer Configuration and User Configuration settings of Local Group Policy objects can be managed. The Local Security Policy settings are among the security settings contained in the Local Group Policy Editor.

An administrator can use these to set policies that are applied to the computer. In this project, you will view and change local security policy settings.

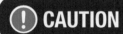 **CAUTION**   You need to be an administrator to open the Local Group Policy Editor.

1. Click **Start**.
2. Type **secpol.msc** in the Search box and then click **secpol**.

NOTE 25

If your computer is already joined to a domain, then searching for secpol.msc might not launch the application. If this is the case, click **Start** and type **mmc.msc**. On the File menu, click **Add/Remove** snap-in and then click **Add**. In **Add Standalone Snap-in**, double-click **Group Policy Object Editor**.

3. First create a policy regarding passwords. Expand **Account Policies** in the left pane and then expand **Password Policy**.
4. Double-click **Enforce password history** in the right pane. This setting defines how many previously used passwords Windows will record. This prevents users from "recycling" old passwords.
5. Change **passwords remembered** to **4**, and then click **OK**.
6. Double-click **Maximum password age** in the right pane. The default value is 42, meaning that a user must change the password after 42 days.
7. Change **days** to **30**, and then click **OK**.
8. Double-click **Minimum password length** in the right pane. The default value is a length of 8 characters.
9. Change **characters** to **10**, and then click **OK**.
10. Double-click **Password must meet complexity requirements** in the right pane. This setting forces a password to include at least two opposite case letters, a number, and a special character (such as a punctuation mark).
11. Click **Enabled**, and then click **OK**.
12. Double-click **Store passwords using reversible encryption** in the right pane. Because passwords should be stored in an encrypted format, this setting should not be enabled.
13. If necessary, click **Disabled**, and then click **OK**.
14. In the left pane, click **Account lockout policy**.
15. Double-click **Account lockout threshold** in the right pane. This is the number of times that a user can enter an incorrect password before Windows will lock the account from being accessed. (This prevents an attacker from attempting to guess the password with unlimited attempts.)
16. Change **invalid login attempts** to **5**, and then click **OK**.
17. Note that the Local Security Policy suggests changes to the **Account lockout duration** and the **Reset account lockout counter after** values to 30 minutes. Click **OK**.
18. Expand **Local Policies** in the left pane and then click **Audit Policy**.
19. Double-click **Audit account logon events**.
20. Check both **Success** and **Failure**, and then click **OK**.
21. Right-click **Security Settings** in the left pane.
22. Click **Reload** to have these policies applied.
23. Close all windows.

Case Projects

Case Project 14-1: Business Impact Analysis

Using your school or organization, develop a brief business impact analysis. What are the impacts? What is the mission-essential function? What are the critical systems? What is the single point of failure? Use the steps outlined earlier in the module. Share your plan with others if possible. What did you learn? Modify your plan accordingly.

Case Project 14-2: Impossible Travel

Impossible Travel detection identifies two user activities originating from geographically distant locations within a time period shorter than the user could travel between locations. Research Impossible Travel. How does it work? How does Impossible Travel learn about a user's normal activities? What are the levels that the sensitivity slider allows administrators to configure to define how strict the detection logic is? What happens if a user regularly uses two more locations on a regular basis? How accurate would you determine Impossible Travel to be? How could the information gleaned by Impossible Travel pose a threat? Write a one-page analysis of your research.

Case Project 14-3: Continuous Data Protection (CDP)

Use the Internet to research continuous data protection (CDP). Identify three different solutions and compare their features. Create a table of the different features to make a side-by-side comparison. Which product would you consider to be the best solution for an enterprise environment? Why?

Case Project 14-4: Personal Disaster Recovery Plan

Create a one-page document of a personal disaster recovery procedure for your home computer. Be sure to include what needs to be protected and why. Does your DRP show that what you are doing to protect your assets is sufficient? Should any changes be made?

Case Project 14-5: RAID Level 6 Costs

Use the Internet to research the costs of adding RAID Level 6 to a computer, which is generally recognized as the best general RAID level. Create a chart that lists the features, costs, and operating systems supported for this level. Would you purchase this for your computer? Why or why not?

Case Project 14-6: Personal Backup Procedures

What are your personal data backup procedures? Write a one-paragraph description of how you back up your data, what data you back up, how often you perform a backup, where your backup is stored, etc. Use the information in this module to compare it with your current backup procedures. Write a second paragraph that identifies the strengths and weaknesses of your current procedures. Finally, write a third paragraph that outlines how you could change your current procedures to make your backups more secure.

Case Project 14-7: Online Backup Services

Several good online backup services can help make data backup easy for the user. Use a search engine to search for *online backup service reviews*, and select three different services. Research these services and note their features. Create a table that lists each service and compare their features. Be sure to also include costs. Which would you recommend? Why?

Case Project 14-8: North Ridge Security

North Ridge Security provides security consulting and assurance services. You have recently been hired as an intern to assist them.

Operation Appreciation is a statewide charity service that assists military veterans who are struggling. Recently, one of its primary servers crashed. When the IT department tried to restore from a recent backup, they found that there was a flaw, and several months' worth of the backups was useless. Fortunately, North Ridge Security was able to restore the server that crashed and obtain a good backup before it was installed on a new system. (North Ridge did this service without charging Operating Appreciation.) Now North Ridge now wants to assist Operating Appreciation with creating a secure backup system. You have been asked to make a presentation to them.

1. Create a PowerPoint presentation for Operation Appreciation about backups, including the types of data backups, where they should be stored, how they should be tested, etc. Your presentation should contain at least 10 slides.
2. After the presentation, Operation Appreciation is most interested in cloud backups and has asked for your opinion. Use the Internet to research cloud backups and then create a memo about your findings and recommendations.

Case Project 14-9: Community Site Activity

The Information Security Community Site is an online companion to this textbook. It contains a wide variety of tools, information, discussion boards, and other features to assist learners. Go to **community.cengage.com/infosec2** and click the *Join or Sign in* icon to log in, using your login name and password that you created in Module 1. Click **Forums (Discussion)** and click on **Security+ Case Projects (7th edition)**. Read the following case study.

Serious issues surround social media analysis of posts made by applicants and employees. For example, while looking at social media posts, employers could easily learn details such as religion, disability, or pregnancy of an applicant. By law, employers cannot take these into account, but just knowing them could introduce bias in hiring decisions. Yet if an employer ignores a history of inflammatory social media posts, it could expose that employer to liability. So should a prospective or current employer read your social media posts? Does that fall outside the boundaries of when you are at work? Or do you represent your employer even when you are away from work? Take your side of this argument, and post your opinions to on the Community Site discussion board.

References

1. Wang, T, "Global economic losses from natural disasters 2000-2019," *Statista*, Jan. 24, 2020, accessed Jul. 30, 2020, www.statista.com/statistics/510894/natural-disasters-globally-and-economic-losses/.
2. "Study: 40% of businesses fail to reopen after a disaster," *Access*, Apr. 14, 2020, accessed Jul. 30, 2020, www.accesscorp.com/access-in-the-news/study-40-percent-businesses-fail-reopen-disaster/.

RISK MANAGEMENT AND DATA PRIVACY

After completing this module, you should be able to do the following:

1. Define risk
2. Describe strategies for reducing risk
3. Explain concerns surrounding data privacy
4. List methods for protecting data

Front-Page Cybersecurity

The COVID-19 pandemic, which is believed to have started in late 2019, caused unprecedented upheaval around the world. Virtually every part of everyone's life was impacted in ways too numerous to mention. One particular area that the virus dramatically changed is personal data privacy. There is concern that these changes will continue well into the future.

One of the three major defenses against COVID-19, along with social distancing and wearing protective masks, is "contact tracing." As the name implies, contact tracing is walking back in time to identify the people a patient infected with COVID-19 may have been in contact with recently. Because infected people may not show any symptoms (they are "asymptomatic") for several days, they could be infecting others without knowing it just by being around them. Those who begin to show symptoms and are then tested as positive would likely have difficulty remembering everyone they came in contact with over several days—especially if they are now sick—in order to warn others.

To stem the tide of the outbreak, governments around the world first turned to smartphones used by the general public to conduct contact tracing. Because COVID-19 was the first global pandemic in the age of the ubiquitous smartphone, these devices gave governments immediate surveillance capabilities. The most aggressive pandemic surveillance using smartphones started in China. Authorities there used cellular phone numbers and location data to trace the identities of thousands of residents who had left Wuhan, the earliest center of the outbreak, over the Chinese Lunar New Year holiday to return home. This information was then passed to local officials and "neighborhood minders," who contacted the targeted individuals and asked them to voluntarily self-quarantine for two weeks, even though many showed no symptoms.

However, the Chinese government soon decided that more drastic measures needed to be taken—and that more data was needed. China turned to travel records and security cameras to identify people who had been in contact with any coronavirus patients on trains, airplanes, and even in passing on street corners. Those individuals were also put in forced isolation.

Other governments soon followed, using both smartphone location data and other means of technology surveillance. In Western Australia, lawmakers approved a bill to install surveillance devices inside the homes of those placed under quarantine to ensure that they did not leave. Authorities in Hong Kong and India used geofencing from smartphones and wearables to create virtual fences around quarantine zones: infected offenders who ventured outside these zones could be sent to jail. The most popular Japanese messaging app regularly sent health-status questions to its users on behalf of the government.

Authorities in Moscow used facial-recognition technology to catch a Chinese woman who broke quarantine and was walking down the street. The police in England used drones to spot residents venturing out to a scenic overlook.

South Korea, after reporting 900 COVID-19 cases per day in early 2020, by mid-April only averaged 30 cases per day, without using lockdowns. Instead, the government heavily relied on technology. After the nation suffered a botched attempt to contain a different coronavirus in 2015, a law was passed that authorized officials to produce dossiers of confirmed patients using smartphone data, credit card transactions, and security video footage. Authorities started using such information to identify people who had come into contact with coronavirus patients to encourage them to get tested or stay home. South Korean government websites also published detailed reports about confirmed coronavirus cases. These online reports include patients' ages, work and home addresses, and personal details such as the restaurants they frequented, trips taken to family get-togethers, and even where they went to get massages. This was done to warn others not to visit these establishments. The South Korean law was expanded during the spring of 2020 to grant both health officials and local governments the power to request more information. The government said it could identify and locate at-risk patients in 10 minutes or less by automating access to personal information.

The United States likewise has used data to monitor the movement of its citizens. For example, the state of Kansas announced it used third-party GPS tracking data to monitor whether suspected infected people were following the advice of phone calls instructing them to stay at home.

In the wake of COVID-19, polls have indicated a dramatic shift in thinking among the general public about the usage of this type of privacy data. In a survey conducted in 2019 prior to the pandemic, Americans indicated data privacy was the biggest issue facing companies. But in a poll taken just weeks after the COVID-19 infections began in the United States, more than half of Americans said they backed anonymized and involuntary use of smartphone and other digital data to conduct contact tracing.

Privacy advocates have expressed concern not only for how this data is used today but also into the future. Will governments continue to collect and use this data after the pandemic? Some advocates have said that COVID-19 may become a watershed moment similar to the September 11, 2001, terrorist attacks, which ushered in new government surveillance powers around the world in the name of protecting public safety. Historically, once such surveillance powers are in place, they rarely are rescinded. Instead, the data continues to be collected and is quietly used for other purposes.

Two elements of cybersecurity are of high importance to both enterprises and users. The first involves risk. Although all organizations as well as users face innumerable risks, many choose to focus only on "putting out the fire" of the most recent incident and do not consider overall risk at a higher level. They often fail to understand their own philosophy toward risk and do not see how this drives their approach to cybersecurity as a whole. Ignoring an understanding of risk can have a significant impact on the overall security posture of an enterprise and user.

A second element of high importance is data privacy. As technology devices gather data on user behavior at an unprecedented rate, users are becoming increasingly concerned about how their private data is being used. Only recently have governments started enacting regulations about what user data can be collected, how it can be used, how the user is informed, and what options are given to consumers about the collection and protection of their data. Enterprises faced with growing government and user concerns over data privacy must wrestle with how they can use private data while responsibly protecting it from falling into the wrong hands.

This module examines these twin elements of high importance to cybersecurity. First, you learn about risk and study strategies for mitigating risks. Next, you explore data privacy and the issues that surround it.

MANAGING RISK

 **CERTIFICATION**

5.1 Compare and contrast various types of controls.

5.3 Explain the importance of policies to organizational security.

5.4 Summarize risk management processes and concepts.

Managing risk is an important task for enterprises and users. Managing risk involves defining what it is, understanding risk types, knowing different methods of risk analysis, and realizing how to manage risk.

Defining Risk

An *asset* is any item that has a positive economic value. In an enterprise, assets have the following qualities: they provide value to the enterprise; they cannot easily be replaced without a significant investment in expense, time, worker skill, and/or resources; and they can form part of the enterprise's corporate identity. Examples of enterprise assets range from people (employees, customers, business partners, contractors, and vendors) to physical assets (buildings, automobiles, and plant equipment).

Obviously, not all assets have the same value or worth. The **asset value** is the relative worth of an asset. Consider the assets in an enterprise's information technology (IT) infrastructure. Some assets have a very high value while others do not. For example, a faulty desktop computer that can easily be replaced is not be considered an asset with a high value, yet the information contained on that computer can be an asset. Table 15-1 describes the elements of an enterprise's IT infrastructure and whether these assets would normally be considered as having a high value.

Table 15-1   Typical IT assets

Asset	Description	Example	High value?
Information	Data that has been collected, classified, organized, and stored in various forms	Customer, personnel, production, sales, marketing, and finance databases	Yes: Extremely difficult to replace
Customized business software	Software that supports the business processes of the enterprise	Customized order transaction application	Yes: Unique and customized for the enterprise
System software	Software that provides the foundation for application software	Operating system	No: Can be easily replaced
Physical items	Computer equipment, communications equipment, storage media, furniture, and fixtures	Servers, routers, and power supplies	No: Can be easily replaced
Services	Outsourced computing services	Voice and data communications	No: Can be easily replaced

Assets are continually under threat, which is a type of action that has the potential to cause harm. Several threat classifications are listed in Table 15-2.

Table 15-2   Threat classifications

Threat category	Description	Example
Strategic	Action that affects the long-term goals of the organization	Theft of intellectual property, not pursuing a new opportunity, loss of a major account, competitor entering the market
Compliance	Following (or not following) a regulation or standard	Breach of contract, not responding to the introduction of new laws
Financial	Impact of financial decisions or market factors	Increase in interest rates, global financial crisis
Operational	Events that impact the daily business of the organization	Fire, hazardous chemical spill, power blackout
Technical	Events that affect information technology systems	Denial of service attack, SQL injection attack, virus
Managerial	Actions related to the management of the organization	Long-term illness of company president, key employee resigning

Organizations must determine how realistic the chance is that a given threat will compromise an asset, called the likelihood of occurrence. This is stated in terms of risk. At a basic level, risk may be defined as a situation that involves exposure to some type of danger. At a more advanced level, risk can be described as a function of threats, consequences of those threats, and the resulting vulnerabilities.

Risk Types

There are many types of risk. Risk types can be grouped into these broad categories:

- *Internal and external.* An internal risk comes from within an organization (such as employee theft), while an external risk is from the outside (like the actions of a hactivist).
- *Legacy systems.* One type of platform that is well known for its risks is a legacy system. A legacy system is no longer in widespread use, often because it has been replaced by an updated version of the earlier technology. Although legacy hardware introduces some risks, more often risks result from legacy software, such as an OS or program.
- *Multiparty.* Often overlooked in identifying risk types is the impact that vulnerabilities of one organization can have on other organizations that are connected to it. These are called multiparty risks that impact multiple "downstream" organizations.

NOTE 1

The results from the vulnerability of one organization rippling downstream are staggering. One study that examined more than 90,000 cyber events found that multiparty risks that were exploited resulted in financial losses 13 times larger than single-party incidents. The number of organizations impacted by multiparty incidents outnumber primary victims by 850 percent, and these multiparty incidents will continue to increase at an average rate of 20 percent annually.

- *Intellectual property (IP) theft.* Intellectual property (IP) is an invention or a work that is the result of creativity. The owner of IP can apply for protection from others who attempt to duplicate it; these protections over IP or its expression are patent, trademark, copyright, and trade secret. Threat actors attempt to steal IP (IP theft) that may include research on a new product from an enterprise so that they can sell it to an unscrupulous foreign supplier who will then build an imitation model of the product to sell worldwide. This deprives the legitimate business of profits after investing hundreds of millions of dollars in product development, and because these foreign suppliers may be in a different country, they are beyond the reach of domestic enforcement agencies and courts.
- *Software compliance and licensing.* Specialized software used by an enterprise is subject to licensing restrictions that protect the rights of the developer. An obvious violation would be for an organization to license software for a single manufacturing plant but then distribute that software to five other plants without paying for its usage. Software compliance and licensing risks are today considered a serious problem for organizations. Most organizations unknowingly violate one or more licensing agreements. Several of the reasons for this are listed in Table 15-3.

Table 15-3 Reasons for software noncompliance

Reason	Example	Explanation
Software licensed for one reason but now used for a different reason	Limited-use license purchased only to be used in nonproduction development environment used in a production environment.	Organizations may purchase limited-use licenses rather than full-use licenses to obtain a pricing discount; a newly hired technician is not aware of the restriction and copies software into the production facility.
Product use rights changed	A third party accesses software purchased by the organization that is used in violation of new product use rights.	Although developers initially allowed third parties approved by the organization to use their software, now this "indirect access" is changed so a new license requires all users to have a purchased license.
Software installed on a virtual machine	Software migrated to a virtual machine and moved to multiple other machines in violation of license.	Some developers restrict software from being installed and then moved among multiple virtual machines without purchasing a new license.

Risk Analysis

It is important for an organization to regularly perform a *risk analysis*, or a process to identify and assess the factors that may jeopardize the success of a project or reaching a stated goal. Following a methodology or process for performing a risk analysis is crucial. Risk assessments and tools for representing risk can be used to assist an organization in a risk analysis.

Methodology

Which is more difficult: identifying a risk or mitigating it? At first glance, it may seem that identifying risks through a risk analysis should be a straightforward process, and the more difficult work would involve addressing that risk. However, that is not always the case. Often simply seeing the risk can be difficult.

This difficulty is due to two factors. First, risks can be elusive and often hard to identify. While obvious risks seem readily apparent (such as a firewall that unplugged), not all risks are so clear (such as the danger of opening an email attachment that appears to come from a friend). Risks, by their very nature, are often hidden below the surface and are not apparent.

A second reason for the difficulty of identifying risks is due to human nature. One recognized reason for this difficulty is *unconscious human biases*.[1] All individuals have their own set of biases developed through preferences, intuition, or past experiences. These biases influence decision making and "vision." They may have a bias toward which foods to eat, what clothes to wear, or even the order of tasks to be tackled each day. Table 15-4 lists commonly recognized biases and effects.

Table 15-4   Decision-making biases and effects

Bias	Explanation
Aggregate bias	Inferring something about an individual by using data that actually describes trends for the broader population
Anchoring bias	Holding onto a specific feature or set of features of information early in the decision-making process
Availability bias	Perceiving how likely an event is to occur given how frequently the event is heard of
Confirmation bias	Making a decision before investigating and then only looking for data that supports the theory
Present bias	Tending to discount future risks and gains in favor of immediate gratification
Framing effect	Deciding on an option based on how the choices are worded
Fundamental attribution error	Viewing the failures or mistakes of others as part of their identity rather than attributing them to contextual or environmental influences

These unconscious biases and effects can influence risk identification. For example, an anchoring bias may cause someone to focus on one of the first risks exposed and then marginalize other risks. People with a confirmation bias could quickly decide that a risk is relatively unimportant—particularly on a system for which they are responsible—and then look for data to support their position. These biases could easily lead to identifying the wrong individual as the source of a risk, making incorrect estimates about the potential impact of a risk, focusing on an unlikely risk, or even spending too much time on incorrect theories.[2]

Research into human behavior has also revealed that most people have difficulty seeing risks and are prejudiced toward particular risks while minimizing others. Generally, when dealing with risks, people tend to

- Overreact to risks caused by intentional actions
- Underreact to risks associated with accidents, abstract events, and natural phenomena
- Overreact to risks that are considered insulting, disgusting, or offensive to our moral standards
- Overreact to immediate risks
- Underreact to long-term risks
- Underreact to risks and changes that occur slowly and over time

Due to the difficulty in identifying risks, a methodology has been developed that can be helpful in identifying risks. This methodology helps to minimize human factors in identifying risk by not relying on a few employees in an organization but instead involving many individuals in the process. As more employees are involved, biases and prejudices are minimized. An analysis of risk that involves a wide array of users is considered the most effective approach. **Risk Control Self-Assessment (RCSA)** is an "empowering" methodology by which management and staff at all levels collectively work to identify and evaluate risks. The goal of RCSA is to not only minimize biases and prejudices but also to integrate risk management practices into the culture of the organization. As staff perform their normal activities and as business units work toward their objectives, the topic of risk permeates all of these activities.

Risk Assessment

An organization that can accurately calculate risk is better prepared to address the risk. For example, if a customer database is determined to be of high value and to have a high risk, the necessary resources should be used to strengthen the defenses surrounding that database.

There are two risk assessment approaches. One is **qualitative risk assessment**. This approach uses an "educated guess" based on observation. For example, if it is observed that the customer database contains important information, it would be assigned a high asset value. Also, if it is observed that this database has been frequently the target of attacks, it would be assigned a high-risk value as well. Qualitative risk typically assigns a numeric value (*1–10*) or label (*High, Medium,* or *Low*) that represents the risk.

The second approach, **quantitative risk assessment**, is considered more formal and systematic. Instead of arbitrarily assigning a number or label based on observation, the quantitative risk calculation attempts to create "hard" numbers associated with the risk of a system element by using historical data. For example, if the customer database has a higher risk calculation than a product database, more resources would be allocated to protecting it.

Quantitative risk calculations can be divided into the likelihood of a risk and the impact of a risk being successful.

Risk Likelihood   Historical data is valuable in providing information on how likely it is that a risk will become a reality within a specific period of time. For example, when considering the risk of equipment failure, several quantitative tools can be used to predict the likelihood of the risk, including the following:

- *Mean Time Between Failure (MTBF)*. MTBF calculates the average (*mean*) amount of time until a component fails, cannot be repaired, and must be replaced. It is a reliability term used to provide the amount of failures. Calculating the MTBF involves dividing the total time measured by the total number of failures observed.

CAUTION   Although MTBF is sometimes used to advertise the reliability of consumer hardware products such as hard disk drives, this value is seldom considered by the purchaser. This is because most consumer purchases are simply price driven. MTBF is considered more important for industries than for consumers.

NOTE 2

MTBF and MTTR are covered in Module 14.

- *Mean Time To Recovery (MTTR)*. MTTR is the average amount of time that it will take a device to recover from a nonterminal failure. Although MTTR is sometimes called *Mean Time To Repair* because in most systems this means replacing a failed hardware instead of repairing it, the Mean Time To Recovery is considered a more accurate term.
- *Mean Time To Failure (MTTF)*. MTTF is a basic measure of reliability for systems that cannot be repaired. It is the average amount of time expected until the first failure of a piece of equipment.
- *Failure In Time (FIT)*. The FIT calculation is another way of reporting MTBF. FIT can report the number of expected failures per one billion hours of operation for a device. This term is used particularly by the semiconductor industry. FIT can be stated as *devices for one billion hours, one billion devices for 1,000 hours each,* or in other combinations.

Other historical data for calculating the likelihood of risk can be acquired through a variety of sources. These are summarized in Table 15-5.

Table 15-5   Historical data sources

Source	Explanation
Law enforcement agencies	Crime statistics on the area of facilities to determine the probability of vandalism, break-ins, or dangers potentially encountered by personnel
Insurance companies	Risks faced by other companies and the amounts paid out when these risks became reality
Computer incident monitoring organizations	Data regarding a variety of technology-related risks, failures, and attacks

Once historical data is compiled, it can be used to determine the likelihood of a risk occurring within a year. This is known as the **Annualized Rate of Occurrence (ARO)**.

Risk Impact   Once historical data is gathered so that the ARO can be calculated, the next step is to determine the impact of that risk. This can be done by comparing it to the monetary loss associated with an asset to determine how much money would be lost if the risk occurred.

> **⊘ CAUTION**   When calculating the loss, all costs must be considered. For example, if a network firewall failed, the costs would include the amount needed to purchase a replacement, the hourly wage of the person replacing the equipment, and the pay for employees who could not perform their job functions because they could not use the network while the firewall was not functioning.

Two risk calculation formulas are commonly used to calculate expected losses. The **Single Loss Expectancy (SLE)** is the expected monetary loss every time a risk occurs. The SLE is computed by multiplying the Asset Value (AV) by the Exposure Factor (EF), which is the proportion of an asset's value that is likely to be destroyed by a particular risk (expressed as a percentage). The SLE formula is as follows:

$$SLE = AV \times EF$$

For example, consider a building with a value of \$10,000,000 (AV) of which 75 percent of it is likely to be destroyed by a tornado (EF). The SLE would be calculated as follows:

$$7,500,000 = \$10,000,000 \times 0.75$$

The **Annualized Loss Expectancy (ALE)** is the expected monetary loss that can be expected for an asset due to a risk over a one-year period. It is calculated by multiplying the SLE by the ARO, which is the probability that a risk will occur in a particular year. The ALE formula is as follows:

$$ALE = SLE \times ARO$$

In this example, if flood insurance data suggests that a serious flood is likely to occur once in 100 years, then the ARO is 1/100 or 0.01. The ALE would be calculated as follows:

$$75,000 = 0.01 \times \$7,500,000$$

Representing Risks

Different tools can be used to represent risks identified through a risk assessment. A **risk register** is a list of potential threats and associated risks. Often shown as a table, a risk register can help provide a clear snapshot of vulnerabilities and risks. A sample risk register is shown in Figure 15-1.

Another tool is called a **risk matrix/heatmap**. This is a visual color-coded tool that lists the impact and likelihood of risks. Figure 15-2 illustrates a risk matrix/heatmap.

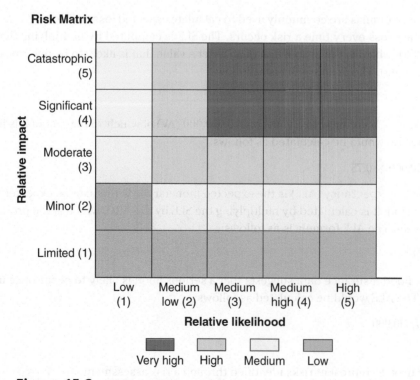

Risk Register											
Risk Id	Risks	Current risk			Status	Owner	Raised	Mitigation Strategies	Residual risk		
		Likelihood	Impact	Severity					Likelihood	Impact	Severity
Category 1: Projecty selection and project finance											
RP-01	Financial attraction of project to investors	4	4	16	Open		01-march	• Data collection • Information of financial capability of investor • Giving them assurance of tremendous future return.	4	3	12
RP-02	Availability of finance	3	4	12	Open		03-march	• Own resources • Commitment with financial institution • Exclusive management of investor.	3	3	9
RP-03	Level of demand for project	3	3	9	Open		08-march	• Making possibility and identification of low cost and best quality material • Eradication of extra expenses from petty balance.	2	3	6
RP-04	Land acquisition (site availability)	3	3	9	Open		13-march	• Making feasibilites • Analysis and interpretation of feasibilities • Possession and legal obligation of land.	2	2	4
RP-05	_High finance costs	2	2	4	Open		15-march	• Lowering operational expenses and transportation expenses • Proper management of current expenses.	1	2	2

Figure 15-1   Risk register

Figure 15-2   Risk matrix/heatmap

Risk Management

The objective of managing risk is to create a level of protection that mitigates the vulnerabilities to the threats and reduces the potential consequences—that is, to reduce risk to a level that is considered acceptable for the organization (called a **risk appetite**). Managing risk involves using specific strategies and control types, addressing third-party risk, and incorporating user training.

Determining a Strategy

There are four strategies for dealing with risks. These can be illustrated through the following scenario. Suppose that Ellie wants to purchase a new motorized Italian scooter to ride from her apartment to school and work. However, because several scooters have been stolen near her apartment, she is concerned about its protection. Although she parks the scooter in the gated parking lot in front of her apartment, a hole in the fence surrounding the apartment complex makes it possible for someone to access the parking lot without restriction.

Ellie has different options when dealing with the risk of her scooter being stolen, and these are the same that can be used by an organization:

- *Acceptance*. Risk **acceptance** simply means that the risk is acknowledged but no steps are taken to address it. In Ellie's case, she could accept the risk and buy the new scooter, knowing there is the chance a thief could steal it by entering the parking lot through the hole in the fence. In a similar fashion, an organization may decide to accept the risk that a flood will engulf its manufacturing plant if that flood is estimated to occur only once every 50 years.
- *Transference*. Ellie could transfer the risk to a third party. She can do this by purchasing insurance so that the insurance company absorbs the loss and pays if the scooter is stolen. This is known as risk **transference**. An organization may elect to purchase **cybersecurity insurance** as an example of transference so that in exchange for paying premiums to the insurance company, the organization is compensated in the event of a successful attack.
- *Avoidance*. Risk **avoidance** involves identifying the risk but making the decision to not engage in the activity. Ellie could decide based on the risk of the scooter being stolen that she will not purchase the new scooter. Likewise, an organization may decide that after an analysis, building a new plant in another location is not feasible.
- *Mitigation*. Risk **mitigation** is the attempt to address risk by making it less serious. Ellie could complain to the apartment manager about the hole in the fence to have it repaired, and an organization could erect a fence around a plant to deter thieves.

Using Controls

A security control is a safeguard or countermeasure employed within an organizational information system to protect the confidentiality, integrity, and availability of the technology system and its data. A security control attempts to limit exposure to a danger. There are three broad categories of controls. These are listed in Table 15-6, using phishing as an example.

Table 15-6   Categories of controls

Control category	Description	Phishing example
Managerial	Controls that use administrative methods	Acceptable use policy that specifies users should not visit malicious websites.
Operational	Controls implemented and executed by people	Conducting workshops to help train users to identify and delete phishing messages.
Technical	Controls incorporated as part of hardware, software, or firmware	Unified threat management (UTM) device that performs packet filtering, antiphishing, and web filtering.

Specific types of controls are found within the three broad categories of controls. These include the following:

- *Deterrent controls.* A **deterrent control** attempts to discourage security violations before they occur.
- *Preventative controls.* A **preventative control** works to prevent the threat from coming in contact with the vulnerability.
- *Physical controls.* A **physical control** implements security in a defined structure and location.
- *Detective controls.* A **detective control** is designed to identify any threat that has reached the system.
- *Compensating controls.* A **compensating control** is a control that provides an alternative to normal controls that for some reason cannot be used.
- *Corrective controls.* A control that is intended to mitigate or lessen the damage caused by the incident is called a **corrective control**.

These control types are summarized along with examples in Table 15-7.

Table 15-7   Control types

Control type	Description	When it occurs	Example
Deterrent control	Discourage attack	Before attack	Posting signs indicating that the area is under video surveillance
Preventive control	Prevent attack	Before attack	Providing security awareness training for all users
Physical control	Prevent attack	Before attack	Building fences that surround the perimeter
Detective control	Identify attack	During attack	Installing motion detection sensors
Compensating control	Alternative to normal control	During attack	Isolating an infected computer on a different network
Corrective control	Lessen damage from attack	After attack	Cleaning a virus cleaned from an infected server

> **(!) CAUTION**   Security professionals do not universally agree on the nomenclature and classification of control types. Some researchers divide control types into administrative, logical, and physical. Other security researchers specify up to 18 control types.

NOTE 3

Inherent risk is sometimes viewed as a negative. That is, it represents the amount of risk that exists in the absence of controls.

Controls change over time as new hardware and software are added and new procedures are implemented. **Inherent risk** is defined as the current risk level given the existing set of controls. **Residual risk** is the risk level that remains after additional controls are applied. A specific type of risk is a **control risk** or the probability that financial statements are materially misstated because of failures in the organization's system of controls. When there are significant control failures, a business's financial statements may reveal a profit when there is actually a loss.

Remember that the goal of security is not to eliminate all risk; that simply is not possible. Instead, the goal in designing and implementing controls is to reach a balance between achieving an acceptable level of risk and expense while minimizing losses. Some assets, however, must be protected irrespective of the perceived risk. For example, controls based upon regulatory requirements may be required regardless of risk (**regulations that affect risk posture**).

Implement Third-Party Risk Management

NOTE 4

Third parties and supply chains are covered in Module 1.

Almost all businesses use external entities known as third parties. These include **vendors** (those from whom an organization purchases goods and services), **business partners** (a commercial entity with whom an organization has an alliance), and those as part of a *supply chain* (a network that moves a product from the supplier to the customer).

There are several risks associated with using third parties. First, with the sheer number of third parties used, it can be difficult to coordinate their diverse activities with the organization. Second, almost all third parties today require access to the organization's computer network to provide these external entities the ability to perform their IT-related functions (such as outsourced code development) and even do basic tasks such as submitting online invoices. Yet one of the major risks of this third-party system integration involves the principle of the weakest link: if the security of the third party has a vulnerability, it can provide an opening for attackers to infiltrate the organization's computer network. Third, the difficulties associated with third-party integration, or combining systems and data with outside entities, is significant. The risks associated with this integration include the following:

- *On-boarding and off-boarding. Partner on-boarding* refers to the startup relationship between partners, while *partner off-boarding* is the termination of such an agreement. Significant consideration must be given to how the entities will combine their services without compromising their existing security defenses. Also, when the relationship ends, particularly if it has been in effect for a significant length of time, work must be done to ensure that as the parties and their IT systems separate, no gaping holes are left open for attackers to exploit.
- *Application and social media network sharing.* How will applications be shared between the partners? Who will be responsible for support and vulnerability assessments? As social media becomes more critical for organizations in their interactions with customers, which partner will be responsible for sharing social media information?
- *Privacy and risk awareness.* What happens if the privacy policy of one partner is less restrictive than that of the other partner? How will risk assessment be performed on the combined systems?
- *Data considerations.* All parties must have a clear understanding of who owns data generated through the partnership and how that data will be backed up. Restrictions on unauthorized data sharing also must be reached.

One of the means by which the parties can reduce risk is to reach an understanding of their relationships and responsibilities is through interoperability agreements, or formal contractual relationships, particularly as they relate to security policy and procedures. These agreements, which should be regularly reviewed to verify compliance and performance standards, include the following:

- A **service-level agreement (SLA)** is a service contract between a vendor and a client that specifies what services will be provided, the responsibilities of each party, and any guarantees of service.
- A **business partnership agreement (BPA)** is a contract between two or more business partners that is used to establish the rules and responsibilities of each partner, including withdrawals, capital contributions to the partnership, and financial reporting.
- A **memorandum of understanding (MOU)** describes an agreement between two or more parties. It demonstrates a "convergence of will" between the parties so that they can work together. An MOU generally is not a legally enforceable agreement but is more formal than an unwritten agreement.
- A **nondisclosure agreement (NDA)** is a legal contract between parties that specifies how confidential material will be shared between the parties but restricted to others. An NDA creates a confidential relationship between the parties to protect any type of confidential and proprietary information.
- A **measurement system analysis (MSA)** uses scientific tools to determine the amount of variation that is added to a process by a measurement system. For example, a third party who manufactures a product for an organization would need to demonstrate that how it measures the size, weight, dimensions, and other properties of the product is both valid and does not contribute to any variation of the product.
- **End of life (EOL)** is a term used by a manufacturer to indicate that a product has reached the end of its "useful life" and the manufacturer will no longer market, sell, or update it after a specified date, although the manufacturer may still offer maintenance options but at a premium price. **End of service (EOS)** indicates the end of support, which is when the manufacturer quits selling a piece of equipment and no longer provides maintenance services or updates after a certain date; EOS is the final phase of a piece of an equipment's life cycle. Organizations should clearly communicate EOL and EOS between themselves and third parties so that there are no sudden surprises that a product or equipment is no longer available.

Provide User Training

An often-overlooked consideration in risk management is the importance of providing training to users. Training results in **risk awareness**, which is the raising of understanding of what risks exist, their potential impacts, and how they are managed. Training can make users aware of common risks and how they can become a "human firewall" to help mitigate these risks.

All computer users in an organization have a shared responsibility to protect the assets of the organization. However, it cannot be assumed that all users have the knowledge and skill to protect these assets. Instead, users need training in the importance of securing information, the roles that they play in security, and the steps they need to take to prevent attacks. Because new attacks appear regularly, and new security vulnerabilities are continuously being exposed, user awareness and training must be ongoing. User training is an essential element of security.

> **NOTE 5**
>
> Education in an enterprise is not limited to the average employee. Human resource personnel also need to keep abreast of security issues because in many organizations, it is their role to train new employees on all aspects of the organization, including security. Even upper management needs to be aware of the security threats and attacks that the organization faces, if only to acknowledge the necessity of security in planning, staffing, and budgeting.

One of the challenges of organizational education and training is to understand the traits of learners. Table 15-8 lists general traits of individuals born in the United States since 1946.

Table 15-8   Traits of learners

Year born	Traits	Number in U.S. population
Prior to 1946	Patriotic, loyal, have faith in institutions	75 million
1946–1964	Idealistic, competitive, question authority	80 million
1965–1981	Self-reliant, distrustful of institutions, adaptive to technology	46 million
1982–2000	Pragmatic, globally concerned, computer literate, media savvy	76 million

In addition to traits of learners, training style also impacts how people learn. The way that one person is taught may not be the best way to teach all others. Most people are taught using a *pedagogical* approach (from a Greek word meaning *to lead a child*). Adult learners, however, often prefer an *andragogical* approach (the art of helping an adult learn). Some of the differences between pedagogical and andragogical approaches are summarized in Table 15-9.

Table 15-9   Approaches to training

Subject	Pedagogical approach	Andragogical approach
Desire	Motivated by external pressures to get good grades or pass on to next grade	Motivated by higher self-esteem, more recognition, desire for better quality of life
Student	Dependent on teacher for all learning	Self-directed and responsible for own learning
Subject matter	Defined by what the teacher wants to give	Learning is organized around situations in life or at work
Willingness to learn	Students are informed about what they must learn	A change triggers a readiness to learn or students perceive a gap between where they are and where they want to be

In addition to training styles, people have different learning styles. Visual learners learn through taking notes, being at the front of the class, and watching presentations. Auditory learners tend to sit in the middle of the class and learn best through lectures and discussions. The third style is kinesthetic, which many information technology professionals tend to have. These students learn through a lab environment or other hands-on approaches. Most people use a combination of learning styles, with one style being dominant. To aid in knowledge retention, trainers should incorporate all three learning styles and present the same information using different techniques. For example, a course could include a lecture, PowerPoint slides, and an opportunity to work directly with software and replicate what is being taught.

Different techniques are employed for user training:

- *Computer-based training (CBT).* **Computer-based training (CBT)** uses a computer to deliver the instruction. CBT is popular for user training due its flexibility (training can be done from any location and at any time) and ability to provide feedback about the progress of the learner. However, CBT is not always considered the best means for training. Instead, a variety of other modalities, such as specialized face-to-face instruction or informal "lunch-and-learn" sessions, may provide better overall learning results.

- *Role-based awareness training.* Many organizations use **role-based awareness training**. Role-based training involves specialized training that is customized to the specific role that an employee holds in the organization. An office associate, for example, should be provided security training different from training provided to an upper-level manager, because the duties and tasks of these two employees are significantly different.

- *Gamification.* The fast-growing field of digital gaming is generally divided into two distinct markets: recreational gaming for entertainment and instructional gaming for training and education. **Gamification** is using game-based scenarios for instruction. User training can often include gamification in an attempt to heighten the interest and retention of the learner.

- *Capture the flag.* When training security professionals, organizations sometimes add an incentive called a **capture the flag (CTF)** exercise. A series of challenges with varying degrees of difficulty is outlined in advance. When one challenge is solved, a "flag" is awarded, and the points are totaled once time has expired. The winning player or team is the one that earns the highest score.

- *Phishing simulations.* Because phishing is the primary means by which threat actors initially launch an attack, many organizations use **phishing simulations** to help employees recognize phishing emails. These tools can be highly customized and provide detailed feedback on a dashboard, as seen in Figure 15-3, which shows a phishing simulation dashboard from gophish. Phishing simulators can be one part of an entire **phishing campaign** that uses a variety of other tools (such as email reminders, printed posters, and points earned to be redeemed for prizes) to counteract phishing attacks.

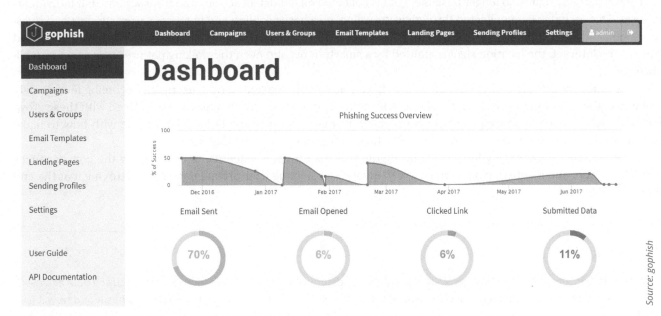

Figure 15-3   Phishing simulation dashboard

TWO RIGHTS & A WRONG

1. At a basic level, risk may be defined as a situation that involves exposure to some type of danger, while at a more advanced level, risk can be described as a function of threats, consequences of those threats, and the resulting vulnerabilities.
2. The Annualized Loss Expectancy (ALE) is the expected monetary loss that can be expected for an asset due to a risk over a one-year period.
3. Risk avoidance uses cybersecurity insurance.

See Appendix B for the answer.

DATA PRIVACY

✔ CERTIFICATION

2.1 Explain the importance of security concepts in an enterprise environment.

2.7 Explain the importance of physical security controls.

4.1 Given a scenario, use the appropriate tool to assess organizational security.

5.5 Explain privacy and sensitive data concepts in relation to security.

Privacy is defined as the state or condition of being free from public attention, observation, or interference to the degree that the person chooses. In short, privacy is the right to be left alone to the level that you want.

Prior to the current age of technology, almost everybody (with the exception of media celebrities and politicians) generally could choose the level of privacy that they desired. Those who wanted to have open and public lives could freely provide information about themselves to others. Those who wanted to live quiet or even unknown lives could limit what information was disseminated. In short, both those wanting a public life and those wanting a private life could choose to do so by controlling information about themselves.

However, today that is no longer possible. Data is collected on almost all actions and transactions that individuals perform. This includes data collected through web surfing, purchases (online and in stores), user surveys and questionnaires, and smartphone apps. Data is also collected on benign activities such as the choice of movies streamed through the Internet, the location signals emitted by a smartphone, and even the walking path recorded by a surveillance camera.

As technology devices gather data on user behavior at an unprecedented rate, users are becoming increasingly concerned about how their private data is being collected, used, and stored. Organizations are faced with these growing user concerns and increasing government regulations over data privacy. They must wrestle with how to make legitimate use of user data while responsibly collecting, using, and protecting that data.

Understanding data privacy includes knowing the reasons for user concerns, understanding the consequences of a data breach, and identifying data types. It also involves protecting user private data and destroying it at the end of its life cycle.

NOTE 6

Sometimes a distinction is made between data protection and data privacy. Data protection involves securing data against *unauthorized* access, while data privacy is concerned with the *authorized* access of data, namely who has it and how it is being used. Data protection is a technical issue whereas data privacy is a legal issue.

User Concerns

Users are increasingly concerned over the collection, usage, and protection of their personal data, whether that data is collected with or without their authorization. These user concerns revolve around the risks associated with the use of their private data. This falls into three broad categories:

- *Individual inconveniences and identity theft.* Data that has been collected on individuals is frequently used to direct personalized ad marketing campaigns. These campaigns—which include email, direct mail marketing promotions, and telephone calls—generally are considered annoying and unwanted. In addition, personal data can be used as the basis for identity theft.

> **NOTE 7**
>
> Identity theft is covered in Module 1.

- *Associations with groups.* Another use of personal data is to group what appears to be similar individuals. One data broker has 70 distinct segments (*clusters*) within 21 consumer and demographic characteristic groups (*life stages*). These groups range from *Boomer Barons* (baby boomer–aged households with high education and income), *Hard Chargers* (well-educated and professionally successful singles), and *True Blues* (working parents who hold blue-collar jobs with teenage children about to leave home). Once a person is placed in a group, the characteristics of that group are applied, such as whether a person is a "potential inheritor" or an "adult with senior parent," or whether a household has a "diabetic focus" or "senior needs." However, these assumptions may not always be accurate for someone placed within a group. Individuals might be offered fewer services or the wrong types of services based on their association with a group.
- *Statistical inferences.* Statistical inferences are often made that go beyond groupings. For example, researchers have demonstrated that by examining only four data points of credit card purchases (such as the dates and times of purchases) of 1.1 million people, they could correctly identify 90 percent of the people. In another study, the *Likes* indicated by Facebook users can statistically reveal their sexual orientation, drug use, and political beliefs.

The concerns raised regarding how private data is gathered and used are listed in Table 15-10.

Table 15-10   Concerns regarding how private data is gathered and used

Issue	Explanation
The data is gathered and kept in secret.	Users have no formal rights to find out what private information is being gathered, who gathers it, or how it is being used.
The accuracy of the data cannot be verified.	Because users do not have the right to correct or control what personal information is gathered, its accuracy may be suspect. In some cases, inaccurate or incomplete data may lead to erroneous decisions made about individuals without any verification.
Identity theft can impact the accuracy of data.	Victims of identity theft often have information added to their profile that was the result of actions by the identity thieves, and even the victims have no right to see or correct the information.
Unknown factors can impact overall ratings.	Ratings are often created from combining thousands of individual factors or data streams, including race, religion, age, gender, household income, zip code, presence of medical conditions, transactional purchase information from retailers, and hundreds more data points about individual consumers. How these different factors impact a person's overall rating is unknown.
Informed consent is usually missing or is misunderstood.	Statements in a privacy policy such as "We may share your information for marketing purposes with third parties" is not clearly informed consent to freely allow the use of personal data. Often users are not even asked for permission to gather their information.
Data is being used for increasingly important decisions.	Private data is being used on an ever-increasing basis to determine eligibility in significant life opportunities, such as jobs, consumer credit, insurance, and identity verification.

> **NOTE 8**
>
> Unlike consumer reporting agencies, which are required by federal law to give consumers free copies of their credit reports and allow them to correct errors, those who collect data are not required by federal law to show consumers information that has been collected about them or provide a means of correcting it.

Data Breach Consequences

Once a data breach occurs, specific actionable steps must be taken by the organization. When required, it must notify those impacted by the breach (**public notifications and disclosures**) along with relevant stakeholders. It must also outline the actions that are being taken. Depending upon the severity of the breach, a regulatory agency may even require that a breach be classified as a "major incident" and that additional steps be taken (**escalation**).

The consequences to an organization that has suffered a data breach are not insignificant. These consequences include the following:

- *Reputation damage.* The bad publicity surrounding an organization that has been the victim of a data breach usually results in a tarnished reputation (**reputation damage**). This has been evidenced by the loss of customers and a drop in the stock price of publicly traded organizations following a breach.
- *IP theft.* Another consequence of a data breach is the theft of IP that the organization or its customers may own.
- *Fines.* A financial penalty (**fine**) may be assessed against the organization following a data breach. Several federal and state laws have been enacted to protect the privacy of electronic data, and businesses that fail to protect data they possess may face serious financial penalties. Some of these laws include the Health Insurance Portability and Accountability Act of 1996 (HIPAA), the Sarbanes-Oxley Act of 2002 (Sarbox), the Gramm-Leach-Bliley Act (GLBA), the Payment Card Industry Data Security Standard (PCI DSS), the Family Educational Rights and Privacy Act (FERPA), and various state notification and security laws. Organizations in nations that belong to the European Union (EU) face two tiers of fines due to a data breach based on the General Data Protection Regulation (GDPR). The first tier is a fine of up to 10 million euros or 2 percent of the firm's worldwide annual revenue from the preceding year, whichever amount is higher. The second tier is 20 million euros or 4 percent of worldwide annual revenue.

NOTE 9

Many users are surprised to learn that the rules regarding a breach of a small number of medical records are not strong. The HIPAA Breach Notification Rule requires that data breaches of 500 or more records must be reported to the Secretary of the Department of Health and Human Services (HHS) no later than 60 days after the discovery of a breach. Breaches of fewer than 500 records can be reported to the Secretary at any time, but no later than 60 days from the end of the calendar year in which the data breach was experienced. That means a breach of 450 records that occurred in January 2021 would not have to be reported until March 2022.

Data Types

Different data types require protection besides customer data, financial information, and government data. Several of these are listed in Table 15-11.

Protecting Data

An organization may take various steps to protect consumer data. It is important to begin with an **impact assessment**, which is a means for measuring the effectiveness of the organization's activities. The impact assessment can help reveal any shortcomings around the use and protection of privacy data.

In most instances, organizations fall short of informing users of what is being collected and how it is being used. Organizations should have a **privacy notice** that outlines how the organization uses personal information it collects. A typical privacy notice for consumers is shown in Figure 15-4.

A **terms of agreement** document sets out what is expected from both the organization and its users. This agreement can be used to manage users' activity and expectations and also to protect the organization from legal issues.

Different technologies can be used to enhance the protection of privacy data. These include the following:

- *Data minimization.* **Data minimization** is limiting the collection of personal information to that which is directly relevant and necessary to accomplish a specific task. In other words, the collection of privacy data should be adequate, relevant, and not excessive in relation to the designated purpose. Organizations should periodically review their privacy data collection to ensure that the collection is following the principle of data minimization.

Table 15-11   Data types

Data type	Description	Recommended handling
Confidential	Highest level of data sensitivity	Should only be made available to users with highest level of pre-approved authentication
Private	Restricted data with a medium level of confidentiality	For users who have a need-to-know basis of the contents
Sensitive	Data that could cause catastrophic harm to the company if disclosed, such as technical specifications for a new product	Restricted to employees who have a business need to access the data and have been approved
Critical	Data classified according to availability needs; if critical data not available, the function and mission would be severely impacted	Critical data must be rigorously protected
Proprietary	Belongs to the enterprise	Can be available to any current employee or contractor
Public	No risk of release	For all public consumption; data is assumed to be public if no other data label is attached
Personally Identifiable Information (PII)	Data that could potentially identify a specific individual	Should be kept secure so that an individual cannot be singled out for identification
Protected Health Information (PHI)	Data about a person's health status, provision of health care, or payment for health care	Must be kept secure as mandated by HIPAA

- *Data masking.* **Data masking** involves creating a copy of the original data but obfuscating (making unintelligible) any sensitive elements such as a user's name or Social Security number. Data masking should replace all actual information that is not absolutely required. Because data masking involves replacing data elements, it is also called **data anonymization**: there is not a means to reverse the process to restore the data back to its original state. Data masking is one way to perform **data sanitization**, which is the process of cleaning data to provide privacy protection.
- *Tokenization.* Similar to masking, tokenization obfuscates sensitive data elements, such as an account number, into a random string of characters (token). The original sensitive data element and the corresponding token are then stored in a database called a token vault so that if the actual data element is needed, it can be retrieved. Unlike encryption, which requires using an algorithm and a key, tokenization can hide the data while making the retrieval process more seamless. Because it is possible to restore the original data, tokenization is also called **pseudo-anonymization**.

> *In general, you can visit us on the Internet without telling us who you are and without giving any personal information about yourself. There are times, however, when we or our partners may need information from you. You may choose to give us personal information in a variety of situations. For example, you may want to give us information, such as your name and address or e-mail, to correspond with you, to process an order, or to provide you with a subscription. You may give us your credit card details to buy something from us or a description of your education and work experience in connection with a job opening for which you wish to be considered. We intend to let you know how we will use such information before we collect it from you. You may tell us that you do not want us to use this information to make further contact with you beyond fulfilling your request. If you give us personal information about somebody else, such as a spouse or work colleague, we will assume that you have their permission to do so.*

Figure 15-4   Privacy notice

NOTE 10

Data masking and tokenization are covered in Module 9.

A final consideration is to know the country-specific government regulations that apply to protecting data. However, these regulations are not necessarily those where the organization is headquartered. **Data sovereignty** is the country-specific requirements that apply to data. Generally, data is subject to the laws of the country in which it is collected or processed. In many instances, the data must remain within its borders. Countries such as Russia, China, Germany, France, Indonesia, and Vietnam require that citizen data must be stored on physical servers within the country's borders, arguing that it is in the citizens' (and government's) best interest to protect private data against any misuse from foreign governments, and this is not possible if the data is outside of that country's jurisdiction.

NOTE 11

Many countries have had laws on the books for decades that data of its citizens must be stored within its borders, but it was less of an issue and was not always enforced. However, new privacy laws such as the GDPR in the European Union is now making data sovereignty and data privacy more prominent. With the rising popularity of cloud computing and Software as a Service (SaaS) solutions, data sovereignty issues have taken on even greater importance.

Data Destruction

The information life cycle is the flow of an information system's data (and metadata) from data creation to the time it becomes obsolete. Once data is no longer useful, it should be properly destroyed.

Because data itself is intangible, destroying data that is no longer needed involves destroying the media on which the data is stored. If any data is on paper and is not labeled as public, that media should never be thrown away in a dumpster, recycle bin, or trash receptacle. Paper media can be destroyed by burning (lighting it on fire), shredding (cutting it into small strips or particles), pulping (breaking the paper back into wood cellulose fibers after the ink is removed), or pulverizing ("hammering" the paper into dust).

If data is on electronic media, the data should never be erased using the operating system's "delete" command (*purging*). Deleted data can still be retrieved using third-party tools. Instead, data sanitation tools can be employed to securely remove data. One technique is called *wiping* (overwriting the disk space with zeroes or random data). For a magnetic-based hard disk drive, degaussing permanently destroys the entire drive by reducing or eliminating the magnetic field. Normally, degaussing is a third-party solution because it is a specialized technique requiring special equipment.

NOTE 12

There is no universal agreement on the differences between purging and wiping.

Consideration on which data destruction technique to use may hinge upon the need to verify the destruction for regulatory purposes. Some techniques cannot provide this verification. For example, degaussing cannot verify that the drive was destroyed. In this instance, it may be necessary to first wipe the drive to verify that all data has been destroyed and then degauss the drive to destroy the data completely and permanently.

TWO RIGHTS & A WRONG

1. The data type "confidential" has the highest level of data sensitivity.
2. Tokenization is a process that is part of data anonymization.
3. "Pulverizing" is hammering paper into dust.

See Appendix B for the answer.

 **VM LAB**   You're now ready to complete the live, virtual machine labs for this module. The labs can be found in the Practice It folder in each MindTap module.

SUMMARY

- A risk is a situation that involves exposure to some type of danger. There are many different types of risk. An internal risk comes from within an organization (such as employee theft), while an external risk is from the outside (such as the actions of a hacktivist). One type of platform well known for its risks is a legacy system. Although legacy hardware introduces some risks, more often risks result from legacy software, such as an OS or program. Often overlooked in identifying risk types is the impact that vulnerabilities of one organization can have on other organizations connected to it. Intellectual property (IP) theft involves threat actors who attempt to steal IP and profit from it. Specialized software that an enterprise uses is subject to licensing restrictions to protect the rights of the developer. Software compliance and licensing risks are today considered a serious problem for organizations. Most organizations unknowingly violate one or more licensing agreements.

- It is important for an organization to regularly perform a risk analysis, or a process to identify and assess the factors that may jeopardize the success of a project or reaching a stated goal. Identifying risks can be difficult due to the elusive nature of risks, unconscious human biases, and prejudices toward certain types of risks. Risk Control Self-Assessment (RCSA) is an "empowering" methodology by which management and staff at all levels collectively work to identify and evaluate risks. The goal of RCSA is to not only minimize biases and prejudices but also to integrate risk management practices into the culture of the organization.

- There are two approaches to risk calculation: qualitative risk calculation, which uses an "educated guess" based on observation, and quantitative risk calculation, which is considered more scientific. Quantitative risk calculations can be divided into the likelihood of a risk and the impact of a risk being successful. The tools used for calculating risk likelihood include Mean Time Between Failure (MTBF), Mean Time To Recovery (MTTR), Mean Time To Failure (MTTF), Failure In Time (FIT), and the Annualized Rate of Occurrence (ARO). Risk impact calculation tools include Single Loss Expectancy (SLE) and Annual Loss Expectancy (ALE).

- Several approaches are used to reduce risk. An organization can accept, transfer, avoid, or mitigate risks. A security control is a safeguard or countermeasure employed within an organizational information system to protect the confidentiality, integrity, and availability of a technology system and its data. It attempts to limit exposure to a danger. There are three broad categories of controls: managerial, operational, and technical. Specific types of controls are found within these three broad categories. Inherent risk is defined as the current risk level given the existing set of controls. Residual risk is the risk level that remains after additional controls are applied. A specific type of risk is a control risk or the probability that financial statements are materially misstated because of failures in the system of controls used by an organization.

- Several risks are associated with using third parties. One of the means by which the parties can reduce risk is to reach an understanding of their relationships and responsibilities through interoperability agreements, or formal contractual relationships, particularly as they relate to security policy and procedures. These agreements should be regularly reviewed to verify compliance and performance standards.

- An often-overlooked consideration in risk management is the importance of providing training to users. Training results in risk awareness, which is the raising of understanding of what risks exist, their potential impacts, and how they are managed. When conducting training, all users should be involved. Understanding the traits of learners and different learning styles is important. Different techniques are used for user training. Computer-based training (CBT) uses a computer to deliver the instruction. It is popular for user training due its flexibility (training can be done from any location and at any time) and ability to provide feedback about the progress of the learner. However, CBT is not always considered the best means for training. Role-based training involves specialized training that is customized to the specific role that an employee holds in the organization. Gamification is using game-based scenarios for instruction. User training can often include gamification in an attempt to heighten the interest and retention of the learner. When training security professionals, sometimes organizations add an incentive called a capture the flag (CTF) exercise. A series of challenges with varying degrees of difficulty is outlined in advance. When one challenge is solved, a "flag" is given to the participant, and the points are totaled once time has expired. The winning player or team is the one that earns the highest score. Because phishing is the primary means by which threat actors initially launch an attack, many organizations use phishing simulations to help employees recognize phishing emails.

- Privacy is defined as the state or condition of being free from public attention, observation, or interference to the degree that the person chooses. Today data is collected on almost all actions and transactions that individuals perform. As technology devices gather data on user behavior at an unprecedented rate, users are becoming increasingly concerned about how their private data is being collected, used, and stored. Organizations are faced with these growing user concerns and increasing government regulations over data privacy. They must wrestle with how to legitimately employ user data while responsibly collecting, using, and protecting that data.

- Once a data breach occurs, an organization must take specific actionable steps. When required, it must notify those impacted by the breach (public notifications and disclosures) along with relevant stakeholders. It must also outline the actions that are being taken. Depending upon the severity of the breach, a regulatory agency may even require that a breach be classified as a "major incident" and that additional steps be taken (escalation). The consequences to an organization that has suffered a data breach are significant. These include reputation damage, IP theft, and fines.

- Different data types require protection besides customer data, financial information, and government data. These types are confidential, private, sensitive, critical, proprietary, public, personally identifiable information (PII), and protected health information (PHI). An organization may take various steps to protect consumer data. It is important to begin with an impact assessment, which is a means for measuring the effectiveness of the organization's activities. Technologies that can be used to enhance data protection include data minimization, data anonymization, data sanitization, and pseudo-anonymization. Data sovereignty is the country-specific requirements that apply to data. Generally, data is subject to the laws of the country in which it is collected or processed.

- Once data is no longer useful, it should be properly destroyed. Because data itself is intangible, destroying data that is no longer needed involves destroying the media on which the data is stored. Data on paper that is not labeled as public should never be thrown away in a dumpster, recycle bin, or trash receptacle. Paper media can be destroyed by burning (lighting it on fire), shredding (cutting it into small strips or particles), pulping (breaking the paper back into wood cellulose fibers after the ink is removed), or pulverizing ("hammering" the paper into dust). If data is on electronic media, the data should never be erased using the operating system "delete" command (purging). Deleted data can still be retrieved by using third-party tools. Instead, data sanitation tools can be employed to securely remove data. One technique is called wiping (overwriting the disk space with zeroes or random data). For a magnetic-based hard disk drive, degaussing will permanently destroy the entire drive by reducing or eliminating the magnetic field.

Key Terms

acceptance	external risk	pseudo-anonymization
Annualized Loss Expectancy (ALE)	fine	public
Annualized Rate of Occurrence (ARO)	gamification	public notifications and disclosures
asset value	impact assessment	pulping
avoidance	information life cycle	pulverizing
burning	inherent risk	qualitative risk assessment
business partners	internal risk	quantitative risk assessment
business partnership agreement (BPA)	IP theft	regulations that affect risk posture
capture the flag (CTF)	likelihood of occurrence	reputation damage
compensating controls	managerial controls	residual risk
computer-based training (CBT)	measurement system analysis (MSA)	risk
confidential	memorandum of understanding (MOU)	risk appetite
control risk	mitigation	risk awareness
corrective controls	multiparty	Risk Control Self-Assessment (RCSA)
critical	nondisclosure agreement (NDA)	risk matrix/heatmap
cybersecurity insurance	operational controls	risk register
data anonymization	Personally Identifiable Information (PII)	role-based awareness training
data masking	phishing campaign	sensitive
data minimization	phishing simulations	service-level agreement (SLA)
data sanitization	physical controls	shredding
data sovereignty	preventative controls	Single Loss Expectancy (SLE)
degaussing	privacy notice	software compliance and licensing
detective controls	privacy	technical controls
deterrent controls	private	terms of agreement
end of life (EOL)	proprietary	third-party solution
end of service (EOS)	Protected Health Information (PHI)	transference
escalation		vendors

Review Questions

1. Which of the following threats would be classified as the actions of a hactivist?
   a. External threat
   b. Internal threat
   c. Environmental threat
   d. Compliance threat

2. Which of these is NOT a response to risk?
   a. Mitigation
   b. Transference
   c. Resistance
   d. Avoidance

3. Which of the following is NOT a threat classification category?
   a. Compliance
   b. Financial
   c. Tactical
   d. Strategic

4. In which of the following threat classifications would a power blackout be classified?
   a. Operational
   b. Managerial
   c. Technical
   d. Strategic

5. Which of the following approaches to risk calculation typically assigns a numeric value (*1–10*) or label (*High, Medium,* or *Low*) to represent a risk?
   a. Quantitative risk calculation
   b. Qualitative risk calculation
   c. Rule-based risk calculation
   d. Policy-based risk calculation

6. What is a list of potential threats and associated risks?
   a. Risk assessment
   b. Risk matrix
   c. Risk register
   d. Risk portfolio

7. Giovanni is completing a report on risks. To which risk option would he classify the action that the organization has decided not to construct a new a data center because it would be located in an earthquake zone?
   a. Transference
   b. Avoidance
   c. Rejection
   d. Prevention

8. Which of the following control categories includes conducting workshops to help users resist phishing attacks?
   a. Managerial
   b. Operational
   c. Technical
   d. Administrative

9. Emiliano needs to determine the expected monetary loss every time a risk occurs. Which formula will he use?
   a. AV
   b. SLE
   c. ARO
   d. ALE

10. Enzo is reviewing the financial statements and has discovered a serious misstatement. What type of risk has he found?
    a. Control risk
    b. Financial risk
    c. Reporting risk
    d. Monetary risk

11. Simona needs to research a control that attempts to discourage security violations before they occur. Which control will she research?
    a. Deterrent control
    b. Preventive control
    c. Detective control
    d. Corrective control

12. Which of the following is NOT a legally enforceable agreement but is still more formal than an unwritten agreement?
    a. BPA
    b. SLA
    c. MOU
    d. MSA

13. Angelo has received notification that a business partner will no longer sell or update a specific product. What type of notification is this?
    a. EOA
    b. EOP
    c. EOL
    d. EOS

14. Which of the following is NOT a concern for users regarding the usage of their privacy data?
    a. Associations with groups
    b. Individual inconveniences and identity theft
    c. Timeliness of data
    d. Statistical inferences

15. Which of the following is NOT a consequence to an organization that has suffered a data security breach?
    a. Reputation damage
    b. IP theft
    c. De-escalation of reporting requirements
    d. Monetary fine

16. Which of the following data types has the highest level of data sensitivity?
    a. Private
    b. Secure
    c. Sensitive
    d. Confidential

17. Sergio has been asked to make a set of data that was once restricted now available to any users. What data type will Sergio apply to this set of data?
    a. Open
    b. Unrestricted
    c. Public
    d. Available

18. Which of the following uses data anonymization?
    a. Tokenization
    b. Data masking
    c. Data minimization
    d. Data obfuscation sanitization (DOS)

19. Which of the following is NOT true about data sovereignty?
    a. Data sovereignty is a concept that until recently was less of an issue.
    b. Generally, data is subject to the laws of the country in which it is collected or processed.
    c. Governments cannot force companies to store data within specific countries.
    d. Regulations are not necessarily on where an organization is headquartered.

20. Bob needs to create an agreement between his company and a third-party organization that demonstrates a "convergence of will" between the parties so that they can work together. Which type of agreement will Bob use?
    a. SLA
    b. BPA
    c. ISA
    d. MOU

Hands-On Projects

 **CAUTION**   If you are concerned about installing any of the software in these projects on your regular computer, you can instead use the Windows Sandbox or install the software in the Windows virtual machine created in the Module 1 Hands-On Projects. Software installed within the virtual machine will not impact the host computer.

Project 15-1: Viewing Your Annual Credit Report

Time Required: 25 minutes

Objective: 5.5 Explain privacy and sensitive data concepts in relation to security.
   • Organizational consequences of privacy breaches

Description: Security experts recommend that consumers reduce personal risk and protect their identity by receiving a copy of their credit report at least once per year to check its accuracy. In this project, you access your free credit report online.

1. Use your web browser to go to **www.annualcreditreport.com**. Although you could send a request individually to one of the three credit agencies, this website acts as a central source for ordering free credit reports.
2. Click **Request your free credit reports**.
3. Read through the three steps and click **Request your credit reports**.
4. Enter the requested information, click **Continue**, and then click **Next**.
5. Click **TransUnion**. Click **Next**.
6. After the brief processing completes, click **Continue**.
7. You may then be asked personal information about your transaction history to verify your identity. Answer the requested questions and click **Next**.
8. Follow the instructions to print your report.

9. Review it carefully, particularly the sections of "Potentially negative items" and "Requests for your credit history." If you see anything that might be incorrect, follow the instructions on that website to enter a dispute.
10. Follow the instructions to exit from the website.
11. Close all windows.

Project 15-2: Using a Nonpersistent Web Browser

Time Required: 25 minutes
Objective: 5.5 Explain privacy and sensitive data concepts in relation to security.
- Privacy enhancing technologies

Description: Nonpersistence tools are used to ensure that unwanted data is not carried forward but instead a clean image is used. This helps protect user privacy. One common tool is a web browser that retains no information such as cookies, history, passwords, or any other data and requires no installation but runs from a USB flash drive. In this project, you download and install a nonpersistent web browser.

1. Use your web browser to go to **www.browzar.com**. (If you are no longer able to access the program through this URL, use a search engine and search for "Browzar.")
2. Click **Key Features** and read about the features of Browzar.
3. Click **Help & FAQs** and read the questions and answers.
4. Click **Download now – it's FREE!**
5. Choose one of the available themes and click **Download**.
6. Click **Accept**.
7. Click **Download**.
8. Click the downloaded file to run Browzar. Note that no installation is required and the browser can be run from a USB flash drive.
9. From Browzar, go to **www.google.com**.
10. Enter **Cengage** in the search bar to search for information about Cengage.
11. Click the red **X** in the upper-right corner to close the browser. What information appears in the pop-up window? What happens when you close the browser?
12. Launch Browzar again.
13. Click **Tools**.
14. Click **Secure delete**.
15. Click **More**. What additional protections does Secure Delete give?
16. Close all windows.

Project 15-3: Online Phishing Training

Time Required: 25 minutes
Objective: 5.3 Explain the importance of policies to organizational security.
- Diversity of training techniques

Description: In this project, you will use an online phishing training tool. Note the user awareness training features in this simulation as you proceed.

1. Use your web browser to go to **public.cyber.mil/training/phishing-awareness/**. (If you are no longer able to access the program through this URL, use a search engine and search for "phishing awareness.")
2. Click **Launch Training**.
3. If necessary, adjust your web browser settings, and then click **Start/Continue Phishing Awareness**.
4. Watch the brief video on accessibility features. Click the right arrow button.
5. Read the information. Click either the URL or **Continue**, depending upon your needs.
6. Listen to the video message about your choice. Is this a good learning technique? Why? Click the right arrow button.
7. Continue through the phishing training. Slides 16–18 ask you for answers to questions about what you have learned.
8. How effective was this training? What did you learn? Would you recommend this to others to learn about phishing?
9. Close all windows.

Case Projects

Case Project 15-1: Multiparty Risks

Until recently, multiparty risks have not been considered as serious. Use the Internet to research multiparty risks. Why is there now heightened emphasis on multiparty risks? What are three examples of security incidents that were the result of a vulnerability in one organization affecting multiple other organizations? What were the outcomes of each of these? Should an organization that allows other organizations to be compromised through a multiparty risk be held liable? What should be the penalty? How can these be mitigated? Write a one-page paper on your findings.

Case Project 15-2: Intellectual Property (IP) Theft

Use the Internet to find details on four recent incidents of intellectual property (IP) theft from an organization. What was stolen? What vulnerability did the threat actors exploit? How valuable was the IP? What did the threat actors do with it? What loss did it create for the organization? How could it have been prevented? Write a one-page paper on your findings.

Case Project 15-3: Unconscious Biases in Cybersecurity

How could unconscious biases impact cybersecurity? Review the information in Table 15-4 and select four of the biases. Then create a practical example of how each bias or effect could impact cybersecurity. Now return to the table and list in order what you consider your own biases from most prevalent to least. What can be done to minimize the impact of these biases?

Case Project 15-4: Reacting to Risks

Using the six reactions to risks in this module, identify a specific risk that you would place in each category. This risk should be something that involves you by identifying intentional actions, accidents, etc. Evaluate your reaction to these risks. Could these play a part in how you might evaluate cybersecurity risks in an organization? How could they be addressed? Write a one-page paper on your analysis.

Case Project 15-5: User Awareness and Training

What user security awareness and training is available at your school or place of business? How frequently is it performed? Is it available online or in person? Is it required? Are the topics up to date? On a scale of 1–10, how would you rate the training? How could it be improved? Write a one-page summary.

Case Project 15-6: Privacy Notices

Identify four different privacy notices and read through them. What information do they contain? How easy are they to understand? Who are they intended to protect, the user or the organization? Now assign a letter grade (A–F) for each notice. Finally, using these as a basis, write your own privacy notice that you consider to be thorough and fair. How does it differ from those that you have found? Why? Write a one-page summary.

Case Project 15-7: North Ridge Security

North Ridge Security provides security consulting and assurance services. You have recently been hired as an intern to assist them.

Firm and Fit (FAF) is a regional health and fitness chain that is rapidly expanding. However, a new CIO is concerned that FAF has not been realistic about the cybersecurity risks that they face, yet he is having difficulty convincing the other senior vice presidents (SVPs) of this concern. Because FAF has not been the victim of a major attack, the other SVPs think that the security posture of FAF is fine. The new CIO has contracted with North Ridge Security to help provide information to the SVPs about risk. You have been asked to make a presentation to them.

1. Create a PowerPoint presentation for the SVPs of FAF about managing risk. Include a definition of risk, different risk types, how to perform a risk analysis, and good risk management procedures. Your presentation should contain at least 10 slides.

2. After the presentation, the SVPs have agreed that they need to look more thoroughly into risk at FAF, particularly as it relates to their business partners and other third-party entities. They have asked you how best to implement third-party risk management. Create a memo with your recommendations.

Case Project 15-8: Community Site Activity

The Information Security Community Site is an online companion to this textbook. It contains a wide variety of tools, information, discussion boards, and other features to assist learners. Go to **community.cengage.com/infosec2** and click the *Join or Sign in* icon to log in, using your login name and password that you created in Module 1. Click **Forums (Discussion)** and click on **Security+ Case Projects (7ᵗʰ edition)**. Read the following case study.

Are you concerned about your data privacy? Have you taken concrete steps to limit the exposure of your data? If so, what are they? How far would you go to protect your data? Would you stop using social media if it meant your data was less exposed? What, if any, restrictions should there be on organizations that collect, use, and store your personal information? Should there be government regulations on user data? If so, what should they look like? Post your opinions to on the Community Site discussion board.

References

1. Cunningham, Margaret, "'Thinking about thinking' is critical to cybersecurity," *Forcepoint*, June 10, 2019, accessed June 17, 2019, www.forcepoint.com/blog/insights/thinking-about-thinking-critical-cybersecurity.

2. Zorz, Zeljka, "How human bias impacts cybersecurity decision making," *HelpNetSecurity*, June 10, 2019, accessed June 12, 2019, www.helpnetsecurity.com/2019/06/10/cybersecurity-decision-making/.

COMPTIA SECURITY+ SY0-601 CERTIFICATION EXAM OBJECTIVES

Bloom's Taxonomy is an industry-standard classification system used to help identify the level of ability that learners need to demonstrate proficiency. It is often used to classify educational learning objectives into different levels of complexity. The Bloom's Taxonomy column in the following table reflects the level of coverage for the respective SY0-601 objective domains. In all instances, the level of coverage in *CompTIA Security+ Guide to Network Security Fundamentals, Seventh Edition*, meets or exceeds that indicated by CompTIA for that objective. See the Introduction of this book for more information.

Security+ Exam Domain/Objectives	Module	Section	Bloom's Taxonomy
1.0 Threats, Attacks, and Vulnerabilities			
1.1 Compare and contrast different types of social engineering techniques. • Phishing • Smishing • Vishing • Spam • Spam over Internet messaging (SPIM) • Spear phishing • Dumpster diving • Shoulder surfing • Pharming • Tailgating • Eliciting information • Whaling • Prepending • Identity fraud • Invoice scams • Credential harvesting • Reconnaissance • Hoax • Impersonation • Watering hole attack • Typo squatting	1	Vulnerabilities and Attacks	Understanding

(continues)

Security + Exam Domain/Objectives	Module	Section	Bloom's Taxonomy

• Influence campaigns
  ○ Hybrid warfare
  ○ Social media
• Principles (reasons for effectiveness)
  ○ Authority
  ○ Intimidation
  ○ Consensus
  ○ Scarcity
  ○ Familiarity
  ○ Trust
  ○ Urgency			

1.2 Given a scenario, analyze potential indicators to determine the type of attack.			

• Malware
  ○ Ransomware
  ○ Trojans
  ○ Worms
  ○ Potentially unwanted programs (PUPs)
  ○ Fileless virus
  ○ Command and control
  ○ Bots
  ○ Cryptomalware
  ○ Logic bombs
  ○ Spyware
  ○ Keyloggers
  ○ Remote access Trojan (RAT)
  ○ Rootkit
  ○ Backdoor
	3	Attacks Using Malware	Analyzing

• Password attacks
  ○ Spraying
  ○ Dictionary
  ○ Brute force
    ▪ Offline
    ▪ Online
  ○ Rainbow tables
  ○ Plaintext/unencrypted
	12	Types of Authentication Credentials	Creating

• Physical attacks
  ○ Malicious universal serial bus (USB) cable
  ○ Malicious flash drive
  ○ Card cloning
  ○ Skimming
	5	Securing Mobile Devices	Applying

• Adversarial artificial intelligence (AI)
  ○ Tainted training data for machine learning (ML)
  ○ Security of machine learning algorithms
	3	Adversarial Artificial Intelligence Attacks	Understanding

• Supply-chain attacks • Cloud-based vs. on-premises attacks			

• Cryptographic attacks
  ○ Birthday
  ○ Collision
  ○ Downgrade
	6	Cryptographic Attacks and Defenses	Applying

Security + Exam Domain/Objectives	Module	Section	Bloom's Taxonomy
1.3 Given a scenario, analyze potential indicators associated with application attacks.	3		
• Privilege escalation		Segmenting the Network	Understanding
• Cross-site scripting			
• Injections		Creating Network Deception	Applying
○ Structured query language (SQL)		Implementing Endpoint	Applying
○ Dynamic link library (DLL)		Security	
○ Lightweight directory access protocol (LDAP)			
○ Extensible markup language (XML)			
• Pointer/object dereference			
• Directory traversal		Hardening the Network	Analyzing
• Buffer overflows			
• Race conditions			
○ Time of check/time of use			
• Error handling			
• Improper input handling			
• Replay attack			
○ Session replays			
• Integer overflow			
• Request forgeries			
○ Server-side			
○ Client-side			
○ Cross-site			
• Application programming interface (API) attacks			
• Resource exhaustion			
• Memory leak			
• Secure sockets layer (SSL) stripping			
• Driver manipulation			
○ Shimming			
○ Refactoring			
• Pass the hash			
1.4 Given a scenario, analyze potential indicators associated with network attacks.			
• Wireless	11	Wireless Attacks	Understanding
○ Evil twin			
○ Rogue access point			
○ Bluesnarfing			
○ Bluejacking			
○ Disassociation			
○ Jamming			
○ Radio frequency identifier (RFID)			
○ Near field communication (NFC)			
○ Initialization vector (IV)			
• Man-in-the-middle	8	Attacks on Networks	Applying
• Man-in-the-browser			
• Layer 2 attacks			
○ Address resolution protocol (ARP) poisoning			
○ Media access control (MAC) flooding			
○ MAC cloning			

(continues)

Security + Exam Domain/Objectives	Module	Section	Bloom's Taxonomy

• Domain name system (DNS)
  ○ Domain hijacking
  ○ DNS poisoning
  ○ Universal resource locator (URL) redirection
  ○ Domain reputation
• Distributed denial of service (DDoS)
  ○ Network
  ○ Application
  ○ Operational technology (OT)
• Malicious code or script execution
  ○ PowerShell
  ○ Python
  ○ Bash
  ○ Macros
  ○ Visual Basic for Applications (VBA)			

1.5 Explain different threat actors, vectors, and intelligence sources.			

• Actors and threats
  ○ Advanced persistent threat (APT)
  ○ Insider threats
  ○ State actors
  ○ Hacktivists
  ○ Script kiddies
  ○ Criminal syndicates
  ○ Hackers
    ▪ White hat
    ▪ Black hat
    ▪ Gray hat
  ○ Shadow IT
  ○ Competitors
	1	Who Are the Threat Actors?	Understanding

• Attributes of actors
  ○ Internal/external
  ○ Level of sophistication/capability
  ○ Resources/funding
  ○ Intent/motivation			

• Vectors
  ○ Direct access
  ○ Wireless
  ○ Email
  ○ Supply chain
  ○ Social media
  ○ Removable media
  ○ Cloud
	1	Vulnerabilities and Attacks	Analyzing

• Threat intelligence sources
  ○ Open source intelligence (OSINT)
  ○ Closed/proprietary
  ○ Vulnerability databases
  ○ Public/private information sharing centers
  ○ Dark web
  ○ Indicators of compromise
	4	Threat Intelligence Sources	Analyzing

Security + Exam Domain/Objectives	Module	Section	Bloom's Taxonomy
○ Automated indicator sharing (AIS) 　■ Structured threat information exchange (STIX)/Trusted automated exchange of indicator information (TAXII) 　■ Predictive analysis 　■ Threat maps 　■ File/code repositories • Research sources ○ Vendor websites ○ Vulnerability feeds ○ Conferences ○ Academic journals ○ Request for comments (RFC) ○ Local industry groups ○ Social media ○ Threat feeds ○ Adversary tactics, techniques, and procedures (TTP)	2	Cybersecurity Resources	Analyzing
1.6 Explain the security concerns associated with various types of vulnerabilities. • Cloud-based vs. on-premises vulnerabilities • Zero-day • Weak configurations ○ Open permissions ○ Unsecured root accounts ○ Errors ○ Weak encryption ○ Unsecure protocols ○ Default settings ○ Open ports and services • Third-party risks ○ Vendor management 　■ System integration 　■ Lack of vendor support ○ Supply chain ○ Outsourced code development ○ Data storage • Improper or weak patch management ○ Firmware ○ Operating system (OS) ○ Applications • Legacy platforms • Impacts ○ Data loss ○ Data breaches ○ Data exfiltration ○ Identity theft ○ Financial ○ Reputation ○ Availability loss	1	Vulnerabilities and Attacks	Analyzing

(continues)

Security + Exam Domain/Objectives	Module	Section	Bloom's Taxonomy

1.7 Summarize the techniques used in security assessments.
 	
• Threat hunting
  ○ Intelligence fusion
  ○ Threat feeds
  ○ Advisories and bulletins
  ○ Maneuver
• Vulnerability scans
  ○ False positives
  ○ False negatives
  ○ Log reviews
  ○ Credentialed vs. non-credentialed
  ○ Intrusive vs. nonintrusive
  ○ Application
  ○ Web application
  ○ Network
  ○ Common Vulnerabilities and Exposures (CVE)/Common Vulnerability Scoring System (CVSS)
  ○ Configuration review
• Syslog/Security information and event management (SIEM)
  ○ Review reports
  ○ Packet capture
  ○ Data inputs
  ○ User behavior analysis
  ○ Sentiment analysis
  ○ Security monitoring
  ○ Log aggregation
  ○ Log collectors
• Security orchestration, automation, response (SOAR)
	2	Vulnerability Scanning	Evaluating

1.8 Explain the techniques used in penetration testing.
 	
• Penetration testing
  ○ White box
  ○ Black box
  ○ Gray box
  ○ Rules of engagement
  ○ Lateral movement
  ○ Privilege escalation
  ○ Persistence
  ○ Cleanup
  ○ Bug bounty
  ○ Pivoting
• Passive and active reconnaissance
  ○ Drones/unmanned aerial vehicle (UAV)
  ○ War flying
  ○ War driving
  ○ Footprinting
  ○ OSINT
• Exercise types
  ○ Red team
  ○ Blue team
  ○ White team
  ○ Purple team
	2	Penetration Testing	Evaluating

Security + Exam Domain/Objectives	Module	Section	Bloom's Taxonomy
2.0 Architecture and Design			
2.1 Explain the importance of security concepts in an enterprise environment.			

• Configuration management
  ○ Diagrams
  ○ Baseline configuration
  ○ Standard naming conventions
  ○ Internet protocol (IP) schema
	9	Security Appliances	Understanding

• Data sovereignty	6	Defining Cryptography	Applying

• Data protection
  ○ Data loss prevention (DLP)
  ○ Masking
  ○ Encryption
  ○ At rest
  ○ In transit/motion
  ○ In processing
  ○ Tokenization
  ○ Rights management
	9	Security Technologies	Applying

• Hardware security module (HSM)	6	Using Cryptography	Evaluating
• Geographical considerations			
• Cloud access security broker (CASB)			
• Response and recovery controls	13	Incident Preparation	Understanding
• Secure Sockets Layer (SSL)/Transport Layer Security (TLS) inspection	7	Cryptographic Protocols	Understanding
• Hashing			
• API considerations			

• Site resiliency
  ○ Hot site
  ○ Cold site
  ○ Warm site
	14	Business Continuity	Applying

• Deception and disruption
  ○ Honeypots
  ○ Honeyfiles
  ○ Honeynets
  ○ Fake telemetry
  ○ DNS sinkhole
	9	Security Appliances	Applying

2.2 Summarize virtualization and cloud computing concepts.			

• Cloud models
  ○ Infrastructure as a service (IaaS)
  ○ Platform as a service (PaaS)
  ○ Software as a service (SaaS)
  ○ Anything as a service (XaaS)
  ○ Public
  ○ Community
  ○ Private
  ○ Hybrid
	10	Cloud Security	Applying

• Cloud service providers			
• Managed service provider (MSP)/Managed security service provider (MSSP)			
• On-premises vs. off-premises			

(continues)

Security + Exam Domain/Objectives	Module	Section	Bloom's Taxonomy

• Fog computing
• Edge computing
• Thin client
• Containers
• Microservices/API
• Infrastructure as code
  ○ Software-defined networking (SDN)
  ○ Software-defined visibility (SDV)
• Serverless architecture
• Services integration
• Resource policies
• Transit gateway
• Virtualization
  ○ Virtual machine (VM) sprawl avoidance
  ○ VM escape protection
	10	Virtualization Security	Creating

2.3 Summarize secure application development, deployment, and automation concepts.
 	
• Environment
  ○ Development
  ○ Test
  ○ Staging
  ○ Production
  ○ Quality assurance (QA)
• Provisioning and deprovisioning
• Integrity measurement
• Secure coding techniques
  ○ Normalization
  ○ Stored procedures
  ○ Obfuscation/camouflage
  ○ Code reuse/dead code
  ○ Server-side vs. client-side execution and validation
  ○ Memory management
  ○ Use of third-party libraries and software development kits (SDKs)
  ○ Data exposure
• Open Web Application Security Project (OWASP)
• Software diversity
  ○ Compiler
  ○ Binary
• Automation/scripting
  ○ Automated courses of action
  ○ Continuous monitoring
  ○ Continuous validation
  ○ Continuous integration
  ○ Continuous delivery
  ○ Continuous deployment
• Elasticity
• Scalability
• Version control
	4	Creating and Deploying SecDevOps	Understanding

Security + Exam Domain/Objectives	Module	Section	Bloom's Taxonomy
2.4 Summarize authentication and authorization design concepts.			

• Authentication methods
  ○ Directory services
  ○ Federation
  ○ Attestation
  ○ Technologies
    ▪ Time-based one-time password (TOTP)
    ▪ HMAC-based one-time password (HOTP)
    ▪ Short message service (SMS)
    ▪ Token key
    ▪ Static codes
    ▪ Authentication applications
    ▪ Push notifications
    ▪ Phone call
	12	Authentication Solutions	Evaluating

○ Smart card authentication
• Biometrics
  ○ Fingerprint
  ○ Retina
  ○ Iris
  ○ Facial
  ○ Voice
  ○ Vein
  ○ Gait analysis
  ○ Efficacy rates
  ○ False acceptance
  ○ False rejection
  ○ Crossover error rate
• Multifactor authentication (MFA) factors and attributes
  ○ Factors
    ▪ Something you know
    ▪ Something you have
    ▪ Something you are
  ○ Attributes
    ▪ Somewhere you are
    ▪ Something you can do
    ▪ Something you exhibit
    ▪ Someone you know
• Authentication, authorization, and accounting (AAA)
• Cloud vs. on-premises requirements
	12	Types of Authentication Credentials	Analyzing

2.5 Given a scenario, implement cybersecurity resilience.	14	Introduction to Business Continuity	Applying

• Redundancy
  ○ Geographic dispersal
  ○ Disk
    ▪ Redundant array of inexpensive disks (RAID) levels
    ▪ Multipath
  ○ Network
    ▪ Load balancers
    ▪ Network interface card (NIC) teaming			

(continues)

Security + Exam Domain/Objectives	Module	Section	Bloom's Taxonomy

○ Power
      ■ Uninterruptible power supply (UPS)
      ■ Generator
      ■ Dual supply
      ■ Managed power distribution units (PDUs)
• Replication
    ○ Storage area network (SAN)
    ○ VM
• On-premises vs. cloud
• Backup types
    ○ Full
    ○ Incremental
    ○ Snapshot
    ○ Differential
    ○ Tape
    ○ Disk
    ○ Copy
    ○ Network attached storage (NAS)
    ○ Storage area network (SAN)
    ○ Cloud
    ○ Image
    ○ Online vs. offline
    ○ Offsite storage
      ■ Distance considerations
• Nonpersistence
    ○ Revert to known state
    ○ Last known good configuration
    ○ Live boot media
• High availability
    ○ Scalability
• Restoration order
• Diversity
    ○ Technologies
    ○ Vendors
    ○ Crypto
    ○ Controls			

2.6 Explain the security implications of embedded and specialized systems.
 	
• Embedded systems
    ○ Raspberry Pi
    ○ Field programmable gate array (FPGA)
    ○ Arduino
• System control and data acquisition (SCADA)/ industrial control system (ICS)
    ○ Facilities
    ○ Industrial
    ○ Manufacturing
    ○ Energy
    ○ Logistics
• Internet of Things (IoT)
    ○ Sensors
    ○ Smart devices
    ○ Wearables
    ○ Facility automation
    ○ Weak defaults
• Specialized
    ○ Medical systems
    ○ Vehicles
	5	Embedded and Specialized Devices	Understanding

Security + Exam Domain/Objectives	Module	Section	Bloom's Taxonomy

○ Aircraft
○ Smart meters
• Voice over IP (VoIP)
• Heating, ventilation, air conditioning (HVAC)
• Drones/AVs
• Multifunction printer (MFP)
• Real-time operating system (RTOS)
• Surveillance systems
• System on chip (SoC)
• Communication considerations
  ○ 5G
  ○ Narrow-band
  ○ Baseband radio
  ○ Subscriber identity module (SIM) cards
  ○ Zigbee
• Constraints
  ○ Power
  ○ Compute
  ○ Network
  ○ Crypto
  ○ Inability to patch
  ○ Authentication
  ○ Range
  ○ Cost
  ○ Implied trust			

2.7 Explain the importance of physical security controls.
 	
• Bollards/barricades
• Mantraps
• Badges
• Alarms
• Signage
• Cameras
  ○ Motion recognition
  ○ Object detection
• Closed-circuit television (CCTV)
• Industrial camouflage
• Personnel
  ○ Guards
  ○ Robot sentries
  ○ Reception
  ○ Two-person integrity/control
• Locks
  ○ Biometrics
  ○ Electronic
  ○ Physical
  ○ Cable locks
• USB data blocker
• Lighting
• Fencing
• Fire suppression
• Sensors
  ○ Motion detection
  ○ Noise detection
  ○ Proximity reader
  ○ Moisture detection
  ○ Cards
  ○ Temperature
	8	Physical Security Controls	Applying

(continues)

Security + Exam Domain/Objectives	Module	Section	Bloom's Taxonomy

• Drones/UAV
• Visitor logs
• Faraday cages
• Air gap
• Demilitarized zone (DMZ)
• Protected cable distribution
• Secure areas
  ○ Air gap
  ○ Vault
  ○ Safe
  ○ Hot aisle
  ○ Cold aisle
• Secure data destruction
  ○ Burning
  ○ Shredding
  ○ Pulping
  ○ Pulverizing
  ○ Degaussing
  ○ Third-party solutions
	15	Data Privacy	Evaluating

2.8 Summarize the basics of cryptographic concepts.
 	
• Digital signatures
• Key length
• Key stretching
• Salting
• Hashing
• Key exchange
• Elliptical curve cryptography
• Perfect forward secrecy
• Quantum
  ○ Communications
  ○ Computing
• Post-quantum
• Ephemeral
• Modes of operation
  ○ Authenticated
  ○ Unauthenticated
  ○ Counter
• Blockchain
  ○ Public ledgers
• Cipher suites
  ○ Stream
  ○ Block
• Symmetric vs. asymmetric
• Lightweight cryptography
• Steganography
  ○ Audio
  ○ Video
  ○ Image
• Homomorphic encryption
• Common use cases
  ○ Low-power devices
  ○ Low latency
	6
	
	12
	
	6
	
	6
		Defining Cryptography
		
		Authentication Credentials
		
		Defining Cryptography
		
		Using Cryptography
			Understanding
			
			Understanding
			
			Analyzing
			
			Analyzing

Security + Exam Domain/Objectives	Module	Section	Bloom's Taxonomy
• High resiliency ∘ Supporting confidentiality ∘ Supporting integrity ∘ Supporting obfuscation ∘ Supporting authentication ∘ Supporting nonrepudiation ∘ Resource vs. security constraints • Limitations ∘ Speed ∘ Size ∘ Weak keys ∘ Time ∘ Longevity ∘ Predictability ∘ Reuse ∘ Entropy ∘ Computational overheads ∘ Resource vs. security constraints			
3.0 Implementation			

3.1 Given a scenario, implement secure protocols.
 	
• Protocols
∘ Domain Name System Security Extension (DNSSEC)
∘ SSH
∘ Secure/Multipurpose Internet Mail Exchanger (S/MIME)
∘ Secure Real-Time Protocol (SRTP)
∘ LDAPS
∘ File Transfer Protocol, Secure (FTPS)
∘ Secured File Transfer Protocol (SFTP)
∘ Simple Network Management Protocol, version 3 (SNMPv3)
∘ Hypertext transfer protocol over SSL/TLS (HTTPS)
∘ IPSec
  ▪ Authentication header (AH)/Encapsulating Security Payload (ESP)
  ▪ Tunnel/transport
∘ Secure Post Office Protocol (POP)/Internet Message Access Protocol (IMAP)
• Use cases
∘ Voice and video
∘ Time synchronization
∘ Email and web
∘ File transfer
∘ Directory services
∘ Remote access
∘ Domain name resolution
∘ Routing and switching
∘ Network address allocation
∘ Subscription services
	8
	
	7
	10
		Attacks on Networks
		
		Cryptographic Protocols
		Secure Network Protocols
			Applying
			
			Understanding
			Applying

(continues)

Security + Exam Domain/Objectives	Module	Section	Bloom's Taxonomy
3.2 Given a scenario, implement host or application security solutions.			

• Endpoint protection
  ○ Antivirus
  ○ Antimalware
  ○ Endpoint detection and response (EDR)
  ○ DLP
  ○ Next-generation firewall
  ○ Host intrusion prevention system (HIPS)
  ○ Host intrusion detection system (HIDS)
  ○ Host-based firewall
• Boot integrity
  ○ Boot security/Unified Extensible Firmware Interface (UEFI)
  ○ Measured boot
  ○ Boot attestation
	4	Securing Endpoint Computers	Evaluating

• Database
  ○ Tokenization
  ○ Salting
  ○ Hashing
	12	Authentication Solutions	Understanding

• Application security
  ○ Input validations
  ○ Secure cookies
  ○ Hypertext Transfer Protocol (HTTP) headers
  ○ Code signing
  ○ Whitelisting
  ○ Blacklisting
  ○ Secure coding practices
  ○ Static code analysis
    ▪ Manual code review
    ▪ Dynamic code analysis
    ▪ Fuzzing
	4	Creating and Deploying SecDevOps	Understanding

• Hardening
  ○ Open ports and services
  ○ Registry
  ○ Disk encryption
  ○ OS
  ○ Patch management
    ▪ Third-party updates
    ▪ Auto-update			

• Self-encrypting drive (SED)/full disk encryption (FDE) ○ Opal • Hardware root of trust • Trusted Platform Module (TPM) • Sandboxing	6	Using Cryptography	Understanding
3.3 Given a scenario, implement secure network designs.			

• Load balancing
  ○ Active/active
  ○ Active/passive
  ○ Scheduling
  ○ Virtual IP
  ○ Persistence
• Network segmentation
  ○ Virtual local area network (VLAN)
  ○ DMZ
  ○ East-west traffic
	3	Security Appliances	Analyzing

Security + Exam Domain/Objectives	Module	Section	Bloom's Taxonomy
○ Extranet			
○ Intranet			
○ Zero trust			
• Virtual private network (VPN)			
○ Always on			
○ Split tunnel vs. full tunnel			
○ Remote access vs. site-to-site			
○ IPSec			
○ SSL/TLS			
○ HTML5			
○ Layer 2 tunneling protocol (L2TP)			
• DNS			
• Network access control (NAC)			
○ Agent and agentless			
• Out-of-band management			
• Port security			
○ Broadcast storm prevention			
○ Bridge Protocol Data Unit (BPDU) guard			
○ Loop prevention			
○ Dynamic Host Configuration Protocol (DHCP) snooping			
○ Media access control (MAC) filtering			
• Network appliances			
○ Jump servers			
○ Proxy servers			
▪ Forward			
▪ Reverse			
○ Network-based intrusion detection system (NIDS)/network-based intrusion prevention system (NIPS)			
▪ Signature based			
▪ Heuristic/behavior			
▪ Anomaly			
▪ Inline vs. passive			
○ HSM			
○ Sensors			
○ Collectors			
○ Aggregators			
○ Firewalls			
▪ Web application firewall (WAF)			
▪ Next-generation firewall			
▪ Stateful			
▪ Stateless			
▪ Unified threat management (UTM)			
▪ Network address translation (NAT) gateway			
▪ Content/URL filter			
▪ Open-source vs. proprietary			
▪ Hardware vs. software			
▪ Appliance vs. host-based vs. virtual			
• Access control list (ACL)			
• Route security	9	Security Technologies	Applying
• Quality of service (QoS)			
• Implications of IPv6			
• Port spanning/port mirroring			
○ Port taps			
• Monitoring services			
• File integrity monitors			

(continues)

Security + Exam Domain/Objectives	Module	Section	Bloom's Taxonomy
3.4 Given a scenario, install and configure wireless security settings.			
• Cryptographic protocols ○ Wi-Fi Protected Access II (WPA2) ○ Wi-Fi Protected Access III (WPA3) ○ Counter-mode/CBC-MAC protocol (CCMP) ○ Simultaneous Authentication of Equals (SAE)	11	Wireless Security Solutions	Analyzing
• Authentication protocols ○ Extensible Authentication Protocol (EAP) ○ Protected Extensible Application Protocol (PEAP) ○ EAP-FAST ○ EAP-TLS ○ EAP-TTLS ○ IEEE 802.1X ○ Remote Authentication Dial-in User Server (RADIUS) Federation	11	Vulnerabilities of WLAN Security	Applying
• Methods ○ Pre-shared key (PSK) vs. Enterprise vs. Open ○ Wi-Fi Protected Setup (WPS) ○ Captive portals			
• Installation considerations ○ Site surveys ○ Heat maps ○ Wi-Fi analyzers ○ Channel overlays ○ Wireless access point (WAP) placement ○ Controller and access point security	11	Additional Wireless Security Protections	Creating
3.5 Given a scenario, implement secure mobile solutions.			
• Connection methods and receivers ○ Cellular ○ Wi-Fi ○ Bluetooth ○ NFC ○ Infrared ○ USB ○ Point-to-point ○ Point-to-multipoint ○ Global Positioning System (GPS) ○ RFID	5	Securing Mobile Devices	Understanding
• Mobile device management (MDM) ○ Application management ○ Content management ○ Remote wipe ○ Geofencing ○ Geolocation ○ Screen locks ○ Push notifications ○ Passwords and pins ○ Biometrics ○ Context-aware authentication ○ Containerization ○ Storage segmentation ○ Full device encryption			
• Mobile devices ○ MicroSD HSM ○ MDM/Unified endpoint management (UEM) ○ Mobile application management (MAM) ○ SEAndroid			

Security + Exam Domain/Objectives	Module	Section	Bloom's Taxonomy
• Enforcement and monitoring of: ○ Third-party app stores ○ Rooting/jailbreaking ○ Sideloading ○ Custom firmware ○ Carrier unlocking ○ Firmware over-the-air (OTA) updates ○ Camera use ○ SMS/multimedia message (MMS)/Rich communication services (RCS) ○ External media ○ USB on the go (OTG) ○ Recording microphone ○ GPS tagging ○ Wi-Fi direct/ad hoc ○ Tethering ○ Hotspot ○ Payment methods • Deployment models ○ Bring your own device (BYOD) ○ Corporate-owned personally enabled (COPE) ○ Choose your own device (CYOD) ○ Corporate-owned ○ Virtual desktop infrastructure (VDI)			
3.6 Given a scenario, apply cybersecurity solutions to the cloud. • Cloud security controls ○ High availability across zones ○ Resource policies ○ Secrets management ○ Integration and auditing ○ Storage ▪ Permissions ▪ Encryption ▪ Replication ▪ High availability ○ Network ▪ Virtual networks ▪ Public and private subnets ▪ Segmentation ▪ API inspection and integration ○ Compute ▪ Security groups ▪ Dynamic resource allocation ▪ Instance awareness ▪ Virtual private cloud (VPC) endpoint ▪ Container security • Solutions ○ CASB ○ Application security ○ Next-generation secure web gateway (SWG) ○ Firewall considerations in a cloud environment ▪ Cost ▪ Need for segmentation ▪ Open Systems ▪ Interconnection (OSI) layers • Cloud native controls vs. third-party solutions	10	Securing Cloud Computing	Understanding

Security + Exam Domain/Objectives	Module	Section	Bloom's Taxonomy
3.7 Given a scenario, implement identity and account management controls.			
• Identity ○ Identity provider (IdP) ○ Attributes ○ Certificates ○ Tokens ○ SSH keys ○ Smart cards • Account types ○ User account ○ Shared and generic accounts/credentials ○ Guest accounts ○ Service accounts	13	Incident Preparation	Analyzing
• Account policies ○ Password complexity ○ Password history ○ Password reuse ○ Time of day ○ Network location ○ Geofencing ○ Geotagging ○ Geolocation ○ Time-based logins ○ Access policies ○ Account permissions ○ Account audits ○ Impossible travel time/risky login ○ Lockout ○ Disablement	14	Policies	Analyzing
3.8 Given a scenario, implement authentication and authorization solutions.			
• Authentication management ○ Password keys ○ Password vaults ○ TPM ○ HSM ○ Knowledge-based authentication • Authentication ○ EAP ○ Challenge Handshake Authentication Protocol (CHAP) ○ Password Authentication Protocol (PAP) ○ 802.1X ○ RADIUS ○ Single sign-on (SSO) ○ Security Assertions Markup Language (SAML) ○ Terminal Access Controller Access Control System Plus (TACACS+) ○ OAuth ○ OpenID ○ Kerberos	12	Authentication Solutions	Evaluating
• Access control schemes ○ Attribute-based access control (ABAC) ○ Role-based access control	13	Incident Preparation	Applying

Security + Exam Domain/Objectives	Module	Section	Bloom's Taxonomy
○ Rule-based access control ○ MAC ○ Discretionary access control (DAC) ○ Conditional access ○ Privilege access management ○ Filesystem permissions			
3.9 Given a scenario, implement public key infrastructure.			

• Public key infrastructure (PKI)
  ○ Key management
  ○ Certificate authority (CA)
  ○ Intermediate CA
  ○ Registration authority (RA)
  ○ Certificate revocation list (CRL)
  ○ Certificate attributes
  ○ Online Certificate Status Protocol (OCSP)
  ○ Certificate signing request (CSR)
  ○ CN
  ○ Subject alternative name (SAN)
  ○ Expiration
	7	Public Key Infrastructure (PKI)	Applying

• Types of certificates
  ○ Wildcard
  ○ SAN
  ○ Code signing
  ○ Self-signed
  ○ Machine/computer
  ○ Email
  ○ User
  ○ Root
  ○ Domain validation
  ○ Extended validation
	7	Digital Certificates	Evaluating

• Certificate formats
  ○ Distinguished encoding rules (DER)
  ○ Privacy enhanced mail (PEM)
  ○ Personal information exchange (PFX)
  ○ .cer
  ○ P12
  ○ P7B
• Concepts
  ○ Online vs. offline CA
  ○ Stapling
  ○ Pinning
  ○ Trust model
  ○ Key escrow
  ○ Certificate chaining			

4.0 Operations and Incident Response			
4.1 Given a scenario, use the appropriate tool to assess organizational security.			

• Network reconnaissance and discovery
  ○ tracert/traceroute
  ○ nslookup/dig
  ○ ipconfig/ifconfig
  ○ nmap
  ○ ping/pathping
  ○ hping
	8	Tools for Assessment and Defense	Applying

(continues)

Security + Exam Domain/Objectives	Module	Section	Bloom's Taxonomy
○ netstat			
○ netcat			
○ IP scanners			
○ arp			
○ route			
○ curl			
○ the harvester			
○ sn1per			
○ scanless			
○ dnsenum			
○ Nessus			
○ Cuckoo			
• File manipulation			
○ head			
○ tail			
○ cat			
○ grep			
○ chmod			
○ logger			
• Shell and script environments			
○ SSH			
○ PowerShell			
○ Python			
○ OpenSSL			
• Packet capture and replay			
○ Tcpreplay			
○ Tcpdump			
○ Wireshark			
• Forensics			
○ dd			
○ Memdump			
○ WinHex			
○ FTK imager			
○ Autopsy			
• Exploitation frameworks	13	Incident Preparation	Applying
• Password crackers			
• Data sanitization	15	Data Privacy	Evaluating
4.2 Summarize the importance of policies, processes, and procedures for incident response.			
• Incident response plans	13	Incident Preparation	Applying
• Incident response process			
○ Preparation			
○ Identification			
○ Containment			
○ Eradication			
○ Recovery			
○ Lessons learned			
• Exercises			
○ Tabletop			
○ Walkthroughs			
○ Simulations			
• Attack frameworks			
○ MITRE ATT&CK			
○ The Diamond Model Intrusion Analysis			
○ Cyber Kill Chain			
• Stakeholder management			
• Communication plan			
• Disaster recovery plan			

Security + Exam Domain/Objectives	Module	Section	Bloom's Taxonomy
• Business continuity plan • Continuity of operation planning (COOP) • Incident response team • Retention policies	14	Introduction to Business Continuity	

4.3 Given an incident, utilize appropriate data sources to support an investigation.
 	
• Vulnerability scan output
• SIEM dashboards
  ○ Sensor
  ○ Sensitivity
  ○ Trends
  ○ Alerts
  ○ Correlation
• Log files
  ○ Network
  ○ System
  ○ Application
  ○ Security
  ○ Web
  ○ DNS
  ○ Authentication
  ○ Dump files
  ○ VoIP and call managers
  ○ Session Initiation Protocol (SIP) traffic
• syslog/rsyslog/syslog-ng
• journalctl
• nxlog
• Retention
• Bandwidth monitors
• Metadata
  ○ Email
  ○ Mobile
  ○ Web
  ○ File
• Netflow/sflow
  ○ Echo
  ○ IPfix
• Protocol analyzer output
	13	Incident Investigation	Analyzing

4.4 Given an incident, apply mitigation techniques or controls to secure an environment.
 	
• Reconfigure endpoint security solutions
  ○ Application whitelisting
  ○ Application blacklisting
  ○ Quarantine
• Configuration changes
  ○ Firewall rules
  ○ MDM
  ○ DLP
  ○ Content filter/URL filter
  ○ Update or revoke certificates
• Isolation
• Containment
• Segmentation
• Secure Orchestration, Automation, and Response (SOAR)
  ○ Runbooks
  ○ Playbooks
	13	Incident Response	Analyzing

(continues)

Security + Exam Domain/Objectives	Module	Section	Bloom's Taxonomy

4.5 Explain the key aspects of digital forensics.
 	
• Documentation/evidence
  ○ Legal hold
  ○ Video
  ○ Admissibility
  ○ Chain of custody
  ○ Timelines of sequence of events
    ▪ Time stamps
    ▪ Time offset
  ○ Tags
  ○ Reports
  ○ Event logs
  ○ Interviews
• Acquisition
  ○ Order of volatility
  ○ Disk
  ○ Random-access memory (RAM)
  ○ Swap/pagefile
  ○ OS
  ○ Device
  ○ Firmware
  ○ Snapshot
  ○ Cache
  ○ Network
  ○ Artifacts
• On-premises vs. cloud
  ○ Right-to-audit clauses
  ○ Regulatory/jurisdiction
  ○ Data breach notification laws
• Integrity
  ○ Hashing
  ○ Checksums
  ○ Provenance
• Preservation
• E-discovery
• Data recovery
• Nonrepudiation
• Strategic intelligence/counterintelligence
	13	Incident Investigation	Analyzing

5.0 Governance, Risk, and Compliance			

5.1 Compare and contrast various types of controls.
 	
• Category
  ○ Managerial
  ○ Operational
  ○ Technical
• Control type
  ○ Preventative
  ○ Detective
  ○ Corrective
  ○ Deterrent
  ○ Compensating
  ○ Physical
	15	Managing Risk	Applying

Security + Exam Domain/Objectives	Module	Section	Bloom's Taxonomy

5.2 Explain the importance of applicable regulations, standards, or frameworks that impact organizational security posture.
 	
• Regulations, standards, and legislation
  ○ General Data Protection Regulation (GDPR)
  ○ National, territory, or state laws
  ○ Payment Card Industry Data Security Standard (PCI DSS)
• Key frameworks
  ○ Center for Internet Security (CIS)
  ○ National Institute of Standards and Technology (NIST) RMF/CSF
  ○ International Organization for Standardization (ISO) 27001/27002/27701/31000
  ○ SSAE SOC 2 Type II/III
  ○ Cloud security alliance
    ▪ Cloud control matrix
    ▪ Reference architecture
• Benchmarks /secure configuration guides
  ○ Platform/vendor-specific guides
    ▪ Web server
    ▪ OS
    ▪ Application server
    ▪ Network infrastructure devices
	2	Cybersecurity Resources	Analyzing

5.3 Explain the importance of policies to organizational security.
 	
• Personnel
  ○ Acceptable use policy
  ○ Job rotation
  ○ Mandatory vacation
  ○ Separation of duties
  ○ Least privilege
  ○ Clean desk space
  ○ Background checks
  ○ Nondisclosure agreement (NDA)
  ○ Social media analysis
  ○ Onboarding
  ○ Offboarding
  ○ User training
    ▪ Gamification
    ▪ Capture the flag
    ▪ Phishing campaigns
      ▪ Phishing simulations
      ▪ Computer-based training (CBT)
      ▪ Role-based training
• Diversity of training techniques
• Third-party risk management
  ○ Vendors
  ○ Supply chain
  ○ Business partners
	14
	
	15
		Policies
		
		Risk Management
			Creating
			
			Evaluating

(continues)

Security + Exam Domain/Objectives	Module	Section	Bloom's Taxonomy

○ Service-level agreement (SLA)
 ○ Memorandum of understanding (MOU)
 ○ Measurement systems analysis (MSA)
 ○ Business partnership agreement (BPA)
 ○ End of life (EOL)
 ○ End of service (EOS)
 ○ NDA
 • Data
   ○ Classification
   ○ Governance
   ○ Retention
 • Credential policies
   ○ Personnel
   ○ Third party
   ○ Devices
   ○ Service accounts
   ○ Administrator/root accounts
 • Organizational policies
   ○ Change management
   ○ Change control
   ○ Asset management			

5.4 Summarize risk management processes and concepts.
 	
 • Risk types
   ○ External
   ○ Internal
   ○ Legacy systems
   ○ Multiparty
   ○ IP theft
   ○ Software compliance/licensing
 • Risk management strategies
   ○ Acceptance
   ○ Avoidance
   ○ Transference
     ■ Cybersecurity insurance
   ○ Mitigation
 • Risk analysis
   ○ Risk register
   ○ Risk matrix/heat map
   ○ Risk control assessment
   ○ Risk control self-assessment
   ○ Risk awareness
   ○ Inherent risk
   ○ Residual risk
   ○ Control risk
   ○ Risk appetite
   ○ Regulations that affect risk posture
   ○ Risk assessment types
     ■ Qualitative
     ■ Quantitative
   ○ Likelihood of occurrence
   ○ Impact
   ○ Asset value
   ○ Single loss expectancy (SLE)
   ○ Annualized loss expectancy (ALE)
   ○ Annualized rate of occurrence (ARO)
	
	 15
	
	 14
		
		 Managing Risk
		
		 Business Continuity
			
			 Analyzing
			
			 Understanding

Security + Exam Domain/Objectives	Module	Section	Bloom's Taxonomy

• Disasters
  ○ Environmental
  ○ Person-made
  ○ Internal vs. external
• Business impact analysis
  ○ Recovery time objective (RTO)
  ○ Recovery point objective (RPO)
  ○ Mean time to repair (MTTR)
  ○ Mean time between failures (MTBF)
  ○ Functional recovery plans
  ○ Single point of failure
  ○ Disaster recovery plan (DRP)
  ○ Mission essential functions
  ○ Identification of critical systems
  ○ Site risk assessment			

5.5 Explain privacy and sensitive data concepts in relation to security.
 	
• Organizational consequences of privacy breaches
  ○ Reputation damage
  ○ Identity theft
  ○ Fines
  ○ IP theft
• Notifications of breaches
  ○ Escalation
  ○ Public notifications and disclosures
• Data types
  ○ Classifications
    ▪ Public
    ▪ Private
    ▪ Sensitive
    ▪ Confidential
    ▪ Critical
    ▪ Proprietary
  ○ Personally identifiable information (PII)
  ○ Health information
  ○ Financial information
  ○ Government data
  ○ Customer data
• Privacy enhancing technologies
  ○ Data minimization
  ○ Data masking
  ○ Tokenization
  ○ Anonymization
  ○ Pseudo-anonymization
• Roles and responsibilities
  ○ Data owners
  ○ Data controller
  ○ Data processor
  ○ Data custodian/steward
  ○ Data protection officer (DPO)
• Information life cycle
• Impact assessment
• Terms of agreement
• Privacy notice
	15	Data Privacy	Creating

TWO RIGHTS & A WRONG: ANSWERS

MODULE 1

Two Rights & A Wrong 1-1

1. A security manager works on tasks identified by the CISO and resolves issues identified by technicians.
2. Since 2015, the number of unfilled cybersecurity positions has increased by 10 percent.
3. The relationship between security and convenience is inversely proportional: as security is increased, convenience is decreased.

Answer: The wrong statement is #2. Since 2015, the number of unfilled cybersecurity positions has increased by 50 percent.

Two Rights & A Wrong 1-2

1. Script kiddies are responsible for the class of attacks called Advanced Persistent Threats.
2. Hacktivists are strongly motivated by ideology.
3. Brokers sell their knowledge of a weakness to other attackers or a government.

Answer: The wrong statement is #1. State actors are responsible for the class of attacks called Advanced Persistent Threats.

Two Rights & A Wrong 1-3

1. Spear phishing targets specific users.
2. "I'm the CEO calling" is an example of the psychological principle of authority.
3. The goal of impersonation is often prepending, which is obtaining private information.

Answer: The wrong statement is #3. Pretexting is obtaining private information.

MODULE 2

Two Rights & A Wrong 2-1

1. The Purple Team is made up of the referees who enforce the rules of a pen test.
2. One advantage of using external pen testing consultants is their credentials.
3. White box testers are given full knowledge of the network.

   Answer: The wrong statement is #1. The White Team is made up of the referees who enforce the rules of a pen test.

Two Rights & A Wrong 2-2

1. The purpose of a vulnerability scan is to reduce the attack surface.
2. SIEMs generate alerts and automate incident response.
3. The Common Vulnerabilities and Exposures (CVE) vulnerability feed identifies vulnerabilities in operating systems and application software.

   Answer: The wrong statement is #2. SOARs generate alerts and automate incident response.

Two Rights & A Wrong 2-3

1. The two NIST frameworks are the NIST Risk Management Framework (RMF) and NIST Cybersecurity Framework (CSF).
2. The Center for Internet Security (CIS) has published a Cloud Controls Matrix.
3. The European Union General Data Protection Directive (GDPR) is a regulation regarding data protection and privacy in the EU and the European Economic Area (EEA).

   Answer: The wrong statement is #2. The Cloud Security Alliance (CSA) has published the Cloud Controls Matrix.

MODULE 3

Two Rights & A Wrong 3-1

1. It is a common tactic for cryptomalware attackers to not send the decryption key after the ransom has been paid.
2. Fileless viruses take advantage of native services and processes that are part of the operating system (OS) to avoid detection and carry out its attacks, and these native services used in a fileless virus are called living-off-the-land binaries (LOLBins).
3. A remote access Trojan (RAT) can monitor what the user is doing, change computer settings, browse and copy files, and use the computer to access other computers connected on the network.

   Answer: The wrong statement is #1. When victims pay the ransom, a decryption tool is delivered 99 percent of the time.

Two Rights & A Wrong 3-2

1. In an XSS attack, a website that accepts user input without sanitizing it and uses that input in a response can be exploited.
2. An SSRF takes advantage of a trusting relationship between a web browser and web servers.
3. A time of check/time of use is a vulnerability that causes a race condition.

Answer: The wrong statement is #2. A server-side request forgery (SSRF) takes advantage of a trusting relationship between web servers (as opposed to a CSRF, which manipulates the trust from a user's browser to a server.)

Two Rights & A Wrong 3-3

1. Artificial intelligence (AI) may be defined as technology that imitates human abilities.
2. AI is already being used broadly in cybersecurity defenses.
3. A recognized subset of ML is AI.

Answer: The wrong statement is #3. A recognized subset of artificial intelligence (AI) is machine learning (ML).

MODULE 4

Two Rights & A Wrong 4-1

1. Two concerns about public information sharing centers are the privacy of shared information and the speed at which the information is shared.
2. Two tools that facilitate AIS are STIX and TAXII.
3. Security professionals consider threat maps a vital source of information.

Answer: The wrong statement is #3. Many threat maps claim that they show data in real time, but most are simply a playback of previous attacks. Also, threat actors usually mask their real locations so what is displayed on a threat map is incorrect. As a result, many cybersecurity professionals question the value of threat maps.

Two Rights & A Wrong 4-2

1. In a Trusted Boot, the endpoint's firmware logs the boot process to the OS can send it to a trusted server to assess the security.
2. Dynamic analysis uses heuristic monitoring.
3. Cookies are a work-around of the stateless protocol HTTP.

Answer: The wrong statement is #1. A Measured Boot logs the boot process so it can be sent to a trusted server.

Two Rights & A Wrong 4-3

1. A goal of software diversity is to reduce the probability that errors created by different compilers will influence the end results.
2. Provisioning is removing a resource that is no longer needed.
3. SecDevOps has elasticity and scalability.

Answer: The wrong statement is #2. Provisioning is the enterprise-wide configuration, deployment, and management of multiple types of IT system resources, of which the new application would be viewed as a new resource.

MODULE 5

Two Rights & A Wrong 5-1

1. Due to its slow speed and other limitations, infrared capabilities in mobile devices are rarely found today.
2. COPE allows users to use their own personal mobile devices for business purposes.
3. Circumventing the installed built-in limitations on an Apple iPhone is called jailbreaking.

Answer: The wrong statement is #2. BYOD allows users to use their own personal mobile devices for business purposes.

Two Rights & A Wrong 5-2

1. Multiple SCADAs are controlled by an ICS.
2. Power, compute, and network are all security constraints for embedded systems and specialized devices.
3. RTOS is tuned to accommodate very high volumes of data that must be immediately processed for critical decision making.

Answer: The wrong statement is #1. Multiple ICS are managed by a larger supervisory control and data acquisition (SCADA) system.

MODULE 6

Two Rights & A Wrong 6-1

1. Steganography hides the existence of information.
2. Unencrypted data that is input for encryption or is the output of decryption is called cleartext.
3. Entropy is the measure of randomness of a data-generating function.

Answer: The wrong statement is #2. Unencrypted data that is input for encryption or is the output of decryption is called plaintext.

Two Rights & A Wrong 6-2

1. A digest of a short set of data should produce the same size as a digest of a long set of data.
2. SHA-1 is considered a secure hash algorithm.
3. Asymmetric cryptography keys can work in both directions.

Answer: The wrong statement is #2. SHA-1 is no longer considered suitable for use.

Two Rights & A Wrong 6-3

1. In a downgrade attack, an attacker forces the system to abandon the current higher security mode of operation and instead "fall back" to implementing an older and less secure mode.
2. Post-quantum cryptography is comprised of algorithms that are secure against an attack by a quantum computer.
3. The basis of a quantum computer is a bit.

Answer: The wrong statement is #3. The basis of a quantum computer is a qubit.

Two Rights & A Wrong 6-4

1. Modern OSs provide encryption support natively.
2. Opal is a standard for FEDs.
3. An HSM is external while a TMP is internal.

Answer: The wrong statement is #2. Opal is a standard for SEDs.

MODULE 7

Two Rights & A Wrong 7-1

1. A digital certificate is a technology used to associate a user's identity to a public key and that has been digitally signed by the owner of the private key.
2. A certificate repository (CR) is a publicly accessible centralized directory of digital certificates that can be used to view the status of a digital certificate.
3. Root digital certificates are self-signed.

   Answer: The wrong statement is #1. A digital certificate is a technology used to associate a user's identity to a public key and that has been digitally signed by a trusted third party.

Two Rights & A Wrong 7-2

1. The hierarchical trust model assigns a single hierarchy with one master CA called the root.
2. An OID, which names an object or entity, corresponds to a node in a hierarchy tree structure. OIDs can name every object type in an X.509 certificate.
3. When a digital certificate is revoked, the user must update internal records and any CRL with the required certificate information and time stamp.

   Answer: The wrong statement is #3. When a digital certificate is revoked, the CA updates its internal records and any CRL with the required certificate information and time stamp.

Two Rights & A Wrong 7-3

1. SSL is a replacement cryptographic protocol for TLS.
2. A cipher suite is a named combination of the encryption, authentication, and message authentication code (MAC) algorithms that are used with TLS.
3. S/MIME is a protocol for securing email messages.

   Answer: The wrong statement is #1. TLS is a replacement for SSL.

Two Rights & A Wrong 7-4

1. Three primary characteristics determine the resiliency of the key to attacks (called key strength).
2. Counter (CTR) mode requires that both the message sender and receiver access a counter, which computes a new value each time a ciphertext block is exchanged.
3. A block cipher mode of operation specifies how block ciphers should handle streams.

   Answer: The wrong statement is #3. A block cipher mode of operation specifies how block ciphers should handle blocks.

MODULE 8

Two Rights & A Wrong 8-1

1. The goal of an MITM attack is to either eavesdrop on the conversation or impersonate one or both of the parties.
2. A session ID is a unique number that a web browser assigns for the duration of that user's visit.
3. In a MAC cloning attack, a threat actor will discover a valid MAC address of a device connected to a switch, spoof that MAC address on his device, and send a packet onto the network.

Answer: The wrong statement is #2. A session ID is a unique number that a web server assigns a specific user for the duration of that user's visit.

Two Rights & A Wrong 8-2

1. The tools tracert (Windows) and traceroute (Linux) show the details about the path a packet takes from a computer or device to a destination.
2. Nessus is from Kali Linux.
3. The Linux text file manipulation tool logger adds content to the syslog file.

Answer: The wrong statement is #2. Nessus is from Tenable.

Two Rights & A Wrong 8-3

1. A barricade is a short but sturdy vertical post that is used to as a vehicular traffic barricade to prevent a car from "ramming" into a secured area.
2. An electronic lock is a combination lock that uses buttons that must be pushed in the proper sequence to open the door.
3. A DMZ is also called a physical air gap.

Answer: The wrong statement is #1. A bollard is a short but sturdy vertical post that is used to as a vehicular traffic barricade to prevent a car from ramming into a secured area.

MODULE 9

Two Rights & A Wrong 9-1

1. The bypass firewall rule action is designed for media-intensive protocols or traffic from a trusted source.
2. A stateless packet filter looks at packets and permits or denies it based solely on the firewall rules.
3. A forward proxy is a computer or an application program that intercepts user requests from the internal secure network and then processes that request on behalf of the user.

Answer: The wrong statement is #2. A stateful packet filter looks at packets and permits or denies it based solely on the firewall rules.

Two Rights & A Wrong 9-2

1. There are two types of ACLs: filesystem ACLs filter access to files and directories on an endpoint and networking ACLs filter access to a network. Network ACLs are often found on routers.
2. The Layer 2 Tunneling Protocol (L2TP) is a VPN protocol that does not offer any encryption or protection, so it is usually paired with IPSec.
3. Tokenization is used for creating test data.

Answer: The wrong statement is #3. When the data is used only for testing purposes, such as determining if a new app functions properly, masking may be used.

MODULE 10

Two Rights & A Wrong 10-1

1. A community cloud is a cloud that is open only to specific organizations that have common concerns.
2. The fog computing location is performed at or very near the source of the data instead of relying on the cloud or on-prem for processing.
3. A serverless infrastructure is one in which the capacity planning, installation, setup, and management are all invisible to the user because they are handled by the cloud provider.

Answer: The wrong statement is #2. The edge computing location is performed at or very near the source of the data instead of relying on the cloud or on-prem for processing.

Two Rights & A Wrong 10-2

1. A host system runs a VM monitor program that supports one or more guest systems that run applications.
2. SDV allows network administrators to automate multiple functions in a network infrastructure.
3. Type II hypervisors run directly on the computer's hardware instead of the underlying operating system.

Answer: The wrong statement is #3. Type I hypervisors run directly on the computer's hardware instead of the underlying operating system.

Two Rights & A Wrong 10-3

1. The current version of SNMP is SNMPv2.
2. SFTP is considered more secure than FTPS.
3. A mail gateway can automatically and transparently encrypt outbound email messages.

Answer: The wrong statement is #1. The current version of SNMP is SNMPv3.

MODULE 11

Two Rights & A Wrong 11-1

1. Bluetooth LE also supports a many-to-many topology, known as a mesh.
2. Most RFID tags are active and require their own power supply.
3. An AP primarily consists of an antenna and a radio transmitter/receiver to send and receive wireless signals, special bridging software to interface wireless devices to other devices, and a wired network interface that allows it to connect by cable to a standard wired network.

Answer: The wrong statement is #2. Most RFID tags are passive and do not have their own power supply.

Two Rights & A Wrong 11-2

1. An initialization vector (IV) is a 24-bit value that changes each time a packet is encrypted.
2. There are three common WPS methods.

3. Filtering by MAC address has several vulnerabilities, most notably that MAC addresses are initially exchanged between wireless devices and the AP in an unencrypted format.

Answer: The wrong statement is #2. There are two common WPS methods.

Two Rights & A Wrong 11-3

1. There are two modes of WPA2, WPA2 Professional and WPA2 Enterprise.
2. The encryption protocol used for WPA2 is the Counter Mode with Cipher Block Chaining Message Authentication Code Protocol (CCMP) and specifies the use of CCM (a general-purpose cipher mode algorithm providing data privacy) with AES.
3. EAP-TLS uses digital certificates for authentication.

Answer: The wrong statement is #1. There are two modes of WPA2: WPA2 Personal for individuals or small offices and WPA2 Enterprise for larger enterprises, schools, and government agencies. There are two common WPS methods.

MODULE 12

Two Rights & A Wrong 12-1

1. Password crackers differ as to when candidate digests are created.
2. Online brute force attacks are considered impractical.
3. An HMAC-based one-time password (HOTP) password is "event driven."

Answer: The wrong statement is #1. Password crackers differ as to how these candidates are created.

Two Rights & A Wrong 12-2

1. A salt is a random string that is used in hash algorithms.
2. Two popular key stretching password hash algorithms are bcrypt and PBKDF2.
3. A complex password (*xi8s7$t#6%*) is more secure than a long password (*thisisalongpassword*).

Answer: The wrong statement is #3. Long passwords are more secure than complex passwords.

MODULE 13

Two Rights & A Wrong 13-1

1. Any shared account (an account used by more than one user), generic account (an account not tied to a specific person), or guest account (given to temporary users) should be prohibited.
2. A data privacy officer (DPO) is someone to whom day-to-day actions have been assigned by the owner.
3. An access control scheme is embedded in the software and hardware.

Answer: The wrong statement is #2. A data privacy officer (DPO) is someone who oversees data privacy compliance and manages data risk.

Two Rights & A Wrong 13-2

1. A runbook is a linear style checklist of required steps and actions required to successfully respond to specific incident types and threats.
2. SOAR platforms have different pre-configured playbooks that are based on industry best practices and recognized standards.
3. When an incident occurs, isolation is then used to segregate both the attacker and the infected systems from reaching other devices.

   Answer: The wrong statement is #1. A playbook is a linear style checklist of required steps and actions required to successfully respond to specific incident types and threats.

Two Rights & A Wrong 13-3

1. A DNS service is the most important network-based device log to examine.
2. A multi-platform log management tool that supports various platforms, log sources, and formats is nxlog.
3. IPFIX (IP Flow Information Export) is similar to NetFlow but with additional capabilities, such as integrating Simple Network Management Protocol (SNMP) information directly into the IPFIX information.

   Answer: The wrong statement is #1. A firewall log is the most important log file to examine.

MODULE 14

Two Rights & A Wrong 14-1

1. A business continuity plan (BCP) is the development of a strategic document that provides alternative modes of operation for business activities that, if interrupted, could result in a significant loss to the enterprise.
2. Mean time to recovery (MTTR) is the average amount of time that it will take a device to recover from a failure that is not a terminal failure.
3. RAID can be implemented only through hardware.

   Answer: The wrong statement is #3. RAID can be implemented through either software or hardware.

Two Rights & A Wrong 14-2

1. A policy is a collection of suggestions that should be implemented.
2. Risky IP address examines the IP address that was used to attempt a login and compares it against a list of IP addresses involved in malicious activities.
3. Employee offboarding entails actions to be taken when an employee leaves an enterprise.

   Answer: The wrong statement is #1. A guideline is a collection of suggestions that should be implemented.

MODULE 15

Two Rights & A Wrong 15-1

1. At a basic level, risk may be defined as a situation that involves exposure to some type of danger, while at a more advanced level, risk can be described as a function of threats, consequences of those threats, and the resulting vulnerabilities.
2. The Annualized Loss Expectancy (ALE) is the expected monetary loss that can be expected for an asset due to a risk over a one-year period.
3. Risk avoidance uses cybersecurity insurance.

   Answer: The wrong statement is #3. Risk transference uses cybersecurity insurance.

Two Rights & A Wrong 15-2

1. The data type "confidential" has the highest level of data sensitivity.
2. Tokenization is a process that is part of data anonymization.
3. "Pulverizing" is hammering paper into dust.

   Answer: The wrong statement is #2. Data masking is a process that is part of data anonymization.

GLOSSARY

.cer The file extension for an X.509 certificate that is stored in a binary file.

.P12 The file extension for a Personal Information Exchange Syntax Standard based on PKCS#12 that defines the file format for storing and transporting a user's private keys with a public key certificate.

.P7B The file extension for a Cryptographic Message Syntax Standard based on PKCS#7 that defines a generic syntax for defining digital signature and encryption.

5G The fifth-generation cellular wireless standard.

A

acceptable use policy (AUP) A policy that defines the actions users may perform while accessing systems and networking equipment.

acceptance Acknowledging a risk but taking no steps to address it.

access control list (ACL) A set of permissions or rules attached to an object that administer its availability by granting or denying access.

access control scheme A framework embedded in hardware and software that can be used for controlling access.

access policy A policy that allows a network administrator to create the privileges that the user is given based on a role-based access control scheme.

Account Audits An account setting that audits user connections and events.

account permissions The privileges that a user is given.

accounting A record that is preserved of who accessed the network, what resources they accessed, and when they disconnected from the network.

active-active A configuration in which all load balancers are always active.

active-passive A configuration in which the primary load balancer distributes the network traffic to the most suitable server while the secondary load balancer operates in a "listening mode."

ad hoc mode A WLAN functioning without an AP.

Address Resolution Protocol (ARP) Part of the TCP/IP protocol for determining the MAC address based on the IP address.

admissibility Evidence that can hold up to judicial scrutiny and can be entered as evidence.

advanced persistent threat (APT) A class of attacks that use innovative attack tools to infect and silently extract data over an extended period of time.

adversarial artificial intelligence Exploiting the risks associated with using AI and ML in cybersecurity.

adversary tactics, techniques, and procedures (TTP) A database of the behavior of threat actors and how they orchestrate and manage attacks.

agentless A NAC system that does not require additional software to be installed on endpoints.

agents Software that is installed on endpoints to gather information for a NAC.

aggregators Network devices that combine multiple network connections into a single link.

air gap An area that separates threat actors from defenders.

alarm An audible warning of an unexpected or unusual action.

algorithm Consists of procedures based on a mathematical formula used to encrypt and decrypt the data. Also called a *cipher*.

always-on VPN A VPN that allows the user to stay connected at all times instead of connecting and disconnecting from it.

Annualized Loss Expectancy (ALE) The expected monetary loss for an asset due to a risk over a one-year period.

Annualized Rate of Occurrence (ARO) A calculation for determining the likelihood of a risk occurring within a year.

anomaly monitoring A monitoring technique used by an intrusion detection system (IDS) that creates a baseline of normal activities and compares actions against the baseline. Whenever there is a significant deviation from the baseline, an alarm is raised.

antimalware   A suite of software intended to provide protections against multiple types of malware, such as ransomware, cryptomalware, Trojans, and other malware.

antivirus (AV)   Software that can examine a computer for file-based virus infections as well as monitor computer activity and scan new documents that might contain a virus.

Anything as a Service (XaaS)   A broad category of subscription services related to cloud computing.

API inspection and integration   A service for authentication, authorization, encryption, availability, and policy compliance of APIs.

appliance firewall   A separate hardware device designed to protect an entire network.

application program interface (API) attack   An attack that targets vulnerabilities in an API.

application security   Protecting cloud-based applications.

application whitelisting/blacklisting   Requiring preapproval for an application to run or not run.

Arduino   A controller for other devices.

ARP poisoning   An attack that corrupts the ARP cache.

artifacts   Technology devices that may contain evidence in a forensics investigation.

asset management policy   A policy that provides the guidelines and practices that govern decisions about how assets should be acquired, maintained, and disposed.

asset value   The relative worth of an asset.

asymmetric cryptographic algorithm   Cryptography that uses two mathematically related keys.

attack vector   A pathway or avenue used by a threat actor to penetrate a system.

attestation   A key pair that is "burned" into a security key during manufacturing and is specific to a device model that can verify authentication.

Attribute-Based Access Control (ABAC)   An access control scheme that uses flexible policies that can combine attributes.

attributes   Characteristic features of the different groups of threat actors.

authentication app   A smartphone application that can be used to verify a user's login attempt.

Authentication Header (AH)   An IPsec protocol that authenticates that packets received were sent from the source.

authentication mode of operation   An information service that provides credentialing by a block cipher mode of operation.

authentication   Proving that a user is genuine and not an imposter.

authentication servers   Servers that facilitate authentication of an entity to access a network.

authority   A social engineering principle that involves directing others by impersonating an authority figure or falsely citing their authority.

authorization   Granting permission to take an action.

automated courses of action   Developing code as quickly and securely as possible.

Automated Indicator Sharing (AIS)   A technology that enables the exchange of cyberthreat indicators between parties through computer-to-computer communication.

Autopsy   A digital forensics platform.

auto-update   The automatic download and installation of patches as they become available.

availability loss   The loss that results from making systems inaccessible.

avoidance   Identifying a risk but making the decision to not engage in the activity.

B

backdoor   Malware that gives access to a computer, program, or service that circumvents any normal security protections.

background checks   Examining the history of a job candidate.

backup copy   A copy of the original data backup.

badge   A token that indicates the wearer has been approved.

barricade   Objects generally designed to block the passage of traffic.

baseband   The original frequency range of a transmission signal before it is converted to a different frequency range.

baseline configuration   A set of security settings that are the initial starting point and the minimum settings.

Bash   The command language interpreter for the Linux/UNIX OS.

behavioral monitoring   A monitoring technique that uses the normal processes and actions as the standard and compares actions against it.

benchmark/secure configuration guides   Guidelines for configuring a device or software usually distributed by hardware manufacturers and software developers.

binary Machine code.

birthday attack A statistical phenomenon that makes finding collisions easier.

Black box A penetration testing level in which the testers have no knowledge of the network and no special privileges.

black hat hackers Threat actors who violate computer security for personal gain or to inflict malicious damage.

blacklisting Creating a list of unapproved software so that any item not on the list of blacklisted applications can run.

block cipher A cipher that manipulates an entire block of plaintext at one time.

block cipher mode of operation How block ciphers handle blocks of ciphertext by using a symmetric key block cipher algorithm to provide an information service.

blockchain A shared, immutable ledger that facilitates the process of recording transactions and tracking assets in a business network.

Blue Team A penetration testing team that monitors for Red Team attacks and shores up defenses as necessary.

bluejacking An attack that sends unsolicited messages to Bluetooth-enabled devices.

bluesnarfing An attack that accesses unauthorized information from a wireless device through a Bluetooth connection.

Bluetooth A wireless technology that uses short-range radio frequency (RF) transmissions and provides rapid ad hoc device pairings.

bollard A short but sturdy vertical post used as a vehicular traffic barricade to prevent a car from ramming into a secured area.

boot attestation The process of determining that the boot process is valid.

bot An infected computer placed under the remote control of an attacker for the purpose of launching attacks.

BPDU guard A feature on a switch that creates an alert when a BPDU is received from an endpoint.

bring your own device (BYOD) Allows users to use their own personal mobile devices for business purposes.

broadcast storm prevention Steps that can be taken to avert a broadcast storm.

brute force attack An attack in which every possible combination of letters, numbers, and characters is combined to attempt to determine the user's password.

buffer overflow attack An attack that occurs when a process attempts to store data in RAM beyond the boundaries of a fixed-length storage buffer.

bug bounty A monetary reward given for uncovering a software vulnerability.

burning Lighting paper on fire to destroy the data on it.

business continuity plan (BCP) A strategic document that provides alternative modes of operation for business activities that, if interrupted, could result in a significant loss to the enterprise.

business impact analysis (BIA) A process that identifies the business functions and quantifies the impact a loss of these functions may have on business operations.

business partners Commercial entities with whom an organization has an alliance.

business partnership agreement (BPA) A contract between two or more business partners that is used to establish the rules and responsibilities of each partner.

C

cable lock A device inserted into the security slot of a portable device to prevent its theft.

cache A type of high-speed memory that stores recently used information so that it can be quickly accessed again at a later time.

call manager A platform used to provide telephony, video, and web conferences.

Canonical Encoding Rules (CER) An X.509 encoding format.

captive portal AP An infrastructure on public access WLANs that uses a standard web browser to provide information, and gives the wireless user the opportunity to agree to a policy or present valid login credentials to provide a higher degree of security.

capture the flag (CTF) An exercise in which a series of challenges is planted as a competition between participants.

card cloning Unauthorized duplication of smart cards.

carrier unlocking Uncoupling a phone from a specific wireless provider.

cat   A Linux text file manipulation tool for displaying an entire file.

cellular telephony   A communications network in which the coverage area is divided into hexagon-shaped cells.

Center for Internet Security (CIS)   A nonprofit community-driven organization.

certificate attributes   Fields in an X.509 digital certificate that are used when parties negotiate a secure connection.

certificate authority (CA)   The entity that is responsible for digital certificates.

certificate chaining   Linking several certificates together to establish trust between all the certificates involved.

Certificate Revocation List (CRL)   A list of certificate serial numbers that have been revoked.

Certificate Signing Request (CSR)   A user request for a digital certificate.

chain of custody   A process that shows evidence was always under strict control and no unauthorized person was given the opportunity to corrupt the evidence.

Challenge-Handshake Authentication Protocol (CHAP)   A weak authentication framework protocol that has been replaced by more secure versions.

change control policy   A policy that stipulates the processes to be followed for implementing system changes.

change management policy   A written document that defines the types of changes that can be made and under what circumstances.

channel overlays   Conflicting frequency channels in a Wi-Fi network.

chmod   A Linux text file manipulation tool for changing file permissions.

choose your own device (CYOD)   Employees choose from a limited selection of approved devices, but the employee pays the upfront cost of the device while the business owns the contract.

Cipher Block Chaining Message Authentication Code (CBC-MAC)   A component of CCMP that provides data integrity and authentication.

cipher suite   A named combination of the encryption, authentication, and message authentication code (MAC) algorithms that are used with TLS and SSL.

clean desk space   A policy designed to ensure that all confidential or sensitive materials, either in paper form or electronic, are removed from a user's workspace and secured.

cleanup   Returning all systems back to normal following a penetration test.

client-side execution and validation   Input validation that is performed by the user's web browser.

client-side request forgery   An attack that takes advantage of an authentication "token" that a website sends to a user's web browser to imitate the identity and privileges of the victim.

closed circuit television (CCTV)   Activity captured by video surveillance cameras that transmit a signal to a specific and limited set of receivers.

closed source   Proprietary information owned by an entity that has an exclusive right to it.

cloud   A remote facility for computing.

cloud access security broker (CASB)   A set of software tools or services that resides between an enterprise's on-prem infrastructure and the cloud provider's infrastructure.

cloud computing   An on-demand infrastructure to a shared pool of configurable computing resources that can be rapidly provisioned and released.

Cloud Controls Matrix   A specialized framework of cloud-specific security controls.

cloud native controls   A cloud security control that is inherent to the cloud computing platforms and offered by the cloud computing providers to their customers.

cloud platforms   A pay-per-use computing model in which customers pay only for the online computing resources they need.

Cloud Security Alliance (CSA)   An organization whose goal is to define and raise awareness of best practices to help secure cloud computing environments.

cloud security audit   An independent examination of cloud service controls.

cloud service providers   Entities that offer cloud computing resources.

code reuse of third-party libraries and SDKs   Using existing software or software development kits (SDKs) in a new application.

code signing digital certificate   Certificate used by software developers to digitally sign a program to prove that the software comes from the entity that signed it and that no unauthorized third party has altered it.

code signing Digitally signing applications.

cold site A remote site that provides office space; the customer must provide and install all the equipment needed to continue operations.

collectors Network devices that gather traffic.

collision When two files have the same hash.

command and control (C&C) A structure that sends instructions to infected bot computers.

common name (CN) The name of the device protected by the digital certificate.

Common Vulnerabilities and Exposures (CVE) A tool that identifies vulnerabilities in operating systems and application software.

Common Vulnerability Scoring System (CVSS) A numeric rating system of the impact of a vulnerability.

communication plan A formalized plan that outlines the internal and external constituents who need to be informed of an incident, how they should be informed, and when it should take place.

community cloud A type of cloud that is open only to specific organizations that have common concerns.

compensating controls Controls that provide an alternative to normal controls that for some reason cannot be used.

competitors Threat actors who launch attacks against an opponent's system to steal classified information.

compilers Programs that create binary machine code from human source code.

computer-based training (CBT) Using a computer to deliver instruction.

conditional access Dynamically assigning roles to subjects based on a set of rules.

confidential The highest level of data sensitivity.

configuration review An examination of the software settings for a vulnerability scan.

consensus A social engineering principle that involves being influenced by what others do.

constraints Limitations that make security a challenge for embedded systems and specialized devices.

container A more reduced instance of virtualization.

container security Protecting containers from attacks.

containerization Separating storage into separate business and personal "containers."

containment An incident response plan step for limiting the damage of the incident and isolating those systems that are impacted to prevent further damage.

content management Tools used to support the creation and subsequent editing and modification of digital content by multiple employees.

content/URL filtering A process used by a firewall to monitor websites accessed through HTTP to create custom filtering profiles.

context-aware authentication Using a contextual setting to validate a user.

continuity of operation planning (COOP) A federal initiative that is intended to encourage organizations to address how critical operations will continue under a broad range of negative circumstances.

continuous delivery Moving the code to each stage as it is completed.

continuous deployment Continual code implementation.

continuous integration Ensuring that security features are incorporated at each stage.

continuous monitoring Examining the processes in real-time instead of at the end of a stage.

continuous validation Ongoing approvals of code.

control risk The probability that financial statements are materially misstated because of failures in the system of controls used by an organization.

controller AP An AP that is managed through a dedicated wireless LAN controller (WLC).

corporate owned A mobile device that is purchased and owned by the enterprise.

corporate owned, personally enabled (COPE) Employees choose from a selection of company approved devices.

corrective controls Controls that are intended to mitigate or lessen the damage caused by an incident.

counter (CTR) A block cipher mode of operation that both the message sender and receiver access a counter, which computes a new value each time a ciphertext block is exchanged.

Counter Mode with Cipher Block Chaining Message Authentication Code Protocol (CCMP) The encryption protocol used for WPA2 that specifies the use of a general-purpose cipher mode algorithm providing data privacy with AES.

credential harvesting   Using the Internet and social media searches to perform reconnaissance.

credential policies   Policies that address requirements for authentication credentials, such as the length and complexity of passwords.

credentialed scan   A scan in which valid authentication credentials, such as usernames and passwords, are supplied to the vulnerability scanner to mimic the work of a threat actor who possesses these credentials.

criminal syndicates   Threat actors who have moved from traditional criminal activities to more rewarding and less risky online attacks.

critical   Data classified according to availability needs so that the function and mission would be severely impacted if compromised.

crossover error rate (CER)   The biometric error rate in which the FAR and FRR are equal over the size of the population.

cross-site request forgery (CSRF)   An attack that takes advantage of an authentication "token" that a website sends to a user's web browser to imitate the identity and privileges of the victim.

cross-site scripting (XSS)   An attack that takes advantage of a website that accepts user input without validating it.

cryptography   The practice of transforming information so that it is secure and cannot be understood by unauthorized persons.

cryptomalware   Malware that encrypts all the files on the device so that none of them can be opened until a ransom is paid.

Cuckoo   An automated malware analysis system.

curl   A Linux command-line utility used to transfer data to or from a server.

custom firmware   Firmware that is written by users to run on their own mobile devices.

Cyber Kill Chain   An exploitation framework that outlines the steps of an attack in an integrated and end-to-end process like a "chain."

cybersecurity insurance   Insurance that protects an organization by monetary compensation in the event of a successful attack.

D

dark web   Part of the web is beyond the reach of a normal search engine and is the domain of threat actors.

data anonymization   Changing data so that there is not a means to reverse the process to restore the data back to its original state.

data at rest   Data that is stored on electronic media.

data backup   Copying information to a different medium and storing it so that it can be used in the event of a disaster.

data breach notification law   A law that requires user notification of a data breach.

data breach   Stealing data to disclose it in an unauthorized fashion.

data classification policy   A policy that outlines how to assign data type labels to data.

data controller   The principal party for collecting data.

data custodian/steward   An individual to whom day-to-day actions have been assigned by the owner.

data exfiltration   Stealing data to distribute it to other parties.

data exposure   Disclosing sensitive data to attackers.

data governance policy   A policy that defines who is responsible for the data, how it can be accessed, how it should be used, and how its integrity can be maintained.

data in processing   Data actions being performed by "endpoint devices," such as printing a report from a desktop computer.

data in transit   Actions that transmit the data across a network.

data loss prevention (DLP)   A system of security tools used to recognize and identify data that is critical to the organization and ensure it is protected.

data loss   The destruction of data so that it cannot be recovered.

data masking   Creating a copy of the original data but obfuscating any sensitive elements.

data minimization   Limiting the collection of personal information to that which is directly relevant and necessary to accomplish a specific task.

data owner   The person responsible for the data.

data privacy officer (DPO)   A manager who oversees data privacy compliance and manages data risk.

data processor   A proxy who acts on behalf of data controller.

data retention policy   A policy that specifies how long data should retained after it has fulfilled its initial purpose.

data sanitization The process of cleaning data to provide privacy.

data sovereignty Country-specific requirements that apply to data.

data storage Third-party facilities used for storing important data.

dd An imaging utility used for generating a physical copy.

dead code A section of an application that executes but performs no meaningful function.

decryption The process of changing encrypted text into the original text.

default settings Settings that are predetermined by the vendor for usability and ease of use (but not security) so the user can immediately begin using the product.

degaussing Permanently destroying an entire hard drive by reducing or eliminating its magnetic field.

demilitarized zone (DMZ) An area that separates threat actors from defenders.

deprovisioning Removing a resource that is no longer needed.

detective controls Controls designed to identify any threat that has reached the system.

deterrent controls Controls that attempt to discourage security violations before they occur.

development stage A stage of application development in which the requirements for the application are established and it is confirmed that the application meets the intended business needs before the actual coding begins.

device driver manipulation An attack that alters a device driver from its normal function.

DHCP snooping A security technology in a switch that drops unacceptable DHCP traffic.

diagram A visual mapping of security appliances.

Diamond Model of Intrusion Analysis A framework for examining network intrusion events that uses four core interconnected elements that comprise any event.

dictionary attack A password attack that creates encrypted versions of common dictionary words and compares them against those in a stolen password file.

differential backup A backup that copies any data that has changed since last full backup.

dig A Linux command-line utility used for DNS diagnostics.

digital certificate A technology used to associate a user's identity to a public key and that has been "digitally signed" by a trusted third party.

direct access An attack vector in which a threat actor can gain direct physical access to the computer.

directory service A database stored on the network itself that contains information about users and network devices.

directory traversal An attack that takes advantage of vulnerability so that a user can move from the root directory to other restricted directories.

disablement An action by an administration to suspend an account.

disabling unnecessary open ports and services Turning off any service that is not being used and closing any unnecessary TCP ports to enhance security.

disassociation attack A wireless attack in which false deauthentication or disassociation frames are sent to an AP that appear to come from another client device, causing the client to disconnect.

disaster recovery plan (DRP) A written document that details the process for restoring IT resources following an event that causes a significant disruption in service.

Discretionary Access Control (DAC) An access control scheme that is the least restrictive, giving an owner total control over objects.

distance considerations The process of making location selections of where backups should be stored.

Distinguished Encoding Rules (DER) An X.509 encoding format.

distributed denial of service (DDoS) An attack that uses many computers to perform a DoS attack.

diversity The ability to include different technologies, third-party vendors, controls, and cryptographic solutions in a BCP.

DLL injection An attack that inserts code into a running process through a DLL to cause a program to function in a different way than intended.

DNS hijacking An attack that infects an external DNS server with IP addresses pointing to malicious sites.

DNS poisoning   An attack that substitutes DNS addresses in a local lookup table so that the computer is automatically redirected to an attacker's device.

DNS sinkhole   A technique that changes a normal DNS request to a preconfigured IP address pointing to a device that will drop all received packets.

dnsenum   A Kali Linux utility that lists DNS information of a domain.

domain name resolution   Mapping computer and device names to IP addresses.

Domain Name System Security Extensions (DNSSEC)   A protocol that adds additional resource records and message header information for improved security.

domain reputation   An attack in which the status of a site is manipulated to earn a low domain reputation score.

domain validation digital certificate   Certificate that verifies the identity of the entity that has control over the domain name.

downgrade attack   An attack in which the system is forced to abandon the current higher security mode of operation and "fall back" to implementing an older and less secure mode.

drone   An unmanned aerial vehicle (UAV) without a human pilot on board to control its flight.

dual power supply   A specialized computer power supply that can provide redundancy.

dump file   A snapshot of the process that was executing and any modules that were loaded for an app at a specific point in time.

dumpster diving   Digging through trash receptacles to find information that can be useful in an attack.

dynamic code analysis   Examining code after the source code is compiled and when all components are integrated and running.

dynamic resource allocation   Deprovision computing resources when they are no longer needed.

E

EAP-FAST   An Extensible Authentication Protocol that securely tunnels any credential form for authentication (such as a password or a token) using TLS.

EAP-TLS   An Extensible Authentication Protocol that uses digital certificates for authentication.

EAP-TTLS   An Extensible Authentication Protocol that securely tunnels client password authentication within Transport Layer Security (TLS) records.

east-west traffic   The movement of data from one server to another server within a data center.

Echo   Request packets used by the TCP/IP Internet Control Message Protocol.

edge   Computing that is performed at or very near to the source of data instead of relying on the cloud or on-prem for processing.

e-discovery   Identifying, collecting, and producing electronically stored information (ESI) in response to a request in an investigation or lawsuit.

efficacy rate   The benefit achieved of a biometric identifier.

elasticity   Flexibility or resilience in code development.

electronic lock   A type of lock that uses buttons that must be pushed in the proper sequence for opening.

eliciting information   Gathering data.

elliptic curve cryptography (ECC)   An algorithm that uses elliptic curves instead of prime numbers to compute keys.

email digital certificate   A certificate that allows a user to digitally sign and encrypt mail messages.

embedded system   Computer hardware and software contained within a larger system that is designed for a specific function.

Encapsulating Security Payload (ESP)   An IPsec protocol that encrypts packets.

encryption   The process of changing plaintext into ciphertext.

end of life (EOL)   A statement that a product has reached the end of its "useful life" and the manufacturer will no longer market, sell, or update it after a specified date.

end of service (EOS)   A statement that the end of support has been reached and no maintenance services or updates are provided.

endpoint detection and response (EDR)   Robust tools that monitor endpoint events and take immediate action.

enterprise method   Authentication for the WPA2 Enterprise model.

entropy   The measure of randomness of a data-generating function.

environmental disasters Disasters such as floods, hurricanes, and tornados that can impact an enterprise.

ephemeral key A temporary key that is used only once before it is discarded.

eradication An incident response plan step for finding the cause of the incident and temporarily removing any systems that may be causing damage.

error handling A programming error that does not properly trap an error condition.

errors Human mistakes in selecting one setting over another without considering the security implications.

escalation Adding steps as the result of a data breach being classified as a "major incident."

European Union General Data Protection Directive (GDPR) A regulation regarding data protection and privacy in the European Union and the European Economic Area (EEA).

evil twin An AP set up by an attacker to mimic an authorized AP and capture transmissions, so a user's device will unknowingly connect to the evil twin instead of the authorized AP.

exercises Simulated activities used to test an incident response plan.

expiration The date of a digital certificate when it ceases to function.

exploitation frameworks A series of documented processes that serve as models of the thinking and actions of threat actors.

Extended Validation (EV) certificate Certificate that requires more extensive verification of the legitimacy of the business than does a domain validation digital certificate.

Extensible Authentication Protocol (EAP) A framework for transporting authentication protocols that defines the format of the messages.

eXtensible Markup Language (XML) A markup language designed to store information.

external disasters Disasters such as environmental disasters that are outside the organization.

external media access A device with a USB connection that can function as a host (to which other devices may be connected such as a USB flash drive) for access to media.

external risk A risk from outside an organization.

external Threat actors who work outside the enterprise.

extranet A private network that can also be accessed by authorized external customers, vendors, and partners.

F

facial recognition A biometric authentication that views the user's face and is becoming increasingly popular on smartphones.

fake telemetry Fictitious data on a honeypot of how certain software features are used, application crashes, and general usage statistics and behavior.

false acceptance rate (FAR) The frequency at which imposters are accepted as genuine when using biometric authentication.

false negative Failure to raise an alarm when there is a problem.

false positive Raising an alarm when there is no problem.

false rejection rate (FRR) The frequency that legitimate users are rejected when using biometric authentication.

familiarity A social engineering principle that portrays the victim as well known and well received.

Faraday cage A metallic enclosure that prevents the entry or escape of an electromagnetic field.

federation Single sign-on for networks owned by different organizations, also called *federated identity management (FIM)*.

fencing A tall, permanent structure to keep out unauthorized personnel.

field-programmable gate array (FPGA) A hardware integrated circuit (IC) that can be programmed by the user.

file and code repositories A storage area in which victims of an attack can upload malicious files and software code that can then be examined by others to learn more about these attacks and craft their defenses.

file integrity monitors A system that detects any changes within the files that may indicate a cyberattack.

File Transfer Protocol (FTP) An unsecure TCP/IP protocol for transferring files.

fileless virus A type of malware that takes advantage of native services and processes that are part of the OS to avoid detection and carry out its attacks.

filesystem permissions A method for protecting files managed by the OS.

financial loss The monetary loss as a result of lost productivity.

fine A financial penalty assessed against an organization as the result of a data breach.

fingerprint A physiological biometric identifier that has become the most common type of authentication.

fire suppression Attempts to reduce the impact of a fire.

firewall Hardware or software that is designed to limit the spread of malware.

firmware OTA updates Mobile operating system patches and updates that are distributed as an over-the-air (OTA) update.

firmware Software that is embedded into hardware to provide low-level controls and instructions.

fog A decentralized computing infrastructure in which data, compute capabilities, storage, and applications are located between the data source and the cloud.

footprinting Gathering information from outside the organization.

forensics The application of science to questions that are of interest to the legal profession.

forward proxy A computer or an application program that intercepts user requests from the internal secure network and then processes those requests on behalf of the users.

framework A series of documented processes used to define policies and procedures for implementation and management of security controls in an enterprise environment.

FTK Imager A package of multiple forensics tools combined into a single suite that has a common user interface and can more easily exchange information among the different tools.

FTP Secure (FTPS) Using Secure Sockets Layer (SSL) or Transport Layer Security (TLS) to encrypt commands sent over the control port in an FTP session.

full backup The starting point for all backups; it copies the entire set of data.

full disk encryption The encryption of all user data on a mobile device.

full tunnel A VPN technology in which all traffic is sent to the VPN concentrator and is protected.

functional recovery plan A plan that addresses the steps to be taken to restore processes if necessary.

fusion center A formal repository of information from enterprises and the government used to share information on the latest attacks.

fuzzing Providing random input to a program in an attempt to trigger exceptions, such as memory corruption, program crashes, or security breaches.

G

gait A person's manner of walking that can be used as a physiological biometric identifier.

gamification Using game-based scenarios for instruction.

generator A device powered by diesel, natural gas, or propane gas to generate electricity.

generic account An account not tied to a specific person.

geofencing Using the mobile device's GPS to define geographical boundaries where an app can be used.

geographic dispersal Spreading sites across a larger area to mitigate the impact of an environmental disaster.

geographical consideration Firewall rules that are in effect depending on the location of an endpoint.

geolocation The process of identifying the geographical location of a device.

Global Positioning System (GPS) A satellite-based navigation system that provides information to a GPS receiver anywhere on (or near) the earth where there is an unobstructed line of sight to four or more GPS satellites.

GPS tagging (geo-tagging) Adding geographical identification data to media such as digital photos taken on a mobile device.

Gray box A penetration testing level in which the testers are given limited knowledge of the network and some elevated privileges.

gray hat hackers Attackers who attempt to break into a computer system without the organization's permission to publicly disclose the attack and shame the organization into taking action.

grep A Linux text file manipulation tool used for searching for keyword.

guest account An account given to a temporary user.

H

hacker A person who uses advanced computer skills to attack computers.

hacktivists A group of attackers that is strongly motivated by ideology.

hardware firewall A firewall that runs on a separate device.

hardware root of trust Security checks that begin with hardware checks.

Hardware Security Module (HSM) A removable external cryptographic device.

hash An algorithm that creates a unique digital fingerprint.

hashing The process of creating a digital fingerprint.

head A Linux text file manipulation tool for displaying the first 10 lines of a file.

heat map A software tool that provides a visual representation of the wireless signal coverage and strength.

heating, ventilation, and air conditioning (HVAC) Environmental systems that provide and regulate heating and cooling.

heuristic monitoring A monitoring technique that uses an algorithm to determine if a threat exists.

high availability across zones Using multiple geographical cloud zones and regions to provide reliability and resiliency.

high availability The ability to withstand all outages while providing continuous processing for critical applications.

high resiliency The ability to quickly recover from resource vs. security constraints.

HMAC-based one-time password (HOTP) A one-time password that changes when a specific event occurs.

hoax A false warning often contained in an email message claiming to come from the IT department.

honeyfiles Software and data files on a honeypot that appear to be authentic but are actually imitations of real data files.

honeynet A network set up with intentional vulnerabilities.

honeypot A computer located in an area with limited security that serves as "bait" to threat actors and is intentionally configured with security vulnerabilities.

host intrusion detection system (HIDS) A software-based application that runs on an endpoint computer and can detect that an attack has occurred.

host intrusion prevention system (HIPS) Software that monitors endpoint activity to immediately block a malicious attack by following specific rules.

host-based firewall A software firewall that runs as a program on the local device to block or filter traffic coming into and out of the computer.

hot aisle/cold aisle A layout used to reduce the heat in a data center by managing air flow.

hot site A duplicate of the production site that has all the equipment needed for an organization to continue running, including office space and furniture, telephone jacks, computer equipment, and a live telecommunications link.

hotspot A location where users can access the Internet with a wireless signal.

hping A Linux command-line utility that sends custom TCP/IP packets.

HTML 5 The current version of HTML that can be used as a "clientless" VPN on an endpoint so that no additional software must be installed.

HTTP Response Header A header that can inform the browser how to function while communicating with the website.

hybrid cloud A combination of public and private clouds.

hybrid warfare influence campaign Influence campaigns used on social media and other sources.

Hypertext Transport Protocol Secure (HTTPS) HTTP sent over TLS (Transport Layer Security) or SSL (Secure Sockets Layer).

I

identification An incident response plan step for determining whether an event is actually a security incident.

identification of critical systems Recognizing processes that aid the mission-essential function.

identity fraud (also called *impersonation*) Masquerading as a real or fictitious character and then playing out the role of that person with a victim.

identity theft Taking personally identifiable information to impersonate someone.

IEEE 802.1x A standard, originally developed for wired networks, that provides a greater degree of security by implementing port-based authentication.

ifconfig A Linux command-line utility that displays network configuration information such as the IP address, network mask, and gateway for all physical and virtual network adapters.

image backup A backup that captures the entire contents of the disk to enable an entire restoration of the contents of the disk to a new hard disk or computer.

IMAP (Internet Mail Access Protocol) A more recent and advanced electronic email system for managing incoming email; the current version is IMAP4.

impact assessment A means for measuring the effectiveness of the organization's activities.

impersonation (also called *identity fraud*) Masquerading as a real or fictitious character and then playing out the role of that person with a victim.

Impossible Travel Analyzing and denying a second user login attempt based on the time and distance of the prior attempt.

improper input handling A programming error that does not filter or validate user input to prevent a malicious action.

incident response plan A set of written instructions for reacting to a security incident.

incident response process Action steps to be taken when a cyber incident occurs; also serve as the elements of an incident response plan.

incident response team A group that is responsible for responding to security incidents.

incremental backup A backup that copies any data that has changed since last full backup or last incremental backup.

indicator of compromise (IOC) An indicator that malicious activity is occurring but is still in the early stages.

industrial camouflage An attempt to make the physical presence of a building as nondescript as possible so that to a casual viewer, the building does not look like it houses anything important.

industrial control systems (ICS) Systems that control locally or at remote locations by collecting, monitoring, and processing real-time data to control machines.

influence campaigns Using social engineering to sway attention and sympathy in a particular direction.

information life cycle The flow of an information system's data (and metadata) from data creation to the time when it becomes obsolete.

infrared Light that is next to visible light on the light spectrum and was once used for data communications.

Infrastructure as a Service (IaaS) A cloud computing model that provides unlimited computing, storage, and network resources that the enterprise can use to build its own virtual infrastructure in the cloud.

inherent risk The current risk level given the existing set of controls.

initialization vector (IV) A 24-bit value that changes each time a packet is encrypted.

injections Attacks that introduce new input to exploit a vulnerability.

inline A system that is connected directly to the network and monitors the flow of data as it occurs.

insider threat Attackers who manipulate data from the position of a trusted employee.

instance awareness The ability for security appliances to differentiate between different instances of cloud apps.

integer overflow attack An attack that changes the value of a variable to something outside the range that the programmer had intended by using an integer overflow.

integrity measurement An "attestation mechanism" designed to ensure that an application is running only known and approved executables.

intent/motivation Reasons for an attack by threat actors.

intermediate certificate authority (CA) An entity that processes the CSR and verifies the authenticity of the user on behalf of a certificate authority (CA).

internal disasters Disasters such as a fire in a data center that are inside the organization.

internal risk A risk that comes from within an organization.

internal Threat actors who work inside the enterprise.

Internet of Things (IoT) Connecting any device to the Internet for the purpose of sending and receiving data to be acted upon.

Internet Protocol schema   A standard guide for assigning IP addresses to devices.

Internet Protocol Security (IPsec)   A protocol suite for securing Internet Protocol (IP) communications.

Internet Protocol version 6 (IPv6)   The next generation of the IP protocol that addresses the weaknesses of IPv4 and also provides several other significant improvements.

intimidation   To frighten and coerce by threat.

intranet   A private network that belongs to an organization and can only be accessed by approved internal users.

intrusive scan   A vulnerability scan that attempts to employ any vulnerabilities which it finds, much like a threat actor would.

invoice scam   A fictitious overdue invoice that demands immediate payment.

IP theft   Stealing intellectual property such as an invention or a work that the organization or its customers may own.

ipconfig   A Windows command-line utility that displays network configuration information such as the IP address, network mask, and gateway for all physical and virtual network adapters.

IPFIX (IP Flow Information Export)   A session sample protocol similar to NetFlow but with additional capabilities.

iris   A thin circular structure in the eye that can be used for authentication.

ISO 27001   A standard that provides requirements for an information security management system (ISMS).

ISO 27002   A "code of practice" for information security management within an organization and contains 114 different control recommendations.

ISO 27701   An extension to ISO 27001 and is a framework for managing privacy controls to reduce the risk of privacy breach to the privacy of individuals.

ISO 31000   A standard that contains controls for managing and controlling risk.

isolation   Segregating both the attacker and the infected systems from reaching other devices.

J

jailbreaking   Circumventing the installed built-in limitations on Apple iOS devices.

jamming   Intentionally flooding the radio frequency (RF) spectrum with extraneous RF signal "noise" that creates interference and prevents communications from occurring.

job rotation   The act of moving individuals from one job responsibility to another.

journalctl   A Linux utility for querying and displaying log files.

jump box   A minimally configured administrator server (either physical or virtual) within the DMZ that is used to connect two dissimilar security zones while providing tightly restricted access between them.

K

Kerberos   An authentication system developed by the Massachusetts Institute of Technology (MIT) and used to verify the identity of networked users.

key escrow   A process in which keys are managed by a third party, such as a trusted CA.

key exchange   The process of sending and receiving secure cryptographic keys.

key length   The number of bits in a key.

key management   The administration by PKI of all the elements involved in digital certificates for digital certificate management of public keys and digital certificates.

key stretching   A password hashing algorithm that requires significantly more time than standard hashing algorithms to create the digest.

keylogger   Hardware or software that silently captures and stores each keystroke that a user types on the computer's keyboard.

knowledge-based authentication   Using perception, thought processes, and understanding for a biometric identifier.

L

lack of vendor support   A lack of expertise to handle system integration.

last known good configuration   A Microsoft Windows option for earlier versions in which the OS can be rolled back to the last time that the device properly booted.

lateral movement   Moving through a network looking for additional systems threat actors can access from their elevated position.

Layer 2 Tunneling Protocol (L2TP)   A VPN protocol that does not offer any encryption or protection so it is usually paired with IPsec.

LDAP injection attacks Attacks, similar to SQL injection attacks, that can occur when user input is not properly filtered in an LDAP session.

least privilege A policy that ensures only the minimum amount of privileges necessary to perform a job or function should be allocated.

legacy platform A platform that is no longer in widespread use, often because it has been supplanted or replaced by an updated version of that earlier technology.

legal hold A judicial act that mandates data in an investigation cannot be modified, deleted, erased, or otherwise edited.

lessons learned An incident response plan step for completing incident documentation, performing detailed analysis to increase security and improve future response efforts.

level of capability/sophistication Power and complexity capabilities of threat actors.

lighting Illumination of a secured area so that it can be viewed after dark.

lightweight cryptography A category of cryptography that has fewer features and is less robust than normal cryptography.

Lightweight Directory Access Protocol (LDAP) A directory service that is a simpler subset of the Directory Access Protocol (DAP).

likelihood of occurrence A determination of how realistic the chance is that a given threat will compromise an asset.

live boot media A bootable OS on an external device such as a USB device that contains a complete OS that may be used in recovery.

load balancing A technology that can help to evenly distribute work across a network.

lockout An automatic action that prevents access to an account until a security administrator reviews the incident and removes the lockout.

log A record of events that occur.

log reviews An analysis of log data.

logger A Linux text file manipulation tool for adding content to syslog file.

logic bomb Computer code that is typically added to a legitimate program but lies dormant and evades detection until a specific logical event triggers it.

longevity The useful lifetime of service of a cipher.

loop prevention A technology that uses the IEEE 802.1d standard spanning-tree protocol (STP) to avert a network loop.

low latency A small amount of time that occurs between when a byte is input into a cryptographic algorithm and the time the output is obtained.

low-power devices Small electronic devices that consume very small amounts of power.

MAC cloning attack An attack that spoofs a MAC address on a device so that the switch changes its MAC address table to reflect the new association of that MAC address with the port to which the attacker's device is connected.

M

MAC flooding attack An attack in which the memory of a switch is flooded with spoofed packets to force it to function like a network hub and broadcast frames to all ports.

machine/computer digital certificate Certificate used to verify the identity of a device in a network transaction.

macro A series of instructions that can be grouped together as a single command.

malicious flash drive A USB flash drive infected with malware.

malicious USB cable A USB cable embedded with a Wi-Fi controller that can receive commands from a nearby device to send malicious commands to the connected mobile device.

malware Malicious software that enters a computer system without the user's knowledge or consent and then performs an unwanted and harmful action.

managed security service provider (MSSP) A specialized type of managed service provider (MSP) that can assist with or fully assume the cybersecurity defenses of an organization.

managed service provider (MSP) An entity that delivers services—such as network, application, infrastructure, and security—through ongoing and regular support as well as active administration of those resources.

managerial controls Controls that use administrative methods.

Mandatory Access Control (MAC) An access control scheme that is the most restrictive by assigning users' access controls strictly according to the custodian's desires.

mandatory vacations Requirement that all employees take vacations.

maneuvering Conducting unusual behavior when threat hunting.

man-in-the-browser (MITB) An attack that intercepts communication between a browser and the underlying computer.

man-in-the-middle (MITM) An attack that intercepts legitimate communication to eavesdrop on the conversation or impersonate one of the parties.

man-made disasters Disasters such as industrial accidents, oil spills, terrorist attacks, and transportation accidents that can impact an enterprise.

mantrap An area designed as an air gap to separate a nonsecure area from a secured area.

manual peer reviews Reviews performed by software engineers and developers paired together or grouped in larger teams to laboriously examine each line of source code looking for vulnerabilities.

masking Creating a copy of the original data but making unintelligible any sensitive elements.

mean time between failures (MTBF) A statistical value that is the average time until a component fails, cannot be repaired, and must be replaced.

mean time to recovery (MTTR) The average time for a device to recover from a failure that is not a terminal failure.

Measured Boot A boot attestation procedure in which the computer's firmware logs the boot process so it can be sent to a trusted server to assess the security.

measurement system analysis (MSA) Using scientific tools to determine the amount of variation that is added to a process by a measurement system.

Media Access Control (MAC) address filtering A method for controlling access to a WLAN based on the device's MAC address.

memdump A Linux utility that "dumps" system memory.

memorandum of understanding (MOU) A document that describes an agreement between two or more parties that is not legally enforceable.

memory leak A situation that occurs when, due to a programming error, memory is not freed when the program has finished using it.

memory management Failure of programmers to create secure code, which allows vulnerabilities that manipulate computer RAM.

metadata Data that describes information about other data.

MicroSD HSM A hardware security module in a small consumer-oriented form factor.

microservices APIs Specialized APIs based on a microservices architecture.

microservices architecture Smaller and more specialized elements, each of which manages its own database, generates its own logs, and handles user authentication.

mission-essential function The activity that serves as the core purpose of the enterprise.

mitigation Addressing a risk by making the risk less serious.

MITRE ATT&CK A knowledge base of attacker techniques that have been broken down and classified in detail.

mobile application management (MAM) Tools that are used for distributing and controlling access to apps on mobile devices.

mobile content management (MCM) A system that is tuned to provide content management to mobile devices used by employees in an enterprise.

mobile device management (MDM) Tools that allow a device to be managed remotely by an organization.

moisture detection A sensor that can detect water leaks, dampness, or increased moisture levels.

monitoring service An external third-party service that can provide additional resources to assist an organization in their cybersecurity defenses.

motion detection A sensor that can determine an object's change in position in relation to its surroundings.

motion recognition Using high-end video surveillance cameras that record when they detect movement.

MS-CHAP The Microsoft version of CHAP.

multifactor authentication (MFA) Using more than one type of authentication credential.

multifunctional printer (MFP) A device that combines the functions of a printer, copier, scanner, and fax machine.

multimedia messaging service (MMS) Text messages in which pictures, video, or audio can be included.

multiparty Risks that impact multiple organizations.

multipath A technique for creating more than one physical path between devices and a SAN.

N

Narrowband Internet of Things (NB-IoT)   A low-power wide area network (LPWAN) radio technology standard.

near field communication (NFC)   A set of standards used to establish communication between devices in very close proximity

Nessus   A vulnerability assessment tool.

NetFlow   A session sampling protocol feature on Cisco routers that collects IP network traffic as it enters or exits an interface.

netstat   A Windows and Linux command-line utility that provides detailed information about current network connections as well as network connections for the Transmission Control Protocol (TCP) network interfaces and routing tables.

network access control (NAC)   A technique that examines the current state of a system or network device before it is allowed to connect to the network.

network address translation gateway   A cloud-based technology that performs NAT translations for cloud services.

network hardware security module   A special trusted network computer that performs cryptographic operations.

network intrusion detection system (NIDS)   A technology that watches for attacks on the network and reports back to a central device.

network intrusion prevention system (NIPS)   A technology that monitors network traffic to immediately react to block a malicious attack.

Network Location   A setting that designates the network type (Not Configured, Public, or Private).

network sensors   Sensing devices used to monitor traffic.

network-attached storage (NAS)   A single storage device that serves files over the network.

next generation firewall (NGFW)   A firewall that has additional functionality beyond a traditional firewall such as the ability to filter packets based on applications.

next generation secure web gateway (SWG)   A virtual cloud device that combines several features into a single product.

NIC teaming   Configuring multiple network interface card (NIC) adapters into one or more software-based virtual network adapters for redundancy and speed.

NIST Cybersecurity Framework (CSF)   A measuring stick against which companies can compare their cybersecurity practices relative to the threats they face.

NIST Risk Management Framework (RMF)   A guidance document designed to help organizations assess and manage risks to their information and systems.

nmap   A tool for network discovery and security auditing.

noise detection   A sensor that can detect a suspicious noise through microphones.

non-credentialed scan   A vulnerability scan that provides no authentication information to the tester.

nondisclosure agreement (NDA)   A legal contract between parties that specifies how confidential material will be shared but not disclosed to others without permission.

nonintrusive scan   A vulnerability scan that does not attempt to exploit the vulnerability but only records that it was discovered.

nonpersistent   A characteristic of a system so that any changes or additions are not saved when the system returns to its original state.

nonrepudiation   The process of proving that a user performed an action.

normalization   Organizing data within a database to minimize redundancy.

nslookup   A Windows command-line utility used as a DNS diagnostic utility.

nxlog   A multi-platform log management tool that supports various platforms, log sources, and formats.

O

OAuth (Open Authorization)   An open source federation framework.

obfuscation   Making something obscure or unclear.

obfuscation/camouflaged code   Writing an application in such a way that its inner functionality is difficult for an outsider to understand.

object detection   Using high-end video surveillance cameras that can identify a suspicious objective and sound an alert.

offboarding   Actions to be taken when an employee leaves an enterprise.

offline brute force attack   An attack in which a stolen digest file is loaded onto a computer to be cracked using password cracking software.

offline CA   A certificate authority that is not directly connected to a network.

off-premises   A computing resource hosted and supported by a third party.

onboarding   The tasks associated with hiring a new employee.

online brute force attack   An attack in which the same account is continuously attacked by entering different passwords.

online CA   A certificate authority that is directly connected to a network.

Online Certificate Status Protocol (OCSP)   A process that performs a real-time lookup of a certificate's status.

on-premises   Computing resources located on the campus of the organization.

on-premises platform   Software and technology located within the physical confines of an enterprise, which is usually consolidated in the company's data center.

Opal   A set of specifications for SEDs developed by the Trusted Computing Group (TCG).

Open ID   A federation technology that provides user authentication information.

open method   A wireless network mode in which no authentication is required.

open permissions   User access over files that should have been restricted.

open ports and services   Devices and services that are often configured to allow the most access so that the user can then close those ports that are specific to that organization.

open source   Anything that could be freely used without restrictions.

open source firewall   A firewall that is freely available.

open source intelligence (OSINT)   Publicly accessible information.

Open Source Interconnection (OSI) seven-layer model   A conceptual model that illustrates network functionality.

OpenSSL   A cryptography library that offers open source applications of the TLS protocol.

operational controls   Controls implemented and executed by people.

Operational Technology (OT)   The source of a DDoS attack in which endpoints can be programmed and have an IP address.

order of volatility   The specific order in which evidence from an incident should be examined.

organizational policies   Policies that relate to the management and functioning of the organization as a whole.

OS event logs   Logs produced by an operating system that document incorrect login attempts, system setting modifications, application or system failures, and other events.

out-of-band management   Using an independent and dedicated channel to reach a device for management purposes.

outsourced code development   Contracting with third parties to assist the organization in the development and writing of a software program or app.

OWASP (Open Web Application Security Project)   A group that monitors web attacks.

P

pagefile   A file that contains data moved from RAM to the hard drive due to a lack of RAM space.

pass the hash   An attack in which the attacker steals the digest of an NTLM password and pretends to be the user by sending that hash to the remote system to be authenticated.

passive   A system that is connected to a device that receives a copy of network traffic.

passive reconnaissance   Searching online for publicly accessible information.

password   A secret combination of letters, numbers, and/or characters that only the user should have knowledge of.

Password Authentication Protocol (PAP) A weak version of Extensible Authentication Protocol (EAP).

password complexity   A setting that determines passwords must meet complexity requirements.

password crackers   Software designed to break passwords through matching.

password history   A setting that determines how many days a new password must be kept before the user can change it.

password keys   A hardware-based device to store passwords.

password reuse   A setting that determines the number of unique new passwords a user must use before an old password can be reused.

password spraying   An attack that uses one or a small number of commonly used passwords when trying to log in to several different user accounts.

password vault   A secure repository in which users can store their passwords.

patch   An officially released software security update intended to repair a vulnerability.

pathping   A Windows command-line utility that tests the connection to each hop.

Payment Card Industry Data Security Standard (PCI DSS)   A compliance standard to provide a minimum degree of security for handling customer card information.

payment method   An electronic alternative to using cash or a credit card for payments; also called *contactless payment system*.

penetration testing   A type of test that attempts to exploit vulnerabilities just as a threat actor would.

perfect forward secrecy   Public key systems that generate different random public keys for each session.

persistence   A process in which a load balancer creates a link between an endpoint and a specific network server for the duration of a session.

persistence   The determination, resolve, and perseverance necessary for performing a successful penetration test.

personal identification number (PIN)   A passcode made up of numbers only.

Personal Information Exchange (PFX)   An X.509 file format that is the preferred file format for creating certificates to authenticate applications or websites.

Personally Identifiable Information (PII)   Data that could potentially identify a specific individual.

pharming   Exploiting how a URL is converted into its corresponding IP address to redirect traffic away from its intended target to a fake website instead.

phishing campaign   A broad initiative that uses a variety of tools to train users to resist phishing attacks.

phishing   Sending an email or displaying a web announcement that falsely claims to be from a legitimate enterprise in an attempt to trick the user into surrendering private information or taking action.

phishing simulations   Exercises to help employees recognize phishing emails.

phone call   A process to use a smartphone to verify a user's login attempt.

physical controls   Controls that implement security in a defined structure and location.

physical locks   A type of lock that requires a key for opening.

ping   A Windows and Linux command-line utility that tests the ability of the source computer to reach a specified destination computer.

pinning   Hard-coding a digital certificate within a program that is using the certificate.

pivot   Turning to other systems to be compromised.

Platform as a Service (PaaS)   A cloud computing model of a software platform on which the enterprise or users can build their own applications and then host them.

platform/vendor-specific guides   Guidelines that only apply to specific products.

playbook   A linear-style checklist of required steps and actions needed to successfully respond to specific incident types and threats.

pointer/object dereference   A flaw that results in a pointer given a NULL instead of valid value.

point-to-multipoint   A network topology in which one device is connected to multiple devices.

point-to-point   A network topology in which one device is connected to one other device.

policy   A document that outlines specific requirements or rules that must be met.

port mirroring (port spanning)   A technology on a managed switch that copies traffic that occurs on some or all ports to a designated monitoring port on the switch.

port TAP (test access point)   A device that transmits the send and receive data streams simultaneously on separate dedicated channels so that all data arrives at the monitoring tool in real time.

Post Office Protocol (POP)   A TCP/IP protocol for receiving email messages; the current version is POP3.

post-quantum cryptography   Cryptographic algorithms that are secure against an attack by a quantum computer.

potentially unwanted programs (PUPs)   Software that users do not want on their computer.

power distribution unit (PDU) A device fitted with multiple electrical outputs and designed to distribute electric power, especially to racks of computers and networking equipment located within a data center.

PowerShell A task automation and configuration management framework from Microsoft.

predictive analysis An evaluation used for discovering an attack before it occurs.

preparation An incident response plan step for equipping IT staff, management, and users to handle potential incidents when they arise.

prepending Influencing a subject before an event occurs.

preservation of the evidence Ensuring that important proof is not corrupted or even destroyed.

preshared key (PSK) The authentication model used in WPA that requires a secret key value to be entered into the AP and all approved wireless devices prior to communicating.

pretexting Using impersonation to obtain private information.

preventative controls Controls that prevent the threat from coming in contact with the vulnerability.

Privacy Enhancement Mail (PEM) An X.509 file format that uses DER encoding and can have multiple certificates.

privacy notice A document that outlines how the organization uses personal information it collects.

privacy The state or condition of being free from public attention, observation, or interference to the degree that the person chooses.

private cloud A type of cloud that is created and maintained on a private network.

private information sharing centers Organizations participating in closed source information that restrict both access to data and participation.

private Restricted data with a medium level of confidentiality.

private subnet A VPC for backend servers that are not publicly accessible.

privilege escalation Moving to more advanced resources that are normally protected from an application or user.

privileged access management Technologies and strategies for controlling elevated privilege access.

production stage An application development stage in which the application is released to be used in its actual setting.

proper input validation Accounting for errors such as incorrect user input.

proprietary Data that belongs to the enterprise.

proprietary firewall A firewall that is owned by an entity who has an exclusive right to it.

protected cable distribution A system of cable conduits used to protect classified information transmitted between two secure areas.

Protected EAP (PEAP) An EAP method designed to simplify the deployment of 802.1x by using Microsoft Windows logins and passwords.

Protected Health Information (PHI) Data about a person's health status, provision of health care, or payment for health care.

provenance Evidence in a forensics investigation that can be traced to the very beginning.

provisioning The enterprise-wide configuration, deployment, and management of multiple types of IT system resources.

proximity A sensor that detects the presence of an object when it enters the sensor's field.

pseudo-anonymization Changing data so there is a means to reverse the process to restore the data back to its original state.

public cloud A type of cloud in which the services and infrastructure are offered to all users with access provided remotely through the Internet.

public Data for which there is no risk of release.

public information sharing centers A repository by which open source cybersecurity information is collected and disseminated.

public key infrastructure (PKI) The underlying infrastructure for the management of public keys used in digital certificates.

public notifications and disclosures Contacting relevant stakeholders in the event of a data breach.

public subnet A VPC with a subnet for public-facing web server applications.

pulping Breaking paper into wood cellulose fibers after the ink is removed to destroy the data on it.

pulverizing "Hammering" the paper into dust to destroy the data on it.

Purple Team A penetration testing team that provides real-time feedback between the Red and Blue Teams to enhance the testing.

push notification   A message displayed on a smartphone through an authentication app.

push notification services   Sending SMS text messages to selected users or groups of users.

Python   A popular programming language that can run on several OS platforms.

Q

qualitative risk assessment   An approach that uses an "educated guess" based on observation.

quality assurance (QA)   The process of the verification of quality.

Quality of Service (QoS)   A set of network technologies used to guarantee a network's ability to dependably serve resources and high-priority applications to endpoints.

quantitative risk assessment   An approach that attempts to create "hard" numbers associated with the risk of an element in a system by using historical data.

quantum communication   A subcategory of quantum cryptography used to secure telecommunications.

quantum computer   A computer that relies on quantum physics using atomic-scale units (*qubits*) that can be both 0 and 1 at the same time.

quarantine   The process that holds a suspicious document.

R

race condition   A situation in software that occurs when two concurrent threads of execution access a shared resource simultaneously.

radio frequency identification (RFID)   A wireless set of standards used to transmit information from paper-based tags to a proximity reader.

RADIUS (Remote Authentication Dial-In User Service) An industry standard authentication service with widespread support across nearly all vendors of networking equipment.

RAID (Redundant Array of Independent Drives or Redundant Array of Inexpensive Disks)   A technology that uses multiple hard disk drives for increased reliability and performance.

rainbow tables   Large pregenerated data sets of encrypted passwords used in password attacks.

ransomware   Malware that prevents a user's endpoint device from properly and fully functioning until a fee is paid.

Raspberry Pi   A low-cost credit-card-sized computer motherboard.

real-time operating system (RTOS)   An operating system that is specifically designed for an SoC in an embedded system.

receptionist   A person who staffs a public reception area to provide a level of active security.

reconnaissance   Learning as much about a person as possible in order to appear as genuine while acting as an imposter.

recovery   An incident response plan step for ensuring no threat remains, permitting affected systems to return to normal operation.

recovery point objective (RPO)   The maximum length of time that an organization can tolerate between backups.

recovery time objective (RTO)   The length of time it will take to recover data that has been backed up.

Red Team   A penetration testing team that scans for vulnerabilities and then exploits them.

redundancy   The use of duplicated equipment to improve the availability of the system.

refactoring   Changing the design of existing code.

reference architecture   An authoritative source of information.

registration authority   An entity that is responsible for verifying the credentials of the applicant for a digital certificate.

registry   A database that contains low-level settings used by the Windows OS and for those applications that elect to use it.

regulations   Standards typically developed by established professional organizations or government agencies using the expertise of seasoned security professionals.

regulations that affect risk posture   Controls based upon regulatory requirements that may be required regardless of risk.

regulatory/jurisdiction   A law that governs the site in which cloud data resides.

remote access Trojan (RAT)   Malware that infects a computer like a Trojan but also gives the threat agent unauthorized remote access to the victim's computer by using specially configured communication protocols.

remote access VPN   A user-to-LAN VPN connection for remote users.

remote wipe   A technology used to erase sensitive data stored on the mobile device.

replay An attack that copies data and then uses it for an attack.

replication A copy of a virtual machine that is automatically launched.

reputation damage A tarnished reputation to an organization as the result of a data breach.

reputation Public perception.

request for comments (RFC) Documents that are authored by technology bodies employing specialists, engineers, and scientists who are experts in those areas.

residual risk The risk level that remains after additional controls are applied.

resource exhaustion attacks An attack that depletes parts of memory and interferes with the normal operation of the program in RAM to give an attacker access to the underlying OS.

resource policies Written statements that outline who is the responsible party for cloud computing, what are their duties and responsibilities, and how cloud computing can be used.

resource vs. security constraint A limitation in providing strong cryptography due to the "tug-of-war" between the available resources (time and energy) and the security provided by cryptography.

resources and funding Financial capabilities of threat actors.

response and recovery controls Steps that should be taken when responding to an incident in order to recoup from it.

restoration order The sequence in which different systems are reinstated after a disaster.

retention policy Part of an incident response plan that outlines how long the evidence of the incident should be retained.

retina A layer at the back (posterior) portion of the eyeball that contains cells sensitive to light and can be used for biometric authentication.

reverse proxy A proxy that routes requests coming from an external network to the correct internal server.

revert to known state An OS feature to restore it to an earlier point in time prior to a problem.

rich communication services (RCS) Mobile device communication which can convert a texting app into a live chat platform and supports pictures, videos, location, stickers, and emojis.

right to audit clause A part of a cloud contract that gives the customer the legal right to review logs.

rights management The authority of the owner of the data to impose restrictions on its use.

risk A situation that involves exposure to some type of danger.

risk appetite A level of risk that is considered acceptable.

risk awareness Raising of understanding of what risks exist, their potential impacts, and how they are managed.

Risk Control Self-Assessment (RCSA) A methodology by which management and staff at all levels collectively work to identify and evaluate risks.

risk matrix/heatmap A visual color-coded tool that lists the impact and likelihood of risks.

risk register A list of potential threats and associated risks often shown as a table.

Risky IP address Examining the IP address that was used to attempt a login and comparing it against a list of IP addresses involved in malicious activities.

robot sentries Automated devices that patrol and use CCTV with object detection in public areas.

rogue AP An unauthorized AP that allows an attacker to bypass many network security configurations and opens the network and its users to attacks.

Role-Based Access Control An access control scheme that is considered a more "real-world" access control that based on a user's job function within an organization.

role-based awareness training Specialized training that is customized to the specific role that an employee holds in the organization.

root digital certificate A certificate that is created and verified by a CA.

rooting Circumventing the installed built-in limitations on Android devices.

rootkit Malware that can hide its presence and the presence of other malware on the computer.

route A Linux command-line utility that displays and manipulates IP routing tables to create static routes to specific hosts.

route security The trust of packets sent through a router.

rsyslog   (rocket-fast system for log processing) An open source utility for forwarding log messages in an IP network on UNIX devices.

Rule-Based Access Control   An access control scheme that can dynamically assign roles to subjects based on a set of rules defined by a custodian.

rules of engagement   Limitations or parameters in a penetration test.

runbook   A series of automated conditional steps that are part of an incident response procedure.

S

safe   A ruggedized steel box with a lock.

salt   A random string added to a hash algorithm for enhanced security.

sandbox   A "container" in which an application can be run so that it does not impact the underlying OS.

scalability   Expandability from small projects to very large projects.

scanless   A tool for using websites to perform port scan.

scarcity   When something is in short supply.

scheduling   Protocols that are used in load balancers to distribute the workload among devices.

screen lock   A security setting that prevents a mobile device from being accessed until the user enters the correct passcode permitting access.

script kiddies   Individuals who want to perform attacks yet lack the technical knowledge to carry them out.

SEAndroid   A security-enhanced version of the Android operating system that uses MAC.

secrets management   A process that enables strong security and improved management of a microservices-based architecture.

secure areas   Areas that separate threat actors from defenders.

secure coding practices and techniques   A methodology to create secure software applications.

secure cookie   A cookie that is only sent to the server with an encrypted request over the secure HTTPS protocol.

Secure FTP (SFTP)   A protocol that encrypts and compresses all FTP data and commands.

Secure Real-time Transport Protocol (SRTP)   A protocol for providing protection for Voice over IP (VoIP) communications.

Secure Shell (SSH)   An encrypted alternative to the Telnet protocol that is used to access remote computers.

Secure Sockets Layer (SSL)   An early and widespread cryptographic transport algorithm that is now considered obsolete.

Secure/Multipurpose Internet Mail Extensions (S/MIME)   A protocol for securing email messages.

Security Assertion Markup Language (SAML)   An Extensible Markup Language (XML) standard that allows secure web domains to exchange user authentication and authorization data.

security groups   Segmented computing resources formed into logical groupings to create network perimeters.

security guards   People who patrol and monitor restricted areas.

Security Information and Event Management (SIEM)   A tool that consolidates real-time security monitoring and management of security information with analysis and reporting of security events.

security key   A hardware device inserted into a computer port that contains all the necessary cryptographic information to authenticate the user.

security of the ML algorithms   A risk associated with the vulnerabilities in AI-powered cybersecurity applications and their devices.

Security Orchestration, Automation and Response (SOAR)   A tool designed to help security teams manage and respond to the very high number of security warnings and alarms by combining comprehensive data gathering and analytics in order to automate incident response.

self-encrypting drives (SEDs)   Drives that can automatically encrypt any data stored on them.

self-signed   A signed digital certificate that does not depend upon any higher-level authority for authentication.

sensitive   Data that could cause catastrophic harm to the company if disclosed, such as technical specifications for a new product.

sensors   Electronic devices that supplement the work of security guards.

sentiment analysis The process of computationally identifying and categorizing opinions, usually expressed in response to textual data, in order to determine the writer's attitude toward a particular topic.

separation of duties The practice of requiring that processes should be divided between two or more individuals.

serverless infrastructure A cloud infrastructure in which the capacity planning, installation, setup, and management are all invisible to the user because they are handled by the cloud provider.

server-side execution and validation Input validation that uses the server to perform the validation.

server-side request forgery (SSRF) An attack that takes advantage of a trusting relationship between web servers.

service account A user account that is created explicitly to provide a security context for services running on a server.

service-level agreement (SLA) A service contract between a vendor and a client that specifies what services will be provided, the responsibilities of each party, and any guarantees of service.

services integration The combined management function of multiple services into a single entity.

Session Initiation Protocol (SIP) A signaling protocol that is used to create "sessions" between multiple participants and is widely found in voice telephony products.

session replay An attack in which an attacker attempts to impersonate the user by using the user's session token.

sFlow A packet sampling protocol that gives a statistical sampling instead of the actual flow of packets.

shadow IT Employees who become frustrated with the slow pace of acquiring technology, so they purchase and install their own equipment or resources in violation of company policies.

shared account An account used by more than one user.

shimming Transparently adding a small coding library that intercepts calls made by a device and changes the parameters passed between the device and the device driver.

short message service (SMS) Text messages of a maximum of 160 characters.

shoulder surfing Watching an individual enter a security code on a keypad.

shredding Cutting paper into small strips or particles to destroy the data on it.

sideloading Downloading unofficial apps.

signage Written information on fencing that explains the area is restricted.

signature-based monitoring A monitoring technique that examines network traffic to look for well-known patterns and compares the activities against a predefined signature.

Simple Mail Transfer Protocol (SMTP) A TCP/IP protocol for sending email messages.

Simple Network Management Protocol (SNMP) A popular protocol used to manage network equipment that is supported by most network equipment manufacturers.

simulation A hands-on exercise using a realistic scenario to thoroughly test each step of an incident response plan.

Simultaneous Authentication of Equals (SAE) A component of WPA3 that is designed to increase security at the time of the handshake when the key is being exchanged.

Single Loss Expectancy (SLE) The expected monetary loss every time a risk occurs.

single point of failure A component or entity in a system that, if it no longer functions, will disable the entire system.

single sign-on (SSO) Using one authentication credential to access multiple accounts or applications.

site risk assessment A detailed evaluation of the processes performed at a site and how they can be impacted.

site survey An in-depth examination and analysis of a WLAN site.

site-to-site VPN A VPN connection in which multiple sites can connect to other sites over the Internet.

skimming A process in which a threat actor attaches a small device that fits inside a card reader to capture information.

smart card A card that contains information used as part of the authentication process.

smart meters Digital meters that measure the amount of utilities consumed.

smishing Using short message service (SMS) text messages to perform phishing.

sn1per A penetration testing tool.

snapshot The current state of all settings and data used for forensics and data backups.

SNMPv3 The current version of the Simple Network Management Protocol used to manage network equipment that supports authentication and encryption.

social engineering Gathering data by relying on the weaknesses of individuals.

social media analysis Viewing social media posts of potential candidates to look for important insights.

social media influence campaign An influence campaign exclusively used on social media.

Software as a Service (SaaS) A cloud computing model of hosted software environment.

software compliance and licensing Risks associated with violating software license agreements.

software diversity Software development technique in which two or more functionally identical variants of a program are developed from the same specification but by different programmers or programming teams.

software firewall A firewall that runs as a program or service on a device, such as a computer or router.

software-defined network (SDN) A network that virtualizes parts of the physical network so that it can be more quickly and easily reconfigured.

software-defined visibility (SDV) A framework that allows users to create programs in which critical security functions that previously required manual intervention can now be automated.

someone you know Authentication based on being validated by another person.

something you are Authentication based on the features and characteristics of the individual.

something you can do Authentication based on actions that the user can uniquely perform.

something you exhibit Authentication based on a genetically determined characteristic.

something you have Authentication based on the approved user having a specific item in his or her possession.

something you know Authentication based on something the user knows but no one else knows.

somewhere you are Authentication based on where the user is located.

spam Unsolicited email that is sent to a large number of recipients.

spear phishing Targeting specific users.

spim Spam delivered through instant messaging (IM) instead of email.

split tunneling A VPN technology in which only some traffic is sent to the VPN concentrator and is protected, while other traffic directly accesses the Internet.

spyware Tracking software that is deployed without the consent or control of the user.

SQL injection An attack that inserts statements to manipulate a database server using Structured Query Language commands.

SSAE SOC 2 Type II A standard for reports on internal controls report that reviews how a company safeguards customer data and how well those controls are operating.

SSAE SOC 2 Type III A standard for reports on internal controls that can be freely distributed.

SSL stripping An attack that manipulates SSL functions by intercepting an HTTP connection.

staging stage A stage in application development that tests to verify that the code functions as intended.

stakeholder management Identifying the relevant stakeholders within the organization who need to be initially informed of an incident and then kept up to date.

standard A document approved through consensus by a recognized standardization body.

standard naming conventions Using the same conventions for assigning names to appliances.

stapling A process for verifying the status of a certificate by sending queries at regular intervals to receive a signed time-stamped response.

state actors Government-sponsored attackers who launch cyberattacks against the foes of the state.

stateful packet filtering A firewall that keeps a record of the state of a connection between an internal computer and an external device and then makes decisions based on the connection as well as the conditions.

stateless packet filtering A firewall that looks at the incoming packet and permits or denies it based on specific conditions.

static code A value that never changes.

static code analysis Analyzing and testing software from a security perspective before the source code is compiled.

steganography Hiding the existence of data within another type of file, such as an image file.

storage area network (SAN) A dedicated network storage facility that provides access to data storage over a high-speed network.

storage segmentation Separating business data from personal data on a mobile device.

stored procedure A subroutine available to applications that access a relational database.

strategic counterintelligence Gaining information about the attacker's intelligence collection capabilities.

strategic intelligence The collection, processing, analysis, and dissemination of intelligence for forming policy changes.

stream cipher An algorithm that takes one character and replaces it with one character.

Structured Query Language (SQL) A language used to view and manipulate data that is stored in a relational database.

Structured Threat Information Expression (STIX) A language and format used to exchange cyberthreat intelligence.

Subject Alternative Name (SAN) Also known as a *Unified Communications Certificate* (*UCC*), certificate primarily used for Microsoft Exchange servers or unified communications.

subscriber identity module (SIM) card An integrated circuit that securely stores information used to identify and authenticate the IoT device on a cellular network.

supervisory control and data acquisition (SCADA) A system that controls multiple industrial control systems (ICS).

supply chain A network that moves a product from the supplier to the customer and is made up of vendors that supply raw material, manufacturers who convert the material into products, warehouses that store products, distribution centers that deliver them to the retailers, and retailers who bring the product to the consumer.

swap file A file that contains data moved from RAM to the hard drive due to a lack of RAM space.

symmetric cryptographic algorithm Encryption that uses a single key to encrypt and decrypt a message.

syslog (system logging protocol) A standard to send system log or event messages to a server.

syslog-ng An open source utility for UNIX devices that includes content filtering.

system integration Connectivity between the systems of an organization and its third parties.

system on a chip (SoC) A single microprocessor chip on which all the necessary hardware components are contained.

T

tabletop A monthly 30-minute discussion of a scenario conducted in an informal and stress-free environment.

TACACS+ The current version of the Terminal Access Control Access Control System (TACACS) authentication service.

tags Identifying labels for evidence bags that have a description of the item, a numeric identifier, date, collection location, and other relevant data.

tail A Linux text file manipulation tool for displaying the last 10 lines of a file.

tailgating Following an authorized user through a door.

tainted training data for machine learning A risk associated with attackers can attempt to alter the training data that is used by ML.

Tcpdump A command-line packet analyzer.

Tcpreplay A tool for editing packets and then replaying the packets back onto the network to observe their behavior.

technical controls Controls that are incorporated as part of hardware, software, or firmware.

temperature detection A sensor that can detect a sudden increase or decrease in temperature or the temperature of an object in relation to its surroundings.

terms of agreement A document that defines what is expected from both the organization and its users.

testing stage A stage in which an application is tested for any errors that could result in a security vulnerability.

tethering Using a mobile device with an active Internet connection to share that connection with other mobile devices through Bluetooth or Wi-Fi.

theHarvester A Kali Linux utility that provides information about email accounts, user names, and hostnames/subdomains from public sources.

thin client   A computer that runs from resources stored on a central cloud server instead of a localized hard drive.

third parties   External entities outside of the organization.

third-party app store   A site from which unofficial apps can be downloaded.

third-party solution   A data destruction technique that requires specialized equipment from an outside source.

third-party solutions   Cloud security controls that are available from external sources.

third-party updates   Patch updates for application and utility software.

threat actor   Individuals or entities who are responsible for cyber incidents against the technology equipment of enterprises and users.

threat feeds   Cybersecurity data feeds that provide information on the latest threats.

threat hunting   Proactively searching for cyber threats that thus far have gone undetected in a network.

threat map   An illustration of cyberthreats overlaid on a diagrammatic representation of a geographical area.

time of check/time of use   A software check of the state of a resource before using that resource.

time of day   Restrictions regarding limiting when a user can log in to their account to access resources.

time offset   The amount of time added to or subtracted from Coordinated Universal Time (UTC) to arrive at the current "actual" (called *civil*) time.

time stamp   The recorded time that an event took place irrespective of the location of the endpoint.

time-based login   A user account login that is based on a specific day and time.

time-based one-time password (TOTP)   A one-time password that changes after a set period of time.

token   A small device with a window display.

token key   A hardware device inserted into a computer port that contains all the necessary cryptographic information to authenticate the user.

tokenization   Obfuscating sensitive data elements into a random string of characters and then stores them in a database for retrieval as needed.

traceroute   A Linux command-line utility that shows the details about the path a packet takes from a computer or device to a destination.

tracert   A Windows command-line utility that shows the details about the path a packet takes from a computer or device to a destination.

transference   Transferring the responsibility of a risk to a third party.

transit gateway   An Amazon Web Services (AWS) technology that allows organizations to connect all existing virtual private clouds (VPC), physical data centers, remote offices, and remote gateways into a single managed source.

Transport Layer Security (TLS)   A widespread cryptographic transport algorithm that replaces SSL.

Transport mode   An IPsec mode that encrypts only the data portion (payload) of each packet yet leaves the header unencrypted.

Trojan   An executable program that masquerades as performing a benign activity but also does something malicious.

trust   A social engineering principle to inspire confidence in a victim.

trust model   The type of trust relationship that can exist between individuals or entities.

Trusted Automated Exchange of Intelligence Information (TAXII)   An application protocol for exchanging cyberthreat intelligence over Hypertext Transfer Protocol Secure (HTTPS).

Trusted Platform Module (TPM)   A chip on the motherboard of the computer that provides cryptographic services.

tunnel mode   An IPsec mode that encrypts both the header and the data portion.

two-person integrity/control   Using two security guards to prevent a single guard from acting maliciously.

typo squatting   Purchasing the domain names of sites that are spelled similarly to actual sites.

U

UEFI (Unified Extensible Firmware Interface)   An improved firmware interface developed to replace the BIOS.

unauthentication mode of operation   An information service that provides a non-credentializing service such as confidentiality by a block cipher mode of operation.

unified endpoint management (UEM)   A group or class of software tools has a single management interface for mobile devices as well as computer devices.

unified threat management (UTM) An integrated device that combines several security functions.

uninterruptible power supply (UPS) A device that maintains power to equipment in case of an interruption in the primary electrical power source.

Universal Serial Bus (USB) connectors A port on mobile devices used for data transfer.

unmanned aerial vehicle (UAV) An aircraft without a human pilot on board to control its flight.

unmanned aerial vehicle An aircraft piloted by remote control or onboard computers.

unsecure protocols Also called insecure protocols, using protocols for telecommunications that do not provide adequate protections.

unsecured root accounts Unprotected accounts that give unfettered access to all resources.

urgency A social engineering principle that demands immediate action.

URL redirection An attack in which a user is redirected to another site.

USB On-the-Go (OTG) A specification that allows a mobile device with a USB connection to act as either a host or a peripheral used for external media access.

user account An approved identity between a user and an endpoint, network, or service.

user behavior analysis Looking at the normal behavior of users and how they interact with systems to create a picture of typical activity.

user digital certificate The endpoint of the certificate chain.

V

vault A ruggedized steel box with a lock.

vein One of the "tubes" that form part of the blood circulation system in the human body that carries oxygen-depleted blood back toward the heart.

vendor management The process organizations use to monitor and manage the interactions with all external third parties with which they have a relationship.

vendors Entities from whom an organization purchases goods and services.

version control Software that allow changes to be automatically recorded and, if necessary, "rolled back" to a previous version of the software.

virtual desktop infrastructure (VDI) Storing sensitive applications and data on a remote server that is accessed through a smartphone.

virtual firewall A firewall that runs in the cloud. Virtual firewalls are designed for settings, such as public cloud environments, in which deploying an appliance firewall would be difficult or even impossible.

virtual IP (VIP) An IP address and a specific port number that can be used to reference different physical servers.

virtual LAN (VLAN) A technology that allows scattered users to be logically grouped together even though they may be attached to different switches.

virtual machine escape protection Preventing VMs from directly interacting with the host operating system.

virtual machine sprawl avoidance Combating VM sprawl through using different procedures.

virtual network A cloud virtual network that connects services and resources like virtual machines and database applications with each other via a secure, encrypted, and private network.

virtual private network (VPN) A technology that enables the use of an unsecured public network as if it were a secure private network.

virtualization The means of managing and presenting computer resources by function without regard to their physical layout or location.

vishing Using a telephone call to perform phishing.

visitor log A paper or electronic record of people granted access to a property.

Visual Basic for Applications (VBA) An event-driven Microsoft programming language.

voice A physiological biometric identifier.

voice over IP (VoIP) A technology that uses a data-based IP network to add digital voice clients and new voice applications onto the IP network.

vulnerability database A repository of known vulnerabilities and information as to how they have been exploited.

vulnerability feeds   Cybersecurity data feeds include that provide information on the latest vulnerabilities.

vulnerability scan   A frequent and ongoing process, often automated, that continuously identifies vulnerabilities and monitors cybersecurity progress.

W

walkthrough   A review by IT personnel of the steps of the plan by paying particular attention to the IT systems and services that may be targeted in an attack.

war driving   Searching for wireless signals from an automobile or on foot while using a portable computing device.

war flying   An efficient means of discovering a Wi-Fi signal using drones.

warm site   A remote site that contains computer equipment but does not have active Internet or telecommunication facilities, and does not have backups of data.

watering hole attack   An attack directed toward a smaller group of specific individuals, such as the major executives working for a manufacturing company.

weak configurations   Configuration settings that are not properly implemented, resulting in vulnerabilities.

weak encryption   Choosing a known vulnerable encryption mechanism.

weak key   A key that causes the cipher to behave in unpredictable ways or may compromise overall security.

web application firewall   A firewall that filters by examining the applications using HTTP.

whaling   Targeting wealthy individuals or senior executives within a business through phishing.

White box   A penetration testing level in which the testers are given full knowledge of the network and the source code of applications.

white hat hackers   Also known as ethical attackers, a class of hackers that probe a system with an organization's permission for weaknesses and then privately provide that information to the organization.

White Team   A penetration testing team that enforces the rules of the penetration testing.

whitelisting   Approving in advance only specific applications to run on the OS so that any item not approved is either restricted or denied.

Wi-Fi   A wireless network designed to replace or supplement a wired local area network (LAN). Also called *wireless local area network (WLAN)*.

Wi-Fi analyzer   A software tool that helps to visualize the essential details of the wireless network.

Wi-Fi Direct   The Wi-Fi Alliance implementation of WLAN ad hoc mode.

Wi-Fi Protected Access 2 (WPA2)   The second generation of WPA security from the Wi-Fi Alliance that addresses authentication and encryption on WLANs and is currently the most secure model for Wi-Fi security.

Wi-Fi Protected Setup (WPS)   An optional means of configuring security on wireless local area networks primarily intended to help users who have little or no knowledge of security to implement security quickly and easily on their WLANs.

wildcard digital certificate   Certificate used to validate a main domain along with all subdomains.

WinHex   A hexadecimal editor that can be used for forensics.

wireless access point placement   Placing an AP in the optimum location.

Wireshark   A popular GUI packet capture and analysis tool.

worm   Malicious program that uses a computer network to replicate.

WPA3   The current generation of Wi-Fi Protected Access (WPA) whose goal is to deliver a suite of features to simplify security configuration for users while enhancing network security protections.

X

XML injection   An attack that inserts statements to manipulate a database server using eXtensible Markup Language (XML).

Z

zero day   A vulnerability that is exploited by attackers before anyone else even knows it exists.

zero trust   A strategic initiative about networks that is designed to prevent successful attacks by eliminating the concept of trust from an organization's network architecture.

Zigbee   A low-power, short-range, and low-data rate specification designed for occasional data or signal transmission from a sensor or IoT device.

INDEX

ISBN-13: 978-0357424384
ISBN-10: 0357424387

90000

9 780357 424384